DISCOVERING ARGUMENTS
An Introduction to Critical Thinking and Writing, with Readings

Dean Memering
Professor Emeritus of English
Central Michigan University

William Palmer
Charles A. Dana Professor of English
Alma College

Prentice
Hall

Upper Saddle River, New Jersey 07458

Library of Congress Cataloging-in-Publication Data

Memering, Dean (date)
  Discovering arguments : an introduction to critical thinking and writing with readings/
Dean Memering, William Palmer
    p. cm.
  Includes bibliographical references and index.
  ISBN 0-13-759614-0
  1. English language—Rhetoric. 2. Persuasion (Rhetoric). 3. Critical thinking. 4. College
readers. 5. Report writing. I. Title: Introduction to critical thinking and writing with
readings. II. Palmer, William (date) III. Title.

PE1431 .M49 2002
808'.0427—dc21   2001021858

AVP, Editor in Chief: Leah Jewell
Acquisitions Editor: Corey Good
Assistant Editor: Vivian Garcia
Editorial Assistant: Jennifer Collins
VP, Director of Production
  and Manufacturing: Barbara Kittle
Senior Managing Editor: Mary Rottino
Production Liaison: Fran Russello
Project Manager: Linda B. Pawelchak
Manufacturing Manager: Nick Sklitsis

Prepress and Manufacturing Buyer:
  Mary Ann Gloriande
Cover Director: Jayne Conte
Cover Design: Bruce Kenselaar
Cover Image: ARTVILLE LLC
Marketing Manager: Brandy Dawson
Copy Editing: Katherine Evancie
Proofreading: Kathleen Lafferty/Roaring
  Mountain Editorial Services

Credits begin on page 706, which constitutes
a continuation of this copyright page.

This book was set in 10/12 Janson Text by Lori Clinton
and was printed and bound by RR Donnelley & Sons Company.
The cover was printed by Phoenix Color Corp.

© 2002 by Pearson Education
Upper Saddle River, New Jersey 07458

Printed in the United States of America
10 9 8 7 6

ISBN 0-13-759614-6

Prentice-Hall International (UK) Limited, *London*
Prentice-Hall of Australia Pty. Limited, *Sydney*
Prentice-Hall Canada Inc., *Toronto*
Prentice-Hall Hispanoamericana, S.A., *Mexico*
Prentice-Hall of India Private Limited, *New Delhi*
Prentice-Hall of Japan, Inc., *Tokyo*
Pearson Education Asia Pte. Ltd., *Singapore*
Editora Prentice-Hall do Brasil, Ltda., *Rio de Janeiro*

Contents

CHAPTER 2

INTERCHAPTER 2

CHAPTER 3

CHAPTER 5

INTERCHAPTER 5

CHAPTER 6

CHAPTER 7

CHAPTER 8

Evaluating Evidence   510

CHAPTER 9

CHAPTER 10
Writing Your Research Paper   606

Preface

<u>Discovering Arguments: An Introduction to Critical Thinking and Writing, with Readings</u> encourages you to discover the critical powers of your mind. By "thinking" we mean not only analyzing a text but also extending from the text, using it as a springboard for your own interpretation, imagination, and insight.

At the end of the year 2000, the media were full of interviews, articles, and talking heads discussing the candidates, then Governor George Bush of Texas and Vice President Al Gore, and the issues of the presidential election: vouchers for private schools, prescription drugs for the elderly, the future role of the military, gun control, stem-cell research, and so on. Most viewers had simple responses to the arguments: "I agree" or "I disagree." Many responded with analytical statements: "it will never work . . . it will cost too much . . . it benefits only the rich." Some people had more detailed responses: "Why don't we try that program for the medical use of marijuana in a few states to see how well it works?" To argue well, you need to know some history of an issue, but you don't have to be a genius to recognize strategies of argument and persuasion (recognizing similarities and differences for example). Most students can learn them. <u>Discovering Arguments</u> will help you do this.

We use the terms <u>argue</u> and <u>persuade</u> in their several meanings. One common meaning is "to fight or dispute with words," as in a heated argument on whether same-sex marriages should be legal. Another is "to offer reasons or evidence," as does a lawyer who argues that eyewitnesses can identify an accused. Also, an argument can mean a theory, a philosophy, or hypothesis, as in the argument that "all life is based on self-interest." In composition classes, argument often means writing a paper in which you construct an argument for or against, or both for <u>and</u> against, a thesis by giving reasons, examples, facts, and other evidence.

<u>Discovering Arguments</u> is a book about using your mind, making thoughtful applications of reading, writing, and persuasion. One of the significant differ-

ences between <u>Discovering Arguments</u> and other books is our emphasis on audience and persuasive appeals: logos (using reasons), pathos (using emotions), and ethos (using ethics). These appeals offer powerful tools that form the center of thinking, reading, and writing activities in the book. Classroom experience shows that students find this approach useful, and it quickly influences the quality of their thinking and writing.

Except for our collection of logical fallacies (which we call "problems in reasoning"), we have made little use of the premises and conclusions of formal logic; instead, you will discover that there are ample resources for argumentation using informal reasoning. Among these we have included a simplified presentation of philosopher Stephen Toulmin's general theory: most arguments are similar; they make some claim that must be supported by credible evidence.

Writing awakens the mind. It causes you to search for ideas, to construct and analyze thoughts that connect with your audience. Overall, this book values reading and writing for their relationships with thinking. You can view essays, books, newspapers, magazines—any text—as the thoughts of other men and women reaching out to their readers. Reading and writing are like a conversation between you and your readers: a conversation that awakens your mental powers as you work through details, facts, library materials, probable arguments, contradictions, paradoxes, and the search for truth.

<u>Discovering Arguments</u> incorporates both product and process approaches to learning. As a reader analyzing an essay, poem, or story, you may see a selection as a product—a fusion of thought and form. Or, as a writer working on a report or an argument, you may see your task as a process of planning, composing, and revising. Process approaches help you find subjects that matter to you and to a real audience. Your process approach can assist you with finding information to assemble your thoughts and, eventually, to reach the revision stages, when your thoughts and language skills come together.

THE BOOK IS MULTIFUNCTIONAL

<u>Discovering Arguments</u> can be used as a <u>rhetoric</u>: it presents a variety of strategies for communicating clearly and persuasively. It can be used as a <u>reader</u>: you will find a variety of papers from our students; published student essays (from <u>Newsweek</u>'s "My Turn" column); and essays, articles, poems, and stories by professional writers such as Mitch Albom, Ellen Goodman, Richard Selzer, Thomas Sowell, Deborah Tannen, Martin Luther King Jr., and many others. Although the book contains a few poems and fiction pieces, the majority of the readings are nonfiction. The book can be used as a <u>handbook</u> on research writing: it features comprehensive sections on library strategies, evaluation of evidence, documentation—including electronic sources from the Internet—and detailed guidelines for writing reports as well as persuasive papers using both MLA and APA styles. Finally, <u>Discovering Arguments</u> can be used as a proofreading guide. The Concise Handbook on Grammar, Mechanics, and Usage

after the chapters can help you understand and correct the errors that plague many writers. Errors in sentence construction such as fragments; problems with punctuation, capitalization, and other "mechanics"; and usage problems such as the differences between <u>who</u> and <u>whom</u>, <u>lie</u> and <u>lay</u>, and others are explained in brief, simple language.

UNIQUE COMPONENTS OF THE BOOK

Active-Discovery Learning

The book is a balance between traditional, deductive teaching, which tells students in advance what they are to learn, and a newer, inductive approach in which students infer for themselves the underlying strategies of composition. In chapter 1, for example, we ask you to write an essay while you read the chapter instead of reading the whole chapter first and then writing your essay. "What you really learn is what you discover," says writing teacher Ann Berthoff (9). Our goal is to help you discover and apply tools of critical thinking that will benefit you whenever you read and write.

An abundance of pedagogy provides students with a variety of ideas and skills to learn, and instructors with **a variety of materials** to teach. Because there are many ways to think, we have included several strategies to help you respond thoughtfully. <u>Discovering Arguments</u> contains many more activities and assignments than are usually provided in similar books.

Interchapters

The interchapters are brief presentations of matters of style and voice. The book provides an interchapter after each of the first five chapters so that learning and practice can begin early in the semester and can be sequenced to correspond with your work as you revise your own writing. You learn tools of style one at a time, discovering patterns of diction, sentences, and punctuation.

Our emphasis on the relationship between style and thought offers insights into language as an instrument of persuasion. We present a holistic view of content and style. You learn to excel at what you say as well as how you say it. At the heart of this view is a paradox: how you say something colors what you mean, and what you mean can be clarified by the way you say it. With a minimum of grammatical jargon, the interchapters help you develop an effective style while learning to communicate persuasively.

Thinking with Contraries

Contradictions, paradoxes, and other forms of reversal offer rich possibilities. Statements such as "love your enemies" or "the indirect is just as real as the direct" stimulate thought. Contraries require exploration and explanation for understanding and, therefore, make an excellent inclusion for careful thinking, reading, and writing. Contraries enable you to discover and to evaluate ideas and information. With contraries you learn to develop a high tolerance for ambiguity and a low tolerance for either/or thinking. You learn ways to use creative thinking skills (such as humor, analogy, and empathy) to complement critical thinking skills (such as analysis, argumentation, and evaluation).

SECTION I: ARGUMENTATION

Chapter 1: Communication and Persuasion: Logos, Pathos, Ethos

Chapter 1 introduces the essential skill of observation: noticing details, examples, ideas, problems, arguments, and structures. You learn to use specific, concrete evidence to support your opinions. Chapter 1 presents the appeals of logos, pathos, and ethos used throughout the book as a unifying foundation for persuasive, argumentative writing. The chapter also offers guidelines for finding a subject, creating thesis statements in persuasive essays, and engaging an audience with effective titles, introductions, and conclusions. You learn to read actively by annotating an essay—a skill that helps to evaluate essays. The appeals not only give you tools to communicate persuasively but also to evaluate how well other writers communicate and persuade.

Interchapter 1: Style and Voice

The first interchapter introduces style and voice and related matters of diction and sentence patterns. Activities here help you use effective diction: the effects of monosyllables or multisyllables, and using specific or general, concrete or abstract, literal or figurative words. You learn the effects of precise words, natural writing, and pretentious writing; and you learn the uses of voice—the sound of your writing personality on the page. You learn about objective writing, persuasive writing, and tone—your attitudes toward audience, subject, and self. Interchapter 1 also introduces you to the use of short sentences for emphasis, joining two complete thoughts for coordination, and using semicolons.

Chapter 2: Arguments and Controversies

Chapter 2 teaches you to examine both or many sides of disputes through careful reading: by asking questions; noticing insights, assumptions, overgeneralizations; and by withholding judgments until you have considered various points of view. The chapter includes analyzing writing situations; using appeals to logos, pathos, ethos; responding to opposing arguments; and using outlining and summarizing as analytical tools. A comparison of articles by Mitch Albom and Thomas Sowell on the issue of gun control enables you to analyze and evaluate writing about a controversy and to write your own essay or letter about a controversy. You learn tools for writing a report and for writing an essay with sources. You learn about kinds of evidence—examples, reasons, authorities, and statistics; Rogerian argument; and ways to organize argumentative papers. The chapter contains readings on gun control, abortion, gambling, creationism versus evolution, same-sex partners, hate speech and the First Amendment, and racial profiling.

Interchapter 2: Voice and Emphasis

Interchapter 2 presents additional matters of diction. You learn to use forms of repetition, such as careful alliteration to make ideas sound emphatic and clear. You learn to use subordination to join complete and incomplete thoughts; to use colons, dashes, underlining (italics), and parentheses; and to analyze the effects of punctuation on a writer's voice and persuasive ability. The interchapter presents the pros and cons of sentence fragments, and the importance of omitting needless words to fine-tune sentences.

Chapter 3: Strategies of Argumentation

Chapter 3 presents strategies writers use to discover, develop, and defend their ideas: induction, deduction, illustration, narration, description, refutation, comparison and contrast, classification, cause and effect, and definition. By analyzing and evaluating these strategies of argumentation, you learn how they complement appeals to logos, pathos, and ethos. Chapter 3 presents a simplified introduction to the Toulmin strategy of argumentation—claims, grounds, warrants—and invites you to analyze an essay using the Toulmin strategy.

Interchapter 3: Strategies of Repetition

Interchapter 3 presents sentence tools involving different kinds of repetition: parallelism (-ing phrases, -to phrases, -of phrases), anaphora, epistrophe, the power of threes in sentences, and varying sentence beginnings (-ing phrases, -ed phrases, to phrases).

Chapter 4: Thinking with Contraries

Chapter 4 teaches you to use contraries in critical ways: to notice and analyze contradictions and paradoxes, and to generate and evaluate ideas. You also learn to use contraries in creative ways: for entertainment, for explaining complex ideas or processes, and for developing empathy through imagination. The chapter invites you to write about your mind (how you think you think) and to evaluate an essay by examining its use of contraries.

Interchapter 4: Style and Contraries

Interchapter 4 presents tools of style involving contraries: loose and periodic sentences, antithesis, antithesis and balanced sentences, active and passive verbs, and fine-tuning sentences by omitting empty words (expletives).

Chapter 5: Problems in Reasoning

Chapter 5 presents a full collection of fallacies and reasoning errors, starting with differences between facts, implications, assumptions, and inferences. The fallacies are categorized as problems of insufficient evidence, problems based on irrelevant information, problems of ambiguity, and problems of faulty reasoning. The chapter contains many activities to help you analyze fallacies, and you are asked to write your own examples of fallacies. At the end of the chapter, we invite you to analyze the use of reasoning in a published essay, "How the Web Destroys the Quality of Students' Research Papers."

Interchapter 5: Analyzing Style

Interchapter 5 reinforces the connection between style and thought, credibility and persuasion. It presents guidelines for analyzing style and voice, a review of the tools of style in the preceding interchapters, and guidelines for organizing an essay that analyzes style. The interchapter contains a lively essay for analysis, "The Swooshification of the World" by Sports Illustrated columnist Rick Reilly (concerning Nike's trademark "swoosh") and a model student analysis of Reilly's essay. You are asked to select an essay or a speech and to analyze how a writer's stylistic choices reinforce content or persuasive appeals.

Chapter 6: Critical Thinking about Poetry, Fiction, Literary Nonfiction, and Film

Because poems, stories, literary essays, and films are artistic, they challenge students to think deeply. Chapter 6 engages you with these special challenges for thoughtful reading and writing. You learn to pay close attention to meaning (what is expressed) and to style (how it is expressed), as well as to make associative discoveries and to respond to felt resonances. The chapter presents concise explanations of the basic elements of each genre along with guidelines for helping you write essays analyzing, interpreting, and evaluating a text from the many selections in the chapter.

SECTION II: RESEARCH

Because persuasive writing requires finding the background and evidence for your subject, you need to become a skillful research writer. Modern library and research skills are so demanding that we have provided a full section devoted to these skills based on the guidelines of the Modern Language Association (MLA) and the American Psychological Association (APA). Building on the theme of cloning and the strategies of analysis and argumentation used throughout the book, the research section contains comprehensive chapters on library use (including virtual libraries), evaluation of evidence (especially Internet sources), documentation, and guidelines for reports and persuasive research papers. Chapter 10 culminates in a model research paper on cloning humans.

Chapter 7: Library Strategies

Chapter 7 introduces students to two main forms of research writing: the informational report and the two-sided (or many-sided) persuasive paper. You explore research questions that matter to you. The chapter presents library work divided into strategies that help you find information from appropriate standard resources: encyclopedias, bibliographies, indexes and online electronic databases, government documents, and other kinds of specialized information. You learn to do preliminary reading, keep a research notebook, and construct a master bibliography. By guiding you through the stages of writing a research proposal, chapter 7 makes a strong connection between thoughtful planning and effective research.

Chapter 8: Evaluating Evidence

Chapter 8 helps students evaluate data. All research information—and especially information from the Internet—requires careful analysis and evaluation of content, source, author, and credibility. The chapter emphasizes the importance of determining the reliability of information. You examine the relationship between evidence and reasoning with many conventions of evaluation: primary versus secondary information, weight of evidence, Occam's Razor (the rule of simplicity), impartiality, objectivity, accuracy, and more. This chapter assists you in applying critical thinking to a research problem: "A Test Case on Cloning Humans." You can analyze several excerpts from various sources and evaluate them for application to the question, "What conclusions should a researcher draw from this evidence?"

Chapter 9: Documentation

Chapter 9 contains a full presentation of documentation rules and problems based on the latest MLA and APA guides to in-text documentation. You learn common problems of documentation: how much to document, what to document, and how to document various kinds of quotations from sources. You learn about different forms of plagiarism and how to avoid plagiarism. You learn to use in-text rules governing authors' names and titles as well as citation forms for books, periodicals, and many other sources, including those on the Internet.

Chapter 10: Writing Your Research Paper

Chapter 10 presents student models of a report (on GHB, a date-rape drug), a persuasive two-sided paper (on whether or not humans should be cloned), and guidelines for writing reports and multiple-sided papers. The chapter includes models for formal outlines, abstracts, and various sections of a research paper (titles, introductions, presentation of evidence, conclusions), as well as guidelines for preparation of the finished paper based on both MLA and APA research guides.

The Concise Handbook on Grammar, Mechanics, and Usage functions as a condensed handbook for you to refer to when you encounter common problems with language: comma splices and run-on sentences, pronoun agreement, avoiding sexist language, subject and verb agreement, appropriate verb tenses, faulty parallelism, and misplaced modifiers. The chapter includes a collection of punctuation and mechanics guidelines and a glossary of usage.

We have written <u>Discovering Arguments: An Introduction to Critical Thinking and Writing, with Readings</u> to be accessible, stimulating, and useful. While you follow your instructor's assignments in this book, we encourage you to use the book recursively. For example, while you write an essay on a contradiction in chapter 4, you can return to chapter 1 to review guidelines for good titles, introductions, and conclusions. We hope you return to earlier chapters for review and jump ahead to any chapter you need—such as chapter 9 on documentation. We hope you will use the book as a ready reference tool, referring to any section you need to help you think, read, and write critically. If we have achieved our goals, you may decide to keep <u>Discovering Arguments</u> and use it throughout your college years and possibly beyond.

ACKNOWLEDGMENTS

We extend our gratitude to our families—to Joan and Bonnie, and especially to the younger members, Ryan, Ean, and Brenden—who patiently endured the time we devoted to the project.

Thanks to the Prentice Hall staff, ever professional and polite:

Vivian Garcia, Assistant Editor, English
Corey Good, Acquisitions Editor, English
Leah Jewell, Editor in Chief, English
Mary Rottino, Senior Managing Editor
Fran Russello, Production Liaison
Mary Ann Gloriande, Prepress and Manufacturing Buyer
Brandy Dawson, Marketing Manager
Phil Miller, President, Humanities and Social Sciences

Linda B. Pawelchak, Editorial/Production Services—Many thanks to Linda and the copy editor, Katherine Evancie, for their precise and exacting work

Jill Dougan, Permissions Specialist—Thanks for helping with the time-consuming work of tracking down permissions

Barb Tripp—Faculty secretary at Alma College for helping us with permissions

Special recognition to the librarians who helped us track down references: Jane Nowak, Department Manager, History, Los Angeles Public Library; Priscilla Perkins, Steven Vest, Peter Dollard, and Larry Hall, Alma College Librarians

Many thanks to special research assistants—Joan Memering and Bonnie Palmer for their comments and suggestions on the manuscript while maintaining house, home, and family in addition to their own work

Thanks to members of the profession who provided useful suggestions and constructive criticism: Barbara Fowler (Longview Community College), Paul J. Voss (Georgia State University), Alison Warriner (California State University–Hayward), Dan Damerville (Tallahassee Community College), Anne Laskaya (University of Oregon), Sandra Marshburn (West Virginia State College), Suzanne C. Padgett (North Lake College), William E. Sheidley (University of Southern Colorado), P. Douglas McKittrick (DeVry Institute of Technology–Atlanta), Wallis Leslie (DeAnza College), Ivonne Lamazares (Miami–Dade Community College), Jeffrey Vail (University of Delaware)

Dean Memering
William Palmer

Chapter 1

Communication and Persuasion: Logos, Pathos, Ethos

NOTICING AND THINKING

Here is your ticket for noticing things—
how sunlight is wide and democratic, how the rain
doesn't care who you are, how sounds will follow you home
and become songs that play back whenever you want them to.
    Adapted from William Stafford, You Must Revise Your Life 62

Please take this ticket. It's a ticket for a ride that can last your whole life. Noticing things is what critical thinkers do: they notice details, ideas, arguments. They notice bits of the world and try to make sense of what they see.

What do you notice in Stafford's lines? Do his images stir your thoughts at all? Stafford's images are more poetic than logical, yet do they make sense? Is sunlight "wide and democratic"? Often yes—it can shine on anybody. Does the rain care who you are? Not really, unless you imagine rain having a mind of its own. Do sounds follow you home and become songs? They can, yes, though not always. Stafford noticed these images, but as a critical thinker you can question them.

Suppose your capacity for noticing things were severely limited. Suppose you couldn't move your arms or legs or head. You couldn't point or wave, walk or run, talk or sing. How would you communicate your thoughts and feelings? Would you want to communicate at all?

This dramatic situation happened in 1995 to Jean-Dominique Bauby, a 43-year-old man, editor of Elle magazine in France, and father of two children.

One day he suddenly suffered a stroke to his brain stem. Afflicted by locked-in syndrome, he could move only his left eye. But, remarkably, this was enough for him to notice things and to communicate. His brain unimpaired, he created a system of blinking: someone would slowly recite the new alphabet Bauby had devised (in which the most common letters in French came first). Then he would blink when a certain letter he wanted was said. This way an observer could write down the letters and form Bauby's words and sentences. Through this method Bauby dictated a memoir about his experience called <u>The Diving Bell and the Butterfly</u>.

By contrast, you can communicate so easily: you can read and write and talk with others. Yet you can learn to notice more than you already do and to notice how your own mind works as well. You can develop thoughtful ways to explore your world and your own mind, persuasive ways to communicate. Our aim in this book is to help you develop these skills.

This book concerns critical thinking and its relationship to writing and reading. It's about thinking carefully. It's about using language that persuades readers, that moves them, that has effects on them—effects you intentionally create. Most of all, critical thinking means finding your own ideas, expressing them in appropriate language, and writing (or speaking) them so that others will respond the way you intend. In this book you will learn much about using words and sentences to help readers respond to your ideas.

COMMUNICATING CLEARLY AND EFFECTIVELY

How do writers create their effects? Why is some language effective and some not? If you want your readers to do something, what language should you use? Because all writers attempt to create effects with their words and sentences, you can say that, in general, all writing is to some degree persuasive. You may not want your readers to get up and do something physical like clean up the local river or park, but there are many other "effects" of language. Writers may seek agreement from their readers. They may seek acceptance.

You were born with the ability to think. But skilled thinkers have learned a procedure for thinking that the unskilled lack: the ability to notice problems, to reduce a problem to its components, and to examine possible solutions.

Thinking, communicating, persuading—they all go together when writers are in control of their writing. But how? Read the following essay by Amy Wu, a 20-year-old history major at New York University. <u>Newsweek</u> published her essay "Stop the Clock" for its My Turn column on 22 January 1996. As you read, consider how Amy Wu notices things, how well she communicates and persuades.

Stop the Clock

Amy Wu

My aunt tends to her house as if it were her child. The rooms are spotless, the 1
windows squeak, the kitchen counter is so shiny that I can see my reflection
and the floors are so finely waxed that my sister and I sometimes slide across
in socks and pretend that we are skating.

Smells of soy sauce, scallions and red bean soup drift from the kitchen 2
whenever I visit. The hum of the washing machine lulls me to sleep. In season,
there are roses in the garden, and vases hold flowers arranged like those in a
painting. My aunt enjoys keeping house, although she's wealthy enough to hire
someone to do it.

I'm a failure at housework. I've chosen to be inept and unlearn what my 3
aunt has spent so much time perfecting. At 13, I avoided domestic chores as
my contribution to the women's movement. Up to now, I've thought there were
more important things to do.

I am a member of a generation that is very concerned with saving time 4
but often unaware of why we're doing it. Like many, I'm nervous and jittery without a wristwatch and a daily planner. I am one of a growing number of students
who are completing college in three years instead of four—cramming credits in
the summer. We're living life on fast-forward without a pause button.

In my freshman year, my roommates and I survived on Chinese takeout, 5
express pizzas and taco take-home dinners. We ate lunch while walking to class.
Every day seemed an endless picnic as we ate with plastic utensils and paper
plates. It was fast and easy—no washing up. My girlfriends and I talked about
our mothers and grandmothers, models of domesticity, and pitied them. We
didn't see the benefits of staying at home, ironing clothes and making spaghetti
sauce when canned sauces were almost as good and cleaning services were so
convenient. A nearby store even sold throwaway underwear. "Save time," the
package read, "No laundry."

We baked brownies in 10 minutes in the microwave and ate the frosting from 6
the can because we were too impatient to wait for the brownies to cool. For a
while we thought about chipping in and buying a funky contraption that makes
toast, coffee and eggs. All you had to do was put in the raw ingredients the night
before and wake up to the smell of sizzling eggs, crispy toast and rich coffee.

My aunt was silent when I told her about utensils, microwave meals and 7
disposable underwear. "It's a waste of money," she finally said. I was angry as
I stared at her perfect garden, freshly ironed laundry and handmade curtains.
"Well, you're wasting your time," I said defensively. But I wasn't so sure.

It seems that all the kids I know are time-saving addicts. Everyone on 8
campus prefers e-mail to snail mail. The art of letter writing is long gone. I know
classmates who have forgotten how to write in script, and print like 5-year-olds.

More of us are listening to books instead of reading them. My roommate last year jogged while plugged in. She told me she'd listened to John Grisham's The Client. "You mean read," I corrected. "I didn't read a word," she said with pride.

My nearsighted friends opt for throw-away contacts and think the usual 9 lenses are tedious. A roommate prefers a sleeping bag so she doesn't have to make her bed. Instead of going to the library to do research, we cruise the Internet and log on to the Library of Congress.

Schoolkids take trips to the White House via Internet and Mosaic. I heard 10 that one school even considered canceling the eighth-grade Washington trip, a traditional rite of passage, because it's so easy to visit the capital on the Information Highway. I remember how excited my eighth-grade classmates and I were about being away from home for the first time. We stayed up late, ate Oreos in bed and roamed around the Lincoln Memorial, unsupervised by adults.

It isn't as if we're using the time we save for worthwhile pursuits like 11 volunteering at a soup kitchen. Most of my friends spend the extra minutes watching TV, listening to stereos, shopping, hanging out, chatting on the phone or snoozing.

When I visited my aunt last summer, I saw how happy she was after baking 12 bread or a cake, how proud she seemed whenever she made a salad with her homegrown tomatoes and cucumbers. Why bother when there are ready-made salads, ready-peeled and -cut fruit and five-minute frosting?

Once, when I went shopping with her, she bought ingredients to make a 13 birthday cake for her daughter. I pointed to a lavish-looking cake covered with pink roses. "Why don't you just buy one," I asked. "A cake is more than a cake," she replied. "It's the giving of energy, the thought behind it. You'll grow to understand."

Slowly, I am beginning to appreciate why my aunt takes pleasure in cook- 14 ing for her family, why the woman down the street made her daughter's wedding gown instead of opting for Vera Wang, why the old man next door spends so much time tending his garden. He offered me a bag of his fresh-grown tomatoes. "They're good," he said. "Not like the ones at the supermarket." He was right.

Not long ago, I spent a day making a meal for my family. As the pasta 15 boiled and the red peppers sizzled, I wrote a letter to my cousin in Canada. At first the pen felt strange, then reassuring. I hand-washed my favorite skirt and made chocolate cake for my younger sister's 13th birthday. It took great self-control not to slather on the icing before the cake cooled.

That night I grinned as my father and sister dug into the pasta, then the 16 cake, licking their lips in appreciation. It had been a long time since I'd felt so proud. A week later my cousin called and thanked me for my letter, the first handwritten correspondence she'd received in two years.

Sure, my generation has all the technological advances at our fingertips. 17 We're computer-savvy, and we have more time. But what are we really saving it for? In the end, we may lose more than we've gained by forgetting the important things in life. (14) □

Why did <u>Newsweek</u>'s editors choose to publish Amy Wu's essay? Wu communicates an important truth: obsessed with saving time, she and her generation don't spend their extra time usefully. Consequently, they have forgotten the value of doing simple activities with their own hands, like gardening, making meals, and writing letters. Her argument applies to many older people in our culture as well. Thus, her essay appeals to a wide audience.

How exactly does Wu communicate her truth? How does she use careful reasoning? What effects does she create through her choice of words and sentences? First, try contrasting Wu's essay with this condensed version of it:

> I don't understand why some people spend hours cooking and cleaning. I hate doing these things. I'm always in a rush. I eat fast food. I'm squeezing four years of college into three. I mean, my friends are the same—we're always hurrying. But we don't do much of anything useful with the time we save. It's pretty crazy really. But I do have a relative who likes to clean and cook, and she's been rubbing off on me. Recently I cooked a home-made meal for my family. They really liked it. I even wrote a letter instead of using e-mail. I think I'm going to start slowing down and start spending my time in more productive ways.

How is this paragraph different from Amy Wu's essay? Although the basic idea is essentially the same, is it clear and persuasive? Not really. It's general and vague, less convincing. Its language does little to create effects in readers—to engage readers, to make them interested or surprised, to move them to say, "Yes, that's exactly how it is with me too." The condensed version lacks reason and emotion; it lacks any real sense of the writer's personality or voice. Except for the main idea, possibly, there isn't much for readers to remember in this condensed version: there aren't any images.

Specific, Concrete Evidence

Having a valid opinion is not enough for clear communication and persuasion. An opinion or idea must be supported with specific evidence: convincing reasons, examples, and details. Amy Wu goes to great lengths to use specific, concrete evidence to prove her point. As a reader you can "see" what she means because she uses language that appeals to your senses of sight, smell, sound, touch, and taste. You can see her aunt's house in Wu's first paragraph, feel Wu sliding across the "finely waxed" floors, and smell her aunt's "soy sauce, scallions and red bean soup." You can sense Wu's own handmade meal too—"the pasta boiled and the red peppers sizzled."

Wu notices and shares so many details that she makes it hard for readers to miss her point—her thesis: "I am a member of a generation that is very concerned with saving time but often unaware of why we're doing it." You can appreciate the VCR metaphor which restates her thesis: "We're living life on fast-forward without a pause button." You can see that at the end of her essay

Wu cares more about slowing down and enjoying the pleasure of making things instead of buying them. Through her essay you can follow her reasoning as she moves from an obsession with saving time to an appreciation of savoring time.

When a writer like Amy Wu communicates clearly, she takes the time to defend her ideas with evidence that will persuade readers to identify with her and to consider whether they too are "time-saving addicts." Critical thinkers take time to support their ideas with details. When Wu asked her aunt why she didn't buy a cake instead of making one, her aunt replied, "A cake is more than a cake [. . .]. It's the giving of energy, the thought behind it." Excellent writing and thinking also require such giving of energy and thought—a commitment to clarity and to persuasion.

When you talk, do you always communicate clearly and persuasively? Suppose you are walking on campus and see a friend. She asks how you are, and you reply, "Fine, and you?" She smiles and responds, "Great." In this brief exchange, does your friend know what you mean by "fine"? Do you know what she means by "great"? Perhaps you weren't feeling fine at all but said so anyway. When you talk to people, you often give general responses. But when you write and want to communicate clearly and persuasively, you need to give reasons, examples, and details as Amy Wu does. Clarity is a hallmark of communication and critical thinking. In order to make a point or to defend an argument, you need to use clear and convincing evidence. Although this may sound simple, it's difficult to practice because people often speak in general language.

ACTIVITY 1

To practice communicating clearly, write two paragraphs about a quality of a person you know well: perhaps your roommate is caring, a friend is funny, or your father is generous. In the first paragraph try to communicate poorly—that is, intentionally be general and vague. In the second paragraph, try to communicate clearly—present sound reasons and specific, concrete evidence. Bring these paragraphs to your next class to share with other students.

Here is another My Turn essay written by a college student, Brian A. Courtney from the University of Tennessee, that <u>Newsweek</u> published on 13 February 1995. As you read it, consider how Courtney communicates and persuades. Also, notice what he does with words to create certain effects in readers.

Freedom from Choice

Brian A. Courtney

As my friend Denise and I trudged across the University of Tennessee campus 1
to our 9:05 a.m. class, we delivered countless head nods, "Heys" and "How ya'
doin's" to other African-Americans we passed along the way. We spoke to people
we knew as well as people we didn't know because it's an unwritten rule that
black people speak to one another when they pass. But when I stopped to greet
and hug one of my female friends, who happens to be white, Denise seemed a
little bothered. We continued our walk to class, and Denise expressed concern
that I might be coming down with a "fever." "I don't feel sick," I told her. As
it turns out, she was referring to "jungle fever," the condition where a black
man or woman is attracted to someone of the opposite race.

This encounter has not been an uncommon experience for me. That's why 2
the first 21 years of my life have felt like a never-ending tug of war. And quite
honestly, I'm not looking forward to being dragged through the mud for the rest
of my life. My white friends want me to act one way—white. My African-American friends want me to act another—black. Pleasing them both is nearly impossible and leaves little room to be just me.

The politically correct term for someone with my racial background is 3
"biracial" or "multiracial." My mother is fair-skinned with blond hair and blue
eyes. My father is dark-complexioned with prominent African-American
features and a head of woolly hair. When you combine the genetic makeup
of the two, you get me—golden-brown skin, semi-coarse hair and a whole
mess of freckles.

Someone once told me I was lucky to be biracial because I have the best 4
of both worlds. In some ways this is true. I have a huge family that's filled with
diversity and is as colorful as a box of Crayolas. My family is more open to
whomever I choose to date, whether that person is black, white, biracial, Asian
or whatever. But looking at the big picture, American society makes being biracial feel less like a blessing than a curse.

One reason is the American obsession with labeling. We feel the need to 5
label everyone and everything and group them into neatly defined categories.
Are you a Republican, a Democrat or an Independent? Are you pro-life or pro-
choice? Are you African-American, Caucasian or Native American? Not everyone
fits into such classifications. This presents a problem for me and the many biracial people living in the United States. The rest of the population seems more
comfortable when we choose to identify with one group. And it pressures us to
do so, forcing us to deny half of who we are.

Growing up in the small, predominantly white town of Maryville, Tenn., 6
I attended William Blount High School. I was one of a handful of minority
students—a raisin in a box of cornflakes, so to speak. Almost all of my peers,

many of whom I've known since grade school, were white. Over the years, they've commented on how different I am from other black people they know. The implication was that I'm better because I'm only <u>half</u> black. Acceptance into their world has meant talking as they talk, dressing as they dress and appreciating the same music. To reduce tension and make everyone feel comfortable, I've reacted by ignoring half of my identity and downplaying my ethnicity.

My experience at UT has been very similar. This time it's my African-Amer- 7
ican peers exerting pressure to choose. Some African-Americans on campus say I "talk too white." I dress like the boys in white fraternities. I have too many white friends. In other words, I'm not black enough. I'm a white "wanna-be." The other day, an African-American acquaintance told me I dress "bourgie." This means I dress very white—a pastel-colored polo, a pair of navy chinos and hiking boots. Before I came to terms with this kind of remark, a comment like this would have angered me, and I must admit that I was a little offended. But instead of showing my frustration, I let it ride, and I simply said, "Thank you." Surprised by this response, she said in disbelief, "You mean you agree?"

On more occasions than I dare to count, black friends have made sweep- 8
ing derogatory statements about the white race in general. "White people do this, or white people do that." Every time I hear them, I cringe. These comments refer not just to my white friends but to my mother and maternal grandmother as well. Why should I have to shun or hide my white heritage to enhance my ethnicity? Doesn't the fact that I have suffered the same preju-dices as every other African-American—and then some—count for something?

I do not blame my African-American or white friends for the problems 9
faced by biracial people in America. I blame society for not acknowledging us as a separate race. I am speaking not only for people who, like myself, are half black and half white, but also for those who are half white and half Asian, half white and half Hispanic, or half white and half whatever. Until American soci-ety recognizes us as a distinct group, we will continue to be pressured to choose one side of our heritage over the other.

Job applications, survey forms, college-entrance exams and the like ask 10
individuals to check only <u>one</u> box for race. For most of my life, I have marked BLACK because my skin color is the first thing people notice. However, I could just as honestly have marked WHITE. Somehow when I fill out these forms, I think the employers, administrators, researchers, teachers or whoever sees them will have a problem looking at my face and then accepting a big X by the word WHITE. In any case, checking BLACK or WHITE does not truly represent me. Only in recent years have some private universities added the category of BIRACIAL or MULTIRA-CIAL to their applications. I've heard that a few states now include these cate-gories on government forms.

One of the greatest things parents of biracial children can do is expose 11
them to <u>both</u> of their cultures. But what good does this do when in the end society makes us choose? Having a separate category marked BIRACIAL will not

magically put an end to the pressure to choose, but it will help people to stop judging us as just black or just white and see us for what we really are—both. (16) ☐

Like Amy Wu, Brian Courtney writes about something that matters to him and to many others. If the problem of being biracial affected only him or a few people, <u>Newsweek</u> might not have published his essay. How does Courtney communicate and persuade clearly and effectively?

He focuses his essay on an important issue—being biracial and having to choose to be black or white.

He states a clear thesis: "American society makes being biracial feel less like a blessing than a curse." He introduces this thesis in his second paragraph in which he refers to his life feeling "like a never-ending tug of war" between being black or white.

He supports his thesis with sound reasons: being biracial is difficult because of our country's "obsession with labeling." To cope with this problem, he has tried to "reduce tension [. . .] by ignoring half of my identity and downplaying my ethnicity." The problem is severe, he argues, because society does not "acknowledge us as a separate race." Then, he offers a reasonable solution to the problem: our society should recognize biracial people as a separate race by including "biracial" or "multiracial" categories on all forms that require people to mark their race.

He supports his thesis with convincing evidence: specific examples and details. His introduction serves as an interesting example—while he walks on campus his friend Denise is bothered because he greets a white female friend. Later he describes his parents and himself so you can visualize them: "My mother is fair-skinned with blond hair and blue eyes. My father is dark-complexioned with prominent African-American features and a head of woolly hair. When you combine the genetic makeup of the two, you get me—golden-brown skin, semi-coarse hair and a whole mess of freckles."

He uses language well to create certain effects in readers. His comparisons help readers see what he means: "I have a huge family that's filled with diversity and is as colorful as a box of Crayolas," and "I was one of a handful of minority students—a raisin in a box of cornflakes, so to speak." These images and others make Courtney an appealing and friendly person. His voice—the sound of his personality—is believable, credible, honest, friendly, sincere. You sense you can trust him.

He persuades readers that the problem of being biracial is real and important.

WRITING AN OPINION ESSAY

Writing opinion essays is useful because as a citizen of any community—whether school, work, town, or state—you will be asked to express your opinions and to defend them with persuasive arguments. How much of your daily life involves expressing your opinions? Much of it. Yet writing an opinion essay enables you to think more deliberately and carefully than you would in normal conversation. This, in turn, will strengthen your ability to express and defend your opinions when you talk.

ACTIVITY 2

Write an essay in which you support an opinion about something that matters to you, something that concerns you and other people. What do you value that you believe other people could benefit from reading and thinking about? What do you care about that you'd like your readers to care about too?

- To get started, write a page or two of notes in which you explore at least three possible ideas for an essay. Talk to yourself on paper about what's been on your mind lately that you'd like to address to a certain audience. Be prepared to hand in this writing for your next class. Because this is exploratory writing, you don't need to worry about grammar or spelling; instead, try to focus on finding ideas and supporting evidence, details.
- Your audience for your essay should be your classmates and teacher. However, if your final essay works especially well, you might consider submitting it to your school newspaper, your local paper, a national paper such as the <u>Christian Science Monitor</u>, or a magazine such as <u>Newsweek</u> for its My Turn column. Your essay should be 700 to 1,200 words ($2^1/_2$ to 5 pages) and contain an effective title, introduction, body, and conclusion.
- We have used two informal essays so far to show that you need not always write about complex, academic subjects in order to think and write clearly and persuasively. Experienced writers often give this advice: "Write about what you know." Amy Wu wrote about her realization that she and her generation could spend time more wisely; Brian Courtney wrote about the problems of being biracial in our society. They both used convincing reasons, examples, and details from their own experience to support their ideas. We invite you to do the same for your essay.
- Start writing your essay soon—today or tomorrow. After you do your exploratory writing to find possible ideas, begin a draft of your essay. While you write during the next few days, you should read the rest of this chapter and try to apply the principles of persuasion we present. You will benefit more by reading this chapter while you write your essay than you would by reading the entire chapter first.

WRITING PERSUASIVELY

Persuasive writing attempts to move your reader. The persuasive writer uses evidence—reasons, facts, examples, details—to cause readers to respond in some way. You can't force your readers, but you can appeal to them. You can appeal to your reader's mind, emotions, and character.

Persuasive writers attempt to get readers to respond as the writer wishes. To move readers you need facts, information, and evidence. You can't get your readers to accept the claim, for example, that cloning human cells would be immoral, if you don't know the facts about cloning. You can tell people the truth about cholesterol, tobacco, drugs, and death, and readers may even agree with you. Still, all that may not produce the desired change in their behaviors. Speakers and writers have known since ancient times that truth and logic alone are not always sufficient to move people. People sometimes rebel at being told what to do, even when they recognize that the advice is in their best interests. Many people are suspicious of anyone who seems to be trying to manipulate them.

Philosophers and orators of ancient Greece and Rome struggled with this conflict. Some philosophers insisted that argumentation should be concerned only with facts, logic, and absolute statements with which all reasonable people must agree. They admired statements such as, "Socrates is a man; all men are mortal—therefore Socrates is mortal." The beauty of such reasoning could be shown with mathematics, the philosophers said, "A is B; B is C—therefore A is C." The philosophers believed that such "truth" would persuade people. The orators, however, said such statements seem not very useful in real life. For one thing, you can't always know what the truth is; in most cases, you can only say what is <u>probably true</u>, not what is "absolutely true." If two people accuse each other of wrong doing, each denying what the other says, it's difficult to say what "truly" happened. You may have seen examples of cases in which much evidence could not prove absolutely what happened. The ancient orators knew that to persuade people it was often necessary—in addition to giving reasons and facts—to stir people's emotions and to convince them of the morality of both the argument and the speaker.

Even now many people believe only verifiable facts should constitute evidence. Our courts are founded on that presumption. Anything else is considered mere trickery. To get the facts, however, our courts are founded on the adversarial system. Thus, you can find even today courtroom scenes awash more in emotion than facts and reason, tearful witnesses and shocked, enraged lawyers (who learned their courtroom theatrics from those passed down from the ancients). In addition to emotion, modern lawyers, legislators, and politicians often rely heavily on moral arguments. "The defendant is a moral person," the jury is told, "with a family to support; this person is a regular churchgoer, a solid member of the community. What a shame for the community that such a fine, upright citizen should be dragged into court," the lawyers argue.

Instead of sticking to factual evidence that could be verified, ancient orators introduced emotions and morality into arguments. But philosophers insisted that students must be taught to use only logic and reason. Persuading audiences through emotional pleas or ethical presentations, the philosophers thought, was manipulation. One of the most important philosophers of the time, however, Aristotle, said speakers needed all three appeals in order to move audiences. Today we know that persuasion often requires all three appeals: logos, pathos, and ethos (appeals to reason, emotion, and character).

Objective Writing and Persuasive Writing

To understand persuasive writing, try contrasting it with "objective" writing. Objective means not expressing an opinion, not attempting to sway the reader one way or the other. News reporting, for example, often reports just the "facts," expressing no opinions. For this kind of writing reporters need to be clear and concise. The objective report is usually described as serious and restrained, rejecting humor and irony and imagination. It is limited to the essential facts. Readers identify this sort of writing as accurate and trustworthy—the language of information. For example:

> In a two-vehicle accident last night, several residents of our town were seriously injured, according to hospital personnel. Mr. Arthur Hulme and his two young sons suffered internal injuries when their 1998 Ford Taurus was struck head-on in a collision with a bus carrying members of the high school soccer team, six of whom were also badly hurt.

Newspapers are written this way because the "news" is for sale. Ultimately newspapers seek to make money. If the public doesn't like what they read or the way it is written, they won't buy. Scientific writing, too, is often called factual or "objective." For example:

> Scientists at Genetics Institute have successfully developed a method for producing human Factor IX without the need for human plasma or plasma proteins. This method, which uses a copy of the human Factor IX gene, is based on what is called recombinant DNA technology. [. . .] DNA contains all the genetic information that parents pass on to their children. The genes serve as the pattern or template with which the body makes cells, hormones, and proteins, such as Factor IX. (The Coalition for Hemophilia B 1)

And science, too, is expensive. Here, money can be lost if the writing isn't satisfactory. Scientists are tied to their publications, most of which are informative, factual, and objective. Objective writers give the impression that they present pure information without regard for an audience.

Persuasive writing, on the other hand, is clearly aimed at readers. Persuasive writing also uses facts. But whereas the news writer needs only to record the facts, persuasive writers must use the facts to move their readers. And persuasive writers often need to add more than facts to their arguments. Objective writers can ignore readers, but persuasive writers can't. To find a writer's awareness of readers, you should ask questions like these:

1. To whom is the writer speaking [writing]? What, if anything, does the writer want from the reader?
2. What are the writer's assumptions about readers?
3. What is the writing situation—why did the writer write this in the first place?
4. What is the writer's point—the thesis?
5. Why is the writer supplying these specific examples and details? (Why not just give a short summary)?
6. Why has the writer selected this or that particular word?
7. Why is the writer using sentences like these?

ACTIVITY 3

Look at the draft of the essay you're writing. On a separate page, ask yourself the preceding questions and write answers to them. As you revise your essay, doing different drafts of it, look back at your answers and add to them if you can.

The primary quality of persuasive writing is the interaction between writers and their readers. The persuasive writer attempts to move the reader—to cause the reader to understand the writer, to believe and trust the writer, to respond in some way the writer intends—mentally, emotionally, or physically. For the reader's sake, a writer uses one sort of language and not another. Amy Wu and Brian Courtney use persuasive writing in their <u>Newsweek</u> essays.

THE PERSUASIVE APPEALS

Reaching readers, getting them to respond to your writing, requires control of all of the elements of persuasive writing: selecting an appropriate subject, determining suitable language for your readers, and projecting an appealing personality. Writers cannot force or command readers to do anything. Skillful writers must appeal to their readers: to their minds, their emotions, and their ethics. You can reach your reader's mind with <u>logos</u> (reason), your reader's emotions with <u>pathos</u> (emotions), and your reader's ethics with <u>ethos</u> (morality).

Logos

To appeal to your reader's mind, you must give reasons, examples, and details. If your reasons are good and your examples and details are appropriate, your logos will be convincing. However, critical thinkers know that people can (and often do) resist logos. Writers can show facts and evidence yet still fail to move people. Suppose you were hired to write a flyer for a campaign aimed at getting more people to keep fire extinguishers in their homes. You might explain all the reasons why every home should have an approved fire extinguisher, why all adults and older children should be trained to use it, and why a law should be proposed making it illegal not to have one. You can show pictures of fires destroying homes, fires that could have been stopped with a home extinguisher. All these reasons and more could make a strong argument for the home fire extinguisher. Nevertheless many readers might do nothing. Logic alone often fails to move people. Critical thinkers know that people can be shown factual evidence and can even seem to agree with intelligent reasoning—yet still fail to do the right thing.

Using all the appeals together, effective writers convince through good reasoning, through a careful stirring of emotions, and through their own character. Logos is most powerful when it deals with absolute or "certain" information. Unfortunately, most of the time you have only "probable" evidence. You can't say the house will <u>certainly</u> burn down if you have no fire extinguisher, nor can you say your house is absolutely safe from fire if you do have an extinguisher. Logos is an important element of persuasion, but often you need other elements—especially in human affairs—to convince readers.

How reasonable is Deborah Prothrow-Stith, MD, in this passage from her book <u>Deadly Consequences</u>?

> While much about human aggression is not known, one fact is indisputable: Among all races, all classes, and in every corner of the globe men are more violent than women. This truth had led researchers to look for a particular male substance that explains violent outbursts. Discredited work done in the 1970s attempted, but failed, to establish the presence in violent males of an extra Y chromosome. Researchers today believe it is the male hormone testosterone that causes male violence. Testosterone courses through the bloodstream of all males. Do violent males have more testosterone than peaceful ones? This question has not yet been fully answered, but according to a small study done by the respected Swedish psychologist Dan Olweus, they do. "Testosterone poisoning," is the term Olweus uses to describe displays of male aggression. What is not clear, however, is whether testosterone causes violence or whether aggressive feelings and violent acts cause increased amounts of testosterone to be produced.
>
> I think there is a likelihood that testosterone plays some not yet fully understood role in male sex-role differentiation and aggression. However, I feel certain that neither this hormone, nor any hormone, is totally responsible. Presumably males in all nations possess reasonably equal amounts of testosterone, and yet rates of violence are far from equal worldwide. Socialization is the factor that differs from place to place. Some societies, like our own, clearly encourage young males to enact their violent feelings. Other societies convey to their young that non-violent outlets must be found for aggressive feelings. (9–10)

In this passage Prothrow-Stith asserts an argument that men are more violent than women—she claims this is a "fact" and "indisputable." We don't have the scientific data that supports her statement—all men everywhere are more violent than women—but neither can we dispute it. She summarizes some research that has attempted to build on this idea. Questioning the role of testosterone, she wonders if it causes violence or whether violence causes it to increase. She concludes that this hormone cannot by itself cause male aggression (else we cannot explain differences in male behavior around the world)—socialization also plays a significant role. We can infer, on the whole, that Prothrow-Stith appears to use effective logos: her appeals to reason make sense, and she seems fair-minded.

You may question her statement that our society "clearly encourage[s] young males to enact their violent feelings." This seems a broad generalization; however, on further reflection, you may agree that many popular movies and television shows do tend to glorify violence, and you may have observed peer groups encouraging violent behavior among males. In this passage Prothrow-Stith doesn't attempt to stir emotions in readers; she offers arguments and reasons. Her material here appeals to logos.

By contrast, later in her book, Prothrow-Stith combines pathos—the appeal of emotion—with logos:

> Why shouldn't the movie hero enjoy using violence? Why not, indeed, when only bad guys, never heroes, get hurt. You won't see Bruce Willis or Arnold Schwarzenegger shot through the spine, a quadriplegic, a paraplegic, a young man without sexual function, a young man with a permanent breathing tube who can only whisper his words from a hospital bed where he will pass the rest of his life. Who, then, if not the mass media, will tell our young that these are the true consequences of violence? (31)

Again Prothrow-Stith displays her questioning mind. Her long third sentence, however, appeals to your emotions: the image of a young man whispering from a hospital bed is sad and real; it seems odd to consider Bruce Willis or Arnold Schwarzenegger in this situation. Prothrow-Stith makes readers think about and feel violence.

Then too, readers can catch a glimpse of the author's ethos in her effort to be fair-minded. Prothrow-Stith acknowledges that media do not always promote violence:

> It ought to be noted, however, that not all of television's lessons are violent ones. Social learning does not just involve the modeling of negative behaviors. Researchers have shown that positive behaviors can be modeled, too. The people who produce <u>Sesame Street</u> and <u>Mr. Rogers</u> do a great job of providing models of desirable social behavior for young kids to emulate. Concern for others. The willingness to delay gratification. The capacity to compromise. All these behaviors and many more are made available to small

children who watch these programs. These lessons will not become patterns of behavior, however, unless home and schools provide reinforcement. When a child sees another child sharing on <u>Sesame Street</u> and then tries sharing at home, parents need to be vigilant. Positive behavior needs reinforcement or it will not reoccur. It is not enough for parents to say all the don'ts. "Don't hit your brother." "Don't take his toys." They must provide positive praise. "Gee, that was good sharing." "You did a good job helping your brother." "I know it's hard to share, but I can see you are really trying." The kind words, a friendly pat, and a smile reinforce and help cement the child's fledgling efforts to be a good citizen. (45)

In showing different points of view, Prothrow-Stith conveys the impression that she is a careful, critical thinker and is fair to both sides.

What might you infer about Prothrow-Stith's ethos? Does she seem trustworthy, believable, credible? We believe the fact that she cares about the complex problem of violence in our culture is a reason to respect her. If you knew more about her background, would her ethos have more persuasive appeal? Prothrow-Stith is a physician and former Massachusetts commissioner of public health who is now a professor at Harvard University. She has worked in emergency rooms and witnessed firsthand the deadly consequences of violence. If she were not a doctor of medicine and a public health expert, you might not accept her appeals to reason and emotion. Even without this biographical information, readers can hear the voice of a concerned individual discussing a serious problem in our society—the relationship of males and violence, hormones and socialization. Further, she seems fair. Prothrow-Stith does not overdo the pathos; she does not exaggerate the reality. Overall, she uses the restrained voice of the objective writer, a scientist, yet she persuades readers to care about this problem.

Logos, pathos, and ethos interplay with each other differently in any given act of communication. Critical thinkers pay attention to persuasive appeals. Noticing these appeals will enable you to use them intentionally while you write and to analyze them while you read.

Recognizing Logos

<u>Logos</u> is Greek for <u>word</u>, by which the Greeks meant "divine words," reason, the word of God. From <u>logos</u> comes our word <u>logic</u>. An appeal to <u>logos</u> is an appeal to reason: the writer tries to reach the reader's mind with rational arguments and evidence. <u>Logos</u> relies on reasons, examples, and facts. For example, consider this thesis: Mothers know they should not leave pots and pans with handles protruding over the edge of the stove. Reason [because]: Curious children may reach for the handles and pull hot cookery down on themselves.

Analyzing logos usually requires careful listening (or reading) and thinking, but you can improve your ability to listen, read, and think if you have some guidelines to help you: "A Critical Thinker's Guide for Analyzing Logos."

**A CRITICAL THINKER'S GUIDE
FOR ANALYZING LOGOS**

- What clues are there that the writer is trying to be logical?
- Is the writer's thesis reasonable and one worth considering?
- Is the writer's supporting evidence clear and convincing?
- Does the writer use sound reasons that make sense?
- Does the writer use accurate facts, examples, and details?

Read the following passage from S. I. Hayakawa's book <u>Language in Thought and Action</u>. As you read, consider Hayakawa's use of persuasive appeals—especially logos.

Language in Thought and Action

S. I. Hayakawa

People who think of themselves as tough-minded and realistic, among them influ-   1
ential political leaders and businessmen as well as go-getters and small-time
hustlers, tend to take it for granted that human nature is selfish and that life is
a struggle in which only the fittest may survive. According to this philosophy,
the basic law by which man must live, in spite of his surface veneer of civilization, is the law of the jungle. The "fittest" are those who can bring to the struggle superior force, superior cunning, and superior ruthlessness.

    The wide currency of this philosophy of the "survival of the fittest" enables   2
people who act ruthlessly and selfishly, whether in personal rivalries, business
competition, or international relations, to allay their consciences by telling themselves that they are only obeying a law of nature. But a disinterested observer is
entitled to ask whether the ruthlessness of the tiger, the cunning of the fox, and
obedience to the law of the jungle are, in their <u>human</u> applications, actually
evidences of <u>human</u> fitness to survive. If human beings are to pick up pointers
on behavior from the lower animals, are there not animals other than beasts of
prey from which we might learn lessons in survival?

    We might, for example, point to the rabbit or the deer and define fitness to   3
survive as superior rapidity in running away from our enemies. We might point to
the earthworm or the mole and define it as the ability to keep out of sight and
out of the way. We might point to the oyster or the housefly and define it as the
ability to propagate our kind faster than our enemies can eat us up. In Aldous
Huxley's <u>Brave New World</u>, we see a world designed by those who would model
human beings after the social ants. The world, under the management of a
superbrain trust, might be made as well integrated, smooth, and efficient as an

ant colony and, as Huxley shows, just about as meaningless. If we simply look to animals in order to define what we mean by "fitness to survive," there is no limit to the subhuman systems of behavior that can be devised: we may emulate lobsters, dogs, sparrows, parakeets, giraffes, skunks, or the parasitical worms, because they have all obviously survived in one way or another. We are still entitled to ask, however, if <u>human</u> survival does not revolve around a different kind of fitness from that of the lower animals. (8–9) □

Hayakawa appeals to reason in this passage. He doesn't give emotional examples; he doesn't stir your feelings. Rather he stirs your thoughts, helping you to consider the familiar idea of "survival of the fittest" in a new way. He questions whether only "beasts of prey" apply to human fitness. He offers readers a different perspective from which to see, describing less predatory kinds of animals and the ways they survive. In using this contrast, he enables you to see a problem in the notion of survival of the fittest. In his book Hayakawa presents this thesis: "Human fitness to survive means the ability to talk and write and listen and read in ways that increase the chances for you <u>and fellow-members of your species</u> to survive together" (17). Thus, what distinguishes humans from other animals is our ability to cooperate with each other through our use of language.

Because Hayakawa uses effective logos or reasoning, many readers are also impressed with his ethos or character: he seems intelligent, knowledgeable, and believable. It happens that Hayakawa was a professor of semantics (the study of human interaction through communication), president of San Francisco State College, and then a U.S. senator from California. This information might further impress you about his character, which in turn might help you find his thinking more credible and persuasive.

However, you don't always have biographical information about writers. You must rely on the ethos you infer or sense in the writing. In Hayakawa's work you can sense the ethics of a man that challenges people who use slogans like "survival of the fittest" and "the law of the jungle" to justify their own selfish behavior. He challenges by asking which animal is appropriate if people must make analogies for human survival? Animal analogies omit the important fact that humanity has survived all these eons, not with claw or fang, but with mind, language, and cooperation.

ACTIVITY 4

Look over the draft of your opinion essay. Examine your use of logos. Make a mark wherever you have used solid reasoning. How might you use reason more effectively? Make a different mark anywhere you believe you could supply additional reasons: write the additional reasons, facts, and examples on your draft.

Pathos

Any single appeal by itself may not be enough to move people. If you just want people to "think about" a problem, logos is a good appeal. But if you want people to do something or stop doing something they enjoy, many writers believe that pathos is essential.

Suppose a group of city engineers presents this argument:

> The old bridge out of town is weak and may soon collapse. It should be repaired or replaced. We need taxes to pay for this work.

The engineers report the truth. Except for the implication in "collapse" there is no emotion here. However, though the argument may be true, the voters are reluctant to vote themselves a tax increase. You can see the <u>logic</u> of the engineers' argument; nevertheless, that may not move the taxpayers. The old bridge has lasted this long; it will probably last a while longer. It's difficult to get the public to respond . . . until you involve their emotions. What is needed is a passionate speech writer who can create images. Using pathos and logos together, writers may be able to reach an otherwise reluctant audience:

> The old bridge is not safe! The school bus must cross it twice daily. Think of it—a busload of our children crossing over the steep ravine under that shaky bridge. The bridge is old and rusting. It creaks and groans. It moves! One of these days it <u>will</u> give way. Our kids may soon crash through and fall screaming to their death. A small increase in taxes can prevent an enormous tragedy. If we don't act now, we will be guilty, responsible for what is sure to happen.

<u>Pathos</u>, the ancients discovered, could overthrow logic. You have to think about reasons and examples, but your emotions stir you automatically: fear, pity, hope, anger, guilt. Officials try to get people to use seatbelts in their cars, but the statistics and logical data don't have as much impact on people as fear does.

In short, people can be moved with emotional appeals, and pathos is often stronger than logos. However, the early philosophers recognized there were dangers in pathos, too. They knew people might be "persuaded" to act against their better judgment. If a speech could be delivered with enough pathos, the emotions of a jury might be moved in sympathy with a criminal. Pathos is an appeal that is easy to abuse. Critical thinkers must beware of arguments aimed at their emotions. You must not let others use guilt, fear, and pity to manipulate you. And you must take care in using pathos yourself. You must be sure the pathos is legitimate, appropriate, and used with restraint.

Here is a selection by a surgeon who became a writer, Richard Selzer, from his book <u>Mortal Lessons: Notes on the Art of Surgery</u>. Notice how Selzer uses pathos:

I stand by the bed where a young woman lies, her face post-operative, her mouth   1
twisted in palsy, clownish. A tiny twig of the facial nerve, the one to the muscles
of her mouth, has been severed. She will be thus from now on. The surgeon had
followed with religious fervor the curve of her flesh; I promise you that. Nevertheless, to remove the tumor in her cheek, I had cut the little nerve.

Her young husband is in the room. He stands on the opposite side of the   2
bed, and together they seem to dwell in the evening lamplight, isolated from me,
private. Who are they, I ask myself, he and this wry-mouth I have made, who
gaze at and touch each other so generously, greedily? The young woman speaks.

"Will my mouth always be like this?" she asks.   3

"Yes," I say, "it will. It is because the nerve was cut."   4

She nods, and is silent. But the young man smiles.   5

"I like it," he says. "It is kind of cute."   6

All at once I <u>know</u> who he is. I understand, and I lower my gaze. One is not   7
bold in an encounter with a god. Unmindful, he bends to kiss her crooked mouth,
and I so close I can see how he twists his own lips to accommodate to hers, to
show her that their kiss still works. I remember that the gods appeared in ancient
Greece as mortals, and I hold my breath and let the wonder in. (45–46) □

Through his description Selzer enables you to imagine and visualize the
young woman whose facial nerve like "a tiny twig" has been severed. Although
she appears "clownish," her husband shows his love (and his moral character)
for her by claiming he likes her new mouth and by forming his lips to kiss hers.
The scene is at once sad yet full of love. Selzer's use of emotion can help you
think about how you might act if someone you loved suddenly changed physically. Would you be as supportive as the young man in this scene?

Consider Selzer's ethos. What does this little story reveal about his moral
character? Is he uncaring, disinterested, cold? Not at all. When he was a doctor,
he witnessed this act of love and was moved both emotionally and intellectually.
When it happened, he had a eureka moment (a sudden insight): he compares the
husband to a god from ancient Greece. Readers respond to Selzer's ethos because
he cares about this young couple. Selzer illustrates an appropriate use of pathos.

Each piece of writing has a different combination of logos, pathos, and
ethos. Some writing, such as objective reports or summaries, appeal entirely to
logos. Other writing, such as personal essays, may appeal more to pathos than
to logos. Even within the same essay, speech, or book, the combination of
appeals may change. Martin Luther King Jr.'s renowned "I Have a Dream"
speech contains powerful logos, pathos, and ethos; however, he appeals most
strongly to pathos at the end when he repeats "I have a dream." His emotional
refrain stirred his audience to action: to demonstrate nonviolently for civil rights.

Pathos is a powerful tool you can use to put your audience into a receptive
mood, to help them feel your messages. But if your audience senses that you are
manipulating their emotions, your pathos will backfire and cause your audience
to question your moral character (ethos). For example, some critics of Vice President Gore's speech during the Democratic National Convention in 1996 accused

him of being too heavy-handed with pathos. In her essay, "Gore's Tear-Jerking Speech Belies Tobacco Background," columnist Joan Beck writes about the speech:

> Those delegates to the Democratic convention who were moved to tears by Vice President Al Gore's poignant story about his sister's death from lung cancer might not have been so misty-eyed if they knew about Gore's long and profitable relationship with tobacco.
>
> With uncharacteristic emotion, Gore told the audience that he was called to the hospital one day in 1984 as his sister, Nancy, lay dying.
>
> "All of us had tried to find whatever new treatment or new approach might help," Gore said, "but all I could do was to say back to her with all the gentleness in my heart, 'I love you.' "
>
> Gore went on: "Tomorrow morning, another 13-year-old girl will start smoking. I love her, too. Three thousand young people in America will start smoking tomorrow. One thousand of them will die a death not unlike my sister's. And that is why, until I draw my last breath, I will pour my heart and soul into the cause of protecting our children from the dangers of smoking."
>
> Gore comes late to the fight against tobacco. He and his family made money by raising tobacco on their Tennessee farm for years—profiting from a product that killed lots of other people's sisters. (9A)

Joan Beck also acknowledges in her essay that Gore's family stopped producing tobacco after his sister died, but she asserts they "didn't stop when the surgeon general issued his sharp warning linking tobacco with illness and death in 1964." Critical of government officials taking campaign contributions from the tobacco industry, Beck raises questions about Gore's ethos because of the pathos in his speech.

Lawyers often use pathos to persuade juries; other lawyers warn juries not to be swayed by emotion. In the O. J. Simpson trial, jurors saw many gruesome photographs of Nicole Brown and Ronald Goldman. They heard intensely tearful testimony from Brown's sister and Goldman's father. But the defense persuaded the jury not to convict by pointing to the emotional and prejudicial nature of the evidence against the defendant.

In the case of Timothy McVeigh, convicted in the Oklahoma City bombing, the prosecutor used pathos when referring to the victims killed in the blast:

> Using McVeigh's own words against him, prosecutor Larry Mackey said the 168 people who died in the April 19, 1995 blast were not "tyrants whose blood had to be spilled to preserve liberty."
>
> "And certainly the 19 children that died that day were not storm troopers who had to die because of their association with an evil empire," he said. [. . .]
>
> Mackey described how McVeigh set the fuse on the truck bomb and could see the toys and cribs in the federal building's day-care center on his way to his getaway car, with only a "wall of windows" to protect the children from the blast.
>
> "America stood in shock. Who could do such a thing?" he said. "It has fallen to you, members of the jury, to answer this question [. . .] . The answer is clear— Tim McVeigh did it."

> [. . .] By the end, one juror and more than a dozen bombing survivors and relatives were crying. ("McVeigh Attorney" 13)

The defense attorney used logos in the following extract to counteract the effect of Mackey's emotional appeals:

> But in the defense summation, lead attorney Stephen Jones said the prosecution based much of its case on emotion. He urged jurors not to be swayed by sympathy the way the O. J. Simpson jury was swayed by race.[. . .] Rather, Jones argued, jurors should focus on the prosecution's evidence, which he said was badly flawed. (13)

When people's lives are at stake, the use of pathos and logos can make a dramatic difference in finding an accused person guilty or innocent. Whoever sends you messages—lawyers, TV reporters, essayists, advertisers—shapes their messages with persuasive appeals of logos, pathos, and ethos. After the Oklahoma bombing, many TV reports ended with a picture of the fence at the bomb site, a shrine of flowers in remembrance of the dead—an emotional appeal no one could miss.

Recognizing Pathos

"Pathos" comes from the Greek word for "suffering"; we use it to mean appealing to the emotions. From <u>pathos</u> comes the word <u>sympathy</u>: to have appropriate feelings for another person's emotions, to "feel for" that person. We also have <u>empathy</u>, which means to feel the same or similar emotion as another person. The word <u>pathetic</u> means pitiable, sad. Emotions are important components of the human psyche. Without emotions, people seem cold, mechanical, and less than human. But unscrupulous speakers can take advantage of emotions, and many people believe that emotions should be ruled out when you try to determine truth. Did the defendant commit the crime, yes or no? The fact that the defendant sits in court weeping piteously should have no bearing on the question. (The defendant may be faking anyway.)

Certainly critical thinkers must be aware that emotions may or may not have anything to do with "truth." In many cases emotions can be essential. Critical thinkers know it's possible to tell people all the scientific data about HIV and AIDS and how they are transmitted, but until you move people, nothing will change. Critical writers must recognize not only "logical or factual" truth but "emotional" truth as well. The breadth and depth of our emotions are part of the human miracle; we list a few here.

> Pathos: affection, anger, contempt, delight, despair, disgust, embarrassment, envy, excitement, fear, guilt, hope, horror, humiliation, humor, jealousy, joy, love, loyalty, passion, pity, pride, remorse, ridicule, sadness, shame, shock, shyness, sorrow, vengeance.

Human emotions can be difficult to analyze: "crying for joy" can look similar to crying for sorrow; silence might indicate anger, fear, or "hurt feelings." Experience will help you develop your ability to identify human emotions. For guidelines that can help you to analyze a writer's use of pathos, see "A Critical Thinker's Guide for Analyzing Pathos."

A CRITICAL THINKER'S GUIDE
FOR ANALYZING PATHOS

- What clues are there that the writer is trying to reach the reader's emotions?
- What emotions do you think the writer is trying to rouse: fear, guilt, anger?
- Is there any biased, slanted, or "loaded" language? (See Ambiguity in chapter 5.)
- Are there any controversial <u>ideas</u>, emotional subjects that will stir up passions?
- Who does the writer think the reader is—an average citizen, a loyal American, someone else? How can you tell?
- Is the pathos legitimate and appropriate (not faked or forced in order to influence an audience)?
- Is the pathos used with restraint (not exaggerated or overdone, such as wild hysterics)? With pathos, a little can go a long way. However, the opposite can work against a person as well. A speaker or writer absent of any emotion can give the impression of indifference.

Please read the following essay by <u>Chicago Tribune</u> columnist Bob Greene. As you do, look for any signs of pathos in it.

His Name Was Eric; He Wouldn't Steal, So His Life Was Stolen

Bob Greene

We may run out of names before we come up with an answer. Joseph, Lattie, 1
Robert, Delenna, Eric, Sarah, Richard, Shavon, Terrell . . . using the first names of the children, often in headlines, has become a signal that we realize children deserve to be treated gently, even in death, and even when the most unspeakable things are done to them.

So when something so horrid that it makes us ache is done to a child, 2
something that rises above the other daily horrors and makes the news, we refer
to the child by his or her first name.

The death of Eric Morris last week in Chicago would seem to be the one 3
case that defines heartbreak once and for all, the one case with the power to
crush us—but the truly crushing thing is that Eric's name soon will be
supplanted by another name.

Five years old, thrown out of a fourteenth-floor window as punishment, 4
police say, for refusing to steal. Five years old and—if the reports are accurate—
sentenced to death for wanting not to commit a crime. The question has been
posed: Was this a gang incident?

The instinct to talk in terms of gangs is an effort to explain the unex- 5
plainable, to create a distance, a barrier. You could do away with all the gangs,
you could even do away with all the guns, and you wouldn't begin to answer
the most difficult question. Which is: Where do we now turn in a world where
an 11-year-old boy and a 10-year-old boy are accused of forcing an 8-year-old
boy to loosen his grip on his 5-year-old brother, thus dropping the child 14
stories to his death? Where do we turn to extinguish the meanness and to fill
the utter, screaming emptiness?

If there is even a whisper of an answer, perhaps it is, against all odds, to 6
be found in the very circumstance of Eric's murder. For—if the official version
of why Eric was killed is, indeed, correct—a rather amazing thing happened.

Which is that this little boy—this little boy who reportedly was born with 7
heroin in his veins, this little boy who was beaten up before he died, this little
boy who went looking for a clubhouse as he was lured to the window from
which he was tossed—this little boy somehow learned, somehow understood,
that it was wrong to steal. This little boy, who we are told, was ordered to steal
candy for the older boys and was executed when he said no, knew the difference between right and wrong.

The worst thought, the thought that makes you lie awake, is the thought 8
of Eric's 8-year-old brother desperately holding onto his hand, trying to pull him
back into the window—and of the other boys biting and scratching at the older
brother's hand until he is forced to let go. The worst thought is the anguish of
Eric's brother, for the rest of his life, knowing that he did everything he could
possibly do to hold on, to rescue, and that he couldn't. That's our anguish, too,
all of us, as we see the list of first names grow longer, and don't know what to
do. That's our nightmare: that we want to hold on, want to help, want to rescue,
and that we can't, that we have failed. (19D) □

ACTIVITY 5

Make a list of any clues you find that suggest Greene is using pathos in his article. Then briefly explain how his use of pathos strengthens or weakens his

persuasion. Discuss whether Greene overdramatizes to stir your emotions. Should he have used more restraint?

Ethos

The most important attribute of any writer or speaker, Aristotle said, is ethos, the writer's character. Nothing is more important than the writer's <u>credibility</u>. You must believe writers in order for them to persuade you.

If readers don't trust a writer's character, they won't trust that writer's appeals to reason or to emotion. Richard Selzer expresses his concern and awe in his scene about the young couple; however, in other essays his ethos may appear less sensitive and more ironic. Much depends on the subject matter and Selzer's tone. Thus, you should not assume that the ethos of a writer in a particular essay will be the same ethos of that writer in another essay. Nor should you assume that a writer's ethos is an absolute reflection of the writer. The ethos or "voice" in writing is the person you hear talking to you in that given situation.

"Voice" is the sound of a writer's personality you hear in a text. The writer's character is part of that voice and has much influence on readers. When you write, your "voice" becomes a dominant element of what you write. Critical thinkers are aware of this. Aristotle wrote, "The whole affair of Rhetoric is the impression [to be made on an audience]." This means that writing strategies can be abused. To create a favorable impression on an audience, irresponsible persons can present themselves as responsible, and immoral persons can present themselves as moral. Critical thinkers know that ethos can be exploited to serve unethical ends. Several television ministers of the past found themselves ruined, even jailed, when the media discovered money collected "for God's work" really had been for the ministers' private use: expensive cars, mansions, high living. While pretending to be moral, honest preachers, they were really pulling an old-fashioned swindle on the public.

Ethos tells you whether the writer shares your morality. This was Aristotle's solution to the potential for abuse—"the problem"—in persuasion. Aristotle said that persuasion could be misused unless the speaker was a <u>vir bonum</u>, a good person. The writer has an obligation to be of the highest moral character, a person of good intentions, someone dedicated to truth, accuracy, and good will. That is, as a reader you need to believe the writer is moral and that the ethos you hear is true and honest. Your readers must also believe that you know your subject, that you offer sound reasons, that you are fair-minded, and that if you use an emotional appeal it is justified by the writing situation. Losing credibility with your readers is easy. But once lost, it is nearly impossible to recover.

Recognizing Ethos

The Greek word <u>ethos</u> means character. From it we have the word <u>ethics</u>. When you say that speakers or writers have "good" character, you imply that you approve of their morals, their sense of right and wrong; you share their values. What writers say and how they say it can be clues to their character. Most people respect writers who have a strong moral character, even if they don't agree with everything the writers say. The audience perceives whether the speaker is fair, honest, trustworthy, well-prepared (showing respect for the audience), and intelligent. It doesn't matter what speakers or writers say if you don't believe them.

As a critical thinker, you should be concerned about character, how others see your ethos. Here are a few of the attributes of character that most people recognize.

Ethos: benevolence, courage, credibility, decency, dedication, dignity, enthusiasm, good will, honesty, honor, idealism, intelligence, morality, nobility, patriotism, resolve, respect, responsibility, seriousness, sincerity, trustworthiness, valor, wisdom.

See "A Critical Thinker's Guide for Analyzing Ethos" for guidelines that can help you identify a writer's ethos.

A CRITICAL THINKER'S GUIDE FOR ANALYZING ETHOS

- What clues—words, phrases, sentences—in the writing make you believe this ethos is sincere, honest, trustworthy, and credible?
- What clues, if any, make you believe this ethos may be insincere, dishonest, untrustworthy, or not credible? (Remember that actors can project any ethos needed for the situation.)
- What is the writer's tone (attitude) toward the audience? Friendly? Concerned? Arrogant? Positive? Negative? Condescending? Humble? Something else?
- What is the writer's tone (attitude) toward the subject? Sincere? Insincere? Caring? Criticizing? Ironic? Sarcastic? Objective? Scientific? Others?
- Who is the writer? Is it someone famous or someone not well-known? How does that information affect the reader's reaction to the writing?
- What authority does the writer have on this subject? How can you tell whether the writer has experience with the subject?
- What is the author's attitude toward him- or herself? Arrogant? Self-important? Self-pitying? Self-Aggrandizing? Serious? Playful? Something else?

In August 1963 at the civil rights rally in Washington, D.C., hundreds of thousands of people gathered at the Lincoln Memorial to hear Martin Luther King Jr.'s "I Have a Dream" speech. Different people hear different things in that speech, but King's ethos comes through in many places. For example

> [T]here is something that I must say to my people who stand on the warm threshold which leads into the palace of justice. In the process of gaining our rightful place we must not be guilty of wrongful deeds. Let us not seek to satisfy our thirst for freedom by drinking from the cup of bitterness and hatred. We must forever conduct our struggle on the high plane of dignity and discipline. We must not allow our creative protest to degenerate into physical violence. Again and again we must rise to the majestic heights of meeting physical force with soul force. The marvelous new militancy which has engulfed the Negro community must not lead us to a distrust of all white people, for many of our white brothers, as evidenced by their presence here today, have come to realize that their destiny is tied up with our destiny and their freedom is inextricably bound to our freedom. We cannot walk alone.

Calling for unity with "white brothers," King reveals his concern for moral responsibility by asking all who desire justice not to seek their "rightful place" through "wrongful deeds." He believed nonviolence could be a moral power. In his call for blacks and whites to work together, King showed that the civil rights movement affected not only the oppressed but the entire nation: the ethos or character of all America was at stake.

Some readers might challenge some of the reasoning in "I Have a Dream," and certainly it is an emotional, passionate speech. But to recognize the ethos in it, ask yourself these questions:

1. What kind of a person is this "voice" you hear?
2. Is there anything specific that suggests a good or bad person to you?
3. Can you describe the ethos in "I Have a Dream"?
4. What do you <u>not</u> hear in King's voice? Analyze the speech using a contrary perspective.

Exploring these questions will help you understand why this speech is considered a masterpiece of logos, pathos, and ethos working together. (See Interchapter 5 for the full speech.)

A writer's appeals aren't always right or wrong, yes or no choices with which all readers can immediately agree. There is usually room for more than one interpretation; disagreements over interpretations are normal. But as a critical reader you should be able to cite evidence and provide reasonable explanations for your interpretation of a writer's appeals.

ACTIVITY 6

By now we hope you have written a rough draft of your persuasive essay. Analyze your own appeals to logos, pathos, ethos. Look for any clues that you are appealing to your readers' reasoning, emotions, and moral character. Jot notes to show where and how you might strengthen or tone down your appeals.

WRITING A PAPER

Finding Your Subject

Writers usually don't find writing subjects: the subjects find the writers. The subject comes from <u>the writing situation</u>. If you happen to be standing by when there is a traffic accident, the "situation" presents your writing subject. Depending on your point of view, you could write about irresponsible drivers, traffic congestion, the need for a sign or signal, or the tragedy of accidental death.

Observation is a writer's major skill. When you notice things—small details, big ideas, any surprising differences or likenesses, anything distinctive in some way, problems, possible solutions, or different perspectives—you can't help but think about them, about what they suggest or mean. Amy Wu in "Stop the Clock" noticed contrasts between herself and her aunt, contrasts in how they spent their time and behaved. Brian Courtney in "Freedom from Choice" noticed his own and other people's problems of being biracial. Amy and Brian both felt a need to write about their situations. Keep your eyes and ears open: noticing things will generate ideas for you. See "A Critical Thinker's Guide for Finding a Subject" for guidelines that can help you discover writing ideas.

Keeping a Notebook for Ideas

Writing is like other skills: you must keep practicing. If you don't exercise, your muscles will lose their tone, and if you don't write, your writing skills will lose their tone. Writing in a notebook can help you keep toned, and it can help you generate ideas as well:

1. Write to explore ideas and possible supporting evidence and persuasive appeals.
2. Write to reflect on your own process of writing—to evaluate your drafts, your title, introduction, conclusion.
3. Write to talk to yourself on paper about what you think and feel; about what's important to you, to your school, team, or club; to your town or city; to your country or your environment.

4. Most of all, write to keep a record of things you see, hear, smell, and feel. Use your notebook as an encyclopedia of what you observe. The more you write about your observations, the more you will discover how much there is to observe.

You can use an actual notebook, or separate pages, or a legal pad for your notes. As you read this book, we will often ask you to write notes, to explore, and to reflect.

The writing situation motivates you to write. For students, the beginning of a writing situation is often the writing assignment; however, you must look beyond the assignment for something in the real world, something that concerns you, someone you care about, or some group you value. Writing involves something that strikes a real vibration with you, the writer.

A CRITICAL THINKER'S GUIDE
FOR FINDING A SUBJECT

There are no definite rules about what is or is not worth writing about, but we offer these guidelines.

1. Write about something that matters to you, something that you honestly care about, something that concerns you and other people, something that might benefit others from reading. It's no good trying to write about things you're <u>not</u> interested in; you will bore yourself and your readers. If you are genuinely interested, not faking it, you can usually get your reader interested as well.

2. Some students say, "Nothing interesting has ever happened to me. I have nothing to write about." Try to find something where others find nothing. Writers must be able to see the invisible and hear the inaudible. Make yourself alert to potentialities.

3. What do readers want from the writer? They hope you will tell them some <u>truth</u>, something new, something different, and, if possible, something interesting, entertaining, or enlightening. Nobody wants to read about what is already obvious. Brian Courtney in "Freedom from Choice" educates readers who never thought about the problems of being biracial in our society. Readers also want writers to remind them of some important truth or value—as Amy Wu does in "Stop the Clock." Her idea that we should savor time is not entirely new, but her presentation of the idea is uniquely hers—her own combination of ethos, logos, and pathos makes her essay new. But new and different needn't mean extraordinary or fantastic. Consider Dr. Selzer's story

(box continues)

---

about the woman whose mouth was distorted because he had cut a nerve in her face. Most of the essays in our book aren't about big, unusual events. Most of them are based on small events in which writers paid attention.

4. How much evidence do you need? How many reasons, facts, examples, or details? Usually the best answer is the more the better, although it's possible to wear a reader down with minutiae. The quantity of evidence depends on the writing situation: if your boss asks you to write a one-page memo about a problem in your department, you must condense what you know. In a persuasive essay or a letter to an editor, you can present more specific information. Writers must decide how much is enough information in whatever they write. How many examples and details do Amy Wu and Brian Courtney use in their essays? Many. How much is enough evidence depends on the quality of the evidence and what kind it is—for example, firsthand observations, secondhand reports, or library material. The writer's problem is much more likely to be not enough detail rather than too much. There isn't any right answer here, but see "The Power of Threes" in interchapter 3.

ACTIVITY 7

Reflect in your notebook on the persuasive essay you are writing as you read this chapter. (1) How exactly did you discover your thesis, supporting evidence, and use of persuasive appeals? If you've tried more than one subject for this essay, reflect on why your first effort didn't satisfy you. (2) Evaluate how well you have communicated so far in your essay. What problems do you notice in your work?

Developing Your Thesis

In a well-developed paragraph or essay, or nearly any kind of writing, a subject is not enough. To reach readers, writers need a point they wish to make. A thesis is a statement of the writer's opinion. The writer implies, I want to explain something; I want to make a point. A thesis requires an opinion about a subject. The subject is <u>what</u> you write about; your thesis is <u>so-what</u> about it. For example

The Subject, The What	Point of View, The So-What
Our need for immediate gratification	produces time-saving addicts who ironically don't use time well.
Being biracial in our society	is a tug-of-war between being white or black . . . or red, brown, or yellow.

Critical thinkers know they can't write everything about anything; they need a way to limit the subject. The thesis serves this purpose: it limits your writing to only one aspect of the subject. Then too, with the thesis as a guide, your readers can see how well you have accomplished your <u>purpose</u>—to communicate clearly and to persuade your readers to agree with you.

Not every paper needs a thesis statement, especially when you have made your subject so clear that the thesis is obvious.

Evaluating Your Thesis Statement

Amy Wu and Brian Courtney both wrote thesis papers. When you try to persuade readers, a thesis statement presents and clarifies your position. It can be a helpful tool for your readers.

Your thesis is the point of your composition. It is the idea you want your readers to accept. For example, in 1999 NATO conducted an air attack on Yugoslavia. A good thesis might be, "It was wrong for NATO to attack Yugoslavia in 1999." What is the subject of this statement? <u>The NATO attack on Yugoslavia in 1999</u>. What is the view of this subject? <u>It was wrong</u>.

If you present a thesis, you must support it with evidence. Most readers will want to know why you say it was wrong. What are your reasons? Some readers may say, "I disagree. Bombing Yugoslavia was the right thing to do." Then you should ask, "Why? What are <u>your</u> reasons?" In short, reasonable people may discuss with each other what they believe about issues if (and only if) they can give evidence that supports their beliefs.

You can write your thesis statement so that it commits you to only one side, "It was wrong to bomb Yugoslavia." Or, if you prefer, you can discuss both sides: "Bombing Yugoslavia in 1999 was both right and wrong."

In some cases you may have a point to make that is not argumentative, for example, a historical paper, a process paper, or a news report:

> President Clinton and the Lewinsky Affair (a historical paper)
>
> How to Crash a Computer (a process paper, humorous)
>
> Tiger Woods: Golfing Wonder, 2000 (a news report or biography)

Some writers describe these as "statements of intent," meaning they identify the paper's main point when there is no arguable thesis.

For persuasive papers, however, you need a thesis, an opinion you can support with evidence. For help with your thesis statement, see "A Critical Thinker's Guide for Thesis Statements in Persuasive Essays" (p. 33).

ACTIVITY 8

Where do Amy Wu and Brian Courtney place their thesis statements in their essays? Where do they both restate their theses? How does the placement of each of their thesis statements affect their readers?

ACTIVITY 9

In your notebook, give your opinion about each of these thesis statements for a persuasive essay. Is each thesis statement good? (Why or why not?)

1. Psychologists believe they can detect "signals" that may identify potentially violent behavior, especially in the young.
2. Smoking tobacco causes cancer.
3. The president's line-item veto is good for the country.
4. TV and movies must accept some of the blame for the violence in our country.
5. America is becoming a second-rate country.

ACTIVITY 10

Look at your own persuasive essay. How well does your thesis work? Where do you state it? Would it help readers if you restated it? Write an evaluation of your own thesis statement according to the preceding criteria.

Appealing to an Audience

If you can't get readers to finish your introduction, you can't persuade them. You need to motivate them to start and to finish reading your essay.

It's a good idea to assume readers are as intelligent, educated, mature, and skillful at detecting fluff and baloney as you are. Generally, most readers are

A CRITICAL THINKER'S GUIDE FOR THESIS STATEMENTS IN PERSUASIVE ESSAYS

1. A thesis statement is an arguable opinion that can be supported with evidence.

2. A thesis statement must be clearly worded, without ambiguous language. A writer cannot argue that Stephen King's novels are <u>gruesome</u> unless that term can be unambiguously defined.

3. A thesis should not be so broad that it's pointless, such as "College is an interesting experience."

4. A thesis should not be a statement of your personal preferences. There is no point in claiming you like chocolate ice cream better than vanilla. A writer might use personal preferences as a strategy for comparing and contrasting, but few readers will be satisfied to learn that you "prefer" chocolate. You must find a way to show that the reader too should prefer one or the other flavor. Better yet might be to find a different thesis.

5. A good thesis statement should not argue the obvious: Racism is wrong. Criminals must be punished. A thesis should not argue simple matters of fact. Factual information is available in reference books—dictionaries, encyclopedias, or almanacs.

6. A good thesis statement should be worth thinking or arguing about. In a persuasive essay you should try to get your readers to say, "I never thought about it that way; you may be right."

7. Most readers prefer to find your thesis statement early, followed by your evidence. However, in less formal writing situations, you could place the thesis later in your paper, or even last. Occasionally, writers may use two sentences to state their theses: the second sentence clarifies the first. Also, writers may restate their thesis in different words. Restatements of a thesis often occur in conclusions.

8. A good thesis statement should not commit writers to more than they can deliver. An enormous subject, such as "The History of the Soviet Union Made Its Collapse Inevitable," may sound interesting but will require at least a book—perhaps more than one—to deal with it adequately. For a paper of a thousand words or less, such enormous subjects commit the writer to a shallow overview instead of a thorough treatment.

open-minded and willing to read your message. Writers deserve a "fair reading," and most readers are willing to give it. However, as soon as readers detect that your intention is aimed at them, the shields go up. Because you're trying to get readers to react in certain ways, you must get and keep their attention.

Analyzing Your Audience

It's your job to help your readers identify with you, to help them know that you are like them: a good person who has something worthwhile to say. Who are your readers? Why don't they agree with you already? What do you need to teach them?

Step One: Engage your reader right away. The introduction is a crucial part of the paper if you want readers to continue reading.

Step Two: Seek as many points of identity with your readers as possible. The philosopher Kenneth Burke said we trust those who are like us, who can see things through our eyes. Therefore, your best strategy is to convince readers that you understand them, that you are like them and share their values. Most readers will continue reading a writer who accepts their point of view and validates their ideas.

Step Three: Use effective appeals for your audience: logos, pathos, and ethos (reason, emotion, and character).

Step Four: Writers who appear insensitive or seem unjust cannot persuade. Some people have a powerful impulse to fudge, trick, or deceive. However, the point of persuasion is not to win but to change the situation. Writers who are caught fudging lose credibility and with it all power to persuade.

Step Five: You must structure all this within your allotted space. Much depends on the writing situation. Most teachers will specify the number of words to write, for example 500 words (about 2 pages). If you submit your writing for publication, persuasive essays for newspapers and magazines can run from 500 to 1,000 words, or more. Letters to an editor are usually limited to 250 to 500 words.

Step Six: What comes first; what order of presentation should you use? Traditional journalism uses the strongest-first strategy, because journalists assume readers may quit reading after the first paragraph (maybe after the first sentence or two). To prevent that, you must help your readers. Except in journalistic writing, modern writers say, start easy: move from the simplest, most readily acceptable supporting idea to, finally, the biggest, hardest ones. Hitting your reader between the eyes with your first shot is usually not a good strategy. If you use your heaviest material first, whatever comes next may sound anticlimactic. Your paper winds down like a spring losing energy: it gets weaker and finally ends on its least important point. Instead, go the other way: build in strength.

Step Seven: Writers must keep their tools clean and sharp. Your tools are primarily words and sentences. After you write a rough draft or two of your essay (be sure to number or date each draft to avoid confusion), carefully analyze your diction (word choice) and your sentence patterns. If readers discover many errors in grammar and spelling, they will assume a writer doesn't care much about communicating clearly—this, in turn, reflects poorly on the writer's ethos.

- Are your words precisely chosen and more specific than general?
- Could you omit any needless words?
- Have you checked your spelling?
- Are your sentences easy for readers to follow and understand?
- Do you use variety in punctuation and in sentence patterns?

- Have you proofread your sentences for mistakes such as comma splices, run-on sentences, pronoun disagreements? (See Interchapter 1 and the Concise Handbook.)

ACTIVITY 11

In your notebook reflect on the audience for your persuasive essay. Who exactly is your audience? How do you appeal to them? How do you help them identify with you? How do you keep their interest?

Engaging Your Audience

You can engage your audience by paying close attention to your title, introduction, and conclusion. Each of these important components can motivate your readers to care about what you have to say.

Features of Good Titles

- Good titles suggest or state the point of an essay.
- Good titles avoid too many words or too few words. Your title should be concise but informative.
- Good titles catch readers' attention.
- Good titles stir thought, often raising small questions for readers: "Well, how can that be?" " 'Freedom from Choice' from what?" "Stop the Clock" . . . why stop it?

Titles to Avoid

- Avoid general, boring titles, such as "An Interesting Problem" or "School and Work."
- Avoid renaming the assignment, such as "Essay 1" or "Persuasive Essay."
- Avoid titles that strain for effect, such as "Suppose You Were a Toe."

Some writers compose the title first; others wait until the paper is finished before deciding on the title. Some titles present themselves like eurekas midway through a draft.

Features of Good Introductions

- Like titles, good introductions need to catch the attention and interest of readers.
- The main purpose of an introduction is to present a writer's thesis statement announcing what the essay will illustrate. The thesis may be stated in the first

sentence. Some instructors like to see the thesis as the last sentence of the introduction as a transition to the rest of the paper. Although this strategy works
well for academic essays, less formal essays—such as Amy Wu's and Brian Courtney's—may take a little longer before stating a thesis. An informal essay may
spend two or three paragraphs describing a scene or telling a story before stating a thesis.

- Your introduction, like the paper itself, depends on your situation: What are you
  writing about, who are you writing to, what is your purpose? If your situation is
  formal, such as addressing the board of trustees at your school for money to
  increase the library's book holdings, your introduction is likely to be serious and
  direct.

- Your introduction reveals your voice right away—the sound of your personality
  that you want to project. If your essay is humorous, your introduction should
  convey a humorous <u>tone</u> or attitude toward your subject and your audience. Do
  you want to sound friendly, concerned, angry, grateful? Use your voice to project
  your attitude.

Please compare the following two introductory excerpts. How can you
account for the differences in them?

The Way We Were

Mark Schoofs

It was an experiment that could have come from a horror movie. Geneticist   1
Walter Gehring took a gene that controls the development of eyes in mice and
inserted it into fruit fly embryos, among the cells that normally develop into
legs. Legs they became—but with eyes all over them.

Researchers at the National Eye Institute recently repeated the experiment,   2
this time splicing in the eye gene from a squid. The flies grew eyes on their wings,
legs, and antennae—eyes that could actually respond to light. But because they
were not wired to the brain, the flies could not see through them.

Such grotesque flies are more than insect versions of Frankenstein's   3
monster. They are dramatic evidence that many genes are interchangeable among
species, that vastly different organisms use similar genetic building blocks. In
fact, the gene for eyes—called <u>Pax-6</u> in mice and squid—helps form the eyes
of humans, too. (36–38) □

Schoofs uses dramatic examples of genetic engineering to catch readers' attention, to pull you into his article, which examines the commonality of genes
between different species. The <u>Village Voice</u> is a New York newspaper that
appeals to a diverse audience of readers, most of whom are well-educated.

Human Cloning: Assessing the Ethical and Legal Quandaries

Lori B. Andrews

When the physicist Richard Seed announced in December that he intended to   1
clone humans, he was denounced by President Clinton and labeled a "mad scientist" by Donna Shalala, Secretary of Health and Human Services. Yet his controversial plan, along with recent advances in animal cloning, indicates that we may be closer to the cloning of humans than we previously had thought. Seed's announcement, and the subsequent scramble by policy makers—from state legislators to the Acting Commissioner of the Food and Drug Administration—to stop him, points out major problems in our current approach to regulating technologies used in human reproduction. (B4) □

Andrews uses a more traditional kind of introduction, which is suitable for her audience of academics. After referring to the Richard Seed controversy, she ends her paragraph with a clearly stated thesis. You can infer that Andrews will examine "major problems" in regulating reproduction technologies.

Introductory Strategies

<u>Start with a dramatic incident</u>, such as Mark Schoofs's description of splicing eye genes into different species.

<u>Start with a story relevant to the subject</u>, such as Brian Courtney's introduction in "Freedom from Choice."

<u>Start with a description</u>, such as the appearance of refugees in resettlement camps in a paper on foreign aid, a description of an airline disaster in a paper calling for rigorous maintenance of commercial airplanes, or Amy Wu's introduction in "Stop the Clock."

<u>Start with a contrast</u>, such as this: "It's one thing to mull over the possibility of cloning superstars such as Michael Jordan and to daydream about the effects on the NBA. It's quite another task to think about cloning yourself." (Deardorff and Buchanan)

<u>Start with a question or problem</u>, such as "What if you have leukemia and cloning your own bone marrow could save your life?" in a paper on the benefits of human cloning.

<u>Start by explaining the thesis</u>, such as "Cloning is not only less fun than sex, it would freeze evolution and destroy our chances for survival in the future." (Mautner 68)

<u>Start with a historical review</u>, such as the first sentence from an essay in the science journal <u>Nature</u>: "The history of science suggests that efforts to block its development are misguided and futile." ("Human Cloning Requires" 1)

Start with <u>unusual facts</u>, such as this:

> There are 435 members of the House of Representatives and 417 are white males. Ten of the others are women and nine are black. I belong to both of these minorities. That makes me a celebrity, a kind of side show attraction. I was the first American citizen to be elected to Congress in spite of the double drawbacks of being female and having skin darkened by melanin. (Chisholm, xi)

Start with a <u>quotation</u>, such as a relevant quote you know or you find. In her book <u>Clone</u>, Gina Kolata begins with this quote: "Many people wonder if this is a miracle for which we can thank God, or an ominous new way to play God ourselves." (Duff 1)

Start with a <u>definition</u>, such as the definition of the key term or some significant concept in your paper. Here is an example that defines a key term as well as provides data:

> More than three-quarters of the US public would consider a xenotransplant— the transplant of an animal organ into a human—for a loved one "if the organ or tissue was not available from a human," according to a poll carried out on behalf of the US National Kidney Foundation (NKF). (Butler 315)

Start with an <u>idea to be refuted</u>, such as a misconception, myth, or stereotype:

> Race and genetics form their own double helix, twisting together through history. The Nazis, as everyone knows, justified the death camps on the grounds that Jews and Gypsies were genetically inferior—but what is less known is that the Nazis took their cue from eugenics legislation passed in the United States. Here, race is defined primarily by skin color. Since that's a genetic trait, the logic goes, race itself must be genetic, and there are differences that are more than skin deep. [. . .] But that's not what modern genetics reveals. (Schoofs, "Myth of Race" 35)

Introductions to Avoid

- Avoid empty introductions that wander vaguely around the subject without saying anything, such as this: "Critical thinking is very interesting. There are many people who think critically. The rewards of critical thinking can be tremendous. There is nothing like witnessing a true critical thinker."
- The one sentence introduction rarely works well in essays, especially in academic writing where readers expect a full introduction (of one or more paragraphs) starting or ending with a thesis.
- Avoid boring conventional openings such as "In this paper I will . . . "
- Avoid apologizing: "I'm not really an expert on this subject, but I'll try to explain it."

Trying to make rules for "good conclusions" is a little like trying to make rules for good clothes: it is a highly individualistic activity. And there are many more kinds of papers and conclusions than we can make rules for. Here we can provide only a few of the general concepts writers use for papers that end with formal conclusions. You may not be able to use all of these features, but try to use those that seem appropriate for your paper.

Features of Good Conclusions

- The conclusion brings the essay to completion and gives the reader a sense of closure.
- The conclusion is memorable—the writer saves something interesting for the end.
- The conclusion reminds readers of the thesis or restates it in different words.
- The conclusion provides a brief but well-worded analysis of the point of the paper.
- The conclusion ends with a distinctive sentence: it may be a short sentence; it may be an especially well-worded or thoughtful sentence; it may be an image that stays with readers.

Concluding Strategies

<u>End by reflecting on the importance or implications of your thesis</u>, as Amy Wu does.

<u>End with a call to action</u>. James Baldwin calls for an end to the injustices of racism in his conclusion to <u>Notes of a Native Son</u>: "One must never, in one's own life, accept these injustices as commonplace but must fight them with all one's strength." (102)

<u>End with a hook</u>. Refer back to an idea, image, or question with which you began your essay. This gives your readers a satisfying sense of closure like a circle coming round. If, for example, you start an essay with a brief story about your mother's kindness, you can refer back to her kindness in your conclusion. Brian Courtney uses a hook from his title "Freedom from Choice" when he uses the word "choose" twice in his conclusion.

<u>End with a vivid image or picture</u> that reinforces your thesis and helps readers feel what you mean.

<u>End with a quotation</u> that reinforces your thesis in a memorable way.

<u>End with a question</u> that leaves readers pondering the significance of your essay. In her essay "Television and Free Time," Marie Winn argues that television programs what a child experiences. Her last sentence is, "When, then, is he going to live his <u>real life?</u>" (Winn 155)

<u>End by offering a solution to a problem</u> your essay concerns, as Brian Courtney does.

<u>End by striking a note of reasonable hope</u> that a problem or an issue will get better.

<u>End with a prediction</u> that logically follows from your thesis and evidence.

Conclusions to Avoid

- Avoid the one-sentence or very short conclusion. Like the one-sentence introduction, the one-sentence conclusion suggests there may be something wrong with the structure of your paper. The conclusion has a real purpose. It is the place where you should evaluate your evidence. In your conclusion you should tell your reader what the evidence means—what insights you draw from your paper.
- Avoid merely summarizing your paper or restating your thesis. The summary ending is a cliché that is so overused it seems amateurish.
- Avoid using an overused phrase, such as "In conclusion" or "To sum up." Try to be original.

- Avoid drawing attention to yourself instead of drawing attention to your point: "Now that I have reached the end of this time-consuming paper . . . "
- Avoid raising any new or irrelevant subjects in the conclusion.

By using effective titles, introductions, and conclusions, you will engage your audience more fully—you will help them pay attention to your thesis and supporting evidence as well as your appeals to logos, pathos, and ethos.

ACTIVITY 12

In your school's library, browse several magazines and newspapers for three examples each of titles, introductions, and conclusions that work well or don't work well. Photocopy the best three examples to share with the class. On the back of each example, briefly explain why you selected it. Also, be sure to document your sources, including the author's name; the title of the essay, editorial, or column; magazine or newspaper name; date of publication; and page number.

ACTIVITY 13

Evaluate the title, introduction, and conclusion of your own persuasive essay. Do they work well? If not, how can you improve them?

The art of persuasive communication is complex, yet with thoughtful practice you can strengthen your critical thinking, writing, and reading abilities. You have far fewer limitations than Jean-Dominique Bauby had when he composed <u>The Diving Bell and the Butterfly</u>. Yet in some ways you too may feel constrained. Perhaps you aren't noticing as much as you could. Maybe you aren't seeing different points of view. Maybe you aren't reasoning or arousing appropriate emotion as well as you'd like. However, you <u>can</u> work on these skills. Using logos, pathos, and ethos, you can learn to communicate persuasively.

ACTIVITY 14

ACTIVELY READING AN ESSAY

1. Make a photocopy of the essay "Bigger, But Not Better" by Ryan Grady Sample, a student at Duke University. Or go to your library and try to find the original print version of the essay, which fills one complete side of a page, and photocopy it.

2. Remember the line "Here is your ticket for noticing things"? We invite you to notice as much as you can in Sample's essay. To do this, <u>annotate</u> your photocopy, that is, write notes on it. Or write notes on a sheet of paper about the essay. Write what you notice about the following issues:

   —How Sample communicates his message—how does he do it? How does his title work? How does he present his thesis? How does his introduction work? How does his conclusion work? What do you think of his conclusion?

   —How Sample uses logos—clear reasoning, factual evidence, and statistics to help him argue his point.

   —How Sample uses pathos—appeals to his readers' emotions, their likes and dislikes, their sense of duty or patriotism.

   —How Sample uses ethos—appeals to his readers' ethics or morality, what they value as right and good, how he creates appeals to his own character. Where do you like him, trust him, perhaps respect him or not?

   —How Sample uses words and sentences—what do you notice about his style? What phrases or sentences catch your attention? Do you like them? Why? Why not? What does Sample do with words to create certain effects in readers?

3. At the bottom of the page or on the back of it, write a brief paragraph giving your opinion of "Bigger, But Not Better." Would you say it is an excellent, more or less okay, or a weak essay? Why? Bring your annotated photocopy (or page of notes) to the next class for discussion.

How to Annotate

When you annotate, you're free to create your own style. You can underline important sentences, such as the thesis statement. You can write brief or expansive comments in the margins on why you like or dislike something. Note any clues you see of Sample's use of logos, pathos, and ethos. Put stars above or beside any words or lines you like. Use braces {braces} in margins to mark key supporting evidence. Put question marks wherever you have a question or beside any place you're confused. Write out some of those questions. Put exclamation marks where you're surprised by something as you read— anytime you have a little eureka and say "oh!" or "wow!" Be aware of your biases: must you be a fisher in order to enjoy Ryan's essay?

Bigger, But Not Better

Ryan Grady Sample

I grew up a fisherman. It was predetermined. My father was a fisherman, my 1
grandfather and his father, too. I could tie flies before I could tie my own shoes.
I could catch a feisty cutthroat trout long before a baseball, and for second-grade
show and tell, I brought mounted fish instead of teddy bears. I was raised on
Saturday-morning fishing shows, not cartoons, and I'm still a sucker for spinning-
lure infomercials. I was out-fishing my eldest brother by the time I was nine.

Of course, the biggest contributor to my premature fishing prowess wasn't 2
my heredity or the Saturday-morning tutorials. It was that I grew up amid some
of the best freshwater fishing in the world. I'm a Montanan, and proud of it,
despite the Unabomber, the Capitol gunman and the Freemen.

Today, despite my big beginnings, I'm no Bill Dance or Bud Lilly. I'm not 3
even my dad. I fish for the love of it and I catch-and-release as much as I catch-
and-feast. I go home happy with nothing and I tell fish-fibs like every other
self-respecting fisherman.

Four years ago, on a fishing foray with my father, he told me about an 4
"invasion" of lake trout (which are approximately three times larger than the
cutthroat trout indigenous to the lake) in one of America's most prized fisheries:
Yellowstone Lake. At the time, an invasion seemed too strong a word to describe
anything a species of fish could do. I remember thinking, "Who cares?" I knew
the exotic lake trout were bigger than the cutthroats, and what's a few more
big fish for a fisherman?

Several summers later, having hooked my fair share of cutthroats, lake 5
trout and sticks, I asked myself again, "Who cares?" I do. And so should you,
if you have any interest—not necessarily in fishing—but in wildlife in general,
in environmental preservation or outdoor recreation. If none of that baits you
(attention, politicians), does money? Yellowstone Lake isn't just the premier
surviving inland trout fishery in North America, it's a big industry. In 1994, it
was estimated that the cumulative 30-year value of the fishery, if lake trout were
absent, was more than a billion dollars. The estimated value depreciates $640
million if the lake trout remain.

To the novice fisherman, the notion of a big fish's being somehow bad is 6
foreign. The only thinking such a fisherman does while in his element is: "Small
fish, good. Big fish, great." It may well have been one of these novice fishermen
who introduced the lake trout to Yellowstone Lake. The Park Service is sure that
someone transferred the lake trout from a nearby lake. It's not possible that the
lake trout's presence is the result of anything except human meddling.

Why will these bigger fish lessen the value of the fishery? The first concern 7
is that the lake trout prey on the smaller cutthroats. The cutthroats, having evolved
without any water-dwelling predators, make for easy meals for the lake trout, and

because they are so plentiful, the lake trout's population will continue to flourish until the cutthroat population is all but demolished. This isn't scientific speculation; it's been well documented. Similar introductions of lake trout into large, northwestern cutthroat fisheries have rendered them former cutthroat fisheries.

The lake trout, if allowed to dethrone the cutthroats, will then proceed 8 to rule Yellowstone Lake's ecosystem in a very different manner. Experts have designated the lake trout a keystone predator, likely to drastically alter the energy flow from the aquatic to terrestrial ecosystems of the Yellowstone valley. Because lake trout dwell in significantly deeper waters than do cutthroats, they are almost entirely unavailable to terrestrial predators. Grizzly bears, bald eagles, river otters, osprey—a total of 42 species—will suffer greatly with the loss of cutthroat abundance.

The decline in such a significant food source will force species to feed 9 elsewhere, putting an enormous amount of pressure on an already delicate balance of resources in the park. Eventually, those species less apt to change will die out. It's as if the lake trout, not the grizzly bear or the wolf, is the park's greatest predator. Its presence preys upon the well-being of the park as a whole.

Experts have assigned the Yellowstone fishery a value of "a billion dollars" 10 in an attempt to put a conceptual price tag on the priceless. But if you've ever hiked, fished or even driven in Yellowstone National Park, then a billion dollars doesn't seem to pick up the tip, much less the tab, when you consider the adverse effects the loss of the cutthroat trout will have on the entire park.

I'm not an environmental fanatic. Sometimes I throw aluminum cans in regu- 11 lar garbage containers when the recycling bin imposes a 10-step detour. I'm a fisherman. I've never called myself an "angler" because I manage to disobey the most practical laws of physics while fishing. I've purchased fishing equipment at Kmart, I always misremember either the size or number of fish I've caught in an outing, and I always tell my fishing-mates I "had a bite" when I didn't feel a tug.

But I'm not worried about me. I'm happy fishing in a wading pool under 12 a Montana sky if you tell me there are fish in there. I'm worried about my children and yours. Yellowstone Lake (and its surrounding ecosystem) is one of an uncountable number of natural areas humans have already altered or destroyed in ignorance, but it is one of the few we can still repair.

After considering many potential solutions, including those as farfetched as 13 introducing seals to prey on the lake trout, the Park Service prescribed a dose of good old-fashioned fishing to fend off the invading species. While fishermen are limiting the lake trout, park experts will be evaluating other means of eradication.

So, I don't know about you, but there's lake trout out there that need to 14 be caught. I just bought a new lure for my rod from a Saturday-morning infomercial, and I'm armed with some experience, limited skill and a lot of desire.

Chances are good that something is invading where you live. It might be 15 zebra mussels, it might be a coal-mining project, and such things may not make for easy fishing. But do what you can. I'll walk back to that recycling bin next time if you will. (14) □

ACTIVITY 15

Evaluate your own persuasive essay once more by annotating it. Make notes on it as you did for Ryan Grady Sample's essay. Then revise it once more, proofread, and edit it. Bring three copies to your next class to share with other students.

You can share copies in class or out, as your instructor thinks best. Either way, try to read each essay three times:

1. For content (thesis and evidence).
2. For appeals (any signs of logos, pathos, or ethos).
3. For style (use of word choice and sentences).

To evaluate classmates' essays and your own, consider the following advice:

> Point out at least three features that you like about each essay.
>
> Point out one or two features (no more) that you think could be improved in each essay. Suggest possible solutions to the problems.
>
> Underline any misspellings or problems in grammar, mechanics, or usage (see following section). Don't correct these problems for your classmates; point them out for the writers to fix.

Remember that you don't need to be hypercritical. It doesn't help to point out every little flaw; in fact, too much criticism is usually more harmful than helpful. Look first for what works well. Writers need some applause before taking a little criticism. For help with your evaluation, see "A Critical Thinker's Guide for Evaluating Writing."

A NOTE ON DEFINING GRAMMAR, MECHANICS, AND USAGE

Grammar refers to the way sentences are constructed. Is a certain sentence a complete thought . . . or a fragment? (See Handbook.)

Mechanics includes correctness of words and punctuation; for example, are there errors such as comma splices? Are there spelling errors or problems with apostrophes, hyphens, underlining, or capitalization? (See Handbook.)

Usage refers to words or phrases well-educated people believe are used either correctly or incorrectly. Is there awkward wording? Is parallel structure used carefully? Do verbs agree with their subjects? Do pronouns agree with their antecedents? Should you use "effect" or "affect," "imply" or "infer"? (See Handbook.)

A CRITICAL THINKER'S GUIDE
FOR EVALUATING WRITING

	Weak	*Okay*	*Strong*
Quality of thesis			
Quality of supporting evidence: reasons, examples, details, facts			
Quality of overall organization			
Title			
Introduction			
Conclusion			
Paragraphing			
Quality of persuasive appeals			
Logos			
Pathos			
Ethos			
Quality of stylistic tools			
Diction			
Punctuation variety: semicolons, colons, dashes			
Sentence variety			
Quality of sentence skills			
Grammar			
Mechanics (including spelling)			
Usage			

Interchapter 1

Style and Voice

DICTION

> How you say your message is part of what you say.

Diction means <u>word choice</u>: the words you choose when you write and speak. Your diction depends on your writing situation. If you write about a rock concert you attended and your audience is your peers, your language will be informal; if you write a letter to your college president arguing that tuition should not be increased, your language will be more formal.

Language can be compared to styles of clothing. <u>Informal language</u> is like wearing comfortable, everyday clothes; <u>formal language</u> is like wearing a suit or a dress. Yet you have various degrees of formal and informal diction:

> "Hey." "Hi." "Hello." "How do you do?" "Nice to make your acquaintance."

When you use formal language, you try to use correct grammar, and you avoid slang and informal expressions you might use when relaxing with close friends. In short, when writing formally, you use your best manners with words.

What does all this have to do with critical thinking? It is true that "I ain't got no money" conveys a similar thought to "I'm broke," "I don't have any money," and "I am out of funds." But these language choices also convey information about the writer. Your diction—word choice—enables readers to interpret your meaning as well as get a sense of you (your ethos). Inappropriate language may distort a writer's intent. It can add unexpected and undesirable information to a message. <u>How</u> you say your message is part of <u>what</u> you say.

Clarity and accuracy are two criteria of careful writing. To write clear and accurate sentences, you must pay attention to diction. Choosing the right words is an absolute law for writers.

Monosyllabic Words

Before we discuss monosyllabic words, we'd like you to do the following.

ACTIVITY 1

Write a fully developed paragraph of at least half a page (it may be longer).

1. Use only words of one syllable. (You can have up to three exceptions.)
2. Try to express something that has meaning or truth. Don't settle for "See Spot run." Spend at least 10 to 15 minutes writing a draft of this paragraph in your notebook. Then type the paragraph and bring it to class.[1] Please do not read ahead until you are finished.

ACTIVITY 2

Answer the following questions below your paragraph:

1. What problems did this activity pose for you?
2. What did you realize about diction from writing your paragraph?
3. Agree or disagree with each of the following statements:
    a. Nothing sophisticated can be addressed in words of one syllable.
    b. There is no way to make such a paragraph interesting.
    c. No one talks like this.

Please don't read ahead until you have finished this activity.

There are no "right" answers to the questions in the preceding activity. The answers depend on the paragraph you wrote and your experience writing it. Most

[1]Activity adapted from Dona J. Hickey, Developing a Written Voice (Mountain View, CA: Mayfield Publishing, 1993) 31–32.

students in our classes write paragraphs that are more meaningful and interesting than they had thought possible. Consider the diction and voice in this writing by a student.

```
Using One-Syllable Words

Kristine Stariha
```

He stamps a hoof while his eyes roll back. The late sun pours   1
gold on his red flank and hip. I trace the long line of his
strong back--my light hand meets the silk of his coat and
rests there. The smooth slope of his great side bids me mount.
He waits. I run deft hands up his taut chest, up through a
mass of coarse red mane. I take hold and pull my weight up. My
leg slides with ease down the broad bulk of flesh. I search
for reins that hide in the mounds of mane and grasp their
cracked old ends. He chews his bit--clank, clank. I feel him
strain and tense as he waits for my cue. When I turn him
loose, he breaks free in a surge of speed and strength, and
I'm lost in a mess of hair, dust, and the sweet smell of fresh
cut hay. We race at the vast orb of light. I grip tight with
weak knees and bend low to the arch of his huge neck--a whirl
of eyes and teeth and hair, and the hooves that pound, pound
the blurred ground. We chase the swift wind, my heels deep in
his sides. In great leaps and bounds we plunge toward the end
of the sky. And then I know God.

   When I rein him in, he stands still. His large chest   2
heaves up and down. I let loose my hold of mane and sweat and
fall back to earth.

Despite the limitations of monosyllabic words, Kristine's writing contains a clear voice—the sound of her personality. She sounds knowledgeable about horses, riding, nature. Her tone is clear as well: her attitude toward her audience shows that she wants readers to experience the joy she did during this ride. This is why she carefully uses concrete, specific details. Her attitude toward her subject shows that she loves this horse, is awed by him—she feels a sense of God when she rides.

We asked you to try this activity of writing with one-syllable words because we believe contrast produces awareness: we want you to think more about diction, to see that monosyllabic words can often replace multisyllabic words. One-syllable words can sound down to earth and real. You talk like this—at times.

Why (in your opinion) did Martin Luther King Jr. choose "I have a dream" instead of other ways to express his thought?

I possess an aspiration.
I have a vision of the future.

Martin Luther King Jr.'s sentence resonates. Our own eight-syllable and nine-syllable versions don't. With King's sentence of four syllables, less is more. Perhaps Dr. King thought <u>aspire</u> could suggest "ambition"; perhaps he believed <u>vision</u> could suggest "illusion" or "ghost." The short word <u>dream</u> carried his meaning without negative connotations. Then too, King was speaking to a vast audience of thousands and the short, simple <u>dream</u> was easiest to understand. Short words can give power and clarity.

Simplicity can also be elegant. According to Richard Selzer, this is the most beautiful sentence in the English language:

There but for the grace of God go I. (<u>Down from Troy</u> 88)

Why would Selzer make such a claim about a string of monosyllabic words? He values the simplicity of the words and the power of the message. What does it mean? If it weren't for God, the writer might not exist, might not be able to appreciate each day. (Selzer was a surgeon.) This short sentence expresses a powerful idea and implies others in just nine syllables.

Indeed, you can write well with many words of one syllable. Monosyllabic words can clarify and emphasize thoughts and feelings.

Multisyllabic Words

Although strings of monosyllabic words often contain power, your writing will sound elementary if you rely on them too much. What are the effects of using multisyllabic words?

ACTIVITY 3

Write a fully developed paragraph of at least half a page (it may be longer).

1. Use as many long multisyllabic words as you can to see what they do to your voice.
2. Use as few monosyllabic words as you can.
3. Try to express something that has meaning or truth.

Spend at least 10 to 15 minutes writing a draft of this paragraph in your notebook. Type the paragraph and bring it to class. <u>Please don't read ahead until you are finished</u>.

ACTIVITY 4

Answer the following questions below your paragraph:

1. What problems did this activity pose for you?
2. What did you realize about diction from writing your paragraph?
3. How would you describe your voice in your paragraph?
4. What differences in your voice do you hear in the two paragraphs—the one with monosyllabic words and the one with mostly multisyllabic words? Which voice do you prefer? Why?

Please don't read ahead until you have finished this activity.

Pretentious Writing

When you write and speak, you naturally use a combination of multi- and monosyllabic words. But using an abundance of long words does change a writer's voice. Consider this paragraph by a student.

```
Precipitation

Dan Scripps


Linguistically, the English language offers speakers fewer          1
varieties in expressing the concept of precipitation--what is
commonly referred to as "snow"--than many Eskimo languages.
Perhaps this stems from the reality that snow occupies a
greater importance to the people of the Eskimo community than
those living closer to the equator. Critics argue that the
variety of expressions for this particular concept indicates
that Eskimos are unable to process thoughts abstractly and
therefore have an inherently inferior language to standard
English. Others disagree, arguing that this variety indicates
far greater capacity and therefore a superior language. Still
others argue that it indicates nothing more than a difference   2
in reality, and the amount of snow in regions occupied primar-
ily by speakers of these Eskimo languages necessitates a
greater number of options for expressing this seemingly unin-
teresting English word.
```

This paragraph does not represent Dan's natural voice; he wrote it to satisfy his writing situation—this assignment. Dan's writing sounds more "intellectual" than Kristine's paragraph using only single-syllable words. Although he makes and supports an interesting point, his writing sounds stuffy and pretentious.

Pretentious writing is a kind of overstatement: through inflated diction and complex sentences, the writer "pretends" that the writing is more important than it really is. Dan writes about snow, but his language is full of words like precipitation.

Although children enjoy saying super long words like "antidisestablishmentarianism," writing and thinking can sound humorous or foolish if diction is inflated too much, as student Gavin McMacken shows in a sentence that uses big words just for fun:

> I was disgruntled after perceiving that the indicator on the gasoline calculator neighbored the bottom marking.

Gavin is playing with language here, his voice extremely artificial. But he succeeds in using many big words to see what they can do to his voice—the sound of his personality.

You don't need pretentious writing. Using big words to impress readers is a sure sign of amateur writing. Choose any word because it is the most accurate word to express your thought. Dona Hickey explains that big words often cause separation between a writer and readers:

> Multisyllabic words are often used to create wide distance between speaker and audience, sometimes for the sake of objectivity and high seriousness. But at other times, they are used to create intentional ambiguity, to establish superiority, and to exclude a general audience—those listeners who are not insiders, not members of a profession. (37)

George Will writes his Newsweek column for a wide general audience, but he sometimes uses diction that many readers find hard to understand:

> Postmodernism is the degenerate egalitarianism of the intelligentsia. ("Torricelli's Larger Point" 78)

Why does Will do this? His diction reflects his voice—the sound of his personality. Well educated and intellectual, he knows what he means and doesn't always care if some readers don't. His tone toward his audience may seem superior or elitist at times.

Scientific language is often multisyllabic. Students studying anatomy and physiology, for example, must know words concerning hamstring muscles, such as semitendinosus and semimembranosus. As a boy Richard Selzer loved to read his father's medical textbooks. They introduced him to long words in a positive way:

> It was then and there that I first became aware of the rich, alliterative language of medicine. I remember that some of the best words began with the letter

C. "Cerebellum," I said out loud and let the word drip off the end of my tongue like melted chocolate. "Carcinoma"—it sounded rather like that aria from <u>Rigoletto</u> that Mother used to sing. And then I learned the word that made a surgeon of me—"Choledochojejunostomy." All those syllables marching across the page, ending in that terminal <u>y</u>. It didn't matter what it meant— if that was the way surgeons talked, I was going to be one of them. (<u>Down from Troy</u> 13–14)

To be a writer, you must be a reader—like Richard Selzer. You must learn to care about words. To write with care, you must choose words to express your thoughts and to persuade your audience. Do you own a good dictionary? It's important to find the accurate, precise words you need, and it's important to replace difficult words with simpler ones. Thoughtful writers want their voice to be heard, not suffered through. You need the best words to suit your thoughts.

A comment by a student reveals an important lesson about diction and voice: "Big words make BS-ing instructors easier." But critical thinkers should not use words to con people because other critical thinkers can usually detect "BS." Using inflated diction to impress others reflects poor ethos. Credibility is easy to lose and difficult to recover. In the world of reading and writing, ethos is central.

When you write essays, your voice should sound natural. Even though your voice changes, depending on your writing situation, the personality expressed through your voice should sound like you. Choose words to express yourself clearly and concisely—not to impress others. Careful attention to diction will help you present your ideas the way you want them to be heard.

ACTIVITY 5

Look at your diction—your word choice—in your current writing. Notice the following:

Do you use any strings of monosyllabic words for emphasis?

Do you use any needlessly complex (multisyllabic) words that you could replace with simpler words?

Do you present your voice the way you want it to be heard?

Choose one of your paragraphs and rewrite it to improve its diction.

OTHER FEATURES OF DICTION

We have focused so far on monosyllabic and multisyllabic words to show how diction can strengthen meaning and voice. Other features of diction you should know are specific or general, concrete or abstract, literal or figurative, and the power of precise words.

Specific or General

A specific word is one that refers to particular things, persons, or events. Specificity involves precise details: black cherry ice cream, Mark McGwire, Battle of the Little Bighorn. A general word, however, is one that refers to a group or class; it "generalizes" where we wish the writer would be specific: dessert, athlete, conflict. Specific details help readers visualize and comprehend information.

General: Many species will suffer greatly without the smaller fish.
Specific: Grizzly bears, bald eagles, river otters, osprey—a total of 42 species—will suffer greatly with the loss of cutthroat abundance. (Sample)

General: It can cost a lot to hire lawyers to defend your pets in court, some people are discovering.
Specific: Nainan Ko, a businessman in Lincoln, Mass., paid $20,000 for the legal defense of his St. Bernards, Baubei and Shingan. (Larrabee 1–2)

General language often will cause readers to ask, "What do you mean? Can you give an example?"

General: Earplugs are cheap and come in different styles.
Specific: For roughly the cost of <u>bus fare</u>, anyone can buy a pair of <u>drugstore earplugs</u>. Their noise-reduction levels (ranging from about <u>20 dB</u> to <u>30 dB</u>) and styles (<u>foam, silicone and wax</u>) aren't all that important. (emphasis ours) (Kalb 76)

Too much generalizing robs your writing of clarity and power. Then too, writing in generalities can suggest writers don't respect their readers. Giving specific details makes your writing sound informed; it tells your reader you know what you're talking about. The more specific your language is, the clearer your communication will be.

ACTIVITY 6

In your notebook write two paragraphs of several sentences on the same topic—perhaps a quality of your school that you like or dislike a lot. In one paragraph use very specific language. In the other use very general language. Type both and bring them to class.

Concrete or Abstract

Concrete means physical or sensory: words referring to sight, sound, smell, taste, and touch. They bring to mind <u>images</u>.

> The frog wasn't <u>green</u> at all, but the color of <u>wet hickory bark</u>. (Dillard, <u>Pilgrim at Tinker Creek</u> 18)

> As the <u>pasta boiled</u> and the <u>red peppers sizzled</u>, I wrote a <u>letter</u> to my cousin in Canada. At first the <u>pen</u> felt strange, then reassuring. I <u>hand-washed</u> my favorite <u>skirt</u> and made <u>chocolate cake</u> for my younger sister's 13th birthday. It took great self-control not to <u>slather</u> on the <u>icing</u> before the <u>cake cooled</u>. (Wu)

> My mother is <u>fair-skinned</u> with <u>blond hair</u> and <u>blue eyes</u>. My father is <u>dark-complexioned</u> with prominent African-American features and a <u>head of woolly hair</u>. When you combine the genetic makeup of the two, you get me—<u>golden-brown skin</u>, <u>semi-coarse hair</u> and a whole <u>mess of freckles</u>. (Courtney)

Abstract means ideas and qualities we cannot detect with our physical senses, such as <u>loneliness</u>, <u>freedom</u>, <u>democracy</u>, <u>cognition</u>, <u>colonialism</u>, <u>education</u>.

> The philosophy of existentialism is transformational.

Abstract diction is similar to general diction: both operate at the level of ideas. Concrete diction is similar to specific diction: both operate at the level of supporting evidence. However, the more abstract writing is, the harder it is to read and understand. Without concrete evidence, your readers may feel you haven't thought through your ideas.

Should you never use abstract language? There are legitimate uses for such language: philosophy, scientific discussions, legal documents, governmental documents, language about ideas, and so on. Is there a common denominator in these? Yes, educated writers communicating with educated readers:

> Congress is considering impeachment proceedings against the president. The report and other evidence submitted by the independent counsel suggest that the president may have committed impeachable offenses.

When educated writers write to educated readers, they may resort to abstract language like this, though not for long. To clarify abstractions, writers must use specific and concrete evidence.

ACTIVITY 7

In your notebook write a least three ideas you think the class should consider, such as more recycling on campus, more lighting at night on campus, or more help with computers. Select one of these and write a paragraph using specific and concrete language to illustrate your idea.

Literal or Figurative

Literal Language

The literal meaning of a word is its plain sense. It is the objective or dictionary meaning. A literal, or denotative, meaning of <u>chair</u> is a seat, furniture for sitting, traditionally supported by four legs and a back piece, though there are a number of variations today (such as beanbag chairs).

In addition to denotation, many words have <u>connotation</u>: implied or associative meanings. Words can acquire positive or negative connotations—overtones of meaning not listed in a dictionary. "Chair" carries connotations of <u>electric chair</u>, <u>wheel chair</u>, and <u>dental chair</u>. The word <u>dog</u> indicates a canine animal, but it can be used to indicate people as well. "You dirty dog" has a negative implication; "you old dog" can imply a positive meaning. The word <u>home</u> carries connotations of shelter, security, and love for most people, but it can carry negative associations of abuse as well. These associations and especially the emotions they invoke are what is meant by connotations.

Figurative Language

Comparisons can show what you mean and give your writing energy. You can make <u>literal</u> comparisons: Nelson Mandela, the former president of South Africa, spoke with all the dignity and nobility of any other world leader.

You can also make figurative comparisons. Metaphors and similes are the most common figures of speech.

Metaphor: A metaphor is an implied comparison ("implied" because writers don't say they are making a comparison).

We're living life on fast-forward without a pause button. (Wu 14)

The mind is not a piece of blotting paper that absorbs and retains automatically. It is rather a living organism that has to search for its food. (Dewey, <u>How to Think</u> 261–62)

Simile: A simile is a direct comparison using the word <u>like</u> or <u>as</u>.

> ALS is like a lit candle: it melts your nerves and leaves your body a pile of wax. (Albom, <u>Tuesdays with Morrie</u> 9)

> The landscapes of all our lives become as full of craters as the surface of the moon. (Quindlen, "Whoever We Are" 11A)

(See "Creativity and Explanation" in chapter 4 for more on metaphors and similes.)

Avoid Clichés

As a critical thinker you should notice and avoid <u>clichés</u>: old familiar expressions considered trite and no longer forceful. They are the opposite of effective figures of speech. Avoid clichés such as the following:

a chip off the old block	end of my rope	ripe old age
anything and everything	few and far between	rude awakening
as busy as a bee	gentle as a lamb	short but sweet
as soft as silk	going down the drain	sigh of relief
a spoiled brat	hard as a rock	sight for sore eyes
at a loss for words	in this day and age	sink or swim
at the crack of dawn	last straw	stand in awe
clear as day	needless to say	tried and true
crying shame	nipped in the bud	white as snow
drop in the bucket	pain in the neck	

Clichés are signs of weak or lazy thinking. They suggest a writer's inexperience with using careful diction. If you cannot think of another way to say something, it may be better not to say it at all than to use a cliché.

Style isn't simply a matter of fixing up words after ideas have been written. Ideas are composed of words, and when the words are not accurate, the ideas will not be accurate. Pay close attention to words: make your language say what you mean.

ACTIVITY 8

Try writing some metaphors and similes about yourself or someone you know. Write three of each in your notebook. For example, "When I'm depressed, I'm like a car without fuel." "When I'm tired, I'm like a library with its lights out." Bring them to class to share.

Precise Words

Well-chosen words are not simply ornaments. They bring energy and strength to your sentences. They can help your readers listen and understand. Jennifer Woodruff, a student, wrote this:

> I was taught that it was better to be analytical than personal. So I began to saturate my work with long sentences and big words to make my writing sound more intelligent.

Her precise verb <u>saturate</u> works well; it suggests drenching. It's a stronger word than <u>fill</u> because of its associations with heavy soaking. Note what happens when Stephen Jay Gould uses an ordinary word in an unexpected context:

> DiMaggio dribbled one down the third-base line, easily beating the throw because the third baseman, expecting the usual, was playing far back. (470)

You don't usually hear or read <u>dribbled</u> in reference to baseball, but this word helps readers visualize the ball. Here are some other examples of precise words:

> Experience, particularly in childhood, <u>sculpts</u> the brain. (Goleman, <u>Emotional Intelligence</u> 224)

> I remember the air <u>carved</u> by bees. (Selzer, <u>Confessions of a Knife</u> 14)

> Fireflies <u>throbbed</u> in the heavy blackness, sending out ardent messages. (Erdrich 19)

Some students assume they should try to find new and unusual words to plant in their writing. That's a serious mistake. Never use a word you haven't learned thoroughly and made part of your vocabulary. It's easy to make yourself look pretentious and foolish:

> You guys are so supercilious; can't you ever be serious?

The word <u>supercilious</u> sounds like it might have something to do with being silly, but it really means contemptuous (showing contempt). If you want to increase your vocabulary, increase your reading and keep a vocabulary notebook. But don't use new words until they feel familiar and right for the thoughts you want to express.

All writing, all reading, all speaking is composed of diction—word choice. Although you usually take words for granted because you speak, hear, and read them so often, as a critical thinker you should pay fresh attention to words, to the ways you use them, and the ways other people use them.

They are building blocks of thought: you construct meaning with them; you create your voice on the page with them.

ACTIVITY 9

In your notebook write a paragraph explaining how to do some process you are familiar with, such as playing a particular instrument or sport or making something. Choose as many precise words as you can. Bring your paragraph to class to share.

LANGUAGE AND THOUGHT

Every message has two components:

1. The information conveyed
2. The style of the language used

Most people are unaware of the second component unless it is very distinct or clashes with the information. For example, President Lincoln's Gettysburg Address begins

> Four score and seven years ago our fathers brought forth on this continent a new nation, conceived in liberty, and dedicated to the proposition that all men are created equal.

The information is fairly clear, but the message has an old-fashioned sound. It was written in the nineteenth century, during the time of the American Civil War. President Lincoln uses a style that seems different from present-day English:

> Eighty-seven years ago, our ancestors created a new nation on this continent. The new nation was free and dedicated to the idea that all people are born with equal rights.

We cannot say the second version contains exactly the same information, but it is close enough that most readers will recognize it as a version of the first. But how the information is given is certainly very different. The style of the message has changed. Much has been written about Lincoln's Gettysburg Address. Some critics believe it is a kind of poetry. Our second version attempts to convey the information in Lincoln's speech with a very plain style.

It's fair to ask, what difference does it make? As long as readers get the information, why care about the style? The answer is to remember that <u>the style of a message is part of the message</u>. Lincoln was at Gettysburg to dedicate a cemetery in honor of the many thousands of northern and southern people who died at Gettysburg (more than 40,000 by some calculations). Gettysburg was a terrible battle. The president's style is somber and appropriate to the occasion. The audience needed to hear the president's tone of voice, the words he chose, and his sorrow for the death of so many.

As a writer you must care about the words you choose and the way you form them into sentences. Sentences are thoughts. To excel as a critical thinker, you must examine the style in which thoughts are expressed. Style is the way a writer uses language—especially words and sentences. Consider again the different ways people address each other. The greetings "Hi" and "How do you do" represent a difference in style.

All writing requires choices about language. You need to chose words carefully to convey your message, especially when you try to be thoughtful and when you want your readers to believe what you say. Suppose you write (or dictate to your secretary if you have one) a short business letter or a memo, such as the following:

Memo to K. Edwards, Director of Purchasing
Re: Printed Forms
From: J. Doe

K. Edwards, you seem not to know that we have been spending very large sums of money each year in order to get printed forms. We use all sorts of different forms in this business, which we tend to purchase from various printers. Some of which are local, others of which come from across the country.

Yet are you unaware that we have right here high-quality computers and printers on these premises? And this expensive equipment is being used mainly just for letter writing.

I propose to you that instead of purchasing business forms from printers who use only very similar equipment, that we could print our own forms right here on the premises using our own equipment. And the savings in costs to us would be extensive.

I recommend that we stop purchasing expensive preprinted forms from printers and begin producing forms with our own equipment at very significant savings in costs to us.

The memo is a proposal that the company start producing its own forms with the computers and printers they already have. However, J. Doe has paid little attention to the style of this memo. It is longer than it needs to be, perhaps in an attempt to impress K. Edwards. Then too, the memo would be better without phrases such as "you seem not to know" and "are you unaware," which seem to accuse K. Edwards of not knowing the job. Finally J. Doe's sentences seem wordy and carelessly written. Yes, you can understand this version of the memo, but J. Doe makes you work for it. Yet it is J. Doe who should do the work here. You get J. Doe's idea, but you also get an idea about J. Doe's ethos—careless, not concerned about audience, undiplomatic. Here is a revised attempt:

Memo to: K. Edwards, Director of Purchasing
Concerning: Printing Our Own Forms
From: J. Doe

We spend a lot on forms we could produce right here with our own high-quality computers and printers.
    I recommend that we try printing our own forms. We should save money and gain more control over forms that we frequently revise and update.

That may not be the best memo on this subject, but you get the idea. The style of a message can be as important as the information, especially when the style is not good.

ACTIVITY 10

Find a paragraph of four sentences or more in one of the news magazines (<u>Time</u>, <u>Newsweek</u>, <u>BusinessWeek</u>, or <u>U.S. News & World Report</u>); avoid picture and gossip magazines, such as <u>People</u>, <u>Life</u>, and <u>TV Guide</u>. Copy the paragraph you find, and then try to write a revision that is easier to read without losing clarity, accuracy, and without increasing length.

VOICE

Writing <u>with voice</u> is writing into which someone has breathed. (Elbow, <u>Writing with Power</u> 299)

Voice is the sound of a writer's personality on the page. In nonfiction writing, "voice" is usually the writer's voice. Readers hear this voice talking to them, telling them about the subject matter. You hear Lincoln's voice telling you about Gettysburg. In some cases (fiction), writers may attempt to disguise their voices or to hide them altogether. However, it isn't possible to hide your writer's voice entirely. Your information—your subject matter—is carried in your writer's voice.

Instead, many writers adopt the so-called "objective" voice, a voice in which writers can present themselves as knowledgeable and authoritative. Such writing is often called information-dominated. Why would writers use this voice? It's a way to emphasize the importance of the information. It's a way writers can keep readers' attention on the credibility of the information. In such writing, writers make little mention of themselves; they make sure that only logic and facts are presented. Information-dominated writing tends to sound serious because writers avoid anything that might lighten the presentation of their information.

> Scientists have been able to clone mammals from fetal cells for two decades. Wilmut said he had cloned Dolly using the nucleus from the cell of an adult sheep that had died three years earlier, the first time that a genetically identical mammal had been created from an adult cell. ("Was Fetal Cell Used?")

For several decades this style has been called "objective" writing.

Features of Objective Writing

Objective writing

- Makes no mention of the writer
- Usually concerns a serious subject
- Expresses no opinions. It reports only the facts. It makes no attempt to entertain or appeal to the reader.

Writers and editors, however, have increasingly come to realize that objective writing can sound false. Just because writers report scientific work doesn't mean they should sound like robots, artificial and unnatural. Many of the traditional notions about technical, scientific, and academic writing are now passing out of favor, if they have not gone already. Rules such as "never use the pronoun I," "never use an adjective or a metaphor," and "never end a sentence with a preposition" are now old-fashioned notions generally ignored by modern writers.

ACTIVITY 11

Read the following two paragraphs. What differences do you "hear" in them? What can you infer about the authors? What kinds of persons do you hear? Why are they writing this way? In your notebook, write your opinions of these voices.

A. Psychologists are increasingly interested in the effects of computers on human behavior. Because the machines are so widespread in our world, we need to understand the ways we interact with them. They may have influences on us of which we are not aware. Children are especially interesting to study on the question of how computers affect them. Behavioral psychologists are working with children to see how they react to computers.

B. It is summer. Robert, seven, is part of a play group at the beach. I have been visiting the group every day. I bring a carton filled with small computer toys and games and a tape recorder to capture the children's reactions as they meet these toys. Robert is playing with Merlin, a computer toy that plays tic-tac-toe. Robert's friend Craig has shown him how to "beat" Merlin. There is a trick: Merlin follows an optimal strategy most of the time, and if neither player makes a bad move every game will end in a draw. But Merlin is programmed to make a slip every once in a while. Children discover a strategy that will sometimes allow them to win, but then when they try it a second time it usually doesn't work. The machine gives the impression of not being "dumb enough" to let down its defenses twice. Robert has watched Craig perform the "winning trick" and now he wants to try it himself. He plays his part perfectly, but on this round Merlin too plays a perfect game, which leads to a draw. Robert accuses it of being a "cheating machine." "And if you cheat you're alive." Children are used to machines being predictable. The surprising is associated with the world of the living. But this is a machine that surprises. (Turkle 29)

We wrote the first paragraph. We used the so-called "academic" or "scientific" style, making it sound impersonal and objective. You encounter such writing often in textbooks (not all textbooks), in reference books, and in scientific journals. Many readers associate this style with scholarly or academic writing. The objectivity of this style is achieved through a kind of distance, a generalizing of the subject, in which authors attempt to elevate their data into a general law.

Sherry Turkle, however, reports her first person observations of children playing with a special computer programmed to "cheat" (periodically it behaves in a surprising manner). She maintains a certain amount of distance in her writing—you are aware that she is reporting, but the paragraph is not about her. She reports her own actions because they are part of the event. This writer sounds credible; she knows what she is talking about. Her "authority" comes from her easy familiarity with her subject. She sounds well informed about children interacting with computers.

Unlike the language in our paragraph, Turkle's language sounds simple and easy—natural. She uses specific details, such as <u>beach</u>, <u>carton</u>, <u>tape recorder</u>, <u>Merlin</u>, and <u>tic-tac-toe</u>, that help readers see what she means. She provides a clear example of a young boy, "Robert, seven," playing with a computer toy and accusing it of "cheating" or being alive. Most students (and some teachers) tend to think difficult language is sophisticated writing. But by humanizing and personalizing her subject, Turkle produces a paragraph not only more readable but more interesting.

However, we can't reduce writing to simple rules, such as "personalize your writing" or "write in the first person." A great deal of writing is not written in the first person—much journalistic writing, for example. Consider the voice in this news report.

Medicine Attacks Cold Virus

A cure for the common cold? Not quite. But perhaps the next best thing is on the way: A medicine that helps you feel only half as rotten as you ordinarily would when the sniffles strike. 1

Researchers on Tuesday described the successful human testing of the first medicine that eases cold symptoms by attacking the cold virus itself. 2

It's still several years away from the drugstore, cautioned Dr. Ronald B. Turner, who said he could not be more specific. "We've got a ways to go before we're willing to say the word 'cure.'" 3

What Turner is willing to say, though, is that a genetically engineered medicine called ICAM-1 clearly seems to make colds less severe if sprayed into the nose around the time of infection. 4

And that's nothing to sneeze at. 5

Standard cold remedies try to tone down the body's reaction to the cold virus rather than thwart the germ itself. (12) □ 6

Although no author is named for this article, you can hear a person speaking behind the written words. The writer uses informal language with a light, almost humorous tone, such as the phrase "sniffles strike," the fragment "Not quite," and the pun "And that's nothing to sneeze at." The distance between writer and reader is not far.

The Writing Situation and Voice

When you write different papers, you will often change your voice. The voice you use will depend on your <u>writing situation</u>.

FOUR ELEMENTS OF A WRITING SITUATION

<u>Your motivation</u>: a problem, an assignment, a personal need.

<u>Your audience</u>: your instructor may require you to vary your audience—to write a letter to the editor of your college paper, for example, or a letter to a former employer. You may choose to write a letter to your parents about a problem or an issue you'd like them to consider before you discuss it in person.

<u>Your subject</u>: if you write a film review of the comedy <u>The Nutty Professor</u> for an Internet site, your voice might be informal. If you write a research paper on cloning, your voice will be more formal, more distant from your regular voice.

<u>Your purpose</u>: what you intend to do in your writing: inform, evaluate, persuade, argue, move, entertain, or some combination of these.

TONE

What you write and how you write depend on your <u>tone</u> of voice: your attitude toward audience, subject, and self. Writers can't afford the attitude that readers don't matter. You have an obligation to communicate with the reader. You must anticipate the reader's reactions. J. Doe's memo reveals little attention to K. Edwards, who will receive the memo.

Analyzing Attitude toward Readers

Please read the following two letters, one by President Abraham Lincoln and one by Kaiser Wilhelm. What attitudes toward their readers can you infer from the letters?

Executive Mansion,
Washington, Nov. 21, 1864.
To Mrs. Lydia Bixby [Boston, Mass.]

Dear Madam,—I have been shown in the files of the War Department a statement of the Adjutant General of Massachusetts that you are the mother of five sons who have died gloriously on the field of battle.
    I feel how weak and fruitless must be any words of mine which

(box continues)

should attempt to beguile you from the grief of a loss so overwhelming. But I cannot refrain from tendering to you the consolation that may be found in the thanks of the Republic they died to save.

I pray that our heavenly Father may assuage the anguish of your bereavement, and leave you only the cherished memory of the loved and lost, and the solemn pride that must be yours, to have laid so costly a sacrifice upon the altar of Freedom. Yours, very sincerely and respect-fully, [A. Lincoln][2]

His Majesty the Kaiser hears that you have sacrificed nine sons in defense of the Fatherland in the present war. His Majesty is immensely gratified at the fact, and in recognition is pleased to send you his photo-graph with frame and autograph signature.

Try to imagine what might have caused the two men to use such words. Consider the recipients of the letters. We don't know anything about Mrs. Bixby or the German mother of the nine sons who died. But unless these are highly unusual mothers, you can imagine mothers reacting to such news: all their sons have died in the war.

Look again at President Lincoln's letter. Lincoln was a man who had read a great deal and that fact may give his letter a somewhat formal sound, but ask yourself whether Lincoln understands the situation—does his letter seem appro-priate? Does it seem from what he says that the president understands Mrs. Bixby's loss? Try to imagine yourself in Lincoln's situation. Suppose you were the one who had to write that letter. Suppose it was your mother who received the letter from the War Department.

The president's tone is sad, respectful, and heartfelt; he speaks of Mrs. Bixby's grief, her bereavement. The president's voice is eloquent with words and phrases like "tendering," "solemn pride," and "altar of freedom." It isn't easy to find words of sympathy for someone who has lost a loved one, much less five loved ones. But Lincoln tries, ending his message with a prayer that "our heav-enly Father" may soften her anguish and leave her with "only the cherished memory of the loved and lost."

Later historians tell us that President Lincoln was misinformed. As some-

---

[2]Source for Lincoln's and Kaiser's letters: M. Lincoln Schuster, ed., <u>A Treasury of the World's Great Letters</u>, 2nd ed. New York: Simon & Schuster, 1960. Lincoln letter on pp. 320–21; Kaiser letter on p. 319.

times happens in war, messages are not always accurate. Historians now believe (Schuster, for example) that not all five of Mrs. Bixby's sons died. Nevertheless, you can hear in Lincoln's words his feelings for a mother he believes to have suffered so terribly. He is thinking about <u>her</u>.

By contrast, the brief note from Kaiser Wilhelm—apparently not from the Kaiser himself but some member of the war office—during World War I barely acknowledges the tragedy with the use of the single word "sacrifice." Instead of compassion from one human being to another, the nameless bureaucrat sends the Kaiser's photograph. This message sounds impersonal, like a machine response: a mass produced letter. The Kaiser's letter sounds inappropriate because it ignores or fails to appreciate the situation—of sending a meaningful condolence. The Kaiser's short note shows no concern for the parent who has lost nine sons. "His Majesty's" note is about His Majesty and the war.

ACTIVITY 12

Write a brief letter to two different people. Write about the same subject for both readers—perhaps your impression of college so far as compared to high school. The point of the activity is to show the effect of audience on tone, so please don't simply write the same letter twice. Select readers you might actually change your writing for, such as a close friend or relative versus someone more distant, such as a school administrator, a teacher, or a coach.

Analyzing Attitudes toward Subject and Self

When we speak of "tone" in writing, we mean not only a writer's attitude toward audience but also a writer's attitude toward the subject, such as taking the subject seriously or lightly. Lincoln takes his subject seriously in his condolence to Mrs. Bixby. Also, what we hear tells something about the writer's self-image. Who do these writers think they are? Read again the Kaiser's note to the German mother who "sacrificed nine sons." What kind of person writes such a note? Who tells the mother of nine that "His Majesty" is "gratified" that she has lost so many sons? We cannot answer that question, but words like "immensely egotistic," "inhuman," and "indifferent" occur to us.

Writing requires not only <u>what</u> to write about but also "<u>what about it</u>?" Your tone tells readers whether you like, dislike, or are indifferent to them and/or the subject, and also what you think about yourself.

Your words and sentences create your voice. Your voice carries your attitudes, and your appeals to logos, pathos, and ethos. How you use words and sentences—style—to create your meaning, your voice, your tone, and your appeals is the central purpose of these interchapters.

ACTIVITY 13

Review Amy Wu's essay "Stop the Clock" or Brian Courtney's essay "Freedom from Choice" in chapter 1. In your notebook write your thoughts about the writer's voice and tone. Then write a page in which you explain how Wu's or Courtney's voice and tone help create one of their persuasive appeals: logos, pathos, and ethos.

SENTENCE TOOLS

Sentences embody thoughts.

All decisions about diction take place within sentences. Just as you need to use a variety of diction, you need to use a variety of sentence structures. The more aware you are of the sentence patterns you use, the more you can control them. In some respects, sentences are like diction: there are simple forms and complex forms.

Simple Sentences

Let's start simple and build toward complexity. As we go, we will ask you to practice sentence tools and to apply them directly to your own writing.

ACTIVITY 14

In your notebook write as many short sentences as you can in three minutes. Try to make the sentences complete grammatically, but keep them short. The shorter the better. Bring your list to class to share some. <u>Please don't read ahead until you have done this activity.</u>

Short sentences help readers stop and think. They work. They can add variety and vitality to your writing. Writers use short sentences to add emphasis and surprise to their thoughts.

I disagree.
Trust me.
So what?
Think critically.
"Lies confuse." (Peck 66)
"Omit needless words." (Strunk 259)

Short sentences can say a lot, and many long sentences can say little. Thus, short sentences often have persuasive power. They can, of course, occur anywhere in a paragraph. Here psychologist Mary Pipher begins and ends a paragraph with a short sentence:

> Volunteers are happy people. The person who turns off daytime TV and teaches an immigrant to read feels better about his/her life. Sometimes volunteers unite against a common enemy, such as tornadoes, floods or fires. Sometimes they unite around a desire to do good work—to build a trail, paint a house or do health screenings for children. Working with others can rekindle idealism and rebuild a sense of community. Work cures despair. (252)

Pipher concisely states a point, supports it with specific evidence, and repeats her point with a short sentence.

Daniel Goleman begins the conclusion to his essay "The New Thinking on Smarts" with a short sentence that contrasts with his thesis:

> IQ matters. But if we want to give our children the strongest foundation for life, we can't ignore EQ [emotional quotient or intelligence]. (7)

Short sentences, as Goleman shows, help writers make points clearly and concisely. By definition, they are <u>simple sentences: complete thoughts containing a subject and a verb</u>. Useful tools for style, they often contain monosyllabic words. Short sentences shift rhythms of thought—at a glance readers can see and comprehend them. Use short sentences occasionally: they will give your writing more variety, emphasis, and power. Experiment. See how they work for you. Keep your eye out for them when you read.

ACTIVITY 15

In your notebook try writing two pairs of sentences. Each pair should have a long and a short sentence that work together. Try one pair with the short sentence first and the other pair with the short sentence last. Bring these to class. Also, review your most recent writing to see if you can add an occasional short sentence for emphasis.

_____

Joining Complete Thoughts: Coordination

What comes to your mind when you think of <u>coordination</u>? A dancer? An Olympic gymnast? A juggler? These are all forms of coordination. Certain types of sentences are classified under the term <u>coordination</u> for similar reasons—they contain a balancing of some kind.

ACTIVITY 16

In your notebook try to write one compound sentence. If you aren't sure how to do this, don't worry, you will learn how soon. <u>Please don't read ahead until you have finished this activity</u>.

_____

You use various sentence patterns every day when you speak, but you probably aren't aware of them. With more awareness you will have more control, and with more control you will be a more effective critical thinker and writer. A pattern that builds on a simple sentence is the <u>compound sentence</u>: a sentence <u>containing two complete thoughts</u>. Grammatical labels such as "coordination" and "compound" often confuse students. The labels, however, are not what's most important; what's important are the patterns.

Three sentences in the preceding paragraph are compound—the first two and the last. They all contain two complete thoughts. The sentences are different because the thoughts within them are joined in different ways. In this section you will learn how to write sentences like those.

The most basic pattern of a compound sentence is combining two complete thoughts with one of these connecting words (called coordinating conjunctions): <u>and</u>, <u>but</u>, <u>or</u>, <u>for</u>, <u>nor</u>, <u>yet</u>, and <u>so</u>.

The blue jay is an opportunist, <u>and</u> opportunists are survivors in every sense. (Erdrich 159)

Try hard to find good arguments for your position, <u>but</u> then try even harder to find arguments to refute yours. (Elbow, <u>Embracing Contraries</u> 201)

You can write a draft without using an outline, <u>or</u> you can use an outline to write a draft.

Comma Rule: Put the comma <u>before</u> the connecting word, never after.

ACTIVITY 17

In your notebook write three more compound sentences, each using a different connecting word.

Using Semicolons to Join Complete Thoughts

Many people don't know how to use semicolons because they were never taught how. But using semicolons can add variety and power to your writing.

ACTIVITY 18

In your notebook write a sentence using a semicolon. If you aren't sure how to do this, you are about to learn a distinctive tool of style. If you already know how, prove it. <u>Please don't read ahead until you have finished Activity 18</u>.

How do semicolons function in the following sentences?

> I reel in confusion; I don't understand what I see. (Dillard, <u>Pilgrim at Tinker Creek</u> 24)

> We do not "come into" this world; we come <u>out</u> of it, as leaves from a tree. (Watts 8)

> Thinking is seeing relationships; rhetoric is the art of representing that "seeing." (Berthoff 137)

Each of the preceding sentences contains two complete thoughts joined by a semicolon instead of a connecting word such as <u>and</u>, <u>but</u>, or <u>or</u>. A semicolon is a hybrid of a period and a comma; like a period it signals a stop between two complete thoughts, but the stop is not as full or definite. The advantage of using a semicolon is that it shows a close relationship between thoughts.

Some writers feel that the semicolon is more formal than a comma, suggesting a more sophisticated use of language. It takes a little more thought about language to decide whether a semicolon is appropriate.

Semicolon Rule: You need a complete thought on each side of a semicolon, and both thoughts should closely relate to each other in meaning.

ACTIVITY 19

In your notebook write three sentences that contain semicolons. Compare these sentences to the one you wrote at the beginning of this section. Did you use a semicolon properly then? Look at your recent writing to see if you can connect two closely related sentences into one sentence with a semicolon. When you write new entries in your notebook or fresh drafts of papers, use some semicolons. Practicing this tool is the best way to learn it.

Using Semicolons with Formal Transition Words

Another way to use semicolons can add more formality to your voice. How are the following sentences different from the ones you've seen so far?

> Some people brush off Tommy Boy as a "no-brainer" and snicker at the suggestion that the film might contain societal values; however, these values are easy to find. (Marisa Proctor, student)

> We do not live in a black and white world; therefore, we should not experience life in a cut and dried manner. (Kelly Battles, student)

> He knew that his son might choose differently than he had wished; nevertheless, he and his wife resolved to love their son unconditionally, regardless of his choice. (Covey 200)

Each of these sentences contains a semicolon followed by a transition word. This structure is useful because it shows cause and effect relationships between thoughts. It also gives the impression of formal reasoning. This sentence tool is useful in any formal essay, essay exam, or research paper. If you wrote a letter to a prospective employer, this tool could help you sound professional. Here is a list of common transition words (or conjunctive adverbs) that can follow a semicolon to join two complete thoughts:

also	furthermore	instead	otherwise
anyway	hence	likewise	still
besides	however	moreover	then
consequently	in addition	nevertheless	therefore
finally	indeed	next	thus

This sentence tool is useful for academic writing, for anytime you want to sound more formal, and for joining closely related thoughts.

As a writer you have many options on how to connect complete thoughts. For example, you can usually exchange <u>however</u> with <u>but</u> and keep the same meaning. Consider this example and revision:

I'm considering a vegetarian diet; however, I'm unsure of the health risks.

I'm considering a vegetarian diet, but I'm unsure of the health risks.

The original sentence sounds more formal, but the revision expresses the same (or a very similar) thought. The word <u>but</u> is monosyllabic and simpler. When you want your voice to sound more formal, choose <u>however</u>. "Also, these transition words provide variety, so that you don't overuse 'But'"

Comma Rule: A comma usually follows a transition word in a sentence containing a semicolon. However, the comma may be omitted for less emphasis.

ACTIVITY 20

In your notebook write three sentences that contain semicolons followed by transition words. Bring them to class to share the one you like best. Then look at your recent writing. See if you can use this sentence tool.

———————

You have used coordination in your sentences since you began to talk: you naturally combine complete thoughts. But with practice you can begin to gain formal control over the effects of your sentences and control in expressing your thoughts, with the help of formal connectors such as semicolons and transition words.

What difference does all this make? Imagine applying for a bank loan (a house mortgage, for example) when you are dressed in your sloppiest most comfortable old clothes. Then imagine applying for that same loan in your sloppiest most casual English. Our clothing and our language give people ideas about us but not always the ideas we might wish.

SOLVING TWO COMMON SENTENCE PROBLEMS

Comma Splices and Run-On Sentences

Comma Splices

Connecting two complete thoughts properly can help you solve two common sentence errors. Consider this sentence:

My sister watched <u>Titanic</u> five times, she bought the music soundtrack too.

What's the problem? This mistake is called a <u>comma splice</u>. In formal writing the comma is not considered strong enough to separate complete thoughts. Connecting complete thoughts requires <u>both</u> a comma and a connecting word, such as <u>and</u>, <u>but</u>, <u>or</u>, <u>for</u>, <u>nor</u>, or <u>yet</u>.

My sister watched <u>Titanic</u> five times, and she bought the music soundtrack too.

Another way to revise a comma splice is to use a semicolon.

My sister watched <u>Titanic</u> five times; she bought the music soundtrack too.

Following the advice of generations of writers—to omit any unnecessary words—a better solution is to revise the sentence.

My sister watched <u>Titanic</u> five times and bought the music soundtrack too.

Run-On Sentences

Another sentence problem is called the <u>run-on</u> or <u>fused sentence</u>. This punctuation error has nothing to do with a sentence rambling on and on with needless words. The error involves two complete thoughts <u>fused</u> together without punctuation or a connecting word. For example:

Critical thinking is important creative thinking is important too.

In this example one complete thought runs into another complete thought. You need some punctuation to connect two complete thoughts. Here are some options:

Critical thinking is important. Creative thinking is important too.
Critical thinking is important, but creative thinking is important too.

Critical thinking is important; creative thinking is important too.

Critical thinking is important; however, creative thinking is important too.

As with the comma splice, we recommend that critical thinkers revise their sentences for conciseness. What is it this writer wants to say?

Both critical and creative thinking are important.

Although critical thinking is important, so is creative thinking.

Critical thinkers need to be creative too.

Comma splices occur more frequently than run-on sentences. As a critical thinker you should know what comma splices and run-on sentences are and identify and repair them in your own writing and in other people's writing. An essay, report, business letter, or research paper containing these errors will not reflect well on your ethos. Readers may infer that you don't proofread carefully—or don't think carefully.

ACTIVITY 21

Look at your recent writing. Notice whether you have any comma splices or run-on sentences. Repair them if you do by using (1) a comma and a connecting word (and, but, or), (2) a semicolon, (3) a semicolon and a transition word, or (4) one complete thought instead of two by omitting needless words.

Chapter 2

Arguments and Controversies

CRITICAL READING AND WRITING: AGREE, DISAGREE, OR MAYBE BOTH?

Should it be legal or illegal? Is it moral or immoral? Will it help or hurt the community? Excuse us, but should these questions be phrased as either/or dilemmas?

The word <u>controversy</u> means "discussion of a question in which opposing opinions clash" (<u>Webster's New World</u>). A controversy involves two or more conflicting views for which there is no easy agreement, as, for example, the conflict between Israel and Palestine. The more extreme the disagreement, the more controversial the issue. A controversy usually goes beyond the experience of one person—it affects many people. It often has profound implications for society.

Reading an essay about a controversial topic involves considering different views of a debatable issue. Writing an essay about a controversial topic does also. Careful attention to logos is essential for both, yet logos is usually not enough to persuade readers. You need to appeal to pathos and ethos as well to persuade readers to see an issue as you do.

You may <u>assume</u>—take for granted—that you know what we mean when we use words such as <u>controversy</u>, <u>argument</u>, and <u>assumption</u>, but unless we tell you what they mean to us, you might misunderstand. When you think of the word <u>argument</u>, what connotations does it have for you? A fight? A way of reasoning? A body of convincing evidence? Is the word positive or negative—or both?

Let us define <u>argument</u> as giving reasons for or against an opinion—or for some middle perspective. Middle perspectives are vital for critical thinkers: without them, we have nothing but extremes—yes/no, either/or, for or against. The middle perspectives, however, can provide much truth, truth not oversimplified by widely divergent either/or views.

Can you argue without fighting—and without concentrating on what you're going to say next instead of listening closely to another person's view? In this chapter we examine such questions and present strategies for you to use whenever you argue about controversial issues.

Critical thinkers analyze what they read. Most often critical thinkers wonder as they read whether they agree or disagree with an author—they may agree with certain ideas and examples but disagree with others. Before we present some essays concerning controversial issues, read the following article by Deborah Tannen, a professor of linguistics at Georgetown University and author of The Argument Culture from which this article is adapted. As you read, notice where you agree and disagree with Tannen.

How to Turn Debate into Dialogue

Deborah Tannen

Balance. Debate. Listening to both sides. Who could question these noble American traditions? Yet today, these principles have been distorted. Without thinking, we have plunged headfirst into what I call the "argument culture."   1

The argument culture urges us to approach the world, and the people in it, in an adversarial frame of mind. It rests on the assumption that opposition   2 is the best way to get anything done: the best way to discuss an idea is to set up a debate; the best way to cover news is to find spokespeople who express the most extreme, polarized views and present them as "both sides"; the best way to settle disputes is litigation that pits one party against the other; the best way to begin an essay is to attack someone; and the best way to show you're really thinking is to criticize.

More and more, our public interactions have become like arguing with a   3 spouse. Conflict can't be avoided in our public lives any more than we can avoid conflict with people we love. One of the great strengths of our society is that we can express these conflicts openly. But just as spouses have to learn ways of settling their differences without inflicting real damage, so we, as a society, have to find constructive ways of resolving disputes and differences.

The war on drugs, the war on cancer, the battle of the sexes, politicians'   4 turf battles—in the argument culture, war metaphors pervade our talk and shape our thinking. The cover headlines of both Time and Newsweek one recent week are a case in point: "The Secret Sex Wars," proclaims Newsweek. "Starr at War," declares Time. Nearly everything is framed as a battle or game in which winning or losing is the main concern.

The argument culture pervades every aspect of our lives today. Issues from global warming to abortion are depicted as two-sided arguments, when in fact most Americans' views lie somewhere in the middle. Partisanship makes gridlock in Washington the norm. Even in our personal relationships, a "let it all hang out" philosophy emphasizes people expressing their anger without giving them constructive ways of settling differences. 5

Sometimes You Have to Fight

There are times when it is necessary and right to fight—to defend your country or yourself, to argue for your rights or against offensive or dangerous ideas or actions. What's wrong with the argument culture is the ubiquity, the knee-jerk nature, of approaching any issue, problem or public person in an adversarial way. 6

Our determination to pursue truth by setting up a fight between two sides leads us to assume that every issue has two sides—no more, no less. But if you always assume there must be an "other side," you may end up scouring the margins of science or the fringes of lunacy to find it. 7

This accounts, in part, for the bizarre phenomenon of Holocaust denial. Deniers, as Emory University professor Deborah Lipstadt shows, have been successful in gaining TV air time and campus newspaper coverage by masquerading as "the other side" in a "debate." Continual reference to "the other side" results in a conviction that everything has another side—and people begin to doubt the existence of any facts at all. 8

The power of words to shape perception has been proved by researchers in controlled experiments. Psychologists Elizabeth Loftus and John Palmer, for example, found that the terms in which people are asked to recall something affect what they recall. The researchers showed subjects a film of two cars colliding, then asked how fast the cars were going; one week later they asked whether there had been any broken glass. Some subjects were asked, "How fast were the cars going when they bumped into each other?" Others were asked, "How fast were the cars going when they smashed into each other?" 9

Those who read the question with "smashed" tended to "remember" that the cars were going faster. They were also more likely to "remember" having seen broken glass. (There wasn't any.) This is how language works. It invisibly molds our way of thinking about people, actions and the world around us. 10

In the argument culture, "critical" thinking is synonymous with criticizing. In many classrooms, students are encouraged to read someone's life work, then rip it to shreds. 11

When debates and fighting predominate, those who enjoy verbal sparring are likely to take part—by calling in to talk shows or writing letters to the editor. Those who aren't comfortable with oppositional discourse are likely to opt out. 12

How High-tech Communication Pulls Us Apart

One of the most effective ways to defuse antagonism between two groups is to   13
provide a forum for individuals from those groups to get to know each other
personally. What is happening in our lives, however, is just the opposite. More and
more of our communication is not face to face, and not with people we know. The
proliferation and increasing portability of technology isolates people in a bubble.

Along with the voices of family members and friends, phone lines bring   14
into our homes the annoying voices of solicitors who want to sell something—
generally at dinnertime. (My father-in-law startles phone solicitors by saying,
"We're eating dinner, but I'll call you back. What's your home phone number?"
To the nonplused caller, he explains, "Well, you're calling me at home; I thought
I'd call you at home, too.")

It is common for families to have more than one TV, so the adults can   15
watch what they like in one room and the kids can watch their choice in
another—or maybe each child has a private TV.

E-mail, and now the Internet, are creating networks of human connection   16
unthinkable even a few years ago. Though e-mail has enhanced communication
with family and friends, it also ratchets up the anonymity of both sender and
receiver, resulting in stranger-to-stranger "flaming."

"Road rage" shows how dangerous the argument culture—and especially   17
today's technologically enhanced aggression—can be. Two men who engage in
a shouting match may not come to blows, but if they express their anger while
driving down a public highway, the risk to themselves and others soars.

The Argument Culture Shapes Who We Are

The argument culture has a defining impact on our lives and on our culture.   18

- **It makes us distort facts**, as in the Nancy Kerrigan–Tonya Harding story. After
  the original attack on Kerrigan's knee, news stories focused on the rivalry
  between the two skaters instead of portraying Kerrigan as the victim of an attack.
  Just last month, Time magazine called the event a "contretemps" between Kerrigan and Harding. And a recent joint TV interview of the two skaters reinforced
  that skewed image by putting the two on equal footing, rather than as victim
  and accused.

- **It makes us waste valuable time**, as in the case of scientist Robert Gallo, who
  co-discovered the AIDS virus. Gallo was the object of a groundless four-year
  investigation into allegations he had stolen the virus from another scientist. He
  was ultimately exonerated, but the toll was enormous. Never mind that, in his
  words, "These were the most painful and horrible years of my life." Gallo spent
  four years fighting accusations instead of fighting AIDS.

- **It limits our thinking.** Headlines are intentionally devised to attract attention,
  but the language of extremes actually shapes, and misshapes, the way we think
  about things. Military metaphors train us to think about, and see, everything in

terms of fighting, conflict and war. Adversarial rhetoric is a kind of verbal infla-tion—a rhetorical boy-who-cried-wolf.

- **It encourages us to lie.** If you fight to win, the temptation is great to deny facts that support your opponent's views and say only what supports your side. It encourages people to misrepresent and, in the extreme, to lie.

End the Argument Culture by Looking at All Sides

How can we overcome our classically American habit of seeing issues in   19
absolutes? We must expand our notion of "debate" to include more dialogue. To do this, we can make special efforts not to think in twos. Mary Catherine Bate-son, an anthropologist at Virginia's George Mason University, makes a point of having her class compare three cultures, not two. Then, students are more likely to think about each on its own terms, rather than as opposites.

In the public arena, television and radio producers can try to avoid, when-   20
ever possible, structuring public discussions as debates. This means avoiding the format of having two guests discuss an issue. Invite three guests—or one. Perhaps it is time to re-examine the assumption that audiences always prefer a fight.

Instead of asking, "What's the other side?" we might ask, "What are the   21
other sides?" Instead of insisting on hearing "both sides," let's insist on hear-ing "all sides."

We need to find metaphors other than sports and war. Smashing heads   22
does not open minds. We need to use our imaginations and ingenuity to find different ways to seek truth and gain knowledge through intellectual inter-change, and add them to our arsenal—or, should I say, to the ingredients for our stew. It will take creativity for each of us to find ways to change the argu-ment culture to a dialogue culture. It's an effort we have to make, because our public and private lives are at stake.

20 Ways to Talk, Not Argue

Battle of the sexes	Relations between women and men
Critique	Comment
Fight	Discussion
Both sides	All sides
Debate	Discuss
The other side	Another side
Having an argument	Making an argument
The opposite sex	The other sex
War on drugs	Solving the drug problem
Litigation	Mediation
Provocative	Thought-provoking
Most controversial	Most important
Polarize	Unify

Attack-dog journalism	Watchdog journalism
Automatic opposition	Genuine opposition
Focus on differences	Search for common ground
Win the argument	Understand another point of view
The opposition party	The other party
Prosecutorial reporting	Investigative reporting
The argument culture	The dialogue culture

(4–5) ☐

Do you think Tannen's argument makes sense? Do you agree with her thesis and supporting evidence? Does she persuade you? Yes? No? Sort of? To analyze and evaluate any text, you should read it a second time more actively.

ACTIVITY 1

Photocopy Tannen's essay and annotate it. In particular, write notes in the margins about things with which you agree and disagree. Consider using these notations:

Write "T" beside any statement you find <u>true</u> and a "?" beside any statement you <u>question</u> or doubt.

Underline any key sentences that surprise you with their <u>insight</u> or seem especially well worded. Put a star by these in the margin.

Underline any sentences that contain problems of reasoning like overgeneralizations. Put a question mark by these in the margin.

Write comments in margins if you remember a personal example that <u>supports</u> or <u>questions</u> what Tannen says.

Go on. Read and annotate Tannen's article. Interact with it once more. See if you notice more of her reasoning. <u>Please don't read ahead until you have annotated Tannen's article.</u>

———

Critical thinkers often read a text more than once, especially if it challenges their usual way of thinking. They try out ideas on themselves—wear them around for a while in their minds. They also reflect on their own experience by asking themselves questions: Do I argue the way Tannen claims most people argue? Have I, at times, had to "fight" to defend myself or someone else? When? What happened? Do I know anyone who argues in a mean-spirited or violent way? Who? Do I know anyone who argues the way Tannen recommends, who is able to create a dialogue of connections during an argument?

READING TOOLS

Suppose your instructor asks you to write an essay in which you analyze and evaluate Tannen's article. In addition to annotating it, what could you do? To analyze (to take apart) and to evaluate (to judge) any essay, ask yourself questions about it and notice insights, assumptions, and overgeneralizations in it.

Asking Questions

Critical thinkers ask questions. It's natural. To think is to notice and to inquire. What questions did you ask yourself as you read Tannen's essay? Here are some questions we asked ourselves:

> Is it true that in our culture, "'critical' thinking is synonymous with criticizing"? We think this is true for most people. However, like Tannen, we aim in this book to present other perspectives on critical thinking—positive ones.
>
> Is it true that "in many classrooms, students are encouraged to read someone's life work, then rip it to shreds"? We're not sure about this claim. Although the word "many" qualifies the statement somewhat, Tannen provides no example to show what she means here.
>
> Is it possible not to view controversial issues as heated debates or wars of words? Do most people "always prefer a fight" as Tannen claims? If true, then changing people's methods of argument is no easy job.

Noticing Insights

One of the pleasures of reading is noticing statements of truth or insight: statements that surprise you with their wisdom and concise expression. We like Tannen's sentence in her conclusion, "Smashing heads does not open minds." This restatement of her thesis closes her essay well along with her metaphor of a "stew" of various views rather than an "arsenal"of one view.

If you notice insights often enough when you read, the process will become a habit: you will experience moments of <u>eureka</u>—the aha! feeling, as if a small light turns on in your mind. The more reading eurekas you experience, the more you will enjoy and value what you read.

Noticing Assumptions

In using the word <u>assume</u> in the following sentences, Tannen notices what people <u>take for granted</u> when they argue:

> Our determination to pursue truth by setting up a fight between two sides leads us to <u>assume</u> that every issue has two sides—no more, no less. But if you always <u>assume</u> there must be an "other side," you may end up scouring the margins of science or the fringes of lunacy to find it. (Tannen)

Critical thinkers notice assumptions—unstated beliefs or values that people take for granted. Our assumptions often limit our thinking: we may assume that gun control is either good or bad, or that drugs are either good or bad, that cloning humans is either good or bad. But truth often exists in the complex middle ground of extreme views.

Try to notice assumptions when you read. You will find that analyzing and evaluating ideas and supporting evidence will soon follow naturally. Noticing assumptions will enable you to go underneath arguments, to see how they are constructed.

Noticing Overgeneralizations

> "TV is the enemy of reading." True? Do children's shows like <u>Reading Rainbow</u> cause kids not to read?
>
> "I think interacting with the elderly is always a refreshing experience." Always? You don't know my Great Uncle Frank who . . .
>
> "All students in college love to learn." All? Surely many students find learning difficult and don't "love" to learn, and learn what? Doesn't loving to learn depend on what is being learned?

An overgeneralization is an extremely broad statement that covers too many cases; it assumes that exceptions don't exist. Critical thinkers notice overgeneralizations as sweeping statements that contain weak reasoning.

You can spot overgeneralizations easily by noticing certain key words: <u>all</u>, <u>always</u>, <u>anything</u>, <u>everybody</u>, <u>everyone</u>, <u>everything</u>, <u>no one</u>, and <u>nothing</u>. <u>All</u> kids love ice cream. <u>Everyone</u> enjoys college. <u>No one</u> ever proofreads papers anymore. <u>Nothing</u> my parents say makes sense. Wealthy people can get away with <u>anything</u>. Old people <u>always</u> have a wealth of knowledge to share with young people.

To disprove or refute an overgeneralization, you need only a single exception. (But see chapter 5 for a qualification of <u>this</u> overgeneralization.) A popular country-western song by Ray Stevens goes "Everything is beautiful in its own way." <u>Everything</u>? What about the Holocaust?

Please don't assume that we're arguing that it is wrong to generalize. People can't help but generalize—that is, state conclusions or opinions. As a critical thinker, however, you must learn to qualify your generalizations. Thoughtful writers qualify any generalization that seems too sweeping or that is likely to create doubt in a reader's mind. Qualifiers, such as <u>many</u>, <u>some</u>, and <u>a few</u>, work well, usually. The word <u>most</u> is a common qualifier, yet it too might be difficult to justify. "Most men love to shop for clothes." This is someone's opinion that is impossible to verify. How many does "most" mean? 55%? 75%? 95%? The statement needs more qualification, for example, "Many men don't like to shop for clothes" or "Most men <u>I know</u> don't like to shop for clothes." The ability to qualify generalizations is a hallmark of critical thinking.

Consider this statement by Tannen: "In the argument culture . . . nearly everything is framed as a battle or game in which winning or losing is the main concern." Her word <u>nearly</u> does qualify <u>everything</u>, but <u>everything</u> is a tremendously broad word that literally means every thing. Is walking down the street a battle or game? Is reading the weather report? Is eating your favorite dessert?

In sum, when you read an essay or article carefully, you can analyze and evaluate it by asking questions about it and by noticing a writer's insights, assumptions, and overgeneralizations. These same reading tools will also help you analyze and evaluate your own writing.

ACTIVITY 2

Make a list of 5 to 10 overgeneralizations—ones you've heard before or said. Then rewrite them by adding a qualifying word or words. Bring your list to class and share with others.

ANALYZING AND EVALUATING TWO ESSAYS ON A CONTROVERSY

Because controversial issues involve extreme disagreements, they often involve extreme emotions. How writers control their emotions in an essay is one way for readers to evaluate that essay. One of the most emotional issues today is gun control. A strictly logical presentation of facts and figures—how many guns there are and how many people die in gun related incidents—makes little impact. Writers usually need to appeal to pathos and ethos as well.

Analysis and Evaluation of Mitch Albom's Essay

Please read the following essay by Mitch Albom.[1] As you read, consider how well Albom argues. What is his thesis and how well does he support it? How does

---

[1]Author of the bestseller <u>Tuesdays with Morrie</u> and voted number one sports columnist in America 11 out of 12 years.

he use logos, pathos, ethos? Does he persuade you to consider his arguments or to agree with him? Try to practice the reading tools we have presented so far in this chapter: asking questions and noticing insights, assumptions, and overgeneralizations.

Don't Shoot Holes in Gun Control Bills

Mitch Albom

Maybe they had an argument. I don't really care. All I know is a man was driving a Ford Bronco on the Lodge Freeway last week and a Cadillac pulled alongside him with several passengers inside and next thing you know, someone in the Cadillac was firing bullets. Three of those bullets hit the driver of the truck. He veered off the highway and began to die. 1

An hour later, there was one less person in our city. 2

Tell me again about how gun control is a stupid idea. Tell me again how all it will do is take guns away from innocent people who want to protect themselves. Tell me again how guns don't kill people, people do. 3

Alan Johnson, the dead man, was killed by a gun. Sure, a person fired it—in a day and age when all we see are guns, everything we watch has guns, every story we hear involves guns. Alan Johnson is not the first man to have an argument with someone. But not so long ago, people settled arguments by yelling louder, or ignoring one another, or, if they were crude, taking a swing. 4

Nowadays they pull up alongside your car and open fire. 5

Bang, bang. Take that, jerk. 6

This is hardly an isolated tale. People in Los Angeles can tell you how their highways have turned into shooting ranges. Cut someone off, they pop you with a bullet. In Detroit, just a few months ago, a guy didn't like his Rally's hamburger, so he threw it back through the pickup window. The female worker threw a drink at him. He drove off, came back with a gun and shot her. 7

Bang, bang. Take that, jerk. 8

We live in an age of hair-trigger tempers—and that is no place for hair-trigger weapons. Yet guns, guns, they seem to be everywhere, even places we once considered perfectly safe, like a busy highway during rush hour. What if the bullets meant for Alan Johnson had sprayed into a passing car instead? The gun used, police say, was an AK47 assault rifle, one of the weapons specifically banned in the previous year's crime bill. 9

This is the same measure opponents said was a waste of time, an unfair burden, the one they are trying to get repealed. 10

Tell me again. 11

Frontier Justice

Am I the only one bothered by this? That you can't honk your horn on the 12
highway anymore without wondering whether the driver is some maniac you
just pushed over the edge, and now he's coming after you, rolling down his
window and taking aim?

Are we not moving back to the days of frontier justice, the Wild Wild 13
West, where getting upset over a card game was reason enough to kill a man?
Think about it. In June, a Detroit firefighter was shot while putting out a blaze.
Nobody knew why. Someone just shot him. In January, gunmen rode past a
house in southwest Detroit, allegedly angry at a young man who lived there,
and sprayed the place with bullets. One of them hit a visiting relative, a 16-
year-old boy, and killed him.

He had been sleeping on the couch. 14

Just a few weeks ago, friends and family were sobbing for a young man 15
who was killed for his Jeep. It wasn't enough that they took the vehicle. They
had to shoot him, dump him, let his body rot while they rode around town.

Where does this stop? Because there is no bottom, folks, there is no lowest 16
level at which things don't get any worse. It keeps getting worse as long as we
allow it. Who's to say we don't go back to the Old West? We lived that way once.
What makes us so different now?

Well, one thing that might is legislation. Stop allowing guns to be as 17
easy to buy as cigarettes. Yes, I know the problem begins at home. And until
parents teach their children to respect life, to be shamed by violence and until
we stop glorifying TV shows that bring us "real life crime drama" and music that
brags about killing cops—until that happens, we will never stomp the killing
gene in our society.

But you have to start somewhere. 18

Memories Linger

Ten years ago, when I first arrived in this town, I went to a Southfield dry 19
cleaners to pick up a jacket. I saw no one in the store except a customer at the
counter. He had his back turned to me. I asked whether anyone was working
and he turned around and pointed a gun at my face. He was robbing the place.
He told me to get in the closet, or he'd shoot me dead, right there.

I survived that, but for weeks I saw the gun in my sleep. I thought there 20
could be no worse horror, to enter an innocent situation and be looking down
the barrel of a gun. Now I realize I was wrong. The worst horror is to look down
the barrel just before it fires.

Alan Johnson died that way, and I don't care what might have precipi- 21
tated it. We cannot live where disputes are solved by bullets. And until we take
the guns away, we will make no dent in this. We just keep arguing, until another
window rolls down. (1F) ☐

Many writers have attempted to argue for or against gun control with little success. There are powerful groups on both sides of this question, and there doesn't seem to be much left for writers to say on either side. Mitch Albom doesn't attempt to deal with the standard arguments concerning the Constitution (does the Second Amendment give individuals the right to have guns?) nor does he cite factual data concerning how many millions of weapons there are in the United States.[2] But he does cite several cases of gun-related crime. He insists that we need to pass laws that restrict gun ownership. Is he right?

Amendment II

A well-regulated Militia being necessary to the security of a free State, the right of the People to keep and bear Arms shall not be infringed.

ACTIVITY 3

In your notebook, write a response to Albom's essay. Do you agree or disagree with him—or perhaps both?

Albom's Writing Situation

Note the "situation" that prompted this article was the death of a man on the Lodge Freeway (in Detroit), a drive-by shooting by someone in another car. The death of Alan Johnson motivated Albom to address the controversy of gun control, to relate other similar examples, and to share his own frightening experience facing a gun. His thesis is that no matter what provocation may exist between individuals, we must not accept guns and killing as the way to resolve a dispute.

Albom's Introduction

Albom uses the power of first-person narration, storytelling, to pull the reader into the events. He does not distance himself from the topic of gun control by trying to be purely objective. Instead, he does all he can to pull the reader into the story, to remove the safe distance between the reader and the

---

[2]The Bureau of Alcohol, Tobacco and Firearms (ATF) reports there were more than 211 million firearms privately owned in the United States in 1991, of which approximately 70,666,000 were handguns. Each year since 1983, an average of 3.5 million guns has been added to the U.S. firearms market. Thus, "there is approximately one gun for each adult and half the children in America" <www.gunfree.org>. Access date: 16 Jan. 1998.

subject. His first sentence, "Maybe they had an argument," causes readers to wonder—an argument about what? But then readers may conclude it doesn't matter what it was about. His second sentence says just that. Albom's first paragraph ends with a powerful sentence: "He veered off the highway and began to die." Alan Johnson's death was not instantaneous. The appeal to pathos builds toward the end of his introductory sequence: "An hour later there was one less person in our city." He sets this sentence off in its own paragraph, for emphasis. He uses one-sentence or one-line paragraphs eight times for emphasis in the article; this is a feature of Albom's style.

Noticing Albom's Insights, Assumptions, and Overgeneralizations

Mitch Albom insightfully writes, "We live in an age of hair-trigger tempers—and that is no place for hair-trigger weapons." The repetition of "hair-trigger" works well to emphasize his point. The statement provokes thought.

Albom assumes—takes for granted or believes—that guns are everywhere in our culture: "in a day and age when all we see are guns, everything we watch has guns, every story we hear involves guns." This assumption is an overgeneralization or exaggeration. Surely not every TV show or movie you watch involves guns—many do, but not all. Not every story you hear involves guns—the cloning of Dolly the sheep involved no guns. Although his assumption is questionable, it is true that guns are a dominant feature of our culture.

Albom assumes that abolishing guns will help solve the problem of violence: "And until we take the guns away, we will make no dent in this." He may be right; he may not be. Albom assumes that we, the people, have power to change chronic violence: "It keeps getting worse as long as we allow it." He assumes that if we motivate our legislators to enact tougher gun laws, this "might" help. He assumes there is a "killing gene" in our society. Would you say this killing gene—if it exists—is related solely to guns?

Responding to Other Arguments

How important is it for a writer to respond to other or opposing arguments? It is crucial. If Albom did not represent the other side, he would not appear fair-minded—his ethos would be less credible. How much does Albom present the other side? Not in depth. Instead, he <u>acknowledges</u> opposing arguments with an ironic attitude:

> Tell me again about how gun control is a stupid idea. Tell me again how all it will do is take guns away from innocent people who want to protect themselves. Tell me again how guns don't kill people, people do.

His repetition of "Tell me again" suggests that he has heard these pro-gun arguments countless times from those who fear they will lose their guns and who fear some conspiracy exists against which guns are their only protection. Later he writes

> The gun used, police say, was an AK47 assault rifle, one of the weapons specifically banned in the previous year's crime bill.
>
> This is the same measure opponents said was a waste of time, an unfair burden, the one they are trying to get repealed.
>
> Tell me again.

Again he briefly acknowledges the pro-gun view that the crime bill was "a waste of time."

Many people want so much to win their argument that they find it difficult to concede anything to the opposing side. Yet the ability to concede to an opponent increases your credibility. Your audience (readers) can see whether you are fair, whether you give the opposing argument its due. Your readers will see that there is no basis for an argument if one side is entirely right and the other is entirely wrong. See "Different Ways to Present Other or Opposing Arguments."

DIFFERENT WAYS TO PRESENT ARGUMENTS

As a writer you have various options in presenting other arguments:

- Briefly acknowledge them while trying to be objective and fair-minded.
- Briefly acknowledge them while conveying your own disagreement and opinion (as Albom does).
- Summarize other positions while trying to be objective and fair-minded.
- Summarize other positions while conveying your own disagreement and opinion.
- Fully and fairly present other positions, pointing out their merits and weaknesses before presenting your own position and evidence.
- Not acknowledge them at all, as if other views don't exist. This is not a wise strategy.
- Misrepresent other positions, exaggerating their weaknesses, making up examples and other kinds of evidence to make the writer appear wrong or foolish. <u>Note:</u> This option is, of course, dishonest—a sign of fatally bad ethos.

Albom's Use of Logos, Pathos, and Ethos

Using logos, Mitch Albom shows that the gun problem isn't just happening in Detroit. He cites Los Angeles where you can get "popped" with a bullet on the highways for cutting someone off. But it's not only driving that can get you killed. Albom cites a Detroit fast-food place where a worker was shot because the customer didn't like his burger. Again he repeats, "Bang, bang. Take that, jerk" [emphasis ours], sounding like a child playing with guns. This switch from narrator to participant puts you momentarily in the story. As an emotional appeal, it helps you think. You read from the shooter's point of view—but the logic of the shooter seems incomprehensible. What is going on? How are you to understand this epidemic of murders over trivial disagreements?

Albom uses logos and pathos in asking probing questions. "What if the bullets meant for Alan Johnson had sprayed into a passing car instead?" "Are we not moving back to the days of frontier justice, the Wild Wild West, where getting upset over a card game was reason enough to kill a man?" People are getting killed for no apparent reason—like the Detroit firefighter shot while battling a blaze and the 16-year-old boy sleeping on a couch. Albom's use of specific examples and details stirs readers' emotions and makes them think about the problem. "Where does this stop?" he asks.

Although Albom's article combines appeals to logos and pathos, the most important appeal for persuasion is ethos. None of the appeals works unless you believe the writer. The writer's credibility is crucial. Not another unknown victim, Mitch Albom is a prize-winning author, well known throughout the country. It doesn't hurt to have external information about the writer, but the ethos in an essay must be built in—you must try to judge from the writing itself whether Albom is a man of good will, a moral person, someone who deserves your respect.

There is no way for you to know absolutely, of course, whether Mitch Albom is being truthful; it's possible that he could have invented much of his evidence. But unless there are obvious clues in the writing that make you suspect the author's truthfulness, you owe the writer a fair reading. Authors have the right to presume you believe them, until you come across something that makes you think otherwise.

Assuming the author is truthful, you can see that he has taken the trouble to put all this information together carefully, skillfully, so that you can follow it and be open to his point of view. Albom's concern for the individuals killed and his concern for society as a whole suggest a thoughtful, compassionate person.

You have to ask yourself—is this a reasonable man? Do you believe him? You may not agree with his position, but it's hard not to accept his presentation of the problem.

What Is the Solution?

Because the gun problem appears to be getting worse, Albom claims we need legislation that will make it harder to buy guns. "Stop allowing guns to be as easy to buy as cigarettes." He argues we need parents to teach children respect for life, and we need to stop glorifying TV shows and music that feature guns and killing. We need a change in attitudes about guns. Albom invokes a metaphor: we must "stomp the killing gene in our society." Loose in our society is a mad impulse to assert one's dominance with a lethal firearm. He calls for action from readers: more legislation and more respect for life.

Albom's Conclusion

Albom could have ended his article with the sentence "But you have to start somewhere." Instead, he ends with a personal experience, describing his own encounter with a gunman holding up a dry cleaners. He explains the horror he felt facing the gun and seeing the gun in his sleep afterward. His personal example at the end of his essay stirs pathos, logos, and ethos. Readers feel and think about Albom's personal experience; he and his arguments become even more credible.

Hooking his last paragraph to his first by referring to Alan Johnson again, the drive-by shooting victim, Albom ends his article with this prediction: "We cannot live where disputes are solved by bullets. And until we take the guns away, we will make no dent in this. We just keep arguing, until another window rolls down." His last image is a haunting reminder that another drive-by shooting is bound to occur soon.

Analysis and Evaluation of Thomas Sowell's Essay

Thomas Sowell is a well-known newspaper columnist who has written several columns about the myths and dangers of gun control. Please read the following essay by Sowell, and, as you do, notice whether his arguments are convincing and whether he appeals to your emotions and ethics. Does he persuade you to consider his view, to agree with him? Ask yourself questions as you read; look for any insights, assumptions, and overgeneralizations.

Mass Shootings and Mass Hysteria

Thomas Sowell

In a world of emotional-outburst TV shows and dumbed-down education, it may not be so surprising that the deaths of 15 people have stampeded Congress toward laws affecting more than a quarter of a billion Americans and their descendants.   1

That stampede is called "gun control."   2

The tragic irony is that such laws are much more likely to increase shooting deaths than to reduce them. For those of us old-fashioned enough to think that facts still matter, comprehensive research has shown that allowing law-abiding citizens to carry concealed weapons reduces gun violence, as well as other kinds of violence.   3

Unfortunately, facts may carry very little weight politically, in the midst 4 of an emotional orgy with rhetorical posturing. Yet the evidence is overwhelming that allowing law-abiding citizens to be armed has reduced violence in general and mass shootings in particular.

For those to whom facts still matter, John Lott's book More Guns, Less 5 Crime presents overwhelming evidence. Another study of his, with Professor William Landes of the University of Chicago as co-author, addresses mass shootings, such as those which have been taking place in schools, post offices and other public places. These shooting rampages have been far more common in places where there are strong gun control laws. No matter what other factors these authors take into account—poverty, race, population density, etc.—the results are still the same. Places with many armed citizens have fewer mass shootings. Their data cover mass shootings in every state and the District of Columbia, going back nearly two decades.

Congress would do well to call Lott and Landes as witnesses who could 6 provide some much-needed education for the public and the media, as well as for the legislators who are being rushed toward ill-considered legislation. Gun control laws have a bad track record, however popular they may be in some quarters.

Think about it: People who are committing illegal acts are not going to 7 be stopped because guns are illegal. What does stop them then? Often it is somebody else with a gun. Indeed, such shootings may not occur at all in places where there is a high probability of encountering armed resistance, either from an intended victim or from someone else on the scene in a public place. If those who are asking emotionally, "How can we stop these school shootings?" were serious, they might discover that some of these shootings have in fact been stopped by an armed adult at the school. None of them would have been stopped by the kinds of gun control laws that Congress is currently being stampeded into passing.

Waiting periods? The young murderers in Colorado waited longer than any 8 waiting period ever suggested before carrying out their well-planned orgy of death. "Assault weapons" ban? Such bans would not have applied to the kinds of guns that were used. Nor would the Columbine High School tragedy have been prevented by programs for "troubled youths." The Columbine killers had already been given a clean bill of health by shrinks running such programs. So had the young killers in another school mass shooting. The track record of psycho-babble is miserable, however popular it may be in the media.

Some people support gun control laws simply because they are opposed 9 to guns. We may all agree that the world would be a better place if guns had never been invented. The same could be said for everything from bows and arrows to nuclear weapons.

But there is no way to unring the bell. The only options available to us 10 today involve choices about what to do now, given that all these deadly things exist and cannot be made to disappear, no matter what kinds of words we put on paper.

In a country where there are millions of guns available illegally to crim- 11
inals, the real question is whether we should allow potential victims to be
armed as well. Even people who never carry a gun are less likely to become
victims in a community where concealed weapons are widely permitted to law-
abiding citizens, because the criminal has no way of knowing who is armed and
who isn't.

Statistics on gun accident deaths need to be weighed against statistics 12
on reduced murders where gun ownership is widespread. The latter far more
than balance the former—but only if facts matter. □

Two Methods for Analyzing an Essay: Outlining and Summarizing

To help you understand anyone's thesis and supporting evidence—especially someone whose position you disagree with or oppose—you can make an
outline or a summary of the person's essay.

Outline of Sowell's Essay

I. Antigun laws promote killing (paragraphs 1–4)
    A. Fifteen deaths in Littleton, Colorado, will affect all Americans if gun
       control is "stampeded" in Congress.
    B. Facts show that gun laws increase shootings deaths.
    C. Research shows that concealed weapons, lawfully owned, reduce gun
       violence.
II. Supporting evidence (paragraphs 5–9)
    A. John Lott's book <u>More Guns, Less Crime</u> "presents overwhelming
       evidence."
       1. Mass shootings happen more often in states with restrictive gun
          laws.
       2. Mass shootings happen less often when citizens are armed with
          guns.
       3. Lott and co-writer Landes should testify before Congress to
          educate lawmakers and the media.
    B. Sowell questions three common arguments that favor strong gun
       control.
       1. If guns were illegal, this would not stop criminals; guns stop
          criminals.
       2. Waiting periods will not stop murderers.
          a. The two Littleton students waited and planned their act.
          b. They had received counseling, which did not stop them.
       3. Some people oppose all guns and, therefore, support total gun
          control, but their view is unrealistic.
III. Concealed weapons reduce murder (paragraphs 10–12)
    A. We must choose to act now on how to deal with violence.

B. Should potential victims be allowed to arm themselves? This is the essential question in the gun control controversy.

C. More concealed weapons owned by lawful citizens will reduce violence because criminals will not know who is armed and who is not.

For some tips about outlining, see "Features of Outlining."

FEATURES OF OUTLINING

- Outlines should be objective, without showing your own agreement or disagreement with the author.
- Use your own wording as much as possible; use quotation marks whenever you use direct quotes.
- Outlining gives you a skeletal view of an argument: you and other readers can quickly view it.
- Making an outline helps you think clearly about your own position.
- You will usually not include an outline within your own analysis of an essay; rather, an outline aids you in understanding an essay so you can write about it later.

Summary of Sowell's Essay Writing a summary, like making an outline, is an aid for understanding. It is useful because it enables you to condense an essay into a paragraph. Also, when you write your own essay on a controversial issue, if you can present summaries of other sources opposing your view, you will appear more fair-minded. Here is a summary of Sowell's essay:

> In his essay "Mass Shootings and Mass Hysteria" (10 June 1999), Thomas Sowell argues that gun control fails to protect lawful citizens from criminals who have guns. He cites John Lott's book <u>More Guns, Less Crime</u> as presenting factual evidence that mass shootings don't happen in states with "armed citizens." States where lawful citizens can own concealed weapons have less mass violence because murderers don't know who is armed or not. After 15 deaths at the high school in Littleton, Colorado, a "mass hysteria" for more gun control swept the nation. But history shows that gun control laws don't work: criminals get guns; waiting periods don't prevent anyone intent on murder; and people who support gun control because they oppose guns in general don't help solve the problem. What matters is whether lawful citizens should have the right to conceal weapons for their own protection. This question is more important than whether Congress should pass more gun control laws.

See "Features of Summarizing" for useful advice.

FEATURES OF SUMMARIZING

- Condense without showing your own agreement or disagreement with the author. Make no references to yourself. In a summary your own opinion does not matter—later, when you analyze and evaluate an argument, you can state your opinion and support it.
- Start your summary by referring to the author's name and the title of the source and by stating what you think is the author's thesis.
- Use your own wording as much as possible; use quotation marks whenever you use direct quotes.
- Follow the organization of the source you summarize: note the main reasons and examples the author uses.
- A summary should be a condensed re-creation of the author's thesis and evidence. A summary the length of a well-developed paragraph will usually suffice.
- A summary should show that you are accurate and careful in presenting an author's thesis and evidence.

Outlining and summarizing are extremely useful tools for critical thinking. Condensing an essay into your own words requires analysis (breaking the essay into component parts) and synthesis (reassembling the parts). Whenever you want to understand an author's argument, you can use these tools.

ACTIVITY 4

For practice, outline and summarize either Mitch Albom's essay "Don't Shoot Holes in Gun Control Bills," Deborah Tannen's essay "How to Turn Debate into Dialogue," or Ryan Grady Sample's essay "Bigger, But Not Better" (chapter 1).

Sowell's Writing Situation

Sowell wrote this essay a few weeks after two students at Columbine High School had killed 14 students and a teacher. This violence generated a wave of support for greater gun control across the nation. This motivated Sowell to argue his belief that tragedy should not prevent us from examining factual evidence: we should not be swayed by our emotions when such tragedies occur. Like many debaters, Sowell believes only logos can lead to truth.

Sowell's Introduction

Sowell uses the strategy of contrast to catch his reader's attention: "In a world of emotional-outburst TV shows and dumbed-down education, it may not be so surprising that the deaths of 15 people have stampeded Congress toward laws affecting more than a quarter of a billion Americans and their descendants." Sowell bluntly states his thesis that the deaths of a few people should not determine the fates of everyone else. His <u>tone</u>—attitude— is clear in this one sentence introduction: he dislikes the exhibition of emotions on TV and dislikes the watering-down of education. In such a culture it's natural for masses of people to feel more emotional than logical about gun violence.

The word <u>stampede</u> works well to express Sowell's opinion that like a stampede the fervor for gun control is out of control. Sowell's one word metaphor is loaded with suggestions. "Stampede" refers to "1. a sudden, headlong running away of a group of frightened animals, esp. horses or cattle 2. a confused, headlong rush or flight of a large group of people 3. any sudden, impulsive, spontaneous mass movement" (<u>Webster's New World</u>). His word may offend staunch believers of gun control. But Sowell gets to his point immediately while conveying his tone about gun control and about those people who support it. He may risk alienating many readers who strongly oppose his view, but he also may persuade other readers who are uncommitted.

Noticing Sowell's Insights, Assumptions, and Overgeneralizations

Sowell's statement that "facts may carry very little weight politically" is insightful. Facts should carry weight—for politicians and nonpoliticians alike. However, facts are open to interpretation, which creates much of the tension in the gun control issue. Sowell assumes that the gun control argument has become irrational as the media focus on the emotions of the events and do not examine the facts. He assumes that facts should carry great weight. Would you disagree? Sowell also assumes that gun control is a "stampede"—not any systematic, orderly quest for solving the complex problem of gun violence. His metaphor of "stampede" may be an overgeneralization, but it effectively questions the character of gun control enthusiasts. Sowell assumes the gun control movement is "an emotional orgy with rhetorical posturing." Loaded with negative meanings, this phrase may also be considered an overgeneralization. Surely not all advocates of gun control base their arguments on emotion and inflated language. Sowell also assumes gun control is like trying to "unring the bell." Like many who oppose him, Sowell knows the power of metaphor. The "unrung bell" makes an image, appeals to senses—and it can seem like a fact. He invokes a silent comparison: once a bell is rung, it can't be unrung: so many guns exist in the hands of so many criminals that this problem can't be undone.

Responding to Arguments

Sowell questions three common arguments that favor strong gun control. (1) If guns were illegal, this would not stop criminals—guns stop criminals. (2) Waiting periods will not stop murderers. (3) Some people oppose all guns and therefore support total gun control, but their view is unrealistic. Sowell chooses to respond to these opposing arguments <u>after</u> he presents his supporting evidence. He doesn't first acknowledge other views and then present his view. It's as if Sowell's message is urgent. He is direct, confident in his beliefs and assumptions. Placing the most important information first is a standard journalistic strategy. This has the effect of diminishing the opposing view, especially because Sowell does not concede anything to the opposition. His organization helps him convey the idea that his is the truthful, logical view, and the opposing view is only "an emotional orgy" which has no truth.

Sowell's Use of Logos, Pathos, and Ethos

Sowell appeals to logos much more than Mitch Albom does. He criticizes extreme emotion in our culture. What Sowell does in this essay that Albom doesn't do is present authorities as evidence: John Lott and William Landes, both professors at the University of Chicago. Lott wrote a controversial book called <u>More Guns, Less Crime</u>, which Sowell adopts as his thesis in his essay. Sowell doesn't cite statistics from Lott's book; rather, he says the book "presents overwhelming evidence." Sowell also offers reasons why the quest for gun control is dangerous for our society.

Sowell uses pathos through repetition. He repeats "stampede" three times, and he repeats the idea that facts matter or should matter four times:

> "For those of us old-fashioned enough to think that <u>facts still matter</u>, comprehensive research has shown . . ." (paragraph 3)
>
> "Unfortunately, <u>facts may carry very little weight</u> politically [. . .]" (4)
>
> "For those to whom <u>facts still matter</u> [. . .]" (5)
>
> "[. . .] but only if <u>facts matter</u>." (12)

This repetition serves as an echo, reinforcing Sowell's conviction that facts should matter, and if facts do matter, then readers should follow Sowell's conclusion that more concealed guns will produce less crime.

Although we believe Sowell's use of logos is his strongest appeal, his appeal to ethos is also strong. He cares deeply about the issue of gun control and about the American public not being unduly swayed by the media's blitz of emotional appeals. Sowell is credible: he believes facts are vital for informed problem solving. His reasoning sounds logical, his arguments plausible, and his supporting evidence verifiable. He persuades readers to consider his thesis. Although he may offend staunch advocates of gun control with his negative tone toward them, he acknowledges some of their leading arguments as he tries to refute them.

What Is the Solution?

Clearly, Sowell argues that more gun control is not the solution. According to Sowell, more guns mean less crime. Most people would assume that more guns would mean more crime. But this is not so, claim John Lott and Sowell. Sowell believes lawful citizens should have the right to own and carry concealed weapons, because this reduces violent crime.

Sowell's Conclusion

Sowell uses a hook strategy to return to the contrast he sets up in his introduction between victims of gun violence and the rights of law abiding citizens: "Statistics on gun accident deaths need to be weighed against statistics on reduced murders where gun ownership is widespread. The latter far more than balance the former—but only if facts matter." This in effect restates his thesis. His essay has led to this conclusion. His last sentence also reinforces his idea that facts should persuade people polarized by the gun control controversy.

Albom and Sowell: What Do You Conclude?

Which essay do you find most persuasive: Mitch Albom's "Don't Shoot Holes in Gun Control Bills" or Thomas Sowell's "Mass Shootings and Mass Hysteria"? Or might you argue that both writers persuade you or that neither writer persuades you? Yes. Perhaps each persuades you somewhat, but also each fails to persuade you in other ways. Much depends on your own interest, knowledge, and experience with guns.

You will notice that these discussions have attempted to be fair to both Albom and Sowell. One way to be fair is to avoid finding fault with either view. This is one of the strategies of reconciliation in controversies. If both or all sides can agree to discuss only the valid points of the opposing view, without fault-finding, they will have taken a step toward reconciling their differences. There can be no persuasion as long as hostility remains and both sides believe the other is at fault.

If you were asked to write an essay in which you support a thesis regarding gun control, you could defend or challenge Albom and Sowell. You could look for middle grounds—any ideas that might bridge the extreme positions of being either for or against gun control. You could do research and gather more information on the issue. You could read Lott's book, <u>More Guns, Less Crime</u>.

<u>Newsweek</u> focused on gun control in its 23 August 1999 issue titled "America under the Gun." In an effort to bridge the opposing sides, <u>Newsweek</u> published an editorial called "What Must Be Done." The editors wrote,

> It is time, as Franklin Roosevelt said long ago, to try <u>something</u>. The anti-gun movement must accept that the United States realistically will not, and should not have to, abolish handguns or any reasonable sporting weapon. At the same time, the pro-gun forces ought to acknowledge that the Second Amendment is not

unconditional and be open to reasonable restrictions. If the warring camps can make that tentative peace, there may be a path out of this bewildering debate. (24)

But what constitutes "reasonable restrictions" is itself debatable. As more episodes of gun violence occur, the need for some decisive action mounts in urgency. Controversies by their very nature are difficult to resolve, but in matters of life and death and freedom, citizens must try to resolve them.

WRITING A REPORT TO ANALYZE AND EVALUATE AN ARGUMENT

We invite you now to apply what you have read in this chapter. To apply means to show that you can put to good use what you are learning.

ACTIVITY 5

Choose one of the selections in the Readings on Controversial Issues section at the end of this chapter and examine it using the accompanying "Guidelines for a Report."

GUIDELINES FOR A REPORT

After you decide which selection to write about, read it again carefully: consider photocopying and annotating, outlining, or summarizing it. Use these reading tools: ask questions, and notice insights, assumptions, and overgeneralizations. In a report you should "report" on what you find. Please address these questions:

1. What is the writing situation and what is the writer's thesis?
2. How does the introduction work?
3. What insights, assumptions, and overgeneralizations do you notice?
4. How does the writer respond to other or opposing arguments?
5. How does the writer appeal to logos, pathos, and ethos?
6. What is the writer's solution to the problem?
7. How does the conclusion work?
8. How do you rate the essay overall: excellent, good, so-so, weak? Why?

(box continues)

Notes

- Within your report you should quote directly from your selection to demonstrate your points. (For information on how to quote, see "Quotation Marks: How to Quote from Sources" in Concise Handbook.)
- Please read the section on Kinds of Evidence for Arguing: Examples, Reasons, Authorities, Statistics later in the chapter. This information will help you analyze and evaluate the evidence the writer uses.
- Your report should be 2 to 4 pages long. Consider your audience to be your class members and your instructor.
- For models of a report, review the discussions of Albom's essay and Sowell's essay earlier in this chapter.

WRITING AN ESSAY WITH SOURCES ABOUT A CONTROVERSY

Writing an essay with sources is similar to writing an opinion essay, as you did in chapter 1. However, writing an essay with sources requires that you pay close attention to academic style and carefully use direct quotes and cite page numbers.

ACTIVITY 6

Write an essay about one of the controversial issues presented in this chapter: gun control, abortion, gambling, creationism and evolution, same sex partners, hate speech and the first amendment, or racial profiling. See "Guidelines for an Essay" for helpful advice for activity 6.

GUIDELINES FOR AN ESSAY

1. Browse through the sets of readings.
2. Choose an issue and set of readings that matter to you. Take a stand on the issue—explain whether you are for or against it or whether you take another perspective on it.

(box continues)

3. Read the selections again, more carefully. Consider photocopying and annotating them. Use the reading tools presented in this chapter: ask questions, and notice insights, assumptions, and overgeneralizations.

4. Within your paper discuss and quote from at least two sources from the readings on the issue. (For information on how to quote, see "Quotation Marks—How to Quote from Sources" in Concise Handbook.)

5. Your essay should be 2 to 5 pages long. Consider your audience to be your class members and your instructor.

Notes:

- Writing this essay is more demanding and complex than writing a report. Pay close attention while you read the following section on Organizing an Essay about a Controversial Issue.

- Please also read the section, Kinds of Evidence for Arguing: Examples, Reasons, Authorities, Statistics. This information will help you defend your own position as well as help you analyze and evaluate the evidence other writers use.

Organizing an Essay about a Controversial Issue

Present the Other Side First

Most students believe they should present their own side of an argument first and that the opposing side should come last if at all. But that organization offers little help in establishing a climate in which people can reason together to reconcile their differences. Rather, it seems to say that "my side" is the truth, and your side is inferior. Imagine saying this in a face to face confrontation. It would not lead to cooperation, much less reasoning together.

A primary rule of persuasion is to avoid stirring up negative reactions during the discussion. You must not start with assumptions about an opponent's intelligence. You must not send any signal that you think you are superior or that the opponent is inferior. It is important that your readers believe you respect them. At the end of an argument, if you've succeeded, enlightened readers will say, "You're right—I never saw it that way."

The road to reason begins where you and others agree, not where you disagree. To present yourself as fair and unbiased, you must convince others that you understand their side of the argument. You must remember that, in fact, it is often impossible to persuade others. The real audience for your discussion, in that case, is the uncommitted, those who haven't made up their minds about the issue. For their sake, you must appear reasonable. Ask yourself, whose mind do you have any chance to reach? Whom can you possibly encourage to see matters as you do?

Rogerian Argument

Writing an essay about a controversy often takes two main forms:

Form A	Form B
Introduction and thesis statement	Introduction and thesis statement
Present other view(s)	Present your supporting evidence
Present your supporting evidence	Present other view(s)
Conclusion and restatement of thesis	Conclusion and restatement of thesis

Mitch Albom follows Form A; Thomas Sowell follows Form B. Form B involves more risks because the writer, like Sowell, can give the impression that his argument is most important. The form reinforces Sowell's tone of harshly judging the arguments of gun control advocates.

Carl Rogers, a well-known psychologist, developed a method of argumentation that he claimed helped his patients communicate in nonthreatening ways. He argued that his method could help any opposing groups create bridges of understanding—even the United States and the Soviet Union at that time in the cold war.

The Rogerian method of argument follows Form A in which writers always present an opposing side before presenting their own. The reason for doing this is to reduce the sense of threat an audience might feel. If you show others you understand their position and if you point out what is valid in their reasoning, then you will reduce the level of threat they feel. If you present an opposing view as well as the opponents themselves would present it, they will in turn try to show that they understand your position. The audience will perceive that you are being fair and reasonable and will expect your opponent to do the same. After fully acknowledging each other's positions, you both are more likely to reach some bridge of understanding.

Rogers believed that people have a natural tendency to judge each other—to approve or disapprove what other people say and do. This continual judging threatens most people when they engage in discussions or arguments. Rogers claims that when emotions run high—as with any controversial issue—the tendency to judge others intensifies. To help people avoid this common problem, Rogers advocates "real communication" in which people "listen with understanding" and try to see and feel an idea "from the other person's point of view" (84).[3] For Rogers, communication should involve "understanding with a person, not about" that person (85).

In his essay "Communication: Its Blocking and Its Facilitation," Rogers invites readers to do an experiment based on listening to others:

> The chances are very great indeed that your listening has not been of the type I have described. Fortunately I can suggest a little laboratory experiment which

[3]Carl Rogers, "Communication: Its Blocking and Its Facilitation," A Review of General Semantics 9 (1952): 83–88.

you can try to test the quality of your understanding. The next time you get into an argument with your wife, or your friend, or with a small group of friends, just stop the discussion for a moment and for an experiment, institute this rule. "Each person can speak up for himself only <u>after</u> he has first restated the ideas and feelings of the previous speaker accurately, and to that speaker's satisfaction." You see what this would mean. It would simply mean that before presenting your own point of view, it would be necessary for you to really achieve the other speaker's frame of reference—to understand his thoughts and feelings so well that you could summarize them for him. Sounds simple, doesn't it? But if you try it you will discover it one of the most difficult things you have ever tried to do. (85)

If you can listen with understanding to arguments different from yours, and if others can listen with understanding to your argument, then together you may reach a level of cooperation. Such "mutual communication tends to be pointed toward solving a problem rather than toward attacking a person or group" (88).

ACTIVITY 7

Try Carl Rogers's experiment. Afterward, in your notebook describe what happened—if the experiment was easy or difficult. Also, when you attend classes, try to notice what happens when people argue. See whether people acknowledge or summarize the position of the person who spoke before them. Take notes on what you observe and bring them to class to share.

The Rogerian method of argument offers a sensible formula that you can use when you write argument papers or when you argue with someone or some group. Many writers are eager to present their own arguments first, but see "Advantages of Presenting Other Points of View First."

Ending Your Essay

Inexperienced writers tend to use up all their material in the body of their paper and then have nothing left for the end of the paper. The end of the paper, however, should be the <u>point</u> of the paper. Here you can briefly explain the arguments and points of agreement on both sides. It's good advice to save something for the end. Otherwise, the end seems unimportant. But if that's true, then the paper hasn't been composed properly. Both Ryan Grady Sample and Mitch Albom save something for the end. Sample gives two brief examples of environmental problems other readers are probably facing now: "It might be zebra

---

ADVANTAGES OF PRESENTING OTHER POINTS OF VIEW FIRST

1. You cause others who hold different views to pay closer attention to your view.
2. You establish yourself as fair. Your audience can see (hear) that you are not diminishing or distorting anyone's arguments. Your goal is to show the audience how well informed you are about the other side's arguments.
3. You create the grounds for reasoning together by conceding whatever must be conceded. You lose nothing by making concessions, and you imply to others that they should do the same for you. (The audience will see whether they are fair.)
4. The other side will feel the necessity to extend to you the same courtesy (the audience will see whether the other side, too, is courteous). Thus you start off with a positive ethos, instead of trying to "defeat" your "opponent."

---

mussels, it might be a coal-mining project [. . . .]" Albom describes his own close call with a gun. The reason some papers seem not to have any real conclusion is that the writer has used up the conclusion in the preceding parts of the paper. It is partly a matter of structure.

There is no standard or routine way to write an argument paper (or shouldn't be), but the Form A pattern we described earlier is useful for college writers. Instructors of various disciplines know it well. See "Guidelines for Essays on Controversies" for some tips.

GUIDELINES FOR ESSAYS ON CONTROVERSIES

1. Present introduction and thesis statement.
2. Present other view(s): acknowledge briefly, summarize, or present them fully and fairly.
3. Present your own supporting evidence: provide examples, reasons, authorities, statistics, and direct quotes from sources.
4. Present the conclusion and restatement of the thesis.

When students use this form, instructors can follow an essay's structure easily and concentrate on the meaning expressed and persuasive appeals used: logos, pathos, and ethos.

WRITING AN ESSAY ABOUT A LOCAL ISSUE

Unless you can use what you are learning about critical thinking and persuasive arguments, then what you're learning will not take root and grow. As a member of your academic community, your workplace, your town, your state, you can use the information in this chapter to address a problem or an issue facing you and others. You can use your writing to work for some common good.

ACTIVITY 8

Deborah Tannen writes, "There are times when it is necessary and right [. . .] to argue for your rights or against offensive or dangerous ideas or actions" (The Argument Culture 4–5). Do you feel any need to defend yourself, to argue for your rights, or to argue against offensive or dangerous ideas? Write an essay about a controversial issue at your school or in your town or state. You must care about the issue: it must matter to you. If you write about a campus issue, consider submitting your essay to your school newspaper. If you write about an issue concerning your town or state, consider submitting your essay to a local or state newspaper. The following section on kinds of evidence will help you defend your position.

KINDS OF EVIDENCE FOR ARGUING: EXAMPLES, REASONS, AUTHORITIES, STATISTICS

Whenever you try to support your position on a controversial issue—indeed on any issue—you need convincing evidence.

Using Examples

The example is the most basic, specific form of evidence. It clarifies, dramatizes, and vitalizes the reality behind any idea. You need specific examples and details to show what you mean. Examples—when well chosen and clearly explained—can persuade readers. They help readers pay attention and understand. They make you seem reasonable, credible, and trustworthy.

Most examples come from real life—based on fact or on what a writer has experienced, witnessed, read, or heard.

SPECIFIC	GENERAL
Wu: "In my freshman year, my roommates and I survived on Chinese takeout, express pizzas and taco take-home dinners."	"My roommates and I survived on fast food."
Tannen: "We can make special efforts not to think in twos. Mary Catherine Bateson, an anthropologist at Virginia's George Mason University, makes a point of having her class compare three cultures, not two. Then, students are more likely to think about each on its own terms, rather than as opposites."	"Teachers should not always think in twos."
Albom: "In June, a Detroit firefighter was shot while putting out a blaze. Nobody knew why."	"An innocent person was shot."

Note the difference between the specific and general examples. Specific examples and details show meaning so readers can see and understand.

Examples can also be <u>hypothetical</u>; that is, they can be imagined in order to suggest or demonstrate an idea. For example, suppose your mother at age 50 finds herself pregnant, and she decides to keep the baby. Her age could pose a health risk to herself and to her child. Would you think she was right not to abort the child?

Biologist Dr. Lee Silver uses hypothetical examples in his book <u>Remaking Eden</u>, which examines the scientific world of reproductive technologies.

> Sometime in the not so different future, you may visit the maternity ward at a major university hospital to see the newborn child or grandchild of a close friend. The new mother, let's call her Barbara, seems very much at peace with the world, sitting in a chair quietly nursing her baby, Max. Her labor was—in the parlance of her doctor—"uneventful," and she is looking forward to raising her first child. You decide to make pleasant conversation by asking Barbara whether she knew in advance that her baby was going to be a boy. In your mind, it seems like a perfectly reasonable question since doctors have long given prospective parents the option of learning the sex of their child-to-be many months before the predicted date of birth. But Barbara seems taken back by the question. "Of course I knew that Max would be a boy," she tells you. "My husband Dan and I chose him from the embryos we made. And when I'm ready to go through this again, I'll choose a girl to be my second child. An older son and a younger daughter—a perfect family. (1)

Hypothetical examples are useful when the argument concerns matters of the future, things that have not yet happened but likely could or will.

Although using specific examples will clarify and energize your writing, examples do not necessarily prove an idea—rather, they show and support an idea. Persuasive examples will not only help readers understand what you mean, but readers also will appreciate your ability to be clear and interesting. Examples and ethos go together.

Using Reasons

Reasons are statements that support or explain an opinion. They give coherence to arguments. Without reasons, arguments would have no power—they would be examples and details with no idea to unify or justify them.

Why did you choose the college or university you are attending? To answer this, you would give reasons such as these: (1) <u>Because</u> I like State's program in health fitness; I hope to get a job as a physical therapist. (2) <u>Because</u> I like small classes. (3) <u>Because</u> I like State's beautiful campus. Notice that each of these reasons could be a topic sentence for a paragraph that you could support with specific examples and details.

To answer questions, you naturally give reasons, which you then explain further with examples and details. Reasons answer the question "why?"

> Tannen: "The argument culture shapes who we are." [Why?] "[<u>Because</u> it] makes us distort facts. [. . .] It makes us waste valuable time. [. . .] It limits our. [. . .] It encourages us to lie."

> Albom: "I thought there could be no worse horror, to enter an innocent situation and be looking down the barrel of a gun. Now I realize I was wrong. [Why?] [<u>Because</u> the] worst horror is to look down the barrel just before it fires."

> Sowell: Gun control causes more problems than it solves. Why? "[<u>Because</u>] places with many armed citizens have fewer mass shootings."

Reasons often sound as if they start with an implied "because." Reasons call for examples and details to help writers communicate clearly and persuade convincingly. Without solid reasons, readers will question your logos as well as ethos. When you present sound reasons, readers find you credible.

Using Authorities

When you argue, you can use authorities to support your claims. An authority is an expert who is respected, reliable, and trustworthy in a given field. Statements by authorities carry weight and can be persuasive.

Deborah Tannen uses authorities in her article. She cites Deborah Lipstadt, a professor from Emory University, who examined how "deniers" of the Holocaust gain media exposure by presenting themselves as "the other side." She cites psychologists Elizabeth Loftus and John Palmer, who conducted research on how language shapes perception, although Tannen doesn't mention their university affiliation. Thomas Sowell cites John Lott and his book <u>More Guns, Less Crime</u> for supporting evidence. He also cites a colleague of Lott's, Professor William Landes. Sowell doesn't supply much information about Lott and Landes. But mentioning the University of Chicago, a highly respected university, lends credence to his claim. The University of Chicago also published Lott's book. Sowell believes that Lott is a credible authority, and we find it hard to disagree.

As a critical thinker you can cite authorities to support or to challenge opinions. If you write an essay arguing that juveniles who commit murder should receive capital punishment, you can try to find experts with informed opinions to support your position. If you want to show your readers that you are fair-minded and consider various sides of an issue, you can cite experts who disagree with you. Authorities often disagree. Both sides at the infamous O. J. Simpson trial used authorities who claimed they had reliable scientific evidence; both sets of experts tried to persuade the jury with opposing testimony.

Arguing from authority is appropriate when a person is an expert on the topic you are discussing; however, part of your job as a critical thinker is to determine whether a person truly is an authority. Consider the scientist Linus Pauling, who won two Nobel prizes—for chemistry and for world peace. Although he was a well-respected authority in chemistry, he was not as well respected in medicine and nutrition. Many scientists found Pauling controversial, even crazy, for promoting vitamin C. He argued that people should take 2,000 to 18,000 milligrams per day of vitamin C instead of 60 milligrams per day as recommended by the National Academy of Sciences. He consumed the maximum dose himself, the equivalent of 240 oranges a day. He lived to be 93 and believed his intake of vitamin C contributed greatly to his longevity (Discover [Jan. 1993]: 54). To evaluate an authority, see "Guidelines for Using Authorities."

GUIDELINES FOR USING AUTHORITIES

1. What are the person's credentials? What achievements is the person well known for? Is the person affiliated with well-respected universities or other organizations? What do other experts say about the person?

2. Is the person an expert in the area you are writing about? If not, using that person as an authority will reflect poorly on your own judgment.

3. Is the testimony from the person relevant? Does the reference or quote you use truly contribute to your argument? If you're using it for padding, to show that you've done "research," then you're putting your own ethos on the line.

4. Is the authority biased? If you claim that studies show the herb Saint Johnswort alleviates depression, your claim will have more credence if the research was done by the Harvard School of Medicine than by the Saint Johnswort Institute. (Note that an authority can be an organization.)

5. Try not to overuse authority. If you cite many experts, your argument may seem like a compilation of their opinions rather than a synthesis of your own understanding.

ACTIVITY 9

Find at least two authorities who hold different positions on the controversial issue your essay concerns. Then in a brief paper explain how these experts disagree. Try to cite a quotation from each of them. Be sure to cite your sources. (See chapter 9, Documentation.)

Using Statistics

Statistics are numerical facts. That Linus Pauling took the equivalent of 240 oranges a day is a single statistic—showing his deep conviction in Vitamin C's power. As a fact it is objective and verifiable: so much vitamin C equals so many oranges. Statistics are often persuasive; they express information clearly and concisely. Numbers have power. However, because statistics can be manipulated easily to fool readers, critical thinkers need to judge whether the numbers have been used appropriately.

When you find useful statistics to support your argument, they usually come from some authority. Jonathan Kozol, an authority on education and literacy, uses many statistics in his book <u>Illiterate America</u>, published in 1985:

> Twenty-five million American adults cannot read the poison warnings on a can of pesticide, a letter from their child's teacher, or the front page of a daily paper. An additional 35 million read only at a level which is less than equal to the full survival needs of our society.
>
> Together, these 60 million people represent more than one third of the entire adult population.
>
> The largest number of illiterate adults are white, native-born Americans. In proportion to population, however, the figures are higher for blacks and Hispanics than for whites. Sixteen percent of white adults, 44 percent of blacks, and 56 percent of Hispanic citizens are functional or marginal illiterates. Figures for the younger generation of black adults are increasing. Forty-seven percent of all black seventeen-year-olds are functionally illiterate. (4)

What is the effect of these statistics? They illuminate the problem, which is why Kozol uses them. He wants to arouse concern in readers. Notice how Kozol carefully classifies illiterate adults. He qualifies his data with "in proportion to population," explaining that more blacks and Hispanic adults are illiterate compared to white adults. Statistics as such appeal to logos and pathos. Kozol's fair-minded use of statistics reinforces his ethos as well.

Statistics rarely stand alone. They usually require someone—not always an expert—to interpret them, to draw inferences from them. In a review of the book <u>The Slave Trade: The Story of the Atlantic Slave Trade: 1440–1870</u> by Hugh Thomas, <u>Baltimore Sun</u> columnist Gregory Kane cites statistics to catch the attention of readers and to provoke thought about the book:

> Some 11.3 million Africans were transported to the New World during the years 1440–1870. Some 4 million went to Brazil, 2.5 million to countries ruled by Spain, 2 million to the British West Indies and 1.6 million to the French West Indies. Only 500,000 went to the country that eventually became known as the United States of America.
>
> [. . .] The figure of 500,000 of Africa's children making it to the United States is especially revealing. For too long egocentric Americans—black and white—have obsessed about the sordid history of slavery as if the scourge were ours alone. [. . .] But the numbers speak for themselves. Just under 4 percent of the blacks taken from Africa ended up in the United States. So in the guilt department, there are clearly countries that should have much more than the United States. (33D)

Although Kane writes that "the numbers speak for themselves," he interprets them. He infers from the facts that Americans should feel less guilt about slavery, because compared to other parts of the world the United States received fewer slaves. You must decide for yourself whether his inference makes sound sense.

Notice how Kane's diction conveys his attitude about the statistics he uses: "Only 500,000" and "Just under 4 percent." His use of "only" and "just under" suggests that Kane diminishes the seriousness of the numbers. Although statistics are objective facts, writers usually wrap their opinions around them. In an advertisement for the car Avenger, Dodge used the word "enormous" to exaggerate a fact: "Avenger offers enormous 17″ wheels and tires for grip and stability." To infer writers' opinions of the numbers they use, pay attention to words that introduce statistics.

Statistics may be misleading. Most people believe what they hear and read, but as a critical thinker you must learn to question statistics. Numbers often sound believable until you analyze them. What if 50% of young women playing high school football in the United States quit during the last 5 years? This number sounds large, but if 20 women played football this means that 10 quit but 10 played. These numbers more accurately reflect the truth, whereas 50% sounds larger—more inflated and dramatic. When you see a percentage, such as 50%, you should ask, "Fifty percent of how many?"

As you should question the credentials and bias of an authority, you should also question the source of their statistics. When Wonder Bread claims it builds strong bodies in 12 ways, is this claim based on their own research or on research performed by impartial scientific organizations?

Many advertisers now include their Web addresses so readers can investigate their claims and statistics in depth. Consider the nutrition bar Balance—"Tastes too good to be good for you." In an ad Balance uses these statistics: "Based on the clinically proven 40–30–30 nutrition concept (40% of calories from carbohydrates, 30% from protein and 30% from dietary fat), Balance bars provide all the essential nutrients to keep you going for the day." At the bottom of the ad Balance invites readers to inquire for more information about their 40–30–30 formula and provides their Web address: <www.balance.com>.

Finding statistics usually requires research in a library or on the Web. In his essay (see chapter 1), Ryan Grady Sample reports the following:

> In 1994, it was estimated that the cumulative 30-year value of the fishery, if lake trout were absent, was more than a billion dollars. The estimated value depreciates $640 million if the lake trout remain.

Notice, however, that Sample does not specify who or what organization "estimated" these values. Is it the Yellowstone park service? Some federal environmental group? If Sample were writing this essay for a college class, his teacher would probably require that he cite sources for these statistics. Still, Sample presents himself as a credible and knowledgeable person. Because of his ethos, you may surmise that his information is accurate, but see "Guidelines for Using Statistics" for suggestions on evaluating statistical data.

GUIDELINES FOR USING STATISTICS

1. Are the statistics reliable? Do they come from credible, trustworthy sources? Are they biased or misleading?
2. Are the statistics clear and relevant? If you use too many numbers, readers soon may feel overloaded. To condense statistics, you can present them in tables or charts.
3. Consider your audience. If your statistics are too technical, you will lose not only your readers but your point. Technical statistics are fine if your audience has the knowledge to understand them: "Chi square is a nondirectional test. Since the statistic is arrived at by squaring the difference between observed and expected frequencies, it has no sign. Consider the .05 value for one degree of freedom in Table IV. This value is 3.841 and the square root of this is ± 1.96 which is the .05 value for $\underline{z}$ for a two-tailed test. Similarly, from this same table for the same number of degrees of freedom we find the .01 value of $\underline{z}$ to be 6.635. The square root of this is ± 2.58, the .01 value of $\underline{z}$ for a two-tailed test." (Downie and Heath 169)

ACTIVITY 10

Try to find some statistics concerning the controversial issue about which you are writing your essay. Consider browsing through a reference book such as <u>Facts on File</u>, <u>FBI Statistics</u>, or <u>Statistical Abstract of the United States</u>. The Internet also provides many sources for statistics. You might look for a chart or table of statistics that interests you and interpret it. Then in a brief report explain how these statistics are useful or not useful in understanding the controversy. Cite your sources at the end of the paper. (See chapter 9, Documentation.)

ACTIVITY 11

When you have a rough draft of your essay, examine your use of evidence. Evaluate your use of examples—are they specific, important, and true? Evaluate your use of reasons—are they clear, sound, and logical? Evaluate your use of authorities and statistics. Do you use them carefully? If you don't use any, would your essay be more persuasive if you did?

READINGS ON CONTROVERSIAL ISSUES

Gun Control

You may use Mitch Albom's "Don't Shoot Holes in Gun Control Bills" and Thomas Sowell's "Mass Shootings and Mass Hysteria" along with the following writings.

Standing Guard

Wayne LaPierre

In the year 2000 elections, the media is hyping the notion that "gun control" 1 should be the central issue of politics. A recent headline in the <u>Atlanta-Journal Constitution</u> is typical: "Make Firearms' Carnage Central to Campaign."

November may seem like a long way off, but in reality, we have precious 2 little time to educate candidates and the public in our simple, yet proven, message: "Make Safety Matter—jail armed criminals!"

We want candidates to understand that they never have to be at cross 3 purposes with firearms owners. The issue of gun control—from registration to licensing to bans—is pointless in the presence of strict application of existing federal law against criminal possession and use of guns. Period. Candidates don't have to tread on any American's rights. They can stand for something positive—jail time for armed criminals.

We'll meet anybody head-on with the choice. On our side is the proven 4 truth about using tough federal laws against criminals with guns, versus Clintonesque government "control" over the rights of innocent citizens to own firearms and be secure in their homes.

The picture that emerges with respect to the Bureau of Alcohol, Tobacco 5 and Firearms (BATF) enforcement of federal firearms law against armed violent criminals shows an anemic performance. Overall, BATF criminal referrals are down by 44 percent since the beginning of the Clinton Administration, according to a Syracuse University study. A city-by-city analysis showed that major jurisdictions such as San Francisco, Los Angeles, Chicago and Bridgeport, Conn. were rated at the very bottom of federal law cases referred and prosecuted.

Under the watch of Bill Clinton and Al Gore, and with the active consent 6 of anti-firearms congressmen and senators, thousands of criminals are allowed to walk away daily from multiple felonies committed when they attempt to buy a gun or are caught possessing a gun. Virtually nothing happens at the main Justice Department level.

It is a national scandal. And it should indeed be the central theme of this 7 election campaign.

Look at news files in any city from the past seven years and you will find 8 the names of innocent victims of the Clinton-era federal firearms law enforcement policy—people who have been murdered, maimed, raped, robbed and cursed with a lifetime of fear. They have families. They have children. The people who did evil to them could have been stopped in time if the law simply had been enforced and criminals had been jailed in sure and timely fashion.

For a three-time convicted felon, the federal law says simple possession 9 of any firearm brings at least a 15-year mandatory prison term. The Clinton-Gore Administration and Janet Reno's Justice Department have blood on their hands every time someone is harmed by a felon, violent juvenile or drug dealer who could have been taken off the streets under existing law.

Drugs and guns can bring down a lifetime of jail for offenders arrested and 10 convicted. It's the law.

Candidates for public office can point to the success of Project Exile in 11 Richmond, Va., where prosecution for violation of existing federal felon-with-a-gun provisions is absolute and the use of existing enhanced penalties for guns and drugs has caused criminals to disarm themselves rather than risk a sure thing—long prison terms.

In Richmond, murder is down. Robbery is down. All crimes of armed 12 violence are down dramatically. Because criminals are off the streets. In fact, Richmond had more BATF-instigated prosecutions under federal felon-with-a-gun laws in 1998 than California, New Jersey, New York and Washington, D.C. <u>combined</u>.

Richmond Deputy Police Chief Teresa Gooch told the U.S. Congress, 13

> Has it worked? Our city residents think so. The daughter of an elderly woman who lives in one of the city's communities thanked us recently. She said she witnessed her mother do something the other day that she'd never seen her do before—walk by herself to the corner grocery. The woman's mother had never felt safe enough to walk just a few blocks along before. She does now.
>
> The attitude of Richmond's would-be criminals is changing, too. When a Richmond detective recently questioned a suspect about whether he was carrying a gun, the suspect was quick to reply—"Carry a gun in Richmond? I don't want to go to jail for five years."

The Administration's national response has been to call the violent criminals who are being prosecuted in Richmond "guppies" not worthy of their attention. These armed "guppies" kill, maim and rape. Project Exile takes them off the streets.

Today, Project Exile—partly through the efforts of NRA—is statewide in 14 Virginia through the leadership of former Attorney General and now Governor Jim Gilmore. Attorneys General in Pennsylvania and South Carolina are pushing statewide Exile legislation. Texas Governor George W. Bush declared major cities Exile zones. And the American people want it because it works.

So what is the continued drumbeat for "gun control" all about? It's about 15 making guns illegal in the hands of peaceable citizens. It's about peeling away our rights to defend our families, homes, children. It's about the media demonizing good people. It's about invasion of privacy, about databases with the names and photos of the innocent. It's about lists of private property and who owns it.

To frame this debate in this high-stakes election year, we need to educate 16 people and especially candidates as to the facts about current law, and about the kinds of "gun control" being pressed by the likes of presidential candidates Al Gore and Bill Bradley.

Let friends, neighbors and open-minded candidates know there is already 17 existing law with respect to firearms registration. It is the law of the land, which will never be mentioned in the media or by the likes of publicity-driven anti-gun-owner politicians.

Federal law on registration was defined by the United States Supreme 18 Court in <u>Haynes v. U.S.</u> when it declared that arresting a criminal for not registering an illegally owned gun is unconstitutional. It would violate the Fifth Amendment right against self-incrimination.

So existing federal case law says with great finality that gun registration 19 only applies to the law-abiding. The same argument holds true with licensing. A recent court decision determined that a criminal couldn't be forced to apply for a firearms owner license, and he couldn't be prosecuted for not having one.

So if criminals can't be arrested and tried for breaking a law that only   20
applies to you and me, what's the point?

Neither registration, nor licensing, nor any form of law that restricts the   21
rights of the peaceable has ever curbed crime.

When the NRA points to the utter failure of any of these schemes wher-   22
ever they have been tried, the gun rights opponents always say the same things,
"that's only because they've not been applied nationally."

If snake oil fails to cure the criminal ills of, say, Chicago, they demand a   23
liberal application of snake oil nationally. The truth is, what fails locally will fail
everywhere.

The inverse is true of the application of federal criminal laws against crim-   24
inals with guns. Project Exile <u>was applied only in and around Richmond and it
had an immediate and dramatic effect locally. It is good medicine that worked
for Richmond and will work everywhere.</u>

It will work equally in Los Angeles, or New Orleans or Chicago. And the   25
mayors of many cities where the carnage is the greatest are keeping Exile and
federal law a secret. They'd rather press a phony "gun control" agenda.

It's time for citizens everywhere to demand a Project Exile in their own   26
communities, their own states.

If some people in politics and the media want to make "gun control" the   27
issue of the country, we welcome the fight. But our fight is "criminal control."
People are getting to really understand this issue.

It's not just innocent gun owners who are getting sick of the ghoulish,   28
in-your-face media blame for insane violence.

During the 1999 off-year elections in Virginia, "gun control" was touted   29
by the media and anti-gun rights organizations as the critical issue statewide.
In races where candidates hung everything on "gun control" and blamed innocent gun owners for the acts of criminals and the insane, they lost. Pro-firearms
rights candidates in those races were pegged by the media for extinction. They
all won. The public had wide knowledge of Exile. Voters had a choice and they
made it resoundingly.

Nationwide, firearms rights activists and casual gun owners alike are non-   30
partisan in their anger. Democrats or Republicans, it doesn't matter. We are
singularly driven this political year—sick and tired of being blamed for acts of
violence that have no connections to the peaceable exercise of our Second
Amendment rights.

We must get the message out to politicians that gun owners are not   31
passive when it comes to voting rights, either.

We welcome the challenge to bring the truth to the American people and   32
give those running for public office a clear choice. We need your help to do it.
Please copy and handout this column. Talk to friends, family and candidates.
Start now. □

Why I Own a Gun

Linda Chavez

Every time some homicidal maniac with a gun starts shooting people, especially 1 children, I start rethinking my opposition to gun control. Last week's blood bath at Wedgewood Baptist Church in Ft. Worth, Texas, was no exception. I own guns—two handguns, a .357 magnum and a .22, and my husband is considering buying a rifle to hunt deer. But with every mass shooting, I ask myself whether the gun-control advocates aren't right after all.

I purchased my first revolver some 25 years ago, after my husband was 2 mugged on the streets of Washington, D.C. The only time I had occasion to use it to protect myself, I couldn't get to it in time. A young male intruder snuck into my house through a door carelessly left unlocked. He hid in a corner of my front hall while I was putting my newborn son down for a nap in the bassinet in my living room.

Luckily, I saw the man out of the corner of my eye as I walked toward the 3 kitchen, but the gun was upstairs, with a trigger lock on it. Without letting the intruder know I'd seen him, I walked directly to the kitchen, picked up the phone, and called the police. Only then did I turn to face the young man, all 6 feet 4 inches of him, looming over me, now standing in the middle of the living room.

I have no idea what his intentions were. As soon as I informed him the 4 police were on their way, he acted as if I had insulted him grievously and calmly walked out the front door through which he'd entered. When he hit the sidewalk, he began running. The police came a few minutes later, but never caught him, despite my careful, detailed description.

I sometimes wonder what I would have done if my gun had been nearby. 5 I like to think I would have remained calm—even with a gun in hand—and done pretty much what I did without one, which was to summon help from the police. Oddly, even the knowledge that I had a gun upstairs probably emboldened me not to scream when I saw the man lurking in my hall. One of the more careful studies of the subject, by University of Chicago professor John Lott, suggests that some 2 million crimes are averted every year because the potential victim is armed.

Still, the mounting carnage from Wedgewood Baptist Church, the Jewish 6 Community Center in Los Angeles, Columbine High School, and on and on, begs some response. But what? Al Gore and most of the Democrats in Congress blame Republicans for failing to pass new gun-control legislation, as if the bills they propose could possibly have prevented any of these specific tragedies, even if they had been enacted before the killings.

In fact, most of the killers in these high-profile mass murders obtained 7 their guns illegally, even under current law. The one exception—Larry Ashbrook,

who killed seven people at the Baptist church in Ft. Worth last week before 8
taking his own life—would not have been prevented from legally purchasing the
guns he used by any of the proposed bills.

It would be wonderful if we could pass a law that kept guns out of the 9
hands of murderers and other criminals. But I don't know of one that could—
short of a total ban on all firearms in private possession, which would require
repealing the 2nd Amendment to the Constitution and confiscating the more
than 200 million guns now in private hands in the United States.

The prospect of more mass shootings is frightening, but so is the idea of 10
the government attempting to seize every privately owned gun. Even if it were
possible for the government to commandeer every gun in the country, do we
really want the assault on civil liberties such a plan would entail?

Prohibiting guns today would be about as successful as prohibiting alco- 11
hol was in the '20s.

I hope I never have to use my gun for self-protection. But living as I now 12
do, in an isolated rural area, I can't count on the police to come to my rescue
if I ever encounter another intruder. So long as there are criminals out there, I
feel safer knowing that I can protect myself. And until someone can figure out
a way to make all guns magically disappear, I'll keep mine, no matter how guilty
I may sometimes feel. □

Gun Control

The American Civil Liberties Union

"Why doesn't the ACLU support an individual's unlimited right to keep and bear
arms?"

Background

The ACLU has often been criticized for "ignoring the Second Amendment" and
refusing to fight for the individual's right to own a gun or other weapons. This
issue, however, has not been ignored by the ACLU. The national board has in fact
debated and discussed the civil liberties aspects of the Second Amendment many
times.

We believe that the constitutional right to bear arms is primarily a collective one, 1
intended mainly to protect the right of the states to maintain militias to assure
their own freedom and security against the central government. In today's world,
that idea is somewhat anachronistic and in any case would require weapons much
more powerful than handguns or hunting rifles. The ACLU therefore believes that
the Second Amendment does not confer an unlimited right upon individuals to

own guns or other weapons nor does it prohibit reasonable regulation of gun ownership, such as licensing and registration.

In Brief

The national ACLU is neutral on the issue of gun control. We believe that the   2 Constitution contains no barriers to reasonable regulations of gun ownership. If we can license and register cars, we can license and register guns.

Most opponents of gun control concede that the Second Amendment   3 certainly does not guarantee an individual's right to own bazookas, missiles or nuclear warheads. Yet these, like rifles, pistols and even submachine guns, are arms.

The question therefore is not whether to restrict arms ownership, but how   4 much to restrict it. If that is a question left open by the Constitution, then it is a question for Congress to decide.

ACLU Policy

"The ACLU agrees with the Supreme Court's long-standing interpretation of the   5 Second Amendment [as set forth in the 1939 case, U.S. v. Miller] that the individual's right to bear arms applies only to the preservation or efficiency of a well-regulated militia. Except for lawful police and military purposes, the possession of weapons by individuals is not constitutionally protected. Therefore, there is no constitutional impediment to the regulation of firearms" (Policy 47).

Arguments, Facts, Quotes

A well regulated militia, being necessary to the security of a free State, the right of the people to keep and bear Arms, shall not be infringed. (The Second Amendment to the Constitution)

Since the Second Amendment [. . .] applies only to the right of the State to maintain a militia and not to the individual's right to bear arms, there can be no serious claim to any express constitutional right to possess a firearm. (U.S. v. Warin [6th Circuit, 1976])

Unless the Constitution protects the individual's right to own all kinds of   6 arms, there is no principled way to oppose reasonable restrictions on handguns, Uzis or semi-automatic rifles.

If indeed the Second Amendment provides an absolute, constitutional   7 protection for the right to bear arms in order to preserve the power of the people to resist government tyranny, then it must allow individuals to possess bazookas, torpedoes, SCUD missiles and even nuclear warheads, for they, like

handguns, rifles and M-16s, are arms. Moreover, it is hard to imagine any serious resistance to the military without such arms. Yet few, if any, would argue
that the Second Amendment gives individuals the unlimited right to own any
weapons they please. But as soon as we allow governmental regulation of any
weapons, we have broken the dam of Constitutional protection. Once that dam
is broken, we are not talking about whether the government can constitutionally restrict arms, but rather what constitutes a reasonable restriction.

The 1939 case <u>U.S.</u> v. <u>Miller</u> is the only modern case in which the Supreme   8
Court has addressed this issue. A unanimous Court ruled that the Second Amendment must be interpreted as intending to guarantee the states' rights to maintain and train a militia. "In the absence of any evidence tending to show that
possession or use of a shotgun having a barrel of less than 18 inches in length
at this time has some reasonable relationship to the preservation or efficiency
of a well-regulated militia, we cannot say that the Second Amendment guarantees the right to keep and bear such an instrument," the Court said.

In subsequent years, the Court has refused to address the issue. It   9
routinely denies cert.[a] to almost all Second Amendment cases. In 1983, for
example, it let stand a 7th Circuit decision upholding an ordinance in Morton
Grove, Illinois, which banned possession of handguns within its borders. The
case, <u>Quilici</u> v. <u>Morton Grove</u> 695 F.2d 261 (7th Cir. 1982), cert. denied 464 U.S.
863 (1983), is considered by many to be the most important modern gun control
case. □

---

[a][cert. certiorari (ser-she-uh-rare-y) applies when a court is asked to review a case. Cert.
denied means the request for a review is denied.]

GUN CONTROL
Questions/Topics

1. Do you favor more or less gun control, or do you have another position to
   argue?
2. Which selection do you find most persuasive? Why? Analyze the writer's
   appeals to logos, pathos, and ethos.
3. Which selection has the most interesting style? What do you notice about
   the writer's diction and sentence patterns? What do you notice about the
   writer's voice—the sound of his or her personality? How does the writer's
   style reinforce the meaning—the writer's thesis and supporting evidence?
4. One of the original arguments for the second amendment of the Constitution was fear (based on experience) that the government might rule by force.
   What do you think of this as an argument today?
5. Proponents of carrying concealed weapons say their argument would reduce
   gun crimes because criminals would not know who is armed. Is this a good
   argument?

6. Some people believe they need a handgun in their home for protection. Can you find reasons on both sides of the argument?
7. The NRA believes teaching gun safety to elementary school children will reduce gun accident rates (see essay by LaPierre). Is this a good argument?

Abortion

As with many controversies, two or more sides of an issue are in conflict. The pro-choice issue forces us to look at both sides: a woman's right to make choices about herself versus the right of a fertilized egg to develop into a human child.

Young Women and Abortion[4]

National Organization for Women (NOW)

In Congress and the states, anti-abortion forces are restricting teens' access to reproductive health care. These restrictions are dangerous and illogical. Parental involvement laws, under the pretense of promoting family communication, require that teens consult with parents on sensitive issues. Young women have died trying to keep their abortion decisions private. Still, legislators continue efforts to block birth control and emergency contraception from teens.

Key Points

The U.S. Supreme Court in <u>Roe</u> v. <u>Wade</u> recognized that all women have a constitutional right to abortion. Restrictive laws deny this right to young women.

- When facing an unplanned pregnancy, most young women (about 60 percent) talk to their parents. A substantial number of those who do not, cite fear of physical or emotional abuse as the main reason.
- Laws pressuring young women to carry pregnancies to term are dangerous. Teens are 2.5 times more likely to die in pregnancy or childbirth than adult women. In addition, young women between the ages of 15 and 19 are 24 times more likely to die during childbirth than from legal first trimester abortions.
- State laws illogically treat a young woman as mature enough to become a mother, choose adoption or make health care decisions for her child or herself—but not mature enough to make her own abortion and contraception decisions.

[4]The following Issue Report reprinted by permission of the National Organization for Women is a factual document (January 1999) and is not designed to be an opinion piece.

- Judicial bypasses allow a young woman to forego parental involvement if a judge rules that she is mature enough to have an abortion. This process is open to each judge's bias, and many times a judge will refuse to even hear a young woman's request. In addition, judicial approval is time consuming and increases physical, emotional and financial hardship.

NOW's Efforts

Six years before <u>Roe</u> v. <u>Wade</u>, NOW members passed a resolution affirming the right of every woman, regardless of age, to control her reproductive life and calling for the repeal of all laws criminalizing abortion. 3

- In 1998, NOW activists lobbied against, and helped defeat, the "Teen Endangerment Act" and other attempts by Congress to restrict young women's reproductive health services.
- Young Feminist Summits in 1991, 1995 and 1997 underscored the importance of the struggle for teens' reproductive rights.
- In 1991, NOW members resolved to encourage and support young feminist activism against parental notification and consent laws. NOW strengthened this position with the 1993 resolution declaring that the struggle for young women's reproductive rights would be a major part of NOW's agenda.
- Young women's reproductive rights were highlighted at NOW's 1989 and 1992 marches that drew crowds of hundreds of thousands to Washington.

Support for Young Women's Rights

Many leading medical groups oppose mandatory parental consent requirements: The American Medical Association, the American Academy of Family Physicians, the American Academy of Pediatrics and the American Medical Women's Association, among others. 4

Under Attack

Young women are an easy target for anti-abortion legislators and groups. Restrictions on teens' rights to reproductive health services are part of a strategy to deny all women reproductive freedom. 5

- In 30 states a minor must involve at least one parent when making the decision to have an abortion. Fifteen of those states require notification of one or both parents prior to the procedure. The other 15 states require consent (permission) of one or both parents. Only two states and the District of Columbia legally affirm a young woman's right to decide to have an abortion on her own.
- In 1998, anti-abortion forces tried to pass two dangerous pieces of federal legislation. An amendment to an appropriations bill would have required federally-

funded clinics to notify a teen's parents prior to dispensing birth control unless written parental consent was provided. The Teen Endangerment Act sought to criminalize anyone other than a parent who accompanied a young woman across state lines to obtain an abortion. Both measures failed.

- Abortion rights groups are contesting a new parental notification law in Colorado that does not include a judicial bypass or an exception for medical emergencies.

Take Action Now

Contact your member of Congress and urge her or him to vote against any legis- 6 lation restricting young women's access to abortion or contraceptive services. The congressional switchboard number is (202) 224-3121, and the congressional website address is http://www.senate.gov or hittp://www.house.gov. Make sure to communicate your thanks to those members of Congress who vote against restrictions on teens. □

Legal Abortion Not the Salvation That Feminists Claim

Laura Schlessinger

It's the hyperbole that always gets me. The pro-abortion feminists are wrought 1 with it. Take, for example, Gloria Steinem's quote eulogizing Justice Blackmun (author of <u>Roe</u> vs. <u>Wade</u>): "Justice Blackmun saved more women's lives than any other person in history."

Really? More women died in voluntary illegal abortions per year than of 2 breast, ovarian and cervical cancer—none of which required intentional activity on the part of the victim? The developers of the mammogram, Pap smear and CA-blood tests have individually saved fewer lives? You believe that?

The discoverer of the germ theory of infection and disease, as well as the 3 scientist responsible for penicillin, cutting down the risk of deaths from infections during childbirth, have saved fewer women? Really?

The individual responsible for hormone replacement therapy, cutting down 4 the death rate of post-menopausal women from heart disease and osteoporosis, saved fewer lives than Blackmun's act to legalize abortion? Really?

And at what cost? Since abortion was legalized in 1973, close to 40 5 million human beings have been terminated early in their journey toward a potential holy, creative, loving, rewarding life.

Teen-age girls have become more and more casual about their sexuality, 6 knowing abortion is there if "a mistake" happens. Other teen-age girls give birth only to strangle, drown, suffocate, abandon or beat their newborns to death, apparently seeing no difference between killing a newborn or an unborn.

And, as many women have told me through letters, faxes and calls to my 7 radio program, there is the lingering horror, guilt and regret that haunts their later, more mature attempts to be happy and fulfilled in love, children and family.

The crass view of early, developing human life extends even to those who 8 desire nothing more than to conceive. A new advance, "selective reduction," is a technique that promises the joy of family to infertile women. One catch, though—each life heralds death. The woman is given fertility drugs to stimulate the production of numerous eggs. The eggs are combined with sperm (in vitro fertilization) in laboratory glassware and then placed inside the woman's uterus. The hope is that some will implant and begin development.

The nightmare is when too many succeed. The woman is told that unless 9 she wants to give birth to a litter or is willing to accept the possibility that all the fetuses might die from lack of room or nourishment, the physician (you remember, the guy who took the Hippocratic oath to "do no harm") uses instruments to go into the uterus and kill and remove one or more of the precious lives that the infertile couple so longed for—and spent so much money on. Pick one. Any one. Designer mothering.

It is one thing to consider abortion as a "necessary evil" if, for example, 10 the mother's heart is too weak to survive a pregnancy or if she requires serious and severe cancer treatment to save her life. It is quite another thing to celebrate human terminations as a right of reproduction (oxymoron?) and a virtual saving grace for women.

First of all, outside of rape, sexual intercourse (and the potential for preg- 11 nancy) is voluntary; unfortunately, so is responsibility. I have been stunned at the number of young women callers over the years who have told me, after I suggested adoption (the other "A" word) as a solution to their inconvenient pregnancy, that it would be too upsetting for them to give a child up for adoption. "Oh, I couldn't do that," they say. "That would be painful for me." There it is. Life and death are secondary to one's feelings of discomfort or guilt.

I disagree with Gloria Steinem's reverential quote about Justice Blackmun. 12 I think that the number of potential magnificent females killed by abortion far surpasses the number of adult females dead from illegal abortions. Even for an adamantly pro-abortion feminist like Gloria, that's got to be a breath-sucking revelation. □

Aborted Knowledge

Thomas Sowell

A certain professor who teaches students who aspire to become speech pathologists 1 begins by showing them the development of the various organs involved in speech. When he shows his class an ultrasound picture of the development of the palate in an unborn baby, it is not uncommon for one or two women in his class to have tears in their eyes, or to say to him afterward that they have had an abortion and were very much affected by seeing what an unborn baby looks like.

For too long we have been led to believe that an abortion is the removal of some unformed material, something like having an appendix operation. The very expression "unborn baby" has almost disappeared from the language, being replaced by the more bloodless and antiseptic term "fetus."

Many vocal advocates who declare themselves "pro-choice" do not want women to have the choice of knowing just what they are choosing before having an abortion. Ferocious opposition has stopped the showing of pictures of an abortion in process—even in schools or colleges that show movies of naked adults performing various sex acts. Still photographs of aborted fetuses have been banned as well.

The particularly grisly procedure know as "partial-birth abortion" cannot even be referred to in much of the media, where it is called a "late-term abortion"—another bloodless term and one that shifts the focus from what happens to when it happens.

What happens in a partial-birth abortion is that a baby who has developed too far to die naturally when removed from his mother's body is deliberately killed by having his brains sucked out. When this is done, the baby is not completely out of his mother's body because, if he were, the doctor would be charged with murder. There is no medical reason for this procedure, which has been condemned by the American Medical Association. There is only a legal reason—to keep the doctor and the mother out of jail.

All this is smoothly covered over in the media by calling such actions a "late-term abortion" and refusing to specify what happens. Such patterns of determined evasions and obfuscations show that "pro-choice" in practice often really means pro-abortion. Knowledge is the first thing being aborted.

Philosophical questions about when life begins may preoccupy some people on both sides of the abortion controversy. But the raw physical facts of what happens in various kinds of abortion have turned many others, including physicians, from being pro-abortion to being anti-abortion. One doctor who had performed many abortions never performed another one after seeing an ultrasound movie of the baby's reactions.

With most other medical procedures, "informed consent" is the watchword. But, when the issue is abortion, great efforts are made to keep "choice" from becoming too informed.

Politically and legally, the abortion issue is too complex for any easy resolution. We have gone through a quarter of a century of bitter controversy precisely because the Supreme Court went for an easy resolution back in 1973 with the <u>Roe</u> v. <u>Wade</u> decision.

Before then, various states had made differing efforts to wrestle with and balance the weighty concerns on both sides of the abortion issue. But Supreme Court Justice Harry Blackmun rushed in where angels fear to tread, with a one-size-fits-all decision, washed down with the blatant lie that this was based on the Constitution.

Far from settling things, <u>Roe</u> v. <u>Wade</u> has led to polarization and escalat-   11
ing strife all across the country, including bombings and assassinations. It has
corrupted the media, academia and other sources that are supposed to inform us,
but which have instead become partisan organs of political correctness.

However this highly-charged issue is ultimately resolved—and there is no   12
resolution on the horizon today—surely honesty must be part of that resolution. Political catch-phrases like "a woman's right to do what she wants with
her own body" cannot be applied to situations where a baby is killed at the very
moment when he ceases to be part of his mother's body.

One of the few signs of hope for some ultimate resolution is that most   13
people on both sides of this controversy are not happy about abortions. The
women who shed tears at the very sight of an unborn baby may not be politically committed to either side of this issue, but their feelings may be part of
what is needed to bring opposing sides together. □

Facts in Brief

The Alan Guttmacher Institute

Induced Abortion

Incidence of Abortion

- 49% of pregnancies among American women are unintended; $1/2$ of these are
  terminated by abortion.
- In 1996, 1.37 million abortions took place, down from an estimated 1.61 million
  in 1990. From 1973 through 1996, more than 34 million legal abortions occurred.
- Each year, 2 out of every 100 women aged 15–44 have an abortion; 47% of them
  have had a least one previous abortion and 55% have had a previous birth.
- An estimated 43% of women will have at least 1 abortion by the time they are
  45 years old.
- Each year, an estimated 50 million abortions occur worldwide. Of these, 30
  million procedures are obtained legally, 20 million illegally.

Who Has Abortions

- 52% of U.S. women obtaining abortions are younger than 25: Women aged 20–24
  obtain 32% of all abortions, and teenagers obtain 20%.
- $2/3$ of women having abortions intend to have children in the future.
- While white women obtain 60% of all abortions, their abortion rate is well below
  that of minority women. Black women are more than 3 times as likely as white
  women to have an abortion, and Hispanic women are roughly 2 times as likely.
- Women who report no religious affiliation are about 4 times as likely as women
  who report some affiliation to have an abortion.

- Catholic women are 29% more likely than Protestants to have an abortion, but are about as likely as all women nationally to do so.
- $^2/_3$ of all abortions are obtained by never-married women.
- On average, women give at least 3 reasons for choosing abortion: $^3/_4$ say that having a baby would interfere with work, school or other responsibilities; about $^2/_3$ say they cannot afford a child; and $^1/_2$ say they do not want to be a single parent or are having problems with their husband or partner.
- About 14,000 women have abortions each year because they became pregnant after rape or incest.

Safety of Abortion

- The risk of abortion complications is minimal; less than 1% of all abortion patients experience a major complication, such as serious pelvic infection, hemorrhage requiring a blood transfusion or unintended major surgery.
- The risk of death associated with abortion increases with the length of pregnancy, from 1 death for every 530,000 abortions at 8 or fewer weeks to 1 per 17,000 at 16–20 weeks and 1 per 6,000 at 21 or more weeks.
- 1 death occurs in every 150,000 legal abortions, compared with 1 in every 34,000 in 1974.
- The risk of death associated with childbirth is about 10 times as high as that associated with abortion.
- The main reason women give for delaying abortion is that they had not recognized earlier that they were pregnant. Almost half of the women having abortions beyond 15 weeks of gestation say they were delayed because of problems in obtaining abortion services—either in affording the cost or in finding or getting to a provider.
- Teens are more likely than older women to delay having an abortion until after 16 weeks of pregnancy, when medical risks associated with abortion increase significantly.
- There is no evidence of childbearing problems among women who have had a vacuum aspiration abortion, the most common type, within the first 12 weeks of pregnancy.

The data in this fact sheet are the most current available. Most of the data are from research conducted by The Alan Guttmacher Institute and/or published in its peer-reviewed journal, <u>Family Planning Perspectives</u>. An additional source is the Centers for Disease Control and Prevention. □

Remaking Eden

Lee Silver

Weeks 6–14: The Embryo Becomes a Fetus

Between six and eight weeks after fertilization, the embryo turns into—what 1
appears to be—a miniature human being with arms, legs, hands, feet, fingers,
toes, eyes, ears and nose. It is these external humanlike features that cause a
shift in terminology from embryo to fetus. By twelve weeks, the inside of the
fetus has also become rather humanlike with the appearance of all the major
organs. The first trimester of pregnancy is now completed.

Although looks alone can have a powerful effect on how we view something, 2
it is important to understand what is, and what is not, present at this early stage
of fetal development. While most major organs can be recognized, they have not
yet begun to function. Although the cerebral cortex—the eventual seat of human
awareness and emotions—has begun to grow, the cells within it are not capable
of functioning as nerve cells. They are simply precursors to nerve cells without the
ability to send or receive any neurological signals. Further steps of differentiation
must occur before they even look like nerves or develop the ability to make synap-
tic contacts with one another. And in the absence of communication among nerve
cells, there cannot be any consciousness. This means that if a fetus is aborted at
this stage, it cannot feel any pain. [. . .]

Weeks 18–22: The Fetus Kicks

Between eighteen and twenty-two weeks after conception, the pregnant mother 3
usually feels the movement of the fetus within her for the first time. This movement is traditionally referred to as "quickening." But, while quickening may be
an important milestone for a pregnant woman, it is not a milestone of any kind
for the fetus. In fact the fetus has been moving around since the tenth week
of its development. It is only when it has grown sufficiently large, though, that
its movements can be perceived outside the womb. [. . .]

Again, looks and feelings can be deceptive. Fetal limb movements during 4
this period are not caused by conscious decisions made by the fetal brain. They
are simply a consequence of random electrical stimulation of muscle tissue. We
can make such a statement with confidence because we know that the seat of
consciousness—the cerebral cortex—does not yet have interconnected neurons
required for any kind of functionality, even in a primitive way.

In the absence of late twentieth-century scientific knowledge, the move- 5
ment of the fetus would certainly seem to be highly significant, and the common
law in many countries recognizes quickening as the boundary that distinguishes
the emergence of a new human life.

Even with our current understanding, it is hard to escape the thought that 6 the kicking fetus inside a woman is a willful little baby trying to escape its confinement. Such thoughts, however, lie in the realm of emotion, not rationality.

Weeks 24–26: The Fetus Becomes Viable; The Brain Becomes Wired

Two independent milestones occur between the twenty-fourth and twenty-sixth 7 weeks after conception. The first is viability. It is during this period that the fetus develops the ability to survive outside the womb. Survival becomes possible as the fetal lungs begin to function for the first time. Even with the best neonatal technology available, we cannot push the point of viability back any further simply because a younger fetus cannot breathe. A number of other organs are not yet fully functional either, and even in the absence of the lung problem, there would be other roadblocks to earlier survival. [. . .]

The second critical milestone that occurs between the twenty-fourth and 8 twenty-sixth weeks is the emergence of a functional cerebral cortex, and with it, the potential for human consciousness. This process begins at twenty-five weeks and is described in dramatic terms by Morowitz and Trefil in their book, The Facts of Life:

> Most brain cells are produced early in the pregnancy, migrate to their final position, and mature into their final form. During this period, a few synapses form, but there is no large-scale wiring up. Then when most of the cells are in place and all is in readiness, synapses start forming in earnest. It is this burst of synapse formation that we call the birth of the cerebral cortex. It marks the period during which the brain is transformed from a collection of individual cells into a connected machine capable of carrying out human thought.

Based on the developmental and anatomical evidence, Morowitz and Trefil 9 argue that human life [. . .] begins sometime after twenty-five weeks of development. Interestingly, as these authors note, by sheer coincidence, "humanness and the ability to survive outside the womb develop at the same time."

Strictly speaking, it seems unlikely that the newly emergent cerebral cortex 10 has the ability to carry out conscious thought. But there is no simple test, or even definition, of what conscious thought is. Although both synapse formation and organized cerebral electrical activity (measured as recognizable EEG brain-wave patterns) begin at twenty-five weeks, they both continue to change and mature until a child reaches the age of ten! Obviously, consciousness emerges very early on, but when exactly that is, nobody knows. (53–57) □

ABORTION
Questions/Topics

1. Do you favor or oppose a woman's right to make her own reproductive choices, or is there another position you could argue?
2. Which selection do you find most persuasive? Why? Analyze the writer's appeals to logos, pathos, and ethos.
3. Which selection has the most interesting style? What do you notice about the writer's diction and sentence patterns? What do you notice about the writer's voice—the sound of his or her personality? How does the writer's style reinforce the meaning—the writer's thesis and supporting evidence?
4. Would there be fewer teen abortions if children were taught more about pregnancy and fetal development?

For additional readings on abortion, see: "Linking Crime, Abortion Rates Makes Everyone Queasy" by Ellen Goodman (in chapter 3) and "Abortion" by Richard Selzer (in chapter 6).

Gambling

Detroit Will Rue Its Deal with Devil

Mitch Albom

They lined the streets in a hellish heat, on the darkest day in this city's recent 1 history.

And they were smiling. 2

They couldn't wait to hand their money over. 3

They sweated. They sat on the curb. They passed hour after hour in boring 4 humidity, staring at a building, waiting for its doors to open.

They couldn't wait to hand their money over. 5

They weren't shopping. They weren't buying anything. They would not go 6 home with a car, a new dress or even a bag of groceries. Most would go home with nothing more than emptier pockets. Still, they stayed.

They couldn't wait to hand their money over. 7

Down the street were empty lots. Up the street was a potholed highway. 8 A few blocks away were poor citizens who flagged passing cars with cardboard signs, asking for help.

No one in line came to help. 9

Yet they couldn't wait to hand their money over. 10

The object of their generosity was not a charity or a church. The object 11 of their generosity was a corporation already so rich, it makes your head spin.

It is a corporation with no roots in this city. It is a corporation that, had 12
it not been granted a license to make money here, would have been out of this
city faster than a getaway car. It is a corporation that, under other circumstances, these same people would decry as greedy and uncaring.

Yet they couldn't wait to hand their money over. 13

They had come to gamble. To roll dice, pull slots, take cards and believe 14
foolishly—as millions have before them—that they were going to beat the
corporation. It was the beginning of increased crime, corruption, social problems and the siphoning of money from those who can least afford it.

And the mayor called it a "great day"? 15

Remember Atlantic City

Lights do not mean progress. Noise does not mean culture. Traffic does not mean 16
commerce. And casinos do not mean rebirth. I will go to my grave declaring that
the MGM Grand opening last week—the first land-based casino in a major American city—was a horrid blemish on the history of this city, a sign that things have
grown so desperate we will play with devils just to see someone smile at us.

Rebirth? Come on. If MGM were interested in urban renewal, would it have 17
taken over an old building just off the freeway and slapped together a temporary gambling center so quickly it was still nailing things in when the doors
opened? Less than 24 hours after the final legal hurdle, the casino was sucking
in dollars. What does that tell you about its priorities?

You may have noticed there were no movie stars imported—which any 18
big casino would do if competing in the glitz of Las Vegas. Here in Detroit,
which is seen by casinos—they won't admit it—as a great place to suck up poor
people's money, the MGM Grand sent a magician into the street Thursday to do
rope tricks and amuse the suckers.

Rebirth, my foot. 19

If MGM is interested in sparking Detroit business, then why are there three 20
restaurants under its roof? Do you think anyone will leave the building to eat
down the street—especially when they can play Keno from their table?

Of course not. They never do. Anyone who has studied casino gambling 21
knows this. Check out Atlantic City. One huge casino, followed by blocks of
poverty, followed by another casino. You can count on a similar pattern here.

And still, they couldn't wait to hand over their money. 22

Money Not in Our Pockets

"Wait," I hear you say. "A casino creates jobs." Yes. Dealing cards, waiting 23
tables, showing cleavage. Not exactly city-boosting careers.

Meanwhile, study after study shows how families are torn apart when 24
gambling is introduced to a community, how costs rise for fighting crime, how
government officials start doing favors in exchange for that casino generosity.

But this morning, the city buzzes with tales of winners. Sure. Nobody 25
brags about money they lost. These glory stories will spur more and more
people—mostly the poor ones—to try the seemingly fast way to wealth.

It won't work. And the corporation couldn't care less. It is doing its thing: 26
getting money on the table and sweeping it into the pot. MGM Grand earned
$180 million in profit the last two years. Whose money do you think that is?

The answer, for those of you waiting in line, is simple: 27

It used to be yours.   28

It just had a rebirth. □   29

Gaming Industry Myths and Facts

American Gaming Association

The gaming-entertainment industry has undergone many changes in the last 1
decade. Most recently, it has emerged as one of the greatest contributors to our
nation's economy. More than one million Americans work in the gaming industry, either through direct or indirect employment, and a recent study indicates
that the gaming industry provides better and higher paying jobs than other
industries that provide products or services such as the soft drink, cellular phone,
video cassette sales and rentals and cable TV industries. For every $1 million in
revenues generated by the casino industry, 13 jobs are created, and the average casino industry wage is $26,000.

State and local governments have seen a much-needed infusion of taxes 2
(well over $2 billion from casinos alone in 1996). Today, gaming-entertainment
is a growing industry consisting primarily of publicly-traded companies.

Although some form of gaming-entertainment is now legal in 48 states, 3
and there were 154 million visits to casinos in 1995, critics still perpetuate old
stereotypes. Since opening our doors in June 1995, the American Gaming Association has been asked the same questions time and time again. This piece
provides the most recent information covering the most frequently-asked questions and outdated myths about the industry.

Myth

The social costs of gaming far exceed the economic benefits.   4

Fact

The fact is, the gaming-entertainment industry employs more than one million 5
people. Casinos paid more than $1.4 billion in taxes to state and local govern-

ments in 1995 and made nearly $22 million in direct supply purchases for each $100 million in casino revenues.

Tunica, Miss., once referred to by the Rev. Jesse Jackson as the "Ethiopia 6 of the United States" because of its poverty, has experienced a 29 percent drop in the number of local residents receiving welfare payments since the introduction of legalized gaming in 1992.

Since 1993, when the first casino opened its doors in Vicksburg, Miss., 7 more than 600 people have been dropped from the rolls of Aid to Families with Dependent Children, a result of the more than 4,000 jobs generated by the gaming-entertainment industry.

Critics build their argument of a nationwide social impact on a house of 8 cards. The estimates typically are based upon two studies. One is a study of the impact of gaming in Connecticut, conducted in 1991 by Dr. Rachel Volberg. Volberg acknowledges that her statistics were "not based on actual data on the costs of pathological gambling in any reliable sense." Regarding her methodology and results, she said, "I wouldn't stand [before] a peer review journal and defend this approach."

The other study, often referenced by critics, is a 1981 study by Politzer, 9 Morrow and Leavey on the social costs of gambling. The Politzer study was based upon an analysis of only 28 pathological gamblers in treatment at Johns Hopkins University.

Clearly, this is flawed methodology. No reputable estimate of state impact, 10 let alone national impact, can be made based on such a small sample, yet this is exactly what the opponents of gaming have done.

Myth

Pathological gamblers are the main source of revenue for casinos. 11

Fact

The few studies alleging that pathological gamblers are the main source of 12 revenue for casinos are seriously flawed. They are based, in most cases, on the South Oaks Gambling Screen (SOGS). The error rate for SOGS has been found to be as high as 40 percent.

Casino patrons are a slice of America, statistically above the national aver- 13 age in education, income and employment. According to a survey conducted by Harrah's and the Home Testing Institute, casino players have a median income of $39,000 compared to the U.S. median of $31,000; 52 percent of all new players have some college education; and 41 percent of all new players are white-collar employees.

The vast majority of Americans who enjoy gaming experience no problem 14 whatsoever.

However, even one person with a gambling problem is one too many. To 15
address this problem, the American Gaming Association (AGA) has done several
things:

- The industry, through the AGA, recently opened the National Center for Responsible Gaming, a multimillion-dollar national foundation in Kansas City, Mo., to respond to the growing need for accurate information and research concerning problem and underage gambling.
- The AGA has created an industrywide task force to develop a long-range strategy to reduce gambling addiction, raise public awareness and develop assistance programs. The task force recently developed The Responsible Gaming Resource Guide, a reference for creating and implementing responsible gaming programs, and they are also in the process of developing a comprehensive training video.

Myth

There are no positive economic benefits to the community from the gaming- 16
entertainment industry.

Fact

The gaming industry is helping the economy grow by creating jobs, paying taxes 17
and providing economic stability to hundreds of communities across the United
States. Today the industry directly and indirectly employs more than one million
people, from card dealers, construction workers and carpet makers, to ranchers,
dancers and cooks. In 1995, the casino gaming industry alone reported $25
billion in total revenues (double the revenues from 1990).

In 1995, for every $1 million in revenues generated by the casino industry, 18
13 jobs were created, compared to seven in the video cassette sales and rentals
industry, five jobs in the cellular phone and cable TV industries, and three jobs for
the soft drink industry. Casino employees alone received $8.5 billion in salaries, and
another $12.5 billion were paid as a result of indirect jobs, which went to buy
houses, cars and VCRs, directly benefiting other sectors of the economy. Furthermore, the average casino industry wage was $26,000, compared to $20,000 in the
other amusement and recreation industry sectors, $16,000 in the hotel/motel industry, and $22,000 in the motion picture industry.

In 1996, it is estimated the gaming-entertainment industry will have made 19
direct capital investments in excess of $3.25 billion for new construction projects
across the country. For every $1 million invested, approximately 10 to 15 jobs are
directly created in the gaming industry. Annually, more than 40,000 jobs are
created as a result of casino industry capital spending. These investments help to
improve local infrastructure and increase business opportunities.

The positive economic advantages to the state and local communities with 20
gaming-entertainment are remarkable:

- In Mississippi, the industry employs 3 percent of the state's entire work force. Welfare payments have dropped in casino counties (by as much as 29 percent in the town of Tunica), while most non-casino counties have shown increases.

- In Illinois, tax revenues from 10 riverboat casinos reached $236 million in 1995, far exceeding the estimate of $20 million a year made by the Illinois State Legislature before riverboats were legalized. In fact, through October 1996 the boats, which opened in September 1991, have generated a total of $955 million in state and local tax revenues. In Joliet, casinos employ 4,000 people, with an annual payroll of $86 million.

- In Louisiana, direct construction expenditures of $574 million over a one-year period created approximately 10,000 construction jobs. This equates to approximately 17 jobs for every $1 million of capital expenditures. In Shreveport, 20 percent of Harrah's casino workers purchased a new home in 1995, 11 percent got off welfare, and 18 percent stopped receiving unemployment payments.

While gaming opponents may offer vague economic theories about gaming 22 revenues, the facts show empirically that when gaming-entertainment is introduced into a region, it creates jobs and generates tax revenues. □

Sounding the Alarm on Gambling

James C. Dobson

David Beasley was right. The former South Carolina governor called gambling a 1 "cancer" eating away at families and communities in his state. In retribution, gambling operators dumped millions into last fall's gubernatorial race to unseat Gov. Beasley. That is what happens to those who dare cross the lords of luck.

Yet the type of courage displayed by the former governor is desperately 2 needed to re-awaken this country to the dangers of gambling. My eight colleagues on the National Gambling Impact Study Commission and I submitted a final report to the President, Congress, tribal leaders and the nation's governors last week that details many of the harmful effects of gambling's rapid growth. The question is, will policy-makers, many of whom are beholden to the industry, have the guts to respond to our findings?

The statistics are staggering—at least 15 million Americans are already 3 afflicted with a gambling problem, and the numbers are growing. For many, their obsession with gambling will culminate in divorce, bankruptcy, domestic violence, criminal activity, child abuse, and even suicide.

Though gambling proponents attempt to marginalize addicts as rare excep- 4 tions, in reality they are the lifeblood of this industry. Our research found that more than 13 percent of bettors at casinos, racetracks and lottery outlets are either problem or pathological gamblers. Another 18 percent are at risk for developing a gambling addiction. Many of these are lower- and middle-income individuals betting huge sums of money they and their families can ill afford to lose.

State lotteries, in particular, prey on the desperation of the poor. They satu- 5
rate impoverished neighborhoods with outlets and aggressively market a million-
to-one long shot to individuals grasping for a straw of hope. Our research showed
that lotteries rake in more than half their profits from the top 5 percent of heavy
players, who are disproportionately poor and undereducated.

Perhaps even more disturbing, 15 percent of our young people already 6
display signs of severe gambling problems. Many gambling operators and their
accomplices in state government actively attempt to inculcate betting habits
in the next generation of gamblers.

Casinos have become "family fun centers," complete with amusement rides 7
and video arcades featuring casino-style games. Lotteries saturate the airwaves
with seductive advertising, using cartoon characters and other ploys to entice the
young. In South Carolina, 30,000 video poker machines in such places as pizza
parlors and bowling alleys are legally accessible to elementary schoolchildren.

Why has our nation allowed gambling to proliferate without even pausing 8
to count the costs? In a word, money—much of which is directed at our political leaders. Gambling contributions continue to flood into the campaign coffers
of our most prominent politicians. Last month House Minority Leader Richard
Gephardt flew to Las Vegas to collect a $250,000 check. President Clinton
followed in his steps, raising $400,000 for the Democratic National Committee.
During that visit, DNC Chairman Joe Andrew proudly proclaimed to a Las Vegas
newspaper that, in the paper's words, "Democrats in Washington want to be the
party of the gaming industry"!

Both parties are equally guilty: Senators Ted Kennedy (D-MA), Mitch 9
McConnell (R-KY), Slade Gorton (R-WA) and John McCain (R-AZ) have all been
part of a scheduled fund-raising blitz to the nation's gambling capital in recent
weeks. In the last four years, casinos have showered more than $4.2 million on
Republicans in "soft money" contributions, while Democrats have collected $2.3
million. The question we have to ask is, what are casino kingpins getting in
return for such generosity? One does not need to guess! Sadly, those contributions will likely deafen our elected leaders' ability to hear the wake-up call
contained in the commission's final report.

After examining the data, hearing from the most respected authorities, and 10
listening to hundreds of witnesses, our conclusion is this: The United States
should pause in its pell-mell rush into gambling's embrace. For some forms,
such as convenience gambling (placing gambling devices in convenience stores
and other businesses) and lotteries offering casino-style games, we urge a roll-
back. Untold damage has already been inflicted, and more looms unless we take
immediate action.

Some of our other recommendations include warning children and adults 11
about gambling's dangers, eliminating ATM-type machines from casino floors, and
requiring the $50-billion-a-year gambling industry to pay for treatment to try to
help those whom it harms. All of these recommendations, if acted upon, would
undoubtedly help lessen the pain that some individuals would otherwise experience. Such actions could even encourage some not to go down that road.

But they are band-aid solutions to a tourniquet-type problem. Until Amer- 12
icans become informed about gambling's true toll and then force gambling-depen-
dent politicians to stand up to this industry, the carnage will continue unabated.

Gambling is not harmless entertainment, as its defenders contend. It is not 13
like bowling, baseball or backpacking. It is a greed-driven, predatory vice, scientifically designed to squeeze the maximum amounts of money possible from every
single patron. It is by its very nature an enterprise wholly dependent on victims.

The gambling commission has sounded the alarm. Is anyone listening? □ 14

GAMBLING
Questions/Topics

1. Do you favor or oppose gambling, or is there another position to argue?
2. Which selection do you find most persuasive? Why? Analyze the writer's appeals to logos, pathos, and ethos.
3. Which selection has the most interesting style? What do you notice about the writer's diction and sentence patterns? What do you notice about the writer's voice—the sound of his or her personality? How does the writer's style reinforce the meaning—the writer's thesis and supporting evidence?
4. Shouldn't adults be able to gamble if they enjoy it—it's a form of entertainment, isn't it? If state lotteries are OK, what's wrong with casinos?
5. Are casinos good for cities, creating jobs, attracting tourists, paying taxes?
6. Aren't casinos pretty innocuous compared to boxing, football, cockfights, bull fights, and other forms of entertainment on which people bet?

Creationism and Evolution

Dr. Hovind's $250,000 Offer
Formerly $10,000, Offered Since 1990

Kent Hovind

I have a standing offer of $250,000 to anyone who can give any empirical 1
evidence (scientific proof) for evolution. My $250,000 offer demonstrates that
the hypothesis of evolution is nothing more than a religious belief.

Observed Phenomena

Most thinking people will agree that—   2

1. A highly ordered universe exists.

2. At least one planet in this complex universe contains an amazing variety of life forms.
3. Man appears to be the most advanced form of life on this planet.

Known Options

Choices of how the observed phenomena came into being—   3

1. The universe was created by God.
2. The universe always existed.
3. The universe came into being by itself by purely natural processes (known as evolution) so that no appeal to the supernatural is needed.

Evolution has been acclaimed as being the only process capable of caus- 4
ing the observed phenomena.

Evolution is presented in our public school textbooks as a process that: 5

1. Brought time, space, and matter into existence from nothing.
2. Organized that matter into the galaxies, stars, and at least nine planets around the sun. (This process is often referred to as cosmic evolution.)
3. Created the life that exists on at least one of those planets from nonliving matter (chemical evolution).
4. Caused the living creatures to be capable of and interested in reproducing themselves.
5. Caused that first life form to spontaneously diversify into different forms of living things, such as the plants and animals on the earth today (biological evolution).

People believe in evolution; they do not know that it is true. While beliefs 6
are certainly fine to have, it is not fair to force on the students in our public school system the teaching of one belief, at taxpayers' expense. It is my contention that evolutionism is a religious worldview that is not supported by science, Scripture, popular opinion, or common sense. The exclusive teaching of this dangerous, mind-altering philosophy in tax-supported schools, parks, museums, etc., is also a clear violation of the First Amendment.

How to Collect the $250,000

Prove beyond reasonable doubt that the process of evolution (option 3 above, 7
under "known options") is the only possible way the observed phenomena could have come into existence. Only empirical evidence is acceptable. Persons wishing to collect the $250,000 may submit their evidence in writing or schedule time for a public presentation. A committee of trained scientists will provide peer review of the evidence offered and, to the best of their ability, will be fair and honest in their evaluation and judgment as to the validity of the evidence presented.

If you are convinced that evolution is an indisputable fact, may I suggest 8 that you offer $250,000 for any empirical or historical evidence against the general theory of evolution. This might include the following:

1. The earth is not billions of years old (thus destroying the possibility of evolution having happened as it is being taught).
2. No animal has ever been observed changing into any fundamentally different kind of animal.
3. No one has ever observed life spontaneously arising from nonliving matter.
4. Matter cannot make itself out of nothing.

My Suggestion

Proponents of the theory of evolution would do well to admit that they believe 9 in evolution, but they do not know that it happened the way they teach. They should call evolution their "faith" or "religion," and stop including it in books of science. Give up faith in the silly religion of evolutionism, and trust the God of the Bible (who is the Creator of this universe and will be your Judge, and mine, one day soon) to forgive you and to save you from the coming judgment on man's sin. □

Creation Science: A Continuing Threat to Education

Eugenie C. Scott

The teacher from Kansas had a problem. He and the other master teachers and 1 scientists who had written the Kansas Science Education Standards had been tipped off that some religiously conservative school board members had rewritten the Standards with the help of creationists. Would I evaluate these "sub-Standards" and help them to detect the creationist "footprints"?

The Kentucky parent wanted to know what she could do: the superinten- 2 dent of education had recalled the fourth grade science books and glued together the pages on the Big Bang. The reason? The books didn't mention creationism as an "alternative" to science.

The college professor from Ohio had a different problem. Students in her 3 class had never learned the basic classifications of "Kingdom, phylum class [. . .]" and so on, so she had asked the local high school teachers why. "We don't teach that," they told her. "It's too much like evolution."

What's going on? Creationism in public schools? Wasn't all this settled 4 over 75 years ago with the Scopes trial in 1925? Certainly, it must have been settled with the Supreme Court's 1987 decision in Edwards v. Aguillard, striking down a Louisiana law requiring the teaching of creationism whenever evolution was taught. Wasn't it?

No, it was not. And, yes, evolution is a controversial issue in the 21st 5
century. Polls consistently show that only about 45% of adult Americans think
that "Humans evolved from earlier species of animals," whereas the numbers in
other developed nations are routinely above 70%.

All Christians and Jews believe that God created, but the religious view 6
called Special Creationism is a particular view of how God created. In this Bible-
based view, God created stars, galaxies, the Earth, and living things in essentially their present form at one time about 10,000 years ago. Noah's Flood was
an historical event during which geological features such as the Himalayas and
the Grand Canyon were formed. Creation "science" claims that Special Creationism can be supported through scientific fact and theory. Usually when people
use the term "creationism," they have in mind Special Creationism, and that is
how I will use the term here.

During the late 1970s and early 1980s, proponents of creation science 7
attempted to get laws promoting "equal time" for creation science and evolution
passed in more than twenty states. In dozens of books and hundreds of articles,
scientists and philosophers of science analyzed the "evidence" presented by
creation scientists and found them to have no scientific merit whatsoever.
Members of mainstream religious organizations, holding to non-literalist theolo-
gies, objected to the teaching of creation science in public schools. Equal time
laws were declared unconstitutional in 1987 by the Supreme Court in Edwards v.
Aguillard. The creationist movement continues, however.

In response to such legal decisions, creationism has evolved by avoiding 8
the word "creationism." Now, some creationists advocate "balancing" evolution
with "evidence against evolution"—which is indistinguishable in content from
its creation science ancestor. A current creationist euphemism is "Intelligent
Design" (ID), presented in the high school textbook <u>Of Pandas and People</u> and
in anti-evolution books by lawyer Phillip Johnson and others. ID is a sort of
creation science "lite," where few actual scientific claims are made—unlike
creation science, ID doesn't tell us what God did and when He did it. Proponents of ID point to supposedly "irreducibly complex" biochemical structures
claiming that they couldn't have been produced by natural causes, but currently
the only specific ID model is a rather tepid "God did it, somehow, but not
through evolution."

Both traditional creation science and the newer ID view make three claims: 9
that evolution is somehow a weak and vulnerable science; that evolution is
antireligious; and that it is somehow only "fair" to present "both views."

Evolution Is a Theory in Crisis

As far as the scientific community is concerned, evolution is fundamental to 10
astronomy, biology and geology, and of primary importance to many other
sciences. Evolution is concerned with history, that the past was different from
the present. Stars, galaxies, and the Earth have changed over time, and living

things have descended from common ancestors. Scientists argue about how evolution occurred, how fast it occurred, and what creature is descended from what. But whether evolution occurs is just not an issue at the university level. It is noteworthy that in every prominent university or college in the country, including religiously sponsored institutions such as Brigham Young, Notre Dame, Southern Methodist, and Baylor, evolution is a routine part of the science curriculum. Each year, thousands of articles in hundreds of scientific journals and thousands of scientists attending myriad conferences debate the details of evolution. Advances in molecular and developmental biology over the last 20 years additionally have provided new insights into biological evolution. If evolution is a "theory in crisis," it is not apparent to scientists.

Evolution Is Antireligious

The best-kept secret in the creationism controversy is that Catholic and main- 11 line Protestant theology and all but the most orthodox forms of Judaism have no problem accommodating evolution or other scientific ideas. Other religious traditions have not been especially hostile toward evolution, either. The plaintiffs (opponents of creationism) in the famous McLean v. Arkansas federal court decision (1982) included officials of the Methodist, African Methodist Episcopal, Episcopal, Roman Catholic, Presbyterian, and Southern Baptist churches.

It is clear that very many Christians hold that their theology can accom- 12 modate evolution. Statements supporting evolution have been promulgated by most of the mainline Protestant denominations, and in 1996, Pope John Paul II reiterated the Catholic church's acceptance of biological evolution. Evolution may be unacceptable to some branches of some religions, but certainly evolution is not intrinsically irreligious.

It's Only Fair to Teach Both

Most Americans, reflecting our strongly-held cultural values, believe in free 13 speech. All voices should be heard, even if not accepted. If the city council allows the Knights of Columbus to march in the town square, it must also allow the Knights of the Ku Klux Klan. Similarly, in science, especially during the development of a theory, many explanations contend for acceptance.

To the average American, it seems reasonable that if one teaches evolu- 14 tion, one should also teach creationism because it's only "fair." But science is not a democratic process or a matter of opinion or viewpoint: to be accepted, a scientific explanation has to work, or it is discarded. Neither the religious idea of Special Creationism or the pseudoscientific idea of creation science qualify as science and therefore they are rejected. Evolution explains observations in paleontology, biochemistry, comparative anatomy, embryology, biogeography and many other fields. Creationism explains nothing.

It simply is not fair to pretend to students that ideas rejected by schol- 15 ars are still in contention. It is not fair to teach that the world goes around the sun, and then give equal time to the geocentrists. It is not reasonable to teach students that six million Jews were killed by the Nazis, and then to teach that the Holocaust is actually just a propaganda ploy of Zionists—even though there is a constituency for this point of view. We shouldn't teach crackpot history to our students just because someone thinks that it would be fair, and we shouldn't teach crackpot science either.

What we should teach students is how science works, and why it is the 16 best method human beings have developed to understand the natural world. Science per se has nothing to say about whether there is ultimate cause or what it is like—which is why both religious and nonreligious individuals can use the same physics despite their having different metaphysics. And we should be teaching students only good science, science overwhelmingly supported by the evidence and accepted by the scientific community, including evolution. □

Between God and Darwin

R. J. Berry

The recent decision of the Kansas Board of Education to remove references to 1 evolution from the state school curriculum has reignited the debate between the two extremes of the creationist and the death-of-God views of our existence. It's an unfortunate detour down an avenue no one has any real need to travel. Faith and natural selection aren't mutually contradictory. There is no reason a person cannot worship God and also believe Darwin was right about how the beak of the finch evolved.

Consider that the modern American fundamentalist religious movement 2 began in the year 1909, with the initial publication of what became a highly popular series of religious pamphlets called "The Fundamentals." Intended as definitive statements of traditional Christianity, "The Fundamentals" were thick with viewpoints any fundamentalist of today would endorse. Yet these works also accepted the theory of evolution. The authors were entirely happy with the idea that God had used evolution as his method of creation.

Consider that the 1925 Scopes "monkey trial" in Dayton, Tenn., did not 3 pit creationism against evolution, as it has since become standard to say. William Jennings Bryan, who has gone down in history as the anti-evolutionist of that trial, was not a creationist as the term is used today. Bryan, for example, accepted the evidence from geology that the Earth must be immensely old. Bryan also didn't contest evolutionary theory as such; he admitted what appears inarguable, that species adapt to changes in Earth's environment. His issue was with the nature of humans as divine creations. He felt that life and consciousness could not have begun through [a] purely random, spontaneous process; a divine hand must have been involved.

Despite the common misperception, this view does not conflict with Darwinism, since evolutionary theory does not pretend to know how life began. Natural-selection biology only seeks to explain how life that already exists evolves into new forms. Though Darwin mused about whether a prehistoric "warm pond" of chemicals struck by lightning started the chain of biology, this was strictly a musing. Natural selection theory makes no claim of explaining the creation of life.

Thus it is perfectly possible to believe in evolution as a principle of biology and simultaneously believe in a creator God. True, some people who accept evolutionary theory use it to argue against faith. But the theory itself doesn't intrude on divine questions; the theory itself says nothing about how life was first formed. Many evolutionary biologists regard the creation of life as a kind of ultimate mystery—much the way many religious believers do.

In some ways it is understandable that some religious believers are suspicious of evolutionary theory. One reason is that misconceptions abound. For example, historically, almost everyone who's been upset about Darwinian theory seems to believe that it teaches people are descended from apes. Evolution does not teach that; it contends that somewhere in the far past, the ape family and the human family shared a common ancestor. But then the evolutionary lines diverged; apes became apes, and people became people. Our existence is unique and special, even to the most doctrinaire Darwinist.

More generally, modern science seems to tell us the world is an enormous machine kept going by energy from the Sun, and that we are nothing but animals struggling to survive. To this way of thinking, God is unnecessary or irrelevant. Many religious believers argue such an assessment comes from a distorted and incomplete understanding of life, an understanding that itself depends on faith. Their solution is to reject the scientific method. Unfortunately for such attempts at a hook-line-and-sinker rejection of science, the evidence for evolutionary change is now overwhelming.

Radioactive dating shows the world is billions of years old; we know that extinctions have occurred on a vast scale; we know from molecular biology that all living things have at least some aspect of common genetic heritage. But attempts to destroy science in order to preserve God are unnecessary.

Long ago, Aristotle recognized that any happening is likely to have more than one cause. For example, a painting is caused by the distribution of chemicals on canvas, but it is just as much "caused" by the painter who had a plan for his work of art. We can describe the painting either in purely chemical (scientific) terms, or as an artistic (spiritual) event: two very different but noncontradictory explanations for the same thing. God's work in creation and evolution might be described the same way.

Reason tells me evolution has taken place in the way Darwin described it, while my faith tells me God ruled and controlled the process. Indeed, the Bible suggests that the correct approach involves both God and science. In the New Testament we read, "through faith we understand that the worlds were framed by the word of God, so that things which are seen were not made of things which do appear." (Hebrews 11:3)—not much different from the assumptions of modern physics. Biology and religion might not be as far apart as Kansas creationists assume, either.

Science and God, evolution and creation, aren't dueling alternatives. 11 They're complements. The God of the Bible might well be a miracle-worker on occasion, but normally He is to be seen at work through natural processes. It is God the Creator who gives meaning to blind mechanisms of science. God's spirit and God's science should both be taught in our schools. □

CREATION/EVOLUTION
Questions/Topics

1. Should creationism be presented as a viable theory in schools on an equal status with evolution?
2. Which selection do you find most persuasive? Why? Analyze the writer's appeals to logos, pathos, and ethos.
3. Which selection has the most interesting style? What do you notice about the writer's diction and sentence patterns? What do you notice about the writer's voice—the sound of his or her personality? How does the writer's style reinforce the meaning—the writer's thesis and supporting evidence?
4. Select two of the essays on creationism and evolution. Do any of their points agree or disagree with each other, or are they arguing about apples and oranges? Try to explain for someone who hasn't read the essays.

Same Sex Partners

Who Are You Taking to the Prom This Year?

The American Civil Liberties Union

Twenty years ago, Aaron Fricke decided he wanted to go to his senior prom with 1 Paul Guilbert. His principal wouldn't let him. The principal was afraid the other students might be offended, or that it could even get violent.

Aaron thought that was wrong. 2

> "The simple, obvious thing would have been to go to the senior prom with a girl. But that would have been a lie—a lie to myself, to the girl, and to all the other students."—Aaron Fricke

To Aaron, it was a question of free expression. Why shouldn't he be able 3 to be who he was at the prom, like everyone else could?

"He feels his attendance would have a certain political element and would be a statement for equal rights and human rights."—United States District Judge Raymond J. Pettine

Before he could go to the prom, Aaron had to go to court. And he won.   4

The federal court in Rhode Island told Aaron's school that it had to let him attend the prom with Paul. In fact, the court even told the school that it had to provide enough security that Aaron and his date would be safe.

After Aaron went with Paul to the prom, Aaron remembered what he was   5 thinking as he stared at all the reporters who were there.

"I thought of all the people who would have enjoyed going to their proms with the date of their choice, but were denied that right; of all the people in the past who wanted to live respectably with the person they loved but could not; of all the men and women who had been hurt or killed because they were gay; and of the rich history of lesbians and homosexual men that had so long been ignored. Gradually we were triumphing over ignorance. One day we would be free."—Aaron Fricke

That was twenty years ago. Today, the law is still the same. Don't let your   6 school tell you that you can't go to the prom with your sweetheart—or even your best friend—just because the two of you are the same sex. Tell them about Aaron Fricke v. Cumberland High School Principal Richard B. Lynch in U.S. District Court in Rhode Island [<http://www.aclu.org>/court/fricke_decision.html>]. And call your local ACLU if they still refuse. □

Let Gays Marry

Andrew Sullivan

"A State cannot deem a class of persons a stranger to its laws," declared the   1 Supreme Court last week. It was a monumental statement. Gay men and lesbians, the conservative court said, are no longer strangers in America. They are citizens, entitled, like everyone else, to equal protection—no special rights, but ample equality.

For the first time in Supreme Court history, gay men and women were   2 seen not as some powerful lobby trying to subvert America, but as the people we truly are—the sons and daughters of countless mothers and fathers, with all the weaknesses and strengths and hopes of everybody else. And what we seek is not some special place in America but merely to be a full and equal part of America, to give back to our society without being forced to lie or hide or live as second-class citizens.

That is why marriage is so central to our hopes. People ask us why we want   3 the right to marry, but the answer is obvious. It's the same reason anyone wants the right to marry. At some point in our lives, some of us are lucky enough to meet the person we truly love. And we want to commit to that person in front of our family and country for the rest of our lives. It's the most simple, the most natural, the most human instinct in the world. How could anyone seek to oppose that?

Yes, at first blush, it seems like a radical proposal, but, when you think 4 about it some more, it's actually the opposite. Throughout American history to be sure, marriage has been between a man and a woman, and in many ways our society is built upon that institution. But none of that need change in the slightest. After all, no one is seeking to take away anybody's right to marry, and no one is seeking to force any church to change any doctrine in any way. Particular religious arguments against same-sex marriage are rightly debated within the churches and faiths themselves. That is not the issue here: there is a separation between church and state in this country. We are only asking that when the government gives out <u>civil</u> marriage licenses, those of us who are gay should be treated like anybody else.

Of course, some argue that marriage is <u>by definition</u> between a man and a 5 woman. But for centuries, marriage was <u>by definition</u> a contract in which the wife was her husband's legal property. And we changed that. For centuries marriage was <u>by definition</u> between two people of the same race. And we changed that. We changed these things because we recognized that human dignity is the same whether you are a man or a woman, black or white. And no one has any more of a choice to be gay than to be black or white or male or female.

Some say that marriage is only about raising children, but we let child- 6 less heterosexual couples be married (Bob and Elizabeth Dole, Pat and Shelley Buchanan, for instance). Why should gay couples be treated differently? Others fear that there is no logical difference between allowing same-sex marriage and sanctioning polygamy and other horrors. But the issue of whether to sanction multiple spouses (gay or straight) is completely separate from whether, in the existing institution between two unrelated adults, the government should discriminate between its citizens.

This is, in fact, if only Bill Bennett could see it, a deeply, conservative 7 cause. It seeks to change no one else's rights or marriages in any way. It seems merely to promote monogamy, fidelity and the disciplines of family life among people who have long been cast to the margins of society. And what could be a more conservative project than that? Why indeed would any conservative seek to oppose those very family values for gay people that he or she supports for everybody else? Except, of course, to make gay men and lesbians strangers in their own country, to forbid them ever to come home. (26) □

Leave Marriage Alone

William Bennett

There are at least two key issues that divide proponents and opponents of same- 1 sex marriage. The first is whether legally recognizing same-sex unions would strengthen or weaken the institution. The second has to do with the basic understanding of marriage itself.

The advocates of same-sex marriage say that they seek to strengthen and celebrate marriage. That may be what some intend. But I am certain that it will not be the reality. Consider: the legal union of same-sex couples would shatter the conventional definition of marriage, change the rules which govern behavior, endorse practices which are completely antithetical to the tenets of all of the world's major religions, send conflicting signals about marriage and sexuality, particularly to the young, and obscure marriage's enormously consequential function—procreation and child-rearing.

Broadening the definition of marriage to include same-sex unions would stretch it almost beyond recognition—and new attempts to expand the definition still further would surely follow. On what <u>principled</u> ground can Andrew Sullivan exclude others who most desperately want what he wants, legal recognition and social acceptance? Why on earth would Sullivan exclude from marriage a bisexual who wants to marry two other people? After all, exclusion would be a denial of that person's sexuality. The same holds true of a father and daughter who want to marry. Or two sisters. Or men who want (consensual) polygamous arrangements. Sullivan may think some of these arrangements are unwise. But having employed sexual relativism in his own defense, he has effectively lost the capacity to draw any lines and make moral distinctions.

Forsaking all others is an essential component of marriage. Obviously it is not always honored in practice. But it is the ideal to which we rightly aspire, and in most marriages the ideal is in fact the norm. Many advocates of same-sex marriage simply do not share this ideal; promiscuity among homosexual males is well known. Sullivan himself has written that gay male relationships are served by the "openness of the contract" and that homosexuals should resist allowing their "varied and complicated lives" to be flattened into a "single, moralistic model." But that "single, moralistic model" has served society exceedingly well. The burden of proof ought to be on those who propose untested arrangements for our most important institution.

A second key difference I have with Sullivan goes to the very heart of marriage itself. I believe that marriage is not an arbitrary construct which can be redefined simply by those who lay claim to it. It is an honorable estate, instituted of God and built on moral, religious, sexual and human realities. Marriage is based on a natural teleology, on the different, complementary nature of men and women—and how they refine, support, encourage and complete one another. It is the institution through which we propagate, nurture, educate and sustain our species.

That we have to engage in this debate at all is an indication of how steep our moral slide has been. Worse, those who defend the traditional understanding of marriage are routinely referred to (though not to my knowledge by Sullivan) as "homophobes," "gay-bashers," "intolerant" and "bigoted." Can one defend an honorable, 4,000-year-old tradition and not be called these names?

This is a large, tolerant, diverse country. In America people are free to do as they wish, within broad parameters. It is also a country in sore need of shoring up some of its most crucial institutions: marriage and the family, schools, neighborhoods, communities. But marriage and family are the greatest of these. That is why they are elevated and revered. We should keep them so. (27) □

I've Had Enough of Your Anti-gay Venom

Sharon Underwood

As the mother of a gay son, I've seen firsthand how cruel and misguided people   1 can be.

Many letters have been sent to the <u>Valley News</u> concerning the homosex-   2 ual menace in Vermont. I am the mother of a gay son and I've taken enough from you good people.

I'm tired of your foolish rhetoric about the "homosexual agenda" and your   3 allegations that accepting homosexuality is the same thing as advocating sex with children. You are cruel and ignorant. You have been robbing me of the joys of motherhood ever since my children were tiny.

My firstborn son started suffering at the hands of the moral little thugs   4 from your moral, upright families from the time he was in the first grade. He was physically and verbally abused from first grade straight through high school because he was perceived to be gay.

He never professed to be gay or had any association with anything gay,   5 but he had the misfortune not to walk or have gestures like the other boys. He was called "fag" incessantly, starting when he was 6.

In high school, while your children were doing what kids that age should be   6 doing, mine labored over a suicide note, drafting and redrafting it to be sure his family knew how much he loved them. My sobbing 17-year-old tore the heart out of me as he choked out that he just couldn't bear to continue living any longer, that he didn't want to be gay and that he couldn't face a life with no dignity.

You have the audacity to talk about protecting families and children from   7 the homosexual menace, while you yourselves tear apart families and drive children to despair. I don't know why my son is gay, but I do know that God didn't put him, and millions like him, on this Earth to give you someone to abuse. God gave you brains so that you could think, and it's about time you started doing that.

No Choice

At the core of all your misguided beliefs is the belief that this could never   8 happen to you, that there is some kind of subculture out there that people have chosen to join. The fact is that if it can happen to my family, it can happen to yours, and you won't get to choose. Whether it is genetic or whether something occurs during a critical time of fetal development, I don't know. I can only tell you with an absolute certainty that it is inborn.

If you want to tout your own morality, you'd best come up with some- 9
thing more substantive than your heterosexuality. You did nothing to earn it;
it was given to you. If you disagree, I would be interested in hearing your
story, because my own heterosexuality was a blessing I received with no effort
whatsoever on my part. It is so woven into the very soul of me that nothing
could ever change it.

For those of you who reduce sexual orientation to a simple choice, a char- 10
acter issue, a bad habit or something that can be changed by a 10-step program,
I'm puzzled. Are you saying that your own sexual orientation is nothing more than
something you have chosen, that you could change it at will?

If that's not the case, then why would you suggest that someone else can? 11

A popular theme in your letters is that Vermont has been infiltrated by
outsiders. Both sides of my family have lived in Vermont for generations. I am
heart and soul a Vermonter, so I'll thank you to stop saying that you are speaking for "true Vermonters."

Principles?

You invoke the memory of the brave people who have fought on the battlefield 12
for this great country, saying that they didn't give their lives so that the "homosexual agenda" could tear down the principles they died defending.

My 83-year-old father fought in some of the most horrific battles of World 13
War II, was wounded and awarded the Purple Heart. He shakes his head in
sadness at the life his grandson has had to live. He says he fought alongside
homosexuals in those battles, that they did their part and bothered no one. One
of his best friends in the service was gay, and he never knew it until the end,
and when he did find out, it mattered not at all. That wasn't the measure of
the man.

You religious folk just can't bear the thought that as my son emerges from 14
the hell that was his childhood he might like to find a lifelong companion and
have a measure of happiness. It offends your sensibilities that he should request
the right to visit that companion in the hospital, to make medical decisions for
him or to benefit from tax laws governing inheritance.

How dare he? you say. These outrageous requests would threaten the very 15
existence of your family, would undermine the sanctity of marriage.

You use religion to abdicate your responsibility to be thinking human 16
beings. There are vast numbers of religious people who find your attitudes repugnant. God is not for the privileged majority, and God knows my son has committed no sin.

The deep-thinking author of a letter to the April 12 <u>Valley News</u> who 17
lectures about homosexual sin and tells us about "those of us who have been
blessed with the benefits of a religious upbringing" asks: "What ever happened
to the idea of striving . . . to be better human beings than we are?"

Indeed, sir, what ever happened to that? □ 18

SAME SEX PARTNERS
Questions/Topics

1. Do you support or oppose gay rights, or is there some other position to argue?
2. Which selection do you find most persuasive? Why? Analyze the writer's appeals to logos, pathos, and ethos.
3. Which selection has the most interesting style? What do you notice about the writer's diction and sentence patterns? What do you notice about the writer's voice—the sound of his or her personality? How does the writer's style reinforce the meaning—the writer's thesis and supporting evidence?
4. Should gay people have the same rights as "everyone else," or are they so different from everyone else that they require special treatment by the law?
5. Bennett argues that the "function" of marriage is procreation and child rearing. Is it possible to argue for any other "function" of marriage?
6. Can same-sex friends share an apartment without a sexual relationship? How does that affect the argument for same-sex relationships?

Hate Speech and the First Amendment

Attacks on Student Free Speech Rights

First Amendment Cyber-Tribune FACT

Poem Was Protected Speech, Not School Threat

Federal District Judge Barbara Jacobs Rothstein ruled on Feb. 24, that the First Amendment rights of high school student James LaVine were violated when he was expelled from school in October 1998 because of the content of a poem he wrote.

The Blaine School District in Washington expelled James LaVine after his teacher   1 read the poem "Last Words" that he had written and gave to her for review. The poem is a first-person account of a student shooting a classmate. School officials refused to allow LaVine to return to school until he had had a psychiatric evaluation. The psychologist who evaluated LaVine said he posed no danger to himself or to others.

In <u>LaVine v. Blaine School District</u>, Judge Rothstein ruled that "Poetry is   2 one of the classical means for artistic expression of the content of one's mind, and as such, falls within the core speech protected by the Constitution."

The judge wrote: "the record presented permits no finding other than that   3 'Last Words' was not a sincere expression of intent to harm or assault, and the poem therefore falls squarely within the purview of the First Amendment's core protection." □

Hip Hop Homophobe: Armed and Dangerous

Triangle Foundation

June 5, 2000: One of the top recording acts in the country is spreading a hate- 1
ful, violent and provocative message that gays should be killed. Eminem, a hip
hop artist from Detroit, has released one of the most direct and blatant examples of anti-gay vitriol, especially in light of his popularity among adolescent
males, the group most likely to commit acts of violence against glbt [gay,
lesbian, bi-sexual, transgendered] victims.

"The producers and promoters of the record that features Eminem's call to 2
arms is UNI/Interscope Records. They need to consider the ramifications of
promoting these lyrics and pull the product off the shelves," said Jeffrey Montgomery, Executive Director of the Triangle Foundation.

Eminem, whose real name is Marshall Mathers, has been a recent feature 3
in Detroit-area media since his arrest in Warren on possible weapons charges.
He was arrested on June 6th following an altercation at a bar. Mathers may have
been carrying a gun at the time.

Here is a sample of the lyrics: 4

"You faggots keep egging me on
'Til I have you at knifepoint, then you beg me to stop"

"My words are like a dagger with a jagged edge
That'll stab you in the head whether you're a fag or les
Or the homosex, hermaph or a trans-a-ves   5
Pants or dress
Hate fags? The answer's yes

Homophobic? Nah, you're just heterophobic
Staring at my jeans watching my genitals bulging

That's my mother-fucking balls, you'd better let go of 'em   10
They belong in my scrotum, you'll never get hold of 'em.

Hey, it's me, Versace
Whoops, somebody shot me
And I was out checking the mail
Get it, checking the male?"   15

"Les" is a derogatory reference to lesbians, "hermaph" and "trans-a-ves" are 5
meant to demean transgendered people. The reference to Versace is obviously to
make fun of the designer's brutal, cold-blooded murder at the hands of Andrew
Cunanan, a spree killer who murdered four men, including Versace, in 1997.

"The lyrics are repulsive on their face," said Montgomery. "But they become 6
even more terrifying when the guy who spouts this call to bash and attack gays
is also suspected of weapons violations and drawing attention to himself in
violent situations.

"Eminem's audience is impressionable and he is regarded as a role model to   7
his fans. They worship this guy, and he's directing them to stab—possibly kill—
gay people. His mocking of the Versace murder is also unforgivable. It says that
some people deserve to be killed simply because of their sexual orientation.

"Any radio station that airs this music, or stores that sell it must share
in the responsibility of the damage and violence that may result from its promo-   8
tion. We hope that outlets will refuse to carry it, and not give this bigoted artist
the privilege of airtime." □

Popular Music under Siege

The American Civil Liberties Union

Beginning in the 1980s, religious fundamentalists and some parents' groups   1
have waged a persistent campaign to limit the variety of cultural messages
available to American youth by attacking the content of some of the music
industry's creative products. These attacks have taken numerous forms, including a call by the Parents' Music Resource Center (PMRC) for the labeling of
recordings whose themes or imagery relate to sexuality, violence, drug or alcohol use, suicide or the "occult," and prosecutions of record companies and storeowners for producing or selling albums that contain controversial songs.

After years of pressure from the PMRC and a series of Senate hearings in   2
1985, the Recording Industry Association of America (RIAA) introduced, in 1990,
a uniform labeling system using the logo, "Parental Advisory—Explicit Lyrics." The
RIAA initiated this system without providing record companies with any standards,
criteria or guidelines for determining what albums should be labeled.

That decision is left completely up to the companies, which have chosen   3
to label only selected rock and rap albums and not recordings of country music,
opera or musical comedy that may also contain controversial material.

Dissatisfied with the RIAA's labels, many would-be censors have demanded   4
even more limits on the sale of music with controversial lyrics. As a result,
legislators have introduced bills in more than 20 states in recent years that
would require warning labels far more detailed than the RIAA's. Some proposed
laws would go beyond mandatory labeling and actually ban the sale to minors
of music deemed to be objectionable.

Until 1992, none of this legislation had passed, although in 1991 a bill in   5
Louisiana failed by only one vote. In 1992, however, the state of Washington
passed a law that required storeowners to place "adults only" labels on recordings
a judge had found to be "erotic"; the law also criminalized the sale of any labeled
CD or tape to a person under age 18. Fortunately, the law was never enforced
because a few months after passage a state court declared it unconstitutional.

Even though Washington's "erotic music" law failed, the battle over propos-   6
als to label or otherwise restrict certain music sales will probably continue. The

groups and individuals who have been attacking popular music want to impose their personal moral and political standards on the rest of us. The American Civil Liberties Union is working hard to prevent the achievement of that goal, which would imperil the First Amendment rights of musicians, and of all Americans, to create, perform and hear music of our own choosing.

Q: What's wrong with voluntary labeling? Isn't it, like movie rating, a harmless way to give parents consumer information that can help them make intelligent choices for their kids?   7

A: Even "voluntary" labeling is not harmless. First of all, a label on an album is   8 no proof whatsoever that the music inside is in any way harmful or illegal. Yet many music stores, including some of the largest national chains, refuse to sell labeled albums to minors, and some stores refuse to carry them at all out of fear that the wrath of pressure groups will bring bad publicity and possible boycotts. Some people argue that an "explicit lyrics" label, like an "R" movie rating, actually boosts sales by drawing attention to the labeled album. This may or may not be true, but we can say for sure that fans can't buy an album if it's not in the store.

Labeling is a red flag for would-be censors, who want to see the content of   9 popular music regulated as much as possible. Even worse, the RIAA's "Parental Advisory" label is now used as a model for labeling legislation that would establish government censorship of record sales to minors. The RIAA label also has encouraged pro-"decency" prosecutors to target particular albums when threatening storeowners with prosecution, usually in the hope of persuading the storeowners to stop selling those albums. Is labeling truly helpful to parents? No. All a label means is that, in somebody's opinion, some parents might consider the labeled material unfit for their children. The only way parents who want to supervise their children's musical experiences can really learn anything about a tape or CD is to personally examine the package, which often includes printed lyrics. Then, they can decide for themselves whether it's acceptable or not.

Q: What about government labeling or classification of music lyrics?   10

A: "Voluntary" labeling is bad enough, but government labeling would be worse   11 still—worse for musicians, for manufacturers, for listeners and for the Constitution.

The labeling bills proposed to date have offered very vague standards for   12 determining what albums should be labeled, making it impossible for artists, record companies and stores to understand whether or how the laws apply to them. A New Jersey bill, for example, would require a "parental advisory" label on lyrics that discuss "suicide, incest, bestiality, sadomasochism, rape or involuntary sexual penetration, or which advocate or encourage murder, ethnic, racial or religious intimidation, the use of illegal drugs or the excessive or illegal use of alcohol." That list could cover everything from the opera, "La Traviata," to the Beatles' "Lucy in the Sky with Diamonds." Such vagueness makes artists and others in the music industry feel that they must censor themselves to avoid risking criminal prosecution.

Most important of all, labeling requirements are usually coupled with   13
restrictions on sales. Therefore, mandatory labeling laws would bring about
unconstitutional restrictions on the First Amendment right of artists to express
themselves freely, and on their fans' right to hear what the artists express—
whatever the subject might be.

Q: What about laws that keep music with antisocial, misogynistic or violent   14
messages away from minors—doesn't society have an obligation to protect
kids?
A: Courts have ruled that the government does have an interest in protecting   15
children. As a result, many states now have "harmful to minors" laws that are
modified versions of adult obscenity laws. These laws specifically target works
that are sexually explicit and lack serious artistic or other value.

Lyric-labeling legislation, however, doesn't limit itself to sexual material   16
that lacks value; instead of being specific, these bills usually target a wide
range of topics regardless of whether the music has value. Because many of our
elected officials disrespect rock and rap music and its fans, they don't feel it's
necessary to be specific about music that they regard as an amorphous mass of
unsavory images and messages.

For example, the real target of the police groups and others who sought to   17
ban "Cop Killer," claiming that the song advocates the murder of police officers,
appeared to be Ice-T's political viewpoint. "Cop Killer" is a work of musical fiction
that depicts violence against the police as a response to police brutality. It reflects
a radical attitude held by some inner city residents, who are furious about the
police abuse of authority they feel they have witnessed or experienced.

As a practical matter, it's impossible to know exactly what message a   18
particular listener takes from "Cop Killer." But most likely, rather than inciting
violence against the police, as its detractors claim, the rap provides an outlet
for anger and encourages listeners to think about the issue of police miscon-
duct and the antagonism it creates.

Q: But what if someone listens to "Cop Killer" and then murders a police   19
officer? Don't lyrics that deal with sex, violence, drug use, suicide, etc.
cause anti-social behavior?
A: No direct link between anti-social behavior and exposure to the content of   20
any form of artistic expression has ever been scientifically established. Moreover, scapegoating artistic expression as a cause of social ills is simplistic. How
can serious social problems like violent crime, racism or suicide be solved by
covering children's ears? If suppressing creative expression were the way to
control anti-social behavior, where would you stop? The source of inspiration
most frequently cited by criminals has been the Bible.

Singer Ozzy Osbourne was sued three times by parents who claimed that   21
his "Suicide Solution" made their sons kill themselves, and the heavy metal
band, Judas Priest, faced a similar lawsuit in 1990. In all of these cases, the

courts rejected the idea that musicians can be held responsible for the acts of unstable individuals.

Throughout American history, popular music has mirrored the thoughts 22 and yearnings of young people. Performers from the Beatles, Bob Dylan and Aretha Franklin to Arrested Development and Madonna, have often celebrated change and challenged "the establishment." Clearly, the real intentions of the would-be music censors is to impose on all Americans the tastes and values of political powerbrokers who don't connect with the experiences and concerns of the young, the alienated and minorities.

Lyric-labeling, directed almost exclusively at rock and rap music, impover- 23 ishes our culture by muzzling the voices of that music's primarily young fans. Such suppression undermines the bedrock of our freedoms, the First Amendment, and it makes us all less free. □

Lawsuit Pits Two Instructors against Anonymous "Teacher Review" Postings

Scott Carlson

There's a war over words going on at City College of San Francisco, where a 1 teacher-evaluation site has stirred up a debate about how the First Amendment applies to the Internet. A court may have to decide whether the postings on the site are libelous or merely offensive.

Two instructors at the college have filed a lawsuit against a former student 2 who maintains Teacher Review, a Web site that posts anonymous comments about the college's faculty members. Daniel Curzon-Brown, who teaches creative writing, and Jesse David Wall, who teaches physics, say that their reputations and livelihoods are being destroyed by obscene and threatening postings on the site. And they say that other instructors at the college feel pressure to give better grades to avoid bad reviews on the site.

"It's there, hanging over everything now, and it's putting the integrity of 3 the classroom under serious pressure," Mr. Curzon-Brown says. "Grades will become absolutely worthless. They'll be extorted."

According to its mission statement, the Web site is a forum for students 4 and a guide to help them pick the best instructors before enrolling. Anonymity, the site says, ensures that the reviews will be honest and that the students will "be protected from retribution."

However, Mr. Curzon-Brown and Mr. Wall say, the site makes little effort to 5 protect instructors from people who want revenge for bad grades they've received— or who want to strike back at professors who complain about the Web site.

Unlike other teacher-evaluation sites that have irked professors, Teacher 6 Review does not take advertising. On its front page, the site offers links to lists of professors who it says are either "Making the Grade" or "Not Cutting It"—the 15 "best" instructors and the 10 "worst." The site currently features 5,000 reviews of more than 600 City College instructors.

Most professors receive a typical mix of good and bad reviews, although 7 postings on the site tend toward the poles—many reviews characterize instructors as either "the best teacher ever" or "the worst, worst, worst." According to the site's own statistics, half of the reviews posted give instructors A's; almost a third give D's or F's.

Among the pans, some reviews might constitute libel if distributed in any 8 traditional medium. In a mild example, one review says about a music instructor: "SHE'S A CRACKHEAD. I'M SERIOUS ABOUT IT."

Mr. Curzon-Brown, an openly gay teacher of creative writing, has been 9 the subject of several graphic postings that use the word "faggot" frequently, and allege that he raped and molested students in exchange for better grades.

Mr. Curzon-Brown also claims that some of the reviews were written by 10 people who clearly have never taken his courses—especially those submitted after news accounts about his lawsuit began appearing. "I've had tons of reviews about me since I've been in the media, and they're not written by people who know me."

Mr. Wall says he joined Mr. Curzon-Brown's lawsuit after bad reviews shrunk 11 his classes last fall. He says his evaluations on Teacher Review were the usual mix of good and bad until he spoke out against the site at a faculty meeting last spring. After that, he says, the positive reviews were dropped from the site and he received a string of F reviews, and his rating on Teacher Review plummeted. That fall, he says, his courses had half the usual enrollment. Mr. Wall says he's so frustrated about the site and what he sees as a lack of support from the college that he'll retire at the end of the year.

He says the site's backers "like to intimidate their teachers, they're find- 12 ing a way to get good grades at City College, and they like that site."

"Here I am attacking their site, and they're going to get me for it," he 13 says. "And sure enough, they have found a mechanism by which they can destroy my career."

The lawsuit names Ryan Lathouwers, the Teacher Review's Webmaster, who 14 started the site in 1997 when he was a student at City College. Mr. Lathouwers is currently the engineer for a similar site, TeacherReviews.com, which will offer instructor reviews for hundreds of universities across the country. Attempts to reach Mr. Lathouwers for comment were unsuccessful.

Bernard A. Burk, a lawyer who is representing Mr. Lathouwers at the 15 request of the American Civil Liberties Union, says that the obscenity-ridden content about Mr. Curzon-Brown and others "isn't slanderous or libelous," although he acknowledges that "it's disgusting and intemperate hate mail, and it doesn't have anything to do with teaching performance."

The site asks people to avoid posting profane or threatening reviews, and 16 urges users to "Please accept the <u>responsibility</u> that comes with anonymous postings!" But reviews are posted automatically, and many users appear to have ignored the guidelines. Nothing prevents users from posting multiple reviews of the same instructor, and many of the reviews seem to be responses to earlier comments about the professor in question.

"People disregard those guidelines, and when Ryan is informed about those 17 postings, he looks at them and decides whether they comply with the guidelines or not, and whether he's in a position to make a judgment about that," Mr. Burk says. "Is that an imperfection in Teacher Review? I would say that it is an imperfection. Is it a basis for a lawsuit or a reason to close down the open forum? Absolutely not."

In Mr. Lathouwers's defense, Mr. Burk asserts that the Communications 18 Decency Act of 1996 gives immunity to Webmasters like Mr. Lathouwers who maintain open forums online. "We believe that Congress let a garden like that bloom understanding that there would be some weeds," Mr. Burk says. As for the instructors' claims that some of the pans are fake, Mr. Burk says that's a convenient way to silence critics.

"Our Constitution says that open communication is what is demanded by 19 our society," he says. "Otherwise you have to pick a philosopher king that says what communication is allowed. Professor Brown would like to be the philosopher king of the Internet, but the Constitution is not going to allow him."

Mr. Curzon-Brown and Mr. Wall also named City College in the suit, because 20 the college has a link to Teacher Review on its Web site. Philip R. Day Jr., chancellor of the college, says he finds some of the content on the site "disgusting," but he says that the ill effects of the site have been overblown and haven't affected morale among most faculty members.

He says the college is negotiating a settlement with Mr. Curzon-Brown 21 and Mr. Wall. "They won't get a cent," Mr. Day says. Administrators believe that the instructors have no case, and say that the college won't seek to recover the cost of its legal fees from them if the suit is dropped.

Mr. Day bemoans City College's link to the Teacher Review site, adding 22 that it wouldn't have been added to the college's site if the institution had a comprehensive review process for links placed there. The college is in the process of forming such a review.

For now, City College officials say they are stuck with the link because 23 removing it from the college's Web site could bring a First Amendment lawsuit from student groups or the A.C.L.U. "As one of the lawyers involved in the case said to me, 'If you think you've got big problems now, sever the link and you're really in the big time,'" Mr. Day says. □

For more information on this case, see these Web sites:

Teacher Review: <www.teacherreview.com>
ACLU Press Release, "City College Teachers Voluntarily Agree to Dismiss Lawsuit Against 'Teacher Review' Webmaster" <http://www.aclunc.org/pressrel/001003-curzon-brown.html>

Even Ugly Speech Deserves Protection

Franklyn Haiman

Hardly a week passes without some new incident being reported in the press   1
about someone uttering statements that are derogatory of others because of
their race, religion, gender, or sexual orientation.

Sometimes it is an allegedly unconscious slip of the tongue, like House   2
Majority Leader Richard Armey's reference to Congressman Barney Frank as
"Barney Fag."

Sometimes it is an entirely deliberate, explicit, and crude verbal attack,   3
such as those of Nation of Islam Minister Khalid Abdul Muhammed on whites
and Jews in his speeches on college campuses. And sometimes it is the more
thinly veiled but clearly racist messages of a David Duke.

Whatever its source, and whoever its targets, there are those who believe   4
that what they have called "hate speech" or described as "words that wound"
should, at least in some circumstances, be forbidden and made legally punishable.

They claim that the free speech clause of the First Amendment does not   5
or should not provide constitutional protection for neo-Nazis who want to march
in Skokie, Illinois; for Ku Klux Klansmen who seek to espouse their racism on
the state capitol grounds in Columbus, Ohio; for male workers who make sexist
remarks in the presence of female co-workers; or for professors and students who
utter politically incorrect sentiments in the classroom.

They argue that such utterances are not mere speech, but "speech acts"—   6
a kind of "violence by speech" that inflicts injury on its victims every bit as
much as hitting them with a fist, rock, or baseball bat. It is not the sort of
communication, they say, that the Founding Fathers had in mind when they
wrote the First Amendment.

On the other side of this debate are those of us who see great danger in   7
this blurring of the line between speech and action, believing that the First
Amendment has legitimacy only if speech is viewed as essentially different from
action, and is thus provided with a degree of immunity from social control that
is not extended to physical conduct.

We do not deny that words can sometimes wound, but note that the injury   8
is psychological rather than physical, subjective rather than objective. Its severity is dependent on how thin-skinned or thick-skinned, vulnerable or invulnera-
ble, experienced or inexperienced with verbal aggression its victim is.

It is also something that it is impossible for others (including judges and   9
juries) either fully to understand or empirically to verify.

Those who claim that racist, sexist, or homophobic verbal attacks do   10
"violence by speech" are indulging in a metaphor that is self-contradictory.
Violence is by definition not speech. Its impact is instantaneous and it hurts
its victims no matter who they are or what language they speak.

Speech, on the other hand, as well as other symbols, such as American 11 flags, Christian crosses, Jewish Stars of David, Nazi swastikas or KKK white hoods, must have their meaning understood by their audience before any impact is felt.

If the members of that audience speak a different language or have never 12 learned what the particular symbols represent there will be no effect upon them at all. If they feel injured it is because of the message that has been communicated, and that is very different from the injury of a fist, rock, or baseball bat.

Different enough, in fact, that the authors of the First Amendment 13 believed that those who hear such messages can and should be trusted to sort them out for themselves. They decided that a democracy is a place where people should be free to think what they wish to, say or write what they want to and worship or not worship as they please, without the government or a majority of their fellow citizens determining what is beyond the pale.

The remedy for bad speech, they felt, was more and better speech, not 14 rules and laws. Any exceptions that have been made to this principle, such as for personal libel, fraudulent advertising, or threats of murder, have not been made because the speech in question is a "speech act," but because the meaning conveyed by such messages has immediate, measurable, objectively verifiable effects for which more speech is no remedy.

Hate speech does not have these characteristics. Its impact is neither 15 measurable nor objectively verifiable. And the best evidence that more and better speech is an effective remedy is the abundance of verbal condemnation that hate speech receives in our society, not only from its victims but from many others, whenever it rears its ugly head.

So let us continue expressing verbally and vigorously our moral outrage 16 when the haters spew their venom, but let us not turn to the law or to punitive measures as a response. Let us save those remedies, and pursue them diligently, only when, as Thomas Jefferson advised us, "principles break out into overt acts against peace and good order." □

HATE SPEECH AND THE FIRST AMENDMENT
Questions/Topics

1. Should critical thinkers agree or disagree with Judge Rothstein's ruling in "Attacks on Student Free Speech Rights"?

2. Would you agree that all poems, all songs—any work of art—should be protected by the First Amendment, no matter how offensive someone finds them?

3. Do you agree or disagree with the ACLU that voluntary labeling and government labeling of music are more harmful than helpful to society? Or do you have another position to argue?

4. How much free speech does the First Amendment allow?

5. Do you agree that the Teacher Review Web site should be protected by the First Amendment?

6. Would you find a similar teacher review Web site at your school helpful? If so, what guidelines would you suggest to make the review less defamatory to teachers?

7. Should students be able to say or print anything they want about a teacher? Should teachers have the same privilege?

8. Which selection do you find most persuasive? Why? Analyze the writer's appeals to logos, pathos, and ethos.

9. Which selection has the most interesting style? What do you notice about the writer's diction and sentence patterns? What do you notice about the writer's voice—the sound of his or her personality? How does the writer's style reinforce the meaning—the writer's thesis and supporting evidence?

Racial Profiling

"American Skin (41 Shots)"

Bruce Springsteen

> Is it a gun?
> Is it a knife?
> Is it a wallet?
> This is your life
> It ain't no secret It ain't no secret   5
> Ain't no secret my friend
> You can get killed just for living in your American
> skin

Race, Crime and Justice

The Christian Century

When four white New York policemen were accused—and eventually acquitted—   1
of murdering an innocent, unarmed black man, the issue of race could hardly be avoided, though it could not be introduced into courtroom proceedings. The officers had stopped Amadou Diallo in 1999 on a routine patrol in the Bronx and ended up shooting him after they mistook the wallet he pulled from his pocket for a gun. If Diallo were white, the odds are great that he would not have been stopped for questioning, much less have been shot to death for reaching for his wallet.

But the jury in the case was not asked to decide about racial prejudice in the New York City Police Department; it was simply asked to decide if the officers had committed murder. On this point, the jurors (black and white) answered with a reasonable no—the police were guilty of a terrible mistake, but not murder.

Amid the controversy over the Diallo case, and over the shooting of another unarmed black man, Patrick Dorismond, in Manhattan last month, activist Al Sharpton and others assailed the police practice known as racial profiling—targeting suspects on the basis of race. Racial profiling is routinely practiced, often unconsciously, by street cops, highway patrols and drug interdiction officers across the country. Countless black motorists and airline passengers have described being stopped for trivial reasons by police in search of drugs or weapons. The only reason they are under suspicion is that they are black. (They are guilty of "driving while black," as the phenomenon has come to be called.)

The political campaign against racial profiling calls on states to keep data on police behavior that will show whether racial profiling is happening. Since black motorists don't violate traffic laws with greater frequency than white motorists, police should not be stopping them more frequently. Such practices are not only unfair; they are an ineffective and wasteful form of law enforcement.

Racial profiling was subtly at work in the Diallo case: Nothing in Diallo's behavior—he was seen looking both ways out of a doorway—was sufficient cause for the initial intervention by the police. The police in this case were members of the aggressive Street Crimes Unit, which in recent years has expanded its activity. Jeffrey Toobin points out in a recent <u>New Yorker</u> article (March 6) that the number of people frisked by the police has risen dramatically in New York— from 18,000 in 1997 to 27,000 in 1998. Toobin also points out that the number of arrests has remained the same, which means that the increased police activity has mostly meant more mistakes—"stopping more individuals who had done nothing wrong." The more policing mistakes that are made, the more likely it is that mistakes will turn into fatal ones, as in the case of Amadou Diallo.

Everyone stands to gain from vigorous policing, especially the African-American communities that suffer most from crime. But until the police frisk whites with the same vigor that they frisk blacks, their mistakes cannot be said to be entirely innocent. (379)□

We're Hard-Wired to Stereotype

Mark Goldblatt

I was in the Detroit Metro airport, waiting to board a plane back to LaGuardia, making my peace with God—I'm not a good flier—when I noticed two Arab men strolling up to the gate.

Immediately, my heart began to race. A palpable hush descended as the men spoke to the flight attendant. Then, smiling amiably, they walked off.

As I exhaled, the other passengers' conversations resumed, too.   3

I don't know if the Arab men realized that their appearance had triggered   4
a wave of anxiety, but I suspect they did. It struck me that their smiles seemed
a little too fixed. It also struck me how unfair our response was—unfair that the
actions of a hundred or so Arab terrorists could make us wary of another hundred
million well-meaning Arabs who just happen to board planes.

Well, it <u>was</u> unfair—but that's the fault of the Arab terrorists, not the   5
crowd at the airport.

Perhaps you've already inferred where I'm going with this, that I'm about   6
to write about racial stereotyping.

Good.   7

Inferring is a survival mechanism wired into the human brain that compels   8
us to make snap judgments. It's the reason we don't need to lean against too many
hot stoves before we're wary of the next one. Such judgments can be wrong, of
course. Not every stove is hot. But snap judgments spare us from getting burned.

Unfortunately, the reflex to judge does not come with an off switch. We   9
are always drawing inferences about other human beings. Hence, the response
to the Arabs at the airport.

It was unfair, but not completely unfounded, because the historical like-   10
lihood of an Arab man turning out to be a hijacker is disproportionately higher
than the likelihood of an Asian, black or Hispanic man being a hijacker.

However, as painful as it is to write this, the historical likelihood of an   11
Arab man killing a New York City cop is disproportionately lower than the likelihood of a black or Hispanic man.

The statistics are grim. Eleven New York City police officers have been   12
killed in the line of duty since 1991. These incidents involved 19 perpetrators.
Of them, 10 were black males, six were Hispanic males, two were white males
and one was a Hispanic female. So even though black and Hispanic men constitute less than a quarter of the city's population, they have accounted for 16
out of 19 cop killers since 1991.

No amount of egalitarian rhetoric can offset those numbers. No amount   13
of sensitivity training can countermand the adrenaline surging through a cop's
veins as he confronts a black or Hispanic male suspect.

<u>Adrenaline</u>: the unspoken, unsatisfying, unavoidable explanation for 41   14
bullets fired, within seconds, by four white cops at unarmed Amadou Diallo.

Now these cops have been indicted for second-degree murder. No doubt   15
the prosecution will recite a litany of black and Hispanic men gunned down by
New York City police. It will conjure up a racist conspiracy. But if there is a
conspiracy, it is one of human nature and urban reality.

None of this justifies racial profiling—the practice of detaining people   16
with no probable cause, except that they fit a stereotype likely to commit a
crime. Here reforms may be due.

But it is utterly unrealistic to expect police officers, when drawn into a   17
confrontation, to react with perfect calm and to suppress the knowledge that a

black or Hispanic male suspect poses a disproportionately large threat to their well-being.

Police are trained as officers of the law, not Jedi warriors. ☐   18

Those Racist Cabbies

Mona Charen

Actor Danny Glover couldn't get a cab in New York City. Three empty taxis sped   1
past him, Glover recounted, and others were rude. When a cab finally did pick up Glover, his college-age daughter and her roommate, the driver (who must not have recognized the star of <u>Lethal Weapon</u>) declined to let the actor sit in the front seat, even though Glover explained that he had a bad hip.

The difficulty black men experience hailing cabs has become a symbol of   2
continuing American racism, though there is a perfectly obvious alternative explanation. Reporting the story in its "Week in Review" section, the <u>New York Times</u> acknowledged a wrinkle—the cabbie who was rude to Glover was non-white also, an immigrant from the subcontinent. Still, this didn't dent the <u>Times</u>' certitude about racism. "The actor's experience," the <u>Times</u> concluded, "may illustrate not just continuing American racism, but one way its character is subtly changing with demographics."

Translation: even other "people of color" are capable of racist stereotyp-   3
ing. Immigrants from Asia, the Middle East and even Africa are arriving with prejudiced ideas about blacks. The <u>Times</u> attributed these attitudes among new immigrants to the prevalence of American entertainment around the world.

So entrenched is the idea that cabbies who pass by black men are prac-   4
ticing racism that New York's Taxi and Limousine commission has sent under-cover police officers out to keep the cabbies honest.

Stephen and Abigail Thernstrom, authors of the most definitive study of   5
American race relations extant, <u>America in Black and White: One Nation, Indivisible</u>, had an interesting experience in a New York taxi recently.

Their native-born black driver said, "You won't believe what just happened   6
to me!" Two very scruffy and unkempt black men hailed his cab. He stopped and asked where they wanted to go. "Bed-Stuy" they replied (one of the most dangerous neighborhoods in New York).

The cabbie was leery, but he was also aware that undercover cops were   7
out looking for cabbies who engaged in illegal racial profiling. So he told them to get in, secretly planning to use one of his escape strategies (pretending that the cab suffered a breakdown). After only a couple of blocks, however, the two men in the back seat identified themselves as undercover cops, congratulated the cabbie on passing the test and got out. But before they walked away, one of the cops asked the driver to lower his window, brought his face very close and asked, "What are you, crazy?"

Ah, reality! What goes through the minds of New York's cab drivers (an 8 estimated 70 percent of whom are non-white) and those of other cities is not: "There's a black man. I think I'll insult him by passing him by." Or, "There's another one of those people I dislike," but rather, "What are the chances that that fare will rob or kill me?" Cab drivers are not social scientists, they are simply entrepreneurs attempting to make a living and stay alive. They are aware of certain realities.

They may not know that in California, 33 percent of black males between 9 the ages of 20 and 29 are either in jail, on probation or on parole at any given time. They may not know that in Washington, D.C., 42 percent of black males between the ages of 18 and 35 are either in prison or somehow in trouble with the criminal justice system. (See <u>The End of Racism</u> by Dinesh D'Souza.) But they do know that black males commit a disproportionate share of crimes, and many have experienced this first-hand. Driving a taxi is one of the most hazardous jobs in America.

Black women and children do not experience the difficulties with cabs that 10 their male counterparts do unless they are heading for a dangerous neighborhood. It's a shame that the majority of black males who do not commit crimes pay a price for those who do. The fact that even Danny Glover—the possessor of one of the sweetest faces in the Western world—has had to pay this price is sad. But it confuses the issue and unfairly defames cabbies to call this problem racism. It is simple caution, and who among us would do it differently? □

New Facts on Racial Profiling

Jeffrey Prescott

For years, activists, community leaders, and ordinary citizens have said minori- 1 ties in this country are treated unfairly by police and the criminal-justice system. Now, a flood of recent studies and reports are proving them correct.

Last week, the Leadership Conference on Civil Rights released a report 2 suggesting that African-American and Hispanic citizens are treated more harshly than their white counterparts at all levels of the criminal-justice system, from arrests to likelihood and length of imprisonment. And on April 25, a ground-breaking study financed by the Justice Department examining the juvenile justice system reached the same stark conclusion.

These reports, among others, join a growing body of evidence on race and 3 police practices, particularly racial profiling.

Law-enforcement agencies have generally responded to accusations of 4 profiling by arguing for its rationality. Because blacks commit crimes at a higher rate than whites, the argument goes, profiling is justified. A more subtle explanation for profiling suggests that since poverty-stricken communities feel the impact of crime most severely, and because these areas are also composed disproportionately of minorities, use of race as a factor in selecting potential lawbreakers is an inevitable byproduct of sound police practices.

Extensive new research on profiling, however, has exposed this rationale   5
as a myth. In the April 25 juvenile-justice report, minorities were at least twice as likely as whites to be sentenced to prison, even comparing youth with similar criminal histories.

Similarly, a recent General Accounting Office study showed that minorities   6
were far more likely than whites to face intrusive searches by U.S. Customs. In fact, Customs Service searches did not correlate with the likelihood of discovering contraband. In at least one category, the disparity was startling: The report found that black women were 9 times more likely to be x-rayed after a frisk or pat-down in 1997 and 1998, but actually "were less than half as likely to be found carrying contraband as white women."

New York Attorney General Eliot Spitzer's study of the "stop and frisk" prac-   7
tices in New York City, using a complex statistical model, found that 50 percent of all police stops were of black New Yorkers, though African-Americans account for only 25 percent of the city's population. Even taking into account the demographics of each police precinct and the crime rate by race, the report found black New Yorkers were still twice as likely to be stopped and frisked as whites.

These data support one obvious conclusion: Race is not a rational factor   8
to use in law enforcement. When people of color are targeted for stops and searches, police are no more likely—in some cases, much less likely—to find them breaking the law. But by focusing on skin color, the police create a self-fulfilling prophesy, as minorities will be "over policed" compared with their white counterparts. The disparity by race in arrests, convictions, and jail sentences will be exacerbated—and perhaps feed stereotypes that created the disparity in the first place. Deteriorating police and community relations, of course, are the destructive byproduct of this depressing formula.

The need for law-enforcement agencies to collect and make public data   9
about their work is most important in repairing damage done by racial profiling. Strong public interest in evaluating the work of police and duplicating the recent research can help root out irrational or pernicious police practices.

In New Jersey, a lawsuit was necessary to start the process; other states and   10
cities are considering laws to require data collection. The Traffic Stops Statistics Study Act (2000) has been introduced in Congress to provide for collection and analysis of data on traffic violations nationwide. Society gets the type of policing it demands. It is our civic responsibility to make certain political leaders react constructively to these new findings, support further research, and demand law enforcement that focuses on individual suspicion—not group stereotypes. □

The Problem of the Color Line

Anna Quindlen

Here's a riddle: why was the internationally known Princeton professor stopped   1
for driving too slowly on a street where the speed limit was 25 miles per hour?
How come a Maryland state trooper demanded to search the car of a lawyer who
graduated from Harvard? And why were an accomplished actor, a Columbia
administrator, a graduate student and a merchandiser for Donna Karan arrested
together in New York although none of them had done anything wrong?

The answer is elementary: all of the men were black. In some twisted   2
sense, they were the lucky ones. They were only humiliated. Not, like Rodney
King, beaten bloody. Not, like Abner Louima, sodomized with a broken broom-
stick. Not, like Amadou Diallo, killed in a gray blizzard of bullets.

The verdict is in. The jury has spoken. The death of Diallo, a hardworking   3
African immigrant, was adjudged a terrible accident, not murder, not manslaugh-
ter. Louima's assailant is in jail. Two of the officers who beat King went to prison.
There have been commissions, investigations, demonstrations, public reaction,
prayer vigils, op-ed pieces, television segments, classroom dialogues. And so Americans ricochet from event to event, speaking of reasonable doubt and prosecutor-
ial competence and ignoring the big picture, the real thing, the most important
issue in this country that we try not to talk about. That is, race.

"The problem of the 20th century is the problem of the color line,"   4
summed up W. E. B. Du Bois in 1903. How dispiriting to realize it is the problem of the 21st century as well. "Our truncated public discussions of race
suppress the best of who and what we are as a people because they fail to
confront the complexity of the issue in a candid and critical manner," wrote
Cornel West, that suspiciously slow-moving Princeton professor, in his aptly
titled monograph <u>Race Matters</u>. But in truth there are really no public discussions of race. There are discussions of affirmative action, and single parent-
hood, and, in the wake of human tragedies like the Diallo killing, of police training and procedures. These are discussions designed to cause the least amount
of discomfort to the smallest possible number of white people.

Police officers are just us wearing uniforms. The assumptions they make,   5
the prejudices they carry with them, are the assumptions and prejudices of their
roots, their neighborhoods, their society. These are not necessarily the excesses
of the egregious bigots, but the ways in which race changes everything, often
in subtle or unconscious fashion. It is an astonishing dissonance in a nation
allegedly based on equality, that there is a group of our citizens who are
assumed, simply by virtue of appearance, to be less. Less trustworthy. Less
educated or educable. Less moral. What we need to talk about candidly is something more difficult to apprehend than 41 shots in an apartment-house
vestibule. It is the unconscious racial shorthand that shapes assumptions so

automatic as to be a series of psychological tics: that the black prep-school kid must be on scholarship, that the black woman with a clutch of kids is careless instead of devoted to the vocation of motherhood. Not the shouts of "nigger" but the conclusions about everything from family background to taste in music, based on color alone, which blunt the acceptance of individuality and original-ity that is the glory of being human.

Some of this is easy to see, and to deride. A black electrician gets on the 6 train at night and there is the barely perceptible embrace of purses on the laps of women around him. A black lawyer stands with upraised hand and watches the cabs whiz by. A mall security guard trails the only black customer through a store. When police officers looking for drug dealers in New York threw four professional men in jail—including, ironically, the black actor who played Coalhouse Walker, harassed by bigots in the musical "Ragtime"—they became suspects by virtue of color alone. On the highways, being stopped because of race is so commonplace that there's even a clever name for it: DWB, or "driving while black." Amadou Diallo's mother is asked to accept that the police who shot her son thought his wallet was a gun. I have two teenage sons, and when they roam the streets of New York City, I never assume that they will be arrested for something they did not do, or shot, or killed. Their wallets will be seen as wallets.

Poll after poll shows a great gap in understanding, between a white Amer- 7 ica that believes things are ever so much better and a black America that thinks that is delusional. And that gap mirrors a gap more important than numbers, between what many of us believe we believe, and the subtle assumptions that creep into our consciousness, and which we are often unwilling to admit are there. For a long time we blamed this chasm on black men and women. We who are white expected them to teach us what it was like to be them, to make us comfortable, and we complained when they did not. Why Are All the Black Kids Sitting Together in the Cafeteria? Beverly Daniel Tatum called her book about the black experience. America is a nation riven by geographic apartheid, with precious few truly integrated neighborhoods, particularly in the suburbs. The great divide between black and white yawns wide with the distance of ignorance, and the silence of shame.

So the sophistry of the margins continues, the discussions of the LAPD or 8 the foster-care system or the failure of black leadership. The flagrant bigotries are discussed; the psychology of how we see one another and what that does to us too often is not. The most talkative nation on earth falls silent in the face of the enormity of the failure, of being two nations across a Mason-Dixon line of incom-prehension and subtle assumptions. Oscar Wilde once called homosexuality "the love that dare not speak its name." But we speak its name all the time now. Sex. Religion. Politics. We talk about them all. But what race means, in all its mani-festations large and small, is too often a whisper, our great unspoken issue. □

RACIAL PROFILING
Questions/Topics

1. Does the practice of racial profiling target minorities unfairly?
2. Is racial profiling useful and necessary for police?
3. What can be done about racial profiling in our country?
4. What should a critical thinker make of Mark Goldblatt's attitude toward snap judgments?
5. Do you agree or disagree that most people in the American culture are "hard-wired" to stereotype racially and ethnically, or do you have another position to argue?
6. Do you agree or disagree with Anna Quindlen that race is our country's "great unspoken issue" or do you have another position to argue?
7. Do you agree that the police officers in the Diallo case were "drawn into a confrontation" (causing them to pump 41 bullets into an unarmed black man)? What other actions do you think the police might have taken in this case?
8. Which of these essay selections do you find most persuasive? Why? Analyze the writer's appeals to logos, pathos, and ethos.
9. Which selection has the most interesting style? What do you notice about the writer's diction and sentence patterns? What do you notice about the writer's voice—the sound of his or her personality? How does the writer's style reinforce the meaning—the writer's thesis and supporting evidence?

Interchapter 2

Voice and Emphasis

Understanding sentence structure is like using the Reveal Codes option in word processing: you're going underneath your writing to see the structure of your thoughts.

DICTION AND REPETITION

Repeating Words for Emphasis

Critical thinkers know the value of repetition. By repeating a key word or phrase, you can emphasize an idea as well as your attitude (tone) toward your audience, subject, and self. Such emphasis helps readers hear your voice. For example

> There are no cheerleaders for readers, no front-page pictures, no end-zone dance. (Pitts F1)

> We aim to make our magazine even more urgent, more relevant, more immediately useful to our readers. (Loeb)

> A sentence should contain no unnecessary words, a paragraph no unnecessary sentences, for the same reason that a drawing should have no unnecessary lines and a machine no unnecessary parts. (Strunk and White xiv)

Repeating words is an easy and explicit kind of emphasis. But don't rely on this effect too often: if you emphasize many thoughts this way, you may lose the emphasis. As with most tools of style, the paradox of less is more applies: a tool will usually have more power if you don't overuse it. Sometimes a single repetition can be too much:

> A cantankerous boss adds extra stress to a worker's load. Many workers suffer unnecessary anxiety at the hands of a cantankerous supervisor.

Words tend to echo in the reader's mind, especially unusual words, which by definition you don't use often, and readers don't expect to encounter them. Because they are unusual, they stand out longer and stronger—and distract from your meaning.

ACTIVITY 1

Write three sentences in which you repeat a single word or a phrase for emphasis. Bring these to class to share. Also, review your latest writing and see if repeating a word or phrase within a sentence (or group of sentences) will strengthen a point you're trying to make.

Alliteration

Essayists, poets, politicians—writers of all types—use repetition to create effective sound patterns as well as to emphasize key ideas. The skillful use of sounds can make the difference between powerful, persuasive prose and plain, pale prose.

As a critical thinker you should be aware of <u>alliteration</u> in prose: <u>the repetition of consonants at the beginning of words</u>. Sound can reinforce sense—meaning—and strengthen your writer's voice. John F. Kennedy repeats two different consonants in this sentence from his Inaugural Address:

> To those people in the huts and villages of half the globe struggling to break the bonds of mass misery, we pledge our best efforts to help them help themselves.

The <u>b</u> and <u>m</u> sounds of <u>break the bonds of mass misery</u> are forceful, calling attention to the words, making the ideas stand out. The repetition indicates that Kennedy cared about the sound of his language in such an important speech. (Note other repetitions of sounds in his sentence.) Alliteration used well suggests that a writer has control, and this sense of control inspires credibility.

Alliteration usually happens in twos or threes within a sentence.

Emotional <u>lessons</u> <u>learned</u> in childhood stay with us as <u>habits</u> of the <u>heart</u> through life. (Goleman, "The New Thinking on Smarts" 6)[1]

One person's <u>mission</u> is another person's <u>minutia</u>. (Covey 190)

I have a dream that my four little children will one day live in a nation where they will not be judged by the <u>color</u> of their skin but by the <u>content</u> of their <u>character</u>. (King)

With a good conscience our only sure reward, with history the final judge, let us go forth to <u>lead</u> the <u>land</u> we <u>love</u>. (John F. Kennedy, Inaugural Address)

We [Bill and Hillary Clinton] have learned that to raise a <u>happy</u>, <u>healthy</u> and <u>hopeful</u> child, it takes a family. (Hillary Clinton, Democratic National Convention, 1996)

Well-chosen repetitions can help your ideas sound emphatic and clear, but a little can go a long way.

ACTIVITY 2

Practice alliteration by writing three sentences that use it. Try not to overdo it, however. Bring these sentences to class to share. Then review your most recent writing to see if you can use some alliteration for emphasis and to improve the sound of a sentence or two.

ACTIVITY 3

Skim "Bigger, But Not Better" by Ryan Grady Sample at the end of chapter 1. Look for examples of alliteration he uses. How does this tool help convey his voice?

---

[1]All emphasis in these pages is ours unless otherwise noted.

ACTIVITY 4

Read the following selection by Annie Dillard. Then try to identify as many features of diction in it as you can. (Review interchapter 1.) A useful way to analyze diction is to type or photocopy a short selection and then annotate it— underline key words and draw lines to the margins identifying certain tools of style, such as these:

> Strings of monosyllabic or multisyllabic words
> Specific or general words
> Concrete or abstract words
> Metaphors or similes
> Precise words
> Words repeated for emphasis
> Alliteration

Note aspects of Dillard's diction that help produce her meaning. Below your analysis, write a brief paragraph in which you describe Dillard's voice.

> A weasel is wild. Who knows what he thinks? He sleeps in his underground den, his tail draped over his nose. Sometimes he lives in his den for two days without leaving. Outside, he stalks rabbits, mice, muskrats, and birds, killing more bodies than he can eat warm, and often dragging the carcasses home. Obedient to instinct, he bites his prey at the neck, either splitting the jugular vein at the throat or crunching the brain at the base of the skull, and he does not let go. One naturalist refused to kill a weasel who was socketed into his hand deeply as a rattlesnake. The man could in no way pry the tiny weasel off, and he had to walk half a mile to water, the weasel dangling from his palm, and soak him off like a stubborn label.
>
> And once, says Ernest Thompson Seton—once, a man shot an eagle out of the sky. He examined the eagle and found the dry skull of a weasel fixed by the jaws to his throat. The supposition is that the eagle had pounced on the weasel and the weasel swiveled and bit as instinct taught him, tooth to neck, and nearly won. I would like to have seen that eagle from the air a few weeks or months before he was shot: was the whole weasel still attached to his feathered throat, a fur pendant? Or did the eagle eat what he could reach, gutting the living weasel with his talons before his breast, bending his beak, cleaning the beautiful airborne bones? (<u>Teaching a Stone to Talk</u> 11–12)

SENTENCE TOOLS

Joining Complete and Incomplete Thoughts: Subordination

Subordination means one thought is not equal to another. It is sometimes explained as dependence: one thought is not complete—it depends on another thought for complete sense. For example,

> If you never experience sadness, you cannot truly experience happiness. (Kelly Battles, student)

The first thought—<u>If you never experience sadness</u>—is not complete. That thought is subordinate—not finished. It depends on the other thought to make sense. The word <u>If</u> is a signal that the thought is incomplete, even though it has a subject and a verb. Here is a list of <u>common signal words</u> (subordinating conjunctions and relative pronouns) that connect incomplete thoughts to complete thoughts:

after	since	when	who
although	that	whenever	whom
as	though	where	
because	unless	wherever	
before	until	which	
if	what	while	

Kelly's sentence is called a <u>complex sentence</u> because it contains one incomplete thought plus one complete thought. The complex sentence gives writers flexibility. For example, Kelly's thought can be reversed so that the complete thought comes first:

> You cannot truly experience happiness if you never experience sadness.

The thought is the same, but the incomplete thought now comes last—where "sadness" receives emphasis. Here are other examples of complex sentences that begin with incomplete thoughts. Notice the signal words that begin each incomplete thought.

> <u>If</u> I could find no word to express what I intended, I made one up. (Selzer, <u>Mortal Lessons</u> 7–8)

> <u>While</u> we are free to choose our actions, we are not free to choose the consequences of those actions. (Covey 90)

<u>When</u> you learn how to die, you learn how to live. (Albom, <u>Tuesdays with Morrie</u> 104)

Here are examples of complex sentences beginning with complete thoughts and ending with incomplete thoughts. Notice the signal words:

Cold often brings on the most spectacular of dreams, <u>as though</u> the brain has been incited to fevered activity. (Erdrich 173)

Educators can help women develop their own authentic voices <u>if</u> they emphasize connection over separation. (Belenky, Clinchy, Goldberger, and Tarule 229)

A deeper level of thinking can go on <u>when</u> you relinquish your conscious grip on your material. (Elbow, <u>Writing with Power</u> 40)

Comma Rule: If you begin a sentence with an incomplete thought, place a comma after it.

ACTIVITY 5

In your notebook write three sentences beginning with an incomplete thought. Then write three sentences beginning with a complete thought followed by an incomplete thought. You may use the same sentences. For example, "<u>When</u> I write essays, I drink coffee." "I drink coffee <u>when</u> I write essays."

You can use complex sentences to revise your writing for variety and clarity. Too many simple sentences can make your thoughts seem all of the same weight and emphasis. The result is likely to sound like a list:

The president is spending his vacation in Africa.
He is taking a break from the world's many problems.
The first lady is touring the continent with him.
They have been welcomed by the people of Africa.

Instead, you can combine these by using a complex sentence and a compound sentence.

<u>While</u> the president is on his vacation in Africa, he is taking a break from his many troubles. The first lady is touring the continent with him<u>, and</u> they have been welcomed by the people of Africa.

Here is an example of revising a compound sentence into a complex one:

> Cloning animals for human organ transplants will save human lives, but this process raises ethical questions.

Revision:

> Although cloning animals for human organ transplants will save human lives, this process raises ethical questions.

Because subordination places greater weight on certain thoughts, using this pattern will help you express your thinking.

ACTIVITY 6

Look at your recent writing. See how often you use complex sentences. Try to combine some simple or compound sentences, making them complex. See if such revision helps you emphasize certain thoughts as well as provide more variety in your writing.

We don't expect you to identify every sentence you write or read. But if you can see these patterns of coordination and subordination, you will have more control with your writing when you revise it and when you evaluate other people's writing. Understanding sentence structure is like using the Reveal Codes option in word processing: you're going underneath your writing to see the structure of your thoughts.

Colons and Dashes and Voice

We ask that you actively practice the following tools in your notebook and try to apply them immediately to your current writing.

Colons

You have already practiced using semicolons to join two complete thoughts in various ways. Using colons and dashes will give your writing more variety and power.

ACTIVITY 7

Write a sentence using a colon. (Sentences containing time such as 2:15 P.M. don't count.) If you aren't sure, don't worry. Just try. <u>Please don't read ahead until you have done this activity</u>.

———————————

How are colons used in the following sentences?

One thing is clear: I am not the only watcher in the woods. (Erdrich 61)

The relationship between thought and language is dialectical: ideas are conceived by language; language is generated by thought. (Berthoff 47)

The horrors of cloning have not been fully understood by the public: it may be possible to produce headless bodies for the purpose of harvesting organs.

Does the sentence you wrote resemble the preceding sentences? When asked to use a colon, most students write a sentence containing a list:

At the bookstore I bought the following: five textbooks, three pens and pencils, and a college mug.

Colons and lists work well together; they are common. However, you can use a colon to clarify your thoughts: the statement before a colon can introduce an explanation that follows it. This sophisticated use of colons shows your reasoning and carries persuasive power.

When you use a colon to introduce an explanation, what follows the colon can be a complete thought (as the preceding examples show) or an incomplete thought:

The fundamental crisis in black America is twofold: too much poverty and too little self-love. (West 93)

To achieve quality in anything, you need this primary emotion: to care.

In formal writing you should not use a colon after forms of the verb <u>to be</u>: <u>am</u>, <u>is</u>, <u>are</u>, <u>was</u>, <u>were</u>, <u>be</u>, <u>being</u>, and <u>been</u>.

Improper

Some of the scientists behind the cloning furor <u>are</u>: Keith Campbell, Ian Wilmut, W. Bruce Currie, and Colin Stewart.

Proper

Some of the scientists behind the cloning furor are Keith Campbell, Ian Wilmut, W. Bruce Currie, and Colin Stewart.

These are some of the scientists behind the cloning furor: Keith Campbell, Ian Wilmut, W. Bruce Currie, and Colin Stewart.

If you don't have a complete thought before a colon, you shouldn't use a colon.

Because colons connect closely related thoughts, you may wonder sometimes whether to use a colon or a semicolon in a sentence. Consider this

Sometimes an outline serves best as a cage to break out of: it makes you think of ideas that won't fit inside but which otherwise wouldn't occur to you. (Elbow, Embracing Contraries 49)

Elbow could have used a semicolon because both complete thoughts relate closely to each other. But because the second thought explains the first thought, a colon is a better choice.

Colon Rule: To use a colon properly, you need a complete thought before it: whether followed by an explanation, a word or phrase, or a list.

Improper:

Diana wanted: privacy, fame and love.

Proper:

Diana wanted it all: privacy, fame and love. (Thomas and Dickey 39)

ACTIVITY 8

Write three sentences using a colon. At least two of the colons should introduce explanations. Bring your sentences to class to share. Then look at your recent writing. See if you can use some colons to combine sentences—to introduce explanations. For practice, try using this tool the next time you write.

Dashes

Punctuation marks enable you to set up your thoughts in different ways, as a golfer uses different clubs for different shots. You've already practiced using semicolons (in interchapter 1) and colons. Now, the dash.

ACTIVITY 9

Write a sentence using a dash. If you aren't sure, don't worry. <u>Please don't read ahead until you have done this Activity</u>.

How are dashes used in the following sentences?

I am one of a growing number of students who are completing college in three years instead of four—cramming credits in the summer. (Wu 14)

I do not shrink from this responsibility—I welcome it. (John F. Kennedy, Inaugural Address)

They were four girls in church—until a bomb blew them away. (Garrow 37)

You can use dashes in various ways. Less formal than colons, dashes are quick connectors—zaps of emphasis.

Unlike colons, dashes can be used without a complete thought before them:

Semicolons, colons, dashes—these tools help you connect thoughts.

To palm a fevered brow, to feel a thin, wavering pulse at the wrist, to draw down a pale lower lid—these simple acts cause a doctor's heart to expand. (Selzer, <u>Down from Troy</u> 160)

In the examples, a series precedes the dash. Like colons, dashes can be followed with a complete thought or an incomplete thought. How do dashes function in the following sentences?

My white friends want me to act one way—white. My African-American friends want me to act another—black. (Courtney 16)

I must therefore assume that the solution lies in that great and dubious driving force of American society—marketing. (Gould 97)

Clearly a single word follows each—dash. Set-off, the word stands out. The dash emphasizes it. A colon could work in each sentence, but colons are more formal than dashes.

Dash Rule: A typed dash is indicated by two hyphens with no space before, between, or after. The distinction between a dash and a hyphen is essential for skilled readers. The hyphen connects two words: ready-peeled, set-off, hand-washed. In print the dash may look like a single line, but that line is twice the length of a hyphen (dash— hyphen-); when typing, always use two hyphens to indicate a dash.

ACTIVITY 10

Write three sentences using a dash. One sentence should contain a dash followed by one word. One sentence should begin with a series followed by a dash and a complete thought. The other sentence is your free choice. Bring your sentences to class to share. Then look at your recent writing. See if you can use some dashes for emphasis or to combine sentences. For practice, try using this tool the next time you write.

Using Double Dashes

You can use dashes in another way to emphasize thoughts. Consider these examples:

One measure—and perhaps the best measure—of a person's greatness is the capacity for suffering. (Peck 222)

My father—a man with a great sense of humor and no sense of direction—constantly led us on what he referred to as "scenic routes." (Goodman, <u>At Large</u> 130)

Analyze almost any writing you can find—textbook, article, novel, magazine, newspaper, poem—and see how writers use dashes.

These double dashes enclose interruptions in thought. The dashes work like parentheses: they set-off clarifying or explanatory information not essential to the main meaning of the sentence. Peck's main thought is "One measure of a person's greatness is the capacity for suffering." Although what he encloses in dashes is not essential, Peck's sentence is more conversational and emphatic with his double dashes. His voice is clearer. Ellen Goodman's sentence is more interesting and humorous with her dashes. The last sentence provides examples of kinds of writing within two dashes.

Dashes help your voice come alive on the page. But some students become dash happy after learning how to use this tool—whether a single dash or double dashes. The tool loses its power if used too often.

ACTIVITY 11

Write three sentences using double dashes to set-off and enclose information. Bring your sentences to class to share. Then look at your recent writing. See if you can use double dashes for emphasis or to combine sentences. For practice, try using this tool the next time you write.

Underlining (Italics) and Voice

How is underlining used in the following sentences?

> We must <u>care</u> about something to do something about it. (Paul 57)

> "Mitch, I <u>embrace</u> aging." (Albom, <u>Tuesdays with Morrie</u> 118)

> In the last analysis, what we <u>are</u> communicates far more eloquently than anything we <u>say</u> or <u>do</u>. (Covey 22)

In these examples the underlined words signify emphasis.

When you talk, you often emphasize certain words with the sound of your voice: your tone may deepen or rise with extra feeling; you may put a twist of sarcasm on a word (Oh I just <u>love</u> that new song by the Zebras); you may simply call attention to a word or phrase (the word <u>quality</u> is important). In short, using underlining is a good way to add <u>voice</u> to your voice, to make your writing sound like a real person—you. As Peter Elbow argues in <u>Writing with Power</u>,

> Writing <u>without voice</u> is wooden or dead because it lacks sound, rhythm, energy, and individuality. [. . .] Writing <u>with voice</u> is writing into which someone has breathed. (299)

Sometimes writers will underline whole sentences to signify their importance. Mitch Albom in <u>Tuesdays with Morrie</u> writes,

> I remembered what Morrie said during our visit: <u>"The culture we have does not make people feel good about themselves. And you have to be strong enough to say if the culture doesn't work, don't buy it."</u> (emphasis in original) (42)

If Albom were to underline many sentences, the underlinings would soon lose their effect.

Many writers use underlining occasionally. The tool becomes part of their style—to create their writer's voice. Many other writers choose not to use the tool at all, especially in formal writing. Add underlining to your stock of stylistic tools as a way to highlight and emphasize certain words or groups of words. But don't use this or any tool of style too much.

Even if your printer or typewriter does have an italics feature, you should use underlining instead. The underline is standard for italics in MLA style. Ask your instructor before using the italic feature of your typewriter or printer.

ACTIVITY 12

Write three sentences using underlining. Use underlining in a sentence to highlight one word; use it in another sentence to highlight a group of words. The third sentence is your free choice. Bring your sentences to class to share. Then look at your recent writing for places where you might use underlining for emphasis.

Parentheses and Voice

How are parentheses used in the following sentences?

> Particularly in class or alone with my teachers, I chattered. (Talking seemed to make teachers think I was bright.) (Rodriguez 129)

> That night I dream I am dancing to Stevie Wonder's song "Always" (the name of the song is really "As," but I hear it as "Always"). (Walker, <u>In Search of Our Mothers' Gardens</u> 393)

> The patient was asleep. Kneeling, I felt his ears (as you might put your hand on the forehead of a child) and they seemed cool. (White, <u>Essays of E. B. White</u> 20)

> Evil is in opposition to life (is "live" spelled backwards). (Peck 42)

> For the writer (prose or poetry) all words rhyme, sort of; that is, all sounded words are more like each other than any word is like silence. (Stafford, <u>Writing the Australian Crawl</u> 26)

Parentheses are another tool of style you can use to shape your voice on the page. They contain information the writer wants to set off from the main thought of the sentence, yet the information usually helps to complete the meaning within a sentence. Sometimes parentheses contain secondary information or clarification; sometimes they function as asides—additional comments; sometimes they seem to whisper what writers don't want to say out loud.

ACTIVITY 13

Write two sentences using parentheses. Use them in a sentence to enclose a complete thought; then use them in another sentence to enclose a word or phrase. Bring your sentences to class to share. Then look at your recent writing to see if you can use parentheses to combine two sentences or to enclose a comment or information. Try using this tool the next time you write.

FINE-TUNING SENTENCES

Sentence Fragments: Pros and Cons

In academic writing you are expected to write complete sentences. In less formal situations, fragments are more acceptable—to those who accept them at all. You use sentence fragments naturally when you talk as a way to avoid repetition. Professional writers sometimes use fragments intentionally to create certain effects. Consider this fragment by Richard Selzer:

> For the first time we can see into the cavity of the abdomen. Such a primitive place. One expects to find drawings of buffalo on the walls. (<u>Mortal Lessons</u> 93–94)

Selzer's fragment expresses his voice: <u>Such a primitive place</u> suggests an aside of surprise; he could have written "It is such a primitive place," but the complete thought is implied. Like short sentences, fragments can help a writer's voice sound authentic; they give writing an oral English (less formal) sound.

When he was a boy, Richard Rodriguez tried to shave off the dark complexion of his skin. How well do his two sentence fragments work here?

> For as I noted with disappointment, the dark would not come out.
>   It remained. Trapped. Deep in the cells of my skin. (124–25)

The word "Trapped" and the phrases "Deep in the cells of my skin" have dramatic emphasis.

Depending on your writing situation, sentence fragments may be another stylistic tool for you to use: they can reinforce meaning as well as make your voice sound real. Many modern writers have become increasingly liberal about the use of fragments. However, many instructors forbid all sentence fragments: it isn't always easy to tell whether a fragment is intentional or a mistake.

Conciseness

Writers and editors honor concise writing. Usually, the more concise the better. Concise doesn't mean "short," though concise sentences do tend to be short. A good synonym for concise is <u>succinct</u>—saying much in little. One of the most concise statements admired around the world is President Lincoln's Gettysburg Address. At that dedication, Mr. Edward Everett, the speaker before Lincoln, took two hours to deliver his address. Historians tell us that Mr. Everett praised Lincoln, saying he wished he had been able to say as much in two hours as the President had in two minutes.

<u>All</u> readers appreciate concise writing. In revision you must try to remove wordy, repetitious, redundant, loosely written sentences and paragraphs. Reading carefully is a time-consuming task. Your readers will appreciate anything you can do to shorten and lighten their work. Then too, concise language helps your readers' comprehension.

Omit Needless Words I

Do you often think you're being clear when, in fact, you aren't? Cluttered with excess words, sentences become fuzzy: fuzzy sentences come from fuzzy thinking. If you can remove words without loss of meaning, you should probably remove them. Revision skills help cut the fuzz from thinking and writing. Thoughtful writers revise with accurate nouns and strong verbs when possible.

Throughout these interchapters we have advised you to "omit needless words." Will Strunk advised students to do this in <u>Elements of Style</u>. E. B. White, his former student, who revised Strunk's book, says that Strunk's lecture on the importance of brevity was so brief he needed to fill time in class, so he repeated "Omit needless words" three times!

A. Up to this point in my life, choosing what I am going to do for the rest of my life has been the biggest decision I have had to make. (30 words)
B. Choosing what I will do in my life has been my biggest decision. (13 words)

Imagine that you wrote sentence A, that most of your writing is inflated with needless words. Then imagine that you wrote sentence B, that most of your writing is concise and clear. The style of sentence B helps readers receive the thought more easily and quickly.

ACTIVITY 14

Write each of these sentences in your notebook. Then revise them, omitting needless words.

1. In the matter of the death of the mouse, it was the dog that should be blamed or credited as the case may be.
2. Infants of a young age should not be left alone by themselves.
3. My dad has this way of being able to converse with anyone that he meets on a level that is appropriate to the person he is speaking to at the time.

ACTIVITY 15

Look at your recent writing. Examine your sentences for needless words. Cross them out or put brackets around them—use whatever method of editing you like.

Omit Needless Words II

Unnecessary words make your writing sound loose and weak. Avoid adding extra words to reach an assigned paper length. Most teachers would prefer a concise paper to a padded one.

Condense expressions such as the following:

Wordy	Revised
a large number of	many
at the present time	now
for the reason that	because
due to the fact that	because
during the time that	while
in American society today	in America
in light of the fact that	because
in order to	to
in the event that	if
in this day and age	now, today
in view of the fact that	because or since
the modern world of today	today

Avoid redundancies such as these:

advance planning   hurry quickly
basic essentials   orange in color
completely unique   rectangular in shape
disappear from view   revert back
disregard altogether   separate and distinct

She smiles with phenomenal radiance. [Isn't radiance already phenomenal?]

ACTIVITY 16

Write each of these sentences in your notebook. Then revise them, omitting needless words.

1. Due to the fact that cigarette smoke irritated his throat, Joe neither smoked nor spent time in places where other people smoked.
2. The game of basketball is a game that is becoming more and more popular in Europe at this point in time.
3. It has been determined by the board of trustees in separate and distinct rulings that alcoholic beverages of an intoxicating nature be banned and prohibited in those buildings devoted to housing students.

ACTIVITY 17

Look at your recent writing. Examine your sentences for any inflated expressions or redundancies like those in the preceding discussion. Then try to revise by omitting needless words.

Chapter 3

Strategies of Argumentation

Most of us most of the time do not know what is going on in our minds.
(Moffett 152)

As a student of composition, you have to learn how to put [. . .] natural facilities to work. (Berthoff 80)

To learn structure [. . .] is to learn how things are related.
  (Bruner, The Process of Education 7)

To get people to understand, to consider, to respond, wise writers and speakers
use various strategies of argumentation—of critical thinking. You have already
practiced some of these strategies in chapters 1 and 2:

Using the process of communication: making and supporting a point
Using persuasive appeals: logos, pathos, ethos
Using different kinds of evidence: examples, reasons, authorities, statistics
Using Rogerian argument: presenting other arguments before your own

In this chapter you will explore other common strategies that will help you
discover, develop, and defend your ideas. Often this means that logos is the
dominant appeal, but you will see that pathos and ethos also play their parts in
these strategies.

A strategy is a plan of action. The word originally referred to the methods generals in armies devised to defeat an enemy—another war metaphor. But

let's consider the word in a more positive way: a strategy is a plan of action to help you discover ideas and supporting evidence, to help you develop and organize your evidence, and to help you defend your thesis—so you can persuade your audience to consider your idea, to understand it, and to agree with it.

In this chapter you will explore ten strategies: <u>induction</u>, <u>deduction</u>, <u>illustration</u>, <u>narration</u>, <u>description</u>, <u>refutation</u>, <u>comparison-contrast</u>, <u>classification</u>, <u>cause and effect</u>, and <u>definition</u>. Each strategy is a different pattern of arranging thoughts. Each strategy is also a tool to help you analyze and understand whatever you write and whatever you read. How many tools do you need to get a job done? It depends on the job. Many jobs will not require refutation or classification, but some jobs will. What we offer in this chapter is a repertoire of thinking tools to draw on when you write. They are not ends in themselves. Rather, they are useful means to useful ends—helping you communicate clearly and persuasively.

You have been using these patterns of thinking for most of your life. But have you used them consciously—that is, with an awareness that you are using them? Critical thinkers act consciously: they deliberately choose certain words over other words, certain sentences over other sentences, certain strategies over others. This enables critical thinkers to control their writing and to revise it until it does what they want it to do—to persuade others in some way.

USING INDUCTION AND DEDUCTION

Using Induction

When you use examples and reasons, you can arrange them in two different ways, called induction and deduction. Inductive reasoning means you give your evidence first and then make your point about it—a generalization. You may observe that whenever you walk on campus and pass people, they say hello and smile. If it happens often enough, you may generalize that your campus is friendly. This is induction or inductive reasoning. You may have walked on other campuses where passers-by don't greet each other; those campuses feel less friendly. This kind of thinking—observing examples and then generalizing from them—is common. It is also the primary tool of science: scientists observe what happens in their experiments and then draw their conclusions.

Induction, however, never absolutely proves a generalization. Although you may have passed by friendly people on your campus, tomorrow you may find that some people ignore you. It's not possible for you to pass by every person at your school to determine whether they are friendly or not. And though you have visited other campuses you find unfriendly, it's possible you didn't spend enough days there to gather enough observations to justify your claim.

The process of induction can fool you if you're not careful. You may think you're drawing logical conclusions from your observations. Suppose you said the following:

Aunt Betty smokes and is healthy. Mr. Amut next door smokes and is healthy. Everyone I know who smokes is healthy. Therefore, there is no truth to the claim that smoking is dangerous.

Such thinking shows a leap—called an inductive leap—from observations to a generalization. But just because every smoker you know is healthy does not mean that countless other people who smoke are also healthy. Your data is insufficient to justify your claim. Plus, you'd be ignoring warnings from the Surgeon General on cigarette packages as well as an abundance of scientific evidence. Induction provides greater and greater (or lesser) degrees of probability.

Induction, then, is an argument that moves from particular examples to an opinion about them. You often reason from the basis of a few examples. You notice that pencils, pens, and notepaper cost less at WonderMart than at Sam's market in town; therefore, you conclude you can save money at WonderMart. The quality of the items may not be the same. But from induction you conclude that items cost less at WonderMart. Many reports on television news shows proceed from induction. A report on the dating habits of college students may focus on four young people from one school. Is this sample adequate to form a reliable generalization? Probably not. But if the report includes surveys on dating taken from thousands of students across the country, this would substantiate a generalization. Usually, the more examples you have to support a point, the more reliable that point is. But it is seldom possible to include more than a few examples—except through highly statistical sampling methods, which allow TV forecasters to know on the basis of less than 2% of the voters who is going to win an election.

The search for generalizations we can rely on is the goal of scientific knowledge. Scientists draw on their observations to find those "laws of nature" so that they can then use such "laws" in tests and in constructing theories about life and the universe. It is a circle of knowledge—searching for the generalizations, then testing them for validity, and then using them to predict other events and generalizations. You can try it yourself.

ACTIVITY 1

A Brief Experiment

When in class, observe what students are wearing and from this draw your conclusions about what other students will be wearing in your next class or wherever you encounter groups of students. If your generalization is accurate, you will have "proved" or shown how "probable" your reasoning is; if it is not accurate, amend it so that it will be.

Using Deduction

Deduction is the other major strategy of reasoning. Deduction means that general laws <u>predict</u> specific examples or instances. In your travels to various schools, you may conclude that small colleges (of less than 2,000 students) are more friendly than large universities (of more than 40,000 students). When you go to a small college, you can predict that the atmosphere "probably" will feel more friendly. When you go to a large university, you can predict that the atmosphere "probably" will feel less friendly. Your predictions may not hold true. You may find a small college unfriendly and a large school friendly. But the process of deduction involves such prediction: drawing out specific cases from a general law. Likewise, because you know that school supplies are cheap at WonderMart, the next time you need supplies you can predict you will probably save money at WonderMart instead of buying them at Sam's market. Why use the word <u>probably</u>? In the modern world we have discovered that very little can be predicted absolutely: science is much more inclined to deal with degrees of probability.

Consider another example of deduction. Because you know from experience that the quality of YumYum restaurants is variable, you can't predict the quality of the next YumYum's restaurant you visit. But you can predict that you probably will have good food and service at YumYum in Mt. Pleasant because you have been there many times without being dissatisfied.

Robert Pirsig in <u>Zen and the Art of Motorcycle Maintenance</u> clarifies induction and deduction by providing concrete examples:

> Two kinds of logic are used [in motorcycle maintenance and in living], inductive and deductive. Inductive inferences start with observations of the machine and arrive at general conclusions. For example, if the cycle goes over a bump and the engine misfires, and then goes over another bump and the engine misfires, and then goes over another bump and the engine misfires, and then goes over a long smooth stretch of road and there is no misfiring, and then goes over a fourth bump and the engine misfires again, one can logically conclude that the misfiring is caused by the bumps. That is induction: reasoning from particular experiences to general truths.
>
> Deductive inferences do the reverse. They start with general knowledge and predict a specific observation. For example, if, from reading the hierarchy of facts about the machine, the mechanic knows the horn of the cycle is powered exclusively by electricity from the battery, then he can logically infer that if the battery is dead the horn will not work. That is deduction. (99)

You use induction and deduction naturally. But if you can use them more consciously, you will have more power to direct your thoughts logically. You can use induction in a single paragraph or in a whole essay by moving from specific examples to a generalization about them. You can use deduction in a single paragraph or in a whole essay by moving from a generalization to specific examples.

Induction	**Deduction**
Specific example	Generalization
Specific example	Specific example
Specific example	Specific example
Generalization	Specific example

Deduction works best in mathematics and the mathematical sciences because in math you can have absolute premises. But when you are talking about human behavior, it's difficult to find absolute premises. You may believe all blondes are fair-skinned, but it would be foolish to posit that as a working premise: nobody has seen "all blondes."

ACTIVITY 2

Identify whether you think the following examples show inductive or deductive reasoning:

1. Students who think critically evaluate what they read and write. Seymour thinks critically. Therefore, he evaluates what he reads and writes.
2. Seymour reads a lot and gets A's. Roseanne reads a lot and gets A's. Carole does too. Conclusion: Students who read a lot get good grades.
3. Students who take Human Anatomy dissect a cadaver. Franny and Buddy have enrolled in Human Anatomy. Thus, they will dissect a cadaver.
4. I see yellow, orange, and red leaves. I see many leaves turned brown, piled along the curb. Two pumpkins smile on a porch step across the street. I love autumn, but it doesn't last long enough.

ACTIVITY 3

1. Practice induction by writing a paragraph in which you give examples and details of what you see—it may be about this book, the cafeteria, your computer, what you are wearing, the room you are in, what you see outside your window. Conclude by stating a generalization from your examples. For example: "From all these examples I conclude that the cafeteria is as much about socializing as eating."
2. Practice deduction by writing a paragraph in which you state a generalization followed by specific examples or instances:

When students laugh in class, they enjoy learning. For example, Professor Hyde told a joke (describe joke). . . . On another occasion, my friend Alicia had a terrific sneeze during her speech (describe sneeze). . . . And so on. . . .

ARGUING BY ILLUSTRATION

The Paradigm Shift

The general rule for supporting an argument is to provide convincing examples and reasons; however, you can use an illustration to make a point also. An illustration is an extended example. You see this in news stories on TV: a reporter focuses on one woman's struggle with cancer and her battle with a health insurance company that refuses to pay for her treatments. If it represents a widespread problem, one in-depth illustration can be more persuasive than brief examples of several people.

What follows is an illustration to show what we mean by illustration: consider the paradigm shift ("paradigm" rhymes with dime). In <u>The Seven Habits of Highly Effective People</u> Stephen Covey discusses "paradigm shifts" in reasoning. A "paradigm" is a pattern, a standard theory or explanation about some aspect of reality. When you throw a baseball up into the air, you have a "paradigm" about what will happen to the ball. Should the ball for some reason not come down, and then all balls thrown into the air not come down as you expect (as if gravity had been turned off), it would mean that an important part of your understanding about reality was wrong! Your standard paradigm about baseballs in the air would have shifted. Imagine the effect that would have on people. That effect is what is meant by a "paradigm shift." You must "shift" your understanding of reality to make room for this new view of it.

Covey cites familiar examples of paradigm shifts in science: when Copernicus placed the sun at the center of the universe (not the earth as Ptolemy had argued) and when Einstein's relativity theory replaced Newton's theory of physics. Then Covey gives his illustration—an extended personal example—to show what he means.

> I remember a paradigm shift I experienced one Sunday morning on a subway in New York. People were sitting quietly—some reading newspapers, some lost in thought, some resting with their eyes closed. It was a calm, peaceful scene.
>
> Then suddenly, a man and his children entered the subway car. The children were so loud and rambunctious that instantly the whole climate changed.
>
> The man sat down next to me and closed his eyes, apparently oblivious to the situation. The children were yelling back and forth, throwing things, even grabbing people's papers. It was very disturbing. And yet, the man sitting next to me did nothing.
>
> It was difficult not to feel irritated. I could not believe that he could be so insensitive as to let his children run wild like that and do nothing about it,

taking no responsibility at all. It was easy to see that everyone else on the subway felt irritated, too. So finally, with what I felt was unusual patience and restraint, I turned to him and said, "Sir, your children are really disturbing a lot of people. I wonder if you couldn't control them a little more?"

The man lifted his gaze as if to come to a consciousness of the situation for the first time and said softly, "Oh, you're right. I guess I should do something about it. We just came from the hospital where their mother died about an hour ago. I don't know what to think, and I guess they don't know how to handle it either."

Can you imagine how I felt at that moment? My paradigm shifted. Suddenly I <u>saw</u> things differently, and because I <u>saw</u> differently, I <u>thought</u> differently, I <u>felt</u> differently, I <u>behaved</u> differently. My irritation vanished. I didn't have to worry about controlling my attitude or my behavior; my heart was filled with the man's pain. Feelings of sympathy and compassion flowed freely. "Your wife just died? Oh, I'm so sorry! Can you tell me about it? What can I do to help?" Everything changed in an instant. (30–31)

Covey's illustration succeeds as a strategy because it clarifies what he means by "paradigm shift"—it appeals to reasoning. It also helps readers feel the irritation caused by unruly kids and then feel pain and sorrow for that family's situation. Covey's illustration is an ethical appeal as well because it shows his character: honest—naturally frustrated, patient, deeply empathic. Whereas the definition of "paradigm shift" is general and difficult to envision, his illustration is specific and full of life.

Here are two more examples of paradigm shifts. One of our students, Patrick, wrote about a Halloween when some boys pointed a gun in his face and stole his bag of candy. Later that evening he went to a party where there was a costume contest. When Patrick told the kids what had happened to him, another boy let Patrick wear his costume (of "Napoleon Bone Apart") and Patrick won first prize—$20. The shift from intense fear and disappointment to a gift of generosity and thanks made a lasting impression on Patrick. That shift was vivid. In the movie <u>Big</u> Tom Hanks goes to bed as a little boy but wakes the next morning as a young man. His stunned reaction is what we mean by the effect of a paradigm shift—such a transformation would be a major shift! And you can see that although reasoning makes logos dominant, reasons—such as illustrations—may provide pathos and ethos as well.

ACTIVITY 4

Using an illustration to show what you mean, write about a paradigm shift that you have experienced or that someone you know has experienced. Describe what happened and then explain how the experience shifted your understanding. Bring this to class to share.

ARGUING BY NARRATION AND DESCRIPTION

Narration

The personal illustration of the paradigm shift that Stephen Covey uses can also be called a narrative—he tells a story to make his point. Narration means telling events, usually in chronological order. In both formal and informal arguments, stories are useful strategies for stating a claim (making a point) and supporting it. The claimant makes a claim, for example

> <u>Claimant:</u> There is hope for the human race yet—some people are still capable of unselfish acts of kindness.
> <u>Reader:</u> Why do you say that?
> <u>Claimant:</u> <u>I'll tell you a story</u>:

Narrative Illustration

I was shopping in an enormous discount store, one of those places where you can buy anything if you can walk for miles. It was a mad house, everyone intent on his/her own purchases—no one paying attention to anyone else. Even the cashiers were staring at merchandise instead of customers, totaling up the costs as fast as they could whip their little electric wands across the coded numbers on bananas, toilet cleaner, pot holders, raisins, whatever. I thought, if a bomb went off just now, no one would notice. I looked up—just in time to see someone's little white-haired grandmother struggling with a package about the size of two loaves of bread. It must have been too heavy for her; she could hardly hang onto it, and she looked like it was hurting her. I thought she was about to cry. Suddenly the package came apart in her hands: out fell about a half dozen cans and a few little boxes of something. She just stared at it all for a moment, and then she started to pick it all up. It looked like an effort for her, and I was about to go over and help, but she was two aisles away, and the cashiers with lines of customers were between us. Before I could move, the bag boy closest to her grabbed a new bag and was on his knees next to her, smiling, talking to her, and in two seconds, with hands the size of catcher's mitts, scooping her purchases into the bag. He was a big blond kid about the size of a refrigerator—fullback I thought. He carried her bag all the way out of the store to the bus bench, where the elderly wait for transportation, smiling and talking and waiting with her for the bus and refusing the tip she offered. I don't know if anyone else saw that little drama, but I did, and I remember thinking, I hope there are more kids like him somewhere.

Narratives (testimonial evidence) can be difficult to verify. Often the verification is another testimony (if you don't believe me, just ask Granny Hooper). If others saw the event they could testify. Certainly, the bag boy could be interviewed. But essentially, personal experiences are hearsay—what claimants allege to have happened. Narratives are called "anecdotes." As evidence they are "anecdotal" evidence. In many cases, anecdotal evidence is considered light or weak evidence. One of the reasons for understanding anecdotal evidence, however, is so you can detect it in other people's arguments.

Yet narratives are often legitimate strategies: various kinds of reports require an introductory narrative; and histories often use narratives to create drama, emphasis, and realism. For example, Richard Selzer gives a historical account of one of the best-known tales in American medicine: a young fur trapper, Alexis St. Martin, and the doctor who treated him, William Beaumont, in 1822 at Fort Mackinaw, the trading center of Michigan at the time:

> On June 6 of that year, as St. Martin stood by his pile of scooped-out muskrats in the company store, a musket was accidentally discharged no more than a yard away. The shot struck the boy in his left side, blowing open a hole in his stomach—a hole that was never to close, but which, like a stigma of martyrdom, would remain unhealed forever. A steady rivulet of gastric juice welled from the rim of his hole, and at its base could be seen the spongy hillocks of the very lining of the stomach itself. It was a shot to be heard around the scientific world.
>
> William Beaumont was summoned to tend the wound. He knelt beside the pile of skins upon which the boy lay, and gazed long and deep into the bloody mangle, seeing reflected in that crimson swim his power and his glory. [. . .] Beaumont trimmed and patched and stitched with all his considerable art, for he was a good, an honorable, surgeon. And it came to pass that the boy St. Martin recovered. The torn flesh healed, almost, it shrank, threw itself up into hard lips of scar about the permanent shriek of the wound, the new mouth that was to become for St. Martin a trap as toothed as any he had set in the many-beavered forest. For two years, each day, Beaumont tied pieces of meat, potatoes, bread, fruit, and vegetables to a silk string, and these he lowered into the wound, pressing them deep within the entrails of his "patient digester." He would withdraw these tasties at varying intervals, to record in his notebook the exact state of the particle's decomposition.
>
> Imagine poor St. Martin, cowering in a corner, pleading with the demonic doctor, the man who had <u>saved his life</u>—at first silently, not wishing to offend his benefactor (now his master), then openly whimpering: "Oh, not the string. Not the string. Not again, please." (<u>Mortal Lessons</u> 126–27)

Beaumont experimented with St. Martin for several more years and became famous for his scientific inquiry into the human digestive system.

Narratives can be personal experiences and historical accounts. They can be objective reports:

Narrative Report

The new scanners arrived at the loading dock at 10:00 a.m. according to the log. They were uncrated and loaded onto dollies, each marked with the office number and name of the intended recipient. By 11:00 they were on their way out of shipping and on their way up the elevators to the various offices. Henson signed for Mrs. Volster's in room 519. It was taken off the dolly by the delivery kid and, according to him, set up in Mrs. Volster's work area, plugged in, and checked out. Henson saw the machine as the kid was leaving. All this is on file every step of the way. No one now can explain what became of Volster's scanner. When Volster arrived from her morning meeting, the scanner was gone.

Narratives are also used when describing how to do something: "First you open the trunk and make sure you have an inflated spare tire and a jack. Then you remove the hub cap, with the jack handle. After that you can remove the lug nuts."

Narration can stir curiosity and feelings in readers. It can help writers make a point and keep readers interested at the same time.

Description

Description means making visual pictures with words. Richard Selzer uses description so you can see what happened to the young fur trapper St. Martin. In a broader sense description means using <u>concrete details</u> that appeal to your senses of sight, sound, smell, taste, and touch. Such details create images in a reader's mind. Description is a useful strategy of argumentation because, like narration, it can stir an audience's emotions and thoughts.

Consider the following paragraph written by William Laurence, a reporter aboard the flight that dropped an atomic bomb on Nagasaki, three days after the bombing of Hiroshima. This is not fiction. It is the nonfiction account of a journalist describing what he saw for readers without television: the atomic blast is at once horrible and fascinating.

Descriptive Report

As the first mushroom floated off into the blue it changed its shape into a flower-like form, its giant petals curving downward, creamy white outside, rose-colored inside. It still retained that shape when we last gazed at it from a distance of about two hundred miles. The boiling pillar of many colors could also be seen at that distance, a giant mountain of jumbled rainbows, in travail. Much living substance had gone into those rainbows. The quivering top of the pillar was protruding to a great height through the white clouds, giving the appearance of a monstrous prehistoric creature with a ruff around its neck, a fleecy ruff extending in all directions, as far as the eye could see. (1)

Today, most of us have seen pictures of atomic blasts. In 1945 almost no one had. Laurence, a working writer, found himself with the job of trying to tell the rest of the world what it was like. As a writer yourself, you can appreciate Laurence's descriptions of the familiar mushroom shape as first a flower and then a monster. Laurence's sentences are full of information and striking detail, forming a vivid picture of the atomic cloud as it seemed to him.

Through description writers can imply their attitude toward their subject. They can, like Selzer, raise ethical questions about William Beaumont's experiments with St. Martin; they can, like Laurence, convey horror and awe. Writers can convey an attitude by carefully choosing details that create images.

In an essay called "Just One of the Guys," student Annie Grover uses description to show a contrast:

> Imagine a little girl's bedroom, painted in dusty rose and papered with hearts and birds. The plush navy carpet is tracked with leaves, grass and tiny clods of dirt; the pink doll trunk rests in the corner and grows dustbunnies. The child is reveling in the outdoors: she and her brother fry ants with lenses. She races up the crabtree--swifter than the boys--and stands on the highest branch with no hands. Her canvas shoes are scuffed and faded. A threadbare pair of grass-stained overalls droops from her scrawny shoulders. There are tangles, dandelions, and sunbeams in her hair; there are rocks, worms, and leaves in her pockets. She is grubby.
>
> That was me. I was the only female in vacillating groups of "guys" for years. Remaining properly feminine without becoming too masculine--or the least bit girly--was like weighing out exactly forty-six thousandths of a gram of copper chloride. I sometimes swayed toward one side or the other, but managed to find an even keel. I loved it.

Annie uses description for her introduction, a common strategy writers use to catch readers' interest. In the remainder of her essay she examines the "even keel" she achieved, arguing that for her, being one of the guys suited her personality well.

Critical thinkers use narration and description for a purpose—to engage readers' interest and to make a point. Readers like stories that demonstrate an idea, and readers like description when it helps them see, hear, feel, smell, and taste what it is you're trying to communicate.

ACTIVITY 5

Practice narration by writing about an early memory of yours. First make a list of memories that occur to you (from your earliest memory to age ten or so)—quickly jot them down, for example, crossing a street by yourself or racing with your brother through the house. Then select a memory that fits into a pattern of your life. Crossing a street by yourself and getting scolded for it—you see a parallel in your being a rebel, an adventurer; you realize you've often taken risks. Running through the house, and your brother smashing through a glass door—you have been fascinated with injuries ever since and want to become a doctor.

Write one paragraph in which you describe the early memory (the story) so readers can experience it. Then write another paragraph in which you explain how the memory fits into a pattern of your life.[1]

ACTIVITY 6

Write a brief essay in which you describe a person or a place, letting your details convey your attitude of that person or place without directly stating your opinion.

ARGUING BY REFUTATION

Refutation means disproving a person's argument. If Stan argues that life begins at birth, Grace can refute this by arguing that Stan doesn't have enough reasonable evidence to support his claim. At O. J. Simpson's trial, his defense team succeeded in refuting the prosecution's arguments that he had murdered his ex-wife and her friend Ron Goldman. His lawyers pointed out flaws in the state's case, such as the claim that the bloody glove found by the police was Simpson's. Simpson's lawyers refuted this by having Simpson try on the glove. His lawyer, Johnnic Cochran, repeated a catchy rhyme, "If the glove does not fit, you must acquit." The jury found Simpson not guilty.

After Princess Diana's funeral, columnist George Will took the opposite case. Instead of joining the tide of worldwide mourning, he criticized it, using words such as "sheer fakery" and "mass hysteria."

> Evidently many scores of millions of people lead lives of such anesthetizing boredom, emotional aridity and felt insignificance that they relish any opportunity for vicarious involvement in large events. And Princess Diana's death has been a large event precisely and only because the public, in a spontaneous act of mass parasitism, has fastened onto the event for the catharsis of emotional exhibitionism.
>
> Even by the standards of today's confessional culture, people certainly have been remarkably "sharing" with their "feelings" about Diana. They have been sharing them with strangers, and their feelings have been about the death of a stranger who, they say, although she never made laws or poetry or shoes or butter, nevertheless "made a difference" and mattered to them more than they knew until she died. The media have been more than merely dutiful in reporting on the "grief" from which millions have been "suffering." [. . .]

---

[1]Activity adapted from Barbara Drake's <u>Writing Poetry</u> and used here with permission. New York: Harcourt Brace Jovanovich, 1983. 15.

During the 1979 malfunction at Three Mile Island nuclear plant, a hyper-ventilating journalist on TV referred to the event—no deaths; no public-health impact—as a "catastrophe." Viewers were left to wonder what words remained to describe, say, war. The premature death of any young mother is, of course, sad. But when it is the celebrity of the deceased that triggers behavior that gets identified as "grief" and "suffering," what words remain to describe what occurs in, say, a pediatric oncology ward? ("A Week of Sheer Fakery" 84)

George Will not only refutes the worldwide "grief" over the death of Princess Diana, but he establishes the serious writer's need for balance, proportion, and level-headed abstinence from hysterics over the death of a young mother—attractive princess and celebrity figure to be sure. Because Will opposed the public and media onslaught of grief for Diana, many <u>Newsweek</u> readers wrote angry letters to the editor, in turn trying to refute Will's argument.

Refutation is a useful strategy when sides polarize around a controversial issue, such as abortion, gun control, or legalized gambling. It's also useful when you disagree with any claim. However, it's important to keep in mind that refutation does not prove you are right; it only shows that an opponent may be is wrong.

When our students read Deborah Tannen's <u>You Just Don't Understand: Women and Men in Conversation</u>, they evaluated the book. Disagreeing with an author and showing weaknesses in an author's arguments require careful critical thinking. Like all strategies of argumentation, refutation requires making a point and supporting it clearly with specific evidence. This excerpt is by student Mike Slater.

> My major complaint about Tannen's methods is that she takes
> her statement on men's independence and women's intimacy as
> <u>the</u> truth. She assumes that the reader also accepts this
> claim as instant reality. But Tannen fails to consider any
> cases where a male is interested in intimacy, or a female
> toward independence, although she briefly hints that there
> may be a few scattered incidents. By simply dismissing these
> cases, Tannen leads me to believe they could prove evidence
> against her theories. She doesn't want to find herself
> wrong. Through these assumptions, she is able to write
> statements like, "If a man experiences life as a fight for
> freedom, he is naturally inclined to resist attempts to
> control him" without offering cases where men do not resist
> attempts to control them (152).
>
> From my own experience, I don't believe that more men
> are interested in independence and women in intimacy. Take
>
> *(box continues)*

> break-ups for example. I have known many women who have
> broken up with men because they felt "smothered" by the
> male. Is this Tannen's idea of striving for intimacy? Was
> the woman's initiation of the breakup an example of what
> Tannen calls women's "hierarchies more of friendship than of
> power and accomplishment" (25)? By not addressing cases like
> these, Tannen seems to pretend they do not exist.

Mike shows keen critical thinking here by questioning Tannen's assumptions and her method of proving her ideas. He cites quotes, gives reasons, and offers examples from his own experience to refute Tannen's claims.

You could try to refute the following claim by film critic Michael Medved:

> Modern films are technically brilliant, but they are morally and spiritually empty. (2)

To refute the claim, what might you do? You could use examples and reasons to make your case. You could make a list of what you consider moral and spiritual movies: <u>Schindler's List</u>, <u>Ordinary People</u>, <u>Sophie's Choice</u>, <u>Amistad</u>, or <u>The Horse Whisperer</u>. You might realize that three of these were produced after Medved made his claim in 1992. You could focus on one of these films—using illustration—and explain how it deals with moral and spiritual values. You could show that Medved's terms <u>morally</u>, <u>spiritually</u>, and <u>modern</u> lack definition, and therefore, Medved's statement lacks clarity: does Medved mean recent films within the past five or ten years, or does he mean films in 1992 when he wrote his essay? Does he mean films made in Hollywood or foreign films as well? You might argue that Medved's claim should be qualified: that "most" or "many" modern films lack moral and spiritual values, you might agree—but not all.

Refutation is useful. Pointing out counterarguments and flaws requires careful analysis and tact. This strategy, like any other, influences ethos. If your method of refutation seems like an attack on a person, then you may sacrifice your ethical appeal for a logical fallacy. George Will risks alienating grievers of Diana with his harsh tone. If you truly want to persuade your audience to change its mind, you need to refute arguments in such a way that your audience doesn't feel attacked.

ACTIVITY 7

Write a brief essay in which you refute one of these claims:

"Television offers no truly thoughtful shows."

"Doing research on the Internet beats doing research in a library."
"People are inherently selfish. When college students do volunteer work, they do it for themselves and their résumés."

ARGUING FROM COMPARISON-CONTRAST

Comparison-contrast is a common strategy because it is extremely useful and natural. If you claim that Bose speakers have superior sound performance, you can demonstrate this by comparing and contrasting them to Realistic speakers from Radio Shack. If you claim that majoring in communication makes more sense than majoring in English, you can compare and contrast both kinds of majors.

To compare is to point out and analyze similarities and differences; to contrast is to point out and analyze differences. When you use comparison-contrast, you may focus on comparison, contrast, or both. It depends on your purpose. As with all strategies of argumentation, comparison-contrast is not an end in itself. You wouldn't compare or contrast any two objects, people, events, or ideas just to do it (although teachers may have asked you to do this to help you practice comparative thinking). Ordinarily you choose comparison-contrast because you need to do it, in order to help your audience understand a point you're trying to make.

Critical thinkers often can't help using comparison-contrast as a method of shaping their ideas and evidence. When Princess Diana and Mother Teresa died within a week of each other, journalists used this strategy to develop and defend their ideas. They did so to make sense of these deaths and of the intense worldwide mourning.

In "Diana's Real Legacy," Jonathan Alter of <u>Newsweek</u> criticized efforts to compare Diana and Mother Teresa:

> It's not fair to hold Diana up against Mother Teresa; only a selfless few anywhere on earth could stand the comparison. As for the comparative news coverage, sudden death at 36 is quite rightly viewed as bigger "news" than slow death at 87.
>
> Even so, the death of Mother Teresa brought the excesses of the Diana coverage into bold relief. The historian Daniel Boorstin memorably described celebrities as people who become famous for being famous. Acclaim is an ancient idea; what's newer is the disconnection between fame and achievement. Diana is now the first woman to join a tiny group of 20th-century megastars in the English-speaking world: Charles Lindberg, Babe Ruth, Winston Churchill, Muhammad Ali, JFK, Elvis Presley, Michael Jordan, to name most of the list. Her astonishing human touch puts her in their league; her accomplishments do not. In the new global marketplace of fame, popularity has become its own art form. (60–62)

As Alter says, contrast can provide "bold relief." You can understand Diana's acclaim more clearly if you understand that it was not based on achievement as was Mother Teresa's. This contrast provides a context in which Alter can develop and defend his point. Although Alter claimed it was not fair to compare the two women, he and many journalists did—to make their points.

Comparison-contrast often helps writers discover significant ideas. The death of Princess Diana and the intense reactions to it puzzled many people who thought critically about it. In an essay called "World Wide Wake," Steven Levy of <u>Newsweek</u> examined two different kinds of grief:

> For almost all of us, she [Diana] has figured more in our fantasies than our grounded existence. It's as if the globe was suddenly consumed with a form of grief that, while sincere and deeply felt, was different from the experience of losing someone in everyday life: a virtual grief.
>
> When someone physically close to us dies, we are crushed by the loss and overwhelmed at the prospect of picking up the pieces. There is no escape; the loss is intertwined with the threads of our existence. Virtual grief, however, springs from the vicarious connection we make with someone we watch on TV, hear about and read about (even, yes, in the tabloids). While the connection can be powerful, it's one we've bought into. In theory, it can be turned off. (66)

Levy contrasts the idea of "virtual grief" with real grief. Virtual grief is not the same. Important differences exist, he points out.

Organizing Compare and Contrast: Block and Alternate Patterns

You can use comparison-contrast in different forms. To compare or contrast two things, you can discuss one thing first and then the other. This is called the <u>block pattern</u>: you can discuss Princess Diana's appearance, achievements, and death and then discuss Mother Teresa's appearance, achievements, and death. You also can interweave both, which is called the <u>alternating pattern</u>: you can discuss first Diana's and Mother Teresa's appearance, then their achievements, and last their deaths.

Block Pattern	**Alternating Pattern**
Princess Diana's appearance	Appearance of both Princess Diana and Mother Teresa
achievements	Achievements of both Princess Diana and Mother Teresa
death	Death of both Princess Diana and Mother Teresa
Mother Teresa's appearance	
achievements	
death	

Which pattern does Richard Selzer use in this excerpt?

> Having practiced both surgery and writing, I am struck as much by the simi-
> larities between the two vocations as by their differences. A surgeon is apt to
> think of both in terms of instruments and physical activity. In the carrying out
> of each, a tool is held in the hand: In surgery this is a scalpel, in writing, a pen.
> In the use of one, blood is shed; in wielding the other, ink is spilled upon a page.
> In surgery the tissues of the body are sutured; in writing, words are stitched into
> sentences. The resemblance is further heightened in that the subject of my
> writing has so often been my work as a doctor. (<u>Down from Troy</u> 251–52)

The alternating pattern enables Selzer to explain and show the close connections
he sees between surgery and writing. He uses this strategy because he has intertwined both surgery and writing in his life.

Which pattern does Deborah Tannen use in this excerpt?

> More men feel comfortable doing "public speaking," while more women feel
> comfortable doing "private" speaking. Another way of capturing these differ-
> ences is by using the terms <u>report-talk</u> and <u>rapport-talk</u>.
>
> For most women, the language of conversation is primarily a language of
> rapport: a way of establishing connections and negotiating relationships.
> Emphasis is placed on displaying similarities and matching experiences. From
> childhood, girls criticize peers who try to stand out or appear better than others.
>
> For most men, talk is primarily a means to preserve independence and nego-
> tiate and maintain status in a hierarchical social order. This is done by exhibit-
> ing knowledge and skill, and by holding center stage through verbal perfor-
> mance such as storytelling, joking, or imparting information. From childhood,
> men learn to use talking as a way to get and keep attention. So they are more
> comfortable speaking in larger groups made up of people they know less well—
> in the broadest sense, "public speaking." (<u>You Just Don't Understand</u> 76–77)

Tannen uses the block pattern, discussing women's style of speaking in a separate paragraph and then discussing men's style in a separate paragraph. This
approach enables her to discuss at some length each type of talk. You may agree
or disagree with Tannen's claims, based on your own experience and observation. She does, however, qualify her generalizations: "more men," "more
women," "most women," and "most men."

Look at one more example of the strategy of comparison-contrast, an
excerpt from "Letter from Birmingham Jail" written by Martin Luther King Jr.
King wrote the letter from jail in 1963 after he was arrested at a sit-in demonstration in a diner. He addressed fellow clergy who criticized his forms of protest
through civil disobedience.

> You express a great deal of anxiety over our willingness to break laws. This is
> certainly a legitimate concern. Since we so diligently urge people to obey the
> Supreme Court's decision of 1954 outlawing segregation in the public schools,

at first glance it may seem rather paradoxical for us consciously to break laws. One may well ask: "How can you advocate breaking some laws and obeying others?" The answer lies in the fact that there are two types of laws: just and unjust. I would be the first to advocate obeying just laws. One has not only a legal but a moral responsibility to obey just laws. Conversely, one has a moral responsibility to disobey unjust laws. I would agree with St. Augustine that "an unjust law is no law at all."

Now, what is the difference between the two? How does one determine whether a law is just or unjust? A just law is a man-made code that squares with the moral law or the law of God. An unjust law is a code that is out of harmony with the moral law. To put it in terms of St. Thomas Aquinas: An unjust law is a human law that is not rooted in eternal law and natural law. Any law that uplifts human personality is just. Any law that degrades human personality is unjust. All segregation statutes are unjust because segregation distorts the soul and damages the personality. It gives the segregator a false sense of superiority and the segregated a false sense of inferiority. Segregation, to use the terminology of the Jewish philosopher Martin Buber, substitutes an "I-it" relationship for an "I-thou" relationship and ends up relegating persons to the status of things. Hence segregation is not only politically, economically, and sociologically unsound, it is morally wrong and sinful. Paul Tillich has said that sin is separation. Is not segregation an existential expression of man's tragic separation, his awful estrangement, his terrible sinfulness? Thus it is that I can urge men to obey the 1954 decision of the Supreme Court, for it is morally right; and I can urge them to disobey segregation ordinances, for they are morally wrong. [. . .]

I hope you are able to see the distinction I am trying to point out. In no sense do I advocate evading or defying the law, as would the rabid segregationist. That would lead to anarchy. One who breaks an unjust law must do so openly, lovingly, and with a willingness to accept the penalty. I submit that an individual who breaks a law that conscience tells him is unjust, and who willingly accepts the penalty of imprisonment in order to arouse the conscience of the community over its injustice, is in reality expressing the highest respect for law.

King's claim and arguments that people have a moral responsibility to disobey unjust laws like segregation show careful critical thinking. To help his audience understand his idea, he contrasts just and unjust laws. This contrast illuminates and clarifies the problem he examines.

King's strategy of comparison-contrast is sophisticated. Although he uses contrast, he does not use a block pattern of organization, nor does he use a neatly ordered point-by-point pattern of alternation. In the second paragraph he combines his discussion of just and unjust laws: first by defining just law and then unjust law. He continues defining these terms, referring to St. Thomas Aquinas for support. In the remainder of that long paragraph King examines segregation and how it is immoral and therefore unjust. The strategy of contrast enables King to develop and defend his ideas.

When writers use comparison-contrast well, the strategy appeals to logos and ethos. Readers respond to clear, structured reasoning, and they admire writers who make comparisons in a fair-minded way.

ACTIVITY 8

Write a brief essay in which you use comparison-contrast to make a point about two objects, people, events, or ideas. Or choose two related advertisements from magazines (such as an ad from 1919 and an ad from 1999, both promoting cigarettes) and use comparison-contrast to make a point about them (find old magazines in the library and photocopy the ads).

ARGUING FROM CLASSIFICATION

Imagine opening the silverware drawer in your kitchen and finding no tray—the spoons, forks, and knives are all mixed together. Chaos. Hunting for a teaspoon wouldn't be as efficient as if all the teaspoons were nestled on top of each other in one group. A silverware tray is a system of classification: each utensil is separated according to size and function: teaspoons, tablespoons, forks (large and small), butter knives, and sharp-cutting knives. This way you can easily choose what you need, reaching for a butter knife for toast and a teaspoon for coffee.

You could not think without classification, as you could not think without comparison and contrast. You naturally divide things and sort them into categories or groups. As a strategy of argumentation, classification enables you to analyze a subject—to break it down into parts or types and to discuss or evaluate them. How you classify something depends on your purpose.

Silverware is simple, but what about knowledge? How can classification help you organize and understand the world of information and ideas? Imagine trying to find anything in the encyclopedia or dictionary if they were not organized with a system for finding information. Without some system of classification, libraries would be depositories of vast chaos. Imagine trying to find a book in a library if there were no call number on it. Fortunately, libraries use systems of classification to order knowledge: the Library of Congress or the Dewey Decimal system.

The human mind craves patterns: groupings of related ideas, objects, or events. Richard Coe explains how useful classification is regarding numbers and colors:

> Real-world phenomena exist in overwhelming numbers and complexity. The ordinary human mind can handle approximately seven items (give or take two) in short-term memory. If you try to memorize the series "85490341," you will find it helpful to think of it as "854-903-41." Telephone numbers, credit card numbers, student identification numbers, and so forth, are usually so grouped.

> Similarly, when you look at a rainbow, you probably see red, orange, yellow, green, blue, and purple. In other words, you probably divide the spectrum into six basic colors. The human eye is capable of discriminating about 7,500,000 colors; the human mind, however, is not capable of dealing with 7,500,000 distinct colors, so it groups them. (311)

As Coe demonstrates, humans classify numbers and colors to cope with complexity. As such, classification is purposeful.

You argue from classification when you use categories to develop and defend a claim. Like other strategies, classification generates analysis: it helps you see distinctions within a complex topic—an idea, a process, an event, or a group of people.

Classification Example

> For example, why do people continue to smoke, despite the warnings from research? The smokers I know fall into several categories. The tough guys: "Ain't nothing gonna kill me!" The know-it-alls: "Bosh, those studies are so much hog wash!" The deniers: "(hack) I'm fine (cough), just a little (wheeze) flu (cough, cough)." The suicidals: "Good, let them kill me—I'm tired of living!" And the friends of smokers: "I know lots of smokers in perfect health." The one thing they all seem to have in common is "I can't quit." That sounds like fear to me.

A problem with classification is that it can produce stereotyping. A stereotype is a simplistic generalization about an idea, a person, or a group of people, such as football players, gays, feminists. It places things in ready-made categories, ignoring individual differences. Aware that some readers might accuse her of stereotyping, Deborah Tannen addresses this problem in the introduction of her book You Just Don't Understand: Women and Men in Conversation.

> We all know we are unique individuals, but we tend to see others as representatives of groups. It's a natural tendency, since we must see the world in patterns in order to make sense of it; we wouldn't be able to deal with the daily onslaught of people and objects if we couldn't predict a lot about them and feel that we know who and what they are. But this natural and useful ability to see patterns of similarity has unfortunate consequences. It is offensive to reduce an individual to a category, and it is also misleading. Dividing women and men into categories risks reinforcing this reductionism. (16)

Tannen acknowledges an important paradox about classification: although dividing people (or ideas and objects) into types is useful for analysis, it can be misleading as well. That Tannen is aware of this and discusses it strengthens her ethos— her credibility. She believes that classifying people is worth this risk if it helps people communicate more effectively. Her purpose governs her classification.

Although classification can lead to oversimplification and stereotyping, it should enable analysis and interpretation. It should facilitate a rational inquiry into some issue. It should assist you in shaping your arguments. Stephen Covey uses this strategy to examine the importance of listening. He argues that for people to listen well, we need a paradigm shift from thinking about ourselves to thinking and feeling the way another person does:

> When another person speaks, we're usually "listening" at one of four levels. We may be <u>ignoring</u> another person, not really listening at all. We may practice <u>pretending</u>. "Yeah. Uh-huh. Right." We may practice <u>selective listening</u>, hearing only certain parts of the conversation. We often do this when we're listening to the constant chatter of a preschool child. Or we may even practice <u>attentive listening</u>, paying attention and focusing energy on the words that are being said. But very few of us ever practice the fifth level, the highest form of listening, <u>empathic listening</u>. [. . .] The essence of empathic listening is not that you agree with someone; it's that you fully, deeply, understand that person, emotionally as well as intellectually. (240)

To define empathic listening, Covey explains how it is different from other types of listening. This prepares readers to follow him. His classification moves in a logical order: from distant to close listening. His categories make sense because readers have experienced them, especially the first four.

Throughout this book we have classified persuasive appeals:

Logos—appeals to reason
Pathos—appeals to emotion
Ethos—appeals to character

Although these three groupings often work in combination, you can analyze each of them more carefully if you separate them. You can concentrate on one type of appeal at a time when you analyze a piece of writing. This kind of focusing can help you analyze more deeply. However, if you aren't careful, classification can generate uncritical thinking—such as stereotypes.

Classification is an important strategy of argumentation because the way you divide a topic into categories influences the way you think about that topic. Your categories influence the way you interpret your topic. Your classifications also can convey your attitude toward the topic—whether you're serious, sincere, humorous, or resolute. You can use classification to argue and to organize your ideas. You can use it to simplify a complex issue; you can use it to show how complex a "simple" issue is. But avoid trivial classifications: "There are three kinds of cars: big ones, little ones, and sort of in between ones." Use classification to help you make a point, not simply to show that you can classify things.

ACTIVITY 9

Write a brief essay using classification to help you communicate an opinion. Try thinking on paper (in your notebook) first: explore people, places, and things in various groups or types—such as different kinds of love, different kinds of friends, different styles of clothing, different places you enjoy or don't enjoy. Don't rush to find your classification system. Think of the idea you want to write about and the point you want to make. Consider using classification to set up alternatives as Covey does with types of listening; then try to persuade your readers to accept a certain category. Consider persuading readers to accept a new way to classify something—like college students or critical thinkers.

ARGUING FROM CAUSE AND EFFECT

Why did it happen? What could have prevented it from happening? What will be the consequences? Or why didn't it happen? If it had happened, what would have been its consequences? These questions concern cause and effect, a type of reasoning you use so often that you may not be aware of it.

Most people take causes and effects for granted. Suppose you cram for a biology exam the day before you take it, reading chapters, writing notes. The exam causes you to study. Your procrastination or neglect also has caused you stress and fear. You stay up until 2:00 A.M., and when you go to bed, you can't fall asleep. So you lie in bed, restless. The next morning at the exam, you're tired and irritable. You block; you forget some definitions. But you stay and finish and review each of your answers. Later that week you learn you earned a 72%. You know you could have done better; next time you resolve to study earlier before an exam.

Cause and effect occurs in every movie, TV show, and play you see, in every story or novel you read. Every plot depends on cause and effect. Characters need a reason, or cause, to act as they do. Causes and effects are so inherent in life that it's often not possible to consider all the ramifications of them.

The strategy of cause and effect helps you analyze and understand what happened and why, what is happening and why, and what will happen and why. When Princess Diana was killed, millions of people wondered why. What caused her death? The media began a frenzy of cause and effect reasoning. The first supposed cause was the paparazzi: a horde of photographers on motorcycles chased the Mercedes in which she rode, causing the driver to speed and lose control—smashing into a pillar in a tunnel in Paris. Keep in mind that there can be multiple causes that produce an effect, and there may be multiple effects from a cause.

Diana's death generated inquiry—it made police experts investigate as many possible causes as they could find. Through tests they determined that Diana's driver had been drinking—the media reported that police had found more than three times the legal limit of alcohol in his blood. They also found evidence of the antidepressant Prozac. The mixture of alcohol and medications could have blurred the driver's vision and affected his motor control. The car's speed was a factor, going at least 80 miles per hour. That Diana had apparently not worn a seat belt may have contributed to her death.

Seeing causes and effects—like comparing, contrasting, and classifying—is a natural kind of thinking. If you analyze causes and effects, your critical thinking skills will strengthen. Inquiry itself is a system of causes and effects. What causes thinking? Most experts on cognition say that problems do. Something puzzles, intrigues, or bothers you, so that you feel tension, which you then want to relieve by solving the problem. Problems can be small (What should I wear today?). But the bigger the problem, the greater the feeling of tension until you solve it.

In the following excerpt from <u>Language in Thought and Action</u>, S. I. Hayakawa uses an illustration to show what happened to him once during World War II. As you read, consider how he uses cause and effect reasoning to help him solve a problem he found himself facing:

An incident in my own experience illustrates how necessary it sometimes is to give people the opportunity to agree. Early in 1942, a few weeks after the beginning of the war and at a time when rumors of Japanese spies were still widely current, I had to wait two or three hours in a railroad station in Oshkosh, Wisconsin, a city in which I was a stranger. I became aware as time went on that the other people waiting in the station were staring at me suspiciously and feeling uneasy about my presence. One couple with a small child were staring with special uneasiness and whispering to each other. I therefore took occasion to remark to the husband that it was too bad that the train should be late on so cold a night. The man agreed. I went on to remark that it must be especially difficult to travel with a small child in winter when train schedules were so uncertain. Again the husband agreed. I then asked the child's age and remarked that the child looked very big and strong for his age. Again agreement—this time with a slight smile. The tension was relaxing.

After two or three more exchanges, the man asked, "I hope you don't mind my bringing it up, but you're Japanese, aren't you? Do you think the Japs have any chance of winning this war?"

"Well," I replied, "your guess is as good as mine. I don't know any more than what I read in the papers. (This was true.) But the way I figure it, I don't see how the Japanese, with their lack of coal and steel and oil and their limited industrial capacity, can ever beat a powerfully industrialized nation like the United States."

My remark was admittedly neither original nor well-informed. Hundreds of radio commentators and editorial writers were saying exactly the same thing during those weeks. But just because they were, the remark <u>sounded familiar</u> and was <u>on the right side</u>, so that it was easy to agree with. The man agreed at once, with what seemed like genuine relief. How much the wall of suspicion had broken down was indicated by his next question, "Say, I hope your folks aren't over there while the war is going on."

"Yes, they are. My father and mother and two young sisters are over there."

"Do you ever hear from them?"

"How can I?"

"Do you mean you won't be able to see them or hear from them till after the war is over?" Both he and his wife looked troubled and sympathetic.

There was more to the conversation, but the result was that within ten minutes after it had begun they had invited me to visit them in their city and have dinner with them in their home. And the other people in the station, seeing me in conversation with people who <u>didn't</u> look suspicious, ceased to pay any attention to me and went back to reading their papers and staring at the ceiling. (80–81)

What caused Hayakawa to ask questions that prompted the man to agree? Being Japanese, he knew non-Japanese people distrusted him and he could sense "the wall of suspicion" in the train station. What were the effects of Hayakawa's giving the man the opportunity to agree? They began a conversation and formed a connection. The suspicion lifted; the man and his wife invited Hayakawa to their home. In short, they had become sudden friends. The effects of Hayakawa's questions were positive. Hayakawa knew he had a problem and he solved it.

Critical thinkers look for causes. In an editorial following Thanksgiving day, Joe H. Stroud, editor of the <u>Detroit Free Press</u>, focused on causes to argue that our country had much to be thankful for. His thesis is, "America has become a significantly less violent and dangerous place over the years of the 90s." He cited statistics from the FBI that crime overall had dropped by 10%, including a 9% decline in most violent crimes. New York City's murder rate had dropped by more than 50%. "So what has happened?" Stroud asks. He then examines several causes:

1. Prosperity—less unemployment. Michigan's rate of unemployment had dropped from near 20% in the early 1980s to less than 4% in 1997.
2. Moral movements—such as the Million Man March, the Promise Keepers Rally in Washington DC, and community-building programs that emphasize God, brotherhood, responsibility, work.
3. More criminals in prisons.
4. Decrease in drug use and drug trade.
5. Earlier intervention in domestic violence.
6. Gun control legislation.

Stroud acknowledged that "we don't know exactly" why crime dropped so much. But it had, and he tried to persuade readers that they should be thankful for this. By identifying and analyzing causes, he made a convincing case. "We still have much to do, but a drop in crime is reason to celebrate" (16A).

ACTIVITY 10

Write a brief essay in which you focus on the causes of some action or event you have witnessed or performed.

———————————

By using cause and effect reasoning, you can develop and defend your own arguments. In her book <u>Deadly Consequences</u>, Dr. Deborah Prothrow-Stith examines the causes and effects of teenage violence in our society. In the following passage, see whether she focuses more on causes or on effects:

> In real life, the impact of a moment of violence reverberates through time. Years later, parents are still mourning the loss of a child, children are still mourning the loss of a parent, a police officer may still feel the anguish that he was required to use deadly force, even to save his own life. On film or videotape violence begins and ends in a moment. "Bang bang, you're dead." Then the death is over. This sense of action-without-consequences replicates and reinforces the dangerous "magical" way many children think. Do the 12- and 14-year-olds who are shooting each other to death in Los Angeles, Chicago, Washington, D.C. really understand that death is permanent, unalterable, final, tragic? Television certainly is not telling them so. (34)

Prothrow-Stith traces the effects of violence here. Her supporting evidence is persuasive. An act of violence can cause a complex chain of effects in many people that can last through their lives.

You can trace the effects or consequences of a problem in such a way that the effects persuade readers to care about the problem and to address it. Consider the complex problem of illiteracy. Be<u>cause</u> they can't read, illiterate people experience a chain of effects that severely limits their lives. Jonathan Kozol demonstrates this in a passage from <u>Illiterate America</u>:

> Illiterates cannot read the letters that their children bring home from their teachers. They cannot study school department circulars that tell them of the courses that their children must be taking if they hope to pass the SAT exams. They cannot help with homework. They cannot write a letter to the teacher. They are afraid to visit in the classroom. They do not want to humiliate their child or themselves. [. . .]
>
> Illiterates cannot travel freely. When they attempt to do so, they encounter risks that few of us can dream of. They cannot read traffic signs and, while they often learn to recognize and to decipher symbols, they cannot manage street names which they haven't seen before. The same is true for bus and subway stops. While ingenuity can sometimes help a man or woman to discern directions from familiar landmarks, buildings, cemeteries, churches, and the like, most illiterates are virtually immobilized. They seldom wander past the streets

and neighborhoods they know. Geographical paralysis becomes a bitter metaphor for their entire existence. They are immobilized in almost every sense we can imagine. They can't move up. They can't move out. They cannot see beyond. (24–26)

Kozol's list of effects is persuasive, building toward his metaphor at the end. His ethos is persuasive because he seems knowledgeable and concerned. He sounds as if he understands the problem of illiteracy. He cares about Americans who can't read. This helps readers care, appealing to pathos. Thus, focusing on effects as Kozol does can be an effective way to argue about causes and what should be done to address a complex problem.

ACTIVITY 11

Write a brief essay in which you explain the effects of some action you have witnessed or performed, or the effects of some social problem.

Reasoning from cause and effect is extremely useful for critical thinkers. It is another lens through which to see and analyze events, ideas, and people. It appeals to logos. It can contribute to a writer's ethos—credibility. You can use cause and effect in different ways depending on your purpose. You can focus on causes, or you can focus on effects . . . or you can do both. But you don't want to examine so many causes and effects that you tire your audience. Trace major causes and effects.

ACTIVITY 12

Write a brief essay using cause and effect to help you argue a point. Some options are as follows:

What caused you to have a particular misconception or to behave a certain way?

What caused you to have a particular interest, habit, or fear?

What are the effects of a particular interest, habit, or fear you have?

What have been the effects of television on your intellectual development or on your family's closeness?

What are some major consequences (effects) of a choice you have made?

ARGUING FROM DEFINITION

A time-honored strategy is to argue from definition. We have saved this strategy for last so that you can use the previous strategies presented in this chapter to examine and define a word.

Critical thinkers think about words. They notice unusual words and wonder what they mean—for example, "quiescently frozen" on the wrapper of a popsicle. They think about common words like quality that are abstract. If you want to communicate and argue clearly, you need to examine the meanings of words—their semantic nature. Let's explore quality, a word you've seen and heard countless times.

ACTIVITY 13

In your notebook, please complete the following sentence:

Quality is _____.

You may complete the sentence with a word, a phrase, or a description. When you finish, continue reading.

———————————————

What is quality? Is your definition the same as everyone else's? Should you assume this? Suppose you are given two red roses: one is real and freshly cut; the other is plastic. Which rose has more quality? If you think the real one does, fine—but why? You may argue that the real rose once contained life and is more pleasing to our senses of sight, touch, and smell. You might add it is a symbol of love. Surely no one would enjoy receiving a plastic rose on Valentine's Day unless it were a joke, because it would suggest that love was fake. But does the mass produced plastic rose have quality? Yes. It does not wilt and die—that is a measure of quality.

Suppose you are given two rings: a silver ring with a turquoise stone and a bubble gum machine ring—the plastic kind shaped like a tiny wristwatch with a white face that changes time when you tilt it. Which ring has more quality? You might agree that the silver ring has more quality because it is made of precious natural substances and is handcrafted. But many children would prefer the toy ring: the novelty of it would give it more quality. Suppose you consider a third ring—a gold wedding band with two names and a date engraved on the inside. Would this have more quality than the other two? You would assume it would mean more to the person who wears it. But if the person is divorced and no longer wears the ring, it may no longer have much quality.

Consider two sentences. Which one has more quality?

1. Nick saw some fish in the water.
2. Nick looked down into the clear, brown water, colored from the pebbly bottom, and watched the trout keeping themselves steady in the current with wavering fins.

Although sentence 1 is concise, it does not present any specific images as 2 does. Sentence 2 paints a vivid and rich picture. The fish are <u>trout</u>, not general "fish." Also, the sentence contains what appear to be contradictions but aren't: the water is clear yet brown because it's colored from pebbles; the trout keep themselves steady by moving their fins. Some people might argue that 2 is too descriptive; others might argue that 2 exemplifies excellent description. Is quality in the eye of the beholder? (Ernest Hemingway wrote sentence 2, in "Big Two-Hearted River, Part 1," <u>In Our Time</u> 177.)

Notice that you've been thinking critically about this word <u>quality</u>, exploring examples of it (roses, rings, sentences), and analyzing it through comparison-contrast. You have seen how the meaning of quality changes depending on where you find the quality.

However, have you as yet reached a clear definition of the term? You have inferred the existence of quality through the particular examples we have given. But can you prove—in a more logical way—that quality exists? Robert Pirsig in his book <u>Zen and the Art of Motorcycle Maintenance</u> struggles with this question of quality, wondering how people can lead quality lives. After much inquiry he offers this hypothesis, using the strategy of refutation: "A thing exists if a world without it can't function normally. If we can show that a world without Quality functions abnormally, then we have shown that Quality exists, whether it's defined or not" (210).

ACTIVITY 14

In your notebook, write your thoughts on this question: What would a world without quality be like? Try to imagine life without quality. Describe how life would be different. When you finish, continue reading.

Without quality, life would contain none of the people, objects, experiences, or ideas that you consider valuable. Robert Pirsig explains that without quality what you enjoy would no longer exist. Art would disappear: "There's no point in hanging a painting on the wall when the bare wall looks just as good" (Pirsig 210). Music, too, would disappear because you would not be able to differentiate music from noise. All sports would vanish because "scores would no longer be a measurement of anything meaningful, but simply empty statistics, like the number of stones in a pile of gravel" (210). Favorite foods and drinks would become bland; supermarkets would sell ungraded meat and milk. People would no longer enjoy "movies, dances, plays and parties" (210). Pirsig concludes that the world "<u>can</u> function" without quality, "but life would be so dull as to be hardly worth living. In fact it wouldn't be worth living. The term <u>worth</u> is a Quality term. Life would just be living without any values or purposes at all" (211).

For Robert Pirsig the word quality carries "a magnitude of importance" (211). Although you encounter the word daily, you may not consider its far-reaching implications—perhaps because the word has lost much of its power from overuse. Advertisers often exploit it. Ford Motor Company's slogan is "Quality Is Job 1." But should you assume Ford products possess quality because their commercials say they do? Any company, college, or corporation can claim it has quality because the word itself is abstract and ambiguous like "family values." It sounds good. Because "quality" can be used by anyone to elevate anything to importance, the word may at last come to mean nothing. This is why defining the word is necessary: the word is too important not to define.

Let's return to the "Quality is _____" completion activity you wrote at the beginning of this exploration. Does your definition reflect what you think about the word now? Compare yours to this sampling of student responses:

> Quality is the value a person sees in an object.
>
> Quality is hard work and determination.
>
> Quality is excellence.
>
> Quality is a smile coming slowly to your lips because you know the object before you is as good as can be humanly produced short of total perfection.

Would a dictionary provide the best definition of quality? <u>Webster's New World Dictionary</u> lists definitions in historical order: oldest definition first, most modern last. It defines "quality" as "1. any of the features that make something what it is; characteristic element; attribute 2. basic nature; character; kind 3. the degree of excellence which a thing possesses" (1099). The third definition comes closest to what we've examined. Clearly, the dictionary does not provide the best definition. Your definition may mean more because it comes from you.

In <u>Language in Thought and Action</u>, S. I. Hayakawa clarifies the dilemma of definition. He writes, "The meanings of words are <u>not</u> in the words; they are in us" (258). As you have seen, the meanings of any abstract word like "quality" depend on what you choose the term to mean. This is why if you wish to communicate the idea clearly you need to give examples—to refer to specific objects, people, events, and memories that represent quality to you. Hayakawa adds, "Beware of definitions, which are words about words. Think with examples rather than definitions whenever possible" (259).

Although quality does not have a clear definition and its meaning is largely personal, let's delve a little further into the idea of quality—because this directly concerns critical thinking for composition.

ACTIVITY 15

In your notebook, write a response to this question: How do you achieve quality? Assume you want to achieve quality in some process: a skill or talent of yours, playing a sport or an instrument, or writing. When you finish, continue reading.

Perhaps you wrote about hard work, skill, determination, practice, and concentration. These all indeed help people achieve quality. However, Robert Pirsig concludes that there is one primary force in achieving quality: <u>caring</u>. If you care about what you do, you will do a better job. This sounds simple. But what does "caring" mean? You see, once you start defining words and realize how useful definition is for thinking, it's hard to stop. Pirsig defines the word thus: "When one isn't dominated by feelings of separateness from what he's working on, then one can be said to 'care' about what he's doing. That is what caring really is, a feeling of identification with what one's doing" (290). Do you agree? The times when you have performed at your best, did you "care" the most? Did you identify deeply with what you were doing? If Pirsig is correct, "caring" is the force that enables hard work, skill, determination, practice, and concentration.

Let's apply the same question to writing: How do you achieve quality in writing? If Pirsig's claim is true, then when you write well, you don't feel separated from your writing. Indeed, you identify with it: you care about your main idea, your supporting evidence, your organization, your style and voice, your audience and purpose. You care enough to revise, perhaps several times. When you have not written well, did you feel disconnected from your paper? Perhaps you wrote it the night before it was due; perhaps you didn't care enough to proofread it. Granted, you may care intensely about a paper yet still not produce quality writing. (Perhaps the subject is too close and personal; you need more distance from it.) But— usually—if you care enough about your writing, you will keep working on it until it achieves the quality you and your instructor or supervisor want.

Critical thinkers care about words. They know that abstract words, such as <u>harassment</u>, <u>multiculturalism</u>, <u>affirmative action</u>, <u>euthanasia</u>, and <u>intelligence</u>, contain various meanings. They know that meanings are in people, not in words. They know that if they want to communicate clearly they should define key words and provide specific examples. They also know that if they want to understand what somebody means when they use a certain word, they should ask for a definition and an example. Critical thinkers don't assume their audience automatically will know what they mean.

The question of what is quality is central to our aim in helping you develop yourself as a critical thinker, reader, and writer. We have examined quality here because we believe that writing an extended definition of a word is an important skill for critical thinkers.

Digging for Roots of Words

To help you define words, you can research their origins—their etymology. Like an archaeologist digging for arrowheads, you can find interesting and useful information this way. Suppose a friend told you that you have a lot of "sarcasm" in your voice. His remark bothers you because you don't consider yourself sarcastic. Now puzzled, you start to inquire what your friend means by "sarcasm." You open up your dictionary and read the modern meaning: "a taunting, sneering, cutting, or caustic remark" (Webster's New World 1191). Sometimes you taunt people, you agree—but sneering and cutting? Then, you notice the etymology of the word; it is located in brackets: "[LL. sarcasmos < Gr. sarkasmos < sarkazein, to tear flesh like dogs, speak bitterly < sarx (gen. sarkos), flesh]" (1191). You're shocked and wonder if you sometimes talk as if you "tear flesh like dogs." You vow to watch what you say—you don't want to be sarcastic.

As this etymology reveals, words have histories and you can trace their roots. You can learn that "sarcasm" derives from Greek to Latin; you can learn that the meaning was extremely concrete (tearing flesh) but now is more abstract (taunting, sneering, cutting). Digging for roots of words can help you develop arguments. Consider one more example. Suppose somebody calls you "humble," but you don't know what the word really means. Looking up its modern meaning, you find, "1. having or showing a consciousness of one's defects or shortcomings; not proud; not self-assertive; modest 2. low in condition, rank, or position; lowly; unpretentious" (657). Looking at the etymology, you discover "[ME. < OFr.< L. humilis, low, small, slight, akin to humus, soil, earth]" (657). This concrete description helps you visualize the idea of "humble": being down to earth, being the earth itself like humus—helping things grow. You decide you'd rather be humble than sarcastic.

ACTIVITY 16

Find and copy the etymology and meanings of three words from an unabridged dictionary, such as Webster's New World, The Oxford English Dictionary, or the Random House Unabridged Electronic Dictionary. You may need to go to a library to find one of these. Choose words that puzzle or intrigue you or that pertain to your major interests. Try to find words that have interesting or surprising concrete roots. Some suggestions are art, science, planet, touch, and think.

As this chapter has shown, you can use various strategies to develop and support an argument. The strategies you use influence your logos, pathos, and ethos. However, critical thinkers use strategies not as ends in themselves but as means to achieve their overall purpose—to communicate an idea they care about and to persuade readers to care about it as well.

DEFINITION ESSAY USING VARIOUS STRATEGIES OF ARGUMENTATION

Words, meanings, and persuasion—arguments can be more than verbal fights. The strategies of using language to move audiences can help you to change your readers' minds and encourage them to change their behavior. The basic characteristics of skillful writers include a deep interest in, and powerful command of, language.

ACTIVITY 17

Write an essay in which you try to <u>persuade</u> classmates and your instructor to accept your understanding of a word. Your essay should contain a title, an introduction with a clearly stated thesis, a body of at least two or three supporting paragraphs, and a conclusion (2 to 4 pages). Some suggestions may include the following:

1. Write an essay on "quality," making what you think quality is the thesis that the rest of your paper will explain and support. Use examples from your experience, observation, and knowledge.
2. Write about a word that you believe is important, a word that intrigues you, a word that bothers you a great deal, a word that has given you problems, or a word over which you experienced a paradigm shift.
3. Think of a word you use frequently. Define what you mean by it in different situations.

For this essay, use some of the strategies presented in this chapter and the previous two chapters:

Examples and reasons: showing and explaining what you mean

Induction or deduction: arranging evidence from examples to a generalization or from a generalization to examples

Illustration: showing and explaining what you mean

Narration: telling a story to make a point

Description: using concrete details to show what you mean

Refutation: defining a word by explaining what it is not

Comparison-contrast: for example, crazy/insane; knowledge/wisdom

Classification: for example, three types of goodness, of lies, of thinking
Cause and effect: causes of a quality _____; effects of a quality _____
Etymology and modern meanings

ANALYZING AND EVALUATING AN ESSAY

A verbal fight is often a stream of whatever comes to mind, usually with loud and impolite language. An essay is a well-constructed sequence of points that support a thesis. Therefore, to evaluate an essay, it is often useful to find its sequence of points. Structure can help you determine quality.

ACTIVITY 18

Choose one of the following essays by Susan Ager, Stephen King, and Langston Hughes to analyze and evaluate in a report (2 to 4 pages).

A. Analyze and evaluate the essay by newspaper columnist Susan Ager. What is her thesis and how does she succeed in supporting it? What strategies of argumentation does she use, and how are they effective? How do her strategies complement her appeals of logos, pathos, or ethos? Do you agree or disagree with her thesis?

Cool Comfort Steals Summer's Seasoning

Susan Ager

Summer used to be sultry and sensual. Now, most of us spend it entombed.   1

We move like chilled slabs of salmon along the conveyor belt of our lives: 2
Home, car, office, all of them icy. We avoid the muggy heat that used to demand
a certain welcome slowness.

The American Economy is grateful. But I hate air-conditioning, which   3
polishes summer air until there's nothing memorable left.

I remember the sensations of summer as a child, when all we had was real   4
air, heavy and damp. I remember playing in the shade on a bed sheet spread
on the grass. Or reading in my room, sprawled on the floor, my cheek against
the cool wood.

Outside Changes

In the evening, we ate macaroni salad or cold leftovers, with watermelon for 5 dessert. We sat in the dark, convinced lights would heat the house. Or we moved our bodies onto the front porch glider, letting it swing and squeak, watching the fireflies, sipping iced tea.

If it was very hot, we ran the ice cubes up and down our bare arms until 6 they vanished. Sometimes we would hear the clink of a neighbor's silverware as she washed her dishes.

Before bed we took tepid showers. Then, in our thinnest cotton night- 7 clothes, we lay atop our beds as still as we could, listening to crickets, until sleep took us.

Now, it is possible to sleep in August with a down comforter pulled to 8 your chin, in absolute silence, except for the air conditioner's steady hum. Outside, the night sound of summer is a hundred condensers humming a new age mantra.

I have no choice at work: air-conditioning always wins in a democracy. 9 And at home, I live with a man whom I vowed to love and respect, which means I must respect his sweat. He turns on the air when the temperature or humidity top 75.

In the car, he's happy when I turn the air vents in his direction. But a 10 few weeks ago, after our engine overheated, we drove for a couple hours on a rural highway with our windows down and our elbows out, the way people used to do.

The wind snuck up our sleeves and billowed out our shirts. Bugs collided 11 with our arms, stinging. We smelled hay and heard the caw of blackbirds. Trees and sky seemed more brilliant.

Inside Efforts

I thought about a scene from <u>My Dinner with Andre</u>, a 1981 Louis Malle film of 12 a conversation between two friends: Andre, a spiritual adventurer, and Wally, a starving playwright.

Wally is excited about his new electric blanket, although he suspects it is 13 changing his dreams. Andre rejects it as "the kind of comfort that separates you from reality."

Without an electric blanket, you might need to add a blanket to your 14 bed, or even pile coats on top. You will <u>know</u> it's cold, and wonder if the person beside you is cold, and think about others in the world who are cold. You might decide you like the cold, because you can snuggle with your bedmate.

"But turn on that electric blanket," says Andre, "and it's like taking a 15 tranquilizer, or being lobotomized."

Wally, unmoved, says "I would <u>never</u> give up my electric blanket. I mean,   16
our lives are tough enough as it is!"

Warmth in December, cool air in August—small, sweet comforts, yes. But   17
I wonder what it means to live summer no differently than winter, lulled by
machines, oblivious to the night moves of crickets. (1D) □

B. Analyze and evaluate the essay by the popular fiction writer Stephen King. What
is his thesis and how well does he succeed in supporting it? What strategies of
argumentation does he use, and how are they effective? How do his strategies
complement his appeals of logos, pathos, or ethos? Do you agree or disagree with
his thesis?

Why We Crave Horror Movies

Stephen King

I think we're all mentally ill; those of us outside the asylums only hide it a   1
little better—and maybe not all that much better, after all. We've all known
people who talk to themselves, people who sometimes squinch their faces into
horrible grimaces when they believe no one is watching, people who have
some hysterical fear—of snakes, the dark, the tight place, the long drop . . .
and, of course, those final worms and grubs that are waiting so patiently
underground.

When we pay our four or five bucks and seat ourselves at tenth-row center   2
in a theater showing a horror movie, we are daring the nightmare. Why? Some
of the reasons are simple and obvious. To show that we can, that we are not
afraid, that we can ride this roller coaster. Which is not to say that a really good
horror movie may not surprise a scream out of us at some point, the way we
may scream when the roller coaster twists through a complete 360 or plows
through a lake at the bottom of the drop. And horror movies, like roller coast-
ers, have always been the special province of the young; by the time one turns
40 or 50, one's appetite for double twists or 360-degree loops may be considerably depleted.

We also go to re-establish our feelings of essential normality; the horror   3
movie is innately conservative, even reactionary. Freda Jackson as the horrible
melting woman in <u>Die, Monster, Die!</u> confirms for us that no matter how far we
may be removed from the beauty of a Robert Redford or a Diana Ross, we are
still light-years from true ugliness.

And we go to have fun.   4

Ah, but this is where the ground starts to slope away, isn't it? Because   5
this is a very peculiar sort of fun, indeed. The fun comes from seeing others
menaced—sometimes killed. One critic has suggested that if pro football has

become the voyeur's version of combat, then the horror film has become the modern version of the public lynching.

It is true that the mythic, "fairy-tale" horror film intends to take away the shades of gray. .... It urges us to put away our more civilized and adult penchant for analysis and to become children again, seeing things in pure blacks and whites. It may be that horror movies provide psychic relief on this level because this invitation to lapse into simplicity, irrationality and even outright madness is extended so rarely. We are told we may allow our emotions a free rein . . . or no rein at all. 6

If we are all insane, then sanity becomes a matter of degree. If your insanity leads you to carve up women like Jack the Ripper or the Cleveland Torso Murderer, we clap you away in the funny farm (but neither of those two amateurnight surgeons was ever caught, heh-heh-heh); if, on the other hand, your insanity leads you only to talk to yourself when you're under stress or to pick your nose on your morning bus, then you are left alone to go about your business . . . though it is doubtful that you will ever be invited to the best parties. 7

The potential lyncher is in almost all of us (excluding saints, past and present; but then, most saints have been crazy in their own ways), and every now and then, he has to be let loose to scream and roll around in the grass. Our emotions and our fears form their own body, and we recognize that it demands its own exercise to attain proper muscle tone. Certain of these emotional muscles are accepted—even exalted—in civilized society; they are, of course, the emotions that tend to maintain the status quo of civilization itself. Love, friendship, loyalty, kindness—these are all the emotions that we applaud, emotions that have been immortalized in the couplets of Hallmark cards and in the verses (I don't dare call it poetry) of Leonard Nimoy. 8

When we exhibit these emotions, society showers us with positive reinforcement; we learn this even before we get out of diapers. When, as children, we hug our rotten little puke of a sister and give her a kiss, all the aunts and uncles smile and twit and cry, "Isn't he the sweetest little thing?" Such coveted treats as chocolate-covered graham crackers often follow. But if we deliberately slam the rotten little puke of a sister's fingers in the door, sanctions follow— angry remonstrance from parents, aunts and uncles; instead of a chocolate-covered graham cracker, a spanking. 9

But anticivilization emotions don't go away, and they demand periodic exercise. We have such "sick" jokes as, "What's the difference between a truck-load of bowling balls and a truckload of dead babies?" (You can't unload a truckload of bowling balls with a pitchfork . . . a joke, by the way, that I heard originally from a ten-year-old). Such a joke may surprise a laugh or a grin out of us even as we recoil, a possibility that confirms the thesis: If we share a brotherhood of man, then we also share an insanity of man. None of which is intended as a defense of either the sick joke or insanity but merely as an explanation of why the best horror films, like the best fairy tales, manage to be reactionary, anarchistic, and revolutionary all at the same time. 10

The mythic horror movie, like the sick joke, has a dirty job to do. It delib- 11
erately appeals to all that is worst in us. It is morbidity unchained, our most
base instincts let free, our nastiest fantasies realized . . . and it all happens,
fittingly enough, in the dark. For those reasons, good liberals often shy away
from horror films. For myself, I like to see the most aggressive of them—<u>Dawn
of the Dead</u>, for instance—as lifting a trap door in the civilized forebrain and
throwing a basket of raw meat to the hungry alligators swimming around in
that subterranean river beneath.

Why bother? Because it keeps them from getting out, man. It keeps them 12
down there and me up here. It was Lennon and McCartney who said that all you
need is love, and I would agree with that.

As long as you keep the gators fed. □

C. Analyze and evaluate the essay by American poet Langston Hughes. What is his
thesis and how well does he support it? What strategies of argumentation does he
use, and how are they effective? How do his strategies complement his appeals of
logos, pathos, or ethos? Do you agree or disagree with his thesis?

That Word <u>Black</u>

Langston Hughes

"This evening," said Simple, "I feel like talking about the word <u>black</u>." 1

"Nobody's stopping you, so go ahead. But what you really ought to have 2
is a soap-box out on the corner of 126th and Lenox where the rest of the orators
hang out."

"They expresses some good ideas on that corner," said Simple, "but for my 3
ideas I do not need a crowd. Now, as I were saying, the word <u>black</u>, white folks
have done used that word to mean something bad so often until now when the
N.A.A.C.P. asks for civil rights for the black man, they think they must be bad.
Looking back into history, I reckon it all started with a <u>black</u> cat meaning bad
luck. Don't let one cross your path!

"Next, somebody got up a <u>black-list</u> on which you get if you don't vote 4
right. Then when lodges come into being, the folks they didn't want in them
got <u>black-balled</u>. If you kept a skeleton in your closet, you might get <u>black-
mailed</u>. And everything bad was <u>black</u>. When it came down to the unlucky ball
on the pool table, the eight-rock, they made it the <u>black</u> ball. So no wonder
there ain't no equal rights for the <u>black</u> man."

"All you say is true about the odium attached to the word <u>black</u>," I said. 5
"You've even forgotten a few. For example, during the war if you bought some-
thing under the table, illegally, they said you were trading on the <u>black</u> market.
In Chicago, if you're a gangster, the <u>Black Hand Society</u> may take you for a ride.
And certainly if you don't behave yourself, your family will say you're a <u>black</u>

sheep. Then if your mama burns a <u>black</u> candle to change the family luck, they call it <u>black</u> magic."

"My mama never did believe in voodoo so she did not burn no black candles," said Simple. 6

"If she had, that would have been a <u>black</u> mark against her." 7

"Stop talking about my mama. What I want to know is, where do white folks get off calling everything bad <u>black</u>? If it is a dark night, they say it's <u>black</u> as hell. If you are mean and evil, they say you got a <u>black</u> heart. I would like to change all that around and say that the people who Jim Crow me have got a <u>white</u> heart. People who sell dope to children have got a <u>white</u> mark against them. And all the white gamblers who were behind the basketball fix are the <u>white</u> sheep of the sports world. God knows there was few, if any, Negroes selling stuff on the black market during the war, so why didn't they call it the <u>white</u> market? No, they got to take me and my color and turn it into everything <u>bad</u>. According to white folks, black is bad. 8

"Wait till my day comes! In my language, bad will be <u>white</u>. Blackmail will be <u>white</u>mail. Black cats will be good luck, and <u>white</u> cats will be bad. If a white cat crosses your path, look out! I will take the black ball for the cue ball and let the <u>white</u> ball be the unlucky eight-rock. And on my blacklist—which will be a <u>white</u>list then—I will put everybody who ever Jim Crowed me from Rankin to Hitler, Talmadge to Malan, South Carolina to South Africa. 9

"I am black. When I look in the mirror, I see myself, daddy-o, but I am not ashamed. God made me. He did not make us no badder than the rest of the folks. The earth is black and all kinds of good things comes out of the earth. Trees and flowers and fruit and sweet potatoes and corn and all that keeps mens alive comes right up out of the earth—good old black earth. Coal is black and it warms your house and cooks your food. The night is black, which has a moon, and a million stars, and is beautiful. Sleep is black which gives you rest, so you wake up feeling good. I am black. I feel very good this evening. 10

"What is wrong with black?" (146–48) □ 11

USING THE TOULMIN STRATEGY TO ARGUE

Most writers are able to argue from an early age. Even quite young children begin to display the rudiments of argumentation, such as holding adults to their promises (you promised we could go to the movies if we cleaned our rooms . . .). It is the beginning of a well-known formula in logic: if X then Y; and X therefore Y.

What is new is the analysis of written structures, which tend to be longer and more complex than most of the oral arguments of youth. Philosopher Stephen Toulmin has simplified the process of analysis in <u>The Uses of Argu-</u>

ment. In most arguments, he says, you make some claim that you want others to believe; then you give your reasons. Toulmin's view of most arguments is illustrated as follows (Toulmin uses several terms for the same thing):

CLAIM: It should be illegal for people to keep dogs in rental apartments.

GROUNDS: (Because = Support for claim):
(Reasons,   1. Dogs are dirty—they drop waste on carpets and floors, urinate
Data,   everywhere, shed all over, slobber on everything.
Evidence,   2. They carry diseases, ticks, and fleas and have distemper.
Support   3. They reek and leave dog smell everywhere.
for Claim)   4. They are destructive, dig holes, chew on furniture, and scratch
    doors.
    5. They are noisy, barking, whining, and howling day and night.
    6. They can be dangerous, especially to small children.

WARRANT: (What is the connection between your evidence
    and your claim? What has this to do with apart-
    ment living?)
(Conclusion, Inference,   Dogs can be a financial liability. ("We might lose
Policy, Generalization,   renters; we could be sued if we allow dogs."
Principle, "So what?")   "An antidog policy could save us money.")

Whether evidence or "support" comes before or after the claim—that is, whether the reasoning is inductive or deductive—the relationship between the claim and the support remains the same. In persuasive arguments you need to know what claim is suggested and what support for the claim is available. And it's possible to start by listing the grounds, the reasons for your argument, first.

GROUNDS: "Because of all these reasons—dogs are dirty, carry diseases,
    reek, and so forth."

CLAIM: "So therefore dogs should be kept out of rental
    apartments."

Many people looking at the argument about dogs might say, "Yes all those statements are true and so dogs should not be allowed in apartments." But Toulmin asks you not to make up your mind too quickly, not to assume anything is self-evident. He asks the claimant to explain the connection even if the connection seems obvious. So what if dogs are dirty, carry diseases, reek, are destructive, and possibly dangerous? What has all this to do with apartment living? Are these statements facts? How do you know? Do they apply to all dogs? The warrant is Toulmin's way of asking claimants to analyze the kind of reasoning they are using.

What is new in Toulmin's work is his concept of the <u>warrant</u>. The warrant asks "So what?" The warrant is the connection between the support and the claim.

Kinds of Arguments—Kinds of Claims

Laws and Policies

You can argue about laws and policies—things you believe <u>should</u> (could, ought to) be changed. In the recent presidential campaigns, the <u>Roe</u> v. <u>Wade</u> law was an important issue. Prochoice and prolife advocates argue and reargue the abortion issue and what role if any the government should have in the issue. Here is another policy argument:

Ban It?

<u>Claimant:</u> Dirty sex pictures should be banned from the Internet.
<u>Critical Thinker:</u> Why? What has happened? On what grounds do you make your claim?
<u>Claimant:</u> The <u>grounds</u> are that I've discovered children see those pictures.
<u>Critical Thinker:</u> So what? What's the connection? What <u>warrants</u> the action you want to take?
<u>Claimant:</u> Children should not be allowed to see dirty pictures.
<u>Critical Thinker:</u> You've already implied as much. We need to know <u>why</u> you say that. Besides, your claim would cover adults too—no one would be able to see them.
<u>Claimant:</u> No one should see them! But I'll qualify my claim: Children should not see dirty pictures on the Internet.
<u>Critical Thinker:</u> Why?
<u>Claimant:</u> Because they are immoral—they are pornographic.
<u>Critical Thinker:</u> So?
<u>Claimant:</u> So children should be able to grow up with normal, healthy attitudes about sex. Those pictures damage children's right to a normal childhood. Children are not able to deal with distorted, filthy pornography.
<u>Critical Thinker:</u> OK. That might work. Do children have such a right? Note that many of the terms in your warrant are "subjective": <u>normal</u>, <u>pornography</u>, <u>right</u>. Can you define these terms?

The critical thinker here is helping the claimant understand that this is a complex argument. The claim that children should not see dirty pictures on the Internet is supported by the claimant's "evidence" (opinion) that such pictures are immoral ("pornographic"). The thinker asks, "So what?" Suppose, for the moment, that the pictures are pornographic—why shouldn't children see them? The claimant then offers a warrant, a rule that we might apply to children in general: Children have a right to a normal childhood. That's a good warrant if it is true.

ACTIVITY 19

In your notebook, write three claims based on laws or policies concerning changes. Discuss with your class or group the claim you like best; discuss why you like it, why you believe it is desirable. After the discussion, write in your notebook at least three good reasons you could use to support your claim.

Reality, Facts

You can argue about what is real—are there aliens? Is Adolph Hitler dead (or is he still alive somewhere)? Will Jesus return? How can you support such questions? You can "support," though perhaps not "prove," such questions with whatever facts, historical or authoritative data, or other evidence the audience accepts. These are factual—or "referential" matters. They have to do with what you believe was, is, or will be real.

Philosophers say that "trivial" matters of fact are seldom worth arguing about. You have to decide for yourself what is trivial, but arguing about things for which there are simple tests or readily available proof is what we mean. Devices that measure temperature, time, and blood pressure; and historic dates such as Washington's birthday in 1732 (celebrated every February 22) can be found in encyclopedias, almanacs, and other sources. Most people don't find arguing about such facts interesting because the facts can be found in reference works. Then too, facts are often substantiated by authorities, specialists who testify for that purpose.

Facts

<u>Claimant:</u> [claim] The victim died of poisoning.
<u>Critical Thinker:</u> On what grounds do you claim this?
<u>Claimant:</u> [grounds] The victim began to complain of cramps 20 minutes after dinner. He then began to exhibit convulsions in 60-second intervals. The coroner says the victim died from asphyxiation brought on by distress of respiratory muscles.
<u>Critical Thinker:</u> So what?
<u>Claimant:</u> [warrant] Such symptoms are characteristic of death by poisoning, namely strychnine.
<u>Critical Thinker:</u> How do you know this?
<u>Claimant:</u> [backing for warrant] I am an authority in the field of forensic medicine and often called to testify in cases where poisoning is suspected.

Sometimes the warrant itself may need additional support. You can use backing to increase the credibility of the warrant. <u>Backing</u> can be any sort of evidence or support that will help your readers believe the argument. The claimant might have answered, "I'm an undertaker, and I've seen lots of corpses that died of poisoning." Or, "I'm a city groundskeeper. We use strychnine often to keep the rodent population under control." As a critical thinker, you need to make sure you have the most authoritative experts you can find.

ACTIVITY 20

In your notebook write three statements based on reality (facts) you'd like your audience to believe. For example: (1) Not all basketball players need to be extremely tall—seven feet or taller—to excel. (2) Students learn better in small classes. (3) Hollywood presents a distorted, unrealistic view of human life. Discuss the claim that appeals to you most: Why does it appeal to you? Why should readers believe your claim? Last, write at least three good reasons you could use to support your claim.

Values, Morals, Taste

You can argue about values—values are whatever you find desirable or not. Values concern your beliefs about morals—your beliefs about good and evil; and aesthetics (sometimes called "taste" as in artistic taste), which are beliefs about what is beautiful and what is not. These are interesting arguments because we all have our own opinions about such things, and if we include abstract art, art of the grotesque, or folk-art, it becomes more and more challenging to decide whose opinion makes sense. Can you "prove" Picasso was the greatest modern artist? It's a fascinating question, full of depth and breadth, and leading you through the entire world of art. You may or may not be able to "prove" Picasso was the greatest modern artist, but you can offer your reasoning. Here's a different argument based entirely on aesthetic values, or taste:

Aesthetic Values

Claimant: I think that's a really hideous house. [claim]

Critical Thinker: How so? [request for support for claim]

Claimant: The design looks like something out of a cartoon or bad abstract art, and purple and green are violently mismatched colors. [support]

Critical Thinker: Do you have some rule or principle about how things should look? [request for warrant]

Claimant: Yes. A house should be pleasing to the eye; it should complement the surrounding environment; its lines should be symmetrical, balanced, and designed to give the effect of artistic unity. Its colors should complement the owner's notion of domestic tranquility. [warrant]

Critical Thinker: So you have a classical view of art!

The Latin expression <u>de gustibus non disputandum est</u> (there is no point in arguing about taste) suggests that we all have our opinions, especially about what is or isn't attractive. And therefore it is pointless to argue such things. Do you agree? Do you believe that "my opinion is all that matters to me, regardless of what anyone says?" Do you believe that discussion and argument help you deepen and broaden your understanding of what may or may not be seen as attractive? Claims (opinions) without support are mere opinions. It seems pointless to have "art" if only personal opinion (300 million opinions?) guides us.

ACTIVITY 21

In your notebook write three claims based on values you'd like your audience to accept. Discuss the claim you like best: Why do you like it? Why do you believe it is desirable? Last, write at least three good reasons you could use to support your claim.

Warrants

On the surface of it, the dog arguments don't seem limited to apartments. If true, the reasons would be true anywhere. If these doggy problems might happen anywhere, why argue against apartments? The warrant, Toulmin says, must guarantee the relationship between the support and the claim. We are asking the claimant (the landlord) to state the principle that connects the support to the claim. In this case, the landlord's explanation might be something like, "Because dogs are dirty, dangerous animals, they can be a financial liability that may cause landlords to lose renters and/or to be sued."

You could of course challenge the data. How do landlords know these things about dogs? What makes them think dogs are dirty and a liability? In that case, we would want some backing for the landlords' data. Most likely we will discover the data are based on personal experience, hearsay (what others have said), and perhaps media reports. No doubt the landlords have seen evidence to cause them to believe the grounds for this claim. Backing for the warrant itself might be court cases: has there ever been a suit? Has anyone ever sued because a renter's dog caused disease, damaged property, or attacked a child? If so the landlord has a strong case against dogs. If this became a court case, could you find counterarguments?

Yes, perhaps, you could raise your <u>objection</u>. One set of true facts may be confronted with another. The data may not be wrong but simply in conflict with other facts. Some pet owners (prospective renters, let's say) will surely object that these facts do not apply to their dog. You can concede that the landlord may have had bad experiences with some dogs, but is it fair to throw out the entire species for a few bad dogs? Not only is it not fair, but you must consider the effect on a jury or on Congress if they hear that these charges are not accurate. They do not apply to little Pookie at all:

Objection

Our dog is trained. She does not drop waste, urinate, shed, nor slobber. Pookie's hair is kept clipped and does not fall off, and we walk her four times a day so that there will be no waste on the rental property. We keep the dog clean—we take her to the Doggy Boutique once a week to be groomed so she doesn't "reek." We take her to the vet every six weeks for her routine check up. She isn't destructive, does not dig or scratch. She is not noisy, does not bark or whine day or night. Pookie is a tiny, little, toy poodle with the gentlest disposition: she would not attack anyone, and certainly not children, with whom she is especially gentle.

Then too, pets are part of the human experience (we claim). We have all learned to put up with some of the inconveniences in order to enjoy the value (the pleasure) of a pet's company. From a renter's point of view the landlord's rules don't sufficiently appreciate dogs. Therefore the renter asks for the landlord's warrant, an explanation of the connection between the support and the claim. And you can challenge a warrant if you don't think it's well made. There are two ways you can improve a warrant.[2]

A well-made warrant should not be too general; it should not use absolute terms where you can only achieve probability. You can show that not all dogs fall under the landlord's warrant. Some, like Pookie, are so well behaved that they don't exhibit any of the behaviors the landlord fears and thus represent no threat of any kind. The landlord's fear of "dogs" seems unreasonably broad. It condemns all animals of that species, though not all dogs have the problems the landlord cites (Maimon et al.).

Also a well-made warrant should not be too specific; it should not be based on only a few individuals, let alone a single individual. If the landlord's argument is based on a single dog encountered once, that's slim evidence on which to condemn the species. Certainly, if the warrant is based solely on the landlord's suspicions about our dog Pookie, we can show that not only is the warrant too specific, but the grounds don't apply. (Imagine showing up in court with a little, toy poodle feared by the landlord.) It will be helpful if we can cite other cases in which the pet owners (not the landlord) won (Maimon et al.).

---

[2]Adapted from Elaine P. Maimon et al., Writing in the Arts and Sciences (Cambridge, MA: Winthrop, 1981): 44.

Stating the Warrant

The warrant should be stated as a law or rule that critical thinkers can apply in other cases. Here you are faced with a problem. Landlords have their reasons, based on whatever their experience has been with dogs. "All dogs" over-generalizes and makes it easy to show that the "support" really doesn't apply to our dog. But, landlords—unfortunately—don't have to listen to reason. Invested with authority for apartments, landlords are likely to refuse to take a chance on Pookie. Nobody can guarantee 100% behavior of a pet. Sooner or later, the landlord says, there will be a rainy day and the dog will have to stay inside, or there will be an emergency and the dog will be left alone, or a stranger will approach the dog . . . it's just too risky.

Failing all else, it may be helpful if you can cite policy (general rule or law) that applies. For example, it is the nature of renting that landlords must accept certain risks, such as "normal" wear and tear on the property, though how far you can extend that is itself open to debate. Not every renter will meet the landlord's expectations, but there are laws against discrimination, and these may be cited as general policy that supersede the landlord's specific rules.

It's hard enough to argue with landlords when you are standing right in front of them. It's even more difficult to persuade in a letter. Writers are caught in a double bind: to be persuasive you may need to write at length, but the more you write, the more your reader may lose interest and not finish reading your letter. If the letter must be brief, it will need to be extremely well written. Is there anything you could say in a letter that might persuade landlords to change their minds? Perhaps. Can you anticipate a landlord's arguments? You might allege that Pookie is "never" out of the apartment without a leash. You could assure the landlord that Pookie is too tiny and too sweet to harm anyone or anything. You might threaten to sue the landlord. You might offer to sign a quit-claim, holding the landlord blameless for any damage the dog might do, and you might offer a financial incentive, an extra charge you would pay for the privilege of having the dog with you (although that seems unfair). Because the underlying concern is financial, you might show that by welcoming pet owners the landlord could find a new clientele that would increase profits. There are many responses renters could make to try to persuade a landlord; still, you must concede that arguing with a landlord—especially in writing—is a tough task.

ACTIVITY 22

Suppose one of the following were the substance of a renter's letter to the landlord. In your notebook, decide which is more likely to be persuasive and explain why you think so. Include in your answer why the others may not be as persuasive:

1. We understand your fears, but we assure you our dog is well trained, and we will be happy to pay for any damage caused by Pookie.
2. Pookie is a tiny, little, toy poodle incapable of injuring anyone and sweet and docile anyway. She has never so much as growled at anyone.
3. The rental contract we signed makes no mention of pets; therefore, we do not think we are bound by any of your changes to the contract.

Finding the Claim

A claim can appear anywhere in a paper—it need not be first, though it often is. To find the claim, ask yourself: What does the writer want me to believe? Why is USA Today writing about tobacco companies? In the second sentence of the following article you are told that five major tobacco companies filed on "Tuesday" a 2,000-page report concerning federal regulations on cigarette sales to minors. Read the article carefully, twice, and then see if you can say in a single sentence what the writer wants readers to believe.

Blowing Smoke on Teens

If you've ever doubted the sincerity of the tobacco industry's concern for teenage smokers, today you have new reason for suspicion.

The evidence can be found in a quick browse through 2,000 pages filed Tuesday by five major tobacco companies to fend off the proposed toughening of federal regulations on cigarette sales to minors.

The cigarette makers say they agree minors should not smoke. But they want the federal government to butt out of the business of making sure that they don't.

The tobacco industry's quarrel is over new regulations designed by the Food and Drug Administration to address rising underage smoking rates.

In documents filed with the government, company officials accuse the FDA of a "power grab" emanating not from concern about youth smoking but from a hidden agenda to ban cigarette sales to adults.

Quite an accusation from an industry tarnished by questions and lawsuits over its own hidden agendas and credibility.

And quite beside the point. The problem here is not what's being done or why, but what's not being done to reverse this disturbing trend.

The industry's answer has been ineffective, Band-Aid solutions such as pack labels admonishing against underage sales. Meanwhile, advertising with proven appeal among younger audiences continues. Just ask Joe Camel.

The result: In 1995, cigarette smoking again rose among U.S. youth. A widely followed University of Michigan survey found smoking among eighth-graders jumped 30% between 1991 and 1994. In all, an estimated 3.1 million U.S. teens smoke regularly. Those statistics are particularly alarming because other studies show that 80% to 90% of today's adult smokers picked up the habit before age 20.

Teens, like adults, plan to quit, not now but later. The surgeon general says, however, that only 3% of 20 million Americans who try to kick the habit each year succeed.

Some states have tried their own get-tough measures, such as vending machine bans and stiffer penalties for illegal sales to minors. But attorneys general in 25 states want more help and have endorsed FDA's proposed federal crackdown.

Tobacco companies got one thing right. Voluntary action by the industry is preferable to government regulation. But that opportunity has been blown.

Kid smoking is getting worse. It will continue to do so as long as tobacco companies are left to police themselves. (10A)

This article is an editorial, an argument. In any argument you need to know this: What is the <u>claim</u> of this argument and what <u>evidence</u> is used to support the claim? Toulmin says that the point of any argument is what the writer wants you to believe: the claim.

What is the claim here? The claim is expressed directly in the last two sentences: <u>Kid smoking is getting worse [and] will continue to do so as long as tobacco companies are left to police themselves</u>. The "support" (evidence) for this argument is in the statistics:

1. In 1995, cigarette smoking rose among U.S. youth.
2. A University of Michigan survey found smoking among eighth-graders jumped 30% between 1991 and 1994.
3. An estimated 3.1 million U.S. teens smoke regularly.
4. Other studies show that 80% to 90% of today's adult smokers picked up the habit before age 20.
5. According to the Surgeon General, "only 3% of 20 million Americans who try to kick the habit each year succeed."

You can see the claim and the support for it. Toulmin asks you to state the connection between the evidence and the claim. Why is this good evidence? What can you cite that would make it good evidence? The warrant should be a general statement that reasonable people can accept. What is the <u>warrant</u> for this claim? You may believe <u>USA Today</u> is a reliable source of information and so is the University of Michigan: its survey is "widely followed," and "other studies" verify what most of us know from our own experience—that most smokers start before the age of 20. And, finally, you can assume the word of the Surgeon General probably is reliable. In short, the connection between the claim and the support is your belief that this evidence comes from reliable sources. The claim is that "kid smoking" will probably get worse "as long as tobacco companies are allowed to police themselves." The evidence shows not only that kid smoking is on the rise but that the rise occurred while the tobacco companies were (allegedly) self-policing sales to minors.

When the warrant makes the connection between the claim and the evidence explicit this way, you may discover that some aspects of the argument are less solid than you had thought. In order for readers to believe the claim, they must believe that the evidence is accurate, and in order to believe the evidence is accurate, they have to believe the sources are reliable: <u>USA Today</u>, the University of Michigan, the Surgeon General. It is here that you must think carefully. Is there any reason not to believe these sources? On the whole there is little reason to doubt any of these sources, so you can accept the warrant in this case.

What can you conclude from this? If you are going to court to sue the tobacco companies, do you have enough information? Would this data be good enough to win the suit? Maybe not. The sources may be reliable, but statistical data isn't always the best evidence and there isn't very much of it. It would help if you could have real plaintiffs in court, real smokers. The evidence you have may not win a suit for you, nor cause many smokers to quit. But it may make some parents start thinking about their underage children. It may cause some parents to start checking the stores that sell tobacco products to children.

There is no absolute way to win all arguments; arguing is a matter of persuasion, after all. However, you can improve the strength of the arguments you do have. See "Guidelines for Increasing the Credibility of Your Arguments."

ACTIVITY 23

In your notebook write about these questions: At what age should youngsters be allowed to smoke? What reasons can you give for allowing youngsters to purchase and use adult substances? In class, discuss these issues with other students.

GUIDELINES FOR INCREASING THE CREDIBILITY OF YOUR ARGUMENTS

There are no absolute rules or techniques for rebuttals (see "Fallacies" in chapter 5), but research suggests some guidelines for increasing the credibility of your arguments.[a]

1. Avoid weak counterarguments: audiences exposed to weak counterarguments may build up defenses and become less persuaded by stronger arguments later. The alcohol argument (drinking): There's nothing wrong with drinking in moderation. Rebuttal: Young people should avoid the drinking habit because some people find it morally repugnant. The argument is "weak" because it does not address the central complaint against drinking.

(box continues)

2. Those who present both sides of an argument are believed to be more credible (research says), especially among the well educated. The ethos of presenting both sides reveals that the writer is fair and more interested in finding the truth than in imposing his/her own point of view. Even if "the other side" is detestable, it is important that the "uncommitted" audience hears that you are fair, impartial, and <u>knowledgeable</u> (informed). No matter how filthy and deadly smoking tobacco may be, it is important to review all those arguments the tobacco companies will use anyway.

3. Honest, genuine arguments are perceived as more credible than those that seem to be adopted for the moment. We believe those who argue from the heart. It may be more persuasive to discuss one's own hospitalized parent dying with emphysema than to present the conventional litany against tobacco or to invent comparisons with fictional victims of smoking.

4. People perceived as credible are more persuasive than those who don't seem credible. We seem credible when we are knowledgeable, well prepared, well organized, fair to the opponent, willing to consider objections, and able to project an honest, sincere voice. We may be perceived as lacking credibility if we use a harsh, disrespectful, insulting, or insincere tone; when we disregard the opposing view; when we seem not to have done our homework (are not prepared); and, in general, lack knowledge about the subject.

5. Organized arguments are more persuasive than disorganized arguments. The audience (your readers) must be able to follow your presentation. Keep the organization simple and use signals, transitions that tell the reader when you are moving to the next point and present the relationship of one point to another.

6. Evidence, especially evidence produced by others, is more credible than lack of evidence. We have witnessed (on TV) court cases in which lawyers argued that their clients must be found innocent because no credible evidence was brought against them. Outside of court it's a good idea to assume both sides have evidence (if there truly were no evidence on one side or the other, there would be little need for an argument).

7. Research does not agree whether to begin or to end with the statement of the argument, but many teachers and experienced writers believe it is best to start by telling the reader what the case is about. It is possible to start with the reasons first and then end with the argument, but doing so imposes an additional burden on the reader.

8. "Policy-based" law relies on reasons and purposes <u>behind</u> rules—citing a higher authority, "a greater good." For example, an article in the <u>Detroit Free Press</u> by Howell Raines ("<u>Globe's</u> Decision on Barnicle Undercuts Newspaper Credibility" 16 Aug. 98) reports that <u>Boston Globe</u> columnist Mike Barnicle was censured for lifting jokes from a

(box continues)

book he did not write and using them in his column without attribution as if they were his original material. Many of his friends spoke up for him—citing a higher rule (higher than the paper's strict plagiarism rules): it was too severe, his friends said, to end a brilliant 25-year career because of a few borrowed jokes. Thus they appealed to a higher rule—that the penalty should fit the crime. (They won.)

9. <u>Backing</u> makes warrants more persuasive: thus, the need for expertise. Being knowledgeable gives authority: knowing what is relevant and sufficient, recognizing structure in random pieces of information, recognizing what is merely surface and what is structural.

[a]Adapted from Paul T. Wangerin, "A Multidisciplinary Analysis of the Structure of Persuasive Arguments," <u>Harvard Notebook of Law and Public Policy</u> 16.1 (Winter 1993): 195–239.

(Guidelines in John C. Reinard, "The Role of Toulmin's Categories of Message Development in Persuasive Communication: Two Experimental Studies in Attitude Change." American Forensic Association, 1984.)

ACTIVITY 24

Write notes for an argument in your notebook, especially reasons for your claim. Write a brief argument in which you supply two or three reasons (more is better) to support your claim.

THE PSYCHOLOGY OF ARGUMENT

Persuasion is a subtle art. It has been studied for thousands of years, but art doesn't lend itself very well to rules and laws. It's possible to "win" an argument, for example, yet still fail to "persuade" the opponent. Therefore, it's good advice to pick your arguments carefully. Then too, few people are likely to change their mind about their beliefs or values on the basis of a single argument. Often the best audience is the uncommitted—people who haven't made up their minds or who don't have a strong opinion one way or the other. Those who have a strong opposition to your claim are not likely to be convinced no matter what you say.

Critical thinkers know there is much psychology in modern argumentation. Traditionally, we have said that arguments are based on reason—that is, logic. Yet, we know emotions can get involved in a "hot" argument. Many critical thinkers believe that human beings aren't inherently logical anyway. Audiences may resist logic and "reason" even when the argument is to their own benefit and even when resisting the argument can work to their injury—as with people who smoke. For that reason you need to understand the psychology of argument. You can cite physical evidence and other irresistible reasons, but what really moves people is their own psychology. Our reasons are based on values, beliefs, and attitudes—the psychology under our reasoning. We rely on physical evidence whenever we can because it is easiest to prove or disprove. Psychological matters, however, are invisible, hidden within the individual. We must deduce the reader's values, beliefs, and attitudes based on our own experiences with them. However, if we are right about them, these psychological matters can be powerful motivators in an argument. They can "move" an audience when logic cannot.

The process of drawing the audience into the arena where you can reach them begins with your title. There can be no participation and thus no persuasion if you cannot get the audience's attention. Once your reader begins to read your title, instead of tossing your paper aside, the process has begun; like a willing subject, your reader has begun to fall under the spell of your information and style.

Many journalists prefer to use their best material immediately for fear of losing the reader; many other writers say they begin with the best of the opposing material. Either way the participation between writer and reader has begun, and the reader is now participating in the unfolding of the story or report that you are presenting. The bullet theory of communication (message sent, message received) doesn't really work when you are trying to persuade readers. For persuasion you need the reader's cooperation and participation. Throughout your paper there must be invitations to the reader to think about your message, to wonder, and to respond not only with logos but also with emotion.

The conclusion is often called "the climax" because it is the height of reason—it is the point of the paper, toward which you have been leading the reader all along. And the feeling of completion and satisfaction for an appropriate ending should be nearly visceral for the reader. The paper not only ends but leaves the reader with a sense of ending. If the paper has been well written, the writer alternatively acts as teacher—teaching the reader, eliciting responses—and reporter, telling readers what they need to know in order to respond. The credibility and trustworthiness of your character pull the reader on: your ethos makes a bridge across the reader's cynicism. And the sincerity and pathos of your arguments and your voice move your reader ever closer to agreement with you.

Uncovering Hidden Values, Beliefs, and Attitudes

People argue about their values, beliefs, and attitudes. Unfortunately, they tend to be just those things about which people have little agreement. Then too, argumentation is the only way you can establish whatever agreement you can get. In short, critical thinking is linked to argumentation, inescapably. You must argue with yourself and with other reasonable people in an effort to find what you and they believe about the truth, specifically, values, beliefs, and attitudes.

Values are things you admire and desire (or the opposite). Values include your ethics, morals, and standards, the "good" or not good. Opinions about what is beautiful or ugly or simply plain express your values about matters of "taste." Usually, it's difficult to convince others about values. Nevertheless, you are required to explain the grounds on which you make your judgments, whether you can convince others or not. Without explanation, you have only your own opinions. But if you can provide explanations and offer reasoning—support for your values—then at least you have "considered opinions," something others can consider, add to, and agree with, or not. For example, why should you admire the architect Frank Lloyd Wright? Wright was born only two years after the Civil War, in 1867. He became one of America's foremost architects. He developed the American "Prairie Style" which featured large, open rooms, flowing space, and low, expansive roofs. Many of Wright's wide, low buildings built before World War II still have an astonishingly contemporary appearance (Britannica CD, 1997).

Beliefs are assumptions, ideas, opinions, notions, and faith, things you have learned. Beliefs make up your concept of reality. Most of us believe the Earth is round, spherical, not flat. If someone tells you that the Earth is really flat, not round, you're not likely to change your belief. Instead, you are more likely to think there is something wrong with that person. Philosophers and scientists say that a "fact" is merely a belief people agree about. Most of your notions about what is real or not real constitute beliefs about reality. Any facts you can demonstrate to be absolute statements usually are found in the sciences. Facts, which are relative, situational, and probable instead of absolute, you find in the art of persuasion.

Attitudes are temperaments, moods, emotions, and feelings. Attitudes involve your beliefs and values together. Today, someone who has an attitude usually means he or she has a bad attitude, but in psychology, attitude can refer to either good or bad. In argumentation, attitude often suggests bias, a feeling you have for or against something. In writing, a writer's attitude is equated with tone or with that writer's voice—the sound of his or her personality: serious, sincere, sarcastic, comic, and so on. Many Newsweek readers, for example, argued that George Will's attitude about the worldwide grief for Princess Diana was condescending. He considered the mourning "sheer fakery."

Values, beliefs, and attitudes make up the psychology of argumentation. They have power to affect others as much as ethos, pathos, logos. Without "reasoning" behind your values, beliefs, or attitudes, however, you have only opinion and bias, with no more strength than any other:

> "I like fried chicken."
> "Oh yeah? Well, I despise fried chicken!"

Without additional reasoning and explanation (Toulmin's support for your claim), the two opinions simply cancel each other out. You are in a stalemate. Only if you can offer explanations, evidence that holds up your claim, and a warrant that explains the connection between the claim and the evidence do you have more than mere opinion. Personal preferences alone do not offer any way to reason together.

ACTIVITY 25

Write a brief essay on the psychology of a TV show or film. Give examples of the values, beliefs, and attitudes you find in it. Discuss the audience to whom the show or film appeals most.

ACTIVITY 26

Find a picture (not an advertisement necessarily) from a magazine, something large enough to show to the class or your group. List as many reasons as you can think of that explain why, according to you, the picture does or doesn't achieve its purpose. Concentrate on the psychology of the picture. Encourage the group to offer their own comments.

ACTIVITY 27

Find an advertisement from a magazine or newspaper. Choose an ad that is not too small (about a half page or more). Choose an ad that is not too complicated: the more complicated the ad, the more analysis will be required.

1. Use Toulmin's claim, grounds, and warrant to analyze the ad in an essay or for a class presentation. First, point out what you think the ad's claim is. Second, point out the grounds that support the claim. Third, analyze the warrant or warrants you see—answer the "So what" question: discuss the relation of the grounds to the claim.

2. Explain whether you think the ad is persuasive. Who is its most likely audience? (And why do you say so?) Try to be objective. It may be best to select an ad that interests you in the first place. Consider discussing the ad's ethos, pathos, and logos.

3. Discuss any problems with the ad. Could it be improved? Are there any fallacies or weak reasoning?

USING THE TOULMIN STRATEGY TO ANALYZE
AN ARGUMENT

Please read the following essay by Thomas Sowell. Then read the analysis of it.

Human Parasites Are Infesting Society

Thomas Sowell

Why do people contribute money to the degeneration of the very society in   1
which they live, and in which their children will grow up?

It happens every day, on the streets of cities and towns all across the coun-   2
try—in New York subways, in San Francisco parks and in thousands of other places
where begging on the streets has become a full-time occupation. Even in shopping centers with "help wanted" signs in the windows of stores and fast-food
restaurants, people carry signs saying, "Will work for food"—not so that they will
get either work or food, but so that they will be given hard cash.

All this is happening in a society with massive welfare-state programs   3
covering virtually every conceivable problem—or claim of a problem. Begging
provides supplementary income, sustaining drug and alcohol consumption,
among other things.

Can anyone seriously believe that maintaining an army of idle people on   4
the streets makes for a better society? Or that subsidizing irresponsible behavior is the way to get responsible behavior—either by the people involved or by
those who see them getting away with it?

Would so many young people be able to devote so much time to gang   5
activities if they had to make a living? Not all of them are living by selling
drugs. Many are able to indulge their "lifestyle" courtesy of the taxpayers.

Even more remarkable than the growth in numbers—and in boldness—of   6
parasites is the growth of a sickly sense of guilt toward them by people who
pause on their way to work to give money to those who refuse to work.

Perhaps there is some sense of, "There but for the grace of God go I." Even   7
in a secular age, that statement has a ring to it.

It is certainly true that you could have turned out to be a very different   8
person if you had been raised a different way—or not raised at all, but allowed
to grow wild, like a weed. But that is very different from the propaganda line
that the homeless or other parasites are "just like everyone else."

The plain truth is that drugs, alcohol, or an irresponsible, hustling, or   9
criminal mentality have flooded our streets with parasites. Mental illness has put
some of the more heartbreaking cases on the street, instead of in custody.
Perhaps a third of those wandering the streets are prey to the delusions of their
own minds—and to the truly vicious among their fellow "homeless."

How did such a mess suddenly develop, in cities around the country, within   10
the past several years? Indeed, it is a phenomenon also found in the streets of
London and Paris—able-bodied people, often young and speaking in educated
accents, shamelessly asking others for the money they are unwilling to earn to
support themselves.

The most obvious reason is that they can get away with it. There was a   11
time when the police would have put you in jail for pestering decent people as
they went to work or headed home, or went shopping with their own hard-
earned money. Then the courts and the American Snivel Liberties Union came
to the rescue of the parasites.

To the morally anointed, all social outcasts are "victims" to be rescued,   12
even if they were cast out for their own rotten behavior. Adopting wrongos as
mascots puts a special shine on the halo of the anointed, and demonstrates their
moral superiority to the rest of us.

By the same token, the anointed regard the ordinary, decent, law-abid-   13
ing, taxpaying citizen as expendable. John Q. Public can be hustled on the
streets while trying to get to work, or in an airport while trying to catch a plane.
His children can be driven out of the parks that his taxes built by the sleazy
characters who infest parks today, doing all sorts of shameless things in broad
daylight.

Ultimately, however, we cannot blame it all on others. We elect the politi-   14
cians who spend our tax money on parasites and who appoint mushy judges who
create "constitutional rights" out of thin air to make it impossible for a society to defend itself against infestations of parasites.

We must also take responsibility for listening gullibly, to all sorts of "advo-   15
cates" for homelessness and other causes, as they regale us with statistics that
they have generated to serve their own purposes. The media act as megaphones
for all these unexamined numbers and unsubstantiated claims, but ultimately we
are responsible for believing self-serving propaganda from zealots.

Most directly of all, it is we who reach into our pockets and pull out   16
money to contribute to keep this social cancer going.

Worst of all, guilt has so furtively stolen into many hearts and minds that   17
people feel apologetic about being civilized, educated and productive when
others are barbaric, uneducated and parasitic. When civilization apologizes to
barbarism, something has gone very wrong at a very fundamental level. (9A) □

Analyzing Sowell's Argument

One advantage of Toulmin's approach is that it doesn't matter what sort of "argument" is involved. What matters is that there is a claim, grounds, and a warrant.
Sowell's article, "Human Parasites," challenges some basic human assumptions.
Most people were taught to feel compassion for the poor, the deranged, the
afflicted, and the elderly—"the truly needy." Therefore, readers may be shocked

to hear a newspaper columnist call needy people "parasites." But that's his point. He believes these people are not "needy" but lazy.

Sowell's article is written in question and answer form. He believes (assumes) there are more people begging (in 1992) in the streets of our cities. Sowell accepts his own assumption and then attempts to find the <u>cause</u> of this begging. He first dismisses any opposing arguments: he <u>anticipates</u> the arguments of opponents. (1) There are no jobs; times are hard (he points to window signs that say "help wanted"). (2) Many who beg are unable to work (he cites "massive welfare-state programs").

Then what could be the cause of all the begging? Sowell lists 17 possibilities, 17 causes. But ultimately, he says, "we" the public are the cause. We let it happen. We keep it going: we elect judges who will not prosecute these people; we pay for police who will not arrest them; we listen to the liberal propaganda that feels sorry for them—it's our fault because we pay out cash when approached by these people.

Although Sowell has a cause and effect, question and answer structure, there is something else here. If you examine his <u>tone</u>, his <u>attitude</u>, you will discover something other than the cool, calm, academic voice you are used to when writers search for the truth. Exploring an argument can help you hear the writer's voice. Sowell's references to <u>human parasites</u>, his key term, should alert critical readers—as well as the <u>American Snivel Liberties Union</u>, <u>wrongos</u>, the <u>morally anointed</u>, <u>sleazy characters who infest parks today</u>, <u>self-serving propaganda from zealots</u>, <u>social cancer</u>—these terms project the voice of an angry man. As the essay progresses, the tone escalates to moral outrage. Those (the good guys) who are civilized, educated, and productive, he says, are made to feel apologetic for the "others" who are "barbaric, uneducated and parasitic."

This analysis suggests Sowell is venting—letting off steam like a man who has been approached by street beggars once too often. These pathetic people, he assumes, constitute an attack on our society; they are the "social cancer"— they are "barbaric" people who prefer to beg than to work. Yet Sowell has nothing to say about 1992, during which the winning argument (Mr. Clinton won with it) was that times were indeed hard. People were afraid for their jobs. Billionaire Ross Perot in the presidential debates referred to the "giant sucking sound as American jobs were siphoned off to Mexico." About this Sowell has nothing to say.

Sowell's Claim

Sowell's claim is this: more people are begging in the streets because they are too lazy to work. It's a cause and effect argument, and begging in the streets is the effect.

The logos of Sowell's article is his attempt to determine who or what is to blame for this situation. What causes this social dysfunction? Why do people give money to street beggars? Sowell insists that society has acquired a "sickly sense of guilt" toward its beggars. Those who do (did) have jobs feel guilty about those who don't, he says. The truth is (according to Sowell) the beggars <u>refuse</u> to work. The rest of us feel not only guilt but fear it could happen to us. He quotes the old saying, "There but for the grace of God go I." It's possible, of course, that some catastrophe could befall anyone, but Sowell suggests our lives are basically the result of our parents, how we were raised . . . or not raised. And therefore, it's propaganda to say that the homeless or other parasites are "just like everyone else." Those of us who were taught to work and stand on our own two feet are less likely to suffer some catastrophe and become homeless beggars in the streets. Sowell believes, however, those who beg were not taught to be responsible for their own destiny; they know that the easiest way to survive is to beg for money from those that have it.

Sowell blames parents for children that grew up to be beggars, and he also blames "drugs, alcohol, or an irresponsible, hustling, or criminal mentality." The mental institutions, too, he says, have contributed to the problem by allowing the deranged to roam the streets.

According to the essay, this is a problem of the cities: he mentions New York, San Francisco, London, and Paris—where "able-bodied people, often young and speaking in educated accents" shamelessly beg, because they are unwilling to support themselves, that is, work. Why? Because they can. Begging is easier than working and city police no longer arrest such people for vagrancy; they don't get chased from the parks—and the courts are reluctant to punish them.

It's our fault, Sowell says, for the politicians and the mushy judges who create "constitutional rights" that prevent us from defending ourselves against these "parasites." We listen gullibly, he says, to the "advocates" of homelessness and their fictional statistics. The media are much to blame for unexamined numbers and unsubstantiated claims—but "ultimately we [the public] are responsible for believing self-serving propaganda from zealots." We are the ones paying out our cash to sustain this "social cancer."

The Grounds

Sowell offers a lot of support in the form of generalizations (his opinions). He says begging is caused by the following:

1. Drugs (the need to get money with which to purchase drugs)
2. Alcohol (the need to get money with which to purchase alcohol)
3. Subsidized irresponsible behavior
4. Idleness, lack of need to earn a living, lack of jobs, refusal to work
5. Guilt on the part of those who give money to beggars
6. Fear of personal catastrophe ("There but for the grace of God go I")
7. Lack of parental guidance
8. Propaganda: "the homeless or other parasites are 'just like everyone else'"
9. Criminal mentality

10. Mental illness
11. Ability to get away with it, refusal of police to arrest, refusal of courts to punish
12. Opinion of the morally anointed that social outcasts are "victims" to be rescued
13. Opinion of the morally anointed that John Q. Public is expendable
14. We protect parasites with "constitutional rights" <u>we</u> create out of thin air
15. <u>Our</u> gullible listening to advocates for homelessness who generate their own statistics
16. Media use of unexamined numbers and unsubstantiated claims
17. Most directly, perpetuating the problem by giving money to the beggars

In addition to Sowell's reasons, we think there may be an underlying reason—the political and economic climate immediately before and after 1992. Why is (was) Sowell writing this argument (opinion)? What was the event or events that caused him to feel the need for his article? He says there has been (in 1992) an increase in public begging. He mentions the availability of work, "help wanted" signs in the windows of stores and fast-food restaurants. He does not mention—but should—the presidential campaign of 1992. Mr. Clinton and the Democrats were making much of the global recession, using the recession as the reason why the Republicans should lose the White House. The Republicans were trying to convince the public that the American economy was in good condition. Yet by 1994 job loss had become so severe that economists began talking about permanent "structural" unemployment.

Unfortunately, more people were suffering than President Bush [senior] seemed to know. The recession, downsizing, and the perception that American jobs were being moved to Mexico and China made President Bush's reelection a hard sell.

Sowell is arguing a question of policy. He says street begging is very wrong in our society, and we need to do something about it, but what should be done is less clear. It sounds as if Sowell is saying "just say no" to the beggars. If we all stop giving them money, they will stop begging.

Sowell's Warrant

The warrant asks so what? What is the connection between all of Sowell's reasons and the claim? Sowell's claim, what he wants us to believe, is that beggars are simply lazy. Because he believes there are jobs available (though he doesn't say what sorts of jobs nor at what pay) and he believes there are welfare programs for those who cannot work (though he does not say who might be unable to work: the disabled? the elderly? women with children?), Sowell accepts his own claim as established and goes on to search for the causes of begging . . . and finds 17 of them.

However, these grounds don't seem to have much to do with laziness. Number four, "Idleness," can mean laziness but it also means "unemployed" (<u>Webster's New World</u>). The rest? At least 16 of the "grounds" do not directly at fault. Those who give money to the beggars are the real cause. We contribute to the degeneration of our own society: we are the cause.

Is there something wrong with this argument? If you examine the writer's ethos or pathos, you may decide there is more here than logos. The tone of Sowell's essay sounds like that of an outraged man. He is angry and sarcastic ("the American Snivel Liberties Union"). The more you examine the psychology of Sowell's essay, the more it sounds like ranting. The list of reasons seems not to have as much to do with begging as with all those things that anger Sowell. You can find two claims in Sowell's essay. One has to do with street beggars. About that, we think Sowell protests too much. The other has to do with the "social cancer," the "degeneration" of our society: drugs, alcohol, the "morally anointed." About that, we think Sowell has not connected the two strands of this essay. We don't think all the ills of the modern city can be traced back to street beggars. At least we don't think Sowell's argument has shown us how to connect them.

ESSAYS TO ANALYZE USING THE TOULMIN STRATEGY

Please read the following three essays. Then choose one to discuss or write about. Analyze the claim, grounds, and warrant. Consider the author's use of ethos, logos, and pathos. Consider the author's psychology. Then decide whether you think the essay presents a good argument.

```
I Need a Minivan . . . Not!

Dan Olson (student)


It's rush hour. Traffic is slowly inching along bumper to
bumper. People are shaking their fists--cursing the car in
front of them or having deep, in-depth conversations with
themselves. There I am right in the middle of it, cursing with
everyone else, watching all the people around me, or wondering
why people get personalized license plates that don't make any
sense except to themselves. Sure, sometimes driving in heavy
traffic can drive me crazy; however, this doesn't necessarily
mean I would rather be driving a minivan.

    The minivan advertisement in Newsweek states that if I
hate driving in heavy traffic, then I would be crazy not to
drive one of their vans. The ad declares that the van is
designed to feel more like a place I would want to be rather
than have to be. How do they know I would rather be driving a
```

(box continues)

big van during rush hour traffic? If I could be in anything it would be a little sports car. In it, squeezing into narrow spaces would be a breeze, so would be striking up conversations with attractive motorists next to me. These are just two circumstances which are difficult to perform in heavy traffic while driving a minivan. Also, other drivers seem to respect sports cars because the cars look as though they don't belong in heavy traffic. As a result, other motorists tend to let them through more often. Minivans, on the other hand, just look as though they belong creeping along in heavy traffic. Other drivers are well aware that the individual driving the minivan is comfortable, surrounded by ample amounts of leg and head room; therefore, they tend to get stuck in traffic.

The advertisement also boasts of a comfortable, stylish interior with seats for seven that can adjust to practically any position. I don't know about most of America, but I do know that if I were to be stuck in heavy traffic, I definitely wouldn't want six other people with me. Being a teenage male I can, however, see where having seats that can adjust to practically any position might [be] beneficial, but definitely not while driving during rush hour.

There appears to be no real legitimate reason why I would benefit from driving a minivan in heavy traffic. Driving during rush hour may drive me crazy, but I would be even crazier driving a minivan.

Asymmetries: Women and Men Talking at Cross-Purposes

Deborah Tannen

Eve had a lump removed from her breast. Shortly after the operation, talking to 1 her sister, she said that she found it upsetting to have been cut into, and that looking at the stitches was distressing because they left a seam that had changed the contour of her breast. Her sister said, "I know. When I had my operation I felt the same way." Eve made the same observation to her friend Karen, who said, "I know. It's like your body has been violated." But when she told her husband, Mark, how she felt, he said, "You can have plastic surgery to cover up the scar and restore the shape of your breast."

Eve had been comforted by her sister and her friend, but she was not 2 comforted by Mark's comment. Quite the contrary, it upset her more. Not only didn't she hear what she wanted, that he understood her feelings, but, far worse, she felt he was asking her to undergo more surgery just when she was telling him how much this operation had upset her. "I'm not having any more surgery!"she protested. "I'm sorry you don't like the way it looks." Mark was hurt and puzzled. "I don't care," he protested. "It doesn't bother me at all." She asked, "Then why are you telling me to have plastic surgery?" He answered, "Because you were saying you were upset about the way it looked."

Eve felt like a heel: Mark had been wonderfully supportive and concerned 3 throughout her surgery. How could she snap at him because of what he said—"just words"—when what he had done was unassailable? And yet she had perceived in his words metamessages that cut to the core of their relationship. It was self-evident to him that his comment was a reaction to her complaint, but she heard it as an independent complaint of his. He thought he was reassuring her that she needn't feel bad about her scar because there was something she could do about it. She heard his suggestion that she do something about the scar as evidence that <u>he</u> was bothered by it. Furthermore, whereas she wanted reassurance that it was normal to feel bad in her situation, his telling her that the problem could easily be fixed implied she had no right to feel bad about it.

Eve wanted the gift of understanding, but Mark gave her the gift of advice. 4 He was taking the role of problem solver, whereas she simply wanted confirmation for her feelings.

A similar misunderstanding arose between a husband and wife following a 5 car accident in which she had been seriously injured. Because she hated being in the hospital, the wife asked to come home early. But once home, she suffered pain from having to move around more. Her husband said, "Why didn't you stay in the hospital where you would have been more comfortable?" This hurt her because it seemed to imply that he did not want her home. She didn't think of his suggestion that she should have stayed in the hospital as a response to her complaints about the pain she was suffering; she thought of it as an independent expression of his preference not to have her at home. [. . .]

"I'll Fix It For You"

Women and men are both often frustrated by the other's way of responding to 6 their expression of troubles. And they are further hurt by the other's frustration. If women resent men's tendency to offer solutions to problems, men complain about women's refusal to take action to solve the problems they complain about. Since many men see themselves as problem solvers, a complaint or a trouble is a challenge to their ability to think of a solution, just as a woman presenting a broken bicycle or stalling car poses a challenge to their ingenuity in fixing it. But whereas many women appreciate help in fixing mechanical equipment, few are inclined to appreciate help in "fixing" emotional troubles.

The idea that men are problem solvers was reinforced by the contrasting 7 responses of a husband and wife to the same question on a radio talk show. The couple, Barbara and William Christopher, were discussing their life with an autistic child. The host asked if there weren't times when they felt sorry for themselves and wondered, "Why me?" Both said no, but they said it in different ways. The wife deflected attention from herself: She said that the real sufferer was her child. The husband said, "Life is problem solving. This is just one more problem to solve."

This explains why men are frustrated when their sincere attempts to help   8
a woman solve her problems are met not with gratitude but with disapproval. One man reported being ready to tear his hair out over a girlfriend who continually told him about problems she was having at work but refused to take any of the advice he offered. Another man defended himself against his girlfriend's objection that he changed the subject as soon as she recounted something that was bothering her: "What's the point of talking about it any more?" he said. "You can't do anything about it." Yet another man commented that women seem to wallow in their problems, wanting to talk about them forever, whereas he and other men want to get them out and be done with them, either by finding a solution or by laughing them off.

Trying to solve a problem or fix a trouble focuses on the message level   9
of talk. But for most women who habitually report problems at work or in friendships, the message is not the main point of complaining. It's the metamessage that counts: Telling about a problem is a bid for an expression of understanding ("I know how you feel") or a similar complaint ("I felt the same way when something similar happened to me"). In other words, troubles talk is intended to reinforce rapport by sending the metamessage "We're the same; you're not alone." Women are frustrated when they not only don't get this reinforcement but, quite the opposite, feel distanced by the advice, which seems to send the metamessage "We're not the same. You have the problems; I have the solutions."

Furthermore, mutual understanding is symmetrical, and this symmetry   10
contributes to a sense of community. But giving advice is asymmetrical. It frames the advice giver as more knowledgeable, more reasonable, more in control—in a word, one-up. And this contributes to the distancing effect.

The assumption that giving advice can be oneupmanship underlies an   11
observation that appeared in a book review. In commenting on Alice Adams's <u>After You've Gone</u>, reviewer Ron Carlson explained that the title story is a letter from a woman to a man who has left her for a younger woman. According to Carlson, the woman informs her former lover about her life "and then steps up and clobbers him with sage advice. Here is clearly a superior woman. . . ." Although we do not know the intention of the woman who wrote the story, we see clearly that the man who reviewed it regards giving advice as a form of attack and sees one who gives advice as taking a superior position. (<u>You Just Don't Understand</u> 49–53) ☐

Linking Crime, Abortion Rates Makes Everyone Queasy

Ellen Goodman

The whole thing is enough to make John Donohue nostalgic. "Usually what I   1
write languishes in obscurity," the Stanford law professor says drolly. Not this
time.

Donohue and Steven Levitt, a University of Chicago economist, set out   2
innocently enough to look at one of the great puzzles of the research world:
Why has the crime rate dropped so sharply, so widely, so quickly in the 1990s?

The two sleuths found a clue that no one had considered: <u>Roe</u> v. <u>Wade</u>.   3
These two respected scholars came to the wildly provocative conclusion that
the legalization of abortion may explain as much as half of the drop in the
crime rate.

To put it simply, those states that had very high rates of abortion right   4
after the Supreme Court ruling in the 1970s had very large declines in crime in
the 1990s. That's true even when you consider myriad other things that influence crime rates, from prison sentencing to policing to jobs. Fewer offenses are
being committed today by those under 25 years old.

Before Roe, as Levitt says, choosing his words carefully, "women who   5
wanted to abort but were denied that opportunity seem to have given birth to
children more likely to have become criminals." After Roe, to put it bluntly,
some unwanted fetuses at risk of becoming potential criminals were aborted.

This statistical link—or leap—between abortion and crime has set all   6
sorts of teeth on edge. The research was greeted with respect at several academic conferences. But when it became public, the two novices in the politics
of abortion were immediately cast as equal opportunity offenders.

The prolife community is appalled at their notion that abortion—which   7
they regard as murder—reduced crime. As for the idea that every 10 percent
increase in abortion resulted in a 1 percent decrease in crime, Joe Scheidler, the
executive director of the Pro-Life Action League, fumed, "It follows logically
that to really eliminate crime, you simply need to get rid of everybody."

The prochoice community, on the other hand, would rather give the whole   8
subject a good leaving alone. Jeannie Rosoff, president of the Alan Guttmacher
Institute, which does research in reproductive issues, called the study "interesting," "simplistic," "not improbable," and, finally, "explosive."

Prochoice leaders are particularly uneasy at any link between race, class,   9
abortion, and crime. In this case, the women who chose to have abortions in
the wake of Roe were disproportionately teenagers, minorities, and the poor.
What does that say? A way to stop the "breeding" of criminals by class and race
and age?

To anyone with a politically sensitive ear, the implication that abortion can   10
prevent crime carries ugly echoes of the days when Social Darwinists wanted to
improve society by breeding "good families" and not breeding "bad families."

In the 1920s and '30s, eugenicists supported laws that would put the 11
government in charge of reproductive decisions. At one point there were laws
in 31 states to forcibly sterilize the "handicapped" and "feebleminded."

Levitt and Donohue, whose work has been branded with the charge of 12
eugenics, are by no means promoting abortion as a crime prevention policy. In
fact, their research is a counterpoint to eugenics. They looked at what happened
when women—not the state—were finally allowed to make their own choices.

As Levitt says, their work was not "about class or race but about unwant- 13
edness."

After Roe, women who knew they weren't ready or able to raise children 14
had a choice. The children they did have were more likely to be wanted.

Today abortion rates are at their lowest point since Roe. That doesn't 15
mean we're due for a crime wave in 2020. It means there are fewer unwanted
pregnancies today—due in large part to contraceptives. If there's universal
agreement on anything in the world of reproduction, it's that birth control is a
better way to prevent "unwantedness" than abortion.

Levitt and Donohue set out to answer questions about crime and ended 16
up raising hackles about abortion. Their thesis may or may not hold up to further
review. But all in all, it has the whiff of common sense.

As Levitt offers simply enough, "I think children have better outcomes when 17
mothers want them and have the resources and inclination to have them." It's
what family planners have said all along. It's not really such a puzzle. (F7) ☐

Interchapter 3

Strategies of Repetition

With style, little things matter a lot.

SENTENCE TOOLS

Parallelism

Please examine the following sentences. What stylistic pattern do they have in common?

> Losing balance, regaining it, and going on, is the substance of learning.
> (Graves 231)

> For Bill and me, there has been no experience more challenging, more reward-ing and more humbling than raising our daughter.
> (Hillary Clinton, Democratic National Convention, 1996)

> We should be enabling, healing, curing.
> (Christopher Reeve, Democratic National Convention, 1996)

Words ending in -ing are repeated in each of these sentences. <u>Parallelism</u>, or parallel structure, is the intentional repetition of a word ending, a single word, a phrase, or a clause. As a critical thinker, you can use parallelism for emphasis and for making attention-catching patterns of language. By balancing certain words so they have the same structure, you can make sentences clearer, smoother, and easier to read. (Did you notice the repetition of -er endings in that sentence?) Parallel ordering of thoughts suggests a careful mind at work.

ACTIVITY 1

In your notebook write three sentences using a repetition of -ing words. Bring them to class to share. Then look at your recent writing, and see if you can improve any sentence by using parallel -ing words or phrases. Try to use this tool the next time you write.

Please examine the following sentences. What stylistic pattern do they have in common?

> Your economic security does not lie in your job; it lies in your own power to produce—to think, to learn, to create, to adapt. (Covey 304)

> I need to feel strongly, to love and to admire, just as desperately as I need to breathe. (Bauby 55)

> We love occasional reversals of established order, both to defuse the tension of inequity and to infuse a bit of variety into our lives. (Gould 94)

These sentences repeat infinitive verb phrases that begin with to. This repetition provides a clear structure for readers to follow. It also provides a rhythm to the sentences, appealing to your sense of sound. Gould's pair of phrases "to defuse" and "to infuse" are well chosen because of the reversal of thought they convey. As a scientist, Gould carefully chooses his words for meaning as well as sound. You too can choose your words for meaning and sound.

Writers sometimes use more than one form of parallelism within a sentence or group of sentences:

> "Skilled" thinking can easily be used to obfuscate rather than to clarify, to maintain a prejudice rather than to break it down, to aid in the defense of a narrow interest rather than to take into account the public good. (Paul 57)

Here Richard Paul uses parallel structure by repeating <u>to</u> phrases and "rather than." This double repetition gives the impression that Paul controls his thinking well: he can express a complex idea by fastening it to clear parallel structure. His voice sounds authoritative—persuasive.

ACTIVITY 2

In your notebook write three sentences using a repetition of <u>to</u> phrases. For one sentence, consider imitating Richard Paul's use of <u>to</u> phrases and <u>rather than</u>'s. Bring them to class to share. Then look at your recent writing, and see if you can improve any sentence by using parallel <u>to</u> phrases. Try to use this tool the next time you write.

————————

Please examine the following sentences. What stylistic pattern do they have in common?

Diana was the very essence of compassion, of duty, of style, of beauty.
(Earl Spencer, Eulogy for his sister Diana)

Thinking is a matter of seeing relationships—relationships of parts to wholes, of items in a sequence, of causes and effects. (Berthoff 70)

Writing a poem is a process of focusing a topic, of using images, of playing with sounds.

The <u>of</u> phrases smoothly connect different parts of each sentence. They give each sentence a pattern with balance and rhythm. They suggest to readers that the writers know what they are saying and how to say it.

ACTIVITY 3

In your notebook write three sentences using a repetition of <u>of</u> phrases. Bring them to class to share. Then look at your recent writing, and see if you can improve any sentence by using parallel <u>of</u> phrases. Try to use this tool the next time you write.

————————

You have practiced three types of parallel structure: repeating -ing phrases, to phrases, and of phrases. Although these types often occur in writing, countless other types occur as well because writers can repeat almost any word ending or word. Here, for example, psychologist Jerome Bruner repeats the familiar un prefix:

> Our attention is attracted to something that is unclear, unfinished, or uncertain. (Toward a Theory of Instruction 114)

With style, little things matter a lot. A simple repetition of un can make his sentence easy to read and to consider. Such repetition suggests the work of a critical thinker who carefully guides readers with the structure of his thoughts.

Anaphora

Examine the following passages. What stylistic pattern do they have in common?

> We shall fight on the beaches. We shall fight on the landing grounds. We shall fight in the fields and in the streets. We shall fight in the hills. We shall never surrender. (Winston Churchill, Speech on Dunkirk, House of Commons 4 June 1940)

> We need the arts to express ideas and feelings in ways beyond words. We need the arts to stir creativity and enrich a child's way of knowing. We need the arts to integrate the fragments of academic life. We need the arts to empower the disabled. And, above all, we need the arts to create community and to build connections across the generations. (Boyer A18)

This stylistic tool is called anaphora, a favorite of many politicians and writers. Anaphora is the repetition of a single word or phrase at the beginning of clauses or sentences. As a tool of emphasis, it helps an audience follow along and remember key ideas. It shows an audience that the speaker or writer has control and can steer thoughts in parallel ways. It also helps stir an audience emotionally, as Churchill's sentences did to the people of Great Britain. Anaphora strengthens a writer's voice, capturing a tone of conviction.

Anaphora often occurs toward the end of a speech or essay, but you can use it almost anywhere for emphasis. Anaphora usually shows a writer's passion about an idea or problem. Whenever writers use this tool, they want your attention and usually get it. Notice how Hillary Clinton uses anaphora:

> Right now, in our biggest cities and our smallest towns, there are boys and girls being tucked gently into bed, and there are boys and girls who have no one to call mom or dad, and no place to call home. [. . .]
> Right now there are parents worrying: "What if the baby sitter is sick tomorrow?" Or: "How can we pay for college this fall?" And right now there are parents despairing about gang members and drug pushers on the corners in their neighborhoods.
> Right now there are parents questioning a popular culture that glamorizes sex

and violence, smoking and drinking, and teaches children that the logos on their clothes are more valued than the generosity in their hearts. (emphasis ours) (Democratic National Convention, 1996)

Clinton's repetition of "Right now there are" serves as a refrain, reinforcing her point that many parents and children in our country experience homelessness, violence, and drugs and that society must address these problems—now.

Lawyers often use anaphora to catch the ear of jury members and to reinforce key ideas. What is the effect of the anaphora used by Daniel Petrocelli (lawyer for the Goldman family whose son O. J. Simpson was accused of murdering) in this passage?

Petrocelli focused on Simpson's four days of testimony, in which Simpson admitted that he had been unfaithful during his marriage and had been involved in several domestic disturbances.

"What kind of man takes a baseball bat to his wife's car right in front of her and says she was not upset even though she called police for help?

"What kind of man kicks in a door and says it was just a reflex?

"What kind of man says his wife was lying on that tape when she says she was afraid and he was going—in her words—to beat the s––– out of her?

"What kind of man says cheating on your wife isn't a lie?

"What kind of man says his wife's most private writings [. . .] are—quote—a pack of lies? [. . .]

"What kind of man comes into court and says, I never lied about anything in my life?"

Petrocelli answered his own questions: "A guilty man . . . A man with no remorse. A man with no conscience." (Deutsch and Fleeman 5A)

The repetition of "What kind of man" hammers home a question that undermines Simpson's ethos—credibility. Used this way, anaphora can be powerfully persuasive.

As one of the most potent stylistic tools writers can use, anaphora can help you as a critical thinker persuade an audience to feel, to think, and to care about a problem. But if you overuse it, anaphora can lose its power and raise questions about your efforts to persuade.

ACTIVITY 4

Write an example of anaphora. It may be one sentence or several sentences. Experiment. Then write another example. For example, "We learned to support our ideas with specific evidence; we learned to examine paradoxes; we learned to argue about what matters to us." Bring your sentences to class to share.

Epistrophe

What stylistic pattern do the following sentences have in common?

> We here highly resolve [. . .] that government of the people, by the people, for the people, shall not perish from the earth. (Abraham Lincoln, Gettysburg Address)

> What education has to impart is an intimate sense for the power of ideas, for the beauty of ideas, and for the structure of ideas.
> (Whitehead, <u>Aims of Education</u> 18)

> On the wall of my room when I was in rehab was a picture of the space shuttle blasting off, autographed by every astronaut now at NASA. On top of the picture it says, "We found nothing is impossible." That should be our motto. Not a Democratic motto, not a Republican motto. But an American motto. (Christopher Reeve, Democratic National Convention, 1996)

The opposite of anaphora is epistrophe. <u>Epistrophe is the repetition of a single word or phrase at the end of clauses or sentences</u>. Epistrophe creates emphasis at the end of thoughts. This tool, therefore, helps an audience focus on and remember key ideas. Lincoln's sentence helps you focus on <u>people</u>, Whitehead's on <u>ideas</u>, and Reeve's paragraph on <u>motto</u>. Epistrophe is not used by writers as often as anaphora, though it is a highly effective tool of style. Used sparingly, epistrophe can give your writing power and meaning.

Sometimes writers use anaphora and epistrophe within the same group of sentences:

> <u>If women</u> are healthy and educated, <u>their families will flourish</u>. <u>If women</u> are free from violence, <u>their families will flourish</u>. <u>If women</u> have a chance to work and earn as full and equal partners in society, <u>their families will flourish</u>.
> (Hillary Clinton, 1995)

Clinton's group of sentences is well crafted, each beginning with "If women" and ending with "their families will flourish." Her style suggests control, strength, and conviction. It creates her clear and sure voice.

ACTIVITY 5

Write an example of epistrophe. It may be one sentence or several sentences. Experiment. Then write another example. For example, "I value rational people who speak <u>with their heart</u>, listen <u>with their heart</u>, and act <u>with their heart</u>." You may also try combining anaphora and epistrophe. Bring your sentences to class to share.

THE POWER OF THREES IN SENTENCES

True style isn't a collection of tricks you can add to your writing, and we aren't suggesting that you look for gimmicks to give your essays more zip. Once in a while, however, you may find a device you can use for emphasis: the power of threes may be one of them.

ACTIVITY 6

Without looking ahead, list as many sayings or phrases as you can think of that contain three main words. For example, <u>red, white, and blue</u>.

Elements of three are persuasive in thought and style. If you can support an idea with three examples, your argument is usually more convincing than if you use only one. Three is satisfying for patterns within sentences too. Browse through the preceding pages on parallel structure and see how many examples contain elements of three. Most do. Your mind easily processes three.

Susan Ager, columnist for the <u>Detroit Free Press</u>, wrote an essay about threes. As you read it, consider how well she communicates her thesis and supporting evidence. Consider her style: the way she uses words and sentences. Consider her voice (the sound of her personality), her tone (attitude toward her audience, subject, and self), and her use of persuasive appeals—logos, pathos, ethos. Check whether she uses any of the stylistic tools about which you've been learning.

Baby, Baby, Baby, Three Has Its Charms

Susan Ager

1   No ifs, ands or buts about it: Three enjoys a magic and rhythm that two and four lack. John and Michelle Engler [governor and wife of Michigan] will learn what preachers and writers already know: Three is powerful. Memorable. Dramatic. Two is tepid, four overwrought.

2   Three works.

3   Had the Engler triplets been boys, they might have been Larry, Mo and Curly. Or Winken, Blinken and Nod. With mixed genders, they might have been Peter, Paul and Mary.

The girls, by birth order, became Margaret, Hannah and Madeleine. Nick- 4
name two, and you've got a winning team: Hannah, Maddy and Meg.

Three is magical because we think about much of the world in contrast- 5
ing pairs: men and women, body and soul, fire and ice.

Couples make the world go 'round, but trios give it zest: Men, women and 6
children. Red, white and blue. Bacon, lettuce and tomato.

Hop, Skip and a Jump

The musketeers were three. So were the blind mice and the Magi. So were the 7
witches who chanted around a bubbling cauldron in <u>Macbeth</u>.

The genie gave Aladdin three wishes. We give our friends three guesses. 8
Realtors cite the three most important things to look for in a house: Location,
location, location.

Animal, vegetable or mineral? Coffee, tea or milk? Children study readin', 9
'ritin' and 'rithmetic, and learn their ABCs—not ABs or ABCDs.

What's so wrong with two and four? Think about it geometrically: Two 10
points make nothing but a straight line.

Mork and Mindy. Frick and Frack. Black and white. 11

Three points make a triangle, elegant and interesting. 12

The Father, Son and Holy Spirit. 13

The butcher, the baker, the candlestick maker. 14

A loaf of bread, a jug of wine and thou. 15

With four points, you get some variety, but four words or concepts are one 16
too many for graceful recollection.

We can name the Beatles, but each of us chooses a different order. Same 17
with the seasons. I start with winter. My husband starts with summer, because
he remembers the Howdy Doody show and Princess Summerfall Winterspring.

Sun, Moon, Stars

Whoever named the rock group Blood, Sweat and Tears was wise to the magic 18
of three. The name comes from a Winston Churchill pledge to end World War II
with "blood, toil, tears and sweat," but I always have to look up that quote to
remember the correct order.

Advice goes down easiest in threes: Eat, drink and be merry. Healthy, 19
wealthy and wise. Jesus told a lame man, "Arise, take up thy bed and walk."

And more: On your mark, get set, go! 20

Snap, crackle and pop. 21

Rub-a-dub-dub, three men in a tub. 22

I could get carried away with this. Like waltzing, the examples are endless 23
and dizzying: <u>one</u>-two-three, <u>one</u>-two-three, <u>one</u>-two-three. So much more
mesmerizing than the two-step.

Enough. The Engler triplets will see the magic of three all around them 24
as they grow.

I wish them each a good dose of faith, hope and charity. A safe dose of 25
sex, drugs and rock'n'roll. And opportunities for health, wealth and happiness,
every morning, noon and night. (1D) □

Susan Ager tries to persuade you that three is a powerful number in
thought and style. We think she succeeds. Not only does she make an insightful point about three, but she makes it humorously. Her voice is inquisitive and
honest—she sounds excited in this essay, as if she's having fun with her subject
and her language. She writes, "I could get carried away." She does get carried
away, and her voice carries readers with her. Through many clear examples of
threes, Ager enables readers to consider this number more than they had before.

Tricolon

You have seen many sentences containing three elements to create parallel structure. But there is one more tool that employs three. Examine the following
sentences. What do they have in common beside three elements?

> To see, to feel, to discover is all. (Selzer, <u>Mortal Lessons</u> 24)

> <u>Interdependence</u> is the paradigm of <u>we</u>—<u>we</u> can do it; <u>we</u> can cooperate; <u>we</u>
> can combine our talents and abilities and create something greater together.
> (Covey 49)

> Almost all of the world-class athletes and other peak performers are visualiz-
> ers. They see it; they feel it; they experience it before they actually do it.
> (Covey 134)

Notice how Selzer uses three infinitive phrases. Placing "to discover" last may
mean that Selzer believes this is the most important element. <u>When writers
sequence three elements in rising order of importance, this tool of style is called
tricolon</u>. Covey's first example contains a tricolon after his first complete thought:
he joins three short thoughts with semicolons and anaphora (repetition of "we
can"); the last thought is longer, explaining more fully the idea of interdependence. His second example of tricolon is similar: three short thoughts joined with
semicolons, with the last one longer, emphasizing the idea of experience.

However, many sentences use three elements without rising order—and
they too can be effective.

> Will Strunk loved the clear, the brief, the bold, and his book is clear, brief,
> bold. (White, "Will Strunk" 126)

Science probes the factual state of the world; religion and ethics deal with moral reasoning; art and literature treat aesthetic and social judgment. (Gould 100)

While the world celebrated Diana's youth, sense of style and wealth, it was comforted by Mother Teresa's wrinkled face, simple blue-trimmed sari and the vows of poverty her missionary sisters took. (Crumm 1A)

You can use threes to sequence a rising order of elements; you can join three thoughts by using semicolons; you can simply use three details or examples. The pattern of three is an important tool of style, rich in possibilities.

ACTIVITY 7

Write three sentences using threes. One of your sentences should contain a tricolon. For example, "At this school we know what it means <u>to live</u>, <u>to love</u>, and <u>to learn</u>." Write another sentence that contains three complete thoughts joined by semicolons. For example, "Don't push; be patient; be respectful" (Covey 258). Bring your sentences to class to share. Then look at your recent writing. Try to combine and tighten some sentences by using threes. Try to use this tool the next time you write.

Varying Sentence Beginnings: Three Ways

Using -ing Phrases

Please examine the following sentences. What stylistic pattern do they have in common?

Judging by drop-out rates, we see that college does not benefit all students. (Marisa Proctor, student)

Learning to play a flute, she felt as happy as a butterfly. (Emily Schaeffer, student)

Unbuttoning his shirt, he placed the disc over his heart. (Selzer, <u>Down from Troy</u> 133)

The preceding sentences each begin with an <u>-ing phrase</u> (the -ing verb plus its noun or pronoun): <u>Judging</u> refers to <u>we</u>; <u>Learning</u> refers to <u>she</u>; and <u>Unbuttoning</u> refers to <u>he</u>.

Verbs have four forms. For some verbs each form is different:

Present (infinitive)	Past	Past Participle	Present Participle
begin	began	begun	beginning
go	went	gone	going

Other verbs repeat one or more of the forms:

bring	brought	brought	bringing
set	set	set	setting

Other verbs form their past and/or past participle by adding <u>-d</u>, <u>-ed</u>, <u>-n</u>, <u>-en</u>, or other endings:

hammered, opened, waved
given, known, taken
kept, slept, wept

Writers use these forms to indicate verb tenses, such as past, present, future, and also the "perfect" tenses (which require "helping" verbs: <u>have spoken</u>, <u>had fought</u>, <u>will have</u> won). You can also use them in other ways.

The <u>-ing</u> form of a verb (the present participle) can be used like an adjective to describe nouns and pronouns. Like other adjectives these <u>-ing</u> verbs help readers understand who, which, what, or what kind of thing you mean.

Beginning a sentence with an <u>-ing</u> phrase can help you omit needless words and can give your sentences flexibility and variety. Consider this complex sentence and a revision of it:

When I studied his arguments, I realized they made sense.

Revision

<u>Studying</u> his arguments, I realized they made sense.

Sentence variety can help keep your reader's attention and strengthen your ethos as a careful writer. It can also help you achieve concise writing (the preceding revision saves two words). If you find many of your sentences begin the same way, you can change some of those sentences by using <u>-ing</u> phrases. Here's another example:

As I waited for the plane, I read my book.

Revision

> Waiting for the plane, I read my book.
> Or: I read my book, waiting for the plane.

Again you save two words, and you don't need to repeat "I."

You can also use -ing phrases to revise compound sentences. Consider this example and two revisions:

> The instructor watched her students write; she wondered if they were prepared.

Revision

> Watching her students write, the instructor wondered if they were prepared.
> Or: The instructor watched her students write, wondering if they were prepared.

The -ing phrases are flexible; you can often move them around in a sentence. Although commonly used at the beginning or end of sentences, an -ing phrase also can be used in the middle:

> Campuses, being concentrations of young people, are awash with hormones, which are powerful. (Will, "Sex Amidst Semicolons" 92)

George Will could have placed "being concentrations of young people" up front:

> Being concentrations of young people, campuses are awash with hormones, which are powerful.

However, by breaking up his main thought with the -ing phrase, Will gives readers a strong reminder. Also, Will's original version captures his writer's voice, which is often layered with parenthetical comments.

You can also use an -ing phrase after a preposition or other introductory word for even more flexibility and variety.

> By shepherding, guiding and protecting our children's souls, we build a better America. (Vice President Al Gore, Democratic National Convention, 1996)

> Since returning to school, the kids have been navigating ever more densely packed schedules. (Dahl 18)

The -ing phrases are extremely useful tools for you as a writer. They provide variety and often save words by combining and compressing thoughts.

Misusing -ing Phrases: Dangling Modifiers

When writers learn how to use -ing phrases at the beginning of sentences, they sometimes create unintentional meanings—called dangling modifiers:

Using Netscape, my foot fell asleep. [Sounds like a foot was using Netscape.]

Repair: To repair this kind of mistake (dangling modifier) you need to supply a subject:

Using Netscape, I realized my foot had fallen asleep.
Or: While I used Netscape, my foot fell asleep.

By writing a rough draft, my main idea will come to me.
[Sounds like "my main idea" is writing the draft.]

Repair

By writing a rough draft, I will discover my main idea.
Or: When I write my rough draft, a main idea will appear.

Watching Psycho, goose bumps covered my arms.
[Sounds like goose bumps watched the movie.]

Repair:

Watching Psycho, I felt goose bumps cover my arms.
Or: When I watched Psycho, goose bumps covered my arms.

To avoid dangling modifiers, make sure the -ing phrase has a noun or pronoun to modify, and always place the -ing phrase as close as possible to the noun or pronoun to which it refers.

Comma Rule: An initial -ing phrase usually requires a comma after it.

ACTIVITY 8

Write three sentences beginning with -ing phrases. Then write a sentence using an -ing phrase in the middle or at the end. Bring your sentences to class to share. Then look at your recent writing. See how often you use -ing phrases. If you don't have any, try to use some. Try to combine and tighten some sentences. Try to use this tool the next time you write.

Using Past Participle -ed or -en Phrases

ACTIVITY 9

In your notebook, try to revise each of the following sentences using an -ed or -en phrase. For example

Because I was tired from writing, I put down my pen. (11 words)

Revision

Tired from writing, I put down my pen. (8 words)

1. When I was confused about my philosophy paper, I took a walk. (12 words)
2. There are people who work at jobs they hate because they are terrified of losing their livelihoods. (17) (Pipher 265)
3. They were scared about the lump; they didn't know what the doctor would say. (14)
4. Someone broke Tim's new monitor beyond repair; it lay in pieces on the floor. (14)
5. We were given a new perspective on the problem and finally found a solution. (14)

Please don't read ahead until you have finished activity 9.

_____

Each of the sentences in activity 9 is proper grammatically; however, they can be tightened by omitting needless words:

1. Confused about my philosophy paper, I took a walk. (9)
2. Terrified of losing their livelihoods, many people work at jobs they hate. (12)
3. Scared about the lump, they didn't know what the doctor would say. (12)
4. Broken beyond repair, Tim's new monitor lay in pieces on the floor. (12)
5. Given a new perspective on the problem, we finally found a solution. (12)

These -ed and -en phrases function like adjectives: they refer to (or modify) nouns and pronouns. Past participles usually have -ed or -en endings. In the first three examples you used an -ed phrase; in the last two examples you used an -en phrase. Some other verbs that have an -en or -n ending for past participle are chosen, driven, frozen, grown, known, sewn, thrown, and woven.

The -ed and -en phrases may not occur as often as -ing phrases, but they are equally useful in helping writers achieve concise sentences. Here are other examples of their effective use:

Urged to attend medical school by his father, Keats proved a desultory student.
(Selzer, <u>Letters to a Young Doctor</u> 174)

Offered the same menu, people make different choices.
(Tannen, <u>You Just Don't Understand</u> 28)

Paralyzed from head to toe, the patient, his mind intact, is imprisoned inside
his own body, unable to speak or move. (Bauby 4)

Comma Rule: If you begin a sentence with an <u>-ed</u> or <u>-en</u> phrase (past participial phrase), place a comma after it.

ACTIVITY 10

Write three sentences beginning with <u>-ed</u> or <u>-en</u> phrases. Bring your sentences
to class to share. Then look at your recent writing. Try to combine and tighten
some sentences by using past participial phrases. Try to use this tool the next
time you write.

Using <u>to</u> Phrases

What stylistic pattern do these sentences have in common?

To think critically, you must see hidden differences and similarities.
To polish a rough draft, a writer should evaluate each word and each sentence.

To understand how pervasive and surreal the violence in our mass media has
become, we need to step back and look at our own culture as if we were
outsiders. (Prothrow-Stith 31)

Each sentence begins with a phrase made of <u>to</u> and a verb. An <u>infinitive</u> is a
form of a verb beginning with the word <u>to</u>: such as <u>to argue, to persuade,</u> or <u>to
convince</u>. The infinitive is another way to start a sentence: it provides yet
another way to achieve flexibility and variety that can help you hold your reader's
attention.

Comma Rule: A sentence beginning with an infinitive usually requires a comma
after the <u>to</u> phrase.

ACTIVITY 11

In your notebook combine the following sentences, using a <u>to</u> phrase to begin the sentence. Your revision should contain fewer words than the original.

1. Jane Doe wants to change the image of God as male. She refers to God as female. (17 words)
2. Dr. Richard Seed wants to clone the first human. He seeks money from donors to help him. (17)
3. Martin Luther King Jr. wanted to unite blacks and whites. He delivered his speech before the Lincoln Memorial. (18)

<u>Please don't read ahead until you have finished activity 11</u>.

———————————

To combine these sentences, you changed some of the word order and saved a few words, such as

1. To change the image of God as male, Jane Doe refers to God as female. (15)
2. To clone the first human, Dr. Richard Seed seeks money from donors to help him. (15)
3. To unite blacks and whites, Martin Luther King Jr. delivered his speech before the Lincoln Memorial. (16)

Infinitive phrases are useful sentence tools. They create variety for your thoughts.

<u>To</u> phrases (infinitive phrases) can also function as complete subjects themselves.

To argue well requires paying attention to logos, pathos, and ethos.

To be fair-minded is a hallmark of critical thinking.

To dwell upon bone is to contemplate the fate of man. (Selzer, <u>Mortal Lessons</u> 54)

In each of these sentences the subject is an entire phrase: <u>To be fair-minded</u>, <u>To argue well</u>, and <u>To dwell upon bone</u>. Thus, infinitive phrases are versatile. They also add formality to your voice, if this is what you want for a particular situation and audience.

ACTIVITY 12

Write three sentences beginning with a <u>to</u> phrase that refers to the subject of the sentence. Then write a sentence beginning with an infinitive phrase that functions as the subject of the sentence. Bring your sentences to class to share. Then look at your recent writing. Try to combine and tighten some sentences by using infinitive phrases. Try to use this tool the next time you write.

———————————

Chapter 4

Thinking with Contraries

Thinking begins [. . .] in a <u>forked-road</u> situation, a situation that is ambiguous, that presents a dilemma, that proposes alternatives. (Dewey, <u>How We Think</u> 14)

I believe that opposite mentalities or processes can enhance each other rather than interfere with each other if we engage in them in the right spirit. (Elbow, <u>Embracing Contraries</u> 152)

As you have seen, critical thinking involves communicating clearly, persuading readers, arguing different points of view, and analyzing what you read and hear. In chapter 3 you examined various strategies of argumentation. However, there is another important strategy that many artists, philosophers, and scientists use. We call it "thinking with contraries."

To help you discover the principle, let's look at examples of it before we discuss what it is. First, here is an excerpt from <u>Herzog</u>, a novel by Saul Bellow, in which a father is talking with his young daughter.

"Papa?"
"Yes, June."
"Tell me about the most-most."
For an instant he did not remember. "Ah," he said, "you mean that club in New York where people are the most of everything."
"That's the story."
She sat between his knees on the chair. He tried to make more room for her. "There's this association that people belong to. They're the most of every type. There's the hairiest bald man, and the baldest hairy man."
"The fattest thin lady."

"And the thinnest fat woman. The tallest dwarf and the smallest giant. They're all in it. The weakest strong man, and the strongest weak man. The stupidest wise man and the smartest blockhead. Then they have things like crippled acrobats, and ugly beauties."

"And what do they do, Papa?"

"On Saturday night they have a dinner-dance. They have a contest."

"To tell each other apart."

"Yes, sweetheart. And if you can tell the hairiest bald man from the baldest hairy man, you get a prize."

Bless her, she enjoyed her father's nonsense. (295–96)

Is the kind of thinking in this passage "nonsense"? You may argue, "Yes, of course it is. It's not logical." Yet you may also argue, "Well, it does make sense in a playful way. It does involve a kind of logic. Words and ideas are reversed, yet both pairs mean the same thing." What do you think?

Critical thinking often involves noticing and exploring contraries or opposites. Albert Rothenberg reports in "Creative Contradictions" that in 1907, while struggling to make sense of Newton's theory of gravitation, Albert Einstein experienced a eureka: "the happiest thought of my life," Einstein said—"a person falling from the roof of a house was both in motion and at rest <u>at the same time</u>" (qtd. in Rothenberg 55). Although Einstein's idea seemed illogical, it made paradoxical sense and generated his theory of relativity. Scientists James Watson and Francis Crick explored opposites when they discovered that DNA is composed of "<u>identical but spatially opposed chains</u>," which they called "the double helix" (Rothenberg 60).

Does the following statement make sense? "The crystal never sparkles more brightly than in the cavern." It seems contradictory. But if a cave were not dark, it would be difficult to notice a bright crystal or light within it. A small light within a dark place is brighter than a candle flame at noon. Imagine a photograph in which a black bowling ball rests on a white stool in the center of a totally white room. What would you notice more: the black ball or the white room? You would notice <u>both</u> black and white, but your eye would be drawn to the ball, much as your eye would be drawn to a bright crystal in a dark cave. Although these examples are opposites, they suggest the same point: <u>Contrast produces awareness. When you notice contrasts, you think</u>.

Consider this short poem by John Stone, a physician.

Death

I have seen come on
slowly as rust
sand

or suddenly as when
someone leaving
a room

finds the doorknob
come loose in his hand (10)

This poem uses contrast: two different views of death. What kinds of death are slow like the creation of rust or the buildup of sand? Certain forms of cancer, Alzheimer's disease, AIDS, muscular dystrophy. The rust image suggests a gradual falling apart; the sand image suggests a gradual accumulation of earth that covers over or buries someone, perhaps an accumulation of fat in arteries or alcohol in a liver. The other image of sudden death is unsettling to imagine: if you grabbed a doorknob that came off in your hand, you would be surprised or shocked. You might fall back. Perhaps this is how a massive heart attack feels or death by a sudden accident. The contrast in this poem enables you to imagine how death might feel. Although there is a wide middle area of death which is neither slow nor sudden, the poem focuses on the contraries because they provoke powerful emotion and thought in the most concise way.

Thinking with contraries may appear not to make sense at first, but on further analysis, it does make sense: <u>two contrary ideas combine or interplay with each other to express some idea or truth</u>. Such contrary thinking is a way of exploring opposites to help you generate ideas and to evaluate what you read and hear. This strategy can take critical and creative forms, and this chapter helps you examine and practice both.

Thinking with contraries—also called dialectical thinking because it involves a dialogue or give and take between different points of view—is as natural for you as your thumbs. That is, you have <u>opposable</u> thumbs, which exist in opposition to your fingers. If you pull your fingers and thumb together as if making a hand shadow talk on a wall, you see that your thumb opposes your fingers. Your opposable thumbs enable you to grab onto things and hold them. Although you don't have fingers and thumbs in your mind, you do have the ability to think of opposites and to consider how they go or don't go together. As novelist F. Scott Fitzgerald wrote, "The test of a first-rate intelligence is the ability to hold two opposed ideas in the mind at the same time—and still retain the ability to function" (qtd. in Elbow, <u>Embracing Contraries</u> 234).

Figure 4.1. Sally Forth cartoon. (<u>Detroit Free Press</u>) 15 Oct. 1996. Reprinted with special permission of King Features Syndicate.)

This strategy of thought helps you see different perspectives, an essential quality of critical thinking. Consider the "Sally Forth" cartoon in Figure 4.1.

Cartoonist Greg Howard presents a contrast: while you have heard the phrase "Founding Fathers" many times, you have probably never considered the idea of "Founding Mothers." This opposite produces a sudden awareness, helping you realize that American history classes and textbooks often leave out women, as if women did not take part in founding our country. Hilary's point makes her father realize something he did not know before. This is a hallmark of thinking with contraries: you realize viewpoints and ideas you did not consider before.

Writing expert Ken Macrorie expresses the importance of thinking with contraries:

> Strong writers bring together oppositions of one kind or another. [. . .] What they choose to present from life—whether it be object, act, or idea—is frequently the negative and the positive, one thing and its opposite, two ideas that antagonize each other. The result is tension. And the surprise that comes from new combinations. [. . .] The most available and obvious truths are frequently closed to us because we are not open to possible surprise, to seeing the opposite of the common. [. . .] Make a habit to look for oppositions. You will find suddenly that you are wiser than you thought. Do it automatically. If you find yourself putting down <u>hot</u>, consider the possibility of <u>cold</u> in the same circumstances; if <u>simple</u>, then <u>complex</u>; if <u>loving</u>, then <u>hating</u>; etc. The habit will prevent you from oversimplifying people, processes and ideas. (71–74)

ACTIVITY 1

In your notebook, reflect on what you have read so far in this chapter. Does thinking with contraries make sense to you? Do you recall ever noticing opposites or striking differences before? What happened? Describe one example and then explain what you realized or learned from the contrast.

USING CONTRADICTIONS AND PARADOXES FOR CRITICAL THINKING

> Without contraries is no progression. (Blake, "The Marriage of Heaven and Hell" 9)

Contradictions

Writers often discover ideas by noticing contradictions. Imagine you are talking with your mother about school and you say you don't like English classes. On hearing this she says, "But you enjoy reading and writing—how can you not like English classes? This is a contradiction!" Depending on how she vocalizes her last statement, you might interpret it as a criticism or as an invitation for further thought.

Sometimes a contradiction feels like a pickle in baseball: caught between two players, you can be tagged out. But contradictions are useful because they help you think; instead of being called out, you're given an opportunity to keep playing—and the game becomes more interesting. Peter Elbow, author of several composition books including <u>Embracing Contraries</u> and <u>Writing without Teachers,</u> recommends that writers should welcome contradictions.

> Encourage conflicts and contradictions in your thinking. We are usually taught to avoid them; and we cooperate in this teaching because it is confusing or frustrating to hold two conflicting ideas at the same time. It feels like a dead end or a trap but really it is the most fruitful situation to be in. <u>Unless you can get yourself into a contradiction, you may be stuck with no power to have any thoughts other than the ones you are already thinking</u>. (Emphasis ours) (<u>Writing without Teachers</u> 50)

American poet Walt Whitman heartily embraced contradictions. In "Song of Myself" he proclaims:

> Do I contradict myself?
> Very well then . . . . I contradict myself;
> I am large . . . . I contain multitudes. (85)

In developing your own critical powers, try to understand statements such as Whitman's. He embraces the idea of contradiction—saying he embodies many contrary forces within himself. But don't you as well? Don't all humans?

Contradictions spark thought. As a writer you can deliberately look for them, as these students do in their notebooks.

```
You can feel very close to someone who's very far away. My
best friend (actually one of my three best friends) lives in
Switzerland and has had a completely separate life from me
for three years. Despite this, through our frequent letters
I feel just as close to her as I did when we lived in the
same town, let alone the same continent. At times I feel
that I can relate to Sarah even more than I can to my other
two friends here in Michigan. When she moved farther away
physically we became closer mentally and emotionally since
we were forced to evaluate exactly what our friendship meant
to each other. (Allison Topham, student)
```

A contradiction is wise men who are foolish. Consider the biblical story of David and Bathsheeba. David was a wise king who ended up acting very foolishly. He saw Bathsheeba bathing and he gave into his feelings of lust. He had an affair with her despite the fact that he was married. He then proceeded to orchestrate the death of Bathsheeba's husband, so that he could be with her. David was wise but wrong. (Anne Griffith, student)

Everyday in life we tell "true lies." Women ask men for opinions on their appearance, and men reply with "You look wonderful." Even if the man disagrees, he'll say "You look wonderful." Another example is when children take music lessons and ask their parents how they sound. Usually the parents think their child is producing noise--similar to the sound of farm animals being maimed! Despite this, the parents will turn to their child and tell her that she sounds wonderful. Yet, in a way the child does sound wonderful because she is learning to make music. (Anne Griffith, student)

Critical thinkers notice contradictions in meanings of words. Using his own personal experience and observation, student Mike Slater examines contraries to help him define "pride."

Although Grover from <u>Sesame Street</u> tells us "Everybody should be proud of themselves," pride is also one of the seven deadly sins. A contradiction, pride can be a concept of good or evil.

    The main benefit of pride is that it gives people a reinforcement for doing good work. This is one reason why there are so many volunteers in America. My Grandpa Matiyow volunteers at St. Mary's hospital in my hometown. Once he told me that even though he doesn't get paid, the feeling of pride he gets in helping others is more than worth the effort. He also creates birdhouses for his family and

(box continues)

friends. He spends hours each day meticulously perfecting his latest design. Grandpa always leads visitors downstairs into the dark corner of his basement where his birdhouses surround them. The gleam in the old man's eyes when he shows off his craft proves to me the importance of pride.

When is pride a harbinger of evil? In medieval times, pride was seen as putting one's self before God, rather than accepting humility as a way to approach religion. For a modern example, turn to any fashion magazine. Women today are made to think they have to be the picture-perfect super model: thin, glamorous, and sexy. I know extremely good-looking girls who torture themselves and their loved ones in their never-ending desire to achieve what they believe is the perfect weight, look, and body. One of my friends is at her perfect weight, yet she still insists on dieting to lose another <u>eight</u> pounds. Another friend who already weighs less than 100 pounds forces herself to throw up each time she consumes a large meal. Unnecessary plastic surgery on breasts, faces, and hips have permanently damaged countless women all because of pride.

Pride is an ambiguous concept because it holds both positive and negative meanings. I suggest we keep the positive meaning of pride but replace the negative meaning with "vanity." I'd amend the seven deadly sins to replace Pride with Vanity as well. When was the last time you heard someone say, "You should be vain of your accomplishments?" This way, the meaning becomes more clear, and Pride can truly be used in a positive way.

By exploring pride's positive and negative meanings, Mike analyzes the contradictory nature of the word. Pride contains meaningful contraries for him because his grandfather and female friends exemplify the same word in different ways. Mike arrives at an insight by suggesting that "vanity" replace the negative meaning of pride.

ACTIVITY 2

Write a brief essay about a contradiction. First try to generate a list of contradictions that you see in your own life or in your family, friends, education, employment, the media, government, or society. Explore three of these in your notebook. Then select the contradiction that intrigues you most and write about it. Or explore one of these contradictions: how someone or something can be strong yet weak, beautiful yet ugly, kind yet cruel, afraid yet brave, happy yet sad.

PARADOXES

Critical thinkers notice and examine paradoxes such as this:

> We must grasp the topic in the rough, before we smooth it out and shape it. (Whitehead, <u>Modes of Thought</u> 8)

Writers are like artists who work with clay. No one starts out with a finished product (sculpture, apple pie, or essay). Some process must take place first—grabbing an idea and a clump of supporting evidence like a scoop of red clay. The rough idea becomes a precisely stated thesis. Taking away unnecessary words like excess clay, you shape your ideas and polish them.

The words <u>contradiction</u> and <u>paradox</u> are closely related; both involve a joining of contraries or opposites. <u>Webster's New World</u> defines contradiction as "a condition in which things tend to be contrary to each other" (302) and paradox as "a statement that seems contradictory, unbelievable, or absurd but that may actually be true" (979). If you placed a hand on a hot iron but felt no pain, this would be a contradiction. However, the title of the rock song "Hurts So Good" by John Cougar Mellencamp is a paradox.

Although "Hurts So Good" seems contradictory, the test for a paradox is whether it expresses truth. How can anything that hurts be good? Within the song Mellencamp sings that love hurts yet feels good. Does his statement apply to other activities besides love—such as running five miles a day, weight-lifting, or writing? Yes, they may hurt while you perform them but you feel good when finished. To distinguish contradiction from paradox, let's conclude that <u>a paradox is a contradictory statement that involves truth—often a surprising truth</u>.

Critical thinkers pay attention to paradoxes. They notice and explore them, as the following three students do in their notebooks:

"The end is the beginning." It is a common statement that   1
expresses two opposites in conjunction. This paradox seems
to clash unless you look at its true meaning and start
to think about your life. After all, each time we end
something, there is always something else coming after it.

(box continues)

We do not cease to live because one stage in life is over;
we move on to the next stage. I never paid much attention to
this idea until my great-grandmother clarified it for me.
She mentioned that in the natural world another stage always
follows the previous one, such as day to night or winter to
spring. She spoke of hope, for all things end while bringing
fresh starts with them.

Last May, my father and I noticed that half of the
people in my graduating class were referring to the upcoming
ceremony as "graduation" while the other half called it
"commencement." One indicates an ending, the other a
beginning, yet both are correct. (Amy Pardee, student)

2

Tragedy is our greatest opportunity. Only from the depths
of despair can we rise to our greatest heights. Each bad
experience brings with it a chance for hope and joy. Maybe
that could be considered "disgusting optimism" or "pathetic
happiness." When my car got stuck in a snowbank, I had
already had a bad day and was frustrated. As I sat waiting
for a tow, my irritation turned to acceptance, and soon I
was glad I got stuck there. Right across the street two
girls were also stuck. I was strong enough to push their
little Hyundai out of the snow. They couldn't help me, but I
was glad I was there to help them. Last May when we lost
power for a week, it was a nuisance--food spoiled, we cooked
oatmeal on the grill--but we had the greatest week of family
time we'd had since the kids were little. I saw it as an
opportunity to make the best of a bad situation. (Mary
Rosalez, student)

Luke 6:27: "But if you are willing to listen, I say, love
your enemies. Do good to those who hate you. Pray for the
happiness of those who curse you. Pray for those who hurt
you." This passage in the Bible provides great paradox.
"Love your enemies" doesn't seem to make sense when your
enemies are the ones you are taught to hate. To "do good to
those who hate you" seems the opposite of what is pushed
into our minds from a society driven on self-satisfaction.

(box continues)

To pray for the happiness of a person who brings you grief
goes against what seems normal—usually we are told to
get even. Although these statements seem to contradict
themselves, they make perfect sense. Jesus told us to let
love rise above hate. You cannot put out a fire with
gasoline, but with water things can be accomplished. In the
same manner, you cannot disperse someone's anger by adding
your own wrath; only love can rise above the anger.
(Erica Erlewine, student)

By exploring paradoxes, these students show keen critical thinking.
    In this brief essay a student shares her discovery of a paradox.

Quiet's Noise

Kelly Betzold

We think of quiet as being without noise, but it can never   1
really be quiet, for there are <u>always</u> noises if you listen
hard enough.

    One night at home, when I couldn't sleep, I listened to   2
the quiet. Within my own room, I could hear my own breathing
and the thumping of my heart. The sheets rustled as I turned,
and my cat, Yin, purred happily at the end of my bed. My alarm
clock ticked with a systematic rhythm, louder than I could
recall, and the heater periodically turned on and then off
again.

    My room was not the only place where quiet let its sounds   3
escape; the rest of the house held its share of noises as
well. The refrigerator grumbled every once in a while, the
toilet occasionally flushed, and the faint sound of music could
be heard from my brother Brian's stereo. A light switch clicked
on, a door closed, and a creak came from the floor as someone
walked by. Bear, the dog, walked across the linoleum kitchen
floor and slurped up some water. The washing machine churned
away at our clothes, and the dryer hummed warmly.

    Outside I could hear the wind--seeping through my window   4
and blowing through the leaves. Branches rubbed together and

(box continues)

brushed against the roof. A car door slammed. As I lay there
listening, a car passed, a garage door squeaked, and a dog
barked—thus setting off a chorus of neighborhood dogs!

All of these sounds I heard within the quiet, and this is   5
but one example. Most anywhere you may be, it can never truly
be quiet, because if you really listen, there is still noise.
In fact, quiet contains more noise than loud does; it just
contains noises that are seldom noticed. Loudness covers up all
of these usually undetected sounds and so is just one big
noise. Therefore, loud is really quieter than quiet and quiet
is really louder than loud! Confused? Merely try to listen
once, and you won't be any longer. I listened, and I can see
why I couldn't sleep! Shhh! Be very, very quiet . . . and
listen.

Kelly's essay builds to a surprising paradox: "loud is really quieter than quiet and quiet is really louder than loud!" By paying close attention, she moves from describing sounds in her bedroom to throughout her house to outside her house in order to collect supporting evidence for her thesis. Kelly takes a risk in thinking in an unusual way. Some readers may consider her idea foolish. But critical thinkers take the risk of thinking unusual thoughts if they can support them and if they express truth.

Your life contains many paradoxes, though you may not notice them. You may now be living in a paradox regarding your school. On the one hand, <u>life at private colleges is more public than private</u>. True? If you attend a small private college, is there less privacy? On the other hand, <u>life at large public universities is more private than public</u>. True? If you attend a large university, do you have more anonymity? Thinking with contraries can help you identify and explore paradoxes.

Paradox is a common feature of religion and philosophy. That Christ was born from a virgin is a paradox. "A Time for Everything" from Ecclesiastes in the King James version of the Bible is paradoxical, as this excerpt shows:

To everything there is a season, and a time to every purpose under the heaven:
[2] A time to be born, and a time to die; a time to plant, and a time to pluck up that which is planted;
[3] A time to kill, and a time to heal; a time to break down, and a time to build up;
[4] A time to weep, and a time to laugh; a time to mourn, and a time to dance.
(Ecclesiastes 3:1–4)

The ancient Chinese philosophy of yin and yang is paradoxical. Yin is "the passive, negative, feminine force or principle in the universe"; yang is "the active, positive, masculine force or principle in the universe" (Webster's New World 1549, 1546). The moon symbolizes yin; the sun symbolizes yang. According to this philosophy, the contrasting forces of yin and yang complement each other and create balance in the universe. As a critical thinker you may question the validity of yin/yang in today's world. Does this philosophy stereotype women and men?

Paradox and Tolerance for Ambiguity

Thinking with contraries helps you develop a high tolerance for ambiguity and a low tolerance for either/or thinking. Being "ambiguous" means "1. having two or more possible meanings 2. not clear; indefinite; uncertain; vague" (Webster's New World 43). Because paradoxes are ambiguous, they provoke inquiry. Sydney J. Harris, a newspaper columnist, said, "The universe is the same for all of us and different for each of us" (9A). How can this be so? The universe is the same for us because we are all human beings. But the universe is different for each of us because we are individually different and unique.

"For every thing you gain, you lose something," wrote Ralph Waldo Emerson in "Compensation" (58). True? His statement is ambiguous in part because of the generality of the words "every thing" and "something." When you gain something, you lose something of the person you were before you gained it. If you learn how to use semicolons and colons well, you lose much of the uncertainty you felt when you didn't understand how to structure your thoughts in different ways. If you learn how to excel in singing, you lose much of the fear you felt when you didn't sing well—which motivated you to excel. If you learn through painful experience that some people are deceitful, you lose some innocence. Because Emerson's statement generates multiple meanings, it is ambiguous. What examples could you give to support his paradox?

As a critical thinker, try not only to tolerate ambiguity but to welcome it. Many problems are too complex to be solved with only one answer. Look for different perspectives from which to see multiple meanings. Roger von Oech, in a playful book called A Whack on the Side of the Head, teaches readers to think ambiguously. He writes, "What is half of 8? One answer is 4. But if you assume that the question is ambiguous, you'll look for other answers such as 0, 3, E, M, and 'eig,' all depending on how you define 'half' " (76–77). He also uses Figure 4.2.

"What is this figure?" von Oech asks. "If you look at it one way, it's a bird; if you look at it another way, it could be a question mark; if you turn it upside down, it looks like a seal juggling a ball on its nose. By assuming an ambiguous attitude, you generate a variety of ideas" (77).

If you saw a bird in the figure and stopped looking for other images, you shortchanged your thinking. Through the countless multiple-choice tests and quizzes you have taken in school, you have been conditioned to look for "one right answer." The problem with this, explains von Oech, is that "if you think there is only one right answer, then you will stop looking as soon as you find

Figure 4.2. Bird/Question Mark. (From <u>A Whack on the Side</u>
<u>of the Head</u> by Roger Von Oech. Copyright © 1983, 1990, 1998
by Roger Von Oech. By permission of Warner Books, Inc.)

one" (21). He advises instead that you look for <u>plural answers</u> when you explore
questions and problems.

ACTIVITY 3

On the Web or in your library, find at least two quotes that contain contraries
or seem paradoxical. Write each quote down, cite your source, and briefly
explain why the quote is paradoxical. Examples

Eternal life belongs to those who live in the present. (Wittgenstein)

The cut worm forgives the plough. (Blake, "The Marriage of Heaven and
Hell" 11)

If the fool would persist in his folly he would become wise. (Blake, "The
Marriage of Heaven and Hell" 11)

Either/Or Thinking

Either/or thinking is seductive. It often sounds good and makes quick, easy
sense. For example, in the movie <u>Harvey</u> with James Stewart, Stewart plays Elwood
P. Dowd, an eccentric and lovable man whose best friend is a six-foot tall, imaginary rabbit named Harvey. At one point in the movie Dowd says, "My mother
taught me a lesson many years ago [. . .] that in this world you can be oh so smart
or oh so pleasant. I was smart for 35 years. I recommend pleasant." Although this
may sound nice, it's a false dilemma—another term for simplistic either/or thinking. Why can't Elwood P. Dowd and all of us try to be <u>both</u> smart and pleasant?

Thinking with contraries counteracts simplistic either/or thinking. Rather than think black <u>versus</u> white, you can think black <u>and</u> white—and see various shades of gray. Rather than think that scientists are analytical and artists are creative, you can consider that scientists also are creative and artists also are analytical. Rather than stereotype men as fierce competitors and women as nurturers, you can argue that many men are nurturers and many woman fierce competitors—and that it's possible for a person to be both a competitor and a nurturer, depending on the situation.

In a chapter called "Oxygen Deprivation: Bad Intellectual Habits" from her book <u>Fire with Fire,</u> Naomi Wolf identifies either/or views that have hurt feminism: "You are either victim or oppressor; you are either for or against us; you are either a nonsexist woman or a sexist man" (107). The alternative to such either/or thinking is <u>both/and thinking</u>. Thus, both men and women can be victims and oppressors. You can be both for and against feminism (there are various forms of feminism). Both women and men can be nonsexist and both can be sexist, depending on the individual. Thinking with contraries goes beyond simple either/or views.

As a critical thinker, try to notice either/or statements and look for possible middle grounds or "third alternatives" as Stephen Covey calls them in <u>The Seven Habits of Highly Effective People</u> (273). A little alarm should ring or red flag appear when you hear or read them. Consider either/or statements as invitations for further thought—to see what hides between the extremes. If someone says, "It is either day or night," suggest that it may be dawn or dusk. If someone says, "You either write well or you don't," suggest that this assessment depends on each individual paper you write.

Not all either/or statements are false, however. In her song "Diamonds & Rust" folk singer Joan Baez says that memories "bring diamonds and rust." When you recall memories, are they extremely positive or negative? This seems true, for the most part. What happens to the wide majority of your memories in between these extremes? Do they fade? Do they become indistinguishable and thus forgettable?

Critical thinkers enjoy paradoxes and ambiguity but develop warning signals for simplistic either/or thinking. If you see something paradoxical, if you examine it, you may arrive at an insightful understanding of it.

ACTIVITY 4

Please read the following paradoxes. Choose two that intrigue you most. Then write about them in your notebook, trying to make sense of them.

1. Desire causes suffering; therefore, we should desire not to desire. But how can we desire not to desire? (This paradox is at the center of Buddhism.)
2. "What lies behind us and what lies before us are tiny matters compared to what lies within us." (Oliver Wendell Holmes)

3. "The world outside your skin is just as much you as the world inside: they move together inseparably." (Alan Watts 112)

4. "The indirect is always as great and real as the direct." (Walt Whitman 19)

5. "An ounce of experience is better than a ton of theory." (John Dewey, <u>Democracy and Education</u> 169)

6. "No one can be moral [. . .] without coming to a working arrangement between the angel in himself and the devil in himself, between his rose above and his manure below. The two forces or tendencies are mutually interdependent, and the game is a working game just so long as the angel is winning, but does not win, and the devil is losing, but is never lost." (Alan Watts 119–20)

ACTIVITY 5

Write an essay about a paradox. First try to generate some paradoxes that you see in your own life or in your family, friends, education, employment, the media, government, or society. Select a paradox that means the most to you and write about it. Or explore one of these paradoxes:

> Less is more.
> Winning is like losing sometimes.
> You need to lose yourself to find yourself.
> A longer way can be a shorter way.
> The more things change, the more they stay the same.

THINKING WITH CONTRARIES TO EVALUATE WHAT YOU READ

> All things are known by their differences from and likenesses to each other. (Watts 130)

If it is true that you know the world by noticing differences and likenesses, then as a critical thinker you should deliberately look for them not only in your own experience but also in what you read. Doing so will enable you to consider different perspectives—to keep your mind open. Thinking with contraries is a useful strategy for evaluating other people's writing.

Let's look at an excerpt from John Gray's book <u>Men, Women and Relationships</u>. As you read this, look for contrasts and connections—large and small. Consider whether Gray uses critical thinking well, whether what he claims is true.

Wallets and Purses

John Gray

Contrasts in how men and women confront the world are most visually appar- 1
ent when we compare a woman's purse with a man's wallet. Women carry large,
heavy bags with beautiful decorations and shiny colors, while men carry lightweight, plain black or brown wallets that are designed to carry only the bare
essentials: a driver's license, major credit cards, and paper money. One can never
be too sure what one will find when looking into a woman's purse. Even she
may not know. But one thing is for sure, she will be carrying everything else
she could possibly need, along with whatever others may need too.

When looking in a woman's purse the first thing you find is a collection 2
of other, littler purses and containers. It's as though she carries her own private
drugstore and office combined. You may find a wallet, a coin purse, a makeup
kit, a mirror, an organizer and calendar, a checkbook, a small calculator, another
small makeup kit with a little mirror, a hair brush and comb, an address book,
an older address book for really old friends, an eyeglass container, sunglasses
in another container, a package of tissue, several partially used tissues, tampons,
a condom package or diaphragm, a set of keys, an extra set of keys, her
husband's keys, a toothbrush, toothpaste, breath spray, plain floss, flavored
floss (her children like mint), a little container of aspirin, another container of
vitamins and pills, two or three nail files, four or five pens and pencils, several
little pads of paper, a roll of film in its container and an empty film container,
a package of business cards from friends and experts in all fields, a miniature
picture album of her loved ones, lip balm, tea bags, another package of pain-
relief pills, an envelope filled with receipts, various letters and cards from loved
ones, stamps, a small package of bills to be paid, and a host of other miscel-
laneous items like paper clips, rubber bands, safety pins, barrettes, bobby pins,
fingernail clippers, stationery and matching envelopes, gum, trail mix, assorted
discount coupons, breath mints, and bits of garbage to be thrown away (next
spring). In short, she has everything she could need and carries it with her wherever she goes.

To a woman, her purse is her security blanket, a trusted friend, an impor- 3
tant part of her self. You can tell how expanded a woman's awareness is by the
size of her purse. She is prepared for every emergency, wherever she may find
herself.

Ironically, when she is being escorted to a grand ball she will leave this 4
purse at home and bring a little shiny purse with the bare essentials. In this
case, she feels that this night is for her. She is being taken care of by her man
and she doesn't have to feel responsible for anybody. She feels so special and
so supported that she doesn't need the security of her purse. (85–87) □

Although John Gray clearly uses contrast in this excerpt, do you find his connections between women and purses true? In large part, his thinking is either/or, stereotypical, and could be offensive to many women readers—but this depends on how you perceive his tone. Is he serious, mock-serious, or playfully exaggerating? As a critical thinker you can examine his assumptions and generalizations.

Do men's wallets and women's purses accurately reflect the way they "confront the world"? Wallets and purses are simplistic belongings to convey the complexity of men and women. Gray paints in broad strokes: surely all or most women do not "carry large, heavy bags with beautiful decorations and shiny colors." Many women do, but to imply that all women do is a sweeping generalization. Also, many men carry more than the essentials in their wallets—many carry photographs of loved ones.

Readers may infer that Gray is condescending toward women when he claims that "One can never be too sure what one will find when looking into a woman's purse. Even she may not know." When he states, "But one thing is for sure," it is not a certainty that a woman will carry "everything she could possibly need, along with whatever others may need too." But if you find Gray's tone mock-serious or playful, you can accept his statements.

Is Gray's second paragraph reasonable? Although he qualifies his enormously long third sentence with "may" ("You may find . . . "), his list is so long and detailed it soon becomes absurd. Cleverly, however, his sentence reflects what he considers the typical woman's purse: it is bloated with details—with stuff.

In his third paragraph, is Gray correct in stating a woman's purse is "an important part of her self"? Yes, much as a wallet is important to a man—it holds a person's identification. But how logical is Gray in this assertion: "You can tell how expanded a woman's awareness is by the size of her purse"? If this were true, you could infer that the smaller a woman's purse, the smaller her awareness. But awareness of what? Of the needs of other people? Can a woman with a large purse be "prepared for every emergency, wherever she may find herself"? We doubt it. We believe Gray's connection between purse size and awareness is an exaggeration.

By equating women with purses and men with wallets, John Gray heightens a simplistic contrast. If readers consider his logical appeals weak, they may question his ethos or character, especially given his reputation as a best-selling author on the subject of women and men. But if readers consider his logos accurate and insightful, they will likely admire his ethos.

Many writers think with contraries not only to discover their ideas but also to support and defend them. In the following excerpt from You Just Don't Understand: Women and Men in Conversation, Deborah Tannen explains two ideas. As you read, look for contrasts and connections. Consider whether she uses critical thinking well, whether what she claims is true.

Intimacy and Independence

Deborah Tannen

<u>Intimacy</u> is key in a world of connection where individuals negotiate complex   1
networks of friendship, minimize differences, try to reach consensus, and avoid
the appearance of superiority, which would highlight differences. In a world of
status, <u>independence</u> is key, because a primary means of establishing status is
to tell others what to do, and taking orders is a marker of low status. Though
all humans need both intimacy and independence, women tend to focus on the
first and men on the second. It is as if their lifeblood ran in different directions.

These differences can give women and men differing views of the same   2
situation, as they did in the case of a couple I will call Linda and Josh. When
Josh's old high-school chum called him at work and announced he'd be in town
on business the following month, Josh invited him to stay for the weekend. That
evening he informed Linda that they were going to have a houseguest, and that
he and his chum would go out together the first night to shoot the breeze like
old times. Linda was upset. She was going to be away on business the week
before, and the Friday night when Josh would be out with his chum would be
her first night home. But what upset her the most was that Josh had made these
plans on his own and informed her of them, rather than discussing them with
her before extending the invitation.

Linda would never make plans, for a weekend or an evening, without first   3
checking with Josh. She can't understand why he doesn't show her the same
courtesy and consideration that she shows him. But when she protests, Josh
says, "I can't say to my friend, 'I have to ask my wife for permission'!"

To Josh, checking with his wife means seeking permission, which implies   4
that he is not independent, not free to act on his own. It would make him feel
like a child or an underling. To Linda, checking with her husband has nothing
to do with permission. She assumes that spouses discuss their plans with each
other because their lives are intertwined, so the actions of one have consequences for the other. Not only does Linda not mind telling someone, "I have
to check with Josh"; quite the contrary—she likes it. It makes her feel good to
know and show that she is involved with someone, that her life is bound up
with someone else's.

Linda and Josh both felt more upset by this incident, and others like it,   5
than seemed warranted, because it cut to the core of their primary concerns.
Linda was hurt because she sensed a failure of closeness in their relationship:
He didn't care about her as much as she cared about him. And he was hurt
because he felt she was trying to control him and limit his freedom.

A similar conflict exists between Louise and Howie, another couple, about   6
spending money. Louise would never buy anything costing more than a hundred
dollars without discussing it with Howie, but he goes out and buys whatever he

wants and feels they can afford, like a table saw or a new power mower. Louise is disturbed, not because she disapproves of the purchases, but because she feels he is acting as if she were not in the picture.

Many women feel it is natural to consult with their partners at every turn, 7 while many men automatically make more decisions without consulting their partners. This may reflect a broad difference in conceptions of decision making. Women expect decisions to be discussed first and made by consensus. They appreciate the discussion itself as evidence of involvement and communication. But many men feel oppressed by lengthy discussions about what they see as minor decisions, and they feel hemmed in if they can't just act without talking first. [. . .]

Communication is a continual balancing act, juggling the conflicting needs 8 for intimacy and independence. To survive in the world, we have to act in concert with others, but to survive as ourselves, rather than simply as cogs in a wheel, we have to act alone. In some ways, all people are the same: We all eat and sleep and drink and laugh and cough, and often we eat, and laugh at, the same things. But in some ways, each person is different, and individuals' differing wants and preferences may conflict with each other. Offered the same menu, people make different choices. And if there is cake for dessert, there is a chance one person may get a larger piece than another—and an even greater chance that one will <u>think</u> the other's piece is larger, whether it is or not. (26–28) □

Tannen's argument and evidence are more complex and qualified than John Gray's. Although Tannen uses intimacy and independence as contrary behaviors, she does not fall into the either/or thinking trap because she acknowledges that "all humans need both intimacy and independence." Her use of "tend to" further qualifies her idea: "women tend to focus on the first and men on the second."

Tannen defends her idea with examples of Linda and Josh and Louise and Howie. Both men behave in similar ways: they act without discussing their actions with their wives. Both women behave in similar ways: they feel let down and ignored. Whether these two examples are truly representative of women and men in our society is debatable, which helped to make Tannen's book a best-seller.

IRONY AS THINKING WITH CONTRARIES

<u>Irony</u> implies the opposite of what someone means or expects. When asked what you think about mother's new hat, you may believe the hat is atrocious, but not wanting to hurt her feelings, you may say something innocuous, such as "I've never seen such a hat!"

Critical thinkers look for and evaluate ironies. They notice that it is odd when an automobile mechanic drives a car that keeps breaking down, when a fire station burns to the ground, when nurses abuse patients they supposedly care for. A wealthy woman, believing she is about to die, gives away all her wealth, only to learn from her doctor that her malady is trivial, and she will have a long and active life. That's irony.

In The Shelter of Each Other: Rebuilding Our Families, psychologist Mary Pipher points out ironies within many families in our society:

> Honest parents don't always raise honest kids. Abusive parents sometimes have wonderful children. One of the most wholesome girls I know lives with her alcoholic mother in a small apartment. Some of the unhappiest children I know come from the families of sensitive, child-focused parents. [. . .]
>
> Children who are ignored sometimes become as strong, beautiful and resilient as sunflowers and sometimes they turn into dangerous psychopaths. Well-meaning families sometimes have extraordinarily bad luck with their children, while slapdash parents may raise highly successful children. (3)

Although most people might assume that honest parents would raise honest kids, every family is different, and overgeneralizing about families would indicate poor logos and ethos by Pipher. In her book she writes, "It's impossible to capture the diversity or complexity of families" (4).

Edward Tenner's book When Things Bite Back: Technology and the Revenge of Unintended Consequences contains many ironies, which George Will points out through a list of examples in one of his Newsweek columns:

> Nighttime illumination at the Lincoln Memorial attracted millions of midges, and spiders that fed on the midges, and sparrows that fed on spiders. Scrubbing away the bird droppings and spider webs made the marble vulnerable to exhaust particles. A modern technology, the jet airliner, has democratized tourism, enabling millions to travel to see Michelangelo's restored frescoes in the Sistine Chapel, where the heat of the visitors' bodies and the vapor in their breath combine with dust in the air to produce indoor acid rain. Warm, humidified, insulated and carpeted modern homes are comfortable not only for humans but also for fleas, which probably outweigh people on this planet. [. . .] ("A New Level of Worrying" 72)

In his book, Tenner writes that the world has a tendency "to get even, to twist our cleverness against us" (72). Problem solvers need to be aware of possible ironic "unintended consequences" and try to prevent them:

> Federal water projects made America's arid Southwest able to sustain millions of new residents and air conditioning made the region attractive to millions, including many seeking relief from allergies. But the water irrigated lawns, golf courses and wind-pollinated trees and plants that the new residents wanted in order to feel at home. And the allergy-sufferers began to suffer again. ("A New Level of Worrying" 72)

Critical thinkers know that irony is a form of unexpected contrast. They notice when English teachers misuse apostrophes, when Holden Caulfied in The Catcher in the Rye says, "I'm quite illiterate, but I read a lot" (18).

ACTIVITY 6

Make a list of ironies that you see in your own life or in your family, friends, education, employment, the media, government, or society. Select an irony that intrigues you and write about it in your notebook.

THE IMPORTANCE OF INTERDEPENDENCE

> All explicit opposites are implicit allies—correlative in the sense that they "gowith" each other and cannot exist apart. [. . .] With a slight shift of viewpoint, nothing is more obvious than the interdependence of opposites. But who can believe it?" (Watts 133–34)

Thinking with contraries enables you to discover and to evaluate ideas and information. Look for opposites, contradictions, and paradoxes. Guard yourself against the seductive simplicity of either/or thinking. Look for middle grounds between extremes. Discover how contraries might depend on each other.

Thinking and writing involve the interdependence of opposing processes. Discovering an idea and supporting evidence for it is different from criticizing that idea and evidence—but we use both processes when we write. Peter Elbow says excellent writing and thinking "must involve finding some way to be both abundantly inventive yet toughmindedly critical" (Embracing Contraries 60). Although writing involves both creative and critical thinking, Elbow advises students to work on one process at a time, not both: "Since creative and critical thinking are opposite and involve mentalities that tend to conflict with each other, it helps most people to learn to work on them separately or one at a time by moving back and forth between them" (61). He recommends that writers work first on creating ideas and evidence and then on critically analyzing and revising them. Trying to do both at once defeats each process for most people.

To manage your thinking well, you need to be aware of how your mind works. Looking for opposites, contradictions, and paradoxes can help you discover and evaluate ideas. Contrasts and connections are everywhere, and the more you notice them, the more you will think and learn.

READING AND WRITING ACTIVITIES

Reading and writing are opposing ends of the same pole: they are the input and output of communication through print. Writers must read their own work; readers—to think carefully and critically—must write their own thoughts.

Through critical and creative reading and writing, you may surprise yourself with the discovery of ideas you never experienced.

ACTIVITY 7

Please read the student essay "Learn the Hard Way" by Jennifer Peacock. Then in your notebook write responses to the questions following the essay.

Learn the Hard Way

Jennifer Peacock

The dangers in life an adult views with a wary eye are the adventures a child sees with a sparkling eye. Why else is the person who invented the little plastic gadget that plugs an electrical outlet driving a Rolls Royce and eating caviar? It is simply because ever since Mama screamed when baby innocently came within two feet of an electrical socket it has been the secret mystery spot. After all, something must be wonderful and magical about an object that makes Mom scream and Dad turn the same color as the living room walls. Indeed parents can count on this: if they tell their children not to do something, their children will most certainly try to do it. **1**

Take my childhood for instance; I was no angel! I learned every lesson the hard way. My mother warned me that vanilla did not taste as good as it smelled, but as soon as she turned her back I took the bottle and, like a skilled drinker with a bottle of Jack Daniels, tipped my head back to taste that little bit of heaven. She was not kidding at all I realized as I threw up in the sink. Nevertheless, the thrill of blatant disobedience was grand. I know if my mother had banned green beans, liver, and Malt-O-Meal from my diet I would secretly ravage them even now. Instead, I still get the urge to swig vanilla, even when I smell a candle. **2**

Kids will be kids, parents may say, when it comes to such harmless antics. Yet most parents are oblivious to their **3**

(box continues)

children's <u>constant</u> urge to see what really happens when they defy the BIGGIES. These are the rules every child hears: Don't talk to strangers! Don't swear! Don't play ball in the house! Don't play with matches! This is why, with a pounding heart, a child says hi to the cashier at the grocery store. This is why a child sits under Dad's coat in the closet saying "God Damnit!" over and over and over.

And this is why fourteen summers ago (but only yesterday) I snatched a book of ROSELAND BAR AND GRILL matches from my dad's car and sneaked to the park with Erick Woods. We went beneath a large bush and Erick, being the school's resident troublemaker and thus quite good at defying the BIGGIES, lit matches one by one. My heart pounded wildly and my head was dizzy with this <u>great</u> excitement. With my parents just across the street, I was undermining their whole authority system. Just as I was feeling confident, I heard my dad yell my name. It had been too good to be true; of course he must have been able to sense such a grave sin. I ran home, my heart in my throat and the empty match book in my sock. He smiled at me with a "Hi pal! Time for dinner!" And I, weak with relief and jubilation of pulling off such a crime, skipped in to eat.

Kids feel very smart and a bit smug when they defy the framework of their parents' lives. It does not even matter how the vanilla tastes or if the match fizzles out. The glory of it all is the feeling of being one up on Mom and Dad. So, parents, give your children matches, vanilla, and a basketball in the living room. Teach them the worst words you know and beg them to go with a stranger. Just do a dance of horror if they say "please" or "thank you," eat spinach, or practice the piano. Then those kids will be the safest and most polite children around.

Questions/Topics

1. How does Jennifer Peacock use contraries in this essay? Does she express a paradoxical truth?
2. Evaluate how well Peacock communicates by analyzing her ethos, logos, and pathos.
3. What do you notice about Peacock's style: her diction and sentence patterns, her voice (the sound of her personality), how her style reinforces her thesis and evidence?

ACTIVITY 8

Please read the student essay "One Hundred Percent: Unattractive Score" by Hanjun Kwon. Then in your notebook write responses to the questions following the essay.

One Hundred Percent: Unattractive Score

Hanjun Kwon

Last summer I saw an impressive advertisement in the <u>Asian Wall Street Journal</u>. It said, "We are the second company in our industry. That is the reason we are struggling to be the first." The ad impressed me because it was different from what I had normally thought. I had thought that there is nothing better then being ahead of others. At least, I could not be proud of being left behind. However, after thinking about the advertisement I realized this idea: to be the first or to be perfect is not the best.   1

The Roman Empire became corrupted from the time when they became the strongest country which defeated other countries in major aspects: architecture, military, and trade. They were satisfied with their status. With no competition, they paid less attention to their development. They wasted their time on seeking pleasure. When Rome was surrounded by enemies, it was the fastest growing country in the world. When it had no rival to compete with, there was nothing but decline. That is why it is more difficult to remain a champion than to become one.   2

I enjoyed my military service. I still miss that totally different life. But the one thing I really hated was the policy of keeping everything in order. I had to put down my combat shoes along the line on the floor. I had to wear combat fatigues without any wrinkles. I was not even allowed to mess up my personal drawer. I could not understand why my superior criticized me just because my combat hat was put down in the other direction. Though I agree that strict order is necessary in the military, that policy made me extremely   3

(box continues)

uncomfortable. I wanted to oversleep sometimes. I missed my
room at home: I could feel natural when I had to take a few
minutes to find textbooks, pens and backpack. I learned this
policy of strict order better than someone who had no problem
with it.

My father was perfect to me until his retirement. He   4
was a General in the Army. Every position he took was so
important that I could see his picture in newspapers from time
to time. He was very handsome as well as humorous. He was
good at every sport I experienced in my childhood—tennis,
golf, cross country, ice skating, and swimming. I was a little
nervous when I was with him. It seemed almost impossible
for me to be a person like him. In the summer of 1996 when
he retired from the Army, I was embarrassed to be with him
more. With time, I found several shortcomings of his. Since
he had spent thirty-two years in the Army, he was out of
touch with much of the world. It took a few months to teach
him how to use the Internet. He was too conservative in
political and cultural aspects. When I realized he was
not a perfect man, I felt closer than before. I lost my
father who was a General in the Army; however, I gained a
wonderful friend who understood me more and made mistakes
quite often.

I study hard to get the best score. I prefer one hundred   5
percent to ninety-nine. I would be reluctant to show my
weaknesses to others. However, I would take the merits of not
being perfect since I know those steps to one hundred percent
are more valuable than one hundred percent itself. If we go
climbing and reach the summit, the next thing we can do is
only descend. I want to be on the way to one hundred percent
rather than be an uncomfortable perfect.

Questions/Topics

1. How does Hanjun Kwon use contraries in this essay? Does he express a paradoxical truth?
2. Evaluate how well Kwon communicates by analyzing his ethos, logos, and
   pathos.
3. What do you notice about Kwon's style: his diction and sentence patterns,
   his voice (the sound of his personality), how his style reinforces his thesis and
   evidence?

ACTIVITY 9

Please read the student essay "The Best Balance of All" by Eryn Hart. Then in your notebook write responses to the questions following the essay.

The Best Balance of All

Eryn Hart

I studied the scene intensely. Rescuers attempted to breathe the life back into the dead man as we arrived with our lights and sirens, defibrillator, and cardiac stimulating drugs. We were creating a work of art: each of us knew our task and fell to it accordingly. The man was a lump of molded clay. His complexion was a pasty glaze with hints of indigo. His body jolted with every compression of his stiffening chest. We were molding this man's last minutes of life. He died that day. The scene intrigued me. My mind thought of all the physiological changes that his body would complete; however, I also saw the scene as a subject of art--I could draw the feeling of death in the house.

    The opposition between art and medicine has been a component of my entire existence. When I was very young, I would draw rocket ships, planets, and people. I made scientific sculptures of robots and factories. Yet when my parents would take me to the doctor or the hospital I would be filled with inquiry and an undescribable feeling of desire. When an ambulance sped by, my heart raced. I wondered who was in the back and what illness plagued the patient. While in middle school I found my interest in science grow further by receiving praise from my teachers, winning a science fair competition, participating in Odyssey of the Mind, and achieving high scores in Science Olympiad. Meanwhile, the summer before my freshman year of high school I went to Blue Lake Fine Arts Camp and received the top artist award. Despite what appeared to many an obvious talent, I deserted my gift and focused my attentions on college preparatory classes. I needed to make myself an

1

2

(box continues)

attractive candidate to colleges. My desire was focused on
becoming a physician--there was no time for art.

    In the midst of focusing on my journey towards medicine, 3
I rediscovered my lost art. I enrolled in a class to become
an Emergency Medical Technician: I would gain practical
knowledge and determine if medicine was an appropriate career.
I learned more in those four months than in my entire life. My
instructor not only taught me the science of the body. He
opened my eyes to the art I thought I had lost. He is not only
an EMT, but his first love is being an artist: a metalsmith.
He worked as an independent metalsmith for about ten years
until a bicycle accident occurred near his home. He decided
that he wanted to provide care to those experiencing medical
trauma. He found the balance between science and art.
Currently, he works at his metalsmithing shop, volunteers and
works as a Paramedic, and teaches new EMT's and veteran
Paramedics continuing education. He exemplifies the balance I
hope to find: he feels the same contrasts I do. He has shown
me that a balance between many passions is the best balance of
all. When I am discouraged with college, he encourages me to
sketch and think creatively. When art proves a challenge, we
discuss heart arrhythmias (changes in the normal heartbeat) or
a memorable ambulance run. He encourages me to follow medicine
as my vocation and art as my avocation.

    Medicine is often referred to as an art form. I believe 4
that the contrasts between my passion for art and medicine
are more related than I had realized. It will be possible to
integrate my art into my career as a physician. Art will
provide a means of relaxation; medicine will provide a subject
for my art. My love of art and passion for medicine complement
each other in a way that makes me more complete.

Questions/Topics

1. How does Eryn Hart use contraries in this essay? Does she express a paradoxical truth?
2. Evaluate how well Hart communicates by analyzing her ethos, logos, and
   pathos.
3. What do you notice about Hart's style: her diction and sentence patterns, her
   voice (the sound of her personality), how her style reinforces her thesis and
   evidence?

CONTRARIES AND CREATIVITY

> The creative act, by connecting previously unrelated dimensions of experience, enables [you] to attain to a higher level of mental evolution. (Koestler 96)

In addition to using contraries to discover and evaluate ideas, you can use them to create new thoughts and to imagine yourself into other people. Such creative thinking—by contrast— will strengthen your critical thinking.

Suppose a teacher tells a class of college students this story:

> A few months ago I felt depressed after my morning classes had gone badly. Students kept yawning. I went to my office, turned off the light, sat in the dark and put my feet up on my desk. Then I noticed a ray of light through my door window touching the tips of my shoes—and I realized my shoes were frowning at me. How silly, I knew, but if only my shoes could smile, I thought to myself. Then it hit me: no matter how boring my classes may be, there is always at least one level of smiling in the room. No? Well, look down at the tips of your shoes. When we face each other, your shoes smile at me, and my shoes smile at you! You see? There is always at least one level of smiling in the room.

Shoes frowning and smiling? Would you say this teacher's story is <u>creative</u>? What is creativity? Is there some technique that can help you think new thoughts?

ACTIVITY 10

"The ordinary mortal thinks most of the time in clichés—and sees most of the time in clichés," wrote Arthur Koestler in <u>The Act of Creation</u> (377). Do you agree, disagree or both? Write a response in your notebook.

DEFINING CREATIVITY

Creativity has various definitions. Rollo May says it "is the process of <u>bringing something new into being</u>" (<u>The Courage to Create</u>). Yes, like conceiving a child and giving birth. But how does this "bringing" function? Arthur Koestler suggests an answer; he defines creativity this way: "The logical pattern of the creative process is [. . .] the discovery of hidden similarities" (<u>The Act of Creation</u> 27). Koestler's phrase "hidden similarities" describes what usually happens in creativity: someone notices connections that other people don't see. Jerome Bruner says creativity is the joining of "unrelated things" (<u>On Knowing</u> 13). For our purposes, let's use this as our working definition: <u>creativity is the effective joining of unrelated things</u>.

Creativity takes various forms. Advertisers often try to catch your attention by combining things through hidden similarities. The 9 November 1981 issue of Newsweek contains a cover picture of the Earth in the shape of a Rubic's Cube with a pair of hands turning one of its trisections. The headline reads, "U.S. Foreign Policy: The World According to Reagan." That the Earth is suddenly similar to an intellectual puzzle in the hands of one person is a surprising image. Advertisements for a popular brand of vodka join unrelated things: such as an airplane propeller shaped like the product's distinctive bottles or a lemon cut in half with seeds shaped like bottles. In the business world advertisers pay great amounts of money for creative ads that catch people's attention and help them remember their product.

Does any joining of unrelated things produce creativity? Psychologist Jerome Bruner argues that genuine creativity contains "effective surprise." He writes

> Surprise is not easily defined. It is the unexpected that strikes one with wonder or astonishment. What is curious about effective surprise is that it need not be rare or infrequent or bizarre and is often none of these things. Effective surprises [. . .] seem rather to have the quality of obviousness about them when they occur, producing a shock of recognition following which there is no longer astonishment. [. . .] All of the forms of effective surprise grow out of combinatorial activity—a placing of things in new perspectives. (On Knowing 18–20)

As a critical thinker you can judge whether a certain "combinatorial activity" works well or not.

Consider one particular advertising campaign. In the early 1980s a tobacco company ran a series of ads that combined unrelated things. One ad shows a plate of pancakes dripping with syrup—on top of which is a white pack of cigarettes like a pat of butter. Another ad shows a bagel cut in half with a package of cigarettes on it like cream cheese. Yet another ad shows a half-gallon of vanilla ice cream resembling a package of smokes. Although these ads involve unusual combinations, do they contain "effective surprise"? When shown these ads, most students in our classes dislike the thought of mixing cigarettes with food.

ACTIVITY 11

Go to the library and browse through magazines and newspapers looking for advertisements that contain creativity—the effective joining of unrelated things. Find one you like and photocopy it. Cite the source, date, and page number. Bring it to class to show and discuss.

PURPOSES FOR CREATIVITY

Creativity is used for many purposes, including entertainment, explaining complex ideas or processes, and developing empathy by imagining yourself into other people.

Creativity and Entertainment

The effective joining of unrelated things is a feature of word play, cartoons, and humor.

Word Play

A particular form of creative word play is the <u>oxymoron</u>. Examples include pretty ugly, freezer burn, old news, good grief, same difference, alone together, original copy, random order, bittersweet, death benefit, and jumbo shrimp. An oxymoron, then, is a pair of contrary terms that people often use without being aware of their contradictory nature. The word <u>oxymoron</u> is itself an oxymoron: <u>oxy</u> = sharp; <u>moron</u> = dull, stupid. So, oxymorons have a "sharp dullness." Critical thinkers know what oxymorons are and enjoy noticing them.

Many quotes are oxymoronic—contradictory and ironic. For example,

Do not put statements in the negative form.
   Also, avoid awkward or affected alliteration.
   And don't start sentences with a conjunction.
   Never use a long word when a diminutive one will do. (Safire 10, 43, 67, 69)

I'm not going to say, "I told you so."
   "I'll give you a definite maybe." —Samuel Goldwin
   "I am a deeply superficial person." —Andy Warhol
   May I ask a question?
   "Why don't you pair 'em up in threes?" —Yogi Berra
   "Our similarities are different." —Dale Berra[1]

ACTIVITY 12

Surf the Web and find at least three oxymorons. Write them down, citing your sources, and bring them to class to share.

Cartoons

Cartoons by nature are creative, and many involve the effective joining of unrelated things. The new combinations cause surprise and perhaps laughter. Mike Peters's cartoon "When Cannonballs Swim" (Figure 4.3) is creative because Peters reverses the usual: human beings in our culture often jump into water yelling "Cannonball!" But cannonballs do not jump into water yelling "HUMAN BEEEEEE-IIINNNGGG!!" Peters joins unrelated things in a surprising way that is not logical (because cannonballs cannot talk or swim) but fun.

[1]Quotes from <http://www.wordfocus.com/oxymora-quotes.html>

Figure 4.3. "When Cannonballs Swim."
(Cartoon by Mike Peters, <u>Detroit Free Press</u> 14 Aug. 1996. © Tribune Media Services, Inc. All Rights Reserved. Reprinted with permission.)

ACTIVITY 13

Look at the cartoons in Figures 4.4 through 4.7. Then explain how each is creative.

Figure 4.4. "Psst, Leo . . . Your Human's Open."
(Mike Peters, "Mother Goose & Grimm," <u>Detroit Free Press</u> 19 May 1986. © Tribune Media Services, Inc. All Rights Reserved. Reprinted with permission.)

Figure 4.5. "Sorry, Buddy, I'm Baroque."
(Mike Peters, "Mother Goose & Grimm," <u>Detroit Free Press</u> 12 June 1996. © Tribune Media Services, Inc. All Rights Reserved. Reprinted with permission.)

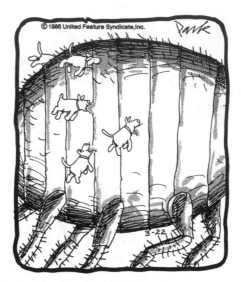

Figure 4.6. "The Body of a Flea Magnified 215 Times."
(W. B. Park, "Off the Leash," <u>Detroit Free Press</u> 22 Mar. 1986. Used with permission.)

Figure 4.7. "Fish Drinking at Bar."
(W. B. Park, "Off the Leash," <u>Detroit Free Press</u> 9 Oct. 1986. Used with permission.)

ACTIVITY 14

Browse through magazines and newspapers or surf the Web for cartoons that involve an effective joining of unrelated things. Find at least one you like, photocopy it, cite its source, and bring it to class to share.

Humor

Humor involves thinking with contraries: the funny joining of unrelated things. The things joined in humor are unexpected; a collision of thoughts occurs, resulting in surprise and laughter. Consider this quip by Steven Wright:

> "I went to a restaurant that serves 'breakfast at any time.' So I ordered French toast during the Renaissance."

Humor produces "effective surprise." Wright takes a common saying—"breakfast at any time"—and presents a new way of looking at it. Here are a few more jokes by Wright:

> "I hate it when my foot falls asleep during the day because that means it's going to be up all night."

> "A lot of people are afraid of heights. Not me, I'm afraid of widths."

> "I got food poisoning today. I don't know when I'll use it."

> "I went to a general store. They wouldn't let me buy anything specific."

> "I have an answering machine in my car. It says, 'I'm home now. But leave a message and I'll call you when I'm out.'"[2]

Wright thinks with contraries much as Einstein did in conceiving that a person can be falling and at rest at the same time. Both play with opposite ideas and combine them in odd, fresh ways.

---

[2]All jokes <www.albrecht.ecr.purdue.edu/~taylor/humor/sw.html>

Here are some jokes by Phyllis Diller. How do they work?

"The top of the piano is always open when I play—actually, it's yawning."

"Fang [her husband] was hurt in a hunting accident. Cut himself on a beer can."

"He's pretty handy though. He did a beautiful job of cementing the hole in our screen door."

"Last week, he was watching the map for me while I drove. He's a big help. He said, 'You stay on Highway 150 for an inch and a half.' "[3]

Diller's humor also joins unrelated things, such as a piano yawning. But her jokes rely on the "punch line"—a final thought that jabs the reader with an ironic surprise.

Humor not only lets you laugh but also presents you with new perspectives. Arthur Koestler argues that humor involves "the ability to break away from the stereotyped routines of thought" (91). "It is an act of liberation—the defeat of habit by originality" (96).

ACTIVITY 15

Look for three examples of humor based on the effective joining of unrelated things that produce surprise. Surf the Internet; browse some magazines and books in the library; watch comedians on TV. Write down the jokes, cite your sources, and bring them to class to share.

Creativity and Explanation

Using Metaphors and Similes

Critical thinkers use metaphors and similes to clarify and enliven what they explain. By joining unrelated things, metaphors and similes arouse thought and feeling. The more the joining contributes to clear and persuasive communication, the more useful it is.

---

[3]All Phyllis Diller jokes from <u>Parade</u> (4 Feb. 1979): 23.

A metaphor is a comparison of two unlike things. Metaphors can be simple, such as this lyric from a Stevie Wonder song: "You are the sunshine of my life." Here some loved one is compared to the sun. The image suggests associations: you bring light into my life so I can see; you nourish me; you keep me warm and alive. Singer/songwriter Sheryl Crow uses a metaphor in her song title "Every Day Is a Winding Road." We don't know where exactly the road—or each day—will take us.

Metaphors can be complex. Peter Elbow often uses them to describe the process of writing:

> To write is to overcome a certain resistance: you are trying to wrestle a steer to the ground, to wrestle a snake into a bottle, to overcome a demon that sits in your head. (Writing with Power 18)

This sentence contains three images, each a comparison between writing and an extremely difficult process. Does it make sense? It does if Elbow persuades you that writing indeed is overcoming great resistance. He could have chosen not to use any metaphors:

> To write is to overcome a certain resistance: you are trying to pull out the words but the mind resists and won't produce your thoughts.

Why not just use these plain, simple words? After all, they get the idea across. But the revision lacks the power and effective surprise that Elbow's original has. Besides, the "plain and simple" words have been used so often they are nearly clichés. They can have the effect of putting readers asleep.

Prose stylist Annie Dillard also uses multiple metaphors to describe writing:

> When you write, you lay out a line of words. The line of words is a miner's pick, a woodcarver's gouge, a surgeon's probe. You wield it, and it digs a path you follow. Soon you find yourself in new territory. Is it a dead end, or have you located the real subject? (The Writing Life 3)

Without her metaphors, Dillard's sentence would lack the images that help readers <u>see</u> and <u>feel</u> what she means.

Similes are similar to metaphors: they are comparisons between unlike things using "like" or "as." With a simile Richard Selzer enables you to feel a doctor's scalpel:

> One holds the knife as one holds the bow of a cello or a tulip—by the stem. (Mortal Lessons 92)

Selzer's image suggests the delicate nature of such an action. Newspaper columnist Ellen Goodman uses a simile to explain how she absorbs life:

I tend to go through life like a vacuum cleaner, inhaling all the interesting tidbits in my path. ("On Being a Journalist" 15)

Metaphors and similes help readers see, feel, and think. They can give spark and surprise to writing, making it more interesting for readers. They can enhance a writer's appeals to logos, pathos, and ethos. However, if overused, they can make readers feel a writer is trying too hard to be clever.

ACTIVITY 16

Complete these statements using metaphors and similes:

"Writing is _____."   "Writing is like _____."
"Reading is _____."   "Reading is like _____."
"Critical thinking is _____." "Critical thinking is like _____."

Using Analogies

An analogy is an extended comparison between unlike things; it shows similarities between two ideas or processes that on the surface may appear to have little in common. Critical thinkers use analogies to clarify complex ideas and to persuade audiences. Analogies provide images that help readers visualize and understand meaning. They can be extremely useful in winning an audience's attention. Yet analogies can fool uncritical readers into assuming that important similarities exist when they might not.

Analogies, like metaphors and similes, can be simple or complex or some state in between. Stephen Covey in The Seven Habits of Highly Effective People uses analogies to explain how people can transform their professional and personal lives. In this excerpt he explains the importance of the "Emotional Bank Account":

> We all know what a financial bank account is. We make deposits into it and build up a reserve from which we can make withdrawals when we need to. An Emotional Bank Account is a metaphor that describes the amount of trust that's been built up in a relationship. It's the feeling of safeness you have with another human being.
>
> If I make deposits into an Emotional Bank Account with you through courtesy, kindness, honesty, and keeping my commitments to you, I build up a reserve. Your trust toward me becomes higher, and I can call upon that trust many times if I need to. I can even make mistakes and that trust level, that emotional reserve, will compensate for it. [. . .]

But if I have a habit of showing discourtesy, disrespect, cutting you off, over-reacting, ignoring you, becoming arbitrary, betraying your trust, threatening you, or playing little tin god in your life, eventually my Emotional Bank Account is overdrawn. The trust level gets very low. Then what flexibility do I have?

None. I'm walking on mine fields. I have to be very careful of everything I say. I measure every word. It's tension city, memo haven. It's protecting my backside, politicking. And many organizations are filled with it. Many families are filled with it. Many marriages are filled with it. [. . .]

Our most constant relationships, like marriage, require our most constant deposits. With continuing expectations, old deposits evaporate. If you suddenly run into an old high school friend you haven't seen for years, you can pick up right where you left off because the earlier deposits are still there. But your accounts with the people you interact with on a regular basis require more constant investment. (188–89)

Does Covey's analogy help you understand trust more clearly? If so, then his analogy is useful and important. As with all strategies of reasoning, analogy is not an end in itself. Writers use it for a purpose—to help them make a point.

The power of an analogy is its ability to help an audience see, feel, and think about an idea. In his "I Have a Dream" speech, Martin Luther King Jr. uses a similar analogy to Covey's. Recall that King spoke to hundreds of thousands of people, mostly African Americans, at the Lincoln Memorial on 28 August 1963.

So we've come here today to dramatize a shameful condition. In a sense we've come to our nation's capital to cash a check. When the architects of our repub-lic wrote the magnificent words of the Constitution and the Declaration of Independence, they were signing a promissory note to which every American was to fall heir. This note was the promise that all men, yes, black men as well as white men, would be guaranteed the inalienable rights of life, liberty, and the pursuit of happiness.

It is obvious today that America has defaulted on this promissory note in so far as her citizens of color are concerned. Instead of honoring this sacred oblig-ation, America has given the Negro people a bad check; a check which has come back marked "insufficient funds." We refuse to believe that there are insufficient funds in the great vaults of opportunity of this nation. And so we've come to cash this check, a check that will give us upon demand the riches of freedom and the security of justice.

King's analogy is rich and compressed. It provides a clear context for his speech and the March on Washington that day: for blacks to cash a check promised to them when our country was founded. Because King's analogy stirs the minds and hearts of his audience, it reflects on his ethos as a person of insight and rhetor-ical power. King shows that analogies can be powerfully persuasive arguments.

Scientists often use analogies to explain complex or abstract processes. They relate something familiar to something unfamiliar, such as comparing a strand of curly hair to the structure of an amino acid. Sir James Jeans, a British physicist and astronomer, used an analogy to explain why the sky is blue. He wrote the following essay "Why the Sky Is Blue" for a general audience, not for a group of scientists. Does his analogy make sense; is it a useful explanation for a general audience?

> Imagine that we stand on any ordinary seaside pier, and watch the waves rolling in and striking against the iron columns of the pier. Large waves pay very little attention to the columns—they divide right and left and re-unite after passing each column, much as a regiment of soldiers would if a tree stood in their road; it is almost as though the columns had not been there. But the short waves and ripples find the columns of the pier a much more formidable obstacle. When the short waves impinge on the columns, they are reflected back and spread as new ripples in all directions. To use the technical term, they are "scattered." The obstacle provided by the iron columns hardly affects the long waves at all, but scatters the short ripples.
>
> We have been watching a sort of working model of the way in which sunlight struggles through the earth's atmosphere. Between us on earth and outer space the atmosphere interposes innumerable obstacles in the form of molecules of air, tiny droplets of water, and small patches of dust. These are represented by the columns of the pier.
>
> The waves of the sea represent the sunlight. We know the sunlight is a blend of lights of many colors—as we can prove for ourselves by passing it through a prism, or even through a jug of water, or as Nature demonstrates to us when she passes it through the raindrops of a summer shower and produces a rainbow. We also know that light consists of waves, and that the different colors of light are produced by waves of different lengths, red light by long waves and blue light by short waves. The mixture of waves which constitutes sunlight has to struggle through the obstacles it meets in the atmosphere, just as the mixture of waves at the seaside has to struggle past the columns of the pier. And these obstacles treat the light-waves much as the columns of the pier treat the sea-waves. The long waves which constitute red light are hardly affected, but the short waves which constitute blue light are scattered in all directions.
>
> Thus, the different constituents of sunlight are treated in different ways as they struggle through the earth's atmosphere. A wave of blue light may be scattered by a dust particle, and turned out of its course. After a time a second dust particle again turns it out of its course, and so on, until finally it enters our eyes by a path as zigzag as that of a flash of lightning. Consequently the blue waves of the sunlight enter our eyes from all directions. And that is why the sky looks blue. (23–24)

Jeans's analogy clarifies the complex process of sunlight and color through our atmosphere. Thinking with contraries, he relates waves of light to waves of the sea, discussing both long and short waves. His analogy is at once logical and creative. He carefully balances his description, first describing sea waves, then waves of sunlight, and then both together.

Jeans's writing is specific and concrete, which are qualities of successful analogies. He enables you to visualize his meaning: you can see "through a jug of water" and "through the raindrops of a summer shower." Within his analogy Jeans uses two similes that further help readers see and understand. He compares waves dividing "as a regiment of soldiers would if a tree stood in their road" and compares a wave of blue light entering "our eyes by a path as zigzag as that of a flash of lightning." It's easy to appreciate his ability as a scientist to use creativity in such a clear and effective way.

Analogies, however, are not always useful. Although they can help you explain a complex process, they can also weaken arguments. Logically, analogies are not considered strong forms of evidence in argumentation because they involve imagination. They cannot be verified. To make sure important similarities exist in an analogy, you need to evaluate the analogies you and other people use.

If an analogy oversimplifies a subject, or if it contains more important differences than similarities, it is considered a <u>false analogy</u> (See fallacies in chapter 5). For example, consider the idea that arguing is like arm wrestling. Similarities exist. Arguing usually involves two people as arm wrestling does, but arguments often involve several people—such as in heated class discussions. Arguing also involves a show of strength: there is a competition for the strongest arguments, for the most convincing logic and supporting evidence. However, the arm wrestling comparison reduces the real complexity of arguing. Important differences exist. In arm wrestling the object is for one person to win and one person to lose. But arguing need not involve a winner or a loser. In many arguments different sides concede that each side has relevant points. The purpose of argument should be understanding; the aim should be the search for truth. Argument is more complex than a contest of arm strength.

Analogies often persuade audiences, but analogies do not prove arguments. An analogy is like a map. It isn't the exact territory it stands for. But like a map it can be extremely useful. Analogies are one of the most creative tools critical thinkers can use.

ACTIVITY 17

Write a brief essay using an analogy. Following are some suggestions:

1. Explain by means of analogy any complex process or idea you have learned recently in one of your classes. Suppose your audience includes fellow students having trouble understanding the process or idea.
2. Write an analogy about learning. Compare learning some process such as writing to another process such as driving a car.

Explaining the Mind

Do you think much about how you think? Is it good to think about thinking? Experts on cognition argue it is. Strong thinkers wonder about how they discover ideas and how they solve problems. They reflect on their thinking and notice patterns, questions, and realizations. They know when they are confused about something. This kind of thinking is called <u>metacognition</u>. Poor thinkers tend not to do this. If they don't understand a class assignment, poor thinkers usually will not ask for clarification. But strong thinkers will ask because they are aware of what's happening in their minds—they feel a need to understand.

How would you describe your mind? Because the mind is mysterious and abstract (you can't see, smell, hear, touch, or taste it), it is impossible to describe the mind with total knowledge and accuracy. Thus, comparing the mind with something more concrete and less complex is natural and can be useful. Using an analogy is a way to represent your mind.

It's common for poets to compare the mind to other things. William Carlos Williams compares the mind to a waterfall rushing with thoughts. Our thoughts "forever strain forward" (<u>Paterson</u> 7). William Stafford writes, "At times in my thinking I take my hands off the handlebars and see what happens. In a poem I do that all the time" (<u>You Must Revise Your Life</u> 59). He compares his mind to riding a bicycle. Usually, people need to hold on well for control, but sometimes we know our mind (bike) so well we can ride without hands and glide. In her poem "The Mind, Like an Old Fish," Diane Wakoski compares the mind to "a rose in a glass paperweight," "a curtain cord blowing in the open-window breeze," and "a caterpillar rolled into a ball against prodding" (34). Consider this last image. Have you ever felt like this caterpillar? Have some teachers prodded your mind with a mental stick? Have other teachers encouraged you to move freely and to transform yourself?

Here are two examples from students who explain how they think.

```
Mind


Bill Antos


My mind is like juggling three balls. The balls are constantly     1
being exchanged from one hand to another. My thoughts
constantly move through my mind.
     Sometimes when I juggle I unexpectedly manipulate the          2
balls or position my body differently and discover a new trick.
I'll drop a ball and then kick it up with my foot, continue to
juggle, and say to myself, "Wow! I didn't know I could do
                                              (box continues)
```

that." Similarly I'll be sitting in my room or walking down the street and bam--I think of something I hadn't thought of before. I might look at a tree and see a lollipop. I might come up with a solution to a calculus problem I was working on an hour before. Simply by accident I have a realization.

In contrast I will purposefully try some new juggling move, like throwing one of the balls behind my back and catching it as it comes over the opposite shoulder, but I usually fail because of a misguided throw or blink of my eye. Likewise, I often fail with my thoughts. I will try to understand a problem or concept, or think of a topic for an English paper, and nothing will come to my mind. I may already have one thought being juggled in my mind, but no matter how hard I try to think new thoughts or ideas, the same old thought remains there. Sometimes, until a ball happens to come over my shoulder in the right place, my thoughts do not appear.

3

Mind

Rebecca Dewald

Last weekend while driving home, I wondered if the mind can be compared to <u>anything</u>.

1

"Well," I told myself as a raindrop hit the windshield and spattered, "the mind certainly is nothing like a water droplet." But I had to admit that my mind was like that raindrop. Often thoughts--like raindrops--fall down upon me so unexpectedly that I'm unable to turn on my wipers or pull out an umbrella. I'm not ready for them. And they can pelt down making it difficult to see, until I adjust my focus to the change.

2

As I heard the growing rumble of the engine, I looked at the speedometer and realized I was well above the speed limit. Then it occurred to me that sometimes my thoughts are like my car--they race along without restriction, until I realize my foot is weighing too heavily upon the accelerator.

3

Well, maybe the mind <u>is</u> like all things in <u>some</u> way I thought as my hand automatically went to the gold chain around

4

(box continues)

my neck as it does so often when a new thought hits me. As my
fingers moved across the smooth metal, I saw my mind as that
gold chain: made of many separate thoughts that somehow link
together.

Before I knew it I had compared my mind to a clump of   5
grapes, a blank piece of paper and pen, split ends, a ring, a
diamond, snowflakes, popcorn, pavement, traffic signals, a mail
box, and a parking lot.

By the time I pulled into my parents' driveway I was   6
quite tempted to accept the notion that the mind is like all
matter. But something kept nagging me at the bottom of my
mind--like one of those popcorn kernels that never pops. I'll
just have to continue working to figure out a way to pop this
idea.

These analogies are maps of the mind—creative representations of an incredibly complex system. Analogies are useful in explaining what seems impossible to explain.

Although scientists know much about the brain, it continues to hold great mystery. As Richard Selzer writes, "The surgeon knows the landscape of the brain, yet does not know how a thought is made" (<u>Mortal Lessons</u> 30). Critical thinkers care about the mind. They care about how they think and how other people think.

ACTIVITY 18

Write a brief essay using an analogy to describe your mind or how you think. Your purpose should not be to discover clever connections but to discover images that truly reflect how you think you think.[4]

Empathy and Imagination

Have you put yourself into somebody else's shoes lately?

Suppose you and your peers in class took off your shoes and tried on three

---

[4]This activity is adapted from D. Gordon Rohman and Albert O. Wlecke, <u>Pre-Writing: The Construction and Application of Models for Concept Formation in Writing</u>, Cooperative Research Project No. 2174, Michigan State University, 1964: 63–65.

different pairs. How would they fit? Would they be comfortable? Some shoes would be too small, too tight— you wouldn't be able to fit your feet into them. Some shoes would be too large; if you walked in them you'd trip. Some shoes might be snug, some a little too big, and some might fit well—as if they were your own.

What's the point? The expression "It's good to put yourself in somebody else's shoes" really means "It's good to put yourself into somebody else's mind." As a critical thinker you need to put yourself into other people's minds to try feeling and thinking as they do. This enables you to know "where they're coming from." This helps you see their perspectives and arguments, which you can later support or challenge. Thinking through someone else's mind widens your own array of perspectives, enabling you to be less self-centered.

Egocentricity and Empathy

Egocentricity is being self-centered, caring only for your own point of view, for your own feelings, reasons, and experience. An egocentric person is like a child who walks into a room and stands in front of the TV set, oblivious to the fact that her or his family is trying to watch it too. We hear egocentric people talk too much at movie theaters or concerts; they don't care if they disturb others trying to listen to the show. Egocentric people care about themselves and their own points of view to a fault.

As a critical thinker you must pay attention to points of view other than your own—because it's easy to be egocentric. Your own perspectives are partial. A classic analogy shows this: imagine there is a large creature behind a huge fence with various peepholes through it. What you see depends on your perspective. You may see a long gray tail and not know the animal has huge floppy ears; you may see only some thick gray skin from its side and not know the animal has a tremendous trunk. The more perspectives you can look through, the more complete your understanding will be.

Critical thinkers can use creativity to imagine themselves into other people, to feel what they feel and think what they think. Doing this is called <u>empathy</u>, defined as "the projection of one's own personality into the personality of another in order to understand the person better; ability to share in another's emotions, thoughts, or feelings" (<u>Webster's New World</u> 445).

To understand the view of a 16-year-old girl who wants an abortion, imagine yourself as that girl in school, in her community. To understand the view of her priest who opposes abortion, imagine yourself as that priest. To understand the view of a scientist who favors human cloning, try to imagine yourself as that scientist excited by possible research opportunities. And imagine yourself as a mad scientist driven by money to clone multiple copies of Princess Diana (what if someone took some of her cells before she died?). Or imagine yourself as a clone of Diana. You can try to imagine yourself into anybody, if you want.

Creativity—joining unrelated things—helps you monitor your egocentricity and develop your ability to empathize with others different from yourself. Bruce Springsteen's song "Streets of Philadelphia" earned him a Grammy and an Academy Award because it gave voice to the drama of AIDS. Springsteen imagined himself into a person with the disease. Complementing the song's haunting melody, the lyrics help people who don't have AIDS empathize with those who do:

I was bruised and battered I couldn't tell what I felt
  I was unrecognizable to myself
I saw my reflection in a window I didn't know my own face
  Oh brother are you gonna leave me wastin' away
On the streets of Philadelphia   5

I walked the avenue 'til my legs felt like stone
  I heard the voices of friends vanished and gone
At night I could hear the blood in my veins
  Black and whispering as the rain
On the streets of Philadelphia   10

  Ain't no angel gonna greet me
  It's just you and I my friend
  My clothes don't fit me no more
  I walked a thousand miles
  Just to slip this skin   15

The night has fallen, I'm lyin' awake
  I can feel myself fading away
So receive me brother with your faithless kiss
  Or will we leave each other alone like this
On the streets on Philadelphia   20

Springsteen's lyrics appeal to emotions. With few words he paints a portrait of a person wasting away with AIDS who asks the listener to "receive" him, to help him in some way. The speaker in the song acutely feels his body's dramatic changes: he can feel the blood in his veins "Black and whispering as the rain." He wants to "slip this skin" and have another body, a healthy body, but he can't. Springsteen's song serves a noble purpose in helping people care more about the disease and those who suffer from it.

  Various kinds of writing aim to create empathy in readers. Fiction writers want readers to empathize with characters in deep conflict. Poets often want readers to imagine themselves into other people. Lucille Clifton wrote "wishes for sons," hoping that men might empathize with women.

i wish them cramps
i wish them a strange town
and the last tampon.
i wish them no 7–11.

i wish them one week early
and wearing a white skirt.
i wish them one week late.

later i wish them hot flashes
and clots like you
wouldn't believe.   let the
flashes come when they
meet someone special.
let the clots come
when they want to.

let them think they have accepted
arrogance in the universe,
then bring them to gynecologists
not unlike themselves.

quilting: poems 1987–1990 60

What do you think about this poem? Does it express truth? Do you suppose women prefer this poem more than men do?

Clifton, an African American poet and author of children's books, likes to tell audiences, "I comfort the afflicted and afflict the comfortable." You might infer that in her poem she tries to afflict men with a greater awareness of how menstruation affects women, and she tries to comfort women with her wishes that men might be more understanding of the physical/emotional problems women face each month. That her title contains "for sons" is noteworthy, not "wishes for men." The word "sons" is parental. The speaker of the poem is like a mother wishing her sons might know how it feels to be a woman—and to be treated by arrogant male doctors who don't empathize with their women patients—because sons might grow into wiser, more caring men, husbands, and fathers if they knew.

As a creative skill, empathy will strengthen your own critical abilities. By imagining yourself into someone else, by wearing somebody else's mind, you will enlarge your own mind.

ACTIVITY 19

Choose one of the following suggestions and write a brief essay:

1. Imagine yourself as someone you know who holds a different view than you do—such as not drinking alcohol on weekends, watching action movies with lots of violence, going to church each Sunday, or some other view you oppose. Write in that person's voice—using that person's point of view and arguments. Write as if that person were trying to persuade you to consider the opposing view.

2. Imagine yourself as your mother or father disagreeing with you about something you're doing at school—taking a certain class or participating in a certain activity. Write in that parent's voice using his or her point of view and arguments.

3. If you disapprove of people smoking cigarettes in restaurants, write from the point of view of a smoker who feels his or her rights are being violated. Or if you approve of people smoking in restaurants, write from the point of view of someone who opposes such smoking.

CONCLUDING REMARKS ON THINKING WITH CONTRARIES

In this chapter you have examined how to think with contraries for two main purposes: to make "critical" sense and to make "creative" sense. You can use contraries in critical ways:

To notice and analyze opposites, contradictions, and paradoxes

To generate ideas and to evaluate ideas

To develop a high tolerance for ambiguity and a low tolerance for either/or thinking

You can use contraries in creative ways:

For entertainment—word play, cartoons, and humor

For explaining complex ideas or processes—metaphors, similes, analogies

For developing empathy by imagining yourself into other people

Contrast produces awareness: when you notice contrasts, you think. But thinking with contraries takes courage. You may want to avoid contradictions and paradoxes because they don't make sense at first. Seeing multiple perspectives on an issue can make it difficult to choose a perspective. Often it's easier not to consider points of view other than your own; however, such egocentricity is a sure sign of poor thinking. To join unrelated things through a metaphor, simile, or an analogy is to risk thinking unusual thoughts—some people may think you're odd. To imagine yourself into another person may feel alien, but you will feel and think more. You will learn more.

READING AND WRITING ACTIVITIES

You see your exact image in a mirror, except that it is reversed. You reach out with your right hand and see your mirror image reaching toward you with its left. This is why we write "ecnalubma" on emergency vehicles—so that your rearview mirror will show you "ambulance." You can often find truth in the reverse of what you think you see.

ACTIVITY 20

Please read the essay "Hate Is Simple, Love Complex" by newspaper columnist Sydney J. Harris. Then in your notebook write responses to the questions following the essay.

Hate Is Simple, Love Complex

Sydney J. Harris

We think of our emotions as being either positive or negative—love, on the one 1 hand, or hate, on the other. But there is another important way in which emotions divide: They are also simple and complex. And this is what creates much of the trouble in the world.

Love, for example, is difficult to sustain not because it is a positive 2 emotion, but because it is a complex one. Hate is easy to maintain for a lifetime, because it is a simple one.

That is, love requires the addition of other elements in order to play its 3 proper role; it needs understanding, patience, tact, the willingness to be hurt or disappointed from time to time. Love alone, in its simplicity, is not enough to carry the burden of relationship.

Hate is a totally different matter; it is not the opposite of love. (As St. 4 Augustine pointed out long ago, indifference is the opposite of love.) Hate is a supremely simple emotion that makes it enormously attractive to a certain type of mind and personality.

First, hate makes no demand on our mental processes, and doesn't call on 5 us to expand or change our views. In fact, it tends to remove doubt, and gives us a sense of decision and a feeling of righteous well-being.

It doesn't call on any of the other emotions for support; indeed, it puts 6 them quite out of court. It rejects understanding, despises tact, condemns patience, and will endure no hurt or disappointment without quick revenge.

Besides being the simplest of emotions, hate can also be the most fulfill- 7 ing for a certain kind of person, because it provides him or her with a meaning to life, something to oppose, to blame, to relieve the sense of frustration or failure.

Most of all, because of its seductive simplicity, hate seems to remove the 8 need for reasoning (an intolerable burden to many people) and for any of its auxiliary efforts, such as reading, analyzing, estimating, and judging. Hate has only one function and only one object.

Love might be compared to the building of a tall and elaborate sandcas-   9
tle, taking many hours of painstaking effort, cooperation, balance, and persistence; and hate might be compared to the foot that comes along and with one vicious or thoughtless kick destroys in a moment what has been built up.

There is so little love in the world compared with the amount of hate—   10
both expressed and latent—not because it is harder for us to be positive than negative, but because it is harder to combine and coordinate a complex emotion in a creative act than to live blindly by blaming and attacking some "enemy" for our dissatisfactions and disappointments. It takes a dedicated genius years to build a great cathedral; any desperado can bomb it to obliteration in a second. Why shouldn't hate, being so much easier, be so much more popular? (Pieces of Eight 108–9) □

Questions/Topics

1. How does Harris use contraries in this essay? Does he express a paradoxical truth? Do you agree with his thesis?

2. How useful are his analogies?

3. Imagine yourself as someone who strongly disagrees with Harris' thesis and some or much of his supporting evidence. Explain why you disagree, giving reasons and examples.

4. Evaluate how well Harris communicates by analyzing his logos, pathos, and ethos.

5. What do you notice about Harris's style: his diction and sentence patterns, his voice (the sound of his personality), how his style reinforces his thesis and evidence?

ACTIVITY 21

Please read the essay "Senior-Teener, A New Hybrid" by Dorothy Noyes. Then read it again to evaluate it, based on the suggestions following the essay.

Senior-Teener, A New Hybrid

Dorothy Noyes

Come next May, there's no denying that fact that I'll have racked up 89 years 1
as an inhabitant of planet earth. One glance and you'd know I'm a Senior. The
hair on my head is white, and although my face is not overly lined, it's obvious that I'm past 50 or 60 or even 70. While I work at standing erect, my shoulders slouch a bit. And, despite regular swim sessions and frequent brisk walks,
I have difficulty hiding my protruding belly. But the inner me, the emotional
me, is so frequently a Teener. I feel much as I did 75 years ago: alone, tremu-
lous and fearful about my future.

Were Charles Darwin to arise from the dead, I'd say to him, "There's a new 2
subspecies abroad today, sir." And I'd tell him about its evolution during the
latter part of the 20th century when humankind—particularly womankind—was
living longer and longer in an amazing state of physical health. But I'd have to
come clean as to the emotional downside: the sense of queasiness that from time
to time overtakes an otherwise reasonably fit body. For today I'm often jittery
and "out of it" as in long-ago days—no special boyfriend or agemates. Three
husbands have predeceased me, and my longtime female intimates have also
made their final exits.

At the start of my adolescence, my self-confidence was on the low side. 3
Because I was born a southpaw, conventional wisdom forced me to learn to
write with the "right" hand. Even now, my friends' exhortations to "type, don't
write" can be amusing but far from uplifting. That I was clumsy was dinned into
me time and again. Well, I still feel clumsy.

Transplant shock also took its toll. When I was 12, and for the next several 4
years, we lived in cities in three different states. This meant four high schools.
I've never succeeded in blocking out the memory of that sense of desolation
when I was 13 ½ and a sophomore in Montclair High School in New Jersey—
far from the kids I knew as a freshman in Evanston, Ill. That unforgettable
moment when I saw the spot on my white skirt: I was a child no longer. How
to blot it out? Where to go?

This is somewhat comparable to one of Seniors' embarrassing problems: 5
the need for protective garments to cope with the unexpected lack of control
over failing body parts. While Senior and Teener are not look-alikes, they're so
often act-alikes.

Obviously, the female bodily changes of Teener and Senior are not the 6
same. Teener's route is onward and upward, though it doesn't always seem so
to her as she deplores some of the external blemishes. For Senior it's mostly
downhill, obliged as she is to spend more and more time in body-repair shops
to compensate for eyes and ears and other organs that malfunction. Our
commonality lies in our need to face up to the inevitable biologic changes with

equanimity—to learn the art of self-mastery, of peaceful acceptance of the inevitable and of our own self-worth as the life cycle spirals on. Living comfortably with one's own body with its limitations and defects is no easy assignment.

One of our most difficult challenges comes from the outside world. It's 7 another factor that makes our struggle to mature so alike: coping with those numerous unsympathetic, contemptuous and sometimes outright hostile others. Like those folk who accuse Teeners of being too self-absorbed, irresponsible, sex-driven, booze-drinking, "no good"; and for those who look upon Seniors with much disdain, not as national treasures.

Virtually from the first moment last spring when I was introduced to the 8 about-to-be 15-year-old stepdaughter of my godson, I remembered how, long ago, I cherished the companionship of an elderly spinster who paid special attention to insecure young me. This probably prompted me to issue a spur-of-the-moment invitation to Christine. She seemed ecstatic at the thought of spending part of a holiday weekend with me. All during the first day as we meandered through Central Park and again at dinner and at the dance theater, I was struck by her apparent maturity—fascinated as she was in studying people's faces. "What do you suppose they're thinking about, Dorothy?" But this confidence—this absorption with others—was not to last. Christine was pondering her trip home the next day: alone in a taxi and the crowd at Penn Station! She hated to bother me, but would I mind coming along as a pal, just in case . . . ? Of course I went. Her scary moment of panic came when she couldn't find the platform for the train's departure. (I experience comparable panicky self-doubt when I'm under pressure.)

In the early '60s, when Doubleday was about to publish my first book, 9 there was great discussion as to the title of this parental "how to" guide. It was understandable that it should be called "Your Child," based as it was in part on my syndicated newspaper column with that title. The big question was: should we add "from birth to maturity"? Not <u>to</u> maturity, I insisted, but rather <u>toward</u> maturity. For who knows when maturity has been reached? And, besides, what kind of maturity are we thinking about?

For Teener, maturity means graduation from kiddom—the search for 10 personhood in her own right, the freedom to find her own worth and her own place. For Senior, maturity means greater acceptance of waning physical powers and the ability to continue to grow in understanding and, yes, in wisdom—to accept death as a part of life. Neither Teener nor Senior can control biological maturity, but each can have much effect over psychological and philosophical maturity.

Many times, the Teener part of this hybrid is thrown by what she feels 11 must be grasped to gain self-mastery and to appreciate what life is all about. So, too, the Senior is frequently non-plussed by how much more there is to discover about our universe. And time is running short—gotta crowd in as much as possible as fast as possible! Each of us must deal with continuing bodily changes and our reactions to them as well as with our changing relationships with our fellow earthlings. Both of us long for many of those Others to appreciate what seems to be the professional consensus that Teeners and Seniors both are almost <u>overendowed</u> with heartfelt compassion for all humankind. □

Questions/Topics

1. How well does Noyes use contraries? What contrasts and connections do you find most interesting or meaningful in her essay? Does she express a paradoxical truth? Do you agree with her thesis?
2. Write a letter to Dorothy Noyes in which you state an opposing argument. Try to challenge her idea and supporting evidence.
3. Evaluate how well Noyes communicates by analyzing her logos, pathos, and ethos.
4. What do you notice about Noyes's style: her diction and sentence patterns, her voice (the sound of her personality), how her style reinforces her thesis and evidence?

ACTIVITY 22

Please read the essay by newspaper columnist and humorist Dave Barry. Then in your notebook write responses to the questions following the essay.

The Evil Eye

Dave Barry

Call me a wild and crazy guy if you want, but recently, on a whim, I decided 1
to—Why not?—turn 48.

It's not so bad. Physically, the only serious problem I've noticed is that I 2
can no longer read anything printed in letters smaller than Shaquille O'Neal. Also, to read a document, I have to hold it far from my face; more and more, I find myself holding documents—this is awkward on airplanes—with my feet. I can no longer read restaurant menus, so I fake it when the waiter comes around.

Me (pointing randomly): I'll have this.
Waiter: You'll have your napkin?
Me: I want that medium rare.

It's gotten so bad that I can't even read the words I'm typing into my computer right now. If my fingers were in a prankish mood, they could type an embarrassing message right in the middle of this sentence HE'S ALWAYS PUTTING US IN HIS NOSE and there is no way I'd be able to tell.

I suppose I should go see an eye doctor, but if you're 48, whenever you 3 go to see any kind of doctor, he or she invariably decides to insert a lengthy medical item into your body until the far end of it reaches a different area code. Also, I am frankly fearful that the eye doctor will want me to wear reading glasses. I have a psychological hang-up about this, caused by the fact that, growing up, I wore eyeglasses for 70,000 years. And these were not just any eyeglasses: These were the El Dork-O model, the ones that come from the factory pre-broken with the white tape already wrapped around the nose part. As an adolescent, I was convinced that my glasses were one of the key reasons why the opposite sex did not find me attractive, the other key reason being that I did not reach puberty until approximately age 35.

Anyway, other than being functionally blind at close range, I remain in 4 superb physical condition for a man of my age who can no longer fit into any of his pants. I have definitely been gaining some weight in the midriff region, despite a rigorous diet regimen of drinking absolutely no beer whatsoever after I pass out. The only lower-body garments I own that still fit me comfortably are towels, which I find myself wearing in more and more social settings. I'm thinking of getting a black one for funerals.

Because of my midriff situation I was very pleased to read recently about 5 the new Miracle Breakthrough Weight Loss Plan for Mice. In case you missed this, what happened was, scientists extracted a certain chemical ingredient found in thin mice, then injected it into fat mice; the fat mice lost 90 percent more weight than a control group of fat mice who were exposed only to Richard Simmons. The good news is that this same ingredient could produce dramatic weight loss in human beings; the bad news is that, before it becomes available, it must be approved by the Food and Drug Administration (motto: "We Haven't Even Approved Our Motto Yet"). So it's going to take a while. If you're overweight and desperate to try this miracle ingredient right away, my advice to you, as a medical professional, is to get hold of a thin mouse and eat it. It can't be any worse than tofu.

But getting back to aging: Aside from the vision thing, and the weight 6 thing, and the need to take an afternoon nap almost immediately after I wake up, and the fact that random hairs—I'm talking about <u>long</u> hairs, the kind normally associated with Cher—occasionally erupt from deep inside my ears— aside from these minor problems, I am a superb physical specimen easily mistaken for Brad Pitt.

Not only that, but I have the mind of a steel trap. Of course very few 7 things in the world—and I include the Home Shopping Network in this statement—are as stupid as a steel trap. What I'm saying is, I have definitely detected a decline in some of my mental facilities. For example, the other day

I was in my office, trying to perform a fundamental journalistic function, namely, fill out an expense report, and I needed to divide 3 into a number that, if I recall correctly (which I don't; that's the problem), was $125.85, and <u>I couldn't remember how to do long division</u>. I knew I was supposed to put the 3 into the 12, then bring something down, but what? And how far down? And would I need the "cosine"?

I was starting to panic, when all of a sudden—this is why you youngsters 8 should pay attention in math class—my old training came back to me, and I knew exactly what to do: Ask Doris. Doris works in my office, and she has a calculator. I guess I should start carrying one around, along with some kind of device that remembers (a) people's names, (b) where I put the remote control, and (c) what I had planned to do once I got into the kitchen other than stand around wearing a vacant expression normally associated with fish.

But so what if my memory isn't what it used to be? My other mental skills 9 are as sharp as ever, and I'm confident that I can continue to do the kind of astute analysis and in-depth research that have characterized this column over the years, which is why today I want to assure you, the readers, that my advancing age will in no way change the fact that MAINLY HE SCRATCHES HIMSELF. (254–57) ☐

Questions/Topics

1. What is Dave Barry's main purpose and how does he succeed or not in achieving it?
2. How does Barry use contraries to create his humor?
3. Imagine yourself as someone who thinks Dave Barry's essay is stupid, not worth reading. Explain this position as if you believe it, giving reasons and examples.
4. Evaluate Barry's logos, pathos, and ethos in this essay.
5. What do you notice about Barry's style: his diction and sentence patterns, his voice (the sound of his personality), how his style reinforces his thesis and evidence?

Interchapter 4

Style and Contraries

Things are best known by opposition, and all the better known when the opposites are put side by side. (The Rhetoric of Aristotle 204)

SENTENCE TOOLS

Loose and Periodic Sentences

You can apply your knowledge of sentence tools to create sentences with more detail. How are the following two sentences similar and different in structure?

> A. We caught two bass, hauling them in briskly as though they were mackerel, pulling them over the side of the boat in a businesslike manner without any landing net, and stunning them with a blow on the back of the head. (White, "Once More to the Lake" 199)

> B. Sitting alone at the witness table, relying exclusively on her command of the details and her brilliance as an advocate, looking outrageously cool and dignified through the long periods in the spotlight, Mrs. Clinton has been showing why her husband and the people of Arkansas have thought so highly of her. (12A)

Please don't read ahead until you've examined the preceding sentences.
What did you notice? Yes, each sentence contains three -ing phrases that refer to the main thought. But where is the main thought in each sentence?

This is the major difference between the two sentences. The main thought comes first in White's sentence, "We caught two bass." However, in the other sentence, the main thought comes last, "Mrs. Clinton has been showing why her husband and the people of Arkansas have thought so highly of her."

E. B. White's example is called a loose sentence. <u>A loose sentence is structured with the main thought first followed by description or explanation.</u> The loose sentence reflects how the mind often works: you have a thought like an outline and then fill it in with further specific thoughts from your memory. Here are two loose sentences with three <u>-ing</u> phrases written by students:

> He skated with the puck, looking for an open man, watching for defenders, waiting to put a shot on net. (Michael Krebs, student)

> She turned the wheel of the car cautiously, looking for oncoming traffic, hoping no one would fly around the corner, deciding to wait for the light to change just in case. (Erica Bachman, student)

ACTIVITY 1

Write three loose sentences using <u>-ing</u> phrases. Bring your sentences to class to share. Then look at your recent writing, and see if you can combine some sentences into a loose sentence. Try to use this tool the next time you write.

Periodic sentences, such as the one about Hillary Clinton, are opposite in form from loose sentences. <u>A periodic sentence is structured so description or explanation comes first and the main thought comes last—toward the "period."</u> This is a useful tool for building up to an idea. The reader has to wait for the main thought in order to understand the entire sentence. Here is a periodic sentence by Alice Walker from her essay "Beauty: When the Other Dancer Is the Self":

> Whirling happily in my starchy frock, showing off my biscuit-polished patent-leather shoes and lavender socks, tossing my head in a way that makes my ribbons bounce, <u>I stand, hands on hips, before my father</u>. (emphasis ours) (385)

In this sentence Walker uses three <u>-ing</u> phrases containing vivid concrete details to show how happy she was as a young girl. Periodic sentences create suspense. They take you for a ride, and you don't know where you're going until the end. Loose sentences tell you where you're going first and then take you for a ride.

You can often convert loose sentences into periodic sentences by reversing their structure:

> Looking for an open man, watching for defenders, waiting to put a shot on net, he skated with the puck.

> Looking for oncoming traffic, hoping no one would fly around the corner, deciding to wait for the light to change just in case, she turned the wheel of the car cautiously.

Loose and periodic sentences are useful tools of style; they can help you communicate complex thoughts in interesting patterns that satisfy the mind. However, loose and periodic sentences don't always require a series of -ing phrases.

Loose

> In time I learned the strength of words, how they could raise you up high, higher than you deserved, how they could convince others to love you, to do your bidding, how they could deflect wrath. (Selzer, <u>Down from Troy</u> 249)

Periodic

> Without the ability to think critically, to differentiate verifiable fact from goofball rantings, to understand what is valuable and what is worthless, information in itself means nothing. (Cantor C6)

Although these examples do not contain -ing phrases, they do contain three parallel groupings of words: Selzer repeats "how they" and Cantor repeats <u>to</u> phrases—"to think," "to differentiate," and "to understand."

Thus, loose and periodic sentences can take various forms. When you use these sentence patterns well, your voice will sound persuasive.

ACTIVITY 2

Write three periodic sentences—two with -ing phrases, one with another form. Also, try writing a loose sentence without -ing phrases. Bring your sentences to class to share. Then look at your recent writing, and see if you can combine some sentences into a periodic sentence.

Antithesis

What do the following sentences from President John F. Kennedy's Inaugural Address have in common?

> If a free society cannot help the many who are poor, it cannot save the few who are rich.

> Let us never negotiate out of fear, but let us never fear to negotiate.

> Let both sides explore what problems unite us instead of belaboring those problems which divide us.

> Ask not what your country can do for you; ask what you can do for your country.

As a sentence tool, <u>antithesis combines contrary thoughts, usually arranged in parallel structure</u>. One reason the last example is famous is because of its balanced opposition:

| Ask not | what your country | can do for you; |
| ask | what you | can do for your country. |

This balanced sentence reflects Kennedy's voice. If a president can structure a clear and insightful sentence like that, if he has that kind of control with language, his audience might assume he can govern as well. Critics believe Kennedy's use of antithesis in his inaugural speech was masterful because one of his purposes was to unite the world by forging connections with the Soviet Union. At that time (1961) the cold war had produced a real threat of nuclear destruction. Kennedy's rhetoric—his use of antithesis—suggests that opposites can work together. His style reinforced his message and purpose.

You may remember Kennedy's famous statement because he unites contraries, and contraries help you think. Aristotle valued antithesis. He said

> This kind of style is pleasing, because things are best known by opposition, and all the better known when the opposites are put side by side. [. . .] The more concise and antithetical the saying, the better it pleases, for the reason that, by the contrast, one learns the more, and, by the conciseness, learns with the greater speed. (<u>The Rhetoric of Aristotle</u> 204, 214)

Politicians like to use antithesis because, as Aristotle says, it appeals to the mind:

> Those who have been <u>left out</u>, we will try to <u>bring in</u>. Those <u>left behind</u>, we will help to <u>catch up</u>. (Richard Nixon, Inaugural Address, 1969)

There is nothing <u>wrong with America</u> that cannot be cured with what is <u>right with America</u>. (Bill Clinton, Inaugural Address, 1993)

We are <u>disgusted</u> by the things we <u>desire</u>, and we <u>desire</u> what <u>disgusts</u> us. (Mario Cuomo, Governor of New York, qtd. in <u>Newsweek</u> [24 Oct. 1994]: 33)

Setting foot on the moon, Neil Armstrong used antithesis in another statement millions of people know by heart:

That's one small step for a man, one giant leap for mankind.

Notice the two major contrasts in this sentence:

That's one small step	for a man,
one giant leap	for mankind.

Armstrong's simple sentence with simple diction (ten monosyllabic words, two two-syllable words) is memorable because of its contrasts and the milestone meaning behind them.

Many writers use antithesis. As a form of thinking with contraries, it allows writers to connect contrasting thoughts, and such connection stimulates thinking in readers. Shakespeare, one of the world's great writers, often used antithesis, such as "To be or not to be." Here are a few more examples from other writers:

When we think we are using language, our language is using us. (Tannen, <u>You Just Don't Understand</u> 243)

If thought corrupts language, language can also corrupt thought. (Orwell 89)

It's not a just world; it's just a world. (Cushman B4)

I don't paint to live; I live to paint. (Willem de Kooning, <u>Detroit Free Press</u> obituary [20 Mar. 1997]: 6B)

Antithesis is useful for juxtaposing contrary thoughts. This tool of style requires more thought than many other tools, but the effect on readers makes antithesis worth your effort. Look for antithesis in other people's writing to see how it affects their meaning, tone, and voice.

ACTIVITY 3

Write three sentences using antithesis. To do this, you might make a list of opposites and then join some together. For example, "Love is constructive; hate is destructive." Or, "It is nice to be important, but it is more important to be nice." Bring your sentences to class to share. Then look at your recent writing, and see if you can use an example of antithesis to help make a point.

Newspaper columnist Sydney J. Harris composed a small book of antitheses called <u>Winners and Losers</u>. As you read these selections, consider whether you agree with them:

A winner listens; **a loser** just waits until it's his turn to talk. (25)

A winner paces himself; **a loser** has only two speeds: hysterical and lethargic. (33)

A winner has a healthy appreciation of his abilities, and a keen awareness of his limitations; **a loser** is oblivious both of his true abilities and his true limitations. (39)

A winner takes a big problem and separates it into smaller parts so that it can be more easily manipulated; **a loser** takes a lot of little problems and rolls them together until they are unsolvable. (41)

A winner seeks for the goodness in a bad man, and works with that part of him; **a loser** looks only for the badness in a good man, and therefore finds it hard to work with anyone. (79)

A winner is sympathetic to weakness in others, because he understands and accepts his own weakness; **a loser** is contemptuous toward weakness in others, because he despises and rejects his own weakness. (113)

ACTIVITY 4

Do you think Harris's statements express truth—some more than others? Which ones? Or do you think some statements are false or stereotypical? Select one of Harris's statements and support and/or challenge it by writing about it in your notebook, giving examples from your own experience to show what you mean. Bring what you write to class to share.

Antithesis and Balanced Sentences

Look at the following sentences. How are they balanced?

> Men have better spatial abilities; women have better verbal abilities. (Goodman, "In the Male Direction" 131)

> **A winner** focuses; **a loser** sprays. (Harris, <u>Winners and Losers</u> 45)

> The sciences are supposed to be objective, intellectual, analytical, reproducible, and useful; the arts are thought to be subjective, sensual, empathic, unique, and frivolous. (Root-Berstein B6)

If you count the number of words in each complete thought of the preceding sentences, you see they have the same number. In Goodman's sentence each thought contains five words, in Harris' three, in Root-Berstein's twelve. This gives each sentence <u>balance</u>, as if both thoughts weigh the same; the semicolon serves as a scale. Because they contain the measurement of thoughts, balanced sentences can suggest to readers that you control your thoughts well. Thus, <u>balanced sentences combine contrary thoughts that have the same number of words</u>.

ACTIVITY 5

Write three balanced sentences using antithesis. Bring your sentences to class to share. Then look at your recent writing, and see if you can use a balanced sentence to help you make a point.

FINE-TUNING SENTENCES

False Starts

Examine the following sentences. What do they have in common?

1. Personally, I believe that both men and women are equally guilty of gossip.
2. There are some arguments that Bruce makes that are not strong.
3. It is through specific examples that we clarify our ideas.

Each of these sentences begins with needless words. You can make them more concise by omitting those words.

1. Men and women are equally guilty of gossip. (Or, Both men and women gossip.)
2. Bruce makes some weak arguments.
3. Through specific examples we clarify our ideas. (Or, We clarify our ideas through specific examples.)

Technically, this problem of beginning sentences with empty words is called <u>expletive</u>, from <u>explere</u>, to fill. Expletives fill sentences with needless words. A clearer name is <u>false start</u>, coined by Stephen K. Tollefson in his booklet <u>Grammar Grams</u>. With ironic humor, Tollefson writes,

> It is true that you should avoid false starts whenever possible. I think that your writing will improve if you do (12). (21 words)

Revised

> You should avoid false starts—your writing will improve if you do. (12 words)

When you revise, look carefully for any false starts: sentences beginning with <u>There are</u>, <u>There is</u>, <u>It is</u>, <u>I think</u>, <u>Personally</u>, <u>I feel</u>, and other needless words.

ACTIVITY 6

Repair the following sentences by omitting false starts and other needless words. Compare your revisions with those of other students in class.

1. Personally I think that it is the combination of fans and team owners that have damaged the game of baseball.
2. There are three options that I am examining the most thoroughly.
3. It is clear that many students' essays are too general.
4. There are too many students who care more about competition than cooperation in school.
5. The point that I wish to make is essentially that people learn best that which they must teach to others.

ACTIVITY 7

Examine the writing you have done so far in this course. Find two or three of your sentences with false starts, copy them, and then revise them, omitting needless words. Bring your work to class.

Active and Passive Verbs

What differences do you notice between these sentences?[1]

1. Great vitality can be added to your style through your verbs—but only if they are wisely chosen.
2. You can add great vitality to your style through your verbs—but only if you choose them wisely.

The two sentences have the same number of words in them. In fact, the sentences are nearly identical. Both speak of adding vitality to your style by choosing verbs wisely. They differ only slightly in their structure. Many readers and writers prefer the second sentence with "active" verbs.

In the second sentence <u>you</u> add the vitality by choosing the verbs wisely. The first sentence does not say who does the adding or the choosing. In passive sentences, either there is no subject at all or the subject comes at the end of the sentence.

Active	Passive
Seymour wrote the essay.	The essay was written by Seymour.
The president addressed the nation.	The nation was addressed by the president.
We considered the book interesting.	The book was considered interesting.

Not only are active sentences more direct, but they are frequently more concise.

However, so-called rules of language often turn out to be stylistic choices. For example, some readers insist that writers must always prefer active verbs over passive.

---

[1]We adapted these pairs of examples on verbs from Robert Miles, Marc Bertonasco, and William Karns, <u>Prose Style: A Contemporary Guide</u> (Upper Saddle River, NJ: Prentice-Hall, 1991) 45–46.

Subject	**Verb**	**Object**

<u>Active:</u>

Franny	drove	the bus.

The verb is called "active" because the subject (Franny) does the acting. The subject is the "doer" of the action. However, writers sometimes turn their sentences around, like this:

<u>Passive:</u>

The bus	was driven	by Franny.

This kind of sentence seems backwards to many readers who expect the <u>subject</u> to come first in a sentence.

Although active verbs are usually clear, concise, and direct, occasionally, you might wish to use a passive sentence to change the rhythm and emphasis of your language. Then too, sometimes you may not know the actor in a situation:

My car has been broken into three times this year.

The vandals were never identified.

Sometimes you may want to deemphasize the actor—who did what may not be important:

The survey was conducted over a two-year period.

The sheep Dolly was cloned in a Scottish laboratory.

Sometimes you may want to hide the actor in a sentence. Instead of naming someone responsible for an error, you may choose to use the passive voice:

Your check amount was incorrectly doubled.

The shattered pieces of the vase were strewn all over the carpet.

Passive verbs aren't always or automatically wrong. Nevertheless, too many passive sentences can make your writing sound abstract and falsely authoritative. Worse than that, you may sound as if you are <u>hiding</u> behind your passive verbs, avoiding responsibility for your own actions, opinions, and conclusions.

Weak Passive

The idea of cloning was not developed in the 1990s. Cloning of plants was known in ancient times. Therefore, this experiment will be a continuation of research with a long history. The intention of this study is to show that modern plant clones can be produced with ancient procedures.

Preferred Active

Ancient farmers used cloning to develop new fruit trees. Continuing this research, my colleagues and I will show that we can produce modern plant clones with ancient cloning procedures.

Passive verbs tend to weaken sentences and give your voice a distant, impersonal sound. In the past, scientists often used passive voice to deemphasize the doer of experiments, to make their writing seem more objective (a practice no longer approved by many editors). Today, however, you should use an active voice in your own writing when you can, unless you have a specific need for the passive.

Pretentious Passive

Experimental chemistry had been dispensed to the subjects in large doses. Sterile, nonpotent chemistry was also administered into the control subjects, whereupon no untoward responses were observed.

Preferred Active

I stuck a syringe full of experimental novocaine into the lab rats—twice the normal dose. I also used a different syringe on the "control rats," but it contained only sterile water. Then nothing happened—nothing we hadn't expected.

When you revise your writing, fine-tune your sentences by examining your choice of verbs.

Writing means anticipating what effects your words might have on your audience. Weak verbs rob your writing of energy, so choose your words carefully. The weakest verbs do not express action at all:

Weak Verbs

am, is, are, was, were, be, being, been
have, has, had, would, should, could

When you tie a weak verb to a strong one, you lose some of the strength of your sentence:

Weak Passive: The church glass <u>had been broken</u> by the kids.
Strong Active: The kids <u>shattered</u> the church glass.

Weak Passive: The party <u>was organized</u> to celebrate Dr. Brown's book.
Strong Active: We <u>organized</u> a party to celebrate Dr. Brown's book.

You must ask yourself, which of these sentences makes a stronger statement?
How would you describe the differences between the following sentences?[2]

1. Verbs are capable of giving life to your sentences but are also capable of having a deadening effect on them.
2. Verbs can enliven your sentences but can just as easily deaden them.

If you count the number of words in each sentence, you find 20 in the first and 12 in the second. Like good gas mileage in a car, the second sentence works efficiently. If you underline the verbs in both sentences, you find <u>are capable</u>, <u>are</u>, <u>capable</u>, and <u>having</u> in the first sentence and <u>can enliven</u> and <u>can . . . deaden</u> in the second. The second sentence wins for clarity and conciseness. Also the second sentence contains a nice stylistic touch: <u>enliven</u> and <u>deaden</u> provide a clear contrast and contain a parallel -<u>en</u> ending.

Try your analysis with one more pair.[3] Which is more effective and why?

1. There are some verbs that are able to give a sentence the strength and resilience of a bullwhip; there are other verbs that are likely to bring about the sort of sentence that has no more life than is possessed by a piece of string.
2. The right verbs can give a sentence the snap and sting of a bullwhip; the wrong verbs can render it as lifeless as a piece of string.

Using the same methods of analysis, you can see that the first sentence contains 45 words, the second 27. The first sentence contains several weak verbs: <u>are</u>, <u>are</u>, <u>to give</u>, <u>are</u>, <u>are</u>, <u>has</u>, and <u>is possessed</u>; the second contains two active verbs: <u>can give</u> and <u>can render</u>. The conciseness of the second sentence gives it clarity. The first sentence's wordiness drags the meaning. The second sentence works well also because it contains a clear contrast between <u>the right verbs</u> and <u>the wrong verbs</u>. In addition, the false starts <u>there are</u> have been deleted from the second sentence, thus enabling a tighter revision. The alliterative string of s's (<u>sentence</u>, <u>snap</u>, <u>sting</u>) of the bullwhip help you hear the sound of the whip. The two images of the bullwhip and piece of string stand out in the second sentence because of the conciseness. The second sentence, therefore, more clearly expresses antithesis.

[2]Miles, Bertonasco, and Karns.
[3]Miles, Bertonasco, and Karns.

ACTIVITY 8

Look at your recent writing. Examine the verbs in your sentences. Underline all the passive verbs you find. Then try to revise sentences by replacing weak passive verbs with strong active ones. See if active verbs help you omit needless words. You might not figure out how to revise some sentences. Don't worry—some sentences may sound better with passive verbs. But you will be able to revise <u>many</u> sentences. Experiment and see. Copy at least three of your passive sentences and write an active revision for each of them. Bring your work to class.

Omit Needless Words III

Often you can omit phrases containing weak verbs in your sentences, such as "that is," "that are" or "it is."

The vivid description <u>that is</u> so prevalent in King's speech stirs pathos.

Revised

The vivid description so prevalent in King's speech stirs pathos.

The use of caffeine can be therapeutic if it is consumed in the right amount.

Revised

Caffeine in the right amount can be therapeutic.

Their bodies change in many ways that are uncontrollable.

Revised

Their bodies change in many uncontrollable ways.

ACTIVITY 9

Write each of these sentences in your notebook. Then revise them, omitting needless words.

1. Magic Johnson is ready to face any obstacle that is placed before him.

2. With the research information that is gathered by scientists, human cloning may happen soon.
3. Many advances in technology that have been made in recent years help senior citizens.
4. Critical thinkers don't ignore problems that are bothering them.
5. George Carlin's humor is full of analogies that are surprising.

ACTIVITY 10

Look at your recent writing. Examine your sentences for any needless phrases, such as "that is," "that are," or "it is." Then try to revise by omitting needless words.

Chapter 5

Problems in Reasoning

FINDING THE FACTS

Finding the <u>facts</u>, said Sherlock Holmes, is the beginning of wisdom. What is a fact? A fact is something real, something you can observe, something you can experience. Critical thinkers define facts two ways: first is primary evidence, those things you can discover with your senses or with tests and measurements of various sorts—science. Also, facts can be secondary evidence: beliefs, ideas, or information you cannot find with your senses but for which there is historical evidence, documents, testimony, or articles related to the fact in question. Was there ever a man named Jesus? The answer is yes, based on secondary (historical) evidence.

We tend to think of "probability" rather than absolute truth in modern science. Primary evidence usually has a higher probability than secondary evidence—but not always. If you find deer tracks in the soft earth, you can accept this as probable evidence of a fact, evidence of deer (that is, if they really are deer tracks and not a trick). Critical thinkers define facts as things you can discover with your senses, or things you believe are "probable." For example, you believe your history books are probably true, based on both physical and secondary evidence. You believe Adolf Hitler was the German "Fuhrer" during World War II, and most thoughtful people agree he ordered the massacre of millions of Jewish people. Why believe these things? Critical thinkers believe them because people are still alive to attest to them; many historians confirm them; and much physical evidence remains of them. A few people say they don't believe the evidence, but the burden is on them to show how else to explain the probable "facts," including all the newspaper and magazine stories at the time, the books, the pictures, and other more appalling evidence of the Holocaust.

Critical thinkers know that if you catch someone whose fingerprints are on the murder weapon, you may or may not have found the guilty individual. Reasoning tells you not to seize the first available answer: critical thinking tells you to explore, to look for other explanations. Fingerprints on a gun don't automatically solve the problem. "Jumping" to the conclusion, before all the facts are in, isn't reasoning. Thoughtful readers and writers must resist drawing conclusions until they are sure of all the facts. Reasoning does not start with guessing an answer. First you must collect and evaluate the facts: then you can attempt to put them together to reach your conclusions.

Facts are verifiable reality, truths you can detect with your own senses or with testimony from witnesses or with instruments and rules of science. In the mathematical sciences, "facts" are demonstrable with numbers and reasoning. It is important to determine facts because without them we have only guessing. And in that case, even careful thinkers are likely to make errors of reasoning. You want to know: did the house burn by accident or was something more deliberate involved? Did the victim die of natural causes . . . or something else? Should we allow developers to build a casino in our town or not? And why? Facts are the foundation of reason.

The purpose of this chapter is to help you learn to recognize problems in reasoning and to avoid them in your own writing and speaking.

IMPLICATIONS, ASSUMPTIONS, AND INFERENCES

Reasoning requires that you sift and weigh your thoughts and make judgments about evidence. Reasoning has an unpredictable quality. It's like fishing or hunting: you seek out the truth by tracking down the facts. Learning principles and techniques of reasoning takes practice. Being able to recognize problems of reasoning will strengthen your critical thinking abilities.

You need to be on the alert for the worst problem of all: self-deception. It's bad enough when you are confronted with faulty evidence; it's worse yet to suspect that you are being deceived by a sly opponent. However, to mislead yourself is the worst problem because it means your own reasoning is not trustworthy. It means you can never be certain whether you have reached a valid conclusion or are merely accepting the answer you want to hear.

Critical thinkers need to be careful when trying to solve a problem because people don't always spell out everything for you in clear, logical language. One of the problems of reasoning lies in the fact that what is <u>not</u> said can be as significant as what is said. For example, the standard "syllogism" states a major premise, a minor premise, and a conclusion: "All men are mortal; Socrates is a man; therefore, Socrates is mortal." But only logicians talk that way. Most of us take shortcuts. Most people can hop and skip through the language, relying on our reader's ability to follow us. We use informal reasoning; we turn things around, skip over the middle part, and sometimes avoid the syllogism altogether: "Of course Socrates was mortal—isn't everyone?"

Therefore, understanding and interpretation rely not only on your ability to recognize what you are hearing or reading but also on your ability to fill in missing information, to use context to supply the missing parts. To analyze problems in reasoning, you need to understand the differences between facts and implications, inferences, and assumptions.

Implications

An implication is a suggestion, an idea expressed with indirect words or an unspoken meaning audiences can detect. For example, you know when your friends don't like your new glasses, even if they say they do like them. Facial expressions, body language, and tone of voice (sarcasm) can negate a message, and so can noncommittal responses ("Yeah, okay I guess"). Such implied messages can mean the opposite of a spoken message: "Your new glasses are . . . very interesting." The speaker seems to say something positive, but most people know this particular message implies something negative. An implication is an unspoken message: "Aunt Lori has done up her hair and put on makeup, perfume, and earrings. She is wearing her blue dress and her hat and gloves. All this <u>suggests</u> (though she doesn't say) she is going somewhere."

Implications, as unspoken messages, may be accurate or inaccurate. When you write 20 pages for your research paper instead of the assigned 10, you may wish to imply (suggest) that you did more work than other students. But length does not equal quality, and most teachers want students to stay within the bounds of the assignment. When you clean your roommate's dishes, you may imply that you are kind. (But the truth might be that you want to borrow your friend's car.) When you volunteer at the local soup kitchen, you may imply to others that you have a social conscience. (But the truth may be you think this will look good on your résumé.)

It's important to be alert to implications because they can lead your reasoning astray. Many people believe the Second Amendment of the Constitution says all citizens have the right to have guns. Many others, however, believe the amendment implies that only a state militia can be armed.

Assumptions

An assumption is an idea or belief you take for granted, a supposition. When you see Aunt Lori dressed up this way, you take for granted that she is going out. Your assumptions are based on your experiences: you've seen Aunt Lori dress this way before. Could there be any other reason for her to dress this way?

Maybe—but if she isn't going out of the house, her hat and gloves seem like overdress. If you are reading <u>Moby Dick</u> at the beach, some people may assume you enjoy serious literature (but you may be reading it for a course you're required to take in the fall, and you're trying to read ahead—and maybe the reading feels like hard work). An assumption is a belief, not necessarily a fact: many religious people assume that Heaven exists and if they lead moral lives they will go there.

Assumptions, as well, can be carelessly or carefully made. You can base your assumptions on prior knowledge: because it's thundering and raining outside, you assume soon there will be lightning. Because the sun just came out, you assume if you go outside you might see a rainbow. Or you can base your assumptions on little knowledge—"I assume that students who attend Michigan State University—where there are more than 40,000 students—are treated like numbers in their classes." This assumption is proven wrong in the case of first year writing classes, which are small and personal.

Not all assumptions are harmless thoughts that you could easily express if you wanted to. Some assumptions are hidden and (some people think) destructive. Although the public may assume school teaches reading, writing, and arithmetic, Jonathan Kozol suggests that the true function of the public schools is to weed out lower class students, to reconcile them to their low position in society, and to direct them toward "suitable" work. In <u>Savage Inequalities</u>, he says,

> A recent emphasis of certain business-minded authors writing about children in the kinds of schools we have examined in Chicago urges us to settle for "realistic" goals, by which these authors mean the kinds of limited career objectives that seem logical or fitting for low-income children. (74)

> Many urban high school students do not study math but "business math"—essentially a very elemental level of bookkeeping. Job-specific courses such as "cosmetology" (hairdressing, manicures) [. . .] are a common item in the segregated high schools and are seen as realistic preparation for the adult roles that 16-year-old black girls may expect to fill. (76)

> A lot of wealthy folks in Texas think the schools are doing a sufficiently good job if the kids of poor folks [. . .] had all the necessary skills to do their kitchen work and tend their lawns. (216)

Kozol's studies were limited to inner city schools, in several large cities. Do such conditions still exist? Are Kozol's conclusions representative of the country at large? If you read his book, might you reach different conclusions?

People assume our schools only teach English, math, history, and science, and most people hold the assumption that it is wrong to use schools to teach any sort of ideology. American education is officially "value free," meaning it doesn't preach any religion and doesn't favor any political party or position. Yet critics say that "value free" has come to mean valu<u>eless</u>. If we take the value out of what students learn, what is left?

ACTIVITY 1

Identify what assumption you think has been made in each of the following statements. Briefly explain your reasoning. (There may be more than one answer.) For example

> After a fine chicken dinner, little Angela became ill. "I'll never serve chicken again," vowed her mother. (Mother assumes the chicken dinner made Angela ill.)

1. Henry opened a letter addressed to his roommate, Bill. The letter said, "Your HIV test was positive." Henry immediately moved out of the dorm.
2. Lonny's father discovered that the family car had a large dent in the rear bumper. "Just wait until I get my hands on that kid," the father said.
3. These IBM computers are too complicated. We better order Apple computers for the students' computer lab.
4. Buddy easily won his event and broke the Olympic record. Another athlete said, "Buddy was lucky he didn't have to take a urinalysis test."
5. Because everyone passed the test, the professor decided to give another, "just to be sure."
6. His father not only took Chris's BB gun away, but he disassembled it because "it's better to be safe than sorry," he said.
7. A recent immigrant to this country, Mr. Pilski went shopping for a new pen. "I want only the best," he told the clerk. After looking at several, Mr. Pilski chose the most expensive.
8. Angry about his stock market losses, Lester cursed, "God is unfair." Suddenly Lester had a stroke. The minister said, "Thou shalt not take the Lord's name in vain."
9. Weeping at his mother's funeral, Arnie said, "It's my fault. Two weeks ago, while playing with an old deck of Tarot [fortune] cards, I dropped the deck, and the 'death card' landed on Mother's picture."
10. Lloyd's loose teeth were a constant embarrassment. At a dinner party Lloyd prepared an after-dinner punch. From the kitchen, the guests could hear a splash, followed by Lloyd saying, "Juth a minute folkth." When the punch arrived, all the guests claimed they were "too full" and quickly departed.

Inferences

An inference is a conclusion, a logical deduction. You infer from your friends' comments that they really don't like your new glasses. You infer that Aunt Lori is going out when she gets "dressed up." If you bring <u>Moby Dick</u> to read at the beach instead of <u>People</u> magazine, some people might infer that you like serious literature. People draw inferences from whatever they notice.

An inference is a conclusion and, therefore, is similar to an assumption, except that an inference usually is based on something you can see or hear, some evidence you can detect with your senses or through premises you believe to be true. Assumptions, however, are usually based on beliefs. For example, Gretchen ended her research paper with the conclusion that there may be Martians, because she could find no evidence against their existence. Gretchen relies on an <u>assumption</u>—she assumes that if there had been any Martians she would have found some evidence of them.

An inference is not a guess—such as "Guess what number I'm thinking of?" An inference is a conclusion you reach because you have evidence that leads you to the conclusion. In <u>The Adventures of Huckleberry Finn</u>, for example, Huck makes an important inference based on footprints in the snow:

> There was an inch of new snow on the ground, and I seen somebody's tracks. They had come up from the quarry and stood around the stile awhile, and then went on around the garden fence. It was funny they hadn't come in, after standing around so. I couldn't make it out. It was very curious, somehow. I was going to follow around, but I stooped down to look at the tracks first. I didn't notice anything at first, but next I did. There was a cross in the left boot-heel made with big nails, to keep off the devil.
>
> I was up in a second and shinning down the hill. I looked over my shoulder every now and then, but I didn't see nobody. [. . .] pap was here again. (19)

Huck's observations about the tracks, where they have come from and where they go, from the stile[1] are inferences based on the shape of a boot. Because a boot has a forward and trailing edge, it's easy to infer the direction of the boot-wearer. But Huck makes one inference most people probably would not: the tracks were made by "pap." The cross on the heel is the evidence from which Huck draws his inference.

Inferences "may be carelessly or carefully made" says S. I. Hayakawa in <u>Language in Thought and Action</u>:

> They may be made on the basis of a broad background of previous experience with the subject matter, or no experience at all. For example, the inferences a good mechanic can make about the internal condition of a motor by listening to it are often startlingly accurate, while the inferences made by an amateur (if he tries to make any) may be entirely wrong. But the common characteristic of inferences is that they are statements [. . .] made on the basis of what has been observed. (37)

---

[1]Stile: steps or stones to help one over a wall.

It isn't always easy to decide between <u>implication</u>, <u>assumption</u>, or <u>inference</u>, especially when, sometimes, more than one answer seems possible. One helpful technique to use is the "rule of simplicity." When there are competing possibilities, the rule of simplicity says to choose the answer that requires the fewest assumptions. That means if you find your pet rabbit dead, the rule of simplicity tells you the rabbit probably wasn't killed by aliens . . . because that answer would require you to introduce an assumption—that there are aliens. You would need additional information before you could reasonably infer that aliens zapped your bunny.

Assumptions, implications, and inferences all rely on your ability to fill in missing information, to make the connection between the information you do have (like the tracks in the snow) and a conclusion, information you don't have. Huck might have been wrong—he lives among superstitious people, and pap might not be the only man with such a mark. However, in this case, Huck's inference was correct, for shortly pap does show up.

ACTIVITY 2

Use the "rule of simplicity" to try to identify which if any of the options is a reasonable inference based solely on the information in the statements. The rule of simplicity tells you the simplest explanation is usually the best one. Using that rule as a guide, select the answer you think is most probable. If none of the answers seems likely to you, select "E. None of the above." Supply your own idea of the correct answer or why you believe the answer should be "E."

1. "It is impossible for me to be pregnant, Dr. Stone," said Mary Doe. "I've been 'on the pill' for two years."

    (A) Dr. Stone is kidding Mary Doe. (B) Mary Doe is sexually promiscuous. (C) Mary Doe believes the "pill" is an infallible birth control method. (D) Mary Doe is having an affair with Dr. Stone. (E) None of the above.

2. More than half the audience left before the film ended.

    (A) Those who left did not enjoy the film. (B) Those who stayed were unable to leave. (C) Those who left had already seen the ending. (D) Those who stayed planned to see the film again. (E) None of the above.

3. If we don't provide study questions, many students will fail.

    (A) The students like study questions. (B) The exam is too easy. (C) Students don't need to study. (D) The exam is very difficult. (E) None of the above.

4. Leroy mixed a drink of odds and ends from his father's liquor cabinet. Shortly thereafter he began to feel "strange." He was found dead soon after.

    (A) Leroy was having a party. (B) The drink killed him. (C) Leroy was an alcoholic. (D) Father had laced the liquor with poison to teach Leroy a lesson. (E) None of the above.

5. Young women of today believe they should not be prevented from doing anything they are capable of doing.

    (A) Young women of today want to be treated as if they were men. (B) Many young women reject the traditional roles of mother and homemaker. (C) Our society is coming apart. (D) Young women believe equality of opportunity should be gender-free. (E) None of the above.

6. The newspaper reported that an old man had been found dead at the foot of a long flight of stairs.

    (A) The stairs had no railing. (B) Someone murdered the old man. (C) A fall down the stairs killed the old guy. (D) The old man had fallen as he started up the staircase. (E) None of the above.

7. Aunt Bess awoke in the night feeling alarmed and smelling smoke. "Quick, Henry," she shouted, "We must save the children."

    (A) Aunt Bess is having a bad dream. (B) Aunt Bess believes the children are smoking. (C) Aunt Bess believes the house is on fire. (D) Aunt Bess believes Henry's smoking is endangering the children. (E) None of the above.

8. The neighbor's newspapers and mail are piling up, their grass needs cutting, and we haven't seen the neighbors in several weeks.

    (A) The neighbors are lazy. (B) The neighbors are dead. (C) The neighbors are not at home. (D) The neighbors have too many newspapers. (E) None of the above.

9. The clouds are getting dark and thick, the skies are getting gray and ominous, the wind is getting stronger—flashes of lightning can be seen.

    (A) It's a nice day. (B) These effects are done with mirrors and other devices. (C) It's a great day to go fishing. (D) We like the wind. (E) None of the above.

10. A holy man doused himself with gasoline and struck a match. After several matches failed to ignite the gasoline, villagers began to kneel and pray to the holy man. The villagers' reaction was the result of which of the following?

    (A) A religious belief about the holy man. (B) Belief in magic. (C) Matches are used in their religious rites. (D) Common sense. (E) None of the above.

ACTIVITY 3

Try to find the best answer for each of the following statements based on what you know about facts, assumptions, implications, inferences, or other reasoning. Using the "rule of simplicity" as a guide, select the answer you think best explains the statement.

1. Uncle Russell reasoned with himself: one vitamin pill is supposed to be good for you, so I will have even more good by taking two pills, and perhaps I shall gain

even more by taking several; no doubt I'll have the greatest good by taking the entire bottle. This reasoning constitutes

(A) A question of fact. (B) An assumption. (C) An inference. (D) Scientific evidence, which says that the more pills the better. (E) None of the above

2. The clues we have found indicate the suspect had long blonde hair, wore bright red lipstick, and wore high-heeled shoes and a green silk material often used in dressmaking.

(A) The suspect lacked good taste. (B) Green silk and bright red don't go together. (C) No one wears high heels anymore. (D) The suspect was dressed as a woman. (E) None of the above.

3. A smiling man dressed in black and wearing a preacher's collar approached people in the shopping mall. He held out a can with the word <u>Help</u> painted on it. Most people dropped some money into the can.

(A) The man was threatening the shoppers. (B) People who gave money may have assumed the man was collecting for a legitimate charity. (C) The man in black was really not a preacher at all. (D) The man was probably working under-cover for the FBI. (E) None of the above.

4. A young woman taking the pill had trouble with vomiting and breathing and had a mysterious pain. She soon died.

(A) The pill killed her. (B) The woman was pregnant. (C) Young women should not take pills. (D) The woman had cancer. (E) None of the above.

5. During the cold war we believed we could prevent a nuclear war by convincing the rest of the world that a holocaust, "a nuclear winter," would follow any attack on us.

(A) We are a warlike people. (B) We want nuclear war. (C) We believe we can prevent war by threatening retaliation. (D) Nuclear war is good for us. (E) None of the above.

6. A man had locked himself in from the inside; there were no windows, no way in other than the locked door. Relatives pounding on the door heard a gun go off, and they broke through the door at that very moment. The man was found with a smoking gun in his hand and a bullet hole in his temple.

(A) Relatives banging on the door caused the gun to go off. (B) There was a secret panel in the room through which the killer escaped. (C) The man had arranged a clever theatrical to convince everyone he was dead. (D) Those who broke down the door lied when they said they heard the gun go off. (E) None of the above.

7. Half the students failed the state's new competency test, so the state ordered a new test.

(A) The new test would certainly get better results. (B) The test was probably boring. (C) This shows that tests are no good. (D) Half the students were mentally limited. (E) None of the above.

8. Betty was reluctant to enter the weight-lifting competition because, she said, "I'll just lose anyway." Her friends forced her to enter, but she lost, just as she had said.

(A) Betty was afraid she would look foolish in the competition. (B) Betty was too shy to enter any competition. (C) Betty believed the other lifters would laugh at her and call her "weakling." (D) Betty may have lost because of her own lack of confidence. (E) None of the above.

9. A man handed the bank clerk a note; the clerk touched a silent alarm button, and suddenly several armed guards surrounded the man with the note.

(A) The guards can hear silent alarms. (B) The man was trying to rob the bank. (C) Something in the note alarmed the clerk. (D) The man was deaf and mute. (E) None of the above.

10. The great magician, Magnifico, performed for the people of a small village. His assistant, Lenore, lying on a table and covered by a cloth, slowly floated up into the air. Suddenly Magnifico whisked away the cloth, revealing . . . empty space. The villagers knelt and began to pray.

(A) The spirit of Lenore had terrified them. (B) The villagers assumed the Great Magnifico had magical powers. (C) Magnifico had turned Lenore into air. (D) Lenore was cleverly hidden within a secret pocket of the cloth. (E) None of the above.

FALLACIES

To reason well, you must word your statements carefully: you must draw your conclusions according to the rules of logic. If worded properly, a logical statement becomes inescapable, which means the conclusion is as near as you can get to absolute truth. And by "worded properly" we mean with true premises arranged according to some rule of logic that reasonable people can accept. Without some training, however, even critical thinkers may accidentally make pseudo statements—statements that may seem logical but which actually contain some error in reasoning.

Most of the errors of reasoning are well known. There may be some exceptions, but on the whole, the fallacies are those we present here. We list them here as "problems" of reasoning because they don't apply automatically. Not all fallacies are fallacious all the time. For example, a self-fulfilling prophecy is a wish, a guess, or a pronouncement about the future that you yourself make come true, or something that is likely to come true, given your premise (a foregone conclusion). For example

There's no sense studying for the test—I'll just fail it anyway.

I won't like the film; it will have no suspense because I already know the butler did it.

Often these "prophecies" are simply our own fears being realized. They sound like excuses (rationalizations) for doing or not doing something. Once in a while, however, the prophecy is a true prediction, not something we ourselves cause: "I can't go to the movies tomorrow. It's my parents' anniversary, and I'll have to stay home and baby-sit my brother and sister."

Some of the fallacies may sound strange to you: many of them still have their Latin names (such as <u>ad hominem</u>). They have English names too, of course, but educated men and women have carried on the tradition of the Latin names for thousands of years. You will have to make up your own mind about that, but once you learn them, you will begin to hear them and see them in print. (Readers tend to skip anything unfamiliar or difficult and thus you may believe that you have never seen or heard these words, but once you learn them you'll discover thoughtful writers have been using them all along.)

PROBLEMS OF INSUFFICIENT EVIDENCE

Problems of insufficient evidence can result in overgeneralizing, cardstacking, ad ignorantium, and post hoc ergo propter hoc. It is the nature of reasoning and research that we rarely have enough evidence. As a result, we find ourselves trying to predict on the basis of small amounts of information. On election night, for example, TV statisticians predict the winners on the basis of only 2% or 3% of the votes. We use general rules and principles to guide us when we can't be absolutely sure of the outcome:

> A horse with a winning record is a safer bet than one that has several losses or one that has never raced before.

> Red is a relatively uncommon hair color in Asia.

Naturally, you can never be absolutely certain about such generalized conclusions; at best you must assume greater or lesser degrees of probability. You can only say that red is "a <u>relatively</u> uncommon hair color" because you really haven't seen many of Asia's billions of people. If you required 100% certainty before making up your mind about anything, you would live in constant indecision. If a two-year-old manages to climb to the top of the jungle gym, what might happen? Most adults would become alarmed and would <u>probably</u> get the child down. We can only say "probably" here because some adults are pretty relaxed and might assume their child was safe. In a court case, you may not have enough information to say absolutely what happened, but you could say the accused is a very small woman weighing less than 100 pounds and has only normal strength and endurance. Is it probable that she could have lifted the victim (a large man who weighs 275 pounds) into a crate, which she then theoretically carried down a flight of stairs and lifted into a truck by herself? It really doesn't seem probable.

However, because you do work with probabilities instead of certainties, you can fall into the habit of casually generalizing without proper sampling and verification techniques. Because we can only predict probabilities, some people develop the attitude that everything is a guessing game and, therefore, "my guess is as good as anyone's," meaning nothing really matters. But clearly this isn't true. Some opinions can get us in trouble (jail). Random guessing is not the technique of critical thinkers. Guessing is allowed, but an "educated guess" is different from a random "shot in the dark."

Experts who have spent years studying and gaining experience with weapons, ballistics, and forensic[2] evidence have expert opinions that are treated differently from yours or ours. They may be giving inferences, but their <u>educated</u> guesses have more influence than average citizens (juries) do. When experts say the victim died of strangulation, we are inclined to believe them.

Overgeneralizing

<u>Overgeneralizing</u> (also called <u>hasty generalizing</u>, <u>faulty generalizing</u>) means drawing a larger conclusion than the evidence supports. Critical thinkers should keep in mind how difficult it is to verify statements about "all" or "most" or even "many" (depending on how many we mean). For example

All robins have red breasts.

The statement isn't exactly true. Young robins are usually speckled. The breasts of adult robins can appear to be more orange than red. In any case, it's highly doubtful that anyone could ever claim to have seen "all" the robins in the world.

Many children die before reaching maturity.

That's a difficult statement at best. The word <u>many</u> is inherently vague—how "many" are we talking about? Further, both "children" and "maturity" are subject to various interpretations.

Men don't cry.

We include this example to show that generalizations can be implicit. The statement doesn't use "all" or "most," but it implies (suggests) a feature of men in general. Depending on how many are included in the statement (some? many? most?), critical thinkers may reject the statement as an overgeneralization. The statement cannot mean that males as a group are biologically incapable of crying: medical information assures us that both males and females have functioning tear ducts. It's possible that the statement refers to the quality of being "manly," and therefore it is even less likely to be true (who makes these rules?).

---

[2]Ballistics: the science of identifying bullets; forensics: accepted in courts of law.

If there are so many exceptions and complications to using generalizations, why do we use them? The answer is that we use them because we must. Most of us will find it difficult to have conversations if we are required to use only scientifically accurate statements. Such information isn't available to most of us and would seriously alter our ability to communicate if it were. Imagine, for example, the statement, "Tall men have big feet." In general, many people would agree—it's a handy generalization you can use in appropriate contexts. But if you had to define exactly what you mean by tall men and big feet, you would be unable to proceed with your discussion and instead would begin arguing about the definitions of these <u>general</u> terms. The ability to generalize is an important part of your ability to think and to communicate. However, critical thinkers need to be alert to overgeneralizations.

If you insist on generalizations, such as "Pigs will eat anything," you make your statements easy to refute. All you need to refute a sweeping generalization such as that one is to produce something some pig somewhere refuses to eat. A single exception can cast doubt on sweeping generalizations and on your credibility. When you stop to analyze a generalization (one that sounds doubtful to you), you may discover that it means something you doubt or that it doesn't mean anything you can verify.

However, there is a limit to how far we can trust this. On the whole it is true that pigs are not very picky, and that's an old and accepted truth. If now someone shows up at the county fair with a pig that won't eat anything but lilacs, we aren't likely to change our old truism about pigs. We are much more likely to conclude that there is something strange about that lilac-eating pig. Established beliefs are those that have stood the test of time and aren't likely to be overturned easily. Despite the rule about big generalizations, it is generally hard to overturn an established rule, and we often require more than a single exception to do it.

Overgeneralizations are one of the most common fallacies of writing and in conversation, for example, "All real men have beards." You know that is not true. Some men do not have beards at all. Many men shave their beards. And, in fact, some women can have surprisingly heavy beards. The generalization between men and beards is too sweeping. It is a fallacy. Be on guard against statements that contain words such as <u>all</u>, <u>everyone</u>, <u>everybody</u>, <u>no one</u>, <u>nothing</u>, <u>everything</u>, <u>anything</u>, and <u>always</u>. Be on guard against statements that imply too many cases, whether they use any of these words or not. Thoughtful writers <u>qualify</u> generalizations that seem too sweeping or that are likely to create doubt in the reader's mind. Qualifiers such as <u>many</u>, <u>some</u>, or <u>a few</u> work well, usually.

As a critical thinker you may qualify as much as you like. Green spots on the bread <u>may</u> indicate spoilage. <u>Most</u> children enjoy school until about second or third grade. <u>Many</u> of the elderly are more concerned with security than with enjoying life. You need to test your generalizations in your mind before setting them in print. However, so much qualifying may give your writing an excessively tentative, indecisive sound, as if you aren't sure of what you want to say. This is one place where reason and style run into each other, a place where you must make decisions about which way to go. How many "maybe's" and "probably's" can readers encounter before they wish you would simply make a good strong statement?

You need to be aware of generalizations—whether they make sense or not, whether they are qualified or not.

ACTIVITY 4

Please read this passage from Richard Paul, author of <u>Critical Thinking: What Every Person Needs to Survive in a Rapidly Changing World</u> (1993). In your notebook, write about these issues: Do you agree with Richard Paul? Evaluate his reasoning (is his reasoning valid?). Does he overgeneralize? How? Write at least a page. Bring your answers to class for discussion.

> Classroom instruction around the world, at all levels, is typically didactic,[3] one-dimensional, and indifferent, when not antithetical to[4] reason. Blank faces are taught barren conclusions in dreary drills. There is nothing sharp, nothing poignant, no exciting twist or turn of mind and thought, nothing fearless, nothing modest, no struggle, no conflict, no rational give-and-take, no intellectual excitement or discipline, no pulsation in the heart or mind. Students are not expected to ask for reasons to justify what they are told to believe. They do not question what they see, hear, or read, nor are they encouraged to do so. They do not demand that subject matter "make sense" to them. They do not challenge the thinking of other students nor expect their thinking to be challenged by others. Indeed, they do not expect to have to think at all. (Introduction ix)

Card Stacking

<u>Card stacking</u> means selecting only data that supports your own point of view and ignoring contradictory data. Card stacking is biased, unfair thinking and writing and should be avoided. For example, suppose we listed these characteristics of former President Clinton:

> During his time in office, President Clinton was a moral man. He was married to a smart and wise woman, Hillary. He loved his daughter and talked a lot about family values. He went to church each Sunday. He often quoted from the Bible.

[3]Didactic: boringly moralistic.
[4]Antithetical to: against.

These statements are one sided; there is no reference to the other side of Mr. Clinton's character, his inappropriate behavior with a young intern. This little report omits a great deal about the president that critical thinkers need in order to make an informed judgment. Stacking the deck means arranging the cards so that it is possible to know the winner or loser in advance. Our little report about the president stacks the evidence to make him seem a winner, but most people know there is more to this story.

Card stacking is especially harmful in research. Researchers who go looking for evidence that supports only one side of an issue—such as evidence that tobacco smoke is harmless—may be able to find an impressive number of people who have smoked all their lives without ill-effect and thus the findings will seem to reinforce the preconceived notion of the thesis. But "stacking" the evidence is of course not research at all; it gives only one side of the evidence. Ignoring evidence, whether deliberately or accidentally, can be considered fraud at worst and amateurish at best. No matter how many healthy smokers can be found, researchers must also account for those who are ill.

As a critical thinker, you must not impose your own bias on the subject or the data. A research paper must examine all sides, all data, and must not be biased toward either side. (A <u>report</u> on healthy smokers is a different matter. See chapter 10.)

Ad Ignorantium

<u>Ad ignorantium</u> is a fallacy based on ignorance. An ad ignorantium writer tells readers something must be true <u>because</u> they can't prove otherwise. "You can't prove there aren't any leprechauns in Ireland; <u>therefore</u> you should assume there are such creatures." (This is false reasoning. The correct wording should be <u>there may or may not</u> be such creatures. In short the statement is meaningless without evidence one way or the other.) The absence of evidence is not proof.

The "ignorant" argument tells you that something must be true if you cannot prove it false, or that something must be false if you cannot prove it true. "You can't prove your candidate will win the race; therefore I assume your candidate won't." A negative premise is not a good basis for concluding anything. The argument assumes that lack of knowledge, "ignorance," can be a source of information.

Except for special cases, most critical thinkers reject the idea that <u>because</u> you don't know something, its opposite must be true. The statement is self-contradictory (because you don't know something, you do know something?). Avoid negative statements. Phrase your claims positively when possible.

Post Hoc Ergo Propter Hoc

<u>Post hoc ergo propter hoc</u> translates as "after this, therefore because of this." That is, it's a fallacy based on time. It is often called <u>post hoc</u> for short. You assume a later event was caused by an earlier event: "The milk was left out all

night and was spoiled the next morning. It should have been put in the refrigerator to keep it fresh." The speaker assumes the first event—leaving the milk out—caused the second event (the milk spoiled). It's a possibility of course: many people would make that assumption. The milk may have spoiled as a result of being out of the refrigerator all night, but you should reject the notion that one thing must cause another. Could there be any other explanation? Yes, it is possible that the milk never was fresh—that it was spoiled before being left out. Many things are possible but few are necessary, especially where causation is concerned. A young man may fall in love with a young woman after she sprinkles a love potion over his cereal, but critical thinkers would be reluctant to say the potion must have been the cause.

To take a more difficult example: "Japan became a great industrial nation after its surrender in World War II; therefore the defeat caused this rise in industry." True? Cause and effect relationships are seldom as simple as people believe; often there are many indirect as well as direct causes of a single effect. It is certainly not true that one thing must have caused another simply because the two things happened sequentially.

ACTIVITY 5

Insufficient Evidence

Identify the fallacy in each of the following statements. Explain why each statement is called an error of insufficient evidence: overgeneralization, card stacking, ad ignorantium, or post hoc ergo propter hoc.

> Example: After he declared an end to our involvement in the Vietnam War, President Nixon was forced out of office: obviously his downfall was the result of his war policy. [Post hoc ergo propter hoc—the later event was not caused by the former. Nixon's downfall was not caused by his war policy.]

1. No one has ever proven that alien life exists elsewhere in the universe; therefore it is foolish to speculate about extraterrestrial beings.
2. Any grizzly bear can outrun any human being.
3. Did women create the great literature of the world? Did they create the great works of art? Paintings? Sculptures and music? Did they invent the sciences, build the cities, create our technological wonders? No they didn't! Clearly women are not equal to men.
4. Some students are blessed with high IQ's, good looks, athletic skills, excellent academic records, and prosperous parents who encourage them to work hard and achieve: no wonder they succeed.
5. It is certain that every college student is committed to reading and writing and diligently studying for years on end to earn a degree.

6. It's a mystery to me why so many Americans mistrust Saddam Hussein. Isn't he good looking? Isn't he smart? The Iraqi people love him—they put his picture up everywhere.

7. Because the library has no books about Eva Braun's sexual intimacies with Adolf Hitler, she must not have had any.

8. We added pure ethyl alcohol to the mixture and immediately there was an explosion; obviously the alcohol had to be the cause of the blast.

9. Everyone loves those old Charlie Chaplin movies.

10. A lab assistant wrote up the results of the professor's experiment. Two dozen mice had been given a substance believed to cause only benign effects. Later 23 mice seemed to be alive and well. However, mouse 24 was dead. The assistant said, "Oh well, never mind. We have enough data with the first 23. We don't need that last one."

ACTIVITY 6

In your notebook write an example of your own for each fallacy: overgeneralization, card stacking, ad ignorantium, and post hoc ergo propter hoc.

PROBLEMS BASED ON IRRELEVANT INFORMATION

Some writing problems occur when a writer bases ideas on irrelevant information. Following are examples of this type of writing:

Ad baculum	Bandwagon
Ad hominem	Plain folks and snob appeal
Fallacy of opposition	Ad verecundiam
Genetic fallacy	Red herring
Guilt by association	Weak opponent [straw man]
Ad misericordiam	Tu quoque
Ad populum	Oversimplification

The largest group of reasoning problems contains the irrelevant arguments. Often these are used in arguments by accident, but sometimes they are the result of faulty thinking. "Irrelevant" here means not related to the point at issue. For example, "A packing company is trying to open a new factory in our town. Is it relevant information that the company president has had psychiatric treatment? A new factory would mean jobs; it would be good for the town. What has the president's medical record to do with that?" Essentially this question asks for the warrant, the connection between the evidence and the claim (see Toulmin, chapter 3). It is the "so what" question. There are several varieties of irrelevance— several ways for an argument to stumble over evidence that doesn't clarify but instead muddies the waters of an investigation. You need to know what it would take to persuade people about the president of the new company. Is there some law against people treated for depression holding positions of power and prestige?

Relevance is an important consideration when evaluating evidence. You can lose a lot of time tracking down and/or evaluating evidence that has no relevance to your case. Opponents can create a lot of confusion by introducing irrelevant data. Critical thinkers must remember that the point of reasoning is not to win arguments but to find the truth of the matter, to the best of your ability. Using irrelevant information not only confuses the issue but may seriously damage your character.

Ad Baculum

Ad baculum comes from the Latin word for a "stick" or "club." The baculum argument is an appeal to force: it may involve threats of physical violence or psychological harm, such as public ridicule and loss of reputation. "My gang and I will beat up anyone who doesn't vote our way." Such crude "appeal to force" may seem laughable today, but even today gangs do make such threats, by implication if not expressly. In the early days of the labor movement, violence was used on all sides—within the unions, between the unions, and between unions and management. Direct threats may be less common today, but the ad baculum appeal is alive and well in the form of extortion, blackmail, and other more psychological appeals. For example, opponents in possession of damaging letters may threaten to make them public if you don't comply with their demands.

There are many different ways to apply force, threats, and pressure. For example, "If you give our cigarettes a bad report, we may lose our smokers and may even go out of business. Then you would lose the source of your grant money!" Here the "force" is indirect. You are being warned not to give a negative report.

Ad Hominem

The Faculty Senate was attempting to decide whether to create a fund for frog cloning research, but the English professors were yelling, "Biomedical researchers are frauds. They don't earn their salaries! They don't do anything productive. They use up all our resources! They're trying to get out of their teaching assignments again! No more money for them!"

Ad hominem translates as "to the person." The ad hominem argument ignores the facts entirely and instead attacks the person presenting them. In the preceding example, nothing is said about the frog cloning research itself. It is the researchers who are called "frauds" who "don't earn their salaries." Ad hominem arguments are often merely insults; they imply that there is something wrong with speakers, which allows us to ignore their arguments: "There is no point debating this question with Halston, a known pathological liar."

Ideally an argument is a close relationship between a claim and its evidence. You claim that lawyer Fastfoot has embezzled from the company, and the evidence is money found in Fastfoot's vacation cottage. The accountants must be able to show that the numbers don't add up, that the accounting has been altered to make it seem the money is still in the bank. Investigators must show that Fastfoot had the opportunity to siphon off the money and alter the numbers. Anything not related to the claim or the evidence is not relevant. Arguments about Fastfoot's personality or character ("he wouldn't do such a thing") aren't relevant to the question, which is not whether Fastfoot could—but whether he did do such a thing. Calling Fastfoot a thief or worse may make the investigators feel better, but such name calling has no bearing on the question.

Ad hominems are ways to avoid dealing with the question at hand. Insults beget insults; name calling can lead to violence. Avoid such irrelevant tactics and stick to the question at hand. It isn't relevant that Fastfoot may cheat on his marriage partner or may be a tax fraud; not even his virtues are relevant to a question of fact (he may be a conscientious churchgoer). The question is, did Fastfoot take the money?

Fallacy of Opposition

The fallacy of opposition is a specific kind of ad hominem. It is name calling based on the assumption that whatever comes from the opposition must be wrong and to your detriment. Such an assumption cuts off all reasoned discourse at the outset. If everything an opponent says is condemned just because the opponent says it, then you have no basis for reasoning together.

"Sure, you favor cloning humans because you're an atheist. I am a believer, and I oppose any tampering with God's natural method of conception." The attack is on the idea of cloning because of the person who supports it. The fallacy of opposition assumes that nothing good can come from those we oppose. In the example, the believer assumes anything an atheist says must be wrong.

Genetic Fallacy

The genetic fallacy is similar to the fallacy of opposition. The genetic fallacy is false because it assumes that where an idea comes from affects its validity. For example, "Can . . . any good thing come out of Nazareth?" the Bible asks (John 1:46). People sometimes attach positive or negative qualities to places. Many of these place attributes are simply biases:

The biomedical research is valid because it was done at Harvard.

You read the <u>Toledo News</u>? I read only the <u>New York Times</u>.

Valedictorians from small midwest towns cannot compete intellectually with valedictorians from New England prep schools.

Oh, he teaches psychology at Springfield Community College. You need to go to a major university to find a real expert in psychology.

You must examine the evidence in any question and not allow yourself to be influenced by faulty genetic assertions.

Guilt By Association

<u>Guilt by association</u> is an assumption that you choose your friends (or they choose you) because you are similar to them: you are like those you associate with. "Birds of a feather flock together." Parents often become alarmed by their children's friends. Friends who lie and cheat, use vulgar language, or smoke dope alarm parents because they fear their own children may be doing such things under the influence of peers. It is possible that peers <u>may</u> influence their friends' decisions, especially among those eager for peer approval.

However, mature people are usually able to withstand pressure to join friends in unwise or illegal activities. Critical thinkers should not make the assumption that people's behaviors must extend to their friends, nor the other way around either. Birds of a feather don't necessarily flock together. A person entering a bar is not necessarily an alcoholic. A person with rowdy friends will not necessarily become rowdy.

Ad Misericordiam

<u>Ad misericordiam</u> is an appeal to pity. Pity is a complex appeal; many people believe it is manipulative. Pity appeals to the emotions (pathos) rather than to the mind (logos). And pathos is frequently used in appeals for charity, for donations to worthy causes. In many cases, pity does seem relevant and does activate thoughtful reasoning.

Aristotle and others have said that pity can be a legitimate appeal—if you can determine that it is really appropriate to the question under consideration. Appeals for veterans wounded in military service, appeals for starving children in impoverished countries, appeals for the aged and the crippled all may be legitimate pathetic appeals for help.

But ad misericordiam can sometimes backfire on those who use it:

> Professor Bertram, please excuse my three absences last week. My grandmother died. She had a horrible stroke two years ago and my mother had to quit her job to care for her. Grandma couldn't talk, eat, or go to the bathroom. But she always smiled when I walked into her room.

In the normal course of events, grandparents do tend to pass on, eventually. However, this message does not explain what Grandma's death has to do with the three absences. There is an implied claim but no support for it. It's sad, of course, that Grandma had to suffer the stroke, but Professor Bertram may get the idea that all this information is simply an attempt to manipulate him. It might have been better if the student had simply asked for permission (before going) to attend Grandma's funeral.

It can be difficult to decide what is appropriate to ethos or pathos:

> Dad, we need to help my friend Jenny. She is in such terrible trouble. She totaled her car last week—a drunk driver ran into her. Her parents refuse to help her. She has no other relatives to turn to. Remember when she went camping with us after her parents' divorce? We all saw how happy she was. Dad, I think it's our ethical duty to help her. She needs a car to get to work.

Would your parents be moved by this appeal? Giving or lending a friend a car is asking for a lot, no matter how tragic the situation. Instead of focusing on the car, your parents, if they really like Jenny, might help by investigating the situation, and they might point out that although you are suggesting an ethical motive, the argument is entirely an appeal to pity.

Ad Populum

Ad populum is an argument "to the people." Ad populum ideas are assumed to be right because they are popular. "Down with big government" is a popular idea, but is it right? Ad populum appeals to biases, prejudices, and slogans. A populist appeal tells people what they want to hear, what they want to believe— such as how great the country is, how wonderful the people are. The populist approach "strokes" the voters with pleasing remarks.

During the Vietnam War a common slogan was "America—love it or leave it." The implication was that if you loved America, you should not criticize the war effort; instead, you should support it. This was a simplistic "ad populum" argument because Americans have the right to disagree with the government and the right not to love this country, especially when loving this country really means loving whatever the government does. Many Americans disagreed with the government's war policy and believed we should not be in Vietnam.

Populists appeal to tradition, oppose change, and call for a return to the values of the past. Populism often relies more on sound bites than on reasoning. Virtues such as "patriotism," "America for Americans," "law and order," "family values," and many others tend to mean whatever people say they mean. These sound bite slogans subvert the reasoning process: people shouting slogans make it difficult to analyze what is happening. Critical thinkers must remember that one of the traditional rules of the reasoning process is to define terms.

Arguments about serious matters are almost never as simple as ad populum slogans would have you believe.

Bandwagon

Bandwagon, a form of ad populum, is an appeal to peer pressure and group identity. An idea is assumed to be valid if many people accept it. "Six million people read the Daily Scandal: it must be an excellent paper."

Bandwagon is an appeal to do things because other people do them. "Get on the bandwagon" comes from the time when big wagons carrying a steam calliope[5] or a band of musicians announced the arrival of the circus in town or some other event. To get on the bandwagon meant to join the parade. Today the expression refers to joining anything that other people are doing. "Twenty million people can't be wrong!" But is that true? Apparently, millions of people still smoke, though research shows the relationship between cancer and smoking. Critical thinkers, obviously, should not do anything just because others do them. Reason is founded on the idea that you can be right no matter how many people oppose you.

Plain Folks and Snob Appeal

The plain folks appeal and the snob appeal are variations of the bandwagon appeal. Plain folks is an appeal that implies you should follow the ordinary citizen, the man in the street, the simple folk. (Avoid the pretensions of snobs.) There are a number of ways to indicate plain folks, for example:

> You can pay a fortune for filet mignon at some fancy restaurant, but ordinary people enjoy the same old steak and potatoes at Downtown Diner.

> Your expensive bar of perfumed soap from Paris may make you smell pretty, but good old brown soap will get folks just as clean.

Snob appeal is the reverse of plain folks. For example, "Your little old Apple II may be workable if you're just using it to type letters. But sophisticated computer users choose the Dynamo Thunderbore VIII." Snob appeal tries to reach the reader's vanity: you should do something because you would then be like one of the beautiful or important people.

> For an automotive experience of real distinction, professional athletes choose the Sportsmobile . . . and so can you.

> For a real education, you should attend Ivy University.

---

[5]Calliope (ka-lī-a-pē): a steam-driven pipe (or whistle) organ, very loud.

Ad Verecundiam

<u>Ad verecundiam</u> is the fallacy of inappropriate use of authority. Experts and authorities in one field are inappropriately cited in other fields, as if their expertise were all-encompassing. For example, "Michael Jordan is a fine athlete, so he might be a good person to ask about the economy." Inappropriate authorities aren't really authorities at all outside their areas of knowledge and experience. For instance, "Professor Novall knows a great deal about computer technology; she teaches at one of the great universities and has published many books and articles on the subject." However, her expertise on computers doesn't make the professor an authority on other matters, such as which stocks to buy on Wall Street (not even which high-tech stocks), a decision which requires an entirely different expertise.

Another ad verecundiam problem concerns the way information is documented in research writing. Readers must be able to find the sources you use—to verify your information if they choose. Will your readers be able to find your source? (Can <u>you</u> find it again?) If not, should you cite it at all? A good rule is to photocopy any source your readers may have trouble finding.

Red Herring

A <u>red herring</u> is an irrelevant point or some side issue leading away from the main point in an argument. According to the legend of the red herring, fleeing prisoners or slaves pursued by dogs would draw a fish across their trail, in the hope that the smell of the fish would lead the dogs away from the main path. There is no truth to this legend, but it illustrates the red herring fallacy.

> Perhaps you're right about integration and busing, but has anyone considered the <u>safety</u> of those buses?

The issue concerns integration and busing, not the safety of buses. The speaker has introduced a red herring, a different subject entirely. Here is another example:

> In order to understand the causes of the Civil War, we must look at the warlike nature of human beings. The history of Europe is full of wars.

Can you explain why we call this example a red herring? Try making an example of your own.

Weak Opponent

A <u>weak opponent</u>, sometimes an imaginary person (or other creature), an opponent made of straw, is someone or something invented for the purposes of an argument, an opponent you can attack without fear of retaliation. For example, many representatives and senators are hard-working, respected government servants, and any unkind or impolite remarks about them could backfire on you. Therefore, speakers and writers may invent a weak opponent: "Those no good politicians spend their time arguing about how to spend our money. Everyone knows politicians have no ethos. All they're interested in is saving their own jobs."

Why do we call this a weak opponent? There is no real person involved. "Politicians" are anyone who might fit under that term. We can insult ("throw stones") at this weak opponent without fearing we will be sued or find ourselves being counterattacked.

The weak opponent isn't merely any group that can be described with a negative label: you must be able to see that the label is unfair, inaccurate, or manufactured just for the sake of the argument. Also, it is possible to have weak opponents that represent allies or those we favor: our heroic military veterans, for example, or the noble immigrants "who came to this country without money or education or skills and not even speaking English, but despite all that have pulled themselves up by the bootstraps, and in the process have made this country what it is!" No specific individual is indicated. The statement is aimed at a handy, if invented, person we have created and can condemn or applaud without fear of backlash. A good example might be "the modern student": we don't want to attack Jenny Hillman nor even "our own students," so we invent someone called the modern student. "The modern student needs to study more and party less," for example.

You need to remind yourself that there are almost always at least two sides to any argument, and often there are more sides than that. Stereotypes such as weak opponents just get in the way of critical analysis. Because neither weak opponents nor stereotypes are real, you need to insist on finding the true subject of an argument. If there really are people labeled "welfare cheats," who are they, and where are they? Who are the "shiftless slackers" who refuse to work according to some critics? Where is the "moral majority"? And what is the source of the information about them? Such labels merely obscure the fact that the argument is really about "people we do or don't like," meaning the argument is based on personal prejudice and bias. Critical thinkers should evaluate whether such an argument is worth indulging. You need to dig under the labels to find who or what is really meant.

Tu Quoque

Tu quoque (too kwo'-kway) means "you did it too." It is used as an argument, or an excuse, when accused persons seek to justify their actions by revealing that their accusers are "guilty" of the same crime. In effect, the accused person says, "You can't accuse me when you yourself are guilty of the same thing!" For example, "So what if I drink at parties on weekends, Dad. You did the same thing in college." The argument is often used by children: "Why can't I stay up late to watch TV—you do!" However, it is a weak argument at any level. We should be able to make the accusation (providing we have the evidence), no matter how many others have done the same or similar things, including ourselves. For example, "cheating" on one's taxes is said to be nearly universal, yet taxpayers have learned to their sorrow that the tu quoque appeal carries no legal weight with the IRS. It carries little moral weight in any case.

Oversimplification

Oversimplification is the tendency to overlook complexity in an argument. For example, "Students can't write well because they watch too much TV." Television could be one of the reasons that some students don't write well—but it's unlikely to be the only reason for all students. Most serious arguments are more compli- cated than people know, but people simplify because it makes problems easier to think about and easier to find a quick solution. (If parents turn off the TV, will students then write better?) Consider the abortion issue. Those on either side of the abortion question wish to reduce the argument to simple questions of a woman's right to control her own body versus a moral prohibition against murder. Yet when the abortion question is examined critically, you discover it is more complicated than either side admits. There are legal, moral, financial, philosoph- ical, religious, psychological, racial, and perhaps many other implications of this question: for example, some people have added "the rights of the unborn child" to this argument. Do you accept the claim that unborn children have rights? Reducing all this to simple pro and con positions is an oversimplification, a fail- ure to understand the complexity of the question. Oversimplification provides simple slogans for groups to yell at each other, but simple slogans can lead to simple actions, such as blowing up the only abortion clinic in South Dakota.

ACTIVITY 7

Irrelevant Evidence

Identify the fallacy in each of the following statements. Explain why each state- ment is called an error of irrelevant evidence: ad baculum, ad hominem, fallacy of opposition, genetic fallacy, guilt by association, ad misericordiam, ad popu- lum, bandwagon, plain folks or snob appeal, ad verecundiam, red herring, weak opponent, tu quoque, or oversimplification. There may be more than one answer for some of these.

1. Because this car was made in a small Balkan country, it can't possibly be popular in the United States.
2. The Second Amendment of the Constitution says all citizens should keep guns for defense of the state; it's as simple as that.

3. It is incredible how many immigrants came to this country with nothing but their native intelligence and willingness to work—and now have become millionaires!

4. So what if I cheat a little on my taxes? So do you!

5. The exam question reads, Is E. A. Poe's "The Raven" a good poem? One student wrote: "Poe, who wrote 'The Raven,' is known to have taken drugs like opium. Opium is an addictive narcotic and may cause many physical and psychological disturbances."

6. For the sake of the poor, starving, dying children of Africa, we must send aid immediately.

7. Professors Memering and Palmer believe our country should vigorously pursue economic cooperation with China.

8. If you don't vote for Vic Jackson for our union rep, you may find yourself out of a job.

9. Don't vote for Kay Malinski for mayor because she lives with a woman and I've seen them holding hands.

10. People can't spell anymore because they use spell checkers on computers.

11. Let's return America to greatness by embracing the tradition of true family values.

12. Corvettes are nice, I suppose, but regular guys do okay with a good, old pickup truck.

13. I admit I was trying to bungee jump off the Empire State building, but so was everyone else.

14. Princess Diana campaigned against land mines, showing pictures of children with no feet as well as farmers and innocent villagers terribly wounded from undetected mines.

15. Political advertisements all over town indicate that if we don't vote for Sitwell, he might have to close his factory and many people would lose their jobs.

16. Aunt Edna says of her neighbor, "I never listen to anything the old bore has to say."

17. The student was kept off the team because someone had seen her going into a gang bar.

18. The company CEO received a "confidential" notice from the CIA that one of the company's employees was known to attend radical, survivalist conventions.

19. Street-corner preachers shouted at anyone who would listen: "America for Americans, down with one-world propaganda, back to the good old days, close the gates on immigrants."

20. "The Dow-Jones keeps going up and up: you too can invest and profit," brokers said in 1999. "Hurry and join the rest of the country before it's too late!"

21. Sent to the Western Division, Mr. Ellis was having a hard time convincing his wife that she would enjoy their new home in Fargo, North Dakota. "There's nothing to do in Fargo," she wept.

22. It won't matter how much technical know-how you have: if you want to get ahead in this world, you need an expensive haircut, handcut Italian suits (several), a Rolex watch, English shoes, and a Lexus to drive. You can't join the winners until you <u>look</u> like a winner.

23. How can you say I'm a bad driver when you've had five accidents yourself?

24. A student said: "It's true, Dean Potter, that we've been making a little noise on Saturday nights and some neighbors have complained. But have you considered the volunteer work we do for senior citizens each year?"

25. Because my parents weren't home, I asked my neighbor Mrs. Benson if I could stay out all night.

ACTIVITY 8

In your notebook write an example of your own for each fallacy in this section: ad baculum, ad hominem, fallacy of opposition, genetic fallacy, guilt by association, ad misericordiam, ad populum, bandwagon, plain folks and snob appeal, ad verecundiam, red herring, weak opponent, tu quoque, and oversimplification.

PROBLEMS OF AMBIGUITY

You may find problems of ambiguity in some writing, including amphibole, begging the question, equivocation, loaded language, and false analogies.

Amphiboly

Amphiboly (am-phib'-o-ly) comes from a Latin word for "ambiguous" and in English means "ambiguity" or "doubt." An amphiboly can be caused by a statement that has more than one meaning. For example, "We had a dog for dinner." In some parts of the world, the sentence may mean serving roast spaniel as the main dinner course. In other parts of the world, the sentence probably means a spaniel was the guest at our evening meal. Or, newspaper headlines could announce, "Girl's slip seen by teammates," suggesting either that the girl fell (slipped) during a game, or she made a mistake (a slip) in some team activity, or some part of her undergarment was exposed.

Sometimes an amphiboly may accidentally result from grammatical misplacement:

> The senators were certain the representatives would understand their duty. [Whose duty—the senators or the representatives?]
> Doctors sometimes think patients would understand them better if they were in their shoes. [If who were in whose shoes?]

Traditionally, amphibolies arise when sentences are inherently vague and capable of more than one interpretation: "Driving our convertible in the mountains, a bear suddenly appeared at an intersection." The sentence seems to say the bear was driving our car. Modern usage applies amphiboly to any ambiguous meaning. For example, statistics, especially percentages, can have vague interpretations: "Of those asked, 75% said they would vote for the president again." If you don't know how many were asked, percentages can be misleading. The 75% figure suggests three-fourths of the electorate, but in fact it can just as well mean three people out of the four who were asked.

Begging the Question

Begging the question means not answering the question. Begging the question is a fallacy in which the conclusion assumes the premise the argument attempts to prove. In effect, the conclusion simply restates one of the premises. One traditional example of begging the question attempts to prove that God exists: "We know that God exists because of all the things that He made!" The answer begs the question. We can't cite anything God made until after we have established that God exists.

Begging the question is sometimes called "circular reasoning." Circular reasoning merely turns the question around. For example, a difficult question for science and religion is, "How can we tell when a fetus is a person?" Nonresponsive, circular answers might include these: A fetus is a person when it is a being, when it is no longer a fetus, when the doctor says it is person, when it has the attributes of a person. These answers beg the question. You must ask further, when is it a being? When is it no longer a fetus? When does the doctor say it is a person? What are the attributes of a person, and when does the fetus acquire them?

The term begging the question is sometimes used in court cases:

Lawyer: Have you ever been in Mr. Crane's apartment?
Witness: I don't know Mr. Crane.
Lawyer: Your answer begs the question. You were asked about the apartment, not the person.

Equivocation

Equivocation (e-kwi-vo-ka'-tion) means quibbling over the meanings of words. It can amount to a form of dishonesty, a deliberate misuse of the definitions of words. For example, "I did not steal your pen; I merely borrowed it." Whether the pen was "borrowed" or "stolen" obscures the issue—namely, that the pen was taken without the permission of the owner. Whether people killed by hand grenades in an Italian airport were killed by "terrorists" or "freedom fighters" depends on point of view—but makes little difference to the material fact that people were killed.

> Humboldt lost his job because his supervisor thought he was <u>obese</u>. "I'm not obese," Humboldt, argued. "I'm a large man, a bit heavy, but not fat."

In general, equivocation suggests trivial distinctions. Yes, it's important to define your terms, but critical thinkers must recognize the difference between thoughtfully defining terms and merely equivocating, a tactic for delaying or distorting. You need to be clear about the terms of an argument, but at some point, you must stop quibbling over the language and get on with the argument. Whether you call it <u>euthanasia</u>, <u>death with dignity</u>, <u>assisted suicide</u>, or <u>ending suffering</u>, the question (let us say) is whether the government should pay for it. You need to define your terms (so we know what you are arguing about), but eventually the argument needs to proceed to consideration of the main point.

Loaded Language

The classic example of <u>loaded language</u> is "Do you still beat your spouse?" Assuming we have only "yes" or "no" answers, there is no good answer to this question. If you answer "yes," you confess you are still a spouse beater; if you answer "no," you confess to having been a spouse beater. The question is pernicious; it has been loaded so that either answer is prejudicial. Loaded language is biased language:

> Must we listen to more of Harvey's idiotic theories?

> Can anyone help us find our way out of this inane problem?

Loading the questions with negative, biased words such as "idiotic" and "inane" ensures that no matter what answer is given, the impression will have been made that Harvey's theories, and perhaps Harvey himself, are idiotic, and that the problem is "inane." A critical thinker should refuse to offer any answer until the questions have been examined and rephrased without the prejudicial, loaded language.

Loaded language is slanted language. But language can also be loaded the other way: "The government has come up with another <u>excellent</u> program for <u>better</u> education programs," we are told. You can assume the writer is using a positive load for this statement. Another writer might use a sarcastic load: "The government has come up with another <u>extraordinary</u> program for the <u>useful</u> distribution of taxpayer money." The writers here may be ironic or sarcastic, depending on readers' interpretations. Writers who use sarcasm suggest that they are superior to the subject matter of the argument. Irony has a slightly better connotation. Sarcasm usually aims to hurt; irony merely notes the truth in a contradiction. Nevertheless, sarcasm and irony in factual and reasoned essays can easily backfire. Thoughtful writing is not a good place to use words that don't mean what they say.

Usually, we expect the claim or thesis of an argument to be as clearly and objectively stated as possible: Should the United States endorse a ban against land mines? When a writer loads an issue or a question with prejudicial language, you should challenge the writer's motives: "Let us consider the idiotic proposition that the United States should render its troops defenseless by banning their protective use of land mines." This writer doesn't want to "consider" the proposition; the writer has already decided the proposition is "idiotic."

False Analogy

An analogy is a comparison. An analogy suggests that because things share one or more points of similarity, we can assume they are similar in other ways too. For example, we have made an analogy between President Roosevelt and a train engine.

> President Roosevelt was a mighty engine pulling the country out of the desert of the Great Depression.

The statement compares President Roosevelt to an engine and the depression of the 1930s to a desert. The statement gives President Roosevelt one of the characteristics of a train engine (its power to pull great weights). And we have given the "Great Depression" (the economy) one or more characteristics of a desert: dry, arid. But, is this a good comparison? No, it is a false analogy. It creates a false impression about the president's relationship to the country. American presidents don't have the power to pull the country. Even popular presidents seldom have more than two-thirds of the country willing to follow them. Furthermore, it might equally have been said that Roosevelt followed the country out of the depression.

Arguing by "analogy" assumes that one thing is similar to another, but such comparisons are often faulty. For example, an argument might suggest that smoking tobacco is like drinking poison. But it is often the case that no two events are very similar. Not everyone who smokes suffers ill effects, but everyone who drinks cyanide will almost certainly die. This is not a defense of tobacco but a reminder to critical thinkers that they undermine their own credibility when they use exaggeration to make a point.

An analogy is a comparison between things that most people think are comparable or that seem reasonable to compare. Ford trucks may be similar to Dodge trucks. But is it reasonable to say "The IRS is an American Gestapo"? This is an extremely harsh criticism, an analogy based on an imagined comparison between American tax collectors (Internal Revenue Service) and the

German Secret Police during World War II, whose ruthless mission it was to eliminate Hitler's enemies and to kill all the Jews in Europe. Americans may be unhappy with the IRS, but a comparison with the Gestapo seems excessive and unfair, and it undermines the writer's credibility. Even if there may be a few superficial similarities in the comparison, there are many dissimilarities. (The IRS does not have the authority to exterminate taxpayers.) The two do not compare. False analogies usually collapse when examined critically.

Even if you have a good case for a comparison, the tactic is at best only suggestive: you can seldom prove a case by comparison. Consider identical twins, who must be very similar indeed—it isn't true that everything one twin does the other must also do. For an analogy to be useful you need some basis for comparison. For example, the common wood saw cuts with its "teeth," so named because they somewhat resemble teeth and serve a similar function. Still, you can see differences between saw teeth and animal teeth. Think of the ways in which saw teeth and human teeth are different and then decide whether they make a convincing analogy.

ACTIVITY 9

Ambiguous Evidence

Identify the fallacy in each of the following statements. Explain why each is an error of ambiguous evidence: amphiboly, begging the question, equivocation, loaded language, or false analogy. There may be more than one answer for some of these.

1. In the old diary was written, "I am not a communist! I am a Marxist!"
2. Given a choice between the current occupant and an escapee from some correctional facility, which do you think the public would rather have in the oval office?
3. The senator was asked whether her "help-the-rich" proposals weren't really an effort to enslave the poor with perpetual debt.
4. The embassy said that these people were no longer "refugees" because the war was over; they were now "illegal immigrants" who must be sent back to their homelands.
5. Anyone who can ride a bike should also be able to ride a motorcycle; they both have two wheels.
6. The reporters asked the chief of staff whether the president's hasty and ill-considered appointment of a shallow and incompetent person wasn't a clue to the sort of slipshod decision making we could expect from her administration.
7. Three out of four doctors recommend Headache Buster to relieve pain.
8. My mother is such a good person because she is so moral.

9. After you've been in love with somebody for a few years, you realize that person is like a record you bought because you liked one or two of the songs. The other songs you never did like.

10. Capital punishment is wrong because killing anybody is not right.

ACTIVITY 10

In your notebook write an example of your own for each fallacy in this section. Try to explain why each is an error of ambiguous evidence: amphibole, begging the question, equivocation, loaded language, or false analogy.

PROBLEMS OF FAULTY REASONING

Some writing may contain problems of faulty reasoning, such as false dilemma (either/or thinking), non sequitur, rationalization, reductio ad absurdum, and slippery slope.

False Dilemma (Either/Or Thinking)

Ordinarily, a <u>dilemma</u> is a choice between two alternatives, both of which are (usually) unpleasant: "pay your taxes or go to jail." Dilemmas are often stated as "either/or" alternatives:

<u>Either</u> America must support her allies <u>or</u> they will perish.

<u>Either</u> we must close our doors to more immigrants <u>or</u> see America overrun with foreigners.

<u>Either</u> you agree with feminism <u>or</u> you don't.

The either/or choice is what makes a dilemma false. You almost always have more than two alternatives. America's allies may find other ways to survive. The notion that America will be "overrun" with foreigners is not only a false dilemma but phrased with loaded language. You might agree with certain aspects of feminism and disagree with others.

Occasionally, however, you may encounter a real dilemma. The car payment is due but you are out of money. The dilemma is pay up or lose the car. That's a real-life dilemma, but you may be able to resolve it—the car dealer probably doesn't want the car back and may be willing to work out some other alternative. Or, you may be able to borrow money to cover the shortage.

A real dilemma may be difficult—maybe too difficult—to resolve. But a "false" dilemma is no dilemma at all if your analysis reveals more than just two options. And most reasonable people assume there may be other alternatives, though they might agree that you have a "predicament." As a critical thinker, you should assume that few situations can be reduced to only two alternatives.

Either/or statements are forms of oversimplification and they can be implied without using "either/or":

If you don't quit smoking, you'll die of lung cancer.

If you don't study, you won't pass.

Exact change only. A familiar warning on city busses: you must have the exact change—or get off the bus (the driver doesn't make change).

Some smokers don't die of lung cancer. Some students pass courses without studying—a dubious achievement that depends on what the course is and who the teacher is. The "exact change" dilemma is a real predicament for which there does not seem to be an alternative—unless one of the other passengers volunteers to "make change." (For more on either/or thinking, see chapter 4.)

Non Sequitur

Non sequitur (non sek'-wi-ter) means "it does not follow." A non sequitur seems unconnected: it is some leap in logic that doesn't make sense. For example, "This photograph appears to show a flying saucer; therefore aliens must have visited earth." The non sequitur often sounds like a faulty conclusion or an error in reasoning: "The president is frequently away from the White House: the vice president must run the country at those times." It doesn't follow that the vice president is in charge just because the president is away. Modern communications keep the president in charge, no matter where he is. Here are a few other examples:

If e-mail is the future, we might as well stop buying envelopes for mail. [A non sequitur because there is still much to send via mail, and many people still prefer handwritten or typed messages.]

Because the Internet has so much information, there isn't any need for libraries. [A non sequitur because many readers prefer actual books, magazines, newspapers, and so on. Also, the Internet has so much information that it has become harder for people to find anything.]

Rationalization

A <u>rationalization</u> is an excuse or a self-serving explanation. Some people can rationalize their way out of almost any difficulty by inventing some self-serving excuse that gets them off the hook:

> The Senate passed a new tax bill, but it was only because they knew the president would veto it. [An excuse for a tax bill: blame it on the president.]

> It's true I don't do well in math, but many creative people have this problem. [Blame a fault on a virtue.]

> Yes I knocked over the crystal vase, but you should have put it away in the cupboard. [Blame the problem on someone else: it's your fault, not mine.]

Reductio Ad Absurdum

<u>Reductio ad absurdum</u> means to reduce to an absurdity. For example, movie critics said that the film was too long and would be stronger if some scenes were removed. But the producer, director, and writer replied, "What nonsense! If removing scenes made the film stronger, perhaps we should remove a few more to make it even stronger. And perhaps it would be strongest of all if we removed all of them!" Or, to use a more familiar example, "If one pill is good for me, two should be better, and best of all may be a whole handful!"

The reductio argument uses the opponent's reasoning against itself. By extending the opponent's argument, you show some ridiculous conclusion it leads to. Revealing absurdity is a good tactic, if true. However, the tactic can be used merely as a way to ridicule the opponent, and in that case it should be avoided by critical thinkers. Here is an example of ridicule:

> A friendly critic wrote: "Last night's concert was excellent, even though one of the drummers dropped a cymbal during the second movement." A later critic responded: "Perhaps we should ask other members of the orchestra to drop their instruments at random moments to produce an even better result!"

The reductio fallacy is based on the assumption that more is better (or that less is better). For example, "If one piece of pie is a good after-dinner dessert, two might be better and maybe three or four would be the best of all!" The reductio can work in reverse too: "If we can save money by firing one of the secretaries, we should save twice as much if we fire two of them. And maybe we can save even more money by firing all of them."

Slippery Slope

The <u>slippery slope</u> is an assumption that one thing leads to another, especially if the "next step" is in the direction of something forbidden. It might be feared, for example, that trying one cigarette would cause youngsters to become addicted to tobacco, or that a single glass of wine would turn you into a wino.

The key to slippery slope isn't only that one thing might lead to another but that one thing <u>must</u> lead to another. Much depends on individual personalities. Some people are lonely and hungry for peer approval. These people may be especially vulnerable to the slippery slope. Thoughtful people, especially young people, should evaluate proposals and suggestions from peers, particularly concerning dangerous proposals (bungee jumping from bridges perhaps, leading to higher and higher jumps). Russian roulette is a suicidal "game" with a loaded pistol. No matter how much pressure peers exert, thoughtful people know it is a deadly slope to start down. Friends don't let friends drive drunk, and friends don't let friends play with a loaded pistol.

ACTIVITY 11

Faulty Reasoning

Identify the fallacy in each of the following statements. Explain why each statement is an error of faulty reasoning: false dilemma, non sequitur, rationalization, reductio ad absurdum, or slippery slope.

1. I could have passed the driving test, but the instructor was making me nervous.
2. Reverend O'Casey drank communion wine all his life and lived to be 90; obviously, wine is good for you.
3. A lot of Dr. Smith's patients have died of cancer, so he must not be a very good doctor.
4. After I broke my arm, my therapist told me to do a few lifts with a one-pound weight to help the bones knit, but if I lift a 10-pound weight, won't I heal even faster? Maybe I should lift a 50-pound weight for the fastest healing of all!
5. Viola refused to visit the opening of the new casino with her friends because, she said, she knew they would all become gambling addicts.
6. It seems obvious that you must either quit being promiscuous or you will get AIDS.
7. A magician had heard of mystics in India who had built up a tolerance to deadly bites. They started with just one drop of venom and gradually built up to more and more. He thought he would try it.

8. Father Piety was faced with the unpleasant choice of declaring how much money he had earned lecturing, and thereby incurring a large additional tax, or forgetting about the extra money, thereby committing tax fraud.

9. A cloned human will not have a mind of its own—his or her thoughts will probably be cloned too.

10. I can't write poetry or fiction, but I don't know any other science major who can either.

11. Father says if I don't get out and find a job soon, I'll become a common slacker, a lazy bum.

12. I didn't proofread my paper carefully because I figured that was my peer-editor's job.

13. If you are moral, you will go to heaven; if you are immoral, you will go to hell.

14. I'm sure I could have done better on the test, if only the professor had been more explicit.

15. You either write well or you don't.

ACTIVITY 12

In your notebook write an example of your own for each fallacy in this section: false dilemma (either/or thinking), non sequitur, rationalization, reductio ad absurdum, and slippery slope. Discuss your examples with your group or class.

REVIEW ACTIVITY

Identify the fallacy (there may be more than one) in each of the following statements. Explain your answer.

Example: "Students love their studies, especially research writing." The statement is an overgeneralization. "Students" implies all or most students, but it is unlikely that anyone could know what so many students do or don't feel about their studies.

1. Either you must memorize the fallacies or you will fail the quiz; there is no other alternative.

2. Defense attorneys in a murder case objected to the eyewitness testimony of the state's star witness on the grounds that the woman was a known prostitute and, therefore, not a credible witness.

3. Blood donors are supposed to go through the door marked "Lab." That man is going through the "Lab" door, so he must be a blood donor.

4. "We must increase welfare spending," the senator argued, "because a great nation must provide for the less fortunate members of society. We cannot aspire to greatness while the poor, the elderly, and the disabled suffer miserably."

5. Two young attorneys were denied membership in an exclusive club because, they were told, they specialized in defending sexual deviants and, therefore, their own sexual preferences were suspect.

6. The President's word can be relied on more than Congress's because one strong beacon casts more light than hundreds of small candles.

7. "It is not necessary to be highly intelligent to enjoy the rewards of this life," a kindly minister said in his speech to the city's administrators. "Nonsense," a cynical administrator responded, "for in that case, those with less intelligence would have more reward, and those with the least intelligence of all would enjoy the most rewards of this life."

8. The officer said the driver had been clocked at 70 miles an hour, but the driver retorted, "You were going just as fast as I was; if I am guilty, so are you."

9. Yak butter may be a culinary delight, but Americans are never going to accept food from a place as far away and strange as Tibet.

10. My client is accused of being immoral, but, in fact, she is really only amoral, for whereas <u>immoral</u> means "not moral," the word <u>amoral</u> really means being "without morals."

11. The case was nearly lost until the prosecutor introduced a medical report published in <u>Reader's Digest</u>, and from this evidence the jury found the defendant guilty.

12. The Speaker of the House was asked whether the rest of the President's idiotic economic policies would be rubber-stamped by the spineless Congress.

13. If God can do anything, can God create a rock so heavy that even God can't lift it?

14. Pointy-headed intellectuals! Government give-away programs! Deficit spending! Endless inflation and taxation! These are not the values for which America stands!

15. Grandfather refuses to watch what he calls "today's vulgar, pornographic, foulmouthed movies."

16. I'm just a poor old country boy trying to make an honest living like you, folks. I know what it means to grow up poor and have to struggle to make ends meet. Send me to Washington and I'll take care of the common man.

17. Elegance is the fragrance of beautiful people: to be one of the elite, use Elegance.

18. Thousands of citizens are speaking out against having another prison built in our community. Let's join this protest today!

19. College students today don't support any social causes. All they care about is partying.

20. You're either a critical thinker, or you're not.

READING AND WRITING ACTIVITIES

ACTIVITY 13

Browse through current magazines and newspapers for any fallacies you can find in advertisements, articles, editorials, or political columns. Write or photocopy the fallacies and cite their sources. Bring two or three examples to class to discuss.

ACTIVITY 14

Please read the essay "How the Web Destroys the Quality of Students' Research Papers" by David Rothenberg. This essay was published in <u>The Chronicle of Higher Education</u>, a weekly newspaper whose audience is professors and administrators across the country. As you read, pay close attention to Rothenberg's logos, especially any assumptions or implications he makes. Then answer the questions in Activity 15.

How the Web Destroys the Quality of Students' Research Papers

David Rothenberg

Sometimes I look forward to the end-of-semester rush, when students' final 1 papers come streaming into my office and mailbox. I could have hundreds of pages of original thought to read and evaluate. Once in a while it <u>is</u> truly exciting, and brilliant words are typed across a page in response to a question I've asked the class to discuss.

But this past semester was different. I noticed a disturbing decline in 2 both the quality of the writing and the originality of the thoughts expressed. What had happened since last fall? Did I ask worse questions? Were my students unusually lazy? No. My class had fallen victim to the latest easy way of writing a paper: doing their research on the World Wide Web.

It's easy to spot a research paper that is based primarily on information 3 collected from the Web. First, the bibliography cites no books, just articles or pointers to places in that virtual land somewhere off any map: http://www.etc.

Then a strange preponderance of material in the bibliography is curiously out of date. A lot of stuff on the Web that is advertised as timely is actually at least a few years old. (One student submitted a research paper last semester in which all of his sources were articles published between September and December 1995; that was probably the time span of the Web page on which he found them.)

Another clue is the beautiful pictures and graphs that are inserted neatly 4 into the body of the student's text. They look impressive, as though they were the result of careful work and analysis, but actually they often bear little relation to the precise subject of the paper. Cut and pasted from the vast realm of what's out there for the taking, they masquerade as original work.

Accompanying them are unattributed quotes (in which one can't tell who 5 made the statement or in what context) and curiously detailed references to the kinds of things that are easy to find on the Web (pages and pages of federal documents, corporate propaganda, or snippets of commentary by people whose credibility is difficult to assess). Sadly, one finds few references to careful, in-depth commentaries on the subject of the paper, the kind of analysis that requires a book, rather than an article, for its full development.

Don't get me wrong, I'm no neo-Luddite. I am as enchanted as anyone else 6 by the potential of this new technology to provide instant information. But too much of what passes for information these days is simply <u>advertising</u> for information. Screen after screen shows you where you can find out more, how you can connect to this place or that. The acts of linking and networking and randomly jumping from here to there become as exciting or rewarding as actually finding anything of intellectual value.

Search engines, with their half-baked algorithms, are closer to slot 7 machines than to library catalogues. You throw your query to the wind, and who knows what will come back to you? You may get 234,468 supposed references to whatever you want to know. Perhaps one in a thousand might actually help you. But it's easy to be sidetracked or frustrated as you try to go through those Web pages one by one. Unfortunately, they're not arranged in order of importance.

What I'm describing is the hunt-and-peck method of writing a paper. We all 8 know that word processing makes many first drafts look far more polished than they are. If the paper doesn't reach the assigned five pages, readjust the margin, change the font size, and . . . <u>voila!</u> Of course, those machinations take up time that the student could have spent revising the paper. With programs to check one's spelling and grammar as standard features on most computers, one wonders why students make any mistakes at all. But errors are as prevalent as ever, no matter how crisp the typeface. Instead of becoming perfectionists, too many students have become slackers, preferring to let the machine do their work for them.

What the Web adds to the shortcuts made possible by word processing is 9 to make research look too easy. You toss a query to the machine, wait a few minutes, and suddenly a lot of possible sources of information appear on your screen. Instead of books that you have to check out of the library, read carefully, understand, synthesize, and then tactfully excerpt, these sources are quips, blips, pictures, and short summaries that may be downloaded magically to the dorm-room computer screen. Fabulous! How simple! The only problem is that a paper consisting of summaries of summaries is bound to be fragmented and superficial, and to demonstrate more of a random montage than an ability to sustain an argument through 10 to 15 double-spaced pages.

Of course, you can't blame the students for ignoring books. When college libraries are diverting funds from books to computer technology that will be obsolete in two years at most, they send a clear message to students: Don't read, just connect. Surf. Download. Cut and paste. Originality becomes hard to separate from plagiarism if no author is cited on a Web page. Clearly, the words are up for grabs, and students much prefer the fabulous jumble to the hard work of stopping to think and make sense of what they've read.

Libraries used to be repositories of words and ideas. Now they are seen as centers for the retrieval of information. Some of this information comes from other, bigger libraries, in the form of books that can take time to obtain through interlibrary loan. What happens to the many students (some things never change) who scramble to write a paper the night before it's due? The computer screen, the gateway to the world sitting right on their desks, promises instant access—but actually offers only a pale, two-dimensional version of a real library.

But it's also my fault. I take much of the blame for the decline in the quality of student research in my classes. I need to teach students how to read, to take time with language and ideas, to work through arguments, to synthesize disparate sources to come up with original thought. I need to help my students understand how to assess sources to determine their credibility, as well as to trust their own ideas more than snippets of thought that materialize on a screen. The placelessness of the Web leads to an ethereal randomness of thought. Gone are the pathways of logic and passion, the sense of the progress of an argument. Chance holds sway, and it more often misses than hits. Judgment must be taught, as well as the methods of exploration.

I'm seeing my students' attention spans wane and their ability to reason for themselves decline. I wish that the university's computer system would crash for a day, so that I could encourage them to go outside, sit under a tree, and read a really good book—from start to finish. I'd like them to sit for a while and ponder what it means to live in a world where some things get easier and easier so rapidly that we can hardly keep track of how easy they're getting, while other tasks remain as hard as ever—such as doing research and writing a good paper that teaches the writer something in the process. Knowledge does not emerge in a vacuum, but we do need silence and space for sustained thought. Next semester, I'm going to urge my students to turn off their glowing boxes and think, if only once in a while.

(David Rothenberg is an associate professor of philosophy at the New Jersey Institute of Technology. He is the author of <u>Hand's End: Technology and the Limits of Nature</u> [University of California Press, 1993] and the editor of <u>Terra Nova: Journal of Nature and Culture</u> [MIT Press].) □

ACTIVITY 15

Does Rothenberg commit any fallacies? If so, which fallacies? In an essay (2 to 4 pages) evaluate Rothenberg's logos. What is his claim? State a clear thesis, and then support it with specific evidence. Try to point out and examine at least three fallacies you see in Rothenberg's reasoning. Toward the end of your essay, explain how his logos affects his appeals to ethos and pathos. Be careful to quote accurately.

ACTIVITY 16

In an essay (2 to 4 pages) use Toulmin's strategy of analyzing an argument: analyze the claim, grounds, and warrant in Rothenberg's essay.

ACTIVITY 17

Please read all four of the following letters to the editor written in response to Rothenberg's essay. As you read them, pay close attention to their logos. Then select one and write a response to its author—Richard Cummins, Sharon Stoerger, Kenneth J. Zanca, or Jere L. Bacharach—agreeing or disagreeing with comments about Rothenberg's essay.

The World-Wide Web and the Quality of Students' Research Papers

Richard Cummins

To the Editor:

David Rothenberg's thoughtful essay includes the common fallacy of giving the   1 World Wide Web far too much power over our lives and consciousness . . . . Too often, the assumption is that this technology somehow induces states of mind for which there is no remedy. But the Web is simply a tool that needs to be used strategically by teachers who have carefully thought through the outcomes they expect from their students. Even the metaphor of a web implies this, and it is up to the student to become either the spider or the fly.

Actually, it is often poor course design that impedes student performance 2 to a far greater extent. Realistically, the Web no more "destroys the quality of students' research papers" than does television, the blackboard, the overhead projector, the way that poorly designed research assignments are routinely handed out to students, or the rote way that some teachers present their materials. In terms of quality, where does the buck stop? I would hope at the professor's desk, where the questions about what is acceptable research need to be discussed and answered for the student's edification, while the professor makes it clear that grades will directly reflect those standards.

Professor Rothenberg's general points, however, are well stated, and I 3 admire his willingness to accept the challenge of what I consider the hard job of <u>real</u> teaching. This includes teaching students "how to read, to take time with language and ideas, to work through arguments, to synthesize disparate sources to come up with original thought . . . [and] how to assess sources to determine their credibility." This is difficult and important work, and it teaches students how to sort the wheat from the chaff in <u>any</u> kind of resource.

In truth, there are as many rotten books and worthless journal articles in 4 libraries as there are rotten sources on the Internet. The particular medium will matter less and less with the preponderance of cheap printers. To suggest that the Web is solely a source of ephemeral advertisements about information is a specious generalization. It sounds great, but closer examination reveals it to be too sweeping an assessment—one that, additionally, fails to account for the Web's future development as a scholarly resource.

We should not allow the spider of popular culture to spin us up in a web 5 of helplessness and despair by allowing the Internet to become so personified that it takes on extraordinary powers. It's just a bunch of interconnected computers. In addition to delineating how it may prevent students (and teachers) from thinking clearly and well, we need to place the onus of education back on the students and insist that they perform to certain standards by intelligently using available tools and technologies: books, journals, computers, and so forth. . . .

These issues will become increasingly important as the waves of the so- 6 called age of information approach flood stage in the years ahead. Among the dikes, sandbags, and navigation equipment that a college can offer are truly rigorous courses in both rhetoric and critical thinking, which all college students should be required to complete. Indeed, the Web may very well turn out to be precisely the burr under the saddle that compels everyone in education to return to our mission, which is teaching people how to think in disciplined ways. (Richard Cummins is Director of Information, Technology Applications at Columbia Basin College, Pasco, WA.) ☐

Response to David Rothenberg's Essay

Sharon Stoerger

To the Editor:

I think David Rothenberg was looking for a scapegoat to explain the poor qual- 1
ity of his students' papers. I cannot believe that this is the first semester he
has received poor papers. Nor do I believe that "students have become slackers" because of the invention of computers.

The problem is not computers. Many students have never been taught how 2
to even begin the research process, let alone produce an acceptable paper. You
cannot assume that your students have been in the library or know the first
thing about finding books or journal articles. Students need to be guided and
taught how to do research. A library instruction session, combined with very
specific requirements for the assignment, will probably result in a higher-qual-
ity product.

Mr. Rothenberg seems to believe that all books contain better information 3
than any other resource, especially any resource on the Web. I work in a library
that has been weeding out books that are so out-of-date that they provide
incorrect data. Certain subjects have changed over the years, such as the role
of women and the portrayal of African Americans. Some students will take any
book off the shelf just as easily as they take information off the Web. Some
believe that if it's in print, it has to be true. Critical-evaluation skills need to
be taught in the classroom and in the library. This is applicable to print as well
as Web resources.

Today's library is rapidly changing because of new technological advances. 4
This is not necessarily a bad thing. Libraries have always been places to retrieve
information. Full-text data bases and the Web supplement existing collections.
This allows patrons to access more resources, not fewer . . . .

I believe librarians and instructors need to work together to help students 5
through the research process and to critically evaluate retrieved resources.
Boundaries and guidelines need to be set in order to have a successful assignment. If you do not want Web resources used, state that in the assignment. We
need to accept the Web as yet another resource rather than deeming it an evil
destroyer. (Sharon Stoerger is the Public Services Librarian at the Learning Resources
Center at Danville Area Community College, Danville, IL.) □

Response to David Rothenberg's Essay

Kenneth J. Zanca

To the Editor:

David Rothenberg might benefit from the following three suggestions before giving any further Internet related research projects:

 Refer students to resources specifically addressing the "how to" of Internet research. I can recommend two print aids—<u>Official Netscape Guide to Internet Research</u> and <u>Internet Homework Helper</u>—and several on-line aids in this area. The latter are less advanced than the former.

 One on-line tutorial—www.digitalthink.com—gives two free lessons on structuring a research query. The Indianapolis-Marion County Public Library also provides a list of free tutorials (see www.imcpl.lib.in.us). Teachers interested in learning how to use the Internet for research can take a look at www.study-web.com and www.teachers.net.

 Not all search engines are created equal. Excite rates "hits," ranking them in order of agreement with search terms. Better to teach students how to use Boolean operators (which are very simple to learn) in making their search requests more focused, thus avoiding the "234,468 supposed references to whatever you want to know."

 I have avoided the demon that snagged Professor Rothenberg by insisting that all research papers have a balance of components: one-third books, one-third periodical literature, one-third Web resources. I grade down for any overloading with Internet sources. If students want to use more Web material, they must also increase their use of other materials.

 I agree with Rothenberg that many students are lazy and look to the Internet as a short cut and "easy way" of getting these kinds of assignments done. This search for short cuts has been going on since "trots" for Caesar's <u>The Gallic Wars</u> and Cliffs Notes. Any tool can be abused. It is imperative that instructors learn how to use the Internet before sending students "out there" to conduct research. If students know that you know how to use the Internet responsibly, there is at least the possibility that they will conform to your standards for its use.

(Kenneth J. Zanca is Professor of Philosophy at Marymount College in Rancho Palos Verdes, CA.) □

Response to David Rothenberg's Essay

Jere L. Bacharach

To the Editor:

David Rothenberg's article ends on the wrong note. Rather than urging his 1
students to "turn off their glowing boxes and think," I would urge him to have
his students turn <u>on</u> their glowing boxes and think. The exercise would start with
his own article or any other article or book in any scholarly field.

The <u>goal</u> would be to establish a set of criteria for evaluating the printed 2
material: Who wrote it, what can we learn about the author, is it dated, where
was it published, is the publication subject to review, etc.? Evaluating criteria
would then be established for the printed piece itself: What is the subject matter
discussed, what are the perspectives or biases of the author(s), can the information be checked for accuracy by comparing it with other examples or data, etc.?

Once the students have established criteria for evaluating the printed 3
material, I would assign them the same task for a Web site. For example, can
they identify the author(s), the date the material was gathered, the biases or
perspectives of the author(s), the accuracy of the material, etc.? Finally, how
would they compare the effectiveness of the evaluating criteria for printed material with their effectiveness for electronic sources? This exercise allows the
students to discover the problems and limitations in using electronic sources.

Jan Alexander (Janet.E.Alexande@widener.edu) and Marsha Tate 4
(Marsha.A.Tate@widener.edu), reference librarians at Wolgram Memorial Library
at Widener University, have developed a series of exercises and criteria for
comparing resources in print with those on the Web (http://www.science
widener.edu/~withers/webeval.htm). I have found their work very helpful. Also
helpful is a class developed at the University of Washington for teaching these
skills (http://weber.u.washington.edu/~libr560/NETEVAL/).

(Jere L. Bacharach is Director of Henry M. Jackson School of International Studies and
Professor of History at the University of Washington, Seattle, WA.) □

ACTIVITY 18

Which of these letters do you agree with most? Why? Explain your position in
a brief essay.

———————————

ACTIVITY 19

Write a letter to David Rothenberg in which you explain whether you agree or disagree with his claim—or both. Within your letter, refer to at least two of the letters to the editor. Be careful to quote accurately.

_____

Interchapter 5

Analyzing Style

Style gives your writing credibility.

Which is more important: <u>What</u> you say or <u>how</u> you say it? We hope that—after studying the previous interchapters, practicing various tools of style, and incorporating these tools into your drafts—you see this question as a false dilemma. <u>Both</u> what you say and how you say it are important. They are inseparable. <u>How you say your message is part of what you say.</u> Each time you write, your style creates your appeals to logos, pathos, and ethos. Your style creates your voice—the sound of your personality. As a critical thinker, you must pay close attention to words and sentences to make your language say what you mean. Style gives your writing credibility—or not—depending on how well you can manage your stylistic choices. Style is ethos.

You can use what you've learned in these interchapters to analyze the style and voice of other writers as well.

GUIDELINES FOR ANALYZING STYLE

When you analyze a writer's style, you should select what you consider the writer's dominant tools of style. The accompanying table presents stylistic tools from previous interchapters.

Tools of Style

Patterns of diction
   Monosyllabic (strings of one syllable words for emphasis) or multisyllabic
   Literal or figurative—metaphors and similes
   Specific or general
   Concrete or abstract
   Precise words (such as strong or surprising verbs)
Patterns of repetition in diction
   Key words
   Phrases
   Alliteration
Patterns of punctuation
   Semicolons
   Colons
   Dashes
   Underlining (or italics)
   Parentheses
Patterns of sentences
   Short
   Compound (coordination)
   Complex (subordination)
   Loose
   Periodic
   Antithesis
   Balanced
   Effective fragments
Patterns of repetition with sentences
   Parallelism (-ing phrases, to phrases, of phrases)
   Anaphora
   Epistrophe
   Tricolon

---

1. When you analyze a writer's style, use this pattern of organization for your essay:

   A. Introduce the essay and state your thesis about the writer's style.

   B. Summarize the essay objectively to show readers you understand it.

   C. Analyze some tools of style the writer uses. Support your analysis with reasons, examples, and details—and direct quotations to show what you mean.

   D. Conclude and restate your thesis.

   Choose patterns of style to analyze that stand out for you, that you can explain by citing at least two or three examples to show what you mean. Don't argue that a writer uses a lot of antithesis if you can only find one example of it.

   Ask yourself questions when you discuss an element of style:

   Why does Louise Erdrich use periodic sentences when she describes birth?

   Why does Rick Reilly use anaphora so much in his Sports Illustrated essay?

   Ask yourself: how does a particular tool of style contribute to the writer's meaning (thesis and support); to the writer's appeals of logos, pathos, and ethos; or to the writer's voice and tone? If you can't find any meaningful answers, look for another element of style to analyze. Write about whatever you find most interesting that sheds light on relationships between meaning and style.

2. When you analyze elements of style, consider one element at a time. You may need to use more than a single paragraph for each element. Try to build up to what you consider is the most important element.

3. Give underline examples of elements of style to show what you mean: quote from the selection. If you quote a passage fewer than four lines, incorporate it within a paragraph of yours. If you use a long quote—more than four lines—set it off: indent it 10 spaces on the left side and double-space. (Do not "justify" or make all the lines the same length on the right side; "ragged right" is standard Modern Language Association [MLA] style.)

4. When you refer to words or letters, underline them:

> E. B. White repeats the word same five times in one sentence.
>
> The long o sound can reinforce emotion in a poem.

5. When you quote, be responsible and accurate. Proofread each quote carefully.

6. Use the MLA style of documentation. The MLA style requires parentheses around documentation within your essay. For example,

> Orwell argues that "ready-made phrases [. . .] think your thoughts for you" (405).

Note that page numbers for material you quote should appear in parentheses before the sentence period. See chapter 9, Documentation, for additional rules about this kind of "in-text" documentation.

ANALYZING THE STYLE OF A PASSAGE

The purpose of stylistic analysis is to show that style is part of meaning. They are inseparable, like the singer and the song.

ACTIVITY 1

For practice analyzing style, please read the following passage by Louise Erdrich from her book The Blue Jay's Dance. Then analyze how one or two of her stylistic choices help create her meaning (thesis and support); her appeals to logos, pathos, and ethos; or her voice and tone (her attitude toward her audience, subject, and self). Look for any patterns of diction and sentence tools presented in the interchapters of this book—see the preceding Tools of Style table. (Consider retyping and annotating the selection to help you see more.) Write a short essay (1 to 2 pages) in which you present and support a clearly stated thesis about an aspect or two of her style.

Rocking, breathing, groaning, mouthing circles of distress, laughing, whistling, pounding, wavering, digging, pulling, pushing—labor is the most involuntary work we do. My body gallops to these rhythms. I'm along for the ride, at times in some control and at others dragged along as if foot-caught in a stirrup. I don't have much to do at first but breathe, accept ice chips, make jokes—in fear and pain my family makes jokes, that's how we deal with what we can't change, how we show our courage.

Even though I am a writer and have practiced my craft for years, and have experienced two natural childbirths and an epidural-assisted childbirth, I find women's labor extremely difficult to describe. In the first place, there are all sorts of labor and no "correct" way to do it. I bow to the power and grandeur of those who insist on natural childbirth, but I find the pieties that often attend the process irritating. I am all for pain relief or caesareans when women want and need these procedures. Enduring pain in itself doesn't make one a better person, though if your mind is prepared, pain of this sort—a meaningful and determined pain based on ardor and potential joy—can be deeply instructive, can change your life. [. . .]

The first part of labor feels, to me anyway, like dance exercises—slow stretches that become only slightly painful as a muscle is pulled to its limit. After each contraction, the feeling subsides. The contractions move in longer waves, one after another, closer and closer together until a sea of physical sensation washes and then crashes over. In the beginning I breathe in concentration, watching Michael's eyes [her husband]. I feel myself slip beneath the waves as they roar over, cresting just above my head. I duck every time the contraction peaks. As the hours pass and one wave builds on another there are times the undertow grabs me. I struggle, slammed to the bottom, unable to gather the force of nerve for the next. Thrown down, I rely on animal fierceness, swim back, surface, breathe, and try to stay open, willing. Staying open and willing is difficult. Very often in labor one must fight the instinct to resist pain and instead embrace it, move toward it, work with what hurts the most.

The waves come faster. Charlotte [a midwife] asks me to keep breathing yes, yes. To say yes instead of shuddering in refusal. Whether I am standing on the earth or not, whether I am moored to the dock, whether I remember who I am, whether I am mentally prepared, whether I am going to float beneath or ride above, the waves pound in. At shorter intervals, crazy now, electric, in storms, they wash. Sometimes I'm gone. I've poured myself into some deeper fissure below the sea only to be dragged forth, hair streaming. During transition, as the baby is ready to be pushed out into life, the waves are no longer made of water, but neons so brilliant I gasp in shock and flourish my arms, letting the colors explode from my fingertips in banners, in ribbons, in iridescent trails—of pain, it is true, unendurable sometimes, and yet we do endure. (42–46)

ANALYZING THE STYLE OF AN ESSAY OR A SPEECH

We invite you to analyze the style of a whole text, not a paragraph or a passage. In a whole essay or speech, you can examine more fully relationships between a writer's meaning and style, between what is expressed and how it is expressed.

ACTIVITY 2

You may choose to analyze one of the essays you have already read in this book (such as the readings on controversial issues in chapter 2) or an essay or a speech not in this book with your instructor's permission. If you choose a selection not in this book, make a copy of it and attach it to your analysis. Or you may analyze one of the selections at the end of this interchapter. Following are some options for analyzing an essay or a speech (3 to 6 pages).

1. Explain how three of a writer's stylistic choices help create the meaning of his or her essay or speech. (See the student paper "Analyzing Rhetoric with a Swoosh.")
2. Explain how three of a writer's stylistic choices help create the writer's appeals to logos, pathos, and ethos.
3. Explain how three of a writer's stylistic choices help create the writer's voice and tone (attitude toward audience, subject, and self).

Please read the following essay. Then read the student analysis of it. This analysis provides you with a model that can help you with your own paper.

The Swooshification of the World

Rick Reilly

Cracking in the face of a marketing behemoth, the author goes loco over a logo

I must get more Swoosh in my life. More, more, more. It's not enough to 1 have the Swoosh on every jersey and scoreboard and dugout roof. It's not enough that the Swoosh is on basketballs, footballs, soccer balls and volleyballs. It's not enough that the Swoosh is slapped all over more than 40 universities, eight NFL teams, six NHL teams (two more next season) and five Major League Soccer teams.

I want the eye black under baseball and football players' eyes to take the 2 form of a Swoosh. I want hockey sticks, nine-irons and yardage markers to be made in the shape of a Swoosh. I want to know who's in the on-deck Swoosh. I want to watch the Swoosh Channel. I want Swoosh condoms (Just Do It).

It's not enough that the Swoosh is on Michael Jordan's beret and Mary 3 Pierce's headband and Gabrielle Reece's beach volleyball top. It's not enough that the center on the Hawaii basketball team had his sideburns shaped into Swooshes. I want a Swoosh tattoo. I want a Swoosh lasered onto my retinas. I want to name my son Swoosh. (If it's a girl, Swooshie.)

I want these things because the Swoosh is the most ubiquitous symbol 4 in sports history. The Swoosh is so huge that the name of the company that goes with the Swoosh doesn't even appear anymore. In the ads, on the shoes, even on the company letterhead, all you get is the Swoosh, and you just <u>know</u>. Try that with Keds, pal.

Happiness is a warm Swoosh. Do you see the way it <u>swooshes</u> upward, a 5 snappy little check mark, letting you know that everything in your life is A-O.K.? It's airy, windswept, uplifting. It's the delighted little final stroke your pen makes when endorsing the biggest check of your life.

But there is not enough of it in our lives yet. From here on in, instead 6 of H-O-R-S-E, I want kids to play S-W-O-O-S-H. I want skis to go <u>Swoosh!</u> I want to get the autograph of Sheryl Swoosh.

Woe to you who underestimate the Swoosh. Tiger Woods, the coolest 7 athlete on Planet Swoosh, has the Swoosh on the front of his hat and the side of his hat and the back of his hat and on his turtleneck and on his shirt and on his sweater and on his vest and on his pants and on his socks and on his shoes. But when Woods arrived in Thailand two weeks ago, he found that his luggage had been misplaced, and he had to play a program without his usual complement of Swooshes. He lasted just 13 holes before heat and exhaustion got to him. Don't you see? The Swoosh is the source of all his powers!

I wasn't always like this. I used to rage against the Swoosh. "Why?" I 8 yelped at strangers. "Why must the Swoosh run the world?" Why, I asked, after almost 30 years, did the Denver Broncos let the Swoosh people redesign the team's uniforms and logo so that they were suddenly uglier than the jerseys of a meat-market softball team? I cried out against the subliminal Swooshing all over the new Denver uniform. "Don't you see it?" I railed, pointing to the Broncos' new logo. "The horse's nostril! It's a Swoosh!"

In protest I determined to go an entire day without getting Swooshed. I 9 made it 14 minutes, just past my Eggo, when my wife came down in her Swoosh sports bra. Something snapped in me that morning. I gave in. You cannot fight the Swoosh.

I want my kids to attend the University of California at Swoosh. I want 10 to get up in the morning and eat a big bowlful of chocolate Swooshios as part of a nutritionally balanced breakfast. I want to meet Carolyn Davidson. She's the graphic designer who, after graduating from Portland State in 1972, came up with the Swoosh for Phil Knight, Zeus of Swoosh, for $35. Thirty-five dollars! When she handed it to Knight, she remembers, he said, "I don't love it, but maybe it'll grow on me." Twenty-five years and a zillion dollars later, you think it's all right now, Phil? (Davidson, who in 1983 was given some Nike stock by Knight and who recently retired, says her second most famous work is the wallpaper she designed for a motel in Yakima, Wash.) Carolyn Davidson, stand up and take your place in world history!

Some experts believe the Swoosh is better known than the McDonald's 11 golden arches. Nine national soccer teams, including Brazil's, wear the Swoosh.

The Tour de France leader wears the Swoosh. When the U.S. played Russia in hockey's recent World Cup, both teams were wearing the Swoosh.

The Swoosh is like Jell-O: There's always room for the Swoosh. I want   12
Swoosh on the periodic table of the elements, right next to boron. I want Swoosh to be the 27th letter of the alphabet. I want to order raw eel at a Swooshi bar.

Do not fight it, brothers and sisters. Trust in the Swoosh. The Swoosh is   13
good and powerful. If our government leaders would only let it, the Swoosh could bail us out of this deficit thing like <u>that</u>. Of course, we would have to make a few small concessions.

<u>Al, does the presidential seal look different to you?</u> (78) □   14

Analyzing Rhetoric with a Swoosh

Gavin McMacken

In his <u>Sports Illustrated</u> essay, "The Swooshification of the   1
World," published February 24, 1997, Rick Reilly questions the overuse of Nike's Swoosh image--a small logo generating such big business it's almost overtaking the world. Reilly's exaggerated style reflects Nike's exaggerated marketing campaign for the Swoosh to appear practically everywhere. Reilly's use of italics, simple yet creative diction, and anaphora enables him to create a playfully ironic voice to question the excess of the Nike Swoosh.

Reilly believes the Nike Swoosh logo has grown out of   2
control, not only in the world of sports but in the whole world. He repeatedly says he wants to see more Swooshes than there already are. Citing various facts, he claims "it's not enough" that many universities and professional sporting teams use the logo. He wants the image to enter his personal life more. The Swoosh is so omnipresent that Nike doesn't need to use its Nike name. Reilly even warns that the Swoosh has supernatural power: Tiger Woods is a great golfer because he wears so many Swooshes. Although Reilly used to question the proliferation of the Swoosh, he no longer fights it. He wants more of it. He wants to celebrate the graphic designer who created it for $35 in 1972. After citing some more facts about how teams around the world use the Swoosh, Reilly concludes by

(box continues)

telling readers to worship the logo because it "is good and powerful." It could also, he suggests, solve our country's deficit problem—and even help run our country.

Reilly's voice is playfully ironic in this essay. He sounds obsessed with the logo to show how our country is obsessed with it. Although he keeps saying he wants more Swoosh, he does not think the logo "is good." He really does not want "a Swoosh lasered onto [his] retinas." He does not want to name his child Swoosh. He does not want "Swoosh condoms." What he wants is for readers to wake up and stop buying into the Swoosh craze. Because his examples are often extreme and foolish, Reilly succeeds in making readers think more about Nike's advertising blitz. Through his playful irony, he appeals to pathos and logos; he helps readers laugh and think. Because he does this so well, readers like Reilly's ethos: he is clever yet insightful--and he uses style to reinforce his sense.

3

Reilly's use of italics contributes to his voice. They help readers <u>hear</u> his voice and exaggerate his point about Swooshification: "Do you see the way it <u>swooshes</u> upward [. . .] ?" "I want skis to go <u>Swoosh</u>!" "[. . .] the Swoosh could bail us out of this deficit thing like <u>that</u>." And the last sentence is completely italicized: "<u>Al, does the presidential seal look different to you?</u>" That Reilly italicizes his last sentence is noteworthy because he raises a question that seems both absurd yet reasonable: Is Nike so rich it could influence or buy the federal government? In one paragraph in which he drops his persona and seems somewhat serious, Reilly writes, "The Swoosh is so huge that the name of the company that goes with the Swoosh doesn't even appear anymore. In the ads, on the shoes, even on the company letterhead, all you get is the Swoosh, and you just <u>know</u>." The word <u>know</u> resonates, and we know what Reilly means.

4

Reilly's use of simple yet creative diction is also effective. Overall Reilly's diction is informal with easy words. Many are monosyllabic as seen in his first two sentences: "I must get more Swoosh in my life. More, more, more." These sentences begin the train of Reilly's exaggeration and playful irony. His heavy use of one-syllable words is fitting because the Swoosh itself is so simplistic in appearance. Throughout his essay Reilly uses eleven sentences containing all monosyllabic words and ten sentences containing all but one monosyllabic

5

(box continues)

word such as "But there is not enough of it in our lives yet."

Reilly maximizes the monosyllabic <u>and</u> in the essay's longest sentence:

> Tiger Woods, the coolest athlete on Planet Swoosh, has the Swoosh on the front of his hat and the side of his hat and the back of his hat and on his turtleneck and on his shirt and on his sweater and on his vest and on his pants and on his socks and on his shoes.

The sentence contains 64 words, 57 of which are monosyllabic. That Reilly repeats <u>and</u> nine times is effective because the word makes the sentence sound slow and tired. The repetition reinforces Reilly's idea that the Swoosh is ridiculously everywhere--especially on star athletes like Tiger Woods whom millions of sports fans emulate.

Yet two important multisyllabic words resonate in the essay. The title contains the five syllable <u>Swooshification</u>. This complex yet playful word suggests Reilly's thesis that the Nike logo has grown out of control. The other word is <u>ubiquitous</u> used in this sentence: "I want these things because the Swoosh is the most ubiquitous symbol in sports history." Here Reilly drops his persona of a Swoosh-crazed guy. He's serious. <u>Ubiquitous</u> is a serious word, one that forces many readers to look at it twice and then possibly run for a dictionary. It means "seeming to be present everywhere at the same time" (<u>Webster's New World</u> 1448). This intellectual word is perfect for describing the Swoosh, and it conveys Reilly's thesis.

Reilly's creative use of diction helps create his voice of playful irony. He says he wants to name his son Swoosh but "(If it's a girl, Swooshie.)" Making a pun on Cheerios, he says he wants to "eat a big bowlful of chocolate Swooshios." And he makes a pun on the word <u>boron</u>: "I want Swoosh on the periodic table of the elements right next to boron." This word works well because it sounds like <u>boring</u> or <u>bore on</u>: Reilly is bored with the Swoosh and thinks we all should be. Reilly's use of assonance also contributes to his playful voice. Notice the long <u>u</u> sound he repeats three times in this sentence: "Woe to <u>you</u> wh<u>o</u> underestimate the Sw<u>oo</u>sh." The assonance reinforces his exaggeration that the Swoosh has magical power. Later he refers to Phil Knight who founded Nike as the "Zeus of Swoosh," again playing on the long <u>u</u> vowel. Reilly uses some alliteration as well, playing on <u>s</u> sounds: "It's not enough

6

7

8

(box continues)

that the center on the Hawaii basketball team had his s̲ideburns
s̲haped into S̲wooshes." "I want to get the autograph of S̲heryl
S̲woosh" and "I cried out against the s̲ubliminal S̲wooshing all
over the new Denver uniform." Reilly doesn't overuse these
sound devices; he doesn't need to because of his strong use of
anaphora through the essay.

    Reilly's use of anaphora is extreme but highly effective.
He uses it throughout his essay. By repeating the same
beginning words in many sentences, he shows how obsessed he   9
and the country are about the Swoosh. He uses two forms of
anaphora. One is "It's not enough":

> It's not enough to have the Swoosh on every jersey
> and scoreboard and dugout roof. It's not enough that
> the Swoosh is on basketballs, footballs, soccer balls
> and volleyballs. It's not enough that the Swoosh is
> slapped all over more than 40 universities, eight NFL
> teams, six NHL teams (two more next season) and five
> Major League Soccer teams.

This repetition at the beginning of the essay enables Reilly to
show his exaggerated obsession--the Swoosh is n̲o̲t̲ "on every
jersey and scoreboard and dugout roof," although it may seem
like it. The three repetitions echo and prepare readers for his
theme: the endless repetition of the Swoosh logo. He uses the
same anaphora in two more sentences in paragraph three.

    Reilly uses his second form of anaphora "I want" seventeen
times throughout the essay. This pattern helps create Reilly's
playfully ironic voice:

> I want the eye black under baseball and football
> players' eyes to take the form of a Swoosh. I want   10
> hockey sticks, nine-irons and yardage markers to be
> made in the shape of a Swoosh. I want to know who's
> in the on-deck Swoosh. I want to watch the Swoosh
> Channel. I want Swoosh condoms (Just Do It).

Reilly not only wants to see more Swoosh in the world of
sports but also in his personal world: "I want a Swoosh
tattoo. I want a Swoosh lasered onto my retinas. I want to
name my son Swoosh. (If it's a girl, Swooshie.)" Toward the
end of the essay his exaggeration reaches climactic heights:
"I want Swoosh on the periodic table of the elements, right
next to boron. I want Swoosh to be the 27th letter of the
alphabet." The logo has taken over Reilly's imagination. He has
seen it so often that he obsessively wants to see it more. It

(box continues)

has taken over the sports' world. By repeating that he wants to see more of it, he causes readers to wonder if the logo is good to see at all.

Reilly's anaphora serves two main purposes. One, the Swoosh exists for people to buy Nike products. Nike wants consumers to say, "I want that baseball cap with the Swoosh." Reilly's refrain of "I want" echoes this. Two, the anaphora skillfully voices Reilly's exaggerated obsession—and the obsession at large in our culture. This is effective because after a while he sounds like a child: the Swoosh has become something to nurse on, which feeds us. But it's not nutritious, Reilly implies; rather, it's full of empty calories that cost consumers too much money. Without anaphora, the essay—and Reilly's voice—would lose much of its power.   11

"The Swooshification of the World" is a hole-in-one, a three pointer basket, a grand slam essay. To achieve his playfully ironic voice, Reilly uses italics, simple yet creative diction, and anaphora. Although his essay is fun to read, he raises a serious question: when is enough Swoosh enough? He wants readers to think about whether the Swoosh logo is good for sports and for people who keep buying Nike products. Reilly cleverly implies his answer: It's not good. It's boring. It's spinning out of control. Through his style, Reilly communicates clearly. Maybe I'll subscribe to <u>Sports Illustrated</u> so I can read more Reilly.   12

ESSAYS FOR ANALYSIS

No Contest: Books Beat Sport Anytime

Leonard Pitts Jr.

"The pride and the presence of a professional football team is far more impor-   1
tant than 30 libraries."

Art Modell, owner of the Baltimore Ravens, formerly the Cleveland Browns,   2
said that in the September issue of <u>Cleveland</u> magazine. Said that a team

provides a town with a "great social common denominator" and has a "tremendous binding effect on the public." He said he spoke with "all due respect to the learning process."

Actually, he spoke with no respect at all. Or humility. Or common sense. 3 Spoke like a poster boy for anti-intellectual America. Memo to Modell: Next time, engage brain before operating mouth.

"The pride and the presence of a professional football team is far more 4 important than 30 libraries."

Right. And hockey teams are more important than schools, I suppose. Basket- 5 ball teams over public parks. Baseball teams more significant than hospitals.

The mind reels. Both at the stupidity of it—and at the thought it might 6 conceivably be true. Hey, at my library they have to set up trash cans to catch the water when it rains. I've never seen a pro sports arena with a leaky roof, so maybe there's something to what he says.

Mind you, that lamentation comes from a sports fan. I've probably spent 7 a cumulative year of my life pacing before the TV set muttering, "C'mon, Lakers, we can do this!"

I love my team as much as anybody. Sport enriches my life. But libraries 8 feed my soul.

And sometimes I watch that water dripping down and wonder: Does 9 anybody care? We say that learning matters, but do we mean it?

When Modell decided to move his team to Baltimore, it was sensational. 10 Fans rallied, columnists railed, negotiators huddled, reporters reported and officials made fiery speeches.

Would they do that if a library were about to shut down? 11

Yes, says Judy Cooper, spokeswoman for my local library. "When politicians 12 start to talk about closing libraries, all hell breaks loose. The library is like the fire station, the police station. It's really . . . the strength of the community."

That's what it boils down to, isn't it? Community. It's heartening to think 13 she might be right, that we haven't completely lost our minds.

Of course, Art Modell believes we have. He believes our priorities are 14 upside down like his.

"The pride and the presence of a professional football team is far more 15 important than 30 libraries."

"If that is Mr. Modell's mentality," says William Urbizu, assistant director 16 of the Miami-Dade Public Library, "I'm sure he would be very proud and pleased to fill his stadium with illiterate fans who would be unable to read the scoreboard or his team's program book."

I'm with him. I'd rather live in a place with no team than one with no 17 books. A library is a place to shape tomorrow, to climb the fertile hills of your imagination and glimpse horizons beyond your own.

There are no cheerleaders for readers, no front-page pictures, no end-zone 18 dance. In a world obsessed with the external and the extraneous, reading is something we do to build the internal and the essential.

And that matters to me, because I believe in the long run. And I believe 19 that in the long run, what you feed your soul determines who you become. That matters a hell of a lot more than any game.

"The pride and the presence of a professional football team is far more   20 important than 30 libraries."

Spoken like a man who hasn't spent nearly enough time in libraries. (1F) ☐   21

Whoever We Are, Loss Finds Us and Defines Us

Anna Quindlen

My great journalistic contribution to my family is that I write obituaries.   1

First my mother's, 22 years ago, listing her accomplishments: two daugh-   2 ters, three sons. Then that of my father's second wife, dead of the same disease that killed his first one.

Last week it was my sister-in-law. "Sherry Quindlen, 41," I tapped out on   3 the keyboard, and then it was real, like a last breath.

"When you write about me," she said one day in the hospital, "be nice."   4

For the obituary, I could only be accurate. The limitations of the form elim-   5 inate the more subjective truths: a good heart, a generous soul, a woman who made her living taking care of other people's children.

My brother's wife, the mother of a teenager and a toddler, who went from   6 a bad cough to what was mistakenly said to be pneumonia to what was correctly diagnosed as lung and liver cancer, from fall to spring, from the day she threw a surprise 40th birthday party for her husband to the day he chose her casket.

Only days after the funeral her two daughters were shopping together   7 when a saleswoman looked at them and said admiringly, "Your mother must have beautiful hair."

"Yes, she does," said the elder, who had learned quickly what is expected   8 of survivors.

Grief remains one of the few things that has the power to silence us. It   9 is a whisper in the world and a clamor within.

More than sex, more than faith, even more than its usher, death, grief is   10 unspoken, publicly ignored except for those moments at the funeral that are over too quickly, or the conversations among the cognoscenti, those of us who recognize in one another a kindred chasm deep in the center of who we are.

Maybe we do not speak of it because death will mark all of us, sooner or   11 later. Or maybe it is unspoken because grief is only the first part of it. After a time it becomes something less sharp but larger, too, a more enduring thing called loss. Perhaps that is why this is the least explored passage: because it has no end.

The world loves closure, loves a thing that can, as they say, be gotten   12 through. This is why it comes as a great surprise that loss is forever, that two decades after the event there are those occasions when something in you cries out at the continual presence of an absence. "An awful leisure," Emily Dickinson once called what the living have after death.

Sherwin Nuland, a doctor and professor at Yale, has become an unlikely 13 best-selling author with a straightforward, unsparing yet deeply human description of the end of life entitled How We Die. In the introduction he explains that he has written the book "to demythologize the process of dying."

But I wondered, reading on, if he was doing something else as well. He 14 wrote: "My mother died of colon cancer one week after my eleventh birthday, and that fact has shaped my life. All that I have become and much that I have not become, I trace directly or indirectly to her death."

Loss as muse. Loss as character. Loss as life. 15

When the president talks of moving some days to the phone to call his 16 mother, who died in January, he is breaking a silence about what so many have felt.

"The hard part is for those of us who've kept silent for decades to start 17 talking about our losses," Hope Edelman writes in her new book, Motherless Daughters. Yet how second nature the silence becomes, so much a rule of etiquette that a 15-year-old knows when her loss is as raw as a freshly dug grave not to discomfit a stranger by revealing it in passing.

All that she and her sister will become, and much they will not, will be 18 traced later on to a time when spring had finally passed over the threshold of winter and the cemetery drives were edged with pink tulips, shivering slightly in a chilly April rain.

My brother and I know too much about their future; both teenagers when 19 our mother died, we know that if the girls were to ask us, "When does it stop hurting?" we would have to answer, in all candor, "If it ever does, we will let you know."

The landscapes of all our lives become as full of craters as the surface of 20 the moon. My brother is a young widower with young children, as his father was before him. And I write my obituaries carefully and think about how little the facts suffice, not only to describe the dead but to tell what they will mean to the living all the rest of our lives.

We are defined by who we have lost. 21

"Don't let them forget me," Sherry said. Oh, hon, piece of cake. (11A) □ 22

Dr. Martin Luther King Jr. delivered the following classic speech at the Lincoln Memorial in Washington DC, 28 August 1963, climaxing the civil rights demonstration of that day.

I Have a Dream

Martin Luther King Jr.

Five score years ago, a great American, in whose symbolic shadow we stand   1
today, signed the Emancipation Proclamation. This momentous decree came as
a great beacon light of hope to millions of Negro slaves, who had been seared
in the flames of withering injustice. It came as a joyous daybreak to end the
long night of their captivity.

But one hundred years later, the Negro still is not free. One hundred years   2
later, the life of the Negro is still sadly crippled by the manacles of segregation
and the chains of discrimination. One hundred years later, the Negro lives on a
lonely island of poverty in the midst of a vast ocean of material prosperity. One
hundred years later, the Negro still languishes in the corners of American society and finds himself in exile in his own land.

So we've come here today to dramatize a shameful condition. In a sense   3
we've come to our nation's capital to cash a check. When the architects of our
republic wrote the magnificent words of the Constitution and the Declaration of
Independence, they were signing a promissory note to which every American was
to fall heir. This note was the promise that all men—yes, black men as well as
white men—would be guaranteed the inalienable rights of life, liberty, and the
pursuit of happiness.

It is obvious today that America has defaulted on this promissory note   4
insofar as her citizens of color are concerned. Instead of honoring this sacred
obligation, America has given the Negro people a bad check, a check which has
come back marked "insufficient funds." But we refuse to believe that the bank
of justice is bankrupt. We refuse to believe that there are insufficient funds in
the great vaults of opportunity of this nation. So we've come to cash this
check—a check that will give us upon demand the riches of freedom and the
security of justice.

We have also come to this hallowed spot to remind America of the   5
fierce urgency of "now." This is no time to engage in the luxury of cooling
off or to take the tranquilizing drug of gradualism. Now is the time to make
real the promises of democracy. Now is the time to rise from the dark and
desolate valley of segregation to the sunlit path of racial justice. Now is the
time to lift our nation from the quicksand of racial injustice to the solid rock
of brotherhood. Now is the time to make justice a reality for all of God's
children.

It would be fatal for the nation to overlook the urgency of the moment.   6
This sweltering summer of the Negro's legitimate discontent will not pass until
there is an invigorating autumn of freedom and equality. Nineteen sixty-three
is not an end, but a beginning. Those who hope that the Negro needed to blow

off steam and will now be content will have a rude awakening if the nation returns to business as usual. There will be neither rest nor tranquility in America until the Negro is granted his citizenship rights. The whirlwinds of revolt will continue to shake the foundations of our nation until the bright day of justice emerges.

But there is something that I must say to my people who stand on the warm threshold which leads into the palace of justice. In the process of gaining our rightful place we must not be guilty of wrongful deeds. Let us not seek to satisfy our thirst for freedom by drinking from the cup of bitterness and hatred. We must forever conduct our struggle on the high plane of dignity and discipline. We must not allow our creative protest to degenerate into physical violence. Again and again we must rise to the majestic heights of meeting physical force with soul force. The marvelous new militancy which has engulfed the Negro community must not lead us to a distrust of all white people, for many of our white brothers, as evidenced by their presence here today, have come to realize that their destiny is tied up with our destiny. And they have come to realize that their freedom is inextricably bound to our freedom. We cannot walk alone. 7

As we walk, we must make the pledge that we shall always march ahead. We cannot turn back. 8

There are those who are asking the devotees of civil rights, "When will you be satisfied?" We can never be satisfied as long as the Negro is the victim of the unspeakable horrors of police brutality. We can never be satisfied as long as our bodies, heavy with the fatigue of travel, cannot gain lodging in the motels of the highways and the hotels of the cities. We cannot be satisfied as long as the Negro's basic mobility is from a smaller ghetto to a larger one. We can never be satisfied as long as our children are stripped of their selfhood and robbed of their dignity by signs stating "For Whites Only." We cannot be satisfied as long as a Negro in Mississippi cannot vote and a Negro in New York believes he has nothing for which to vote. No, no, we are not satisfied, and we will not be satisfied until justice rolls down like waters and righteousness like a mighty stream. 9

I am not unmindful that some of you have come here out of great trials and tribulations. Some of you have come fresh from narrow jail cells. Some of you have come from areas where your quest for freedom left you battered by the storms of persecution and staggered by the winds of police brutality. You have been veterans of creative suffering. Continue to work with the faith that unearned suffering is redemptive. 10

Go back to Mississippi, go back to Alabama, go back to South Carolina, go back to Georgia, go back to Louisiana, go back to the slums and ghettos of our northern cities, knowing that somehow this situation can and will be changed. Let us not wallow in the valley of despair. 11

I say to you today, my friends, even though we face the difficulties of 12 today and tomorrow, I still have a dream. It is a dream deeply rooted in the American dream.

I have a dream that one day this nation will rise up and live out the true 13 meaning of its creed: "We hold these truths to be self-evident; that all men are created equal." I have a dream that one day on the red hills of Georgia the sons of former slaves and the sons of former slave owners will be able to sit down together at the table of brotherhood.

I have a dream that one day even the state of Mississippi, a state swel- 14 tering with the heat of injustice, sweltering with the heat of oppression, will be transformed into an oasis of freedom and justice. I have a dream that my four little children will one day live in a nation where they will not be judged by the color of their skin, but by the content of their character.

I have a dream today. 15

I have a dream that one day, down in Alabama, with its vicious racists, 16 with its governor having his lips dripping with the words of interposition and nullification, one day right there in Alabama little black boys and black girls will be able to join hands with little white boys and white girls and walk together as sisters and brothers. I have a dream today.

I have a dream that one day every valley shall be exalted, every hill and 17 mountain shall be made low, the rough places will be made plain and the crooked places will be made straight, and the glory of the Lord shall be revealed, and all flesh shall see it together.

This is our hope. This is the faith that I go back to the South with. With 18 this faith we will be able to hew out of the mountain of despair a stone of hope. With this faith we will be able to transform the jangling discords of our nation into a beautiful symphony of brotherhood. With this faith we will be able to work together, to pray together, to struggle together, to go to jail together, to stand up for freedom together, knowing that we will be free one day.

And this will be the day . . . this will be the day when all God's children 19 will be able to sing with new meaning. "My country, 'tis of thee, sweet land of liberty, of thee I sing. Land where my fathers died, land of the Pilgrims' pride, from every mountainside, let freedom ring." And if America is to be a great nation this must become true.

So let freedom ring! From the prodigious hilltops of New Hampshire, let 20 freedom ring! From the mighty mountains of New York, let freedom ring, from the heightening Alleghenies of Pennsylvania!

Let freedom ring from the snowcapped Rockies of Colorado! 21

Let freedom ring from the curvaceous slopes of California. But not only 22 that.

Let freedom ring from Stone Mountain of Georgia! 23

Let freedom ring from Lookout Mountain in Tennessee! 24

Let freedom ring from every hill and molehill of Mississippi. From every 25 mountainside, let freedom ring, and when this happens . . . when we allow freedom to ring, when we let it ring from every village and every hamlet, from every state and every city . . . we will be able to speed up that day when all of God's children, black men and white men, Jews and Gentiles, Protestants and Catholics, will be able to join hands and sing in the words of the old Negro spiritual: "Free at last! Free at last! Thank God Almighty, we are free at last!" □

Chapter 6

Critical Thinking about Poetry, Fiction, Literary Nonfiction, and Film

The poet's job is not to tell you what happened, but what happens: not what did take place, but the kind of thing that always does take place. (Frye 63)

Reading literature is a time-honored way to develop critical thinking skills. Because poems, stories, literary essays, and films are artistic, they resist easy analysis. Yet they are persuasive because they <u>move</u> you: literary writers create certain effects that cause you to think, to feel, to consider ethical issues (logos, pathos, ethos). These forms challenge you to question what you read. They require you to slow down and pay close attention to <u>meaning</u> (what is being expressed) and to <u>style</u> (how it is being expressed).

To read critically means to think while you read. The objective is not how many facts you can remember but how well you can understand. Critical reading means

- <u>Analyzing</u>—noticing appeals and arguments, strategies of thinking, insights
- <u>Questioning</u>—wondering why, how, what if, so what
- <u>Inferring</u>—drawing conclusions from what is suggested or implied in a text
- <u>Interpreting</u>—explaining your own understanding of a text
- <u>Evaluating</u>—judging the value or worth of a poem, story, essay, film, or any text

Critical reading matures your ability to think.

READING AND WRITING ABOUT POETRY

Critical thinking helps you read and understand poetry. Let's begin with the following poem, "My Papa's Waltz."

My Papa's Waltz

Theodore Roethke

The whiskey on your breath
Could make a small boy dizzy;
But I hung on like death:
Such waltzing was not easy.

We romped until the pans   5
Slid from the kitchen shelf;
My mother's countenance
Could not unfrown itself.

The hand that held my wrist
Was battered on one knuckle;   10
At every step you missed
My right ear scraped a buckle.

You beat time on my head
With a palm caked hard by dirt,
Then waltzed me off to bed   15
Still clinging to your shirt.

ACTIVITY 1

In your notebook write a paragraph in which you support one of the following interpretations of this poem: (1) "My Papa's Waltz" is a poem about connection and love. (2) "My Papa's Waltz" is a poem about child abuse. (3) Offer another interpretation. Try to cite details from the poem to support your interpretation.

———————————

Poetry—all art—challenges you <u>to think and to feel</u>. To think about what a poem means, you need to pay attention to its words. Usually, there is more than one way to interpret a poem. An interpretation relies not directly on what a poem says but on what it implies through its use of language. Critical thinkers should be able to explain their interpretations. This does not mean, however, that there are right and wrong interpretations—only reasonable and not so reasonable ones, depending on your evidence.

You don't need to know a lot about reading poetry to enjoy Roethke's poem. "My Papa's Waltz" is a favorite in American literature. The image of father, a little drunk, "waltzing" roughly with his child is easy to visualize. And mother's disapproving "countenance"—the look on her face that shows her feelings—that "Could not unfrown itself" is also easy to see. You may recall a childhood moment when your father's behavior with children caused your mother to frown.

Why does she frown? After all, father seems in good spirits. Maybe a little too good? "Romping" around the kitchen, his steps not too steady, the child hanging on . . . she doesn't say it, but many mothers might think it: "Someone's going to get hurt"—a motherly admonition. When he is drunk, father becomes unpredictable, a little rowdy. Then too, something is shared between father and child from which mother is excluded.

If you enjoy the poem, you might ask yourself questions about the way it's constructed. Why is the poem addressed to "you" for example? Why is it written in the past tense? Why does it contain words that rhyme? To understand the poem fully, you must see Papa, smell "the whiskey on [his] breath," enough to "make a small boy dizzy." The poet is telling you something—or rather the narrator in the poem ("I hung on") is—and you must imagine it in your mind if you are to understand the poem.

Whether you can see the images depends on your understanding of the language. Although Roethke's poem is not usually considered difficult (except perhaps for "countenance" in line 7), the poem can present problems of interpretation. Words like "whiskey," "dizzy," "death" may carry negative connotations, as do "hand that held my wrist," "battered," "scraped," "beat time on my head," "palm caked hard by dirt." All these negative words or connotations of words seem to make the poem itself negative. But against the negative ideas, there are three key ideas, unfamiliar to many students: waltzing, romping, and beating time.

Suppose a student claims the poem concerns child abuse, the drunken father "beating" the child while the mother does nothing. In part we think this interpretation is the result of media campaigns against child abuse, wife abuse, and drunkenness. The student's interpretation may be less her own understanding of the poem than an interpretation that fits what she has heard about "beating."

Is this a good interpretation of the poem? Why isn't it sufficient for the student to say, "Well that's the way I see it—that's my interpretation"? Although the student prefers the child abuse interpretation and believes this is a good understanding of the poem, we think this reading could be the result of hurrying through the poem. The "child abuse" interpretation weakens when readers consider the positive connotations in the poem. The key word seems to be "beat" in line 13. That word can mean physical abuse, but here the context suggests something else: "You beat <u>time</u>." A waltz is a formal dance, requiring much twirling in circles—dancers must move in time to the music. The other word that might lead a reader to infer child abuse is "battered" in line 10. But it isn't the child but the adult who is "battered on one knuckle." (Well, maybe his knuckle got battered from beating the child? Possibly, but that requires you to make an assumption based on the interpretation you are trying to defend.)

When you carefully read a poem, you think about its words and sounds and structure. Such critical thinking helps you enjoy and interpret the poem. You can also analyze a poem by its persuasive appeals:

Logos: What does the poem mean? What questions does it raise?

Pathos: How does it make you feel? Are your feelings mixed?

Ethos: What is the character of the speaker of the poem? Is the speaker afraid, having fun? Is the speaker believable and credible?

When you interpret a poem, your job is to make a point and to support it with specific evidence from the poem—examples of words, details, lines. If you believe the poem is about child abuse or about love or something else, you need to defend this view by citing and analyzing parts of the poem that show this. But keep in mind that poems, being works of art, tend to hold some mystery. Poems rarely contain clear topic sentences or thesis statements. Poems suggest meaning: you infer meaning from a poem, and a poem can hold various meanings, even contradictory meanings. Your job is to think about and feel a poem and sort out what it suggests to you.

Might "My Papa's Waltz" concern both love and terror? Might the speaker feel closely connected to his father in the waltz yet feel terrified too—terrified of the father's show of love, his unsteady movements, of the mother's frown and fear, of his own complex feelings toward his father? When he holds on "like death," this could mean that he didn't want to let go of his father physically or let go of his father's love. Thus, the way you interpret this poem depends on the details you cite to support your idea. A "simple" poem, "My Papa's Waltz" is more complex than many readers first think. This is true of most excellent poetry.

The Language of Poetry

We can't do an in-depth study of poetry here; you can find many good books in the library on that subject. Here we present only a brief introduction to some of the major elements of poetry—elements that exist in essays, stories, and plays too. In this section, you will explore how poems convey meanings and how poets use language to achieve those meanings.

Critical reading requires two people—the poet on one end and the reader on the other. Between them is the poem, made of language. But this is true of all reading. Why should poetry be different, harder? Why can't you skim through poetry the way you can skim through a newspaper? Think of champion skaters who do complex yet beautiful twirls—should you forbid them to do anything extraordinary? Can you insist they stick to plain skating? Poets are artists of language. As a critical reader you should try to stay with them, try to appreciate and understand their efforts. If you look for meanings in a poem, you may find different levels of meaning. Poetry often expresses ambiguous truth.

Many poems present images and music to help you feel and comprehend some strong emotion. Read, for example, "A narrow Fellow in the Grass."

A narrow Fellow in the Grass

Emily Dickinson

A narrow Fellow in the Grass
Occasionally rides—
You may have met Him—did you not
His notice sudden is—

The Grass divides as with a Comb—   5
A spotted shaft is seen—
And then it closes at your feet
And opens further on—

He likes a Boggy Acre
A floor too cool for Corn—   10
Yet when a Boy, and Barefoot—
I more than once at Noon

Have passed, I thought, a Whip lash
Unbraiding in the Sun
When stooping to secure it   15
It wrinkled, and was gone—

Several of Nature's People
I know, and they know me—
I feel for them a transport
Of Cordiality—   20

But never met this Fellow
Attended, or alone
Without a tighter breathing
And Zero at the Bone—

What does this poem mean? How might you read it to appreciate it, to interpret it? In his classic book on poetry <u>Sound and Sense</u> (20–23), Laurence Perrine offers three useful questions to help critical thinkers: (1) Who is the speaker and what is the occasion of the poem? (2) What is the poem's central purpose? (3) How does the poet achieve this purpose?

In "A narrow Fellow in the Grass" Emily Dickinson refers to the speaker as a boy: "Yet when a Boy, and Barefoot—." Poets often create the speaker of their poems; you shouldn't assume the poet is the speaker. The speaker of this poem may be a man contemplating being a boy and mistaking a creature as being a "Whip lash." The occasion? The speaker tells about noticing a certain creature of nature.

What is Dickinson's central purpose in the poem? Although she never uses the word "snake," you can infer from Dickinson's images and details that this poem concerns a snake: "narrow Fellow," "spotted shaft," "a Whip lash /

Unbraiding in the Sun." The speaker seems in awe of snakes: they are wonderful creatures yet stir great fear in the speaker and in most people. Dickinson's central purpose may be to capture this contradictory feeling of awe and fear—to help readers feel this same way.

How does Dickinson achieve this purpose? This third question involves analyzing how a poet uses language. You could argue that Dickinson achieves her purpose by using the second person pronoun "you," vivid images, and figures of speech. She involves you as a reader by including you in the poem: "You may have met Him—did you not." Most of us have met snakes unexpectedly. Her second stanza also involves the reader: "And then it closes at your feet / And opens further on" as if a snake in the grass has come near you but left you alone. But after the references to "you," the speaker refers to himself as "I." The poem focuses on the speaker's feelings and thoughts.

Dickinson's images of the snake are visual: "narrow Fellow," "spotted shaft," "a Whip lash / Unbraiding in the Sun." The snake "wrinkled, and was gone"; it seems supernatural. Her simile—"The Grass divides as with a Comb"—conveys the snake's latent power. You can see grass dividing. The whiplash metaphor suggests the snap of a whip like a snake bite. These images create a rising fear in the poem. The speaker does not feel cordial to snakes.

You could analyze other aspects of Dickinson's language, such as her unusual capitalization (is it for emphasis?) or her unconventional punctuation (no periods, and why so many dashes—because they look like snakes?). If you did some research on Dickinson's poem and writing style, you could probably find answers to these questions.

To address the third question of how the poet achieves her purpose, you could also analyze the poem's appeals to ethos, pathos, and logos. The speaker is highly observant and thoughtful; he seems to care about nature, even referring to creatures as "Nature's People." His frank admission of fear makes the speaker honest and credible. You can trust the speaker; you sense he is sharing a truth about snakes and nature with you. Dickinson uses pathos by appealing to your emotions—you may feel awe at imagining a snake riding and dividing the grass; you may feel fear at imagining a whiplash moving and then "stooping to secure it." You have felt cold fear—"a tighter breathing" at seeing a lone snake. Dickinson stirs your feelings of awe and fear, enabling you to identify with the speaker. She appeals to logos or reasoning by moving you to think about snakes and nature and your complex reactions. You may question whether other creatures are like "Nature's People" and whether humans are sometimes like snakes. You might conclude that Dickinson's appeals to the speaker's character and to your own feelings combine to provoke you to think about snakes and your complex relationship with nature.

Elements of Poetry: Diction

Diction means word choice. To analyze a poem, you notice the poem's words and think about what the words do to create meanings and to appeal to your reason, emotion, and character.

Words have denotation and connotation. The <u>denotation</u> is the dictionary meaning of the word, what most people mean by the word. Denotation comes from denote—to "note" the meaning of. "Home" denotes where a person lives when not working.

<u>Connotation</u> is implied meanings and attitudes attached to a word; it is suggestions and associations that color a word with certain meanings.[1] "Home" usually carries connotations of warmth, security, and love. But "home" can carry negative connotations if it calls to mind physical or emotional abuse for somebody. In determining the meanings of poetry, you must be alert to both denotations and connotations of words. The way many readers view Roethke's line "You beat time on my head" depends on whether they consider "beat" as physical violence or making music.

As with any form of writing you read carefully, when you see a word in a poem you don't know or understand, such as "countenance," look it up in a dictionary after you read the complete poem. This bit of research is necessary—and another hallmark of critical thinking. Certain words can unlock a poem for you when you reread it. Certain words hold meanings you aren't aware of until you look them up in a dictionary. This research and discovery of word meaning is part of the pleasure of reading poems—or stories and essays. Of course, if you need to look up many words in a poem to understand it, you may quickly feel overburdened. But most poems don't require such work.

Diction also refers to whether words are <u>simple or complex,</u> <u>specific or general</u>, <u>concrete or abstract</u>, <u>literal or figurative</u>. (See interchapter 1.)

Elements of Poetry: Images

An image is a sensory experience made of words—a detail based on one or more of your senses: sight, smell, sound, taste, and touch. Through images the writer attempts to evoke some sensory event so you can imagine waltzing in a kitchen or witnessing a snake in the grass. Not all poems contain images, but most do. Think about the images presented in "Root Cellar," another poem by Theodore Roethke.

Root Cellar

Theodore Roethke

Nothing would sleep in that cellar, dank as a ditch,
Bulbs broke out of boxes hunting for chinks in the dark,
Shoots dangled and drooped,
Lolling obscenely from mildewed crates,

---

[1]Laurence Perrine, <u>Sound and Sense</u> 7th ed. (New York: Harcourt Brace Jovanovich 1987) asks why Dickinson doesn't use "plain English" at the end of "A narrow Fellow in the Grass." Why doesn't she say she is "frightened" 52?

Hung down long yellow evil necks, like tropical snakes.   5
And what a congress of stinks!—
Roots ripe as old bait,
Pulpy stems, rank, silo-rich,
Leaf-mold, manure, lime, piled against slippery planks.
Nothing would give up life: 10
Even the dirt kept breathing a small breath.

Elements of Poetry: Metaphors and Similes

Metaphors and similes are kinds of comparisons, and poets use them often. A metaphor is a comparison that does not use the words <u>as</u> or <u>like</u>. Consider the metaphors in "Metaphors."

Metaphors

Sylvia Plath

I'm a riddle in nine syllables,
An elephant, a ponderous house,
A melon strolling on two tendrils,
O red fruit, ivory, fine timbers!
This loaf's big with its yeasty rising.   5
Money's new-minted in this fat purse.
I'm a means, a stage, a cow in calf.
I've eaten a bag of green apples,
Boarded the train there's no getting off.

To what do Plath's metaphors refer? (We'll answer this soon.)

Similes are comparisons containing the words <u>as</u> or <u>like</u>. Here's one from "Root Cellar": "Roots ripe as old bait." Dickinson describes the grass dividing "as with a Comb."

Through metaphors and similes, poets join unrelated things to spark your imagination and consider new thoughts. (For more on metaphors and similes, see interchapter 1 and chapter 4.)

Elements of Poetry: Tone

Tone is a writer's attitude toward subject. Tone can be serious, humorous, playful, mock-serious, sad, loving, caring, angry, annoyed, and much more. How would you describe Roethke's tone in "Root Cellar"? Perhaps playful or mock-serious? After his images of rank smells and shoots "like tropical snakes," he ends the poem by suggesting the cellar is incredibly full of life. The speaker seems in awe of nature in a confined space. How would you describe Plath's tone in "Metaphors"? She playfully describes being pregnant, using extreme comparisons to help readers feel this condition.

Elements of Poetry: Speaker

Determining who speaks or narrates a poem can help you understand and interpret it. In "My Papa's Waltz" the speaker addresses his or her father. Although Theodore Roethke, a man, wrote the poem, the speaker could be a son or daughter. You shouldn't always assume that the speaker of a poem is the author of that poem because poets often invent speakers—they adopt personas. In "Root Cellar," the speaker is an observer; you don't know what relationship he has to the cellar, although students doing research on Roethke would find that his family owned a greenhouse in Saginaw, Michigan. In "Metaphors" Sylvia Plath is an exasperated woman fully pregnant. Plath may have been that woman; she did have two children. But she does not announce that she is the woman—the speaker could be any woman close to bearing a child. Analyzing the speaker of a poem aids you in analyzing the appeal to ethos in a poem—the character of the speaker.

Elements of Poetry: Sound Devices

Poems often contain sound patterns. In "Root Cellar" Roethke uses <u>alliteration</u>:

> "<u>d</u>ank as a <u>d</u>itch," "<u>B</u>ulbs <u>b</u>roke out of <u>b</u>oxes," "Shoots <u>d</u>angled and <u>d</u>rooped," "<u>R</u>oots <u>r</u>ipe as old bait"

Alliteration is the repetition of initial consonants of words. Roethke's thick alliteration suggests the thickness of vegetation in the cellar. The sound reinforces the sense or meaning of the poem.

In her snake poem Emily Dickinson uses <u>assonance</u>: the repetition of vowel sounds in words. The long o's in Dickinson's poem echo the fear the speaker feels:

> But never met this Fell<u>o</u>w,
> Attended, or al<u>o</u>ne
> Without a tighter breathing
> And Zer<u>o</u> at the B<u>o</u>ne—

Assonance often reinforces emotion in a poem.

What sound do you hear in this Dickinson line about a snake: "His notice sudden is—"? A hiss sound? Yes. Using words that echo the sound they denote is called <u>onomatopoeia</u>. The word "cricket" makes the sound of the insect; say the word a few times to hear it. But this sound device occurs much less often than alliteration and assonance. Sound devices create the musical quality of poetry and much of the pleasure of listening to poetic language.

Elements of Poetry: Structure

Considering a poem's physical structure can help you understand the poem. In "Metaphors" Plath cleverly structures her poem on the number nine:

the title word has nine characters; each line contains nine syllables; the poem contains nine lines. This pattern is not readily apparent, but once you see it, it helps the poem make sense: a woman nine months pregnant is full term; perhaps such a woman naturally thinks of nines. The number becomes a clue to the poem's meaning. "My Papa's Waltz" contains four-line stanzas, each with two rhymes such as "breath"/"death" and "dizzy"/"easy." These rhymes create a waltzing rhythm in the poem. This structure reinforces the interpretation that the speaker feels connected in a joyful dance with the father.

When you analyze poems, you may not need to consider all of these elements. Certain elements will stand out for you. You can focus on these. But an awareness of all the elements of poetry will help you understand and appreciate any artistic use of language.

READING NOTEBOOKS

A reading notebook is especially worthwhile when you read literature. Your own reading notebook allows you to stop a few moments during or after your reading to reflect, to pull together your own thoughts about a poem or story or essay, to make some record of how it affects you. Reading is most rewarding when you reflect on it. Your personal response to the work of other writers will help you clarify your own ideas and emotions. Reading and writing in this way unites you with an author.

Think of your notebook as your own approach to reading. As you respond to your reading, the notebook contains whatever you notice that catches your attention, puzzles you, or connects with you personally—anything you like or question about a poem's meaning and style. When you begin formal writing, you can draw on your notebook reflections.

ACTIVITY 2

Please read the following poem and in your notebook write a page or so about what you notice in it.

Traveling through the Dark

William Stafford

Traveling through the dark I found a deer
dead on the edge of the Wilson River road.
It is usually best to roll them into the canyon:
that road is narrow; to swerve might make more dead.

By glow of tail-light I stumbled back of the car   5
and stood by the heap, a doe, a recent killing;
she had stiffened already, almost cold.
I dragged her off; she was huge in the belly.

My fingers touching her side brought me the reason—
her side was warm; her fawn lay there waiting,   10
alive, still, never to be born.
Beside that mountain road I hesitated.

The car aimed ahead its lowered parking lights;
under the hood purred the steady engine.
I stood in the glare of the warm exhaust turning red;   15
around our group I could hear the wilderness listen.

I thought hard for us all—my only swerving—
then pushed her over the edge into the river.

Please don't read on until you have written in your notebook about the poem.

Here is an entry about Stafford's poem from Zac's notebook:

Stafford describes a really sad event--or a terrible   1
event, or a non-event, depending on how you feel about nature,
I guess. Are we supposed to "enjoy" this poem? I read that
Aristotle said tragedy was good for us--it purges the soul. If
this is true, I wonder how Stafford's poem purges my soul.

At first "Traveling through the Dark" seems like a routine   2
event, something we can easily deal with. The deer is dead on
the road, but she's pregnant--there's a live fawn inside. If
Stafford just wanted to make us happy, maybe he could have
produced a hunting knife, opened the doe, and delivered the
fawn. Maybe he could have driven the fawn into town, where the
local vet would have cared for it. This would have made a
happy Disney ending.

Instead though the speaker pushes the doe over the edge   3
into the river. It's a shock ending; I didn't expect it. Why
does it happen? There's no mention of a hunting knife in the
poem, nothing to suggest the speaker might have a hunting
knife. Is it hunting season? Even if the speaker could deliver

(box continues)

the fawn, there's no guarantee any vet could be found who
would care for it. A fawn requires a lot of attention, feeding
several times a day. Without its mother, the fawn would almost
certainly die.

Perhaps Stafford is trying to shock us into thinking about   4
a serious problem--civilization's intrusion into the deers'
habitat. The speaker tells us this is not the first deer
killed on this road: "It is usually best to roll them into the
canyon." This suggests he has done this before or knows about
it. As cities expand in urban sprawl, what happens to the
wilderness? What happens to the creatures of the wilderness?
What happens to <u>us</u>?

The speaker "hesitates" but at last decides what must be   5
done. I wonder what I would have done in the same situation.

The more I think about this poem, the more questions come   6
to mind. If the doe had not been "huge in the belly," would I
respond differently? Suppose the deer had been a stag? And does
it make a difference whether the speaker is male or female?

Do I feel purged? I don't know. But I do feel as if I   7
just had this experience with the deer on the road.

I did notice some neat details in the poem. The image "By   8
glow of tail-light"—maybe it suggests blood. Maybe it's a kind
of foreshadowing too. I like how the speaker "stumbled," not
sure of what to do. This seems honest--I'd stumble. I really
feel emotionally caught up in the third stanza. I can imagine
my fingers touching the deer--"her side was warm." I like too
how the poem builds in tension and how Stafford gives the car
human qualities--"The car aimed ahead its lowered parking
lights." And the engine "purred" like an animal. He refers to
the deer and fawn and car and himself as "our group." They are
all united in this awful and somehow precious moment. How can
"the wilderness listen"? Maybe it can--maybe trees and hidden
animals listen when there's tragedy--as if they care.

I think maybe this is what Stafford wants us as readers   9
to do--to care too. Maybe his poem helped purge me of
indifference. Interesting.

WRITING AN ESSAY ABOUT A POEM

We invite you to analyze a poem—to state a thesis about the poem and then to
defend it.

ACTIVITY 3

Choose a poem you like a lot or one that intrigues or puzzles you. Your job is to analyze how the poem works. Look for clues that show a writer's intended effects. Here are two options:

Option 1. Analyze a poem by addressing these questions:
- <u>Who is the speaker and what is the occasion?</u> Is the speaker someone different than the poet? If so, how can you tell? The occasion refers to when and where the poem takes place, as far as you can tell.
- <u>What is the central purpose of the poem?</u> What do you think the poet is trying to do in the poem—to express some emotion or truth, to describe a scene so vividly you never forget it, to help you appreciate what you have . . . ?
- <u>By what means does the poet achieve this purpose?</u> What does the poet do with diction, imagery, figures of speech, tone, sound, structure, and persuasive appeals (ethos, logos, pathos) to achieve his or her purpose? Try to focus on three of these elements. Analyze whatever stands out for you that the poet does to achieve his or her purpose.

Option 2. Analyze the poet's persuasive appeals:
- Examine the use of <u>ethos</u>, the character of the speaker implied in the poem. What does the poet do to make you care or think about the poem's speaker?
- Examine the use of <u>pathos</u>, the stirring of emotions. What does the poet do to make you feel emotionally involved in the poem?
- Examine the use of <u>logos</u>, the logic or reasoning you sense operating. What does the poet do to make you think about ideas or issues?
- In your essay explain how these appeals work together to help create the way you respond to the poem. Which appeals do you think the poet uses most effectively and why? Recall that the use of appeals is usually not balanced. In the poem you analyze, a poet may appeal more to pathos and ethos than to logos.

For help with your analysis, see "Guidelines for Writing an Essay about a Poem," p. 412.

Following is a student paper that illustrates the second option. It is based on "Eye for an Eye" by Anne Caston.

Eye for an Eye

Anne Caston

If I could hate her like they do,
if I could hate her that much, I could want
her dead too, the anger which rises from hatred
rising like a fist, Alpha and Omega, omnipotent,
and maybe then I could forget, in such hard anger as that,

5

the two drowned boys as I imagine they must have been
that day, sleeping, strapped into car seats while she stood
in the Carolina sun, something snapping in her,
and sent the car over into the lake;

like that night when something snapped open in me   10
and, before it snapped shut again, I'd slammed
Earlie Jones' father so hard in the face
it broke his nose, so hard that his head
knocked back and cracked the wallboard behind
and he slid to the floor. The crowd in the E.R. cheered   15
when he went down; he hid
his face in his hands and sobbed.

When the doctor came out to tell him then
his boy had gone unconscious in the next room and died,
the drunk man's face went slack with what he'd done.   20
No one offered him anything then:
not a cloth for his nose, not a word.
So I slid down beside the man and held to him
until he held back to me and we wept and rocked,
like the world must have rocked under her that day   25
when she saw what she had done.

Eye for an Eye--Is It Right?

Jennifer Klaiss

The world was in shock. Who would murder her own children?   1
After Susan Smith fabricated a tale about the man who kidnapped
and killed her children, she admitted it was all a lie--she
had murdered her children. Susan Smith had pushed her locked
car into the lake with her boys inside. There was a great
controversy over whether Susan Smith should be executed for her
actions. Outside the courthouse--where the jury was debating
the issue of the death penalty--protesters picketed with signs
that read "Eye for an Eye." She was convicted to a life
sentence. Now Smith has to live with the decision she made
that fateful day for the rest of her life. In order to make
readers recognize Susan Smith's anguish of murdering her own
children, Anne Caston uses ethos and pathos to reinforce her
logos in her poem "Eye for an Eye."

(box continues)

Caston wrote "Eye for an Eye" about this infamous incident in conjunction with a personal experience. The poem begins with how everyone hated Susan Smith, but the speaker of the poem could not. When Anne Caston visited our class, she said she is the speaker in the poem. She imagines what the two little boys must have looked like when Susan Smith sent the car into the lake. In the next stanza Caston remembers the night when Earlie Jones' father brought him into the ER badly hurt--but she doesn't describe what happened to the boy. Caston loses her professional cool and breaks the abusive father's nose. When the son dies, the father breaks down in his grief. Caston holds him as if he were a child.

Anne Caston appeals to ethos throughout the poem. The reader begins to have a feel for what kind of person Anne Caston is when she compares herself with Susan Smith by writing "something snapping in her, / and sent the car over into the lake; / like that night when something snapped open in me" (8-10). Although Caston compares herself to Susan Smith, the reader sees her as almost heroic. She had broken the nose of an abusive father. No one blamed her for doing it--"The crowd in the E.R. cheered" (15). The reader also senses her to be an honest person for admitting that she surrendered to unprofessional behavior. Her good character is reinforced later in lines 20-25 when she comforts Earlie Jones' father after his son dies. The reader sees that Caston understands what Susan Smith must have dealt with after murdering her children. Caston's empathy is powerful.

Caston appeals to pathos throughout the poem. Almost everyone in the country was aware of the Susan Smith incident because of media reports. People felt emotionally involved when they thought of those two little boys killed that way. Caston uses the reader's foreknowledge of the tragic incident to evoke emotions through her words:

> the two drowned boys as I imagine they must have been
> that day, sleeping, strapped into car seats while she
>   stood
> in the Carolina sun, something snapping in her,
> and sent the car over into the lake. (6-9)

Thinking about someone intentionally murdering both of her children made me furious. Likewise, Earlie Jones's father made me furious. I don't know if the boy was killed by physical

(box continues)

2

3

4

abuse intentionally: his father was drunk. But once Caston pulls me into the story, she guides my emotions to feel sympathy for Earlie Jones's father. When Caston comforts the father, I feel I should look deeper into what the father must have felt.

Caston appeals to logos to persuade readers to recognize 5 Susan Smith's anguish of murdering and losing her children. Caston makes a parallel between herself and Susan Smith in the beginning of the poem. They had both lost control of themselves: Susan Smith killed her children, and Anne Caston punched a man. Because Caston's character was judged to be good even though she had lost control of herself, logos demands readers to consider Susan Smith's character. Her loss of control may have been a one-time incident. Caston also makes the parallel between Susan Smith and Earlie Jones's father. She suggests that Susan Smith must have felt this grief as well.

> So I slid down beside the man and held to him
> until he held back to me and we wept and rocked,
> like the world must have rocked under her that day
> when she saw what she had done. (22-25)

Someone was there to comfort Earlie Jones's father while no one was there to comfort Susan Smith.

Through her use of persuasive appeals, Anne Caston helps 6 readers recognize Susan Smith's anguish of murdering her children. Ethos establishes Caston's character, which changes from feeling contempt to feeling remorse for the father. This shift stirs the reader's emotions which in turn causes the reader to think. Some people may have sympathized with Susan Smith after she realized what she had done; however, when I try to judge Smith fairly, I can not get over the fact that she murdered miracles from God.

Work Cited

Caston, Anne. "Eye for an Eye." <u>Flying Out with the Wounded</u>. New York: New York UP, 1997: 97-98.

GUIDELINES FOR WRITING AN ESSAY ABOUT A POEM

1. Before you write your rough draft, type the poem you want to analyze, double-spaced. This will help you notice details about the poem. Proof-read carefully against the original to catch any errors. Also, in the right-hand margin, number the lines. You may number lines by 5's: 5, 10, 15, and so on, rather than each line. You will need to refer to line numbers when you quote from the poem in your essay.

2. Annotate the poem you typed—write notes on it. In the margins or between the lines write down anything you notice, feel, or think about. Draw arrows or question marks or stars—use whatever system you want to interact with the poem. Annotation helps you see more into the poem to find ideas and connections to write about. As you annotate, ask your-self questions: Why this word? Why this image? Why this structure? Why do I feel this way here in the poem? and so on.

3. Proceed to write a rough draft following this format for your essay:
   A. <u>Title</u>: Give readers an idea of what poem you will analyze, and try to arouse interest. Which of these titles is more effective? "Eye for an Eye—Is It Right?" or "An Analysis of a Poem."
   B. <u>Introduction</u>: Draw readers into your essay. Identify the author and the poem you will analyze. Then state a carefully worded thesis—your main idea—as the last sentence of your introduction.
   C. <u>Body</u>: Defend and demonstrate your thesis.
      1. Present a brief summary of the poem you will analyze, using your own language.
      2. Proceed into your analysis. Use brief quotations—and a long quotation or two if appropriate—for supporting evidence. The body section should be at least three or more paragraphs.
   D. <u>Conclusion</u>: Reassert and clarify your thesis, and briefly discuss the overall quality of the poem.
   E. <u>Works Cited</u>: Provide a complete Works Cited entry for the poem. This need not be on a separate page if there is room to put it on your last page of text. (For information on Works Cited, see chapter 9)
   F. <u>A Typed Copy of the Poem</u>: This should be a clean and accurate copy of the poem you analyze, with line numbers indicated in the right-hand margin. As an option, present the poem toward the beginning of your essay.

4. Your essay should be 2 to 5 pages. Consider your audience to be your fellow classmates and instructor.

Quoting from a Poem

You can quote a word, a phrase, or a stanza—it depends on your purpose. According to the MLA style of documentation, if you quote part or all of a single line from a poem, put it in quotation marks within your text.

> Caston arouses emotion when she describes Susan Smith's boys "sleeping, strapped into car seats" (7).

You may also incorporate two or three lines within your text, using a slash with a space on each side (/) to indicate line breaks:

> Caston never directly states what the father did to his son Earlie. Rather she implies that he abused the boy. The father, who is nameless, suffers more than physical pain after the speaker breaks his nose. Caston implies his guilt: "The crowd in the E.R. cheered / when he went down; he hid / his face in his hands and sobbed" (15–17).

Notice that the numbers at the end of the quotes refer to the line numbers in the poem, not page numbers. You should use line numbers when you quote poetry.

Quotations of more than three lines should be treated like a long quote of prose: indent each line 10 spaces from the left margin and double space between lines, adding no quotation marks that do not appear in the original. (See examples in the student essay on "Eye for an Eye.")

POEMS TO CONSIDER FOR WRITING AN ESSAY

One Time

William Stafford

When evening had flowed between houses
and paused on the schoolground, I met
Hilary's blind little sister following
the gray smooth railing still warm from the sun   5
with her hand; and she stood by the edge
holding her face upward waiting
while the last light found her cheek
and her hair, and then on over the trees.

You could hear the great sprinkler arm   10
of water find and then leave the pavement,
and pigeons telling each other their dreams

or the dreams they would have. We were
deep in the well of shadow by then, and I
held out my hand, saying, "Tina, it's me—
Hilary says I should tell you it's dark,   15
and oh, Tina, it is. Together now—"

And I reached, our hands touched,
and we found our way home. □

Milk Bubble Ruins

Sharon Olds

In the long, indolent mornings of fifth grade
spring vacation, our son sits with the
tag-ends of breakfast, and blows bubbles in his milk
with a blue straw, and I sit and watch him.
The foam rises furiously   5
in a dome over the rim of his cup,
we gaze into the edifice of fluid,
its multiple chambers. He puffs and they pile up,
they burst, they subside, he breathes out slowly, and the
multicellular clouds rise,   10
he inserts the straw into a single globe
and blows a little, and it swells. Ten years ago
he lay along my arm, drinking.
Now, in late March, he shows me
the white light   15
pop and dissolve as he
conjures and breaks each small room of milk. □

Early in the Morning

Li-Young Lee

While the long grain is softening
in the water, gurgling
over a low stove flame, before
the salted Winter Vegetable is sliced
for breakfast, before the birds,   5
my mother glides an ivory comb
through her hair, heavy
and black as calligrapher's ink.

She sits at the foot of the bed.
My father watches, listens for   10
the music of comb
against hair.

My mother combs,
pulls her hair back
tight, rolls it   15
around two fingers, pins it
in a bun to the back of her head.
For half a hundred years she has done this.
My father likes to see it like this.
He says it is kempt.   20

But I know
it is because of the way
my mother's hair falls
when he pulls the pins out.
Easily, like the curtains   25
when they untie them in the evening. □

A Bird came down the Walk

Emily Dickinson

A Bird came down the Walk—
He did not know I saw—
He bit an Angleworm in halves
And ate the Fellow, raw,

And then he drank a Dew   5
From a convenient Grass—
And then hopped sidewise to the Wall
To let a Beetle pass—

He glanced with rapid eyes
That hurried all around—   10
They looked like frightened Beads, I thought—
He stirred his Velvet Head

Like one in danger, Cautious,
I offered him a Crumb
And he unrolled his feathers   15
And rowed him softer home—

Than Oars divide the Ocean,
Too silver for a seam—
Or Butterflies, off Banks of Noon
Leap, plashless as they swim. □   20

Famous

Naomi Shihab Nye

"Everything is famous if you notice it"

The river is famous to the fish.

The loud voice is famous to silence,
which knew it would inherit the earth
before anybody said so.   5

The cat sleeping on the fence is famous to the birds
watching him from the birdhouse.

The tear is famous, briefly, to the cheek.

The idea you carry close to your bosom
is famous to your bosom.   10

The boot is famous to the earth,
more famous than the dress shoe,
which is famous only to floors.

The bent photograph is famous to the one who carries it
and not at all famous to the one who is pictured.   15

I want to be famous to shuffling men
who smile while crossing streets,
sticky children in grocery lines,
famous as the one who smiled back.

I want to be famous in the way a pulley is famous,   20
or a buttonhole, not because it did anything spectacular,
but because it never forgot what it could do. □

The Grocer's Children

Herb Scott

The grocer's children
eat day-old bread,
moldy cakes and cheese,
soft black bananas
on stale shredded wheat,   5
weeviled rice, their plates
heaped high with wilted
greens, bruised fruit,
surprise treats

from unlabeled cans,   10
tainted meat.
The grocer's children
never go hungry. □

I Give You Back

Joy Harjo

I release you, my beautiful and terrible
fear. I release you. You were my beloved
and hated twin, but now, I don't know you
as myself. I release you with all the
pain I would know at the death of   5
my daughters.

You are not my blood anymore.

I give you back to the white soldiers
who burned down my home, beheaded my children,
raped and sodomized my brothers and sisters.   10
I give you back to those who stole the
food from our plates when we were starving.

I release you, fear, because you hold
these scenes in front of me and I was born
with eyes that can never close.   15

I release you, fear, so you can no longer
keep me naked and frozen in the winter,
or smothered under blankets in the summer.

I release you
I release you
I release you   20
I release you

I am not afraid to be angry.
I am not afraid to rejoice.
I am not afraid to be black.   25
I am not afraid to be white.
I am not afraid to be hungry.
I am not afraid to be full.
I am not afraid to be hated.
I am not afraid to be loved, to be loved, to be loved, fear.   30

Oh, you have choked me, but I gave you the leash.
You have gutted me but I gave you the knife.

You have devoured me, but I laid myself across the fire.

I take myself back, fear.
You are not my shadow any longer.   35
I won't hold you in my hands.
You can't live in my eyes, my ears, my voice
my belly, or in my heart my heart
my heart my heart

But come here, fear   40
I am alive and you are so afraid
of dying.   □

jasper texas 1998

Lucille Clifton

    for j. byrd[2]

    i am a man's head hunched in the road.
    i was chosen to speak by the members
    of my body. the arm as it pulled away
    pointed toward me, the hand opened once
    and was gone.   5

    why and why and why
    should i call a white man brother?
    who is the human in this place,
    the thing that is dragged or the dragger?
    what does my daughter say?   10

    the sun is a blister overhead.
    if i were alive i could not bear it.
    the townsfolk sing we shall overcome
    while hope bleeds slowly from my mouth
    into the dirt that covers us all.   15
    i am done with this dust. i am done. □

---

[2]On 7 June 1998, three white men in Jasper, Texas, abducted black hitchhiker James Byrd Jr., 49. After beating him, they chained him by the ankles to their pickup truck and dragged him several miles. The next morning his body was discovered, his head and other body parts strewn across the road. (<http://www.splcenter.org/cgi-bin/goframe.pl?refname=/intelligenceproject/ip-4i2.html> Access date: 30 Dec. 2000)

A Poison Tree

William Blake

> I was angry with my friend;
> I told my wrath—my wrath did end.
> I was angry with my foe;
> I told it not—my wrath did grow.
>
> And I watered it in fears,   5
> Night and morning with my tears,
> And I sunned it with smiles,
> And with soft deceitful wiles.
>
> And it grew both day and night,
> Till it bore an apple bright.   10
> And my foe beheld it shine,
> And he knew that it was mine,
>
> And into my garden stole
> When the night had veiled the pole.
> In the morning glad I see   15
> My foe outstretched beneath the tree. □

When I Heard the Learn'd Astronomer

Walt Whitman

> When I heard the learn'd astronomer,
> When the proofs, the figures, were ranged in columns before me,
> When I was shown the charts and diagrams, to add, divide, and measure them,
> When I sitting heard the astronomer where he lectured with much applause in
>   the lecture-room,
> How soon and unaccountable I became tired and sick,   5
> Till rising and gliding out I wandered off by myself,
> In the mystical moist night-air, and from time to time,
> Looked up in perfect silence at the stars. □

Note: If you'd prefer to analyze a poem not in this book, please ask your instructor for permission. It's important to choose a poem you enjoy, that intrigues you in some way, that you wouldn't mind thinking and writing about. If you'd like, after you write your own analysis of a poem, consider doing research on it—try to find some information about it.

READING AND WRITING ABOUT FICTION

> A story is good when you continue to see more and more in it, and when it continues to escape you. In fiction two and two is always more than four. (F. O'Connor 102)

Short stories and novels contain an artistic use of language—the same elements of poetry presented in the previous section: diction, images, metaphors and similes, tone, speaker, sound devices, and structure. Fiction, however, isn't as musical as poetry because it doesn't employ stanzas and line breaks, which emphasize sound patterns more than paragraphs do. Like meaning in poetry, meaning in fiction is usually suggested or implied, not readily explained. Readers infer meanings from a story based on what characters do, say, and think—and on connotations, details and images a writer uses.

Like poetry, serious or literary fiction requires a slower and more careful kind of reading than skimming through a newspaper or report. Such deliberate reading carries rewards: moments of entertainment and enlightenment. Please read the following vignette—a short literary sketch. After you read it, reflect on it in your reading notebook. What do you notice? What do you like? What questions does it raise for you? What does the vignette mean to you?

Lights

Stuart Dybek

In summer, waiting for night, we'd pose against the afterglow on corners, watch- 1
ing traffic cruise through the neighborhood. Sometimes, a car would go by without its headlights on and we'd all yell, "Lights!"

"Lights!" we'd keep yelling until the beams flashed on. It was usually 2
immediate—the driver honking back thanks, or flinching embarrassed behind the
steering wheel, or gunning past, and we'd see his red taillights blink on.

But there were times—who knows why?—when drunk or high, stubborn, 3
or simply lost in that glide to somewhere else, the driver just kept driving in
the dark, and all down the block we'd hear yelling from doorways and storefronts,
front steps, and other corners, voices winking on like fireflies: "Lights! Your
lights! Hey, lights!" (34) □

Please don't read ahead until you have written in your notebook.

This is a "light" little scene—not heavy, with no definite characters. But there is a conflict. Why does the speaker say that he or she and others yelled "Lights!"? Although the answer is not stated, it is implied: a car without lights on at dusk poses a danger—a driver might not see clearly, and other people might not see a car clearly. A driver without lights on could hit a child; an elderly person could step in front of such a car. Thus, yelling "Lights!" is a community call for caution.

This vignette is taken from Stuart Dybek's book <u>The Coast of Chicago</u>, the city where he grew up. How would you describe Dybek's tone or attitude? He recalls this ritual with fondness: "we'd pose against the afterglow on corners, watching traffic cruise through the neighborhood." The words "pose" and "cruise" suggest a time of ease, of relaxation, on these summer evenings. But if a car didn't respond by turning on its lights, the callers kept calling until a driver honked "back thanks" or "his red taillights" would "blink on." Dybek's images enable you to see, to hear—to experience this setting and situation. The simile "voices winking on like fireflies" is surprising. It suggests that out of concern for others, the people's voices became lights.

ACTIVITY 4

Please read another vignette by Stuart Dybek. When you finish, write about it in your notebook. Try to reflect on what it means and on how Dybek uses language to create certain effects.

Maroon

Stuart Dybek

—for Anthony Dadaro, 1946–58

A boy is bouncing a ball off a brick wall after school. The bricks have been painted maroon a long time ago. Steady as a heartbeat the ball rebounds oblong, hums, sponges back round. A maroon Chevy goes by. 1

Nothing else. This street's deserted: a block-long abandoned factory, glass from the busted windows on the sidewalk mixed with brown glass from beer bottles, whiskey pints. Sometimes the alkies drink here. Not today. 2

Only the ball flying between sunlit hands and shadowed bricks and sparrows brawling in the dusty gutters. The entire street turning maroon in the shadow of the wall, even the birds, even the hands. 3

He stands waiting under a streetlight that's trying to flicker on. Three guys he's never seen in the neighborhood before, coming down the street, carrying crowbars. (4) □ 4

What do you notice about Dybek's use of language? How does his language create his meaning? Here is an entry from Kristin's notebook:

I notice right away the color "maroon" and how it foreshadows   1
blood and the violence that seems implied in the vignette.
The bricks of a wall are painted maroon and so is a car
that drives by. Toward the end the "entire street" turns
maroon-colored as dusk falls.

I notice too that the dedication provides an important   2
clue to the vignette's meaning: "for Anthony Dadaro, 1946-58."
This boy lived only twelve years; he could be the boy in the
vignette that the three "guys," not boys, victimize. Why they
hurt the boy we readers don't know. Dybek doesn't give any
details about their race or if the boy had offended the guys
in some way. Perhaps the guys kill the boy for some kind of
pleasure, as the boy plays catch for pleasure. But the boy is
not a rubber ball.

This is a sad vignette, just the opposite of Dybek's   3
"Lights." There is no concern in this--except the tone. Dybek's
tone seems concerned--his dedication suggests this. I like his
ethos in this.

I'm surprised by Dybek's ability to describe the scene. He   4
notices so much yet uses so few words. I used to play catch
with a rubber ball against a wall at school: "the ball
rebounds oblong, hums, sponges back round." That's exactly what
happens. But the boy doesn't bounce back, and we don't know
why people sometimes commit such brutal acts.

ACTIVITY 5

Please read the following vignette (prose poem) by Anne Caston, the title piece from her book <u>Flying Out with the Wounded</u>. Then in your notebook, write about your reactions: what do you notice, feel, and think; what questions does the piece stir within you?

Flying Out with the Wounded

Anne Caston

When the lightning struck, trees blackened against
a silver sky and the river bruised, the undersides of clouds
wounding its surface. But this was not my work. My work,

pressed into the dark hold of the chopper, was a drunk
man—foul and fuming, restrained against his drunkenness,   5
his abdomen packed with gauze to staunch the bleeding—and
his head-on victims: a woman and a girl whose head had been
bandaged to keep the brain intact.
The girl was dead.
            We lifted off with our cargo. There   10
were scant inches in which to crouch. Jack had to ride in
front. I was airsick and praying that the snarl of blades
overhead wouldn't snag in the electric night.
                      Somewhere
between that stretch of sky and Birmingham, the man caught   15
sight of the woman and girl. "Goddamn," he said, "Goddamn.
Gooks." And then, to me, "In 'Nam we used to throw 'em
out, watch 'em splatter." He laughed and laughed to himself.
The woman flinched. She turned her face from him, went
back to stroking the girl's cheek. The girl's gaze was fixed.   20
Still the woman was making the shushing sound. I leaned
over the man. "Shut up," I said close to his ear so he would
hear me over the noisy blades; "Shut up or I will push you
out." He quieted then and I sat back to ride the airsickness in
me out.   25
    Can I tell you I liked thinking about pushing him
out? Can I say I was imagining how easy it would be for me to
roll the man out into the rumble of thunder and the whirring
blades? I was.
    But then he seized. He arched against his bonds. His   30
eyes rolled back to white. I straddled the man; I called out for
help. Jack grabbed the ambu bag and started the count. I
placed my hands, palms down, against that spot two fingers'
breadth from the tip of the sternum. I pushed: the man's
wound gushed, wet and warm, against my thighs. The smell   35
of blood thickened. I wanted to lift myself from him. Still I
pushed the man's heart to respond. Still Jack counted. Still
the ambu bag wheezed in and out.
               We worked like that the
whole way in, and when we landed someone else took over.   40
They lifted him away; I stepped out to catch a mouthful of
wet, clean air, to drive the blood-drunk smell of him from my
lungs. I looked down then and saw myself: bloodied, where I
had straddled the man, as if I had just given birth. (18–19) □

ACTIVITY 6

After writing in your notebook about Caston's vignette, write a brief essay in
which you analyze Caston's use of persuasive appeals. How does she appeal to

pathos, ethos, and logos? Which of these appeals does she draw on most? State a thesis about one of her appeals and defend it with reasons and specific evidence from the piece.

Elements of Fiction

Although fiction contains elements of poetic language, it contains other elements that characterize fiction as well as plays and movies. Basically, a story involves a main character who experiences a conflict of some kind, minor or major. How the character reacts to the conflict moves the story forward. Usually, the character undergoes some change during a story. This change creates much of the meaning in the story. For serious fiction, character and conflict must be credible and convincing—believable; otherwise, readers will not care what happens.

In Anne Caston's vignette, the speaker is an emergency medical technician. Her character is convincing because she battles to save the life of a drunk man who, in a head-on car accident, has injured a Vietnamese woman and killed her daughter. The major conflict is the speaker's contradictory desire to push the man out of the helicopter and to save his life.

Elements of Fiction: Plot and Conflict

The plot is what happens in a story—the sequence of cause and effect events. The plot hinges on some conflict in which a main character finds him or herself. A story may have a single conflict or several conflicts, even layers of conflict operating at the same time. Usually a story's conflict rises in tension and becomes resolved or not resolved by the end.

Elements of Fiction: Character

In analyzing serious fiction, you can evaluate whether characters are round (complex, contradictory, real) or flat (stereotypical, one dimensional like cardboard cut-outs, artificial). For fiction to work well, the main character must not only be credible but also worth caring about for you to keep paying close attention. Also, what characters say and what they wear reveal their personalities. If a character says "I seen that movie before," you can infer the character speaks ungrammatically and possibly lacks formal education.

But "character" also refers to the ethos or morality of a person in a story. Is the person good, evil, or a mix? Does the person do right, wrong, or both? In short, does the main character have good character?

Elements of Fiction: Point of View

Who is telling the story? In fiction, as in poetry, the "narrator" is generally not the "author"—narrators are characters. Narrators can be

First person ("I" or "We"):	<u>I</u> yelled, "Lights!" <u>We</u> yelled, "Lights!"
Second person ("You"):	<u>You</u> yelled, "Lights!"
Third person ("He," "She," "They," or "It"):	<u>She</u> yelled, "Lights!" <u>He</u> yelled, "Lights!" <u>They</u> yelled, "Lights!"
Omniscient:	The narrator knows the thoughts and feelings of one, some, or all of the characters.

First person, says fiction writer Stuart Dybek, is by nature the most intimate point of view, capable of producing lovable characters, such as Holden Caulfield or Huck Finn. First person encourages the reader to identify with the main character, and to identify is to believe the story, to find it emotionally credible. A story needs to be both emotionally and physically credible. When details are specific, concrete (appealing to the senses), and precise, a reader finds it easy to identify and to participate in the story. Each reading is, after all, a recreation. Reading is like dancing: it's active. A good reader is both artist and mental athlete. A good story is a passionate collaboration between reader and writer (remarks at Dybek's fiction reading, Central Michigan University, 9 Nov. 1999).

Elements of Fiction: Setting

Setting is where the story takes place. It is where a conflict is set in motion. In Dybek's "Maroon" the setting is a rough city street that appears abandoned where a boy plays catch with a rubber ball until three ominous guys approach. In "Flying Out with the Wounded" the story happens within a helicopter and outside the copter when it lands. A story may contain several different settings or scenes and different times of day or year. It may include flashbacks to the past and flash-forwards to the future.

Elements of Fiction: Moral Issues

Serious fiction deals with moral issues, questions of value. Dybek's vignettes concern caring about people not getting hurt. Caston's vignette concerns questions such as "Is it right to help a drunken man whose recklessness has caused irreparable harm?" As a nurse she is obligated to help; as a person she is tempted to push the man out of the chopper. The way characters struggle to deal with moral issues is part of their conflict and a story's meaning.

WRITING AN ESSAY ABOUT A STORY

We invite you to analyze a short story—to state a thesis about the story and to defend it.

ACTIVITY 7

Choose one of the following stories: "The Story of an Hour," "The End of Something," or "Pet Milk." Analyze how the story works. Here are two options:

Option 1. Analyze the story by addressing these questions.

- <u>Who is the narrator and what is the occasion?</u> The occasion refers to when and where the story takes place, as far as you can tell.
- <u>What is the central purpose of the story?</u> What do you think the writer is trying to do and say in the story?
- <u>By what means does the writer achieve this purpose?</u> What does the writer do with diction, imagery, figures of speech, tone, sound, structure, and persuasive appeals (ethos, logos, pathos) to achieve his or her purpose? You might focus on three of these elements. Analyze whatever stands out for you that the writer does to achieve his or her purpose.

Option 2. Analyze the writer's persuasive appeals:

- Examine the use of <u>ethos</u>, the moral qualities of the main character and other characters. What does the writer do to make you care or think about the these characters?
- Examine the use of <u>pathos</u>, the stirring of emotions. What does the writer do to make you feel emotionally involved in the story?
- Examine the use of <u>logos</u>, the logic or reasoning you sense operating. What does the writer do to make you think about ideas or issues?
- In your essay explain how these three appeals work together to help create the way you respond to the story. Which appeals do you think the writer uses most effectively and why?

Note on Quoting from a Story

To communicate clearly, you will need to refer to the story itself. Use some quotations—brief or long—to provide supporting evidence for your points, to show what you mean. With fiction as with nonfiction, a long quote is four or more lines and should be set off 10 spaces from the left margin and double spaced.

STORIES TO CONSIDER FOR WRITING AN ESSAY

The Story of an Hour

Kate Chopin

Knowing that Mrs. Mallard was afflicted with heart trouble, great care was taken   1
to break to her as gently as possible the news of her husband's death.

It was her sister Josephine who told her, in broken sentences; veiled hints   2
that revealed in half concealing. Her husband's friend Richards was there, too,
near her. It was he who had been in the newspaper office when intelligence of
the railroad disaster was received, with Brently Mallard's name leading the list
of "killed." He had only taken the time to assure himself of its truth by a second
telegram, and had hastened to forestall any less careful, less tender friend in
bearing the sad message.

She did not hear the story as many women have heard the same, with a   3
paralyzed inability to accept its significance. She wept at once, with sudden,
wild abandonment, in her sister's arms. When the storm of grief had spent itself
she went away to her room alone. She would have no one follow her.

There stood, facing the open window, a comfortable, roomy armchair. Into   4
this she sank, pressed down by a physical exhaustion that haunted her body and
seemed to reach into her soul.

She could see in the open square before her house the tops of trees that   5
were all aquiver with the new spring life. The delicious breath of rain was in
the air. In the street below a peddler was crying his wares. The notes of a
distant song which some one was singing reached her faintly, and countless
sparrows were twittering in the eaves.

There were patches of blue sky showing here and there through the clouds   6
that had met and piled one above the other in the west facing her window.

She sat with her head thrown back upon the cushion of the chair, quite   7
motionless, except when a sob came up into her throat and shook her, as a child
who had cried itself to sleep continues to sob in its dreams.

She was young, with a fair, calm face, whose lines bespoke repression and   8
even a certain strength. But now there was a dull stare in her eyes, whose gaze
was fixed away off yonder on one of those patches of blue sky. It was not a
glance of reflection, but rather indicated a suspension of intelligent thought.

There was something coming to her and she was waiting for it, fearfully.   9
What was it? She did not know; it was too subtle and elusive to name. But she
felt it, creeping out of the sky, reaching toward her through the sounds, the
scents, the color that filled the air.

Now her bosom rose and fell tumultuously. She was beginning to recog-   10
nize this thing that was approaching to possess her, and she was striving to

beat it back with her will—as powerless as her two white slender hands would have been.

When she abandoned herself a little whispered word escaped her slightly 11 parted lips. She said it over and over under her breath: "free, free, free!" The vacant stare and the look of terror that had followed it went from her eyes. They stayed keen and bright. Her pulses beat fast, and the coursing blood warmed and relaxed every inch of her body.

She did not stop to ask if it were or were not a monstrous joy that held 12 her. A clear and exalted perception enabled her to dismiss the suggestion as trivial.

She knew that she would weep again when she saw the kind, tender hands 13 folded in death; the face that had never looked save with love upon her, fixed and gray and dead. But she saw beyond that bitter moment a long procession of years to come that would belong to her absolutely. And she opened and spread her arms out to them in welcome.

There would be no one to live for her during those coming years; she 14 would live for herself. There would be no powerful will bending hers in that blind persistence with which men and women believe they have a right to impose a private will upon a fellow-creature. A kind intention or a cruel intention made the act seem no less a crime as she looked upon it in that brief moment of illumination.

And yet she had loved him—sometimes. Often she had not. What did it 15 matter! What could love, the unsolved mystery, count for in face of this possession of self-assertion which she suddenly recognized as the strongest impulse of her being!

"Free! Body and soul free!" she kept whispering. 16

Josephine was kneeling before the closed door with her lips to the keyhole, 17 imploring for admission. "Louise, open the door! I beg; open the door—you will make yourself ill. What are you doing, Louise? For heaven's sake open the door."

"Go away. I am not making myself ill." No; she was drinking in a very elixir 18 of life through that open window.

Her fancy was running riot along those days ahead of her. Spring days, 19 and summer days, and all sorts of days that would be her own. She breathed a quick prayer that life might be long. It was only yesterday she had thought with a shudder that life might be long.

She arose at length and opened the door to her sister's importunities. 20 There was a feverish triumph in her eyes, and she carried herself unwittingly like a goddess of Victory. She clasped her sister's waist, and together they descended the stairs. Richards stood waiting for them at the bottom.

Someone was opening the front door with a latchkey. It was Brently 21 Mallard who entered, a little travel-stained, composedly carrying his grip-sack and umbrella. He had been far from the scene of the accident, and did not even know there had been one. He stood amazed at Josephine's piercing cry; at Richards' quick motion to screen him from the view of his wife.

But Richards was too late.   22

When the doctors came they said she had died of heart disease—of joy 23
that kills. (352–54) □

The End of Something

Ernest Hemingway

In the old days Hortons Bay was a lumbering town. No one who lived in it was 1
out of sound of the big saws in the mill by the lake. Then one year there were
no more logs to make lumber. The lumber schooners came into the bay and were
loaded with the cut of the mill that stood stacked in the yard. All the piles of
lumber were carried away. The big mill building had all its machinery that was
removable taken out and hoisted on board one of the schooners by the men who
had worked in the mill. The schooner moved out of the bay toward the open lake
carrying the two great saws, the travelling carriage that hurled the logs against
the revolving, circular saws and all the rollers, wheels, belts and iron piled on a
hull-deep load of lumber. Its open hold covered with canvas and lashed tight,
the sails of the schooner filled and it moved out into the open lake, carrying with
it everything that had made the mill a mill and Hortons Bay a town.

The one-story bunk houses, the eating-house, the company store, the mill 2
offices, and the big mill itself stood deserted in the acres of sawdust that
covered the swampy meadow by the shore of the bay.

Ten years later there was nothing of the mill left except the broken white 3
limestone of its foundations showing through the swampy second growth as
Nick and Marjorie rowed along the shore. They were trolling along the edge of
the channel-bank where the bottom dropped off suddenly from sandy shallows
to twelve feet of dark water. They were trolling on their way to the point to set
night lines for rainbow trout.

"There's our old ruin, Nick," Marjorie said.   4

Nick, rowing, looked at the white stone in the green trees.   5

"There it is," he said.   6

"Can you remember when it was a mill?" Marjorie asked.   7

"I can just remember," Nick said.   8

"It seems more like a castle," Marjorie said.   9

Nick said nothing. They rowed on out of sight of the mill, following the 10
shore line. Then Nick cut across the bay.

"They aren't striking," he said.   11

"No," Marjorie said. She was intent on the rod all the time they trolled, 12
even when she talked. She loved to fish. She loved to fish with Nick.

Close beside the boat a big trout broke the surface of the water. Nick 13
pulled hard on one oar so the boat would turn and the bait spinning far behind

would pass where the trout was feeding. As the trout's back came up out of the water the minnows jumped wildly. They sprinkled the surface like a handful of shot thrown into the water. Another trout broke water, feeding on the other side of the boat.

"They're feeding," Marjorie said.   14

"But they won't strike," Nick said.   15

He rowed the boat around to troll past both the feeding fish, then headed   16
it for the point. Marjorie did not reel in until the boat touched the shore.

They pulled the boat up the beach and Nick lifted out a pail of live perch.   17
The perch swam in the water in the pail. Nick caught three of them with his hands and cut their heads off and skinned them while Marjorie chased with her hands in the bucket, finally caught a perch, cut its head off and skinned it. Nick looked at her fish.

"You don't want to take the ventral fin out," he said. "It'll be all right for   18
bait but it's better with the ventral fin in."

He hooked each of the skinned perch through the tail. There were two   19
hooks attached to a leader on each rod. Then Marjorie rowed the boat out over the channel-bank, holding the line in her teeth, and looking toward Nick, who stood on the shore holding the rod and letting the line run out from the reel.

"That's about right," he called.   20

"Should I let it drop?" Marjorie called back, holding the line in her hand.   21

"Sure. Let it go." Marjorie dropped the line overboard and watched the   22
baits go down through the water.

She came in with the boat and ran the second line out the same way. Each   23
time Nick set a heavy slab of driftwood across the butt of the rod to hold it solid and propped it up at an angle with a small slab. He reeled in the slack line so the line ran taut out to where the bait rested on the sandy floor of the channel and set the click on the reel. When a trout, feeding on the bottom, took the bait it would run with it, taking line out of the reel in a rush and making the reel sing with the click on.

Marjorie rowed up the point a little way so she would not disturb the   24
line. She pulled hard on the oars and the boat went way up the beach. Little waves came in with it. Marjorie stepped out of the boat and Nick pulled the boat high up the beach.

"What's the matter, Nick?" Marjorie asked.   25

"I don't know," Nick said, getting wood for a fire.   26

They made a fire with driftwood. Marjorie went to the boat and brought   27
a blanket. The evening breeze blew the smoke toward the point, so Marjorie spread the blanket out between the fire and the lake.

Marjorie sat on the blanket with her back to the fire and waited for Nick.   28
He came over and sat down beside her on the blanket. In back of them was the close second-growth timber of the point and in front was the bay with the mouth of Hortons Creek. It was not quite dark. The fire-light went as far as the water. They could both see the two steel rods at an angle over the dark water. The fire glinted on the reels.

Marjorie unpacked the basket of supper.   29

"I don't feel like eating," said Nick.   30

"Come on and eat, Nick."   31

"All right." They ate without talking, and watched the two rods and the   32
fire-light in the water.

"There's going to be a moon tonight," said Nick. He looked across the bay   33
to the hills that were beginning to sharpen against the sky. Beyond the hills
he knew the moon was coming up.

"I know it," Marjorie said happily.   34

"You know everything," Nick said.   35

"Oh, Nick, please cut it out! Please, please don't be that way!"   36

"I can't help it," Nick said. "You do. You know everything. That's the trou- 37
ble. You know you do."

Marjorie did not say anything.   38

"I've taught you everything. You know you do. What don't you know,   39
anyway?"

"Oh, shut up," Marjorie said. "There comes the moon."   40

They sat on the blanket without touching each other and watched the   41
moon rise.

"You don't have to talk silly," Marjorie said. "What's really the matter?" 42

"I don't know."   43

"Of course you know."   44

"No I don't."   45

"Go on and say it."   46

Nick looked on at the moon, coming up over the hills.   47

"It isn't fun any more."   48

He was afraid to look at Marjorie. Then he looked at her. She sat there   49
with her back toward him. He looked at her back. "It isn't fun any more. Not
any of it."

She didn't say anything. He went on. "I feel as though everything was   50
gone to hell inside of me. I don't know, Marge. I don't know what to say."

He looked on at her back.   51

"Isn't love any fun?" Marjorie said.   52

"No," Nick said. Marjorie stood up. Nick sat there, his head in his hands. 53

"I'm going to take the boat," Marjorie called to him. "You can walk back   54
around the point."

"All right," Nick said. "I'll push the boat off for you."   55

"You don't need to," she said. She was afloat in the boat on the water   56
with the moonlight on it. Nick went back and lay down with his face in the blanket by the fire. He could hear Marjorie rowing on the water.

He lay there for a long time. He lay there while he heard Bill come into   57
the clearing walking around through the woods. He felt Bill coming up to the
fire. Bill didn't touch him, either. "Did she go all right?" Bill said.

"Yes," Nick said, lying, his face on the blanket.   58

"Have a scene?"   59

"No, there wasn't any scene."   60
"How do you feel?"   61
"Oh, go away, Bill! Go away for a while."   62

Bill selected a sandwich from the lunch basket and walked over to have   63
a look at the rods. (35–41) □

Pet Milk

Stuart Dybek

Today I've been drinking instant coffee and Pet milk, and watching it snow. It's   1
not that I enjoy the taste especially, but I like the way Pet milk swirls in the
coffee. Actually, my favorite thing about Pet milk is what the can opener does
to the top of the can. The can is unmistakable—compact, seamless looking, its
very shape suggesting that it could condense milk without any trouble. The can
opener bites in neatly, and the thick liquid spills from the triangular gouge with
a different look and viscosity than milk. Pet milk isn't _real_ milk. The color's off,
to start with. There's almost something of the past about it, like old ivory. My
grandmother always drank it in her coffee. When friends dropped over and sat
around the kitchen table, my grandma would ask, "Do you take cream and
sugar?" Pet milk was the cream.

There was a yellow plastic radio on her kitchen table, usually tuned to the   2
polka station, though sometimes she'd miss it by half a notch and get the Greek
station instead, or the Spanish, or the Ukrainian. In Chicago, where we lived,
all the incompatible states of Europe were pressed together down at the stat-
icky right end of the dial. She didn't seem to notice, as long as she wasn't hearing English. The radio, turned low, played constantly. Its top was warped and
turning amber on the side where the tubes were. I remember the sound of it
on winter afternoons after school, as I sat by her table watching the Pet milk
swirl and cloud in the steaming coffee, and noticing, outside her window, the
sky doing the same thing above the railroad yard across the street.

And I remember, much later, seeing the same swirling sky in tiny liqueur   3
glasses containing a drink called a King Alphonse: the creme de cacao rising like
smoke in repeated explosions, blooming in kaleidoscopic clouds through the
layer of heavy cream. This was in the Pilsen, a little Czech restaurant where my
girlfriend, Kate, and I would go sometimes in the evening. It was the first year
out of college for both of us, and we had astonished ourselves by finding real
jobs—no more waitressing or pumping gas, the way we'd done in school. I was
investigating credit references at a bank, and she was doing something slightly
above the rank of typist for Hornblower & Weeks, the investment firm. My bank
showed training films that emphasized the importance of suitable dress, good
grooming, and personal neatness, even for employees like me, who worked at

the switchboard in the basement. Her firm issued directives on appropriate attire—skirts, for instance, should cover the knees. She had lovely knees.

Kate and I would sometimes meet after work at the Pilsen, dressed in our proper business clothes and still feeling both a little self-conscious and glamorous, as if we were impostors wearing disguises. The place had small, round oak tables, and we'd sit in a corner under a painting called "The Street Musicians of Prague" and trade future plans as if they were escape routes. She talked of going to grad school in Europe; I wanted to apply to the Peace Corps. Our plans for the future made us laugh and feel close, but those same plans somehow made anything more than temporary between us seem impossible. It was the first time I'd ever had the feeling of missing someone I was still with. 4

The waiters in the Pilsen wore short black jackets over long white aprons. They were old men from the old country. We went there often enough to have our own special waiter, Rudi, a name he pronounced with a rolled R. Rudi boned our trout and seasoned our salads, and at the end of the meal he'd bring the bottle of creme de cacao from the bar, along with two little glasses and a small pitcher of heavy cream, and make us each a King Alphonse right at our table. We'd watch as he'd fill the glasses halfway up with the syrupy brown liqueur, then carefully attempt to float a layer of cream on top. If he failed to float the cream, we'd get that one free. 5

"Who was King Alphonse anyway, Rudi?" I sometimes asked, trying to break his concentration, and if that didn't work I nudged the table with my foot so the glass would jiggle imperceptibly just as he was floating the cream. We'd usually get one on the house. Rudi knew what I was doing. In fact, serving the King Alphonses had been his idea, and he had also suggested the trick of jarring the table. I think it pleased him, though he seemed concerned about the way I'd stare into the liqueur glass, watching the patterns. 6

"It's not a microscope," he'd say. "Drink." 7

He liked us, and we tipped extra. It felt good to be there and to be able to pay for a meal. 8

Kate and I met at the Pilsen for supper on my twenty-second birthday. It was May, and unseasonably hot. I'd opened my tie. Even before looking at the dinner menu, we ordered a bottle of Mumm's and a dozen oysters apiece. Rudi made a sly remark when he brought the oysters on platters of ice. They were freshly opened and smelled of the sea. I'd heard people joke about oysters being aphrodisiac but never considered it anything but a myth—the kind of idea they still had in the old country. 9

We squeezed on lemon, added dabs of horseradish, slid the oysters into our mouths, and then rinsed the shells with champagne and drank the salty, cold juice. There was a beefy-looking couple eating schnitzel at the next table, and they stared at us with the repugnance that public oyster-eaters in the Midwest often encounter. We laughed and grandly sipped it all down. I was already half tipsy from drinking too fast, and starting to feel filled with a euphoric, aching energy. Kate raised a brimming oyster shell to me in a toast: "To the Peace Corps!" 10

"To Europe!" I replied, and we clunked shells.   11

She touched her wineglass to mine and whispered, "Happy birthday," and   12
then suddenly leaned across the table and kissed me.

When she sat down again, she was flushed. I caught the reflection of her   13
face in the glass-covered "The Street Musicians of Prague" above our table. I
always loved seeing her in mirrors and windows. The reflections of her beauty
startled me. I had told her that once, and she seemed to fend off the compli-
ment, saying, "That's because you've learned what to look for," as if it were a
secret I'd stumbled upon. But, this time, seeing her reflection hovering ghost-
like upon an imaginary Prague was like seeing a future from which she had
vanished. I knew I'd never meet anyone more beautiful to me.

We killed the champagne and sat twining fingers across the table. I was   14
sweating. I could feel the warmth of her through her skirt under the table and
I touched her leg. We still hadn't ordered dinner. I left money on the table and
we steered each other out a little unsteadily.

"Rudi will understand," I said.   15

The street was blindingly bright. A reddish sun angled just above the rims   16
of the tallest buildings. I took my suit coat off and flipped it over my shoulder. We stopped in the doorway of a shoe store to kiss.

"Let's go somewhere," she said.   17

My roommate would already be home at my place, which was closer. Kate   18
lived up north, in Evanston. It seemed a long way away.

We cut down a side street, past a fire station, to a small park, but its gate   19
was locked. I pressed close to her against the tall iron fence. We could smell
the lilacs from a bush just inside the fence, and when I jumped for an over-
hanging branch my shirt sleeve hooked on a fence spike and tore, and petals
rained down on us as the sprig sprang from my hand.

We walked to the subway. The evening rush was winding down; we must   20
have caught the last express heading toward Evanston. Once the train climbed
from the tunnel to the elevated tracks, it wouldn't stop until the end of the line,
on Howard. There weren't any seats together, so we stood swaying at the front
of the car, beside the empty conductor's compartment. We wedged inside, and
I clicked the door shut.

The train rocked and jounced, clattering north. We were kissing, trying to   21
catch the rhythm of the ride with our bodies. The sun bronzed the windows on
our side of the train. I lifted her skirt over her knees, hiked it higher so the
sun shone off her thighs, and bunched it around her waist. She wouldn't stop
kissing. She was moving her hips to pin us to each jolt of the train.

We were speeding past scorched brick walls, gray windows, back porches   22
outlined in sun, roofs, and treetops—the landscape of the El I'd memorized
from subway windows over a lifetime of rides: the podiatrist's foot sign past
Fullerton; the bright pennants of Wrigley Field, at Addison; ancient hotels with
TRANSIENTS WELCOME signs on their flaking back walls; peeling and graffiti-
smudged billboards; the old cemetery just before Wilson Avenue. Even without

looking, I knew almost exactly where we were. Within the compartment, the sound of our quick breathing was louder than the clatter of tracks. I was trying to slow down, to make it all last, and when she covered my mouth with her hand I turned my face to the window and looked out.

The train was braking a little from express speed, as it did each time it 23 passed a local station. I could see blurred faces on the long wooden platform watching us pass—businessmen glancing up from folded newspapers, women clutching purses and shopping bags. I could see the expression on each face, momentarily arrested, as we flashed by. A high school kid in shirt sleeves, maybe sixteen, with books tucked under one arm and a cigarette in his mouth, caught sight of us, and in the instant before he disappeared he grinned and started to wave. Then he was gone, and I turned from the window, back to Kate, forgetting everything—the passing stations, the glowing late sky, even the sense of missing her—but that arrested wave stayed with me. It was as if I were standing on that platform, with my schoolbooks and a smoke, on one of those endlessly accumulated afternoons after school when I stood almost outside of time simply waiting for a train, and I thought how much I'd have loved seeing someone like us streaming by. (167–73) □

READING AND WRITING ABOUT LITERARY NONFICTION

Some readers assume stories only occur in fiction. But that isn't true. Biography and autobiography, history, even news events are often presented as stories. They share chronological organization to tell readers <u>what happened</u> and <u>what happens next</u>. For example, when the police arrive at the scene of an accident and want to know <u>what happened</u>, they often get a narrative answer: the witnesses tell their <u>stories</u> or versions of the same <u>story</u>. This kind of storytelling became most popular in the twentieth century—the true story. Some of our finest nonfiction writers have learned not only to tell what happened but also to tell it with techniques normally found only in fiction—dialogue, poetic description, and character development.

You can think critically whenever you read. But how you read depends on your purpose. Often you may want to skim a news article—to get the gist of the information. Or you may read purely for pleasure, as many people do with romance novels. Sometimes you may read for spiritual comfort, as with the Bible. But the purpose of this book is to help you develop yourself as a critical thinker, reader, and writer. Toward this end we have chosen selections that we hope will stir questions within you, that will puzzle you, that will at times surprise or shock you, and that will cause you to consider a writer's appeals to logos, pathos, and ethos.

The following essay "Brute" was written by Richard Selzer. Taken from his book <u>Letters to a Young Doctor</u>, first published in 1982, the essay has stirred controversy for Selzer. Selzer was a surgeon for many years who also taught surgery at Yale University until he retired to write full time. "Brute" is a narrative essay based on an experience of his in an emergency room. As you read "Brute," consider why you think many people have judged this essay as controversial. When you finish the essay, write your reactions to it in your notebook.

Brute

Richard Selzer

You must never again set your anger upon a patient. You were tired, you said, and therefore it happened. Now that you have excused yourself, there is no need for me to do it for you. 1

Imagine that you yourself go to a doctor because you have chest pain. You are worried that there is something the matter with your heart. Chest pain is your Chief Complaint. It happens that your doctor has been awake all night with a patient who has been bleeding from a peptic ulcer of his stomach. He is tired. That is your doctor's Chief Complaint. I have chest pain, you tell him. I am tired, he says. 2

Still I confess to some sympathy for you. I know what tired is. 3

Listen: It is twenty-five years ago in the Emergency Room. It is two o'clock in the morning. There has been a day and night of stabbings, heart attacks and automobile accidents. A commotion at the door: A huge black man is escorted by four policemen into the Emergency Room. He is handcuffed. At the door, the man rears as though to shake off the men who cling to his arms and press him from the rear. Across the full length of his forehead is a laceration. It is deep to the bone. I know it even without probing its depths. The split in his black flesh is like the white wound of an ax in the trunk of a tree. Again and again he throws his head and shoulders forward, then back, rearing, roaring. The policemen ride him like parasites. Had he horns he would gore them. Blind and trussed, the man shakes them about, rattles them. But if one of them loses his grip, the others are still fixed and sucking. The man is hugely drunk—toxic, fuming, murderous—a great mythic beast broken loose in the city, surprised in his night raid by a phalanx of legionnaires armed with clubs and revolvers. 4

I do not know the blow that struck him on the brow. Or was there any blow? Here is a brow that might have burst on its own, spilling out its excess of rage, bleeding itself toward ease. Perhaps it was done by a jealous lover, a woman, or a man who will not pay him the ten dollars he won on a bet, or still another who has hurled the one insult that he cannot bear to hear. Perhaps it was done by the police themselves. From the distance of many years and from the safety of my little study, I choose to see it thus: 5

The helmeted corps rounds the street corner. A shout. "There he is!" And they clatter toward him. He stands there for a moment, lurching. Something 6 upon which he had been feeding falls from his open mouth. He turns to face the policemen. For him it is not a new challenge. He is scarred as a Zulu from his many battles. Almost from habit he ascends to the combat. One or more of them falls under his flailing arms until—there is the swing of a truncheon, a sound as though a melon has been dropped from a great height. The white wedge appears upon the sweating brow of the black man, a waving fall of blood pours across his eyes and cheeks.

The man is blinded by it; he is stunned. Still he reaches forth to make 7 contact with the enemy, to do one more piece of damage. More blows to the back, the chest and again to the face. Bloody spume flies from his head as though lifted by a great wind. The police are spattered with it. They stare at each other with an abstract horror and disgust. One last blow, and, blind as Samson, the black man undulates, rolling in a splayfooted circle. But he does not go down. The police are upon him then, pinning him, cuffing his wrists, kneeing him toward the van. Through the back window of the wagon—a netted panther.

In the Emergency Room he is led to the treatment area and to me. There 8 is a vast dignity about him. He keeps his own counsel. What is he thinking? I wonder. The police urge him up on the table. They put him down. They restrain his arms with straps. I examine the wound, and my heart sinks. It is twelve centimeters long, irregular, jagged and, as I knew, to the skull. It will take at least two hours.

I am tired. Also to the bone. But something else . . . Oh, let me not deny 9 it. I am ravished by the sight of him, the raw, untreated flesh, his very wildness which suggests less a human than a great and beautiful animal. As though by the addition of the wound, his body is more than it was, more of a body. I begin to cleanse and debride the wound. At my touch, he stirs and groans. "Lie still," I tell him. But now he rolls his head from side to side so that I cannot work. Again and again he lifts his pelvis from the table, strains against his bonds, then falls heavily. He roars something, not quite language. "Hold still," I say. "I cannot stitch your forehead unless you hold still."

Perhaps it is the petulance in my voice that makes him resume his strug- 10 gle against all odds to be free. Perhaps he understands that it is only a cold, thin official voice such as mine, and not the billy clubs of half-a-dozen cops that can rob him of his dignity. And so he strains and screams. But why can he not sense that I am tired? He spits and curses and rolls his head to escape from my fingers. It is quarter to three in the morning. I have not yet begun to stitch. I lean close to him; his steam fills my nostrils. "Hold still," I say.

"<u>You</u> fuckin' hold still," he says to me in a clear, fierce voice. Suddenly, I 11 am in the fury with him. Somehow he has managed to capture me, to pull me inside his cage. Now we are two brutes hissing and batting at each other. But I do not fight fairly.

I go to the cupboard and get from it two packets of heavy, braided silk 12 suture and a large curved needle. I pass one of the heavy silk sutures through the eye of the needle. I take the needle in the jaws of a needle holder, and I pass the needle through the center of his right earlobe. Then I pass the needle through the mattress of the stretcher. And I tie the thread tightly so that his head is pulled to the right. I do exactly the same to his left earlobe, and again I tie the thread tightly so that his head is facing directly upward.

"I have sewn your ears to the stretcher," I say. "Move, and you'll rip 'em off." And leaning close I say in a whisper, "Now you fuckin' hold still."   13

I do more. I wipe the gelatinous clots from his eyes so that he can see. And I lean over him from the head of the table, so that my face is directly above his, upside down. And I grin. It is the cruelest grin of my life. Torturers must grin like that, beheaders and operators of racks.   14

But now he does hold still. Surely it is not just fear of tearing his earlobes. He is too deep into his passion for that. It is more likely some beastly wisdom that tells him that at last he has no hope of winning. That it is time to cut his losses, to slink off into high grass. Or is it some sober thought that pierces his wild brain, lacerating him in such a way that a hundred nightsticks could not? The thought of a woman who is waiting for him, perhaps? Or a child who, the next day and the week after that, will stare up at his terrible scars with a silent wonder that will shame him? For whatever reason, he is perfectly still.   15

It is four o'clock in the morning as I take the first stitch in his wound. At five-thirty, I snip each of the silks in his earlobes. He is released from his leg restrainers and pulled to a sitting position. The bandage on his head is a white turban. A single drop of blood in each earlobe, like a ruby. He is a maharajah.   16

The police return. All this time they have been drinking coffee with the nurses, the orderlies, other policemen, whomever. For over three hours the man and I have been alone in our devotion to the wound. "I have finished," I tell them. Roughly, they haul him from the stretcher and prod him toward the door. "Easy, easy," I call after them. And, to myself, if you hit him again . . .   17

Even now, so many years later, this ancient rage of mine returns to peck among my dreams. I have only to close my eyes to see him again wielding his head and jaws, to hear once more those words at which the whole of his trussed body came hurtling toward me. How sorry I will always be. Not being able to make it up to him for that grin. (59–63) □   18

Please don't read ahead until you have written a page of reactions in your note-book.

"Brute" is based on an event that happened to Richard Selzer twenty-five years before he wrote about it. With the book published in 1982, this means the event took place in 1957. It is a personal story, not fiction. But for critical thinkers the essay raises at least two important questions. First, who is the brute? Is the brute the patient or the doctor? Or are there other possibilities—both men? Neither?

Here are some arguments that the patient is the brute:

- He needed to be "escorted by four policeman into the Emergency Room." Four men is a lot to control one man.
- He was extremely drunk and out of control: "The man is hugely drunk—toxic, fuming, murderous."
- He has an awful wound on his forehead but continues to fight in the hospital.
- He is described as less than human: "a great mythic beast," "a netted panther," "a great and beautiful animal" and so on. The connotations of beast and animal are "brutelike." "Brute" is defined as "1. lacking the ability to reason 2. having no consciousness or feelings 3. of or like an animal, specifically brutal, gross, sensual, stupid, etc." (Webster's New World 180).

Here are some arguments that the doctor is the brute:

- He lets his exhaustion and frustration get the better of him.
- He grows angry at the patient when he won't hold still and when he swears.
- He admits he does not "fight fairly" by sewing the man's earlobes to the stretcher.
- He wipes blood away from the patient so he can see Selzer grin: "It is the cruelest grin of my life."

Thus, you could argue that either man is a brute. Although the patient fits the dictionary definition of "brute" in the physical sense, perhaps the doctor is more of a mental brute because he abuses his position as doctor. But did he? Was sewing the man's earlobes necessary? The man was extremely drunk; therefore, administering a drug to quiet him might have killed him. Perhaps nurses and orderlies could have restrained the man, holding down his head; yet it would be difficult for hands to hold a head still, especially with its severe wound. Selzer's solution worked: it calmed the man down so the wound could be stitched. What does seem brutal is Selzer's own anger and grin. Exhaustion cannot justify abusing a patient this way, which Selzer as narrator tells his readers—young doctors and you.

One could also argue that both men are brutes or that the doctor was not a brute. By definition, the doctor was not a brute because he was not irrational. What he did he did with full awareness. Also, the doctor is extremely remorseful for what he did as he suggests at the beginning of the essay and directly states at the end. But being sorry for behavior does not excuse that behavior.

If you wrote an essay about "Brute" in which you argued that one of the men was a brute but the other wasn't, you could use this model for arguing (as presented in chapter 2):

1. Introduce the essay and state your thesis (your position).
2. Summarize "Brute" objectively to show readers you understand it.

3. Briefly acknowledge or summarize the view opposing your own position.
4. Defend your position with reasons, examples, details, and direct quotations.
5. Conclude and restate your thesis.

This way you would show readers you are fair-minded. If you argue that both men are brutes, you could state your thesis, discuss why one man is a brute, and then discuss why the other man is a brute.

Another way to think critically about "Brute" is to analyze Selzer's persuasive appeals. How does he use them? Concerning logos, Selzer presents a dramatic situation that causes readers to think about what will happen next: what will Selzer do to repair his patient's gaping wound? Readers may deem the solution of stitching the man's earlobes to the stretcher as ingenious or inhumane. That Selzer takes pleasure in revealing his own anger with the man makes readers wonder whether this is right. The essay thus raises moral questions for readers to examine. Readers may wonder what they would do in a similar situation: if they were exhausted and confronted by a huge drunken man. Aren't doctors human too? How many hours can we expect doctors to work in an ER before their judgment suffers?

Selzer appeals to readers' emotions or pathos through his vivid description and dramatic technique. It seems as if Selzer wants readers to wince at times. His similes pack emotional punch, such as "The split in his black flesh is like the white wound of an ax in the trunk of a tree." With these 20 simple one-syllable words he shows us the wound and enables us to feel its severity. Another simile stirs emotion as well: "there is the swing of a truncheon, a sound as though a melon has been dropped from a great height." You can hear this awful sound and feel the man's pain. The emotional climax of the essay occurs when Selzer describes in precise detail sewing the man's earlobes with "a large curved needle." Selzer's description draws on emotions; it's as if the reader's earlobes are being sewn as well, and as if the reader is doing the sewing. In this essay readers can identify with the doctor and with the patient; this pull produces emotional tension.

The issue of Selzer's ethos in "Brute" is important. Is he—as a doctor reflecting on this event—credible? The event did happen, and he reports it in vivid literary detail. Did he help his patient? He did succeed in closing the wound. But did Selzer have to taunt the man to move his head? Through his anger, he becomes less credible as a caring doctor. Was his behavior understandable given his exhaustion from working many hours in the ER? It is understandable but still wrong; he lost all compassion for the man until he was finished sewing him. Selzer's character in this essay is complex. What saves his ethos from being completely negative is his honesty and remorse. Although tired "to the bone," he admits he is "ravished by the sight of him, the raw, untreated flesh." He wants to help mend the man's wound. He admits that he's become a brute: "Now we are two brutes hissing and batting at each other. But I do not fight fairly." And he admits that his grin was wrong: "Torturers must grin like that, beheaders and operators of racks." At the end of the essay, twenty-five years after the event, he writes, "How sorry I will always be. Not being able to make it up to him for that grin." Also, Selzer's primary audience for "Brute" is young doctors—to whom his book <u>Letters to a Young Doctor</u> is written. He wants doctors not to make the same mistake he made. He warns them through his own example. This appeal to his character is positive.

As we've shown, "Brute" provokes critical reading and thinking. As authors of this textbook, however, we debated whether to include the essay because it arouses controversy in another way. Thus, the second question: is Selzer racist in this essay? Here are arguments from some students:

Stacy Turschak, on "Brute"

Though he was a brute that night, I do not believe Selzer is a racist in "Brute." His cruelty did not originate in prejudice or hatred; his "Chief Complaint" is fatigue. In fact, Selzer's race is assumed. Do readers really know he is Caucasian?   1

Selzer's references to his patient in animalistic terms could be interpreted as racism, but I do not believe his comparisons are based on ethnic hatred. For example, he writes that the wound makes the man "less a human than a great and beautiful animal." This statement alone does not seem racist. On the other hand, Selzer considers his patient "a netted panther." Panthers definitely have a more positive connotation than parasites--his description of the policemen. Actually Selzer uses positive imagery in his descriptions of the black man throughout the essay. He compares his patient to a Zulu, Samson, and a maharajah--all greatly admired men.   2

I cannot believe Selzer is racist because he makes the reader feel his guilt. "How sorry I will always be. Not being able to make it up to him for that grin." Selzer has not justified his actions. He does not believe the man deserved to be punished. Guilt is not a result of hatred and prejudice; it comes from understanding and regret. Selzer's rage was also short-lived: as the police hauled the man away Selzer called out protectively, "Easy, easy."   3

Tim Jones, on "Brute"

"Brute" troubles me because it does seem to have racist   1
undertones. Selzer says the man "roars something, not quite
language"; he pulls Selzer "inside his cage"; "some beastly
wisdom . . . tells him that at last he has no hope of winning";
Selzer says it is the patient's time "to slink off into high
grass." It's clear that Selzer is a very descriptive writer.
But I'm just not comfortable with the animal references--and
yet I suspect they wouldn't bother me at all if the patient
were white.

        Maybe I'm trying to be too politically correct. I just   2
wish the patient was not African-American.

Lawrence Potter, on "Brute"

We need to distinguish between "racial" and "racist." Racial is
something based on race while racist is one who advocates
racism. I infer from "Brute" that Selzer is addressing issues
of dominance, position, and "race" through the lens of black
and white. In the essay Selzer presents the doctor and the
patient from an action/reaction or cause/effect perspective.
The underlying theme centers on the idea of historical
stereotypes/images of the black male as powerless, uneducated,
inhumane, animalistic, fighter, rageful, and ultimately scarred
for life. The white male has traditionally been in the position
of power/authority, educated, humane, forceful, and ultimately
savior. Selzer does a superb job in referencing the continuous
struggle/plight of the African American male who has been seen
as the progenitor of all ill within society.

In <u>The Doctor Stories</u>, Selzer's recent book of collected writings, he places "Brute" as the final essay in the book. This gives it importance. In his preface, Selzer addresses the controversy of the essay:

> "Brute," written some twenty-five years after the event described, is an act of atonement. It has been woefully misread as racist by some and by others as a "missed opportunity for grace." Neither could be further from the truth. (17)

At a visit to Alma College in 1992, Selzer made the following remarks:

"Timidity is the worst sin of a writer."
"My job is to rouse the reader, to make him weep or laugh."
"I am not ashamed to say I'm fascinated by wounds."
"You write to make sense of yourself."
"One of the blessings for which I am most grateful is that thirty-five years of surgery has not robbed me of my wonder at the human body, my awe of it."

ACTIVITY 8

After reading the arguments by students and quotes by Selzer, what is your position regarding either of the two main questions that "Brute" raises? Write a response in your notebook.

WRITING ABOUT A LITERARY NONFICTION ESSAY

We invite you to analyze a literary nonfiction essay by Richard Selzer.

ACTIVITY 9

Choose "Abortion" or "Toenails." Your job is to analyze how the essay works. Here are two options:

Option 1. Analyze an essay by addressing these questions.
- Who is the speaker and what is the occasion? The occasion refers to when and where the story of the essay takes place, as far as you can tell.
- What is the central purpose of the essay? What do you think Richard Selzer is trying to do and say in the essay?
- By what means does Selzer achieve this purpose? What does Selzer do with diction, imagery, figures of speech, tone, sound, structure, and persuasive appeals (ethos, logos, pathos) to achieve his purpose? You might focus on three of these elements. Analyze whatever stands out for you that the writer does to achieve his purpose.

Option 2. Analyze the writer's persuasive appeals:

- Examine the use of <u>ethos</u>, the moral qualities of the speaker. What does Selzer do to make you care or think about his character?
- Examine the use of <u>pathos</u>, the stirring of emotions. What does Selzer do to make you feel emotionally involved in the essay?
- Examine the use of <u>logos</u>, the logic or reasoning you sense operating. What does Selzer do to make you think about ideas or issues?
- In your essay explain how these three appeals work together to help create the way you respond to the essay. Which appeals do you think Selzer uses most effectively and why?

After you read "Abortion" and "Toenails," please write responses in your notebook.

<u>Note on Quoting:</u> To communicate clearly, you will need to refer to the essay itself. Use some quotations—brief or long—to provide supporting evidence for your points, to show what you mean. Remember that a long quote in prose is four or more lines and should be set off 10 spaces from the left margin and doubled spaced.

   <u>Warning:</u> "Abortion" is powerfully vivid and may upset you as a reader. In using this essay, we do not ask you to choose a position on whether abortion is right or wrong. Rather, we invite you to examine this question: in "Abortion" <u>does Selzer</u> favor abortion, oppose abortion, neither, or both? To answer this question, you need to read closely—to infer Selzer's position based on his description and narration.

Abortion

Richard Selzer

Horror, like bacteria, is everywhere. It blankets the earth, endlessly lapping to find   1
that one unguarded entryway. As though narcotized, we walk beneath, upon, through it. Carelessly we touch the familiar infected linen, eat from the universal dish; we disdain isolation. We are like the newborn that carry immunity from their mothers' wombs. Exteriorized, we are wrapped in impermeable membranes that cannot be seen. Then one day, the defense is gone. And we awaken to horror.

   In our city, garbage is collected early in the morning. Sometimes the bang   2
of the cans and the grind of the truck awaken us before our time. We are resentful, mutter into our pillows, then go back to sleep. On the morning of August 6, 1975, the people of 73rd Street near Woodside Avenue do just that. When at

last they rise from their beds, dress, eat breakfast and leave their houses for work, they have forgotten, if they had ever known, that the garbage truck had passed earlier that morning. The event has slipped into unmemory, like a dream.

They close their doors and descend to the pavement. It is midsummer. You measure the climate, decide how you feel in relation to the heat and the humidity. You walk toward the bus stop. Others, your neighbors, are waiting there. It is all so familiar. All at once you step on something soft. You feel it with your foot. Even through your shoe you have the sense of something unusual, something marked by a special "give." It is a foreignness upon the pavement. Instinct pulls your foot away in an awkward little movement. You look down, and you see . . . a tiny naked body, its arms and legs flung apart, its head thrown back, its mouth agape, its face serious. A bird, you think, fallen from its nest. But there is no nest here on 73rd Street, no bird so big. It is rubber, then. A model, a . . . joke. Yes, that's it, a joke. And you bend to see. Because you must. And it is no joke. Such a gray softness can be but one thing. It is a baby, and dead. You cover your mouth, your eyes. You are fixed. Horror has found its chink and crawled in, and you will never be the same as you were. Years later you will step from a sidewalk to a lawn, and you will start at its softness and think of that upon which you have just trod.

Now you look about; another man has seen it too. "My God," he whispers. Others come, people you have seen every day for years, and you hear them speak with strangely altered voices. "Look," they say, "it's a baby." There is a cry. "Here's another!" and "Another!" and "Another!" And you follow with your gaze the index fingers of your friends pointing from the huddle where you cluster. Yes, it is true! There <u>are</u> more of these . . . little carcasses upon the street. And for a moment you look up to see if all the unbaptized sinless are falling from Limbo.

Now the street is filling with people. There are police. They know what to do. They rope off the area, then stand guard over the enclosed space. They are controlled, methodical, these young policemen. Servants, they do not reveal themselves to their public master; it would not be seemly. Yet I do see their pallor and the sweat that breaks upon the face of one, the way another bites the lining of his cheek and holds it thus. Ambulance attendants scoop up the bodies. They scan the street; none must be overlooked. What they place upon the litter amounts to little more than a dozen pounds of human flesh. They raise the litter, and slide it home inside the ambulance, and they drive away. You and your neighbors stand about in the street which has become for you a battlefield from which the newly slain have at last been bagged and tagged and dragged away. <u>But what shrapnel is this? By what explosion flung, these fragments that sink into the brain and fester there?</u> Whatever smell there is in this place becomes for you the stench of death. The people of 73rd Street do not then speak to each other. It is too soon for outrage, too late for blindness. It is the time of unresisted horror.

Later, at the police station, the investigation is brisk, conclusive. It is the hospital director speaking: ". . . fetuses accidentally got mixed up with the hospital rubbish . . . were picked up at approximately eight fifteen A.M. by a sanitation truck. Somehow, the plastic lab bag, labeled HAZARDOUS MATERIAL, fell off the back of the truck and broke open. No, it is not known how the fetuses got in the orange plastic bag labeled HAZARDOUS MATERIAL. It is a freak accident." The hospital director wants you to know that it is not an everyday occurrence. Once in a lifetime, he says. But you have seen it, and what are his words to you now?

He grows affable, familiar, tells you that, by mistake, the fetuses got 7 mixed up with the other debris. (Yes, he says *other*; he says *debris*.) He has spent the entire day, he says, trying to figure out how it happened. He wants you to know that. Somehow it matters to him. He goes on:

Aborted fetuses that weigh one pound or less are incinerated. Those 8 weighing over one pound are buried at a city cemetery. He says this. Now you see. It *is* orderly. It *is* sensible. The world is *not* mad. This is still a civilized society.

There is no more. You turn to leave. Outside on the street, men are talk- 9 ing things over, reassuring each other that the right thing is being done. But just this once, you know it isn't. You saw, and you know.

And you know, too, that the Street of the Dead Fetuses will be wherever 10 you go. You are part of its history now, its legend. It has laid claim upon you so that you cannot entirely leave it—not ever.

I am a surgeon. I do not shrink from the particularities of sick flesh. 11 Escaping blood, all the outpourings of disease—phlegm, pus, vomitus, even those occult meaty tumors that terrify—I see as blood, disease, phlegm, and so on. I touch them to destroy them. But I do not make symbols of them. I have seen, and I am used to seeing. Yet there are paths within the body that I have not taken, penetralia where I do not go. Nor is it lack of technique, limitation of knowledge that forbids me these ways.

It is the western wing of the fourth floor of a great university hospital. 12 An abortion is about to take place. I am present because I asked to be present. I wanted to see what I had never seen.

The patient is Jamaican. She lies on the table submissively, and now and 13 then she smiles at one of the nurses as though acknowledging a secret.

A nurse draws down the sheet, lays bare the abdomen. The belly mounds 14 gently in the twenty-fourth week of pregnancy. The chief surgeon paints it with a sponge soaked in red antiseptic. He does this three times, each time a fresh sponge. He covers the area with a sterile sheet, an aperture in its center. He is a kindly man who teaches as he works, who pauses to reassure the woman.

He begins. 15

A little pinprick, he says to the woman. 16

He inserts the point of a tiny needle at the midline of the lower portion 17 of her abdomen, on the downslope. He infiltrates local anesthetic into the skin, where it forms a small white bubble.

The woman grimaces. 18

That is all you will feel, the doctor says. Except for a little pressure. But 19
no more pain.

She smiles again. She seems to relax. She settles comfortably on the table. 20
The worst is over.

The doctor selects a three-and-one-half-inch needle bearing a central 21
stylet. He places the point at the site of the previous injection. He aims it
straight up and down, perpendicular. Next he takes hold of her abdomen with
his left hand, palming the womb, steadying it. He thrusts with his right hand.
The needle sinks into the abdominal wall.

Oh, says the woman quietly. 22

But I guess it is not pain that she feels. It is more a recognition that the 23
deed is being done.

Another thrust and he has speared the uterus. 24

We are in, he says. 25

He has felt the muscular wall of the organ gripping the shaft of his needle. 26
A further slight pressure on the needle advances it a bit more. He takes his left
hand from the woman's abdomen. He retracts the filament of the stylet from the
barrel of the needle. A small geyser of pale yellow fluid erupts.

We are in the right place, says the doctor. Are you feeling any pain? he asks. 27

She smiles, shakes her head. She gazes at the ceiling. 28

In the room we are six: two physicians, two nurses, the patient, and me. 29
The participants are busy, very attentive. I am not at all busy—but I am no less
attentive. I want to see.

I see something! It is unexpected, utterly unexpected, like a disturbance 30
in the earth, a tumultuous jarring. I see a movement—a small one. But I have
seen it.

And then I see it again. And now I see that it is the hub of the needle 31
in the woman's belly that has jerked. First to one side. Then to the other side.
Once more it wobbles, is tugged, like a fishing line nibbled by a sunfish.

Again! And I know! 32

It is the fetus that worries thus. It is the fetus struggling against the 33
needle. Struggling? How can that be? I think: that cannot be. I think: the fetus
feels no pain, cannot feel fear, has no motivation. It is merely reflex.

I point to the needle. 34

It is a reflex, says the doctor. 35

By the end of the fifth month, the fetus weighs about one pound, is about 36
twelve inches long. Hair is on the head. There are eyebrows, eyelashes. Pale pink
nipples show on the chest. Nails are present, at the fingertips, at the toes.

At the beginning of the sixth month, the fetus can cry, can suck, can 37
make a fist. He kicks, he punches. The mother can feel this, can see this. His
eyelids, until now closed, can open. He may look up, down, sideways. His grip
is very strong. He could support his weight by holding with one hand.

A reflex, the doctor says. 38

I hear him. But I saw something in that mass of cells <u>understand</u> that it 39
must bob and butt. And I see it again! I have an impulse to shove to the
table—it is just a step—seize that needle, pull it out.

We are not six, I think. We are <u>seven</u>. 40

Something strangles <u>there</u>. An effort, its effort, binds me to it. 41

I do not shove to the table. I take no little step. It would be . . . well, 42
madness. Everyone here wants the needle where it is. Six do. No, <u>five</u> do.

I close my eyes. I see the inside of the uterus. It is bathed in ruby gloom. 43
I see the creature curled upon itself. Its knees are flexed. Its head is bent upon
its chest. It is in fluid and gently rocks to the rhythm of the distant heartbeat.

It resembles . . . a sleeping infant. 44

Its place is entered by something. It is sudden. A point coming. A needle! 45

A spike of <u>daylight</u> pierces the chamber. Now the light is extinguished. The 46
needle comes closer in the pool. The point grazes the thigh, and I stir. Perhaps
I wake from dozing. The light is there again. I twist and straighten. My arms
and legs <u>push</u>. My hand finds the shaft—grabs! I <u>grab</u>. I bend the needle this
way and that. The point probes, touches on my belly. My mouth opens. Could I
cry out? All is a commotion and a churning. There is a presence in the pool. An
activity! The pool colors, reddens, darkens.

I open my eyes to see the doctor feeding a small plastic tube through the 47
barrel of the needle into the uterus. Drops of pink fluid overrun the rim and spill
onto the sheet. He withdraws the needle from around the plastic tubing. Now
only the little tube protrudes from the woman's body. A nurse hands the physician a syringe loaded with a colorless liquid. He attaches it to the end of the
tubing and injects it.

Prostaglandin, he says. 48

Ah well, prostaglandin—a substance found normally in the body. When 49
given in concentrated dosage, it throws the uterus into vigorous contraction.
In eight to twelve hours, the woman will expel the fetus.

The doctor detaches the syringe but does not remove the tubing. 50

In case we must do it over, he says. 51

He takes away the sheet. He places gauze pads over the tubing. Over all 52
this he applies adhesive tape.

I know. We cannot feed the great numbers. There is no more room. I know, 53
I know. It is a woman's right to refuse the risk, to decline the pain of childbirth. And an unwanted child is a very great burden. An unwanted child is a
burden to himself. I know.

And yet . . . there is the flick of that needle. I <u>saw</u> it. I saw . . . I <u>felt</u>— 54
in that room, a pace away, life prodded, life fending off. I saw life avulsed—
swept by flood, blackening—then <u>out</u>.

There, says the doctor. It's all over. It wasn't too bad, was it? he says to 55
the woman.

She smiles. It is all over. Oh, yes.   56

And who would care to imagine that from a moist and dark commence-   57
ment six months before there would ripen the cluster and globule, the sprout
and pouch of man?

And who would care to imagine that trapped within the laked pearl and   58
a dowry of yoke would lie the earliest stuff of dream and memory?

It is a persona carried here as well as a person, I think. I think it is a   59
signed piece, engraved with a hieroglyph of human genes.

I did not think this until I saw. The flick. The fending off.   60

Later, in the corridor, the doctor explains that the law does not permit   61
abortion beyond the twenty-fourth week. That is when the fetus may be viable,
he says. We stand together for a moment, and he tells of an abortion in which
the fetus <u>cried</u> after it was passed.

What did you do? I ask him.   62

There was nothing <u>to</u> do but let it live, he says. It did very well, he says.   63
A case of mistaken dates. (<u>Mortal Lessons</u> 153–60) □

ACTIVITY 10

In his preface to <u>Mortal Lessons</u> Richard Selzer comments on "Abortion." The
following is from the 1996 edition:

> At the time of writing, the subject of abortion had just become a focus of
> contention in American society. Oddly, it happened that I had never seen an
> abortion. I arranged to do so and that night wrote what I had meant to be a
> literary rendition of the event, not an argument against the procedure. (8)

In your notebook write answers to these questions:

1. How does his statement square with your reading of Selzer's "Abortion"? What do
   you think Selzer means by "a literary rendition of the event"?
2. Based on your reading of "Abortion," take a stand and defend it: does Selzer favor
   abortion or oppose abortion? Or are there other options besides these two?
3. If you omitted Selzer's similes and metaphors, how would this affect his appeals to
   logos, pathos, and ethos?

"Toenails" is from Selzer's book <u>Letters to a Young Doctor</u>. His audience
is any young doctor or premed student—as well as any reader interested in the
human body and spirit.

Toenails

Richard Selzer

It is the custom of many doctors, I among them, to withdraw from the practice of   1
medicine every Wednesday afternoon. This, only if there is no patient who demands
the continuous presence of his physician. I urge you, when the time comes, to do
it, too. Such an absence from duty ought not to win you the accusation of lèse
responsibility. You will, of course, have secured the availability of a colleague to
look after your patients for the few hours you will spend grooming and watering
your spirit. Nor is such idleness a reproach to those who do not take time off from
their labors, but who choose to scramble on without losing the pace. Loafing is
not better than frenzied determination. It is but an alternate mode of living.

Long ago I made a vow that I would never again delve away the month   2
of July in the depths of the human body. In July it would be my own cadaver
that engaged me. There is a danger in becoming too absorbed in Anatomy. At
the end of eleven months of dissection, you stand in fair risk of suffering a kind
of rapture of the deep, wherein you drift, tumbling among the coils of intes-
tine in a state of helpless enchantment. Only a month's vacation can save you.
It is wrongheaded to think of total submersion in the study and practice of
Medicine. That is going too far. And going too far is for saints. I know medical
students well enough to exclude you from that slender community.

Nor must you be a priest who does nothing but preserve the souls of his   3
parishioners and lets his own soul lapse. Such is the burnt-out case who early
on drinks his patients down in a single radiant gulp and all too soon loses the
desire to practice Medicine at all. In a year or two he is to be found lying in
bed being fed oatmeal with a spoon. Like the fruit of the Amazon he is too
quickly ripe and too quickly rotten.

Some doctors spend Wednesday afternoon on the golf course. Others go   4
fishing. Still another takes a lesson on the viola da gamba. I go to the library
where I join that subculture of men and women who gather in the Main Reading Room to read or sleep beneath the world's newspapers, and thumb through
magazines and periodicals, educating themselves in any number of esoteric ways,
or just keeping up. It is not the least function of a library to provide for these
people a warm, dry building with good working toilets and, ideally, a vending
machine from which to buy a cup of hot broth or coffee. All of which attributes a public library shares with a neighborhood saloon, the only difference
being the beer of one and the books of the other.

How brave, how reliable they are! plowing through you-name-what inclemen-   5
cies to get to the library shortly after it opens. So unbroken is their attendance
that, were one of them to be missing, it would arouse the direst suspicions of
the others. And of me. For I have, furtively at first, then with increasing recklessness, begun to love them. They were, after all, living out my own fantasies.
One day, with luck, I, too, would become a full-fledged, that is to say <u>daily</u>,

member. At any given time, the tribe consists of a core of six regulars and a somewhat less constant pool of eight others of whom two or three can be counted on to appear. On very cold days, all eight of these might show up, causing a bit of a jam at the newspaper rack, and an edginess among the regulars.

Either out of loyalty to certain beloved articles of clothing, or from scant- 6 iness of wardrobe, they wear the same things every day. For the first year or two this was how I identified them. Old Stovepipe, Mrs. Fringes, Neckerchief, Galoshes—that sort of thing. In no other society does apparel so exactly fit the wearer as to form a part of his persona. Dior, Balenciaga, take heed! By the time I arrive, they have long since devoured the morning's newspapers and settled into their customary places. One or two, Galoshes, very likely, and Stovepipe, are sleeping it off. These two seem to need all the rest they can get. Mrs. Fringes, on the other hand, her hunger for information unappeasable, having finished all of the newspapers, will be well into the <u>Journal of Abnormal Psychology</u>, the case histories of which keep her riveted until closing time. As time went by, despite that we had not yet exchanged a word of conversation, I came to think of them as dear colleagues, fellow readers who, with me, were engaged in the pursuit of language. Nor, I noticed, did they waste much time speaking to each other. Reading was serious business. Only downstairs near the basement vending machine would animated conversation break out. Upstairs, in the Reading Room, the vow of silence was sacred.

I do not know by what criteria such selections are made, but Neckerchief 7 is my favorite. He is a man well into his eighties with the kind of pink face that even in July looks as though it has just been brought in out of the cold. A single drop of watery discharge, like a crystal bead, hangs at the tip of his nose. His gait is stiff-legged, with tiny, quick, shuffling steps accompanied by rather wild arm-swinging in what seems an effort to gain momentum or maintain balance. For a long time I could not decide whether this manner of walking was due to arthritis of the knees or to the fact that for most of the year he wore two or more pairs of pants. Either might have been the cause of his lack of joint flexion. One day, as I held the door to the Men's Room for him, he pointed to his knee and announced, by way of explanation of his slowness:

"The hinges is rusty." 8

The fact was delivered with a shake of the head, a wry smile and without 9 the least self-pity.

"No hurry," I said, and once again paid homage to Sir William Osler, who 10 instructed his students to "listen to the patient. He is trying to tell you what is the matter with him." From that day, Neckerchief and I were friends. I learned that he lives alone in a rooming house eight blocks away, that he lives on his Social Security check, that his wife died a long time ago, that he has no children, and that the <u>Boston Globe</u> is the best damn newspaper in the library. He learned approximately the same number of facts about me. Beyond that we talked about politics and boxing, which is his great love. He himself had been an amateur fighter sixty years ago—most of his engagements having been spontaneous brawls of a decidedly ethnic nature. "It was the Polacks against the

Yids," he told me, "and both of 'em against the Micks." He held up his fists to show the ancient fractures.

The actual neckerchief is a classic red cowboy rag folded into a triangle 11 and tied about his neck in such a way that the widest part lies at the front, covering the upper chest as a kind of bib. Now and then a nose drop elongates, shimmers, wobbles and falls to be absorbed into the neckerchief. Meanwhile a new drop has taken the place of the old. So quickly is this newcomer born that I, for one, have never beheld him unadorned.

One day I watched as Neckerchief, having raided the magazine rack, jour- 12 neyed back to his seat. In one flapping hand the <u>Saturday Review</u> rattled. As he passed, I saw that his usually placid expression was replaced by the look of someone in pain. Each step was a fresh onslaught of it. His lower lip was caught between his teeth. His forehead had been cut and stitched into lines of endurance. He was hissing. I waited for him to take his seat, which he did with a gasp of relief, then went up to him.

"The hinges?" I whispered. 13

"Nope. The toes." 14

"What's wrong with your toes?" 15

"The toenails is too long. I can't get at 'em. I'm walkin' on 'em." 16

I left the library and went to my office. 17

"What are you doing here?" said my nurse. "It's Wednesday afternoon. 18 People are just supposed to die on Wednesday afternoon."

"I need the toenail cutters. I'll bring them back tomorrow." 19

"The last time you took something out of here I didn't see it for six 20 months."

Neckerchief was right where I left him. A brief survey, however, told me 21 that he had made one trek in my absence. It was <u>U.S. News & World Report</u> on his lap. The <u>Saturday Review</u> was back in the rack. I could only guess what the exchange had cost him. I doubted that either of the magazines was worth it.

"Come on down to the Men's Room," I said. "I want to cut your toenails." 22 I showed him my toenail clippers, the heavy-duty kind that you grip with the palm, and with jaws that could bite through bone. One of the handles is a rasp. I gave him a ten-minute head start, then followed him downstairs to the Men's Room. There was no one else there.

"Sit here." I pointed to one of the booths. He sat on the toilet. I knelt 23 and began to take off his shoes.

"Don't untie 'em," he said. "I just slide 'em on and off." 24

The two pairs of socks were another story, having to be peeled off. The 25 underpair snagged on the toenails. Neckerchief winced.

"How do you get these things on?" I asked. 26

"A mess, ain't they? I hope I don't stink too bad for you." 27

The nail of each big toe was the horn of a goat. Thick as a thumb and 28 curved, it projected down over the tip of the toe to the underside. With each step, the nail would scrape painfully against the ground and be pressed into his flesh. There was dried blood on each big toe.

"Jesus, man!" I said. "How can you walk?" I thought of the eight blocks 29
he covered twice a day.

It took an hour to do each big toe. The nails were too thick even for my 30
nail cutters. They had to be chewed away little by little, then flattened out with
the rasp. Now and then a fragment of nail would fly up, striking me in the face.
The other eight toes were easy. Now and then, the door opened. Someone came
and went to the row of urinals. Twice, someone occupied the booth next to
ours. I never once looked up to see. They'll just have to wonder, I thought. But
Neckerchief could tell from my face.

"It doesn't look decent," he said. 31

"Never mind," I told him. "I bet this isn't the strangest thing that's 32
happened down here." I wet some toilet paper with warm water and soap,
washed each toe, dried him off, and put his socks and shoes back on. He stood
up and took a few steps, like someone who is testing the fit of a new pair of
shoes.

"How is it?" 33

"It don't hurt," he said, and gave me a smile that I shall keep in my 34
safety-deposit box at the bank until the day I die.

"That's a Cadillac of a toe job," said Neckerchief. "How much do I owe ya?" 35

"On the house," I said. "And besides, what kind of a boy do you think I 36
am?"

The next week I did Stovepipe. He was an easy case. Then, Mrs. Fringes, 37
who was a special problem. I had to do her in the Ladies' Room, which tied up
the place for half an hour. A lot of people opened the door, took one look, and
left in a hurry. Either it was hot in there or I had a temperature.

I never go to the library on Wednesday afternoon without my nail clip- 38
pers in my briefcase. You just never know. (<u>Letters to a Young Doctor</u> 64–69) □

ACTIVITY 11

Write a brief essay on one of these questions:

1. How different is Selzer's ethos in "Toenails" compared with his ethos in "Brute"
   and in "Abortion"?
2. How does Selzer's description affect his appeals to logos, pathos, and ethos?

READING AND WRITING ABOUT FILM

Do you watch more movies than you read books? Most people in our culture do.
As the most popular art form, film is entertaining and enlightening much like

poetry, fiction, and literary nonfiction. As a critical thinker, you can appreciate and understand film more if you read film reviews and write reviews yourself.

Why read a movie review? This question has been discussed by reviewers on the Web such as Bill and Beth whose Web site "Bill & Beth Go to the Movies" features a collection of past reviews.

> We think that you read a review of a movie to find out whether the movie is entertaining, whether it keeps your interest, and whether it touches you; that is, when you leave the theater, are you glad you've seen it? So we tell you what you want to know, and we tell you what Beth (the woman) and Bill (the man) thought. Sometimes we don't agree! Amazing!
>
> We don't think you read a review to find out what is important to various producers, directors, actors or actresses, to a film class, or to the local newspaper. Whether the movie is too much like another movie strikes us as irrelevant; what's important is whether we like it!
> (<http://www.anet-dfw.com/~billb/> Access date: 2 July 1999)

"Are you glad you've seen it?" This is a good question to examine whenever you see a movie.

Writing a film review is like writing any argument: you make a point and you support it with specific evidence: reasons, examples, and details. As with any paper, a film review requires information. Arguing without information is like trying to serve dinner without any food. To build an informed argument, you need solid and persuasive information about a film. It takes all the skills you possess to put your reasons and examples together so that they convince your readers that your opinion of a film is reasonable and insightful.

Reviews of Fargo, 1996

Memering and Palmer discovered we have different opinions about the film Fargo and have decided to publish our essays to illustrate reviewers disagreeing with each other.

Fargo: Funny Stuff?

Reasoning about art means arguing opinions. No one has the "right" or "wrong" answer, just opinions: reasons and examples readers may accept—or not. Popular art, like movies, can generate much disagreement. For example, the 1996 film Fargo has been much admired by critics. But I don't like Fargo at all.   1

    Roger Ebert, renowned critic of the Chicago Sun-Times, calls Fargo "one of the best films I've ever seen. To watch it is to experience steadily mounting delight. . . . [The Coens] have never [done] a film as wonderful as this one" (1996). Ebert rates Fargo four stars, his highest. Janet Maslin, New York Times   2 film critic, also likes <u>Fargo</u> but gives a more balanced review. <u>Fargo</u> shows, she says, Joel and Ethan Coen "at their clever best" (1996). She finds <u>Fargo</u> "stylish and entertaining." Although, she says, "this tale is fundamentally grim," the filmmakers give it a "winning absurdist humor and beautifully honed storytelling."

These and other reviewers may know more about movies than I do, but I've been viewing movies most of my life, and I have to say I find nothing "wonderful" or "beautifully honed" in this "absurdist humor." Here are two facts for viewers to consider. One is the "cartoonish" violence (Maslin). Into this quiet, snowy Dakota-Minnesota environment, the film introduces two nasty, witless, sadistic killers: one a vicious little rat of a man, the other a silent monster. The killings are so sudden, so horrible, blood-splattered and ghastly that the audience cringes. This is humor? The other point is the film's overall outlook. The film is based on a true story. There really was an unhappy car salesman ("Jerry") who needed money and devised a plan to have his wife kidnapped. And then it all goes wrong and his wife and several other people are brutally murdered. Humor? The plot is hard to accept; so are the sight gags (the hulking killer runs his smaller confederate through a wood chipper). Funny stuff.

No, I think it is the people we are supposed to laugh at. Jerry is a nervous, sad, small man, incapable of dealing with the horrors he has set in motion. Still more humorous, apparently, is the chief of police, Marge. To emphasize how ridiculous it is to have a female chief, Marge is very pregnant and unaccountably cheerful. Most amusing, the film thinks, all these people speak a comic variety of English: a rude parody of the English spoken by the German, Norwegian, and Swedish groups who settled that part of the country. Laughing at the mannerisms and the way these people talk—yumpin' yimminy, yah-sure, dey talk pritty fonny? This is junior high stuff, not humor but <u>mockery</u>, <u>ridicule</u>, <u>derision</u> . . . equating accent with stupidity. Funny that a woman is chief of police? Funny that she is a competent law officer? Funny that the people of Minnesota and the Dakotas do not all speak with an Eastern accent? The film's point of view is mystifying.

The value in this kind of arguing? Important critics think one way, and little old me disagrees. Well, such arguing helps me think better. And when there are enough exchanges of opinions, it helps everyone think about our values and criteria of excellence in art. Maybe then filmmakers will rethink using murder and ridicule for humor.

Works Cited

Ebert, Roger. Rev. of <u>Fargo</u>, by Joel and Ethan Coen. Copyright <u>Chicago Sun-Times Inc</u>. 3 Aug. 1996. 11 Oct. 1998 <http://www.suntimes.com/ebert_reviews/1996/03/1023990.html>.

Maslin, Janet. Rev. of <u>Fargo</u>, by Joel and Ethan Coen. 8 Mar. 1996. 11 Oct. 1998 <http://www.nytimes.com/library/filmarchive/fargo.html>. □

<u>Fargo</u>: A Creative Mix of Humor and Horror

I like <u>Fargo</u>. It's one of the most original and creative movies I've seen. It's odd 1
to watch a mix of graphic violence and humor—a mix with an important moral
within it: that greed causes lots of unforeseen grief.

Creativity is defined as joining unrelated things in ways that cause 2
surprise. Watching <u>Fargo</u>, I felt continuous surprise with the plot and characters. Jerry Lundegaard's conflict is common: he needs money and respect, but
he doesn't know how to earn them honestly. To cover himself from shady business deals, he arranges for two thugs to kidnap his wife so he can collect ransom
money from his wealthy father-in-law Wade, who barely tolerates him. Pushed
to the edge, Jerry sets in motion a sequence of events that he and no one else
can control—like a car without brakes. We know Jerry's scheme will somehow
crash, but we don't know how exactly, and so we watch unprepared for a unique
ride of filmmaking.

Juxtaposition creates much of the film's surprise. Marge Gunderson, the 3
pregnant chief of police, foils Jerry. Whereas he is jumpy and fearful and not in
control of himself or the scheme he hatches, Marge is steady and intelligent,
taking her time as she investigates the murders and motives. Jerry risks his
wife's life, disregarding how his scheme might affect his son; in contrast, Marge
truly loves her husband Norm: she buys him doughnuts and fishing worms; she
reassures him that his fish paintings are special; she persuades him that getting
his fish on a three-cent stamp is an achievement and that he doesn't have to
stand out to be appreciated. Jerry values money and power; Marge values humility, simplicity, and fast food. Jerry explodes emotionally at times, beating his
desk with his calendar and his windshield with his scraper, but Marge is cool,
controlled, and friendly to everyone. Her calm character surprises us as she
observes the murder scene of the policeman and the two people who drove by.
Holding a Styrofoam cup of coffee, she takes in the gruesome scene, inferring
what happened from the size and direction of footprints. Whereas Jerry's life
collapses, Marge's life keeps growing along with the child she carries and the
investigation she pieces together. William H. Macy and Francis McDormand create
these contrasting characterizations with extraordinary acting.

The minor characters of the thugs Carl Showalter (Steve Buscemi) and 4
Gaear Grimsrud (Peter Stormare) also juxtapose each other, producing surprising horror and humor. Carl is short and thin, mouthy, vulgar, and anxious; Gaear
is taller and heavier, intensely quiet, impulsive, and spooky with white hair. Both
thugs get more than they bargain for. Like Jerry they lack smarts. They bungle
the kidnapping, with Jerry's wife wrapped in a shower curtain falling down the
stairs and passing out. When the policeman stops them because their car doesn't
have a license tag, Carl tries to bribe the cop with money, which makes him ask
Carl to get out of the car. Gaear then shoots the policeman, the act that sets
in motion the terrible violence of the movie. A zombie, Gaear drinks beer and
watches fuzzy TV as Carl winds himself tightly with anxiety, ranting at Jerry,

killing Wade, who makes the money drop, and getting shot in the face himself. After Gaear kills Carl with an ax, Marge finds him pushing pieces of Carl through a wood chipper, the snowy ground blown red with blood. We see Carl's leg with his foot sticking up out of the chipper. This scene is at once horrible and comically absurd because we really don't care that Carl has died.

This strange combination of horror and humor is unsettling. I don't 5 consider the violence "cartoonish" as Janet Maslin claims; it is too graphic and real, especially when Carl gets shot in the face and we see him trying to stop the bleeding as he drives. Yet I do agree with Maslin when she argues the film contains "absurdist humor and beautifully honed storytelling." Much of the humor in the story is the exaggerated North Dakota-Minnesota dialect. I don't view it as a "rude parody." Exaggeration often creates humor. The speech helps create the characters of Jerry and Marge. Though unified in dialect, they lead vastly different lives. Without this comic speech to lighten the plot, the film would be too dark and heavy. When Marge says, "Oh yahh, you betcha," it's naturally funny. It suits her friendly personality. Her speech is a little different as she is a little different—cheerful in an odd, fresh way. When Marge talks to a hotel clerk, she asks with a smile, "Is there a phone around here ya think?" The clerk replies, "Yahh!" The humorous dialect is a necessary valve that lets off some of the steam of despair and violence inherent in this true tale.

I don't like violence, and it feels strange to laugh at it sometimes in this 6 movie. But I like <u>Fargo</u>. It took me for an unforgettable ride. Within the frigid, snowy setting where several lives become destroyed, Marge Gunderson's life is warm and happy: she enjoys her job, her husband, and her pregnancy. The murders and the motives don't change her. She's been around; she's seen horror before. She's simple, steady, smart, and moral. In this surprising film, the Coen brothers artfully present the message that extreme greed kills. □

It isn't necessary to use critics such as Roger Ebert and Janet Maslin in your paper, but their reviews may help you understand the film and provide more depth to your appreciation. Then too, sometimes critics can provide you with a point of view to argue against. Here is a review of <u>Fargo</u> in which a student used six reviews.

Fargo: Unique and Worthwhile Despite Divided Reviews

Katie Beam

Starring Frances McDormand as Marge Gunderson; William Macy as Jerry Lundegaard; Steve Buscemi as Carl Showalter; Peter Stormare as Gaear Grimsrud. Written by Ethan and Joel Coen. Produced by Ethan Coen. Directed by Joel Coen.

For years my mother tried to make me watch an Ethan and [1] Joel Coen film. I always refused. I was not interested in watching movies I'd never even heard of. Oddly, the first Coen film I watched, I saw by accident. I rented Fargo one night a couple of years ago--and absolutely loved it! Unfortunately, I was one of the few in my circle of friends and acquaintances who did. I was surprised to hear critics were also divided. However, I have decided that Fargo is an entertaining, worthwhile film to see despite the divided reviews.

Fargo is supposedly the true account of events that [2] occurred in Fargo, North Dakota in 1987. Jerry Lundergaard, a car salesman, has acquired a few outstanding debts. In order to repay these, he has devised a rather outlandish plan. He hires two thugs, Carl (Steve Buscemi) and Gaear (Peter Stormare), to kidnap his wife, Jean (Karen Rudrud). Jerry plans for the kidnappers to demand one million dollars in ransom ($960,000 dollars he plans to keep) and extort this from Jean's rich father, Wade (Harve Presnell). After the kidnapping, Carl and Gaear kill three witnesses, including a state trooper. Enter Chief Gunderson (Frances McDormand). She is an atypical police officer: female, pregnant, and appears somewhat slow-minded. However, she begins to track the kidnappers down and finds Jerry mixed up in the deal. Unfortunately for Jerry, Wade has decided to drop the money off himself. After Carl kills Wade, he opens the bag to find a wee bit more money than he's expecting. He puts aside Gaear's share and hides the rest. He returns to the hideout where he and Gaear fight over who keeps the car. Gaear kills Carl and then tries to dispose of the body, but Marge catches him in the act. At about the same time, Jerry is arrested across town in a hotel.

I selected six reviews to discuss based on their opinions [3] of the strengths and weaknesses of Fargo. The film does have a

(box continues)

few flaws that I feel obligated to mention. For example, Nazgol Shifteh, a reviewer with the <u>College Hill Independent</u>, says, "Somehow, despite multiple killings that seem to occur with the same predictability of deaths in a Shakespearean tragedy, the Coens manage to keep their audiences dry-eyed and smirking" (1). The lack of emotion in the movie is apparent here. This can be disturbing to many viewers. He also says, "The Coens ensure that we in no way empathize with the victim at hand. In fact, the scene prior to the break-in shows Mrs. Lundergaard smiling vacuously at a television show" (1). This scene is unsettling. Why would we not want to sympathize with the victims? The amount of gore is also shocking: the violent scenes are graphic. Anthony Lane, a reviewer from the <u>New Yorker</u>, comments on "a body being fed into a wood chipper, and the wood chipper making an almighty fuss" (99). Disturbing? Yes. Necessary? Yes. John Simon, a reviewer from the <u>National Review</u>, agrees, "The violence, when it erupts, is sudden and grotesque, and all the more convincing" (62). The violence is all the more real because it is so vivid, though still hard to swallow.

However, this is where my agreement with some critics   4
ends. Harsh comments on the movie include these: "<u>Fargo,</u> in addition to being a personal work, is also a fatuous piece of nonsense, a tall cool drink of witless condescension" (McKinney 31) and "The Coen brothers' <u>Fargo</u> is their best film so far, which isn't saying very much" (Simon 60). These comments are exaggerations. First of all, the film is not nonsense; the plot could happen anywhere because greed can create motives as ugly as Jerry's. And secondly, Simon's statement about the film sounds immature.

Other reviews attack the accent/language used in the   5
movie. The Minnesotan dialect is a major aspect of the film. Simon comments, "Marge Gunderson, the pregnant small-town police chief who is the film's hero as well as heroine, manages at one point three <u>jeezes</u> in a row, which is cheesy enough to make you check your cholesterol" (60). Another critic says, "It [<u>Fargo</u>] is littered with nice, plodding Scandinavian citizens, all of whom deliver passionless conversation, as if their batteries were running low" (Lane 99). McKinney states that "the 'yahhh' is ubiquitous, for the screenplay plays it like a mantra" (33). And Corliss comments, "the filmmakers Joel and Ethan Coen, have apparently never got over the giggle value

(box continues)

of their regional dialect" (86). But these critics don't realize that the accents and "yahhs" are hilarious! The characters' dialect is the funniest part of the movie. Without this dialect, the film would not be as fresh and interesting. <u>Magill's Cinema Annual</u> states that "the Coens extol the glories and virtues of dialogue and language. [. . .] The rhythms of the characters' speech, the cadences, nuances, tones and subtleties of their Scandinavian-Canadian heritage drive this project" (182). I could not have said it better myself!

A few reviews claim the characters in <u>Fargo</u> are too superficial, unreal. McKinney says:

> The film's failure is that it mistakes the easy return of ethnic humor for the deeper response engendered by characters who are defined in emotionally or psychologically significant ways, and that it unproblematically offers its heroine's home-and-hearth complacency, her shallows, not her depths, as proof of human substance. (34)

I disagree: we are all "defined in emotional or psychologically significant ways." Why should <u>Fargo</u> be criticized for portraying humans as they are? Shifteh agrees with McKinney: "Excluding Marge, each character can be reduced to a few words, representing a simple idea rather than a complex being. Jerry's father-in-law, for example, can be characterized as a 'stubborn greedy old man, nothing more'" (2). I agree somewhat--the film does use simple characterization, but it fits <u>Fargo</u>. The characters do not need to be more complex. Shifteh and McKinney unfairly expect too much out of the characters. The point is that they carry the movie. Illustration: Frances McDormand won an Academy Award for Best Actress, remember? If her character Marge didn't resonate truthfully, would she have won this award?

Much to my relief, the critics were able the find some points of enjoyment in <u>Fargo</u>. The cinematography is mentioned in a few reviews. Shifteh says, "the film offers creative and aesthetically pleasing cinematography" (2). I agree--the winter scenes are shot beautifully and symbolize the movie's themes. Simon says: "The brothers have good taste in cinematographers, and have acquired one of the best in Roger Deakins. He shoots rural Minnesota as a huge blanket of snow, the image turning fuzzy at the edges to suggest recession into infinity, and even greater desolation" (62). The cinematography sets the tone of the movie--Deakins makes sure he accomplishes this.

6

7

(box continues)

I'd like to see the reviewers enjoy the film for what it [8] is rather than expect it to follow the Coen brothers' usual paths. <u>Fargo</u> may not fit into any particular movie genre, but who says that it has to? The Coens are surprising filmmakers and undoubtedly satisfying. <u>Fargo</u> may not be a favorite among all critics, but it has earned its right to be recognized for its worth--not its shortcomings.

Works Cited

Corliss, Richard. "Swede 'n' Sour." Rev. of <u>Fargo</u>, by Joel and Ethan Coen. <u>Time</u> 18 Mar. 1996: 86.

Lane, Anthony. "The Current Cinema." Rev. of <u>Fargo</u>, by Joel and Ethan Coen. <u>The New Yorker</u> 25 Mar. 1996: 99.

McKinney, Devin. "Fargo." Rev. of <u>Fargo</u>, by Joel and Ethan Coen. <u>Film Quarterly</u> Fall 1996: 31-34.

Rev. of <u>Fargo</u>, by Joel and Ethan Coen. ed. Beth A. Fhaner. <u>Magill's Cinema Annual: A Retrospective of the Films of 1997</u>. New Jersey: Salem Press, 1997: 181-183.

Shifteh, Nazgol. "The College Hill Independent." Rev. of <u>Fargo</u>, by Joel and Ethan Coen. <u>Trapeze Act</u> 1996. 4 Mar. 1998 <http://www.envstudies.brown.edu/indy/issue/ 04-04-96/ arts.html>.

Simon, John. "Forgo Fargo." Rev. of <u>Fargo</u>, by Joel and Ethan Coen. <u>National Review</u> 22 Apr. 1996: 60-62.

WRITING ABOUT A FILM

We invite you to analyze a film that you enjoy or value a great deal. See "Guidelines for Writing a Film Review."

ACTIVITY 12

Write a review of a movie in which you research and synthesize three to six reviews you find in a library and on the Internet. Argue with the critics—disagree and agree with them. In your review, state your opinion in a clear thesis statement and then support and defend it with persuasive evidence—reasons, examples, and details.

> ## GUIDELINES FOR WRITING A FILM REVIEW
>
> - Good reviews briefly sketch an outline of the plot and inform (perhaps remind) readers about the characters.
> - More important, good reviews look at both strengths and weaknesses.
> - Consider whether to address strengths or weaknesses first.
> - If you love a film but see some weaknesses in it, it is usually best to present the weaknesses first and then concentrate on the strengths (as Katie Beam does). Presenting weaknesses first will help persuade your readers that you are fair-minded.
> - If you dislike a film but see some strengths in it, present the strengths first and then concentrate on the weaknesses.
> - You can also offer criticisms and then rebuttals within paragraphs, as Katie Beam does in paragraphs 5 to 7 of her review.
> - Ideally, try to find some insight into the movie that most readers may not have considered before. A good review can help readers have new and deeper understandings.

Here is an excerpt from a student's review of a popular film.

> ```
> The Blues Brothers
>
> Timm Johnson
> ```
>
> Even past the silly and oftentimes far-fetched antics, there is   1
> a deeper side to the movie. Jake and Elwood come to us as two
> hoodlum musicians and despite their casual defiance of the law,
> we find they have big hearts. The truth is we love them
> because they do--and get away with--everything we wish we
> could. They seem to look past the trivial side of our lives
>
> *(box continues)*

```
and bury themselves in the soul of it all--the music, the art,
the spirituality, and paying back those who gave so much.
     Throughout the movie you really get a good sense of the          2
relationship between the two brothers. Jake is played as more
of the irresponsible visionary type while Elwood is more of the
detail man, his brother's keeper. It is always Jake who gets
the big ideas that backfire no matter how well intended, and
it is Elwood that steps up to clean up the mess and get them
out of another jam.
```

Timm's ideas that Jake and Elwood "bury themselves in the soul" of life and that Elwood is Jake's "brother's keeper" go beyond what is obvious about the movie.

What you choose to discuss in your review will depend on your emphasis and purpose. You can discuss the quality of any or some of the items in the accompanying "Elements of Film" box. You may choose to review a movie whose plot, characters, and theme may intentionally not be plausible, believable, or significant—but you love the movie anyway.

Consider your audience. Suppose most of your readers have already seen the movie. Thus, they will read your review to see whether they agree with you. But through your review, you must find something to say beyond "I like it." As a reviewer, you can help readers understand why you like or dislike the film and how your opinion differs from or supports what other reviewers have written. Follow this structure for your film review:

1. Introduction with a clearly stated thesis.
2. Summary of the film; don't spend too much time retelling the plot.
3. Briefly acknowledge or summarize views other than your own.
4. Present your analysis: select only those elements of the film that have an impact on you. Support your ideas with reasons, examples, details from the film, and from the reviews. Try to weave direct quotes from the reviews unobtrusively into your paper.
5. Conclusion with a brief restatement of thesis and a call for readers to see or not see the film.

When many students write film reviews, they spend most of their paper retelling the plot. But the purpose of a review is to analyze a film. Your summary of the film's plot should be a paragraph or two at most.

Your review need not sound like a strictly academic research paper; it can be informal and lively. Don't be afraid to let your personality show. When you write, you present an ethos—a sense of your own character which becomes as much a part of your writing as your appeals to reason (logos) and to emotion (pathos).

ELEMENTS OF FILM

Plot

The sequence of events in a story is the plot; it tells what the story is about. The plot involves some conflict or situation the characters must resolve, some problem that causes tension among the characters. Is the plot credible or plausible? How?

Character

In serious film the characters are realistic, complex human beings with strengths and weaknesses. Real characters are an important part of the plot. The audience must care about the characters and what happens to them. When characters are too predictable or stereotypical, critics say they are flat, cardboard characters. Are the characters believable? How?

Acting

The more realistic an actor's actions and reactions, the better the acting. If audiences think an actor is trying too hard to act, they will not value his or her performance. Is the acting natural, believable, credible? Is the acting particularly interesting or distinctive in some way? How?

Theme

A theme is an author's main idea or subject the film illustrates. Fargo illustrates greed gone awry. Is the theme significant? How?

Setting

The time and place of the story is the setting—anything that helps create the illusion of time and place: clothing, costuming, makeup, buildings, countryside, backgrounds. How does the setting reinforce the plot, the characters, the theme?

Pace

Few viewers enjoy a movie that takes too long to unfold its story. Does the film's pace work well or drag? How? Have you ever seen a film you thought was too fast?

Music/Sound

With advanced technology, sound helps create mood. Sound reinforces special visual effects too—the music in Jaws warns you when the shark is coming. You believe what you see in part because of what you hear. How does the music or sound contribute to the film?

(box continues)

Cinematography/Filming Techniques, Effects

Camera work, lighting, positioning—if you think of a movie as a series of still photographs, each "shot" set up perfectly to illustrate the setting, the plot development at that moment in the film, and so on, it may be easier to understand what the photographers and the technical crew contribute to the film. Movies are rarely filmed straight through from beginning to end, and therefore matching lighting and camera angles becomes important. Special effects, too, involve camera work. How does the cinematography contribute to the film?

Director

The director is usually in charge of everything you see and hear on the screen. Camera shots, for example, are usually set up by the director. The actors cannot see what they are doing, but the director can. Has the director done a skillful job? How?

Value

Does the story have moral, social, psychological, or some other kind of value beyond entertainment? How? Is the entertainment value enough for you to recommend the film?

Your final step should be to work on the style of your review. Remember that a review is partly an intellectual entertainment. Your review needs solid critical judgment and evidence to back it up, but it also needs polish and style. Well-chosen words, well-worded sentences, a sharp criticism or heartfelt praise where you think it is needed—a review can be critical thinking at its best: thoughtful judgments expressed in language that shows a thinker at work. Reviews ought to be fun: fun for the writer and fun for the reader.

Divide your film review project into two parts:

1. A 2- to 4-page paper in which you review a movie without reading other reviews.
2. A 3- to 6-page paper in which you research and synthesize three to six other reviews you find in a library and on the Internet. In this second paper you may incorporate much of what you wrote in the first paper.

You can find many sites on the Web for movie reviews. Among the best are these:

Infoseek Movie Review page: <http://entertainment.go.com/movies/index.html>
Movie Review Query Engine at Telerama: <http://www.cinema.pgh.pa.usmovie/reviews>

New York Times Film Reviews: <http://www.nytimes.com/library/filmarchive>
Roger Ebert's Film Reviews: <http://www.suntimes.com/ebert/ebert.html>

Notes on Sources

1. Evaluate your sources. Examine the assumptions of the writers of the reviews. Question and challenge them: try not to assume they are wise and truthful. Examine their points of view. Look for any <u>insights</u> that reviewers express. Look for hidden <u>assumptions</u>. Look for <u>overgeneralizations</u> and biases.

2. Use the Modern Language Association (MLA) style of documentation: parenthetical text references throughout your paper and a complete Works Cited page at the end of your paper. (See chapter 9.)

3. Provide photocopies of your reviews and <u>highlight</u> or put [brackets] around any direct quotes you use in your paper so your instructor can check their accuracy.

Chapter 7

Library Strategies

RESEARCH WRITING OPTIONS

Research starts with a genuine desire to investigate, to explore, to understand some problem or issue that intrigues you, that matters to you. Without a genuine desire to learn, to investigate your topic, you will find research hard work. But you can make the task easier if you treat it like a process, one that you can divide into stages or phases.

However, unlike other processes, such as cooking or building, for example, researching and writing a research paper is more like following a spiral than a straight line. As you find sources in the library and on the Internet, you may develop a rough outline or start writing brief notes. Later, after you have found information that relates to your purpose and your arguments, you can start adding to your notes; then you may find yourself returning to the library to find more sources, possibly some mentioned in your reading, you may reread various chapters in this book; you may need to reread parts of this chapter. So although you are likely to read chapters 7 to 10 in chronological order, you may also need to refer back to previous chapters, to check again information available in on-line indexes, to check MLA form for documenting journal or magazine articles, and so on. Keep the spiral idea in mind: return to different chapters to answer questions as you do your research and write your paper.

The Informational Report

Research papers can take various forms. Two common forms are the informational report (a "report") and the two-sided position paper.

In a report, you examine a problem or an issue because you want to know more about it, and you think readers can benefit from knowing about it too. For this paper you can explain what something is; explain how something was formed, created, or discovered; or explain how something works. You can offer possible solutions for solving the problem or issue, or to better understand it. Many reports are brief histories. Some reports amount to a one-sided argument (a report on the negative effects of tobacco, for example).

Do you know anyone who could benefit from your research? A relative or a friend? Yourself? Suppose a health problem runs through your family: breast cancer, hemophilia, aneurysms. You can do research to find out more about it: what options can you find for combating the problem?

You may argue against gun control or recreational drugs, but as a researcher, you need to be impartial and fair-minded. You will need to weigh the information you gather and decide which is the clearest, the most helpful. You will need to decide which sources are the most reliable and which authors are truly experts. It is possible to write a report that <u>argues</u> against drinking alcohol, or you can write a paper that only <u>describes</u> the effects of drinking—either way, you must be impartial, fair, and accurate. For an example of an informational report, see Danelle Barber's research paper "GHB: Great Bodily Harm" in chapter 10.

The Two-Sided Paper

In a two-sided paper, the key strategy is to present other or opposing views before you defend your own position. This option requires more research and analysis; it is more challenging than an informational report.

In discussing any issue on which there is more than one position, you should present various sides of it—especially the side most contrary to your own. Presenting the opposing sides of an issue will show your audience that you are fair-minded. If you have presented both sides well, readers should be able to see which side has the stronger support. If you have been fair, your readers will listen more carefully to what you have to say. (See chapter 2 for more on writing about arguments and controversies.) For an example of a two-sided position paper, see Julie Mitchell's research paper "Should Humans Be Cloned?" in chapter 10.

ACTIVITY 1

In your notebook, explore three possible research questions you would like to investigate for your research paper. These questions must intrigue you or matter to you in some way. Keep these possible research topics tentative. You cannot decide for sure what your topic will be until you begin to research what information is available on it. Bring your notebook to class to share ideas with classmates.

MODERN RESEARCH

> I usually have to do five times the amount of research that I will need. [. . .] When I wrote the book about Buffalo Bill (This Old Bill), I had to read four or five books about the pony express because Bill rode the Pony Express when he was 14. I had to find out what kind of spurs he wore as a teenager. One little detail like that can cost you a day or two. (Estelman 8)

Modern libraries store many kinds of information: books, newspapers, magazines, journals, government documents, manuscripts, artworks, film, music, videos, photographs, historic artifacts . . . nearly anything that can be stored, protected, and retrieved. Researchers must work harder than ever to keep up with the constant flow of new research: you barely have time for all the reading you must do. There is so much information that researchers must specialize. Instead of all medicine, for example, medical researchers and doctors specialize in various divisions and subspecialties of medicine. Many doctors specialize in only one organ or only one system or one disease. It's not exactly a joke to say that modern scholars know more and more about less and less.

No matter what subject you choose, you are certain to find dozens of books, magazines, journals, and newspapers with articles about your subject. You may rightly feel appalled at the thought of so many books and articles confronting you: "Must I really read all that?" The answer seems to be yes and no. Most researchers say it's a good rule to read everything you can; therefore, the best tactic is to narrow your research to the smallest question you can. Fortunately, not everything you find is required reading. Much of it is simply repetitious. When one researcher publishes a significant paper, dozens of newspapers, magazines, television and radio news broadcasts repeat the findings, often without adding insight or criticism. For that reason, researchers attempt to find the "significant" or "reliable" sources, and you may be able to weed out some of the items in your working bibliography.

To reduce the amount of work you must do, you need to become knowledgeable about your subject. As you read the research, you will discover what is important and what isn't. It takes only a little reading about "cloning," for example, to come across the name of Ian Wilmut, the Scottish researcher who announced the cloning of "Dolly" the sheep. It takes only a little more reading to discover the name of Richard Seed, of Chicago, who announced his intention to clone a human being (thereby making himself at least a controversial figure in this research). Authors of books such as Lee Silver's Remaking Eden or Leon Kass's article "The Wisdom of Repugnance" in The New Republic are part of the groundwork of this subject. Your research itself will reveal the significant and reliable sources.

START IN THE LIBRARY

The library can help you decide what your project should be. Before making too many important decisions, you need to find out what information is available, what has already been done by other researchers. The library can guide you to material that will help you find a worthwhile project. Research writing starts with research reading. Fortunately, modern libraries have many sources of information that can provide you with ideas, for example, encyclopedias, indexes, or the main catalog. Most big libraries today have converted their catalogs to data banks, which can be searched electronically, and that can be enormously helpful to researchers. Real or virtual (electronic) catalog cards can lead you to useful information. The cards themselves may briefly list subject matter (see Fig. 7.1).

A brief search of the electronic catalog (the library's main catalog) can reveal how many sources—especially recent sources—are available, and the search can suggest whether the subject contains enough research for your purposes. Dolly the cloned lamb was announced in 1997 and by 1999 library data banks already contained dozens of books on the subject of cloning.

Fortunately, information isn't piled up in warehouses. If that were true you'd never have much chance to find anything. Most things in the library have a specific address called a "call" number that matches a shelf address. And powerful "search engines" can help you find material on the Internet. As we write this, google and alltheweb <http://www.alltheweb.com> are two of the fastest, and alltheweb claims to be the most comprehensive search engine, covering the entire Web, hence its name.

Figure 7.1. Catalog Card.

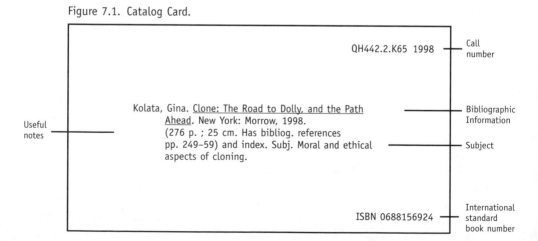

Preliminary Reading

The clearer and simpler your research question, the more likely you are to find an answer. Part of any project is the search for your thesis. Thus, you need a plan for finding your research question. The best procedure is to find your question in the research itself. No matter what your project is, you should start by reading the research. The cloning issue, for example, may include embryology, genetics, the human genome, assisted birthing, assisted fertilization (in vitro), DNA, inherited attributes and defects, microbiology—there is a lot to cover. Before you can make any meaningful decisions as a researcher, you must read. You must teach yourself the background of your project.

It's a mistake to try to decide in advance exactly what point to make— what question to examine or thesis to argue—before you have done the necessary background reading. It's too easy just to accept the conventional ideas everyone hears, such as deciding to write on the evils of smoking. "Conventional" ideas are ideas everyone knows. Knowing people who smoked all their lives without ill-effect isn't evidence.

Before deciding what exactly your research project will be, find out what other researchers have done. The library will show you (for example) what researchers have said about alcohol, tobacco, gun control, smoking, and other subjects. You need to know who favors and who is resisting the research and why. You will find there is more to any subject than you started with. For example, in the face of research against smoking, why do tobacco sales keep going up? What is the role of advertising in this subject? Does the government have a role in this research?

Preliminary reading will give you a background that will help you to evaluate where each new bit of evidence fits into your research. You need a <u>context</u> that will help you to understand the relative importance of the data you find. Preliminary reading gives you an overview of your subject, a context for your research, and an indication of the size of your project.

Locating Your Research Question

We have selected the subject of cloning to illustrate a process for finding a research question. No one, of course, could write everything about cloning. Writing "about" cloning would be a lot like writing "about" sports: the subject is enormous. You need some question about cloning, some subdivision, a smaller and more specific area of research than cloning itself. Strategy one is reading. That is where you will find your research question or topic: in the library. You may find a book in the library that seems just what you need: <u>The Deadly Effects of Smoking</u>. It may seem that someone has already done your research. If that is the case, perhaps you need a different topic.

However, you need to read first and then think about what you have read. Research does not mean copying from the library and pasting together the work of other researchers. Critical thinkers must read and <u>think</u>. How many sources can you find on this topic? You need a topic the research will sustain. Researchers are linked with chains of data in the library, and you need to read some of it before making important decisions about your project. Read encyclopedia entries on cloning; read articles on it; read a book or two about it. Researchers take their work seriously ... and so should you. Perhaps your topic has in fact been researched too much. Perhaps you need to apply more critical thinking to your topic. Read much, write little. And before you write, think, think, think. Make no assumptions about books or articles just because they have been published. Research starts in the libraries: the print library and the virtual libraries online.

STRATEGY ONE: FINDING BACKGROUND MATERIAL

A search strategy will give order to your work. Not all researchers work the same way, of course; eventually you'll work out your own procedures, but at the outset you'll find it helpful to proceed from general to more specific sources.

Look for background material before getting into more serious research. Background material creates a rough map: it doesn't show all the details, but it shows you the area and gives you an idea of how to get where you're going. Background reading can help you evaluate and make informed selections among all those library sources.

The General Encyclopedias

In print or online, the general encyclopedias provide summary backgrounds and histories. A quick look at an encyclopedia such as the Britannica or Americana will reveal that cloning is well known in plant horticulture, genetics and heredity, DNA, genes and genetic engineering, and immunity and acquired immunity. Britannica Online (an Internet site) includes 10,617 articles that mention cloning. Britannica Online[1] contains not only its own articles but links to many other Internet sites that discuss cloning, somatic cell genetics, genetic diseases, the story of Dolly the lamb, and the ethics of cloning. One of the virtues of encyclopedias is that they often contain bibliographies that will help you find reliable sources for your project. The encyclopedias give you an authoritative background. Then too, other researchers may assume you have certainly read the encyclopedia material. You should read the encyclopedias, of course, but how you use this material is a different question.

Always Use the Indexes

The most efficient way to find encyclopedia material is through the indexes. You will discover that encyclopedia subjects can be listed under various names. For example, in the index to the Encyclopedia Americana (1994), the cloning subject is listed as shown in Fig. 7.2, which indicates that genetics is a

---

[1]Spelled "on-line" as an adjective (Webster's New World College Dictionary 947).

Clone (genetics) 7:97.

Figure 7.2. From Index to <u>Encyclopedia Americana</u> (159).

broader category than <u>clone</u>. The index shows that an article on cloning can be found in volume 7, page 97. An excerpt (Figure 7.3, p. 474) from this article contains useful information. Furthermore, encyclopedia articles sometimes include short bibliographies, which means you can begin collecting your preliminary bibliography while still reading general reference works.

ACTIVITY 2

Consider one of the subjects you'd like to research. Find two or three general encyclopedias with articles related to this subject. Write a brief paper (1 to 2 pages) explaining your judgment on how these encyclopedia articles compare with each other and which you think would be the most useful for researchers.

Specialized Encyclopedias

In addition to the general encyclopedias, most libraries also contain specialized encyclopedias that focus on particular subjects. Note that libraries often use the words <u>encyclopedia</u> and <u>dictionary</u> interchangeably.

<u>Encyclopedia of American History</u>
<u>Dictionary of American History</u>
<u>Dictionary of Art</u>

a group of genetically identical cells or whole organisms derived from a single original cell or organism. Clones arise naturally in a number of ways. The body of an adult animal or plant is typically a clone of cells, having arisen by mitosis from a single cell, the fertilized egg. Within the body, a single cell may divide many times to produce a clone of cells with the same function.

Figure 7.3. From <u>Encyclopedia Americana</u> (97).

Encyclopedia of Bioethics
Encyclopedia of Religion
McGraw-Hill Encyclopedia of Science and Technology
New Grove Dictionary of Music and Musicians

Specialized encyclopedias and dictionaries deal with the subjects indicated in their titles. The information they contain is important background material for that subject. Anyone researching genetics, for example, would find the <u>Encyclopedia of Bioethics</u> especially useful. The index example (Fig. 7.4) shows a few of the articles related to cloning.

A brief excerpt from the main topic (reproductive technologies) shows the level of language and the amount of detailed information in this specialized ency-

Reproductive technologies, 2207–2247
    adoption vs., 2218, 2219–2220, 2234 . . .
    artificial insemination, 648, 749
    cloning, 957, 958
    cryopreservation of sperm, ova, and embryos, 436, 474, 475

Figure 7.4. From Index to <u>Encyclopedia of Bioethics</u>, Vol. 4, 1995 (2932).

REPRODUCTIVE TECHNOLOGIES: ETHICAL ISSUES
When the process of fertilization is external, the embryo becomes accessible to many forms of intervention. During the brief extracorporeal, in vitro period, embryos can be frozen, treated, implanted, experimented on, discarded, or donated. Theoretically, embryos that result from IVF could be cryopreserved for generations, so that a woman could give birth to her genetic uncle, siblings could be born to different sets of parents, or one sibling could be born to another. A 1993 experiment in which human embryos were split reawakened concerns about these sorts of possibilities, which had remained dormant since a mid-1970's controversy about cloning human beings (National Advisory Board, 1994).

Figure 7.5. Encyclopedia Excerpt. (Cohen, Cynthia B., "Reproductive Technologies: Ethical Issues." Encyclopedia of Bioethics, ed. Warren T. Reich. 5 vols. New York: Simon & Schuster Macmillan, 1995, 2237.)

clopedia. The Encyclopedia of Bioethics (Fig. 7.5) will help researchers interested in, for example, ethical questions about cloning. The Encyclopedia of Bioethics also has related subject areas, researchers' names, and bibliographic references you can use. Background research such as this should begin to awaken ideas about what your thesis question might be, and with this kind of background material, your bibliography will begin to grow. Note the passing reference to "a mid-1970's controversy about cloning human beings." A researcher should be curious to know what "controversy" is meant, and Cohen provides a reference.

Research is connected to research: you don't have to start from scratch. Background material in encyclopedias will connect you to the work of other researchers so that your project can grow from a context of information. You need to be able to answer questions about your project:

Why do it?
What is the point?
How can readers know your information is reliable?

When your project is supported by the work of other researchers, you will be able to answer such questions with confidence.

ACTIVITY 3

Find one or more specialized encyclopedias related to your research area. Write a page or two of notes on the relevant information.

The Growth Phenomenon: A Research Problem

It's important to keep your thesis restricted. In court a lawyer would not wish to defend the claim that "all street people are worthless slackers." That's an enormous and ill-defined charge. It might serve for an opinion paper, but not research. You need to start small and simple because no matter how simple an idea seems when you start, you may soon discover that your project is growing all by itself. As you delve into the research, you will discover that each new idea leads to others. Good researchers don't skip over all the new ideas they encounter. New ideas can help you refine your project, lead you into unexpected areas of research. For example, you might start by investigating "cloning" in general, learning about the procedures. However, almost from the start other questions will arise. The processes for cloning plants, frogs, mice, and lambs are interesting, perhaps, but the research suggests the important question concerns human clones. Information on how to make a clone soon leads to moral, ethical, and psychological questions. Scientists believe they know how to clone a human, but should they?

Critical Thinking in a Research Notebook

Merely collecting and synthesizing information isn't critical thinking. Summarizing, paraphrasing, and outlining are all useful kinds of note-taking activities, but they don't really require much of your own "thinking." In fact, notes often require you to reduce someone else's words to main- and subpoints, while keeping your own ideas out. Critical thinking is usually defined as "analytical," but that definition ignores its creative side. At the outset in your research, before you get very far into your subject, the research notebook is an essential tool. The notebook will help you to think both analytically and creatively: it can stimulate your own thoughts about what you are reading.

To think critically, you must react to your reading: respond, agree, disagree, challenge the reasoning, find contradictions and exaggerations, pursue side issues, wonder about what authors say. Look for insights, assumptions, and overgeneralizations (see chapter 2). Why does the author say that? What gives her the authority? Notebooks aren't quite the same as "notes," though you can treat them as notes if you wish. Notebooks are more like dialogues between you and the authors you are reading.

In the accompanying research notebook example, notice places where the reader seems to be talking to herself. The notebook illustrates an active, critical response to reading. Critical thinkers <u>react</u> to information. Just because something is published doesn't make it correct, nor does publication make anything too important to criticize. A research notebook encourages you to explore, to question, to think about, and to write about what you read. Think of your notebook as a place in which you can talk to yourself and ask questions about the research. Your notebook can help you find a worthwhile thesis. For help with your notes see "Suggestions for Your Research Notebook."

Mar 23, 2000

Watson, James D. "Moving toward the Clonal Man." <u>Atlantic Monthly</u>
   <www.theatlantic.com/unbound/flashbks/cloning/watson.htm> May
   1971: 50–53.

   Watson discusses the biogenetic mechanics of cloning (cites frog
clone 10 years earlier) and overall—I think—is pretty certain that a human
clone will appear 10 to 20 years from [1971]. The need for babies or
human duplicates will likely override any presumed horrors. The subject (he
says) needs extensive discussion and legislation before anyone tries it.
But, now (2000) seems it is about to work the other way: first will come
the clone and then will come the discussions and legislation (maybe). The
chief problem for America, he points out, is that most of this work is
being conducted elsewhere—England ("There is no American university
which has the strength in experimental embryology that Oxford
possesses" [6/7])—meaning we don't have much control over it. And, also,
it is fairly easy to do, so we can anticipate someone will eventually do it.
Scientists want to do it. People want them to do it. But Watson fears
the reactions that may follow: anti-science reactions, followed by the
cut-off of all funds for genetic research of every kind, maybe. However,
neither the USA nor Great Britain hold a monopoly on this research. We
can expect to see many other countries experimenting in this area. He
suggests tyrants may wish to have heirs for their throne, as well as
"potentialities for misuse by an inhumane totalitarian government" (2/7).

   Watson predicts the first human clone could appear in 20 to 50
years:

>   Thus, if the matter proceeds in its current nondirected
>   fashion, a human being born of clonal reproduction most
>   likely will appear on the earth within the next twenty to
>   fifty years, and even sooner, if some nation should actively
>   promote the venture. (5/7)

His prediction seems reasonable. But I think he has more to say about
the need/desire for children than about the negatives of cloning. Does
he make the assumption others do about what a "clone" means—an
exact duplicate of the donor? Same premise in movie <u>The Boys of
Brazil</u> in which children are cloned from Adolf Hitler's genes?
Assumption that the children will all grow up to be little Hitlers?

   Watson doesn't go very deep into arguments against human
cloning. Spiritual/emotional arguments (I think) should be as important
as mechanical problems involved. What happens, for example, to the
meaning of "human" and our relationship with God—and our respect for
life? We already kill off people by the millions in wars. What will happen
when we can generate them in labs? And make them any way we like?
Will we value that kind of life?

A Research Notebook.

SUGGESTIONS FOR YOUR RESEARCH NOTEBOOK

Give a complete bibliographic reference

If you borrow ideas or quote or paraphrase from your reading, always give a full reference, including page numbers. (See chapter 9.)

> Kass, Leon R. "The Wisdom of Repugnance: Why We Should Ban the Cloning of Humans." The New Republic 2 June 1997. 11 Mar. 1999 <http://web4.searchbank.com/infotrac/session.675/790/12/9966685w3/ !xxrnn-18b6m>.

Write Down Your Thoughts

We've been able to produce babies through "artificial" means for a long time. Farmers have been doing it for decades. Now suddenly cloning seems like something new and troublesome.

Ask Yourself Questions

Why is everyone so hot about cloning humans? If it's all right to clone animals, why not people? Suppose scientists discovered how to regenerate an amputated leg—would we have so much talk of upsetting nature or God's plan? If there were a way to revive a dead accident victim, wouldn't most people say do it? Are naturally born twins controversial?

Propose Answers, Speculate, Theorize

In World War II Hitler tried to produce an "Aryan" super race. Cloning raises fears about race selections and exclusions. If human cloning were a fact, could it be used to "purify" the races? Would there be another Holocaust, more millions of people put to death or sterilized ... ?

Write about Specifics in Your Reading

Kass says you can't have a right to reproduce because it takes two (or did, prior to cloning) and you can't have a "right" for more than one person. I don't think I get this. Don't rights apply to groups as well as individuals? Anyway it sounds kind of old fashioned—technology can overcome most problems of reproduction nowadays.

Your research notebook is a place for letting your mind delve into your reading and into your thoughts. It isn't only a place for summarizing or paraphrasing articles, activities that tend to limit your thinking to other people's thoughts. A stack of summaries doesn't tell you much. What do you think about the information in those summaries? The same can be said of paraphrases. Until you start thinking about the data, all you have is a condensed version of what someone else said. Critical thinking isn't simply memorizing. You need to assimilate information, think about it, respond to it.

ACTIVITY 4

Start a reading notebook for your research. Find an encyclopedia article (or two), a newspaper or magazine article, or a section of a book on one of the subjects that interests you. Interact with your reading. Write your thoughts: respond to your reading; pose questions for yourself. Write 1 or 2 pages in your notebook.

Notes and Note Cards

Research notes, by contrast with notebook entries, usually stick to the subject, though digressions are possible now and then. In your notes (versus your notebook) record information from the source material. "Notes" are summaries, paraphrases, quotes, and always the one absolute rule, the bibliographic information for each and every source you write about: no bibliography, no research (see Figure 7.6). Notes will be of little use if you can't say where they came from. (See chapter 9.) You may add a brief comment or two as a reminder about the source, but usually "notes" indicate what the source says. The rule for notes is read much, write little.

In addition to the bibliographic information, which you must have, you may also have an organizing label (see Figure 7.7, Note Card) to remind your-

17.0

Schwartz, Harry. "Cloning Dolly May Be Biggest News of
Our Lives." <u>Detroit Free Press</u> 28 Feb. 1997:
13A.

Figure 7.6. Bibliography Card with Code Number.

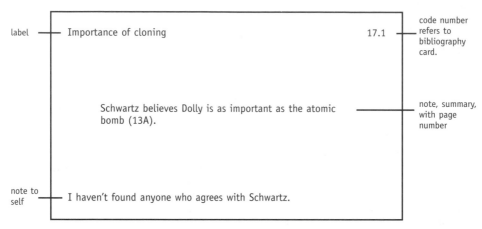

label ——— Importance of cloning   17.1 ——— code number refers to bibliography card.

Schwartz believes Dolly is as important as the atomic ——— note, summary, with page bomb (13A).   number

note to ——— I haven't found anyone who agrees with Schwartz.
self

Figure 7.7. Note Card.

self where the note belongs in your outline. Then too, you may want to use a numbering system so that you don't have to repeatedly write the bibliographic information. For example, you can assign a number (such as 17.0) to each item in your bibliography; Figure 7.7 shows the first note card for Schwartz (17.1). Additional cards for Schwartz need only code numbers (17.2, 17.3, and so on).

<u>Note</u>: Not all researchers use note cards. Some take notes on legal pads, for example, and carefully record information from one source at a time. However, sheets of paper are likely to encourage more writing than is necessary or good. Still, if you do take notes this way, make sure you document your sources: write down all bibliographic information, even if you probably won't use things such as volume and issue numbers, and be careful to quote accurately and cite page numbers.

STRATEGY TWO: LOOKING FOR BOOKS

A little background reading in the general reference works will give you an over-all sense of your subject, and that will help you begin your bibliography. If you aren't quite sure about your thesis, continue reading. You must start making your list of sources, but you can't wait to finish your list before you start read-ing. Researchers seldom have enough time: you must continue adding to your list of sources, but you must also start reading. Furthermore, each source you read may lead you to other sources—your list can soon get longer than you anticipated and longer than you have time to read.

One function of your early reading, therefore, is to help you identify the significant research. The more you read, the more you will understand which books and articles you should read and which ones you can eliminate. In the beginning your bibliography should contain too much rather than too little. A working bibliography isn't the same as the "Works Cited" that will accompany your paper: you probably won't use all the sources you collect nor even all those you read.

Bibliographies

Books in Print—Subject Guide, annual
Bibliographic Index: A Cumulative Bibliography of Bibliographies, 1938–
Cumulative Book Index, 1900–

The library has sources that can lead you to bibliographic information. A classic is Books in Print—Subject Guide—now available electronically. In it you will find an index of all the books currently in print in the United States. You can easily discover how many books have been published on your research topic. The 1996–97 Subject Guide contains 11 books, beginning with Cloning and the Constitution: An Inquiry into Governmental Policy Making and Genetic Experimentation by Ira H. Carmen (1986). Some of these books may look useful; some may not. One may be exactly what you're looking for. Books in Print is available on CD-ROM and in FirstSearch in many libraries. In February 1998 it listed 17 books regarding cloning.

You can find many useful references in these indexes. There are also many specific indexes you can use, such as the MLA International Bibliography for books concerning literature and languages.

Online Databases and Bookstores

If you have access to the Internet, you will find many places where you can search for books by subject, title, author, and sometimes other ways too (keywords for example). Finding book lists isn't the same as finding the books themselves, of course, but you do need to make a list before you can go hunting. Your working bibliography will reveal how much can be found on your subject. If you can't find many sources on the subject you have chosen, you need to rethink the subject. Also, although you might compile an impressive (long) bibliography from various indexes and sources, your library may not contain many items on your list—you should then rethink your subject.

The Library of Congress Online

If you are able to hunt for books online, one of the sites you could visit is the LC (Library of Congress). The Library of Congress, "the largest library in the world," keeps growing at the rate of many thousands of new acquisitions every day (books, manuscripts, maps, magazines, newspapers, music, photos, and so on). As we write this, the LC contains more than 100 million items, of which 12 million are available online. If you can get to the Internet, you can get to the Library of Congress <http://lcweb.loc.gov/> or <www.loc.gov>.

The traditional mission of the Library is to make sure that all branches of government are well informed. Members of Congress and ordinary citizens can reach the Library of Congress Online through its main page, or you can go directly to its online catalog <catalog.loc.gov> all day, any day of the week. The LC also contains the U.S. Copyright Office. In order to register for copyright, writers or their publishers must send at least one copy of any new book to the Copyright Office, and this greatly increases the size of the library over time.

Library of Congress Subject Headings

To find sources related to your subject you should consult the <u>Library of Congress: Subject Headings</u> (Fig. 7.8). This multivolume book is a complete alphabetical listing showing how subjects are organized in the Library of Congress.

Suppose in your research you become interested in transgenics—the process of transferring genes from one organism to another, as from a human to a dog (medical researchers sometimes use animals in seeking treatments for human diseases). If you look up <u>transgenics</u> in the online catalog, you will discover no records for it. For help then, you can look in the <u>LC Subject Headings</u>. Although you may not find <u>transgenics</u>, you will find <u>transgenic animals</u>.

Symbols and abbreviations in an index are usually explained in the front pages of the index. For example, <u>BT</u> in the <u>LC Subject Headings</u>, means "broader term"; <u>NT</u> means "narrower term"; and <u>RT</u> means "related term." To find more subject headings, suppose you decide to look up <u>genetic engineering</u> in the <u>LC Subject Headings</u>. You will find <u>transgenics</u> listed there as well as <u>biotechnology</u>, another useful term you might use. The <u>LC Subject Headings</u> can save you time and effort and may help you find more than enough books to start your research.

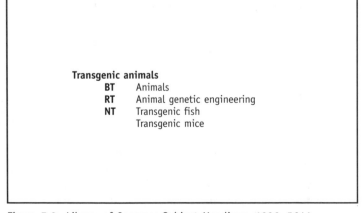

Figure 7.8. <u>Library of Congress Subject Headings</u>, 1996, 5644.

The Library of Congress Main Catalog

If you were researching <u>cloning</u>, you would find interesting facts about Dolly, the sheep that raised so much excitement in 1997, but also areas you hadn't anticipated:

> Cronkite, Eugene P., and A. L. Carsten, eds. "Conference on Application of Diffusion Chamber Culture in Study of Hemopoiesis, Clonal Growth of Tumors, and Cytogenetic and Carcinogenic Effects of Chemicals" (1979: Brookhaven National Laboratory). <u>Diffusion Chamber Culture: Hemo-poiesis, Cloning of Tumors, Cytogenetic and Carcinogenic Assays</u>. Berlin: Springer-Verlag, 1980.

Cronkite and Carsten show that some of this research is technical, related to cancer (tumors, carcinogenic assays), and difficult to read. Should you list this in your master bibliography? No, anything this technical and hard to read is probably too technical to be useful for students and should be excluded from the master bibliography.

However, the Library of Congress can be a good source. On the LC's new on-line search system, a simple search might look like this:

1. http://catalog.loc.gov: This uniform resource locator (URL) takes you directly to the on-line catalog.

2. Subject-name-title-call number: The catalog can be searched four different ways.

3. Name <u>Pence, Gregory</u>:   Type in a name (for example), last name first. Because of certain characteristics of the LOC catalog—you cannot limit a name search; the search automatically truncates entries—a name search is liable to produce all the names that are spelled like the one you want.

4. Result: See Figure 7.9.

The result shows this is the first entry for (several) authors named "Pence," that there are 9 titles for this author, and the "Heading" and the kind of information the Heading represents. These boxes contain "links" to the information: if you click on Pence's name with your pointer, you will see a Titles List, which, in this case, would be a list of Professor Pence's books. If you select one of the

#	*Titles*	*Headings*	*Heading Type*
1	9	Pence, Gregory E.	Personal Name

Figure 7.9. Simulated LC Search Result.

titles, the screen will jump to the appropriate library card (Figure 7.10). Add the book to your list; later, you can look for it in your school library.

Other Online Sources

In addition to the Library of Congress, you can find many other sources on the Internet. With search engines such as FirstSearch and InfoTrac (still listed as SearchBank in some places), you can find other databases online. You can also find online bookstores, such as www.amazon.com or www.barnesandnoble.com. These online bookstores have extensive holdings you can search. For example, at Amazon.com you can find several titles using just the search key, "clone." Among these are

> Kolata, Gina Bari. Clone: The Road to Dolly and the Path Ahead. New York: Morrow, 1998.
>
> McCuen, Gary E., ed. Cloning: Science and Society (Ideas in Conflict Series). Hudson, WI: Gem Publications, 1998.
>
> Pence, Gregory E. Who's Afraid of Human Cloning? Lanham, MD: Rowan & Littlefield, 1998.
>
> Silver, Lee M. Remaking Eden: Cloning and Beyond in a Brave New World. New York: Avon Books, 1997.

ACTIVITY 5

Select a book author from your research area; see what you can find out about the author or author's publications from an online source, such as the Library of Congress. Write a brief notebook entry concerning what you find. If you can't find anything in these sources, try one of the sources in your school library.

The Public Access Catalog

Cards from an online catalog may have information you can use to evaluate whether a source might be useful to you. The online card can provide you with the name of the author and title, whether there is a bibliography, the publisher, date of publication, and subject headings. The public access card in Figure 7.11 shows that the book by Lee M. Silver contains "bibliographic references," which means you can find sources the author used. The screen also gives you the call number you would need to find this book in the library (but note "Status: Checked Out").

If you were researching "cloning," the four subjects listed on the card

```
Who's afraid of human cloning? / Gregory E. Pence.
LC Control Number:
     97038513
Type of Material:
     Book (Print, Microform, Electronic, etc.)
Brief Description:
     Pence, Gregory E.
     Who's afraid of human cloning? / Gregory E. Pence.
     Lanham [Md.] : Rowman & Littlefield, c1998.
     xv, 181 p. ; 24 cm.
CALL NUMBER:
     QH442.2.P46 1998
     Copy 1
—Request in:
     Book Service: Jefferson (main Eur Hisp LHG) or
     Adams 5th fl
—Status:
     Not Charged
```

Figure 7.10. On-Line Library of Congress Catalog Card.

(human reproductive technology, genetic engineering, cloning, human genetics) would suggest that <u>Remaking Eden</u> might be useful to you. You may be able to make a printout of this screen, or make a handwritten bibliography note with the call number (see Fig. 7.12). If you do make a handwritten note, be sure to include all the information you will need to include this book in your bibliography and then look for the book on the shelves.

If you use the online catalogs as well as the print indexes for books, you will soon have a large number of items for your preliminary bibliography. Must you read all these books? No—as a researcher you can learn to skim effectively. A brief overview can tell you a lot: look through the table of contents, the index, and

```
                         Public Access Catalog
Call Number RG133.5 .S56 1997                    Status : Checked Out
     AUTHOR          1) Silver, Lee M.
     TITLE           Remaking Eden: Cloning and Beyond in a Brave New
                     World
     BIBLIOGRAPHY    Includes bibliographical references (pp. 255-306)
                     and Index.
     PUBLISHER       New York: Avon Books, 1997
     EDITION         1st ed.
     COLLATION       viii, 317 p. ; 24 cm.
     SUBJECTS
          1)Human reproductive technology.
          2)Genetic engineering.
          3)Cloning.
          4)Human genetics.
```

Figure 7.11. Example of a Public Access Catalog Card.

Figure 7.12. Handwritten Bibliography Note and Call Number.

any topical headings. An overview can help you decide which books are merely repetitions of information you already have, which are only shallow treatments of the subject, and which are authoritative but not too technical to be useful. You can expect to do a great deal of reading, and you must try to find the best sources available. When you find an unfamiliar book, try the index test: think of three things you believe should be in the index of a good book on your topic; then check to see whether any of them are listed. See if you can find the author listed anywhere. A little preliminary work can help you identify which books you need to read.

Note: Your library probably offers interlibrary loan services; if your library does not have a certain book you need, you may order it through interlibrary loan. A disadvantage of this service is that it may take more time than you can spare to receive the book.

ACTIVITY 6

Start a preliminary bibliography of half a dozen or so books. Use several different sources (don't take them all from Books in Print, for example).

STRATEGY THREE: LOOKING FOR ARTICLES

In the library you can find popular magazines, scholarly journals, and newspapers, collectively referred to as serials or periodicals, meaning published periodically. In addition to print indexes, many libraries now subscribe to on-line data banks such as InfoTrac (which purchased SearchBank), or FirstSearch to find articles. The on-line indexes are fast and easy to use, but the print indexes contain articles from further back in time. In addition, many magazines have their own Web sites from which you may explore their archives. For example

Atlantic Unbound <http://www.theatlantic.com>

BusinessWeek <http://www.businessweek.com>

Discover Magazine <http://www.enews.com:80/magazines/discover>

The New Republic <http://www.enews.com/magazines/tnr>

U.S. News & World Report <http://www.usnews.com/usnews>

In addition to online editions of well-known print magazines, there are a number of electronic magazines on the Web, such as Slate <http://www.slate.com> and The Web Magazine Online <http://www.webmagazine.com>.

Firstsearch

FirstSearch is probably the easiest source to use. FirstSearch allows you to find material in books, newspapers, and magazines and allows you to print out copies of the articles you find.

Readers' Guide to Periodical Literature

The Readers' Guide to Periodical Literature is a useful print index to popular magazines, starting with the year 1900. The Readers' Guide lists articles by author, by subject, and sometimes by title. The Guide is cross-indexed under many different descriptors. Many libraries now have the Readers' Guide online as well. No matter where you start, whether in electronics or in print, the indexes will soon lead you to many useful articles. Then too, the many headings and subheadings in the Readers' Guide can give you ideas for research as well as information for the ideas you already have.

The Readers' Guide to Periodical Literature is a popular source for general magazines in your own library, both in print and on CD-ROM. The Guide is kept up to date with monthly supplements. Many libraries have the Guide all the way back to 1900. Large libraries keep magazines in bound volumes and microform. You will find that many magazines have their own Web sites and maintain online archives; however, magazine archives can differ considerably. Time magazine, for example, <http://www.pathfinder.com/time/magazine/toc> archives back only to 1994.

A researcher using the Guide to find magazine articles on cloning would find an entry such as the one illustrated in Figure 7.13.

CLONES (BIOLOGY)

> See also
> Complementary DNA
> Molecular cloning
> Monoclonal antibodies

Can cloning help save beleaguered species? J. Cohen. il Science v276
p1329–30 My 30 '97
The Dolly debate [sheep cloned in Scotland] B. Wallace. il por
Maclean's v110 p54–8 Mr 10 '97
Spring cloning. S. Begley. il Newsweek v129 p82–83 Je 30 '97
The start of something big? [Aftermath of sheep cloning in Scotland]
T. Beardsley. il Scientific American v276 p15–16 My '97

Figure 7.13. Excerpt from Readers' Guide, Nov. 1997, 189.

Many magazine and newspaper sites can be accessed directly online. In most of them you can search the archives and download articles for a small fee. However, on-line archives differ considerably in their holdings. The New York Times, for example, archives only the previous 365 days; the Christian Science Monitor goes back to 1980. The Washington Post archives go back to 1977. One large online newspaper source is the Newspaper Index, which claims to archive 3,000 U.S. and international papers. The Index lists its top ten papers:

1. New York Times
2. Washington Post
3. Wall Street Journal
4. Los Angeles Times
5. USA Today
6. Chicago Tribune
7. Detroit News
8. Star Tribune (Minneapolis–St. Paul)
9. Christian Science Monitor
10. San Francisco Chronicle

Among those papers that maintain their own web sites are these:

New York Times <http://www.nytimes.com>
Christian Science Monitor <http://www.csmonitor.com>
Los Angeles Times <http://www.latimes.com>
Wall Street Journal <http://interactive.wsj.com>
Washington Post <http://www.washingtonpost.com>

ProQuest

Many libraries now subscribe to ProQuest, a comprehensive newspaper data bank, and some now have the New York Times archives and other data banks on CD-ROM, in addition to their newspaper print indexes. Figure 7.14 provides a brief selection from a ProQuest search for articles, using the search terms "cloning AND humans AND ethics."

To Use Popular Sources or Not

Some instructors believe that students should use only scholarly sources for research, not popular magazines. Others believe that some popular sources should be acceptable. Ask your instructors for their policies. News sources, such as Time, Newsweek, U.S. News & World Report, and others, are often considered responsible sources. Scientific and technical sources, such as Scientific American and Nature, are nearly always considered authoritative publications that you can rely on for scientific information. As always, when you read, evaluate your sources: consider whether the authors are well qualified, fair-minded, and logical. (See chapter 8, Evaluating Evidence.)

Divide your work in the library into steps or phases. Just as with books, you can reduce the time and effort you need in finding articles by first using the periodical indexes. Make yourself a bibliography of periodical articles. Preliminary reading or skimming can help you reduce the number of articles you must read. Follow the researchers' rule that the broader, more general the subject, the more articles you will find, possibly hundreds on a broad subject such as "cloning," which includes plant cloning, animal cloning, human cloning, genetics and heredity, medical ethics, bioethics, embryology, stem cell research, and so on. General subjects are like giant shopping carts into which you can place all the books, articles, and news accounts related to your subject. Even some of

---

At least 50 articles matched your search.
Ethical medicine; [FINAL Edition]; USA TODAY, Arlington; Jun
  22, 1999; pg. 01.D
Embryo Work Raises Specter of Human Harvesting; Medical
  Research Teams Draw Closer to Cloning; [FINAL Edition]; Rick
  Weiss; The Washington Post, Washington; Jun 14, 1999; pg.
  A.01
Animals Are One Thing, Humans Quite Another; Patrick Dixon;
  The Los Angeles Times, Los Angeles, Calif.; Dec 28, 1998;
  Record edition; pg. 5
Cloning a Human Cell; [Editorial]; New York Times, New York;
  Dec 18, 1998; Late Edition (East Coast); pg. A.34
Cloning: Where's the Outrage?; By Brian A. Brown; Wall Street
  Journal, New York; Feb 19, 1998; Eastern edition; pg. 1

Figure 7.14. Partial ProQuest Search Result.

the subdivisions of a topic can be covered by many dozens of periodical articles. Researchers, especially students, need to find a small subdivision of a subdivision. You may start out thinking about a broad, general subject, but you must keep reading and thinking critically until you find a small, specific research question. (See "The Growth Phenomenon" earlier in this chapter.)

Print Indexes for Popular Sources

If you do decide to look for articles in popular magazines and newspapers, here are some of the print indexes you might use:

POPULAR MAGAZINES

Essay and General Literature Index, 1900–
Poole's Index to Periodical Literature, 1802–1906
Readers' Guide to Periodical Literature, 1900–

GENERAL INTEREST NEWSPAPERS

Facts on File: A Weekly World News Digest, 1940–   Current events covered in newspapers
Newspaper Abstracts
New York Times Index, 1913–
Wall Street Journal Index, 1958–

Students are usually limited to those services the school library subscribes to, including services that charge fees to explore their holdings: those that will allow you to print or download full-text articles usually charge hefty fees. A Fax of an article in the British medical journal The Lancet, for which the copyright fee is $19, will cost $29 ($10 for Uncover's service in addition to the copyright). Uncover points out that you can probably find this article in your own library at no cost. The best use of such services is to help build the bibliography. Then use your school library to find the actual articles.

Research librarians can help you find lists of articles pertaining to your research subject as well as the articles themselves. If your library doesn't have all the magazines and journals you require, you may need to go to another library or order what you need through interlibrary loan. However, much use of interlibrary loan is probably a clue that you need to rethink your subject or thesis or both.

Start Where You Are

Research can be a big job, and many students want to know "Where should I start?" In general, the rule is start where you are. Look for the most recent sources first and then work your way back to earlier research. How far back you need to go depends on your project. You will find that recent sources rely on older research. Dolly the cloned sheep was announced in 1997, but questions about the ethics of cloning human beings are much older. Older data may no longer be valid (newer research may invalidate older). Research tends to age. Unless you are doing something historical, such as research about Adolf Hitler, you should seek the most recent information. Unless your project requires information from the past, all research should start in the here and now. Start with today's date: start where (or when) you are.

ACTIVITY 7

Use at least three newspaper and magazine indexes to find half a dozen articles on your research topic. Compile a preliminary bibliography of periodical articles. Don't take all your articles from the same index (don't take them all from the Readers' Guide, for example).

Professional, Technical, and Specialty Journals

In addition to the general magazine and newspaper indexes, there are many specialized indexes covering professional journals and other information not generally found in popular magazines. Many academic disciplines have one or more indexes in which you can find articles written for an audience of well-educated readers. Often journals are intended for members within a particular profession. For example, College English is intended for an audience of college English instructors. The following list shows some of the special indexes available in libraries.

Art: Art Index, Humanities Index

Biology: General Science Index, Bibliography of Bioethics, Biology Digest, Biological Abstracts

Business: Social Sciences Index, Business Periodicals Index, BusinessNews, ABI Inform (American Business Institute)

Chemistry: General Science Index, Chemical Abstracts

Communication: Social Sciences Index, ComIndex, Communication Abstracts

Computer science: ACM Guide to Computing Literature, Microcomputer Abstracts

Dance: Humanities Index, Art Index, Physical Education Index

Economics: Social Sciences Index, Index to Economic Journals, ABI Inform

Education: Education Index, ERIC

Geology: General Science Index, GEOBASE

History: <u>Humanities Index</u>, <u>Historical Abstracts</u>, <u>GPO</u> (Government Publications Office), <u>American History and Life</u>

Humanities: <u>Humanities Index</u>, <u>Arts and Humanities Search</u>

Languages and literature: <u>Humanities Index</u>, <u>MLA International Bibliography</u>

Mathematics: <u>General Science Index</u>, <u>ACM Guide to Computing Literature</u>, <u>Mathematical Reviews</u>

Music: <u>Humanities Index</u>, <u>RILM Abstracts</u>, <u>Music Index</u>

Philosophy: <u>Humanities Index</u>, <u>Philosophers Index</u>

Physics: <u>General Science Index</u>, <u>Current Physics Index</u>

Political science: <u>Social Sciences Index</u>, <u>GPO</u>, <u>Public Affairs Information Service Bulletin</u>, <u>Vital Speeches of the Day</u>

Psychology: <u>Social Sciences Index</u>, <u>General Science Index</u>, <u>PsychINFO</u>

Religion: <u>Humanities Index</u>, <u>Religion Index One</u>

Sociology: <u>Social Sciences Index</u>, <u>Sociological Abstracts</u>

Theater: <u>Humanities Index</u>, <u>Social Sciences Index</u>

Women's studies: <u>Women Studies Abstracts</u>, <u>Contemporary Women's Issues</u>

Find out as much as you can about your library's indexes. The indexes can give you many articles on practically any subject. Pay particular attention to cross-referencing, such as "See also," under subject headings. For example, the <u>Bibliography of Bioethics</u> index (1997) lists two articles on human cloning along with a cross-reference: "<u>See also</u> Reproductive technologies (166)." Under this heading the index lists 10 pages of articles, several of which pertain to cloning.

ACTIVITY 8

Use the indexes for professional journals to find articles related to your research topic. Compile a preliminary bibliography of half a dozen journal articles. Don't take all your references from the same index.

STRATEGY FOUR: LOOKING FOR REPORTS, OTHER SPECIALIZED INFORMATION

Government Documents, Reports

<u>Congressional Directory</u>, 1809–   The <u>Congressional Directory</u> is a "Who's Who" or "Who's Where" in the federal government. The <u>Directory</u> identifies Congress and its committees; the courts and judges; and agencies and officers of the execu-

tive branch; including names, addresses, phone numbers, and so on. To acquire information from any branch of government, you must first find the appropriate person or agency.

Congressional Record Index– The Congressional Record Index is compiled after each session of Congress: there is no cumulative index. To use the CRI, you must know when a subject was discussed in Congress. The Congressional Record contains transcripts (sometimes edited and "expanded") of what was said each day on the floor of the House of Representatives and the Senate.

Statesman's Year-Book, 1864– Statistics and historical annual.

Subject Bibliography Index—The SBI is a list of bibliographies. Many specialized indexes are now on-line or on CD-ROM. GPO Access is the on-line index to all federal government information <http://www.access.gpo.gov/su_docs/index.html>. GPO (U.S. Government Printing Office) can also be accessed through FirstSearch.

United States Government Organization Manual

United States Government Publications: Monthly Catalog, 1895–

Statistical Information

County and City Data Book

Statistical Abstract of the United States, 1879– Prepared by the U.S. Bureau of the Census: Government Printing Office (GPO). The SAUS contains facts and figures about America and Americans. The Statistical Abstract is available through GPO Access, but it does have its own site address: <http://www.census.gov/statab/www/>.

Vital Statistics of the United States

The World Almanac and Book of Facts

Biographical Sources Online

You may need to identify authorities, experts, specialists, and researchers in order to determine whether they are true authorities in their fields. You can find many biographical sources online, many of which are simply advertisements for print sources (such as Who's Who) and it can be difficult to find biographical information on living people, especially if they aren't celebrities.

Academy of Achievement <http://www.achievement.org/autodac/pagegen/gallery-achieve.html>

American Men and Women of Science 1972– <http://palimpsest.stanford.edu/byform/mailing-lists/exlibris/1995/08/msg00255.html>

Available on CD-ROM <http://www.asog.co.at/spcatalog/amwses.htm>

Biographical Dictionary <http://www.s9.com/biography>

Biography <http://www.biography.com> [celebrities]

Biography Master Index <http://library.dialog.com/bluesheets/html/bl0287.html>

Dictionary of Literary Biography <http://www.ottakars.co.uk>

Directories of Scientists from Micro World <http://www.mwrn.com/feature/people.htm>

Directory of American Scholars <http://www.lib.lawrence.edu:8080/LUCIA1/AAR-2256> (Must have Lawrence University ID)

4000 Years of Women in Science <http://www.astr.ua.edu/4000WS>

National Faculty Directory <http://www.lib.lawrence.edu:8080/LUCIA1/AAR-2258> (Must have Lawrence University ID)

PBS History: Biographies <http://www.pbs.org/history/bios.html>

Professors Studying Genetics and Ethics <http://www.ethics.ubc.ca/brynw/profs.html>

Abbreviations and symbols in directories such as American Men and Women of Science, for example, are usually explained in the front of the directory: "Res fel" (Research fellow). Does Lee Silver have solid credentials? Yes, you can see where he graduated, where he has taught, his areas of expertise, and some of his areas of research. He is an authority on genetics, particularly in embryology (Figure 7.15).

If you get an error message at an Internet site, try truncating the address: for example, <http://www.ethics.ubc.ca/brynw/profs.html> can be shortened to <http://www.ethics.ubc.ca>.

Because the Web has become so huge, and search engines so powerful, you may be able to find biographical information simply by searching for names. For example, Gregory E. Pence, author of Who's Afraid of Human Cloning (Rowman & Littlefield, 1998), can be found by searching for "Pence, Gregory E." Using google or www.alltheweb.com, researchers can find articles on Ian Wilmut simply by searching for his name. It's true that most people who are listed on the Web are there because they have written a book, won a prize, or

---

Silver, Lee Merrill, DEVELOPMENTAL GENETICS, MOLEC-ULAR BIOLOGY. Current Pos: PROF, PRINCETON UNIV, 84- Personal Data: b Philadelphia, Pa, Apr 27, 52; m 74; c 2. Educ: Univ Pa, BA & MS, 73; Harvard Univ, PhD(biophys), 78. Prof Exp: Res fel genetics, Sloan Kettering Cancer Inst, 77–79, assoc, 79–80; sr staff investr, Cold Spring Harbor Lab, 80–84. Concurrent Pos: Fel, Pop Coun, 77–78 & NIH, 78–79; asst prof genetics, Med Sch, Cornell Univ, 79–80 & State Univ NY Stony Brook, 80-; vis asst prof genetics, Albert Einstein Col Med, 80; ed, Mammalian Arome, 89- Mem: Am Soc Cell Biol; AAAS; Int Soc Differentiation; Genetics Soc Am. Res: Molecular embryology; molecular biology of spermatogenesis; the mouse T/t complex; chromosomal proteins; cell surface proteins. Mailing Add: 24 Andrews Lane Princeton NJ 08540.

Figure 7.15. Excerpt from American Men and Women of Science, 1995–96 Edition (918).

have been featured in the news for some noteworthy achievement. The ordinary researcher, who has published an article but has yet to achieve a major distinction, can be harder to find. Scholarly journals frequently give a brief identification of authors of articles. If all else fails, you can try calling or writing to the publisher of the article.

ACTIVITY 9

Use two or three sources to find biographical information on an authority in your research. Write approximately a page describing and explaining his or her credentials. Be sure to include source information.

Book Reviews

Book reviews can help you identify research material. Newspapers and magazines often contain reviews. Check major newspapers such as the <u>New York Times,</u> and search the <u>Readers' Guide</u> under the title or the author's name. You can also use special reference works devoted to book reviews:

> <u>Book Review Digest</u>, 1905
> <u>Book Review Index</u>, 1965–
> <u>Technical Book Review Index</u>, 1917–1988
> <u>Book Reviews Online</u> (Mental illness) <http://www.apollonian.com/book/review.asp>
> <u>Book Reviews Online</u> (Best sellers) <http://www.bookspot.com/>
> <u>Book Reviews Online</u> (Various) <http://www.worldlibraries.com/>

Here is part of a review of Gregory Pence's <u>Who's Afraid of Human Cloning?</u> (Rowman & Littlefield, 1998). The review was written by Mary Chitty for <u>Library Journal</u>, Dec. 1997 (143). She gives Pence's book a grade of "B."

Excerpt from a Book Review

With human cloning such a hot topic, there is considerable need for clear explanations of the unresolved and complex science and social and ethical issues. Bioethicist Pence (philosophy, University of Alabama) tackles the subject head on, arguing for human cloning as a reproductive option. Pence's strengths include his take on the much-hyped issue of genetics (over) determinism, useful analogies to in-vitro fertilization, and coherent reasons for preferring regulation over legislative bans. Unfortunately, the flippant and dismissive tone detracts from his arguments and trivializes difficult issues. The focus on babymaking obscures the opportunity to gain insight into basic human physiology.

This review is useful because it offers both strengths and weaknesses in Pence's book, according to Mary Chitty.

STRATEGY FIVE: USING ELECTRONIC SOURCES AND MICROFORM READERS

Modern libraries contain many electronic aids to help you with research. Seated at a computer, you can search databases by subject headings, and in some cases you may be able to download or print out complete texts of the articles you need. If you have your own computer and modem, you might do some research at home, though you will still need to spend time in the library to find many of the books and articles you want.

Not all colleges and universities have the same databases, electronic collections of information, such as bibliographies. Some of the major online and/or CD-ROM databases are FirstSearch (which provides access to 60 databases), InfoTrac (which is still called SearchBank in some places), JSTOR, ProjectMuse, The Electric Library, Uncover, and Lexis-Nexis. As we write this, Lexis-Nexis claims, "Several million documents are added each week to the billions available on Lexis-Nexis" <www.lexis-nexis.com/1ncc/>. Lexis-Nexis charges a fee for its articles, as do most information services. Check with your librarians to find out which services are available to you, the procedures you must follow, and what fees, if any, are involved. If you have access to an on-line service such as aol.com or gte.net, or any of the other Internet services, you can investigate the Internet Public Library (IPL) <www.ipl.org> a popular online virtual library. The IPL offers access to research materials as well as guidelines for writing research papers.

Many databases contain online versions of printed indexes. You can look for indexes on-line, but many are already available in your own library, as printed texts or on CD-ROMs or through subscription to one of the services offering indexes (and full-text copies) of newspaper, magazine, and journal articles, as well as full-text books (see the Gutenberg Project <http://promo.net/pg/>) that you can download to your own machine or a disk. If you planned to compare Dickens's <u>David Copperfield</u> and <u>Great Expectations</u>, you might find it immensely helpful to have both texts on your computer, where you could then search for points of similarity or contrast. The Gutenberg Project stores all the books, carefully checked for accuracy, in plain ASCII text so that they take up very little space and can be read on any computer.

In some cases reference librarians may be able to help you order a computer-generated bibliography on your specific research question (sometimes with a small fee). Most libraries have printed instruction sheets for their standard procedures—especially in the reference library—so that students can find available services.

Microform Readers

Microform is a general term for microfilm and microfiche. Microfilm looks somewhat like photographic film: it's wound on a spool or reel. Microfiche (pronounced "micra-feesh") is a small sheet of film material about the size and shape of a postcard. An entire issue of a newspaper or magazine can be reproduced on a single spool of microfilm or a single microfiche sheet.

Microforms store back issues of newspapers and some editions of magazines. Educational Resources Information Center (ERIC) documents and other kinds of books, pamphlets, and so on are also stored on microform. To find information on microform, you usually need the date of publication. For example, the New York Times Index provides dates on which articles appeared. Using dates from an index, you can locate the microforms you need.

ACTIVITY 10

Using the date of your birth, find the appropriate microform issue of the New York Times; write a brief synopsis of newsworthy events on the day you were born.

_____

The Master Bibliography

In addition to providing you with your research topic, your research thesis, and some background in the research area, your library strategies must help you develop a working or "master" bibliography for your project. Your master bibliography provides a significant control on your project. Before deciding anything too specific about your work, you must first begin to compile a bibliography, and while you are doing that, you must begin to read. You need to know whether there is enough research to support your project.

When you start reading from your bibliography, you will begin to understand what research has already been done, what research needs to be done, what subdivisions exist in the subject, and finally which subdivision interests you and may interest your audience. Because research papers are often planned as semester-long projects, you need to pace yourself and find as much relevant material as you can.

A master bibliography can be many pages long. Part of a master bibliography on cloning appears on the following pages. Most of the items concern the morality and ethics of cloning.

A. Gruenwald
English 101
15 May 2000
Professor Kiely

Cloning Master Bibliography

Andrews, Lori. "Human Cloning: Assessing the Ethical and Legal
    Quandaries." <u>Chronicle of Higher Education</u> 13 Feb. 1998:
    B4-5.
Beals, Gregory, and Larry Reibstein. "A Cloned Chop, Anyone?"
    <u>Newsweek</u> 10 Mar. 1997: 58.
Beardsley, Tim. "A Clone in Sheep's Clothing. <u>Scientific
    American</u> 3 Mar. 1997. 15 Nov. 1998 <http://www.sciam.com/
    explorations/030397clone/030397beards.html>.
Begley, S. "Little Lamb, Who Made Thee?" <u>Newsweek</u> 10 Mar. 1997:
    53-59.
Berreby, David. "Multiplicity Cloning, Nature, and Nurture."
    <u>Slate</u> 1 Mar. 1997. [Part of Slate series: <u>The Week/The
    Clones</u>] 15 Dec. 1998 <http://www.slate.com/Features/
    Multiplicity/Multiplicity.asp.>.
"Biology: Significant Scientific Discoveries in Biology."
    <u>New York Public Library Science Desk Reference</u> 1 Jan. 1995.
Campbell, K. H. S., J. McWhir, W. A. Ritchie, and I. Wilmut.
    "Sheep Cloned by Nuclear Transfer from a Cultured Cell
    Line." <u>Nature</u> 380 (7 Mar. 1996): 64-66.
"Caught Napping by Clones." Editorial. <u>Nature</u> 385 (1997): 753.
"Cloning." <u>Compton's Interactive Encyclopedia</u>. CD. 1997 edition.
"Cloning Isn't Sexy." Editorial. <u>Commonweal</u> 28 Mar. 1997. 27
    Feb. 1998 <http://web3.searchbank.com/infotrac/session/990/
    66/10326127w3/17!xrn_68&bkm_62>.
Coates, James. "The Online Grapevine: Web, Usenet, Spawn Flood
    of Falsehoods." 9 Nov. 1996. 28 May 1999
    <http://www.chicago.tribune.com/news/conspire/conspire.htm>.
"Dutch Pull the Plug on Cow Cloning." <u>Science</u> 279 (1998): 1444.
Human Cloning Foundation. <u>The Benefits of Human Cloning</u> 15 Nov.
    1998. 16 Nov. 1998 <http://www.humancloning.org>.
Kass, Leon, and James Q. Wilson. <u>The Ethics of Human Cloning</u>.
    Washington, DC: AEI Press, 1998.

Gruenwald 2

Kass, Leon R. "The Wisdom of Repugnance: Why We Should Ban
     the Cloning of Humans." The New Republic 2 June 1997. 11
     Mar. 1999 <http://web4.searchbank.com/infotrac/session.675/
     790/12/9966685w3/!xxrnn-18b6m>.

Kolata, Gina. Clone: The Road to Dolly and the Path Ahead. New
     York: Morrow, 1998.

Krauthammer, Charles. "Of Mice and Men: The Ultimate Cloning
     Horror: Human Organ Farms." Time 19 Jan. 1998. 5 Apr. 1999
     <http://www.time.com/time/magazine/1998/dom/980119/
     essay1.html>.

Kuczynski, Alex. "Slate's Coverage of Microsoft Trial Is
     Proving Difficult." New York Times Online Archives 17 Nov.
     1998. 14 June 1999 <http://archives.nytimes.com/archives/
     search/fastweb?search>.

Maloney, Janice. "Gates's Favorite Geek Walks Out the Door:
     After 13 Years, Myhrvold Calls Tt Quits." 1 June 1999. 14
     June 1999 <http://cgi.pathfinder.com/time/daily/
     0,2960,25938,00.html>.

McKinnel, Robert Gilmore. Cloning of Frogs, Mice, and Other
     Animals. Minneapolis: U of Minnesota P, 1985.

Myhrvold, Nathan. "Human Clones: Why Not? Opposition to Cloning
     Isn't Luddism—It's Racism." Slate 13 Mar. 1997. 13 Mar. 1997
     <http://www.slate.com/CriticalMass/97-03-13/
     CriticalMass.asp>.

Nussbaum, Martha Craven, and Cass R. Sunstein, eds. Clones and
     Clones: Facts and Fantasies about Human Cloning. New York:
     Norton, 1998.

Pence, Gregory E., ed. Flesh of My Flesh: The Ethics of
     Cloning Humans: A Reader. Lanham, MD: Rowman, 1998.
     ---, ed. Who's Afraid of Human Cloning? Lanham, MD:
     Rowman, 1998.

Post, Stephen G. "The Judeo-Christian Case against Human
     Cloning." America 21 June 1997: 19-22.

Robertson, John. "Human Cloning and the Challenge of
     Regulation." New England Journal of Medicine 339.2 (1998):
     119-22. 12 Dec. 1999 <www.humancloning.org>.

Rosa, Linda, Emily Rosa, Larry Sarner, and Stephen Barrett. "A
     Close Look at Therapeutic Touch." JAMA 1 Apr. 1998:
     1005-10. 1 Apr. 1998. 10 June 1999 <http://www.ama-
     assn.org/sci-pubs/journals/archive/jama/vol_279/no_13/
     joc71352.htm>.

Tanos, Vasilios, and Joseph G. Schenker. "Is Human Cloning
    Justified?" Journal of Assisted Reproduction and Genetics
    15.1 (1998): 1. 27 Mar. 1999 <http://uncweb.carl.org.80/
    cgi-bin/fullRecord?25267+45+-890150969>.

United States. National Bioethics Advisory Commission. Cloning
    Human Beings: Report and Recommendations of the National
    Bioethics Advisory Commission. Rockville, MD: The
    Commission, 1997.

"U.S. Congress Battles on Human Cloning." The Lancet 351
    (1998): 506. 15 Mar. 1999 <http://uncweb.carl.org:80/
    cgi-bin/fullRecord?25267+103+-890150969>.

Vere, Steven. The Case for Cloning Humans. 16 Nov.1998. 6 Apr.
    1999 <http://www.best.com/~vere/cloning.htm>.

Wachbroit, Robert. "Genetic Encores: The Ethics of Human
    Cloning." Report on Ethics of Human Cloning: Institute for
    Philosophy and Public Policy, Fall 1997. 3 Apr. 1998
    <http://www.puaf.umd.edu/ippp/Fall97Report/Cloning.htm>.

Walliser, Tristanne L. "Scientists and Ethicists Raise Red
    Flags: Too Early to Send in the Clones." 13 Feb. 1998. 17
    Feb. 1998 <http://www.abcnews.com/sections/living/
    DailyNews/clones0213.html>.

Watson, James D. "Moving toward the Clonal Man: Is This What
    We Want?" Atlantic Unbound May 1971. 3 Apr. 1998
    <http://www.theatlantic.com/unbound/flashbks/cloning/
    watson.htm>.

Weiss, Rick. "Ethics Board to Review Cloning's Implications."
    Washington Post Online 25 Feb. 1997. 27 Mar. 1997
    <http://www.washingtonpost.com/wp-srv/wPlate/1997-02/25/
    087L-022597-idx.html>.

Wertz, Dorothy C. "Cloning Humans: Is It Ethical?" The Gene
    Letter 1.5 (1997). 16 Nov. 1998
    <http://www.geneletter.org/0397/cloning.htm>.

Wilmut, Ian. "The Uses and Ethics of Cloning." Britannica
    Online. Book of the Year (1998): The Uses and Ethics of
    Cloning. 10 Mar. 1999 <http://www.eb.com:180/
    cgi-bin/g?DocF=boy/98/L02921.html>.

Wilmut, Ian, A. E. Schnieke, J. McWhir, A. J. Kind, and K. H.
    S. Campbell. "Viable Offspring Derived from Fetal and
    Adult Mammalian Cells." Nature 385 (Feb 1997): 810-13.

Winters, Paul A., ed. Cloning. San Diego: Greenhaven, 1998.

Example Master Bibliography.

ACTIVITY 11

Using strategies from this chapter and as many sources as you can, compile a master bibliography on your research topic. Try to be as thorough and comprehensive as possible: find magazine, newspaper, and journal articles; books, government publications—anything that relates to your research. Look especially for the most recent sources.

WRITING A RESEARCH PROPOSAL

Research projects often start with a proposal. Ask your instructor. Proposals can be helpful: they can reveal a lot about your project before you get very far into it. The bigger the project, the more helpful the proposal, but even small projects can benefit from a proposal. The proposal explains what you plan to do. Proposals allow for critical feedback at the outset, and they may prevent research problems from becoming troublesome.

The point of a proposal, or "prospectus," is to describe your project well enough so that other researchers or an instructor can evaluate your work and, if needed, suggest changes. The proposal ensures that you have done preliminary reading so that your project will be research based. Not all proposals are the same, but in general the proposal tells (1) what you want to do, (2) how you will do it, and (3) what you will do it with. On the basis of the proposal, researchers may be allowed to continue with their project—or not: your proposal must convince readers that you are capable of doing the project and that the project is worthwhile.

Your proposal should be as thorough, accurate, and professionally prepared as you can make it. For that reason we have provided examples of more divisions than you may actually need. Not all students will wish to use all these different components of a proposal, but they could. We have presented these components separately in order to illustrate them clearly, but obviously they would be subdivisions within your finished proposal.

Giving the Background Research

The background in a proposal is often a history—what research has gone before. What research leads to your project (how does your project connect to other research)? The background helps readers understand "why?" Why should anyone do this research? The answer isn't usually "because I like it, I'm interested in it." Your answer should be that something in the research (which you will describe) has led you to your project. The answer should be found in your preliminary reading: for example, genetic researchers are certain that soon it

will be possible to clone humans, but bioethicists are raising powerful objections to such experimentation. The possibility of any such research is already
extremely controversial.

Example Background

Is There Any Value in Human Cloning?

                            Background

     Scientists have been cloning animals (frogs, mice) for   1
decades: many animals' eggs develop outside the animal, where
they are easy to manipulate. But scientific attention was
alerted to the notion of <u>human</u> cloning in 1966 by Nobel
Laureate geneticist, Joshua Lederberg, who felt there were
advantages to be gained from cloning humans (in Kass 17).
However, the development of the human embryo inside the human
uterus causes enough problems that cloning humans did not seem
a realistic option until the discovery of a practical in vitro
[in glass] procedure by Edwards and Steptoe (in Watson 2).

     The public assumed the question was pointless. Scientists   2
continued to claim it was not possible to clone humans, or, if
it was possible, it certainly should not be allowed. But, the
idea of cloning began to catch on, especially in Hollywood
(Begley 58), which offered tales about evil twins, doubles, and
human clones, as in <u>Invasion of the Body Snatchers</u>, 1978, a
sci-fi classic in which aliens arrive in the form of "pods"
capable of producing exact, alien replicas of earthlings.
Hollywood also made a number of films based on cloning, such
as <u>The Boys from Brazil</u>, 1979, in which clones of Adolf Hitler
were raised in secret, and <u>Jurassic Park</u>, 1993, in which
dinosaurs were cultured from genetic material found in mosquito
blood. Hollywood showed that "fooling with Mother Nature" was
usually disastrous, as in the 1931 <u>Frankenstein</u>. Scientists
continued to reassure people that cloning a human was not
possible.

     Then in 1997, "the biggest news of our lives" (Schwartz   3
13A) appeared in media everywhere. Researchers in Scotland--
Keith Campbell and Ian Wilmut et al., at the Roslin Institute--
announced they had cloned a sheep from an adult cell (Begley
58). Cloning a sheep was not news, but using genetic material
from an adult animal was. According to Schwartz, "It's one of

the major events of the 20th Century, right up there with the development of nuclear weapons and the discovery of the nature of DNA" (13A).

Scientists had thought that adult cells could no longer develop. An adult ear cell can no longer be anything but an ear; an adult kidney cell can only be a kidney, they thought. In short, scientists believed adult cells can no longer differentiate: only fetal cells have the ability to differentiate, to develop into entire animals or any parts of them. That's why the news was so big. An adult cell had been used to produce "Dolly" the sheep. Using an adult cell gives scientists the advantage of knowing exactly what the new animal will be like. Schwartz uses the term "crap shoot" to describe the outcome with fetal cells (13A).

4

With an adult cell, Dolly the sheep would not be a guessing game: she would be the twin of the sheep that supplied the genetic material. Cloning lets us know exactly what the clone will and also will not be. The clone won't be, for example, a sickly, diseased, or sterile animal (unless those problems exist in the donor). Dolly gave scientists the ability to produce any sort of animal and to avoid anything they don't want. In short, science seems to have gained an advantage over natural procreation.

5

Describing Your Project

You must describe what you plan to do. The description is used more often in primary, hands-on research, but it can also be useful in library or secondary research. If you plan to use a questionnaire, for example, you must describe the questionnaire: "I'm going to ask people for their opinions on human cloning." If you are going to do a statistical analysis of your questionnaire, you should describe the statistical tests you will use, and why. Much research is done in the library, and in general your proposal for library work should state that you intend to find and collect the available research, analyze it, and then draw conclusions based on your reading. The "description" of your project answers the question, "What will you do?"

You need to pay attention to the language in your proposal: words like "explore," "discuss," and "analyze" mean different things to different people. "My project will be a study of cloning" is too vague. What do you mean by "a study"? (See "Developing Your Thesis" in chapter 1.)

Your proposal should be written as if the project were your own idea. Even if your instructor has given you the assignment, you should describe the project as what <u>you</u> want to do, not what the instructor wants you to do. No matter how the project started, you are responsible for how it turns out. Anyone, not only your instructor, should be able to read your proposal and discover what your project is.

Example Description

```
                           Description

    This research will summarize the presumed bioethical
outcomes of cloning human beings from adult cells. The project
will produce a documented essay of 10 to 12 pages that explain
bioethicists' projections of the consequences of the genetic
breakthrough by Wilmut et al. Because preliminary research
reveals that bioethicists are of different opinions—or that
they report different positions on this question—this report
will take the form of advantages and disadvantages of cloning
adult human cells.
```

Explaining Your Methods and Procedures

Sometimes the "Procedures" section of a proposal merely elaborates on the description; sometimes it is written as part of the description. In some research, however, the procedure can be a separate section called "method." If you are going to use mice or mayflies for genetic experiments, you must explain your methods in detail. For example, "I will randomly divide 100 mice into two groups of 50, which will be kept in separate cages. One group will receive the experimental treatment; the other will be the 'control' group," and so on: and then you would have to explain or describe the "experimental treatment" in detail.

If you plan to use library materials, which ones? How many? How will you find them? What will be your collection technique? It's a good idea to list the different kinds of materials you will seek: books, journals, government documents, reputable magazines, and so on; what indexes you will use, and perhaps why. Your readers need to be assured that you are familiar with library materials and have a plan for using them and that your procedure is likely to produce the result you want. Instructors need to believe that your procedure will lead you to the answer to your question, especially if you plan to search the Web or other parts of the Internet.

Example Methods and Procedures

Methods and Procedures

The data for this research will come from libraries, [1] electronic data banks, and other sources on the Internet. The procedure will be to begin collecting a working or <u>master bibliography</u> of sources on advantages and disadvantages, problems of human cloning, and other relevant descriptors. Library sources for the bibliography will include card catalogs, periodical and journal indexes, and government sources.

In addition, electronic sources will include various [2] Internet sites, such as newspaper and magazine archives, professional journal indexes, perhaps bookstores such as Amazon.com and BarnesandNoble.com, and the Library of Congress (CongressLoc.gov).

The procedure will be to draw up a rough outline based [3] on preliminary reading and then to read and collect notes, following the researchers' rule: read much, write little.

Anticipating Problems and Requirements in Your Project

You must not omit nor diminish research problems. If your project requires money, the use of expensive equipment, or other troublesome problems, you must say so. You must reveal requirements or problems that could cause your instructor to disallow the project if the truth were known. State problems clearly and honestly and explain how you will deal with them.

In library research, the chief problem is usually that you can't find all of the materials you need. Some book you need is out or not owned by the library at all. If it's only a single book, the library should be able to get it for you. If you need to send away for many books or articles, you should probably consider changing your topic. Some libraries charge for online time. If the charges are expensive, a few lessons on efficient Web searching can help. Some Net browsers today will let you plan your search off-line, and then the computer does the search many times faster than you could do it. Learn to use your library. Make friends with the reference librarians. Now that so much research can take advantage of computers, library papers don't usually have a "problems" section.

If your project calls for any special requirements—such as travel to your state capital to interview the governor, for example—you must say so in your proposal and approximate what your expenses would be. Problems concerning historic documents may or may not be solvable. It's important to find out early in your project. Today, computers have nearly done away with the problem of the "distant library." With librarian help, you can find where nearly anything is, and then librarians can send for it. Librarians can download magazine, newspaper, and journal articles, and sometimes there may be a small fee.

Example Problems or Requirements

```
                   Problems or Requirements

      I don't anticipate any problems with this project, except     1
that I don't know much about biology. I'll have to learn more
about human genetics, human procreation at the cellular level,
and cloning.
      Fortunately, much of the research is detailed about the       2
process and most of the information I think I will need. I
don't anticipate needing much more information than is already
available in the school library, though I will check some
Internet sources.
      I've already read some articles, and most of Silver's         3
book, and I was surprised to discover I could understand most
of what I read, so I should not have many problems, and there
should not be any special requirements.
```

Discussing the Significance of Your Project

Is your research question worthwhile? What is its significance? Research is costly and time consuming: you need to think about your project's significance before you start. If you apply for a research grant, for example, you can't present your project as merely "interesting." You may believe that your project is important, but it's your readers who must be convinced. For example, cancer and other severe afflictions are cellular in nature: work in cloning might give us a new window into the cancer process. Cloning might offer another option to childless couples. Your preliminary reading could suggest areas of significance that apply to your research.

By its very nature, research sometimes leads you into unexpected areas of investigation: you can't always know exactly what the outcome may be. Despite what you may think personally, do other researchers seem optimistic about your subject? (Is your idea supported in the research?) The question doesn't call for your guess or private opinion—maybe this, maybe that. Significance is always a call for what the research says about the value of your project.

Example Significance

```
                        Significance
     Some writers believe cloning humans can have serious      1
negative implications for the human race. It may reduce babies
to "commodification" (qtd. in Kass 24), which can be ordered
like vegetables, according to desired attributes, and produced
without "parental" involvement. You could order strong, healthy
sons and beautiful, talented daughters. The entire procedure
might become so impersonal that it hardly seems human. And
what else could you get along with your clone? Those who see
advantages to the process, however, believe it could help us
to strengthen the human race.
     The most immediate and scientifically acceptable answer    2
seems to be the possibility for ending genetic diseases and
afflictions. Other answers include helping infertile couples to
conceive and, possibly, preserving or passing on the desirable
attributes of athletes, artists, and geniuses.
     If Schwartz is right and this question is as important as  3
the atomic bomb, then it is highly significant and needs at
least as much research as went into the bomb. Science has
given us a tool that we can use to improve all human life . . .
or not, as the case may be.
```

Listing Your Works Cited or References

The proposal is an important document. You must provide complete bibliographic data for all references in your proposal. Almost always proposals have a Works Cited or References page where you list the works you have used in your proposal. This relatively short bibliography lets others see how much work you've done, the quality of your sources, how well you know some of the important work in the field, and whether you seem to be headed in the right direction. Both MLA and APA styles insist that you list only those sources you have actually cited in your proposal. You may have read other sources, but if you don't actually cite them, they should be omitted from your bibliography. This list usually begins on a new page, but you can ask your instructor for guidance about that. See chapter 9 Documentation on MLA or APA style.

Example Works Cited for Your Proposal

Works Cited (MLA)

Begley, Sharon. "Little Lamb, Who Made Thee?" <u>Newsweek</u> 10 Mar.
    1997: 53-59.

Kass, Leon R. "The Wisdom of Repugnance: Why We Should Ban the
    Cloning of Humans." <u>The New Republic</u> 2 June 1997: 17+.

Schwartz, Harry. "Cloning Dolly May Be Biggest News of Our
    Lives." <u>Detroit Free Press</u> 28 Feb. 1997: 13A.

Silver, Lee M. <u>Remaking Eden: How Genetic Engineering and
    Cloning Will Transform the American Family</u>. New York:
    Avon, 1998.

Watson, James D. "Moving toward the Clonal Man." (Original in
    <u>The Atlantic Monthly</u> 50-53). <u>Atlantic Unbound</u> (May 1971).

Wilmut, Ian, A. E. Schnieke, J. McWhir, A. J. Kind, and K. H.
    S. Campbell. "Viable Offspring Derived from Fetal and
    Adult Mammalian Cells." <u>Nature</u> 385 (Feb. 1997): 810-13.

Example References for Your Proposal

REFERENCES (APA)

Begley, S. (1997, March 10). Little lamb, who made thee?
    <u>Newsweek, 129,</u> 52-60.

Kass, L. R. (1997, June 2). The wisdom of repugnance: Why we
    should ban the cloning of humans. <u>The New Republic, 216,</u>
    17-26.

Schwartz, H. (1997, February 28). Cloning Dolly may be biggest
    news of our lives. <u>Detroit Free Press,</u> p. A13.

Silver, L. M. (1998). <u>Remaking Eden: How genetic engineering and
    cloning will transform the American family</u>. New York: Avon.

Watson, J. D. (1971, May) Moving toward the clonal man.
    <u>Atlantic Monthly, 227,</u> 50-53.

Wilmut, I., Schnieke, A. E., McWhir, J., Kind, A. J., &
    Campbell, K. H. S. (1997, February). Viable offspring
    derived from fetal and adult mammalian cells. <u>Nature, 385,</u>
    810-813.

<u>Note:</u> As an option, depending on your instructor's preference, you may use hanging indents for APA:

```
Begley, S. (1997, March 10). Little lamb, who made thee?
    Newsweek, 129, 52-60.
```

ACTIVITY 12

Write a proposal for your project. Write the proposal objectively, but without hedging. Avoid vague qualifiers such as "hopefully," "possibly," and "maybe."

Chapter 8

Evaluating Evidence

RESEARCH AND THE INTERNET

The Internet (the Net) is a great treasure trove of everything, however slight, related to human knowledge and curiosity: books, magazines, newspapers, pictures, recordings—information without limit. The Internet is a collection of just about anything and everything that can be stored, retrieved, and conveyed by computers. Furthermore, there is no end to the additions to the Net, day after day, year after year for the foreseeable future. As search engines get faster and more powerful (www.alltheweb.com claims it can sort through 3 million sites in half a minute), our ability to find useful information also increases. So far, the Internet is largely uncontrolled, unregulated. There are few rules about what is available or what you can find. Along with useful information, you can also find silly stuff, trash, pornography, graphics, movies, music, radio and TV programs, writing of dubious value, political speeches, conversations from chat rooms, bulletin boards, hate mail and hate sites preaching various forms of bigotry, quite a lot of advertising, and on and on and on. Almost literally there is no end to what is on the Internet. Skillful researchers can usually separate the wheat from the chaff, but students encountering unfamiliar subjects may have difficulty telling reliable from unreliable information.

EVALUATION AND THE INTERNET

Certainly, you can find excellent sources on the Internet, but there can also be important differences among sites. The ease and speed with which researchers can find material make the Net popular. The Net is a vast virtual (electronic) library with sites all over the world. However, just as with printed sources, Internet researchers need to be alert to problems of evaluation and verification. Because the Internet is open to everyone, it isn't always easy to determine whether material is valid, reliable, or even placed on the Net in good faith. There are guidelines for evaluating Net material, but few guarantees.

You don't absolutely need to know the language of the Internet, but it may be helpful to know what authors are talking about when they use some of the basic terminology. For example, the "Web" (WWW in site addresses) stands for the World Wide Web, one of the most popular resources of the Internet. It is a great "web" of computers throughout the world connected from one to another somewhat like a spider's web. There is no central connection or control over the Web. It was deliberately conceived as a Web of so many connections all over the world that (in case of war or terrorist attack) the communication system cannot be disrupted by destroying any central or controlling site. Following are a few basic terms you may encounter on the Net:

Bookmark:	A feature of your browser that lets you copy site addresses to a list so that you can easily return to the sites without retyping the addresses. "Favorites" used in MS Internet Explorer.
Browser:	A communication program, such as Netscape Communicator or Internet Explorer, for communicating with the Internet.
FAQ:	Frequently asked questions.
HTML:	Hypertext markup language. A machine language telling computers how to display information (such as text and graphics).
HTTP:	Hypertext transfer protocol. A series of commands connecting machines and sending information through the connection.
Protocol:	A series of commands computers use to perform various actions, especially communicating with other computers.
Server:	A computer that connects your machine to the Internet or an Internet service, such as America Online.
Site:	A place on the Web where information (or entertainment) is available. Each site on the Net has its own specific address, or URL.
URL:	Uniform resource locator; an Internet address.

Most people say that the more they learn about the Internet and about their own computer and browser, the more useful and rewarding it all becomes.

Millions of Hits

A general Internet search for a keyword, such as "clone," can turn up thousands, even millions of "hits." Does this mean you have found the mother lode? No, it means your search term is too broad, too general. It has found all those places on the Net that mention the word "clone," not necessarily articles on the subject. Specifying more terms in your search will help you to avoid sites unrelated to your search. The more specific you can be, the fewer extraneous hits you will have, for example

> Searching for <u>clone</u> (in 1999), produces 75,000+ hits.
> Searching for <u>clone human</u> produces 20,000+ hits.
> Searching for <u>clone human ethics</u> produces 1,662+ hits.
> Searching for <u>clone human ethics politics</u> produces 400+ hits.

You will get better results if you spend a few minutes reviewing the "tips" of the search engine you use.

You can winnow out articles that don't contain all the words you specify, but that alone cannot guarantee everything in your resulting hit list will be useful to you. Still, items in the list often contain brief descriptions that can help you decide whether to call up the full article. Clicking on any title in the search list will bring the material to your screen where you can briefly examine it and then either print, download, or click your Back button to return to the list.

Print Out Internet Material

When you find anything useful on the Internet, you need to print out the material. Things can easily go amiss with online transmissions, the simplest being that you can lose the connection . . . and may not be able to find it again, even if you have bookmarked the site. If you are using your own computer, by all means bookmark any useful site. When you do find material that looks promising, it's a wise precaution to print it out as soon as possible. Later you may not be able to find the source or the particular "page," instead getting an error message: "Your browser is unable to locate the site . . . ." You may not be able to find the same URL: it may have been changed or moved or terminated ("The requested URL was not found on this server"). Sources you need for your paper may no longer be available. Readers who need to check your sources may discover your references have evaporated. Printing is your best security against losing information you find on the Net.

WHAT IS A RELIABLE SITE?

Evaluating Web Sites

The more you rely on Internet material, the more you must consider the reliability of the sources. Many sites are meant for entertainment, not research. "Reliability" is a key criterion in research: it is a judgment you must make.

Judging reliability is no simple matter. You might find sites that seem to follow every guideline but still prove unreliable. A reliable site may occasionally contain less than reliable information, even under the best of conditions. You might find excellent material, however, at a site that lacks one or more criteria for reliability. The big academic encyclopedias, <u>Britannica</u> and <u>Americana</u>, are almost always considered reliable sources, but occasionally even they might contain an error. You must use critical thinking to evaluate sources on the Internet.

The main problem is that in some cases it is difficult to separate the site from the sources on the site. <u>Webster's Third International</u> (at Johns Hopkins University Libraries <http://miltonsweb.mse.jhu.edu:8001/dbases/webst.html>) and the great <u>Oxford English Dictionary</u> (<u>OED</u>) are undeniably reliable dictionaries of the English language. (The <u>OED</u> has several sites at Dartmouth; see <http://www.dartmouth.edu/~library.) The <u>OED</u> comes in 20 volumes; though you can get a two-volume set that comes with a magnifying glass. Fortunately, there are also reliable, smaller dictionaries, such as <u>Webster's New World College Dictionary</u> and others. Sources that researchers use with confidence are called "reliable." In general, you should use sources that other researchers use. Suppose you wanted to submit your paper to a conference of scientists. Should you use the little supermarket tabloids or advertising "shoppers" given away free? If you were writing about developments in nuclear energy, would you use the <u>Reader's Digest</u> as a source of information? We have many popular newspapers and magazines, such as the <u>National Enquirer</u> and <u>People</u> magazine, that are not intended for research. Still, it's not always clear what other researchers might or might not use. A paper on contemporary music could cite <u>Rolling Stone</u> or <u>Crawdaddy</u>.

If you find an opinion piece, should you use it? One answer to that could depend on where you find the piece. If an article appears in the <u>American Journal of Human Genetics</u>, that fact could help you to accept the article more than if it had appeared in a children's magazine, such as <u>Jack and Jill</u>. This comparison isn't a question of good, bad, or better: periodicals are aimed at different audiences for different purposes.

You can look for reliable information at government sources, university sources, professional organizations such as the National Education Association, publications of professional organizations such as the <u>Chronicle of Higher Education</u> and the <u>Journal of the American Medical Association</u>, some of the large public libraries such as the New York Public Library or the Los Angeles Public Library or the Internet Public Library (<www.ipl.org> "an initiative of the University of Michigan School of Information"). In addition, of course, there are the Library of Congress and many other excellent sources of reliable information. Still, you must use a reasonable degree of common sense and caution on the Net.

Critical thinkers should also consider the negative side of this question: which sites probably are not relevant or significant for your research? You can quickly eliminate much of the Web if you are only interested in a specific subject, but that still leaves a lot to evaluate. If you were to exclude all "popular" sources, you would further narrow the search, but not all researchers would wish to do that. Anything published on a "professional site" (such as professional journals) should be, by definition, reliable, but you shouldn't use that as a simplistic rule; some popular sites such as <u>Time</u> and <u>Newsweek</u> may also be considered authoritative by some researchers.

Criteria for Web Sites

1. <u>Whose site is it?</u> Who has put this site on the Web? The author? A political group such as People for the American Way <http://pfaw.org>? Harvard University <www.harvard.edu>? A professional organization such as the American Bar Association <www.aba.org>? Some commercial enterprise? Is there any way to tell? (Is there any advertising?) Does the site indicate the source of its information? If you can't find identifying information, should you use the material? If such information is available, what do you learn from it? How much does the site tell you about itself? To see a site that provides a great deal of information about itself and links to many divisions and subdivisions of information, visit the Roslin Institute Online <http://www.ri.bbsrc.ac.uk>.

ACTIVITY 1

Select a Web site at random or one that you particularly want to explore. What does the site reveal about itself? What do you notice? How do you evaluate what the site reveals (or doesn't)?

---

2. <u>Has the site been refereed?</u> Do you find any sort of review or reference to criteria for the site? Is there evaluative information about the site, its origins, its history, and its purpose? Do you find a "mission statement"? The more information you can find about a site the better, usually. A "refereed" or reviewed site is one that has been examined by judges, often experts. Books are previewed by publishers, editors, professional readers, and reviewers. Manuscripts don't become books until they have been carefully read by knowledgeable editors and readers, and they don't get into a school library until librarians or instructors recommend them. The Internet, however, has no such restrictions. Some sites have been rated by various groups, but most sites haven't been rated by anyone other than their authors.

ACTIVITY 2

Find an Internet site that has been reviewed or verified in some way. What in the site suggests that it is legitimate, authoritative research? In your research notebook write a paragraph or two about what you find.

---

3. <u>Can you communicate with the site manager, the author, or whoever sponsors the site?</u> Is there an e-mail address or phone number? Reliable researchers usually assist their readers and welcome questions or comments about their work: for example, the Texas A&M University reported a story concerning a wealthy couple who desired a clone of their aging pet, Missy: The Missyplicity Project. The project includes a Web site <www.missyplicity.com> to answer questions; the site is kept current with monthly reports. Many readers found the story unusual—the project's FAQ begins with the question, "Is this a joke?" At the time, the popular media made the project seem unbelievable, and at least one researcher found it necessary to call A&M for confirmation.

ACTIVITY 3

Find a site that identifies its sponsor or permits you to communicate with the site sponsor or manager. Explain in a brief notebook entry what you find.

---

4. <u>How easy is it to find the site, use it, move around in it, read its information, copy or print from the site?</u> Can you move from the home page to various directories or indexes and from there to useful information, and then back to the home page? Is the organization of the site reasonable and logical? Does the site appear to have been set up for the reader's convenience?

Long URLs can send back error messages (such as error 404) when an address requires too many connections, for example, http://lcweb.loc.gov/adecenter/adecenter.html.

```
HTTP Error 404
404 Not Found
The Web server cannot find the file or script you asked for. Please
check the URL to ensure that the path is correct.
Please contact the server's administrator if this problem persists.
```

You may find it necessary to truncate the URL back to its main site—<http://lcweb.loc.gov>—or to use the new URL for the Library of Congress, http://www.loc.gov.

ACTIVITY 4

Think of a subject you might be interested in learning about. Then see if you can find a Web site on that subject. Explore the site, and report in your notebook on what you find.

---

5. <u>Does the site provide links to other sites?</u> Presumably, the research you seek is in the custody of various specialists and experts who could help you find additional information. Finding a reliable site is like finding a door to the world of information: one thing usually leads to another in research. Specialists, experts, and authorities are often aware of other sources on the Web and can help you to find them. The mere presence of links, however, doesn't guarantee reliability (there are no guarantees in research): the links must lead to reliable, verifiable information. If you need help with the site, is there a Help button, or some way to get assistance? In short, does the site seem to have been well planned, with the reader in mind?

ACTIVITY 5

Look for sites on the Net dealing with your research subject, or select a subject you might be interested in and look for sites on the Net dealing with that subject. Look for a site that offers links or other indicators of reliability as well as concern for readers. Report in your notebook what you find.

---

6. <u>Is there a problem with advertising?</u> There may not be anything wrong with advertising per se, but finding advertising in the "objective," scientific, scholarly world of reliable information raises serious questions. Advertisements might mean that the information is paid for partially or entirely by the advertisers and, therefore, may not be objective.

Then too, the assumption behind much advertising is that the audience is not critical, that it will be entertained by colorful animations no matter how improbable (dancing vegetables), will associate attractive models and athletes with products, will accept without question the alleged virtues of the products, and most of all will remember the name of the product when shopping.

Advertisements are not entirely harmless even if amusing or silly. Neil Postman in <u>Amusing Ourselves to Death</u> (Viking 1985) makes the point that advertisers rely on images, not words, and we cannot debate with images. Others believe advertising may anesthetize critical thinking itself, substituting either cynicism or apathy or both. The fear is that knowing the public's cynicism, advertisers, politicians, and government officials may feel less obligation to be entirely truthful. Advertising is part of the business world: it makes radio, TV, and the Net apparently free to consumers. However, thoughtful writers and researchers need to work without the pressures that corporate sponsors can create. Readers need to believe they are reading reliable information. Advertising on the Web suggests that information exists merely as a lure—to deliver consumers to the advertiser.

True, the money for research must come from somewhere, but it is preferable that it not come with strings attached, not be subverted to other ends (such as selling shoes), and not coincidentally imply dubious messages: "You too can be a superstar!"

Is there anything researchers can do about advertising? You can be alert to the problem while you attempt to find reliable information for your project. Too many intrusive ads (color, sound, animations) may mean that the site is too compromised to be useful. Even subtle, unobtrusive ads (the manufacturer's name discreetly tucked away in some corner) may alert you to a possibility of conflict between what you need and what the source offers. Critical thinkers should examine carefully the relationship between advertisers and Web sites. You need to be aware of biases—slants, implications, exaggerations, distortions, partial truths, "spin" (spinning the truth until it sounds the way you want it to).

ACTIVITY 6

Select two or three Web sites that appeal to you—or select at random if you prefer. Describe any use of advertising you find, especially the absence of advertising, its effects on you, and your evaluation of the site.

WHO IS THE AUTHOR?

Authorship on the Net is similar to authorship in print, except for the Net's greater accessibility. In evaluating information on Web sites, the question of authorship is an important consideration. A single verifiable fact, even if the researcher is not well known, can upset all the experts and established authorities. In such a case the majority does not rule: all the heavy credentials and years of experience do not outweigh the truth. The truth should prevail no matter how many or how powerful are those who disagree. In short, it shouldn't matter who the researcher is, at least in theory.

Questions of authorship and authority can be troublesome for researchers. On the one hand, for example, you could find most scientists saying it isn't possible to regress a mature cell back to a germ-cell state, such that a living clone could be produced from the cell. On the other hand, one lone biologist may sometimes prove that everyone else is wrong. This situation creates a problem for you. In the case of Ian Wilmut et al., who cloned the lamb Dolly, the minority is apparently correct and the majority mistaken. Thus, all the credentials, degrees, memberships in scholarly societies, awards, and publications of the majority should not outweigh the truth.

Still, researchers cannot simply ignore the majority: you must report what you find. The fundamental facts and theories of any discipline are exactly those that have been verified over time. Further, lone geniuses are few, especially those who produce shocking novelties that can upset the foundations of science. Not every lone spokesperson for a different point of view is a genius; some are mistaken, others crackpots. Your problem, then, is to make a judgment: many hundreds of biologists said it could not be done, but Ian Wilmut (not entirely alone but certainly in the minority) said otherwise. What then should you conclude?

The answer to this seeming dilemma, as with so many questions in research, is in your readings. You need to read enough, learn enough, to understand the research. In technical studies concerning embryology and microbiology, you need to be able to understand the reports and the way research works. Seldom is any researcher truly alone in his or her discoveries. Cloning of plants and animals was practiced long before Dolly appeared. Some of the basic components in Wilmut's procedure were known to other researchers (Silver, <u>Remaking Eden</u>). Wilmut may be a genius, but we should all remember that most scientific discoveries are made by "standing on the shoulders of giants." Seldom do we make progress in research by great leaps: it happens, but not often.

In the face of this dilemma, the best rule for you is to assume that credentials are important, but not more important than facts. Otherwise, a paper in which you cite many unknown or unidentifiable researchers can seem to lack authority. If you are unable to establish the authority of those you cite (or many of them), you should probably choose a different subject.

The cloning article by Ian Wilmut et al. lists a bibliography and identifies the Roslin Institute in Edinburgh, where the research was done. As we write this, Wilmut has become recognized as a reliable researcher, and articles by and about him are easy to find. The article announcing his successful experiment appears in <u>Nature</u> (1997), a respected international magazine devoted to science. <u>Nature</u> publishes original research and is read by scientists all over the world. Its editors decide which of the many submissions are most interesting and these are sent to two or three (or more) referees.

Identifying Authors

The Internet's basic characteristic derives from the First Amendment of the Constitution: freedom of speech. The Net, so far, is a public medium: Web pages are not policed; people can post anything they like, making it difficult for you to determine what is reliable information and what isn't. A general rule for critical thinkers is to be suspicious in relation to the amount of information a site offers (or doesn't offer) about itself. An essay with only an author's name for identification isn't necessarily unreliable, but you should avoid unidentifiable, unverifiable information.

To identify Net authors, you can use some of the Web's many biographical sources, or some of the print sources in your library. With a little perseverance, you should be able to identify most authors.

Ian Wilmut was unknown to most American readers when his experiment upset the well-established "rule" that after differentiation a cell cannot return to its undifferentiated state: once a liver cell always a liver cell. Wilmut held the minority opinion in embryology, but his article was a scientific breakthrough. Wilmut's conclusions were quickly accepted as correct.

You should be able to find well-known scholars and scientists in biographical sources. Wilmut's name can be found in newspaper and magazine archives, is listed in some of the biographical sources, and is included in major encyclopedias on-line or off-line. Ian Wilmut is the author of Britannica's article "The Uses and Ethics of Cloning" in the 1997 Year in Review (<www.britannica.com>), which identifies Wilmut as "leader of the research team that produced the first clone of an adult mammal; he is an embryologist at the Roslin Institute, near Edinburgh." In short, depending on how recently researchers have been published, you should be able to find clues to their identities that can then help you infer the reliability of their information. You may be able to find biographical information in one of the biographical reference works; in one of the large encyclopedias; in the archives of a reliable newspaper, magazine, or professional journal; and sometimes by using a simple Web search (www.alltheweb.com and google have been especially effective in our work). The big search engines are excellent for picking up publications, and that tends to mean they find anyone recently published.

Depending on what sources your library has, you may try ProQuest or Lexis-Nexis for newspaper articles and FirstSearch or Uncover for magazine or journal articles. College and university libraries usually have databases for the New York Times, the Readers' Guide, and the Social Sciences and Humanities Index. Your library's Public Access Catalog also may list books relevant to your search.

Some professional organizations maintain biographical information on their members. Even the Library of Congress can help. Preliminary reading in the cloning issue would uncover, in addition to Ian Wilmut, authors such as

Gina Kolata, Lee Silver, Gregory Pence, and others who have written important books or articles on the subject, most of which include bibliographic references. From your preliminary reading you will begin to have information about
whom to look for—and each source you find can lead you to others.

ACTIVITY 7

Based on your research so far, who would you say are two or three important
researchers in your project? Select two and see what you can find about their
credentials.

Caution on the Internet

On the Internet, color and pictures are the rule: it's a visual medium. It is also wide
open to everyone, and, therefore, it isn't always easy to identify authors on the Net.
Albert Einstein may have written the article you are reading, but it's also possible
that someone else has borrowed Einstein's name. Articles that appear out of the
blue—with no indication of who sponsors them or why—can be problematic for
researchers. While researching black holes, for example, suppose you find a Web
site by Professor Soandso in which he presents his own essay on black holes as
the homes of aliens who manage to travel in and out of them. (See Figure 8.1.)
    A black hole is an area of the universe whose gravitational pull is so
powerful that not even light can escape, according to modern science

Whose site is this?	**Black Holes: Home of Aliens**	
	Professor Soandso	Who is this author?
	Nature's great mystery, the black hole has been a favorite tool of science fiction writers. However, science now reveals that the gravitational fields that were thought to prevent anything from escaping a black hole are not as powerful as previously thought. And that fact	Source of this information?
Assumption: "aliens"?	coincides with another great mystery. Where is the home of the aliens who travel in UFO's? How is it so many UFOs can be reported within the Earth's atmosphere, but none can ever be tracked leaving? Where do they go? Where are they from?	
Assumption: "would have the power"?	Black holes are one possible answer. Creatures that can travel the universe would have powers beyond our knowledge, perhaps enough power to enter and leave black holes.	Source of this information?
		Credibility of this article?

Figure 8.1. Illustration of a Doubtful Web Site.

<www.britannica.com> 1999. If this author doesn't identify him- or herself, you must examine the Web page for clues to identity. Without a university, a research institute, some government agency, a professional organization, or some other identifiably reliable sponsor for Professor Soandso, you may find identification difficult. You might try some of the links the professor suggests (if any), but it's possible that those sites may also be doubtful. Before spending much time on this task, you should do two things: first, print out the article. Second, decide what you think of the quality of the information Professor Soandso is offering. If you decide that the information is not something you want to use, you can file the printout and move on to something more promising. Without documentation in the essay, without identifying information on the author, without some kind of sponsorship for this page (The Black Hole Society of America?), nothing about this essay resembles the way authorities publish their work.

Before you spend much time trying to identify hard-to-find people or verifying their expertise, look for those who may be easier to find. The more you read about your subject, the more you will discover the important figures. Then when you come across someone hard to identify, such as Professor Soandso, you will have a context for judging both the author and the information. A critical thinker should ask these questions:

> Does the information fit with the body of research I have been collecting?
>
> Does the information agree with what I already know?
>
> If it disagrees or differs from the research I am collecting, does it offer persuasive reasoning, facts, and believable statements?
>
> Does the author sound knowledgeable?
>
> Does he or she cite sources, and authoritative information?
>
> Is there a bibliography of "Works Cited" or "References"?

Authority

Who is an "expert" witness? There are no easy answers to that question. Experts are usually (but not always) people with advanced degrees and years of experience. However, in court it is fairly common for both sides to provide expert witnesses with impressive credentials, but who disagree, and thus tend to cancel each other out. By definition, the expert witness is one who knows: the expert is the one we can turn to when we need highly specialized, technical information. It is the technical information more than the degrees and diplomas that count. In <u>My Cousin Vinny</u>, a 1992 comedy starring Joe Pesci as would-be lawyer Vinny, the expert witness is Vinny's girl friend (Marisa Tomei), who knows more about cars than anyone else in the film. Her testimony about tire tracks saves the day for Pesci's clients.

Expert testimony can contain problems. The only real solution is to continue reading and studying until you can judge the truth for yourself or until you can find authorities whose judgments you trust.

The Establishment Bias: An Exception

We can't insist that every researcher be well established and well known (the "establishment bias"). One problem for inexperienced researchers could be that Ian Wilmut was himself relatively unknown in this country prior to the birth of Dolly. When his group at the Roslin Institute in Scotland showed that the "rule" about cell differentiation was wrong, the establishment bias should have branded him a crackpot, but it didn't. Wilmut showed without a doubt that the majority opinion was wrong. His experiment was definitive. Though most scientists believed that mature cells could not differentiate, Wilmut and his team had the research to prove otherwise. Thus, the general prejudice in favor of well-established authorities contains an exception. Nothing is more persuasive than proof, and Wilmut had Dolly, the little lamb that had been cloned from an adult donor cell. Now, of course, Ian Wilmut has become well established. Wilmut caused a pardigm shift in embryology (see chapter 3).

The Net is highly accessible. By contrast, print journals have room for only so many articles. Editors receive hundreds of submissions but usually have room to publish only a dozen or so. This state of affairs is difficult for researchers: it can be extremely difficult to get published in the print journals; however, articles in print have at least been read by an editor and may have been submitted to reviewers before publication. Furthermore, journals frequently give brief biographical descriptions of authors.

The Internet, however, can publish and reprint any number of articles online, a fact that can be both good and not so good. There is so much information available on-line that if you must track down every article on your list, you will find research slow work. Instead of looking for everything on the list, a critical thinker should look for information that may be worth finding, based on the criteria in the accompanying Guidelines for Finding Worthwhile Information.

GUIDELINES FOR FINDING WORTHWHILE INFORMATION

1. Based on an abstract you have seen, the information seems important and useful for your research.
2. The article has been discussed or listed as useful in some other source you have read.
3. The author is a well-known authority and should be easy to locate on-line.
4. A reliable Web site like the Biotechnology Information Center (BIC, a center for the National Agricultural Library of the U.S. Department of Agriculture) suggests that the source is worthwhile.

Biographical Information

Journals, and some magazines, typically identify authors, if only briefly. For example (let us imagine), Professor Smith's article "Critical Understanding in Philosophy and Art" appears in a research journal. Before or after the article, the editors provide information as follows:

> Smith is professor of communication
> Department of Speech-Communication
> XYZ State University
> <smithxyz@xyzsu.edu>

Such brief statements don't tell readers how well qualified the professor may be for a paper on philosophy and art, but it does suggest that the professor is likely to be someone trained in the skills and customs of scholarly research and writing. The reference to school and department are leads you can check to locate an e-mail address (if not given in the article) or phone number, where you might contact the author for questions or comments. The fact that the professor's article appears in a research journal also suggests the information may be reliable.

Sources on the Web

You will find many biographical sources on the Web, some of which are advertisements for books or databases available only at libraries or for sale from the publishers. Other sources are restricted to members, fee-paying users, faculty and students of sponsoring universities. Some of these sources cover only particular groups, such as celebrities of the entertainment world, for example. Other sources are clearly vehicles for commercial advertisers: they are ads for print editions of standard biographical sources available in your own library, or they can be advertisements for services providing biographical information for a fee. Unfortunately, using biographical sources to identify recently published researchers or specialists may not provide what you need. Sometimes it can be easier to find researchers through one of the search engines on the Internet itself: www.alltheweb.com (which claims to be the biggest and fastest), www.google.com, Lycos, Excite, and Yahoo for example.

RELIABLE INFORMATION: ON THE NET AND OFF

Step one is to read information and decide what you think of it. There is little to gain by spending much time on information you don't think is good, useful, relevant, or reliable for your project. Background reading can help you to skim through new material and make your judgments about it. While you are building your list of books and articles, you need to start reading and developing a context with which to evaluate material.

Context

Without some <u>context</u> for information, your evaluations must remain general and not very useful. You need a background of fundamental information, a critical thinker's preliminary understanding that can serve as a context for evaluations. What sort of information are you reading: is it fact, fiction, opinion, report, feature item, a human interest story, humor (irony), scholarly, academic, popular, scientific, reliable, . . . something else?

A brief reading or skimming can suggest whether an Internet article might be useful for your research. Other aids can help, if you find them: titles, labels, and headings can give you a quick indication of an article's usefulness. Introductory statements typically contain the thesis or some statement of intent, if there is one: a quick read through the first paragraph or two should give you a fair idea of an author's purpose. Many researchers say they skim through the introduction and then hop to the conclusion to see whether a report may be useful. A context of preliminary readings and a common-sense application of guidelines should help you decide whether an article is likely to be relevant or useful for your project and whether you should print it out.

Timely Data

Researchers tend to believe that newer data are better than old, but that depends on what you are researching. Research about works of art like Shakespeare's <u>Hamlet</u> can be more or less "timely" even if several hundred years old.

Most scientific research, however, requires recent data. You should always seek the most recent data. Recency alone doesn't necessarily carry the day: some data may only confirm, instead of contradicting, earlier data. Studies published in the year 2000 don't automatically mean more than those of 1990. Nevertheless, you should always try to find the most recent data. (Research published prior to 1997 would almost certainly have maintained that adult cells cannot be regressed back to germ-cell state. That research would, of course, be proved wrong in 1997.) Today's researchers would have to justify much use of old research. Information tends to age rapidly, on-line or off. In courts of law, documents 20 years old are considered "ancient." In the computer age, with on-line information available nearly instantaneously, information can be outdated in as little as a year or two. You needn't completely ignore older material, but if you use material from the 1970s, for example, you should look for recent material as well. Omissions or other problems in your documentation must be explained. If you have data for 1998 and 2000 but not 1999, some readers would be curious: what happened to 1999? Some material may not be available at first, but you should keep after it until eventually your research does cover the most recent material, without raising too many questions or creating problems.

Documentation and Credibility

Footnotes, endnotes, or in-text references show readers where your information came from and assist readers in finding relevant material. Research is connected to research, and reliable researchers will help you to find those connections. Documentation is a significant component of scholarly, scientific writing. To say that another way, an important criterion for reliable information is whether the author has provided documentation.

Documentation helps critical thinkers produce thoughtful research, no matter what their credentials may be. For example, the Journal of the American Medical Association (JAMA 279.13 [1998]: 1005–10) once published the science project of a sixth-grade girl concerning "therapeutic touch." Some people believe there is a "human energy field" that can be manipulated without touching the patient. The technique is taught in some nursing schools.

Emily Rosa devised a test for this "energy field." A cardboard screen with hand holes obstructed subjects' view. The subjects put their hands through the holes. Emily held one of her own hands above one of theirs and then asked whether they could "feel" which of their hands she was near. Subjects answered correctly in 44% of 280 trials, a score less than chance. (The significant level for such experiments is typically 95%.) With a little help, Emily's paper found its way to JAMA and was subsequently published, first in print (Rosa et al.) and then online (<http://www.ama-assn.org/sci-pubs/journals/archive/jama/vol_279/no_13/joc71352.htm>).

Research writing, online or in print, whether the work of a scientist or a student, becomes credible when it states a clear thesis and presents clearly documented information on that thesis. Good researchers tell readers where to find that information.

You need verifiable information, careful analysis, reasoning, and documentation. If researchers follow the traditions of academic writing, critical readers can be optimistic about the validity of the research. (Serious researchers don't usually resort to humor, sarcasm, satire, or other "light" tones, but once in a while . . . they may.) As a critical thinker you must remain objective and impartial regardless: it's difficult to challenge carefully documented research, but you should attempt to verify the documentation, especially online references.

Hoaxes, Jokes, Conspiracies, and Frauds

We don't expect scientific research to rely on dubious or obviously fraudulent sources of evidence, but "errors" can happen, even today. In the nineteenth century, the "Cardiff Giant" was a 10-foot fraud: a "petrified man" was planted in the ground until it was discovered and proven a fraud (Britannica Online). "Piltdown Man," discovered in the twentieth century, turned out to be "disguised" fragments from a modern human skull as well as pieces of orangutan and chimpanzee teeth. No one knows the motives behind these hoaxes, but today there is great pressure on scientists, professors, and students to produce successful experiments. The pressure can be so great that individuals may be tempted to "cook" the data a little. Sometimes the results of an experiment can be so close to success, perhaps lacking only a single percentage point, that temptation to add the extra point can be too much. It usually takes highly skilled specialists to discover such cookery.

In the age of information, problems are easy to create and hard to uncover. Research is difficult enough when the information is reliable, but you should be aware that some information is not reliable. The Internet's total democracy can permit all sorts of hoaxes, jokes, phony information, deliberately misleading reports, and disinformation.

Caveat emptor is an ancient warning ("let the buyer beware"): in the computer age, let the researcher beware. In 1996 the Chicago Tribune wrote that a report on the crash of TWA Flight 800 had turned out to be "a long discredited piece of Internet e-mail" (Coates 1) alleging that Flight 800 had been shot down by a U.S. navy ship. Rumors, gossip, conspiracies, and outright frauds await the unwary on the Net.

Here is a good rule for critical thinkers: avoid anything you can't identify or verify. Continue searching until you find data you can rely on. (See the accompanying box, Guidelines for Reliable Data.) For additional information on evaluating Internet sources, you can visit some of these sites on the Web:

http://www.geneseo.edu/~butwell/psy262.htm
http://info.lib.uh.edu/pr/v8/n3/smit8n3.html
http://www.library.cornell.edu/okuref/research/webeval.html
http://www.library.ucla.edu/libraries/college/instruct/web/critical.htm
http://milton.mse.jhu.edu:8001/research/education/net.html
http://www.rrc.mb.ca/library/2evalweb.htm
http://www.tiac.net/users/hope/findqual.html
http://trochim.human.cornell.edu/webeval/webeval.htm
http://www.unc.edu/cit/guides/irg-49.html
http:///www2.widener.edu/Wolfgram-Memorial-Library/webeval.htm

---

GUIDELINES FOR RELIABLE DATA

1. Use reputable sources and Web sites. Avoid sites you're not sure about.
2. Identify researchers when possible. Avoid those you can't identify.
3. Look for documentation of sources. Avoid information you can't verify.
4. Seek confirmation of evidence. Avoid data you can't confirm.

UNDERSTANDING EVIDENCE

Active Reading

Active reading is deliberate reading, reading for a purpose. Active reading means thinking about what authors are saying, interacting with them, making an effort to understand them. For active reading you need to think about meanings. What is the author trying to tell you? Active reading differs from passive reading. Following along with no particular goal in mind is passive reading. Sometimes that's a good way to read. But research calls for active reading; deliberate reading: reading to analyze, understand, and think about evidence.

An Active Reading Technique

Active reading has three steps: (1) Read much, write little. If you find yourself writing a lot, you need to rethink your technique. (2) Make an informal outline of points and supporting materials (examples, arguments). (3) Write briefly in your own words what you think about the information. Ask yourself questions about it. Speculate. Please read the following student review:

The book <u>When Elephants Weep</u> is the "first serious investigation of the subject." The authors Masson and McCarthy are dedicated to their premise: that animals (other than human animals) have emotions. Doing so they contradict scientists who believe animals are machines, "automata," whose behavior can be explained as survival techniques. Pet owners believe their pets frolic in play, exhibit joy when the owner arrives or sets out food. The purrs of house cats and even some of the larger cats are thought to be sounds of contentment. Masson and McCarthy illustrate with many examples that animals express joy, grief, pain, anger, anguish, loneliness, fear, and even mourning—some awareness of death, as illustrated by the strange behavior of elephants when they come upon the corpse of an elephant—picking up the bones, carrying them about, carrying them off a distance from the corpse, and some ritual tossing of weeds and dirt over the carcass. Indian elephants have been observed to "shed tears of grief when a family member is killed."

Thesis: animals have emotions (despite what some scientists believe)

Support: (1) Pets show joy, contentment

(2) Elephants show mourning, tears of grief

Many animals exhibit maternal concern for their young (though some reptiles appear to have no concern for their young). Overall, it is not difficult to believe the other animals have emotions. Anyone who doubts that has only to step on a pet's tail.

(3) Animals have maternal concern

In this short passage you can see the relationship between its components. The thesis is that animals have emotions despite what scientists have said. To "support" (give proof for) this thesis, the writer cites examples from Masson and McCarthy's book: (1) pet cats purr when content; (2) elephants behave strangely in the presence of elephant bones, and Indian elephants have been observed to shed tears; (3) many animals (not all) seem to have a maternal instinct. Active reading helps you to understand the basic concepts in the passage: it reduces the passage to its fundamental components. You can condense the material, turning its words and sentences into thoughts—concepts you can respond to in your mind. Write for yourself in your notebook: ask questions about these ideas; see if you can remember parallel concepts from your own experience. (Why does the cat always want to get into bed with us?)

You can use the technique with anything you read. Here, for example, is a newspaper article that appeared in the <u>Detroit Free Press</u>. Please read the entire article before you make any decisions about it. Then see if you can determine which are the author's main ideas and supporting examples.

Cloning Dolly May Be Biggest News of Our Lives

Harry Schwartz

It's mystifying that so many commentators have been downplaying the significance of the first cloning of a mammal, Dolly-the-sheep in Scotland. 1

It's one of the major events of the 20th Century, right up there with the development of nuclear weapons and the discovery of the nature of DNA. 2

The downplayers betray the short-term mentality that dominates so much of our personal and national thinking. Wall Street didn't seem excited about the event, declared one otherwise thoughtful newspaper, implying the event could not have been all that vital. 3

A financial writer in another top newspaper wrote a long article about how it was unlikely that the advent of mammalian cloning would make profits very soon for the company that did the cloning or for anybody else. 4

And so it went. Astounded by this myopia, I searched for a possible explanation. Then I recalled English economist John Maynard Keynes and his crack, "In the long run we're all dead," a remark he proved a few years later by dying. Keynes left no children; it's understandable he had no interest in the future beyond his life span. 5

But most adults do have children, and if they're old enough, they may have grandchildren and great-grandchildren. Surely the fate of our descendants is of interest to most of us. 6

The point is that cloning a sheep changes all perspectives for the future. If one mammal, a sheep, can be cloned, so can all other mammals, including human beings. 7

And we can be certain that human beings will be cloned, even though some countries have laws against it. Laws can be changed or ignored. 8

A clone is a creature having exactly the same genes as its immediate ancestor. A clone of Albert Einstein would have the same genes and therefore the same potential as the discoverer of relativity. 9

A Babe Ruth clone would have the same genes as the original home-run 10 king. And a clone of Madame Curie would have the same genes as the woman who discovered radium. These outstanding people are all dead, so they cannot be cloned.

But there are geniuses alive today, and more will be born in the years ahead. 11

The thought will undoubtedly occur to people in the future that to let 12 geniuses die is a waste of resources.

And of course, I'm not thinking only about geniuses in science. I'm using 13 the term to cover people of outstanding talent in every field.

Very rich people—such as Bill Gates of Microsoft—will be able in the 14 future to have themselves cloned at their own expense.

Undoubtedly financier J. P. Morgan would have cloned himself if he could 15 have. So would John D. Rockefeller.

The inevitable cloning of people permits creation of a human race that will 16 increasingly include the best of the past—and maybe the worst, too. Surely, Adolf Hitler and Joseph Stalin would have had themselves cloned if they could have.

Today, the quality of future generations is essentially a crapshoot. Couples 17 having children never know what abilities—or lack of abilities—those children will have.

Some children are smarter than their parents or more athletic or better at 18 business, etc. But other children are worse than their immediate predecessors. Cloning opens the way for nations to try to improve their human stock by taking much of the gambling out of their future generations.

I cannot believe that nations will shy away from it. The Chinese govern- 19 ment already limits the number of children Chinese couples can have to one per family. A future China or North Korea might outlaw natural reproduction and insist that future children come only from the best of the current generation.

It is a horrifying prospect but not one we can dismiss because Wall Street 20 couldn't get excited on the day Dolly made news. Wall Street couldn't get excited when Einstein published the theory of relativity, either. (13A)

(Harry Schwartz is a former New York Times editorial writer and has taught at Columbia University's College of Physicians and Surgeons)

There can be disagreement about ideas in an article: disagreements generate thought and discussion, and that is usually helpful for critical thinkers (see chapter 4).

ACTIVITY 8

Use active reading: in your notebook, make an informal outline of Schwartz's article, "Cloning Dolly." What are his main points? What support does he give? You don't need to be correct, just thoughtful. Bring your notebook to class for discussion.

What do you think? Is Schwartz right—is cloning humans "horrifying"? In the following notebook entry, Jill interacts actively with Schwartz's article. She thinks about what Schwartz says. She asks questions and makes comments on certain parts of his article.

```
Thoughts on Cloning Dolly                        Feb 5, 2000
```

    Should we assume that a "genetic clone" would be an   **1**
absolute twin? All the twins I know aren't "identical," even
though they look alike. They were cute when they were little
and hard to tell apart, but as they have grown up, they are
less alike in personality and behavior and they don't really
look like mirror images of each other anymore.

    To produce a "double," wouldn't the clone have to be   **2**
raised the same way, have the same experiences? It doesn't
work with identical twins, so why should it work with clones?
"The concept of eugenics tends to ignore the sizable role that
environment plays in the establishment of human characteristics"
("Eugenics," <u>Britannica CD</u> 1997). Does Schwartz imply
that people will be able to pick and choose among human
characteristics--selecting only the "good" ones and cloning
out the "bad"? No more long noses? No more below-average
intellects? No more tone deaf singing?

    Anyway, who would decide? Some people might think big tall   **3**
musclemen are genetically superior. Who knows what else might
go when we clone out something. Suppose when we clone out
average intelligence or clone in superior intellect, we get not
only a high IQ but a snotty personality. Who knows what else
might get cloned in when we try to change a baby. Suppose
little Eugenia's mother had wanted to be a ballerina. She never
made it, but her sister Consuella had been a dancer. Maybe
Eugenia could have been cloned with Consuella's dancing genes?

    If someone could really create a double, then would a   **4**
Stalin or a Hitler want such a person around? A challenger?
(Of course that's ignoring the fact that we would have to wait
for the genetic double to grow up.) And why would any woman
want to have such a child for heaven's sake?

    I wonder whether Harry Schwartz is being serious in his   **5**
column. He was a teacher at Columbia's College of Physicians
and Surgeons, so he should know the problems involved in trying

(box continues)

to decide what or whose biological characteristics should be preserved, whose should be cloned out. Racists might think cloning could be their opportunity to get rid of races they don't like.

Maybe the answer is in his second paragraph, where he says cloning is as important as the atomic bomb or discovering DNA. I think he means science can change (improve?) the entire human race. At least they could get rid of a lot of genetic diseases.

6

ACTIVITY 9

Write a page or so in your notebook about Jill's response to Schwartz's article. What do you think about their ideas? Bring your journal to class for group discussion.

Some readers accept everything they read as true. "After all," they say, "who am I to question the authorities? If it's in the newspapers it must be true." However, not everything in print is correct. Furthermore, just because you are still learning doesn't mean you shouldn't use your own mind and challenge, with evidence, what you find on-line or in print. Maybe writers are right, maybe not. But relying only on experts, closing your own mind to discovery, isn't good research. Besides, you may soon discover that the "experts" do not agree.

PRIMARY AND SECONDARY EVIDENCE

Thinking about evidence is a critical thinker's most important task. Collecting dozens and dozens of sources means little until you analyze them and decide their relevance or significance. <u>Evidence is the heart of research</u>. Some evidence may be good, but some may be light and of doubtful value. Authorities are one kind of evidence, but they are not necessarily the best kind. Facts make good evidence; theories and arguments can also be good evidence. You can start your research by asking questions: What is evidence? How can you evaluate it? How can you tell what the evidence means? How can a critical thinker know whether evidence is significant? Before you answer such questions, you need to know some basics about evidence.

Primary and Secondary

The skills of primary research are like the skills of the laboratory. The skills of secondary research are more like the skills of the courtroom. But neither the lab nor the courtroom can tell you with absolute certainty the answers to all your questions. In both you may have to do some guess work, even if you do have facts to work with. Courtrooms seldom provide indisputable answers: the lawyers examine, challenge, and contradict each other's evidence. Juries listen and then decide guilt or innocence. Researchers, too, must examine the evidence and then decide what they think it means. Usually, the best a critical thinker can do is to infer reasonable answers based on the data. It's no surprise, then, if later someone else finds other data and reaches different conclusions.

Primary evidence is firsthand. If you are the first one who finds the evidence, through your own investigations, in the lab, in the field, and so on, it is "primary evidence." (Often the first to discover something new gets to name it, like Halley's Comet.) Can students do primary research? Yes. (Consider Rosa's experiment.) Students might do surveys, questionnaires, simple experiments in human behavior, testing reactions to jokes or inkblots; or students might do comparison tests (which is the best restaurant in town? which is the most popular meal on campus?). However, as a critical thinker, you must remember that primary research requires secondary research. Most research starts in the library.

Secondary evidence means you rely on the work of others. Generally, it includes library material and information you find on the Internet. Nearly all research requires at least some secondary material, even if you intend to conduct a primary research experiment. You could plan a project to discover what careers students choose and how well their college major is preparing them for such careers. But, before starting any kind of research, you must go to the library to find out what research has already been done, to examine the projects of other researchers, and to read their conclusions. In research, secondary evidence often comes first, before primary evidence.

At the library, you can discover what other researchers already know about your subject. You will discover what to read, whose projects are important, what critics have said about your topic. In the library, you can look for data on a question such as, "Are college students well prepared for their careers?" However, suppose you don't find anything about careers and education. Does that mean no one knows anything about your topic? Can you then just skip the secondary research and start making a questionnaire and interviewing students? No. If you can't find what you need, you should seek out a reference librarian. If the librarian can't find anything, then you need to modify your question. Before asking librarians to help you, try the Library of Congress and other online sources. If you still can't find anything, you may need to try an altogether different subject.

In secondary research you will discover what other researchers have said. You probably won't find just one, definitive answer to your question; instead, you will find various answers. This leaves your conclusion up to you. From the reading we have already done, we expect to find many authorities who say we must never allow human cloning. We have already discovered that much of the cloning research has a strong bias against human cloning: many researchers consider it unethical. However, we have also found some who don't believe this. So far we have found two sides to our question about cloning. Almost always there are at least two sides to anything—sometimes more than two.

If you plan to write a report, you can take a stance on one side or the other. You can select the side you believe in, for example: "Reasons against Human Cloning." Essentially, such a "report" is an opinion paper. However, research should be unbiased. You should look at both (or all) sides of a research question: "Reasons for and against Cloning."

To analyze secondary research, you must weigh the evidence, analyze the data, and interpret the findings. After all that, you must decide what your evidence is telling you. Often the evidence is inconclusive: you may conclude that there isn't enough data or that the evidence isn't good enough to give a clear, final conclusion. Such research can be valid; it reveals what you don't know. Those results aren't considered failures: they show one more way that doesn't work. Most researchers say it's better to find the mistakes and flaws in research than to believe you know the answers when you don't.

A Problem-Solving Approach to Research

You can use a problem-solving approach to research (and other problems). There is too much variety in research problems for you to reduce them to simple formulas. However, at a general level, problems and projects begin to look alike.

First, something puzzles you, some question irritates you, something raises your curiosity: almost anything can generate this first step. Something awakens your mind, and as a critical thinker you can't just dismiss it. In <u>Gone with the Wind</u>, Scarlett dismisses difficult problems by saying (to herself), "Oh well, I'll think about that tomorrow." Critical thinkers usually can't put off their problem until tomorrow—the problem won't be put off. It will irritate your mind until you find a solution.

Second, you try to come up with an answer. You guess or try to imagine something that will answer the question or explain the puzzle. Perhaps that noise you hear outside is made by some strange bird! Perhaps cloning human cells will yield important medical benefits! First the puzzle, then your possible solution, and then step three.

Third, you test your theory. If you go outside and find the strange bird, you've solved your problem. If you don't find it, you must redo step two: what is making that noise? If scientists can clone human cells to grow new organs, will they do this without cloning complete human beings? This question has no easy answer—you can't verify it right away. You can only speculate, using your best informed judgment.

Critical thinkers, researchers, artists—all sorts of people use this approach to problem solving. They notice problems; they think of possible solutions (eurekas); and they test those possible solutions if they can. Problem solvers are motivated by their curiosity, their need to solve some problem.

Nearly anything can start the mind of a thinker. For example, suppose you watch a magician pour water into a hat and then put the hat on his or her head (usually a volunteer's head). When the hat is whisked away, there is no water. That's the first step. Something is amiss. You know that isn't what should happen. It causes you to think, to puzzle: where is the water? The second step for a thinker is to use your imagination, to visualize, to infer or deduce a possible explanation. However, there is a rule about this second step: your guess must be something you can test, something you can try yourself—no supernatural events in which the magician uses other-worldly powers that only magicians know. Otherwise you can't get to step three—you can't test.

Ruling out things you cannot test, then, suppose in the hat trick you guess that the Great Magnifico pours the water into a funnel connected to a tube running down (or up) a sleeve. In the third step, you can try that yourself to see if it is possible. Unfortunately, you may discover that the funnel and tube are a bit clumsy and don't really correspond with what the magician does. (The Great Magnifico has anticipated your guess and has rolled up both sleeves so you can see there is no tube.) You have found one of the ways the trick doesn't work. (There really is such a trick; it isn't something we invented just to illustrate problem solving. Out of respect for magicians, we won't reveal the answer.)

The Weight of Evidence

When we speak of the "weight" of evidence, we really mean the "amount." But is it true that whoever has the most evidence wins? That notion disregards the kind and quality of evidence. Dragging in dozens of character witnesses—who swear Old Joe is incapable of crime—won't override the bank's security tape, which clearly shows Old Joe pointing a bazooka at the bank teller. Still, all other things being equal, we tend to accept the weight of evidence as an important factor in research.

It's human nature to believe in the weight of evidence. We have laws that try to protect the public, but a single test of a new product is never enough to satisfy the Food and Drug Administration (FDA), which requires many tests before giving its stamp of approval, especially for drugs. And there are other considerations. For example, all the researchers could be wrong, or all partly right. The majority opinion can be the wrong one. Galileo was arrested for defending Copernicus's theory that the Earth is not the center of the universe. Nearly all scholars of the time (including the Pope) believed the Earth was the center of the universe, around which the sun circled each day. Copernicus was right, and Galileo was right to defend him against the majority who believed otherwise. That's the way of research. All the experts swearing that humans can't be safely cloned may be humiliated by one successful cloning. A single definitive[1] piece of evidence may offset all other data: one fingerprint at the scene of the crime may vanquish all the denials that "I was never there." Questions aren't always solved simply by discovering the distribution of the evidence. Nevertheless, you need to know what the weight of evidence does suggest. Is all your evidence of the same quality? Are some facts more convincing than others? Is there more evidence on one side than the other? What is the distribution of evidence?

Magazines and Journals

Popular magazines are colorful, contain pictures and advertisements, and provide entertaining, often short, pieces about celebrities, people recently in the news, and simplified articles about recent events and interesting issues. Popular magazines are often printed on glossy paper and feature large, eye-appealing pictures on the cover, sometimes with bizarre, provocative headlines. Magazines aren't usually too difficult to read, but the reliability of such publications varies. News magazines such as <u>Time</u> and <u>Newsweek</u>, among others aimed at educated readers, are considered reliable by many researchers.

A few periodicals, such as <u>Nature</u> and <u>Scientific American</u>, look like magazines but are well respected among scientists and other educated readers. These periodicals attempt to present valid, accurate articles, but—as they will freely admit—they must have advertisers and subscribers in order to survive. Information they present is generally considered accurate but "popularized," meaning written at a level nonspecialist, educated readers can understand. "Popularization" is frequently considered a negative term, meaning a "dumbing-down" of the information, but without such publications many readers would be uninformed about developments in fields of knowledge other than their own.

What Are Professional Journals?

Journals report research and developments in the academic and technical professions; they don't often use glossy paper, color, or pictures, and they don't usually have advertisements, although that is changing. As the cost of publishing has increased, many journals have had to rely on ads—often from publishers, sometimes from professional organizations. Traditionally, journals have been easy to distinguish from magazines. Magazines look lively, attractive, inviting; journals, at best, look businesslike, plain, without color or pictures, more like reports than entertainment.

The writing itself—serious, objective reports—can suggest that you are reading a journal. Opinions are usually labeled "editorial" or are otherwise designated so that readers will know, especially in scientific writing, that the information is not intended as fact. Often journals are intended only for their own

[1]Definitive: definite, completely reliable, that which defines the truth.

professional membership, and thus they can be more technical and difficult to read than students are prepared for. Professional journals usually do not "dumb down" their articles.

The more you read, the more you will be able to identify which publications are considered reliable and informative, and which are designed for entertainment and profit. Some magazines have good reputations for accuracy and reliable reporting despite their wide public appeal; others have identifiable biases, but are otherwise considered reliable. Some of the larger newspapers like the New York Times also have good reputations.

ACTIVITY 10

Find a journal article for your project. Write a one- or two-page summary of its main points. Then briefly explain why it is or isn't a good source for your project.

Researchers' Rule

You should avoid sources designed as entertainment for mass audiences, gossip magazines, picture magazines, or sources aimed at children. Researchers do not usually look for research information in Jack and Jill, Marybeth's Beanie World Monthly or even in the children's editions of adult magazines such as Sports Illustrated for Kids or Time for Kids. That's not absolute, of course; you might use such sources if your project concerned children's magazines, such as values and biases in children's magazines. However, on the whole, researchers use the sources that other researchers are likely to read. Too many popular sources can raise questions about the credibility of your research. Avoid digests and other sources in which information has been summarized, condensed, or in some other way altered. Always make sure you're reading the original source of information.

Examining Testimony

You should use the best sources available, but there may be problems if you rely too much on only the "best" sources. (See Genetic Fallacy in chapter 5.) Critical thinkers shouldn't assume that the source of evidence always provides unconditional credibility. Researchers at great institutions, such as Duke, Johns Hopkins, Stanford, or the University of Chicago, for example, are not automatically more reliable than researchers at humbler institutions. The research that produced Dolly, for example, was conducted at the Roslin Institute in Scotland, an institute unknown to most Americans. Nor are the larger newspapers, such as the <u>New York Times</u>, the <u>Wall Street Journal</u>, and <u>Washington Post</u>, necessarily always more authoritative than smaller papers.

The great institutions—universities, government agencies, research institutes—are generally reliable and authoritative, but there is no such thing as automatic or constant authority. No place has a permanent lock on the truth. It helps when researchers find evidence from big and powerful institutions with big research grants and Nobel Prize winners on the staff, but you must not disregard evidence just because it comes from a humble source. Research should be impartial, based on facts and evidence, regardless of its source.

Reliable Research

When you quote or cite information, readers need to know this: Is your evidence reliable? Who is your source? Even if you got your information from an expert, readers need to know who that expert is—what are his or her credentials? Some experts are so well respected that few people would question their judgment.

In a democracy the majority rules, usually. But research isn't democratic. One person can be right against all the others. It was the majority opinion that people could not fly . . . until Orville and Wilbur Wright flew a motorized plane at Kitty Hawk, North Carolina, proving that no matter how many people believed the majority opinion, it was not correct.

Can you find out who the authorities are? The best way is through much reading in your research. With much reading you learn your subject, including who the well-known experts are. Who is mentioned in the article you are reading? Who is listed in the bibliography?

You need to find the experts: readers may wonder about your own credibility if you cite only unknown sources. You need to know the experts who are respected by other experts. However, you must make the sources and the evidence balance. Too much interest in the authors can seem more important than the evidence itself. Readers want to believe that you know your field, that you have read the important research and know the credible researchers, but it is your own credibility that is at stake. Your evidence must stand on its own: research must be reliable no matter who the researchers were. Unfortunately, students may sometimes be uncritical about authorities (who am I to challenge the experts?). All "authorities" can seem equally authoritative to inexperienced researchers.

Whether you can identify the authorities or not, you must be careful when reading their testimony. Specialists can sometimes exaggerate or embellish their testimony. You must read carefully and critically. When experts write to other experts, they may take shortcuts. They may refer to research you haven't read. The level of language can be difficult for students when experts take no notice of the effect of style or level of difficulty on their readers. This passage by Dominic W. S. Wong could be difficult reading for many students:

The phage particles are used to infect <u>E. coli</u> cells. Phage transfection results in clear plaques on a bacterial lawn. Each plaque corresponds to a single phage infection. The next step is to screen the plaques for the clone(s) containing the gene of interest. A commonly used technique is DNA hybridization (See Section 7.5). A radio-labeled short DNA probe complementary to the gene sequence is used to identify the particular recombinant clone. (140)

Statements of Fact

Unfortunately, not all experts are careful about documentation. Experts writing to other experts can (and often do) take much for granted. They may assume much information to be common knowledge among the well-informed members of their speciality. However, these aren't permissible assumptions for those who aren't yet specialists. You need to find supporting evidence for information you use, whether or not it was documented. You must read with a critical, enquiring mind. Suppose some historian you are reading alleges that Adolf Hitler is still alive and hiding in Argentina (a post–World War II rumor) or perhaps the historian mentions one of the many Elvis Presley "sightings." You should ask how the historian knows this: where did this information come from? If the writer is quoting or paraphrasing someone, you should try to find the original source.

It's a convention (a custom) in journalistic writing that readers must accept the journalist's word that everything has been checked and verified, usually by more than one source. Published news articles are presumed to be true (columns and editorials follow a different rule because, by definition, they are opinion pieces). Nevertheless, for students, any use of information without attribution (documentation) is a mistake, despite the fact that professionals don't always document fully. Read Mark Schoofs's "Fear and Wonder," for example.

> Tests for drug abuse are now commonplace, but they were first introduced in professions where public safety is at stake. Should genetic tests be used in a similar way? Should someone with a predisposition to, say, Alzheimer's be allowed to become president? Fly an airplane? Drive a school bus? Take custody of a child after a divorce? Genetic fitness has already arisen in a custody battle. (38)

You should ask, where did Mark Schoofs get the information in "Fear and Wonder" concerning a custody battle in which genetic fitness was an issue? His last statement is used as a fact, but he supplies no source for this fact, not here and not at the end of his article. Mark Schoofs is a journalist; he writes for the <u>Village Voice</u>, and readers may accept his word as accurate. However, as a careful researcher, you should not rely on this statement until you can find a valid source for it.

Inferences, Assumptions, and Conclusions

Drawing an inference is seldom as precise as arithmetic. Given evidence, you can make assumptions, draw conclusions, and attempt to infer cause and effect. In the film <u>The Medicine Man</u>, Sean Connery is a scientist working in a Brazilian rain forest. He finds a cure for cancer based on a local flower but then is unable to reproduce his experiment. The tribal medicine man tells him the flower has no magic but is only a house for bugs. Suddenly, Connery has a flash of understanding—eureka!—the bugs are the answer: they carry the cure. Inferences work something like that. They are a kind of guess, a conclusion you reach based on your evidence.

Some authorities have inferred that a clone can never be the exact replica of any person. Testifying before the Science Subcommittee on Technology for the U.S. House of Representatives, Thomas H. Murray (1997), a professor at the Center of Biomedical Ethics at Case Western Reserve University, said there would be "no instant copies." Although a clone of Mel Gibson may look a great deal like Mel, "Mel's charm lies in his personality and wit at least as much as in his good looks." Even though genetic blueprints may be identical, "no two lives are identical," said Representative Murray.[2] His conclusion seems plausible. The myth that human clones would be identical persons has become so disputed now that we can consider it common knowledge: humans can't be replicated (but we would need to clone someone to find out for sure). Clones might resemble each other, but they could be 19 or 20 years younger (let's say) than their "parent," and they would grow up in different times. A clone must be a baby first and then must spend years growing up. No one knows exactly how much of human development is related to genetics and how much to the environment.

"Mere" Opinions versus Critical Judgments

"Mere" opinions are unrelated to particular evidence. In research, opinions without evidence are usually considered editorializing; the researcher is offering his or her own ideas but not citing evidence. If you read that high doses of vitamin C each day are good for your health, you need to ask, "Who says so?" If the writer offers documentation and substantiation, criteria by which you could agree or disagree with the opinion (such as statistics and statements by noted scientists such as Linus Pauling), the statement is no longer a "mere" opinion but a critical judgment.

Considering the Evidence Itself

Eventually, you must examine the evidence itself. Where it came from may suggest something, who it came from can also suggest something, but you can never avoid examining the evidence itself. What is the evidence? If the evidence is testimony of a witness (an "eyewitness" maybe), you can see the importance of who or where the evidence comes from. How much evidence is there? What

[2]<http://www.house.gov/science/murray_3=5.html> Access date: 28 Dec. 1997.

kind of evidence is it? In some cases, important evidence can be historical. Early attempts to induce human conception outside the body encountered religious arguments ("playing God") and arguments suggesting that people feared for the safety of children produced in "unnatural" ways. Fooling with Mother Nature, it was thought, might produce deformed children. Such arguments had to be examined one at a time by serious scientists who treated each argument seriously. The American public was not prepared for non-natural "birth assistance." The first in vitro (in glass) fertilization (IVF)—in which egg and sperm meet in a lab dish—therefore took place not in America but in England, where baby Louise Brown was born healthy and happy through IVF (Silver 78). The arguments raged on, but eventually the public realized that the IVF procedure was safe: today thousands of healthy babies have been born through IVF. The arguments have shifted to cloning. Again, the first results were not achieved in the United States but Scotland. And many of the same objections raised against IVF are being raised against cloning.

It is important to have an accurate understanding of your research subject, especially if it concerns a technical procedure like cloning. For example, proponents can claim that the only "unnatural" part of cloning is the conception of the embryo. Once an adult cell has been received from the donor, it can be made to begin dividing again, as if it were a fetal cell. Within a short time, one cell becomes two, two become four, four become eight, and so on. When the embryo is sufficiently developed it is inserted into the womb, where it would be had conception occurred naturally. From then on it grows and develops. At least that is what happens in animal cloning. Many scientists now believe the same thing would happen with a human embryo. You can see, then, why some scientists are anxious to undertake research on human cloning . . . and why so many others worry about the consequences.

A Priori Reasoning

A priori means "presumptively"; literally it means "from before, from what precedes." A researcher might decide in advance, for example, that cloned people would be less human than naturally conceived babies and then look for data to prove that presumption. The scientific method (induction) relies first on observation and then, based on the observations, afterward reaches a conclusion. A little plover will stagger about dragging her wing any time you approach her nest, but when you move away, she seems to recover and returns to her nest. After several observations of this behavior, you would be right to conclude that the little bird is faking a broken wing to draw you away from her nest.

A priori reasoning (deduction) works the other way around; it is the method of mathematics, in which you may start with a conclusion, some generalization you believe, and then try to find evidence to prove it. However, except for its use in certain areas of science, an a priori presumption is almost always a serious mistake in research. Researchers—a priori—decide first what they will conclude, before they have done any research, and then try to find evidence that will support their presumption, as if you could guess first what the little plover will do and then try to catch her doing it. A priori applies to students most when they decide what their research paper will prove before they have done any research: "I will write a paper to prove that any cloning of human cells is totally bad."

Prima Facie Reasoning

The general meaning of <u>prima facie</u> (pronounced prima fay' she) is "on the face of it," "at first appearance." Legally, prima facie means "sufficient to establish a case." Your fingerprints on the murder weapon is prima facie evidence against you. In research <u>prima facie</u> tends to mean "obvious" or "undisputed." A car full of new merchandise for which the driver has no sales receipts could be prima facie evidence of theft. Typically, a prima facie assumption is strong evidence: that she gave birth to a child is prima facie evidence that she was pregnant.

De Facto Reasoning

<u>De facto</u> means "actually," "in fact," "in reality." Many people believe that without a wedding, no marriage exists, though a couple might live together as de facto man and wife. Also, our language insists that a child is her mother's daughter, but a cloned child could also be accepted as her mother's de facto sister (because they had the same genetic source, the same genetic parentage, they would both be the genetic offspring of the mother's parents). The Chinese government is the de facto ruler of Tibet, though the exiled Dali Lama remains Tibet's spiritual leader and maintains a Tibetan government in exile.

Ex Post Facto Reasoning

<u>Ex post facto</u> means "after the fact," "retroactively." Anyone who assists a criminal fleeing the scene of a crime can be considered guilty of the crime ex post facto. The pressures of research are so great that in order to justify all their time and expense some scientists may "cook" (alter) the data ex post facto. It's easy to tell ex post facto which horse is the winner of the race. One of the fears about human cloning is the fear that something may go wrong ex post facto, when it may be too late to stop it or to repair it.

ACTIVITY 11

In your notebook, write two or three examples of your own for the terms <u>a priori</u>, <u>prima facie</u>, <u>de facto</u>, and <u>ex post facto</u>.

Defining Your Terms

Research often starts in a muddle, but eventually (better sooner than later) your thesis must become clear. It must be clear to everyone, not just you. What are you investigating? It's usually not a good idea to assume readers understand the terms you are using, especially terms such as <u>enzymes</u>, <u>protease</u>, <u>chromosomes</u>, <u>DNA</u>, and so on. Readers may have learned those terms in high school or college, but you should probably explain them anyway. It is especially important to make sure that authors you are reading mean the same thing you do when they use the same terms. If authors discuss human embryos, do they agree on their definition of "embryo"? Do they agree that an embryo is "human" or that it constitutes "human life"? (Actually, some don't. "Embryo" is a loaded term in this research.)

ACTIVITY 12

Select three of the terms in your research and explain in your own words for uninformed readers what the terms mean.

Occam's Razor: The Rule of Simplicity

The rule of simplicity, "Occam's razor," says you should accept the simplest explanation whenever you find competing theories. Researchers have a bias against bizarre, exotic interpretations of evidence. The philosopher Occam said, until you have good evidence one way or the other, choose the interpretation requiring the fewest assumptions. Occam's razor tends to mean you should be skeptical about interpretations and reasoning based on contradictions of accepted fact. Thus, Occam warns you to work hard before accepting things like UFOs, monsters, or ghosts: you must not accept theories or explanations without good evidence. You may hear stories about people who find puddles in the desert and then suggest that an alien must have urinated there. Occam would say such an interpretation requires the prior assumption that there are or were aliens here on Earth . . . and also possibly that they have bodily functions similar to ours.

This isn't to say that you must never accept unusual interpretations, but only that you must work hard to test them before you do accept them. (A simple chemical test should reveal much about those desert puddles.) Extraordinary explanations should be resisted until the evidence for them becomes compelling: a "strange" noise in the house at night could be a monster or it could be the house settling. Occam's razor tells us we should not accept the monster theory until we have powerful evidence for it. Unfortunately, Occam gives strength to the establishment bias, and that is why research isn't usually simply counting the data. If you never accept anything new or unusual, you will not be able to make progress in research. Fortunately, Occam does not tell you never to accept the new or different: his advice is to make sure of your evidence before you conclude that the sky is falling.

Remaining Impartial

Researchers must remain objective and unbiased. You must not let your own emotions influence your judgment. It can be difficult to research alcoholism, drug addiction, or any serious diseases or disorders if someone you know is afflicted. But starting out with an attitude for or against the subject would mean your research is biased from the very beginning.

You can compensate for this by wording your thesis so that either answer is useful: "is drug addiction a genetic problem?" If it is, you know what direction you must take to deal with it; if it isn't, you know you must look elsewhere. Either way you get a useful answer from your research.

Unfortunately, there are other ways impartiality can slip away, especially for students. It isn't easy to remain balanced and nonjudgmental all the way through a project. One of the ways that bias can creep into a project is through unconsciously over- or underresearching one side or the other. If you find much data on one side of your question but little on the other, you will, of course, conclude in favor of the side with the most data. However, it can happen that this difference in the evidence is merely an accident of your procedure. If you find such a problem in your research, ask a reference librarian for assistance. It's possible that you are simply more interested in one side: your bias for one side or the other may have caused you to lose your impartiality. Occasionally, the bias is built into a researcher's thesis. Are aliens similar to humans? There is very little reliable evidence that aliens have ever visited earth, nor should you expect them to be similar to humans if they had. Therefore, this question is likely to be heavily biased in favor of the negative answer. Is cloning dangerous—might it contain harm for children produced this way? There is, so far, little evidence that cloning is more dangerous than natural birth. These questions have built-in biases, and you should examine them carefully before committing yourself to projects based on them. Being impartial can't serve you well when your question itself is biased.

Determining Relevance

Stick to the subject. Avoid side issues. Limit your paper to the relevant facts only. Cloning is a large subject, with connections to other kinds of assisted reproduction. But if your thesis asks whether cloning is morally acceptable, your paper must be restricted to the ethics of cloning. You probably should not, for example, include information on xenotransplantation—animal organs transplanted into humans. Though animal research may be relevant, if you are researching whether human organs should be cloned, you must resist side issues.

Research isn't only routine collecting and summarizing of other people's information. In a sense information is alive: it connects better with some information than with other information. Critical thinkers know they cannot force information into contexts where it doesn't relate. The information resists, changes, becomes unreliable when you try to force it where it does not belong. This aspect of relevance may also resist routine outlining. A thoughtful writer performs complex mental imagery, partly relying on the information of other writers, partly relying on notes and trial outlines on paper, and all the while creating in the mind a vision of the shape of things to come. It is your thoughtful mental image of the subject, including notes, outlines, drafts, and thoughts, that make your project truly yours. Relevance concerns not only the information produced by others, but your own vision of what all that information can be.

Significance

What is the importance of the information, its wider implications for research? Does it signify anything about humanity? Is it worthy, important, not only to you but to others?

Cloning might sound interesting to you, but will it sound interesting to anyone else? Is this a subject that can have meaning for general readers? Will it be so technical that only specialists can understand it? As a researcher you may be able to think of several questions about this subject, many of which may seem to ask whether cloning is a worthwhile subject. Of course, every researcher must answer that question. Yet how can you decide whether your research question is worthwhile? Questions about research are usually answered in the research itself. That is, you can discover the value of your subject by reading about it and thinking about what you read. The more you read and think, the more confident you will be about the value of your research thesis. For example, some researchers stress that cloning may allow scientists to eradicate most genetic diseases and some kinds of cancer. We think nearly all readers would be happy to see genetic diseases disappear from the Earth. This and other promises of cloning make the subject seem worthwhile. You need to keep reading until you find reasons to believe in the worth of your thesis.

As you read about your subject, you will gain a clearer understanding of the relevance and significance of new information. You should become increasingly able to identify what is—or isn't—useful to your research. As a critical thinker, you must decide whether your research subject is worth investigating, whether information may be available on your subject, and whether the information is not only useful for your project but may have an impact on additional research, on society at large, or possibly on certain individuals (those suffering from certain diseases or afflictions for example). A worthwhile subject is one that has implications for the future, one that other researchers can build from and apply to their own research.

ACTIVITY 13

In your notebook write a rough draft of your thoughts on what your research has suggested about the significance of your project.

Objectivity

<u>Objective</u> in research usually means factual, without bias, without slanting or angling the data. Technically, it means that different observers should report the same or similar observations. Researchers should be objective, impartial, open-minded, and without bias.

One kind of bias is presenting only one side of an issue, such as describing only the flaws in an opposing point of view. Another kind of bias is slanting a report. An objective statement:

> Ian Wilmut was the first researcher to demonstrate successfully that it is possible to clone a relatively large mammal from an adult tissue cell.

A biased or slanted statement:

> Ian Wilmut was the first researcher lucky enough to demonstrate that he could clone a relatively large mammal from an adult tissue cell.

The first statement is factual; it is a statement that anyone might make. The second statement contains something in addition to the fact: "lucky enough." The addition changes the statement slightly. It "colors" the information, adding something about the writer. Wilmut might agree—or not—that "luck" had anything to do with it. As a careful researcher, Wilmut might respond, "So <u>you</u> say." The slant expresses an opinion, indicating more about the writer who uses the word <u>lucky</u> than anything factual about Wilmut.

Some words are inherently prejudicial or biased—words that have strong connotations. For example

> A few misguided researchers believe the absurd proposition that cloning provides humanity with the possibility of immortality.

Fortunately, such "loaded" language is obvious and easy to detect, and some readers believe biases are less troublesome when openly stated. However, slants and biases can also be subtle and less openly stated:

> A few researchers believe that cloning offers humanity some sort of immortality.

The comment does not use strong or loaded language; instead, it disparages the idea by implying that the idea ("some sort of immortality") is vague or ill-defined, trivial, or perhaps idiosyncratic (an idea that appeals only to those who believe it). Biases need not be negative. An entirely positive slant on information can express a bias nevertheless: "Cloning has opened a world of possibilities for medical cures and prevention of diseases and afflictions." The statement may be correct, but it is also biased in favor of cloning: not everyone is so uncritical about cloning.

Most readers take the position that there should be no slanting or bias of any kind in research writing, that to bias the information means to produce something other than research. But such a position overlooks the fact that any decision to present information one way rather than another is itself a kind of bias, including the decision to present "objectively." You need to find out what people mean when they use a word like objective.

Accuracy

You must have knowledge of the subject in order to judge accuracy. The more you study your subject, the easier it will become for you to spot problems. Simple factual errors may be easy to find. Errors of reasoning or interpretation may be more difficult. For example

> The Constitution says that we are all equal, yet our country is clearly divided into rich, poor, and middle classes.

Such a statement is based on a misinterpretation of what the Constitution actually says. Then too, questions of law (and the Constitution) are affected by court decisions and precedents. When you believe you have found an error, you should search for confirmation in authoritative sources.

Claim

A research claim is a thesis, a proposition to be inferred or supported with evidence. What does the author want you to believe: what is the claim? Can you find the author's thesis? Critical thinkers take as much care in reporting their work as in doing the research in the first place. You should be able to find a thesis clearly stated or strongly implied at the beginning of most reports, though it can sometimes appear elsewhere. If the author's claim is not clear, it will be difficult, perhaps impossible, to evaluate the effectiveness of the research. However, you must keep in mind that occasionally writers do not provide a written thesis when (they believe) their claim is strongly implied—the claim is obvious enough that the writer doesn't feel the need to write it out explicitly. For example, a writer provides a few examples of fatal automobile accidents and then begins citing research on seat belts. It may not be necessary for the author to explicitly state the claim: seatbelts can prevent automobile fatalities.

Persuasion

How does the writer attempt to persuade you? If there is factual data, is it documented? If it is not documented, should you accept it? If the reasons are theoretical and speculative, do they sound logical and convincing? Can you think of exceptions to the reasons, contradictions, or equally persuasive but contrasting reasons? If you can think of exceptions, how does that affect your assessment of the article? Arguing with reasons as opposed to facts may be theoretical but not, therefore, necessarily less convincing. Such reasoning is an important component of science. It is the way critical thinkers enter into areas for which there are no facts. Speculation is the beginning of theory and leads finally to propositions that can be tested.

Judging Probability

Critical thinkers are seldom able to state results in absolute terms. Is cloning absolutely (100%) harmless? After 100 or 1,000 experiments, you might be inclined to believe cloning is absolutely harmless, but experimenting is a lot like flipping coins: there is always a 50/50 chance that either side will come up, even if you have flipped heads 1,000 times in a row. The odds don't change: you still have a 50/50 chance that the next flip will be tails. Researchers seldom work with absolutes or certainties. Instead you must work with probabilities. At best you can say only that there appears to be a high probability that cloning may (or may not) be harmless.

Mathematics and philosophy (where we can invent "thought experiments") may work with absolute certainties. In the real world, researchers ordinarily work with probable facts and events instead of indisputable evidence. You have no way to know with certainty what will be the outcome of any horse race or where the wheel will stop in a casino. Researchers can only calculate odds and come up with probable answers. In your research paper, you can say only that your conclusion seems probable or reasonable given the data. You can't say that some mad egomaniac will one day clone himself into his own army. Even if that were possible, it isn't probable: cloning only produces embryos—each of which needs a mother's womb in order to develop into a live baby, which would then need many years to grow and develop before being of use in an army.

Probability in research means a chance or trend, the statistical chance (probability) that an event will occur. Young people are sometimes told that because of their age, car insurance will cost many hundreds (sometimes thousands) of dollars. "How unfair," some say. "I do not drive carelessly. Why should I be penalized for someone else's careless driving?" The answer is "probabilities." The insurance company has calculated all the accidents by people of a given age and determined that there is a high correlation between age and accidents. That correlation isn't absolute of course, but the probability is high, especially for young males.

Evaluating Statistical Data

The first law of statistics is beware of statistics. Much research today uses statistics, but many people don't understand statistics and have only a limited ability to do the math required. In fact, the more numbers in your research, the more difficult for your readers. We cannot provide an introduction to statistics here, but we can make a few suggestions. The first is to be critical of statistics. When you encounter them in your research, you may need to find someone who can help you understand them. For example, "If 50% of students have a 30% chance of scoring at 80% or above on the final exam . . . and so on": such statements soon get beyond most readers' ability to calculate.

In addition to arithmetical problems, statistics can bias research simply because of the power of numbers. Numbers tend to carry more weight than other kinds of data. Specific numbers are often more convincing than generalizations about "more" or "less" of anything. "More females than males" could mean 1% more or 27%, or 99%, and so on. If you use mathematical data, you may be perceived as more knowledgeable and trustworthy than researchers who offer only generalizations. However, the downside of that is the likelihood that you may quickly exhaust your readers' ability to deal with numbers. You must make your own judgment concerning how much mathematical information readers can absorb. Unless your readers have studied statistics, you should avoid statistical language like this: "Consider the .05 value for one degree of freedom in Table IV. This value is 3.841 and the square root of this is ±1.96 which is the .05 value of z for a two-tailed test" (Downie and Heath 169).

Critical readers should be suspicious of statistical generalizations. Numbers can be useful, but they don't automatically solve all your problems. The most important fact to remember about statistical research is how many people, rats, or other subjects are you talking about? A sample of 90% seems like a lot— "90% of students in our sample approved of more homework and stricter grading," but that could mean only nine individuals if the total sample was 10 students. Be cautious about using figures to "prove" things (see Amphiboly, chapter 5). Numbers can increase the persuasiveness of research, but inappropriate use of statistical data will have the opposite effect.

Problems of Questionnaires

Questionnaires, among other forms of evidence, usually require statistical analysis. Questionnaires are popular means for gaining information. In the hands of a well-trained pollster, questionnaires can be effective, but they can also be difficult and sometimes more troublesome than helpful, especially in the hands of amateurs.

Your readers may need to know not only where and who you got your information from but also how you got it. Did all your information come from the library or the Internet? Did you perform an experiment? Did you go to Harvard to interview famed science writer, Stephen Jay Gould? Did you send out questionnaires through the mail? If so, were you able to overcome the problems of questionnaires? Following are some problems with questionnaires:

1. <u>Often less than half the recipients will respond</u>. Questionnaires sent by mail are often treated like junk mail, just more unwanted paper that immediately goes into the trash. You might get better results on a street with a lot of foot traffic, but even then your results can be disappointing. Busy people are by definition in a hurry to get where they are going. Even if you could get all of them to stop and answer your questions, you are likely to need a large sample in order to get enough responses to make your results meaningful.

2. <u>Sampling techniques (whether you ask a "random" group or a specific group, such as bus drivers) can be harder than you might think, especially if you need a random sample</u>. A group of anonymous people on the street aren't necessarily random. Randomizing a sample requires a statistical procedure best left to experts.

3. <u>Often people don't understand questionnaire questions</u>. Making a good questionnaire takes training and skill. Wording questions so that they are unambiguous and readily understood may require you to try out your questionnaire on a preview group, sometimes more than one. A question may seem simple and clear when you write it, but our language is full of connotations and ambiguities. Asking whether something is "good" has a variety of meanings, depending on the criteria for "goodness." Has the president done a "good job"? Has the president been "effective"? Do those two questions mean the same thing to you? Do they mean the same thing to everyone?

4. <u>The wording of questions can bias the answers</u>. Slightly different wordings of the same question can produce different results. For example

   Should tobacco products be banned in public places?

   Would you approve of a ban on tobacco products in public places?

   The difference in these two questions is that the first one is aimed at a general audience. The second is aimed at "you," and may cause people to react defensively.

5. <u>People tend to say what they think you want to hear</u>. Some people may respond to the interviewer rather than to the questions. The desire to please or to be liked can bias a respondent's answers. In that case, the interviewer's manner and appearance can have a lot to do with the results. Well-dressed, attractive interviewers may get different responses than do unkempt, unattractive interviewers. An aggressive, intimidating manner may produce different answers than a pleasant, encouraging manner.

6. <u>The order of the questions can bias the answers</u>. It matters which question is first and which is last. "Do you approve of the president's job performance?" If the question is asked first, you will get one answer, but if it is asked last—after a number of other questions concerning the president (Do you approve of the president's tax cut? Aid to the elderly? Reduction in the costs of higher education?)— then you may get a different answer. It isn't easy to create, administer, or interpret a reliable questionnaire.

In addition to biases and other problems concerning validity in the questions, there are technical problems with the calculations and interpretations of the outcome. With the assistance of skilled designers, interviewers, and interpreters, it is possible to obtain useful information through questionnaires, although valid questionnaire construction is a difficult form of data collection, and the results can often be of doubtful validity. Questionnaires are usually considered "soft research" at best.

ACTIVITY 14

Try a group activity. Develop a short list of questions to ask students on campus. Try to make the questions as simple and objective as possible, and then send out two sets of pollsters: one well dressed and one not. Prepare to explain the results you get.

EVALUATING THE DATA: A TEST CASE

The following data represent some of the source material you might find on the question of whether humans should be cloned. If you use the principles of evidence already discussed, it's possible to reach some conclusions about these sources. Please read the excerpts to determine whether you can answer the question:

1. The cloning of Dolly broke the technological barrier. There is no reason to expect that the technology couldn't be transferred to human cells. On the contrary, there is every reason to expect that it <u>can</u> be transferred. It requires only equipment and facilities that are already standard or easy to obtain by biomedical laboratories and free-standing <u>in vitro</u> fertilization clinics across the country and across the world. Although the protocol itself demands the services of highly trained and skilled personnel, there are thousands of people with such skills in the United States alone.

It is not a question of whether human cloning will work, but whether it could be used safely or not. Historical precedent suggests that reprogenetic service providers may not even wait until this question has been resolved. The direct injection of sperm into eggs (ICSI) as a cure for infertility was embraced by the IVF community as soon as the technique was perfected, long before any consequences to the children born could be ascertained. (Silver 93)

2. Why should you be panicked? Because humans are next. "It would almost certainly be possible to produce human bodies without a forebrain," Princeton biologist Lee Silver told the <u>London Sunday Times</u>. "These human bodies without any semblance of consciousness would not be considered persons, and thus it would be perfectly legal to keep them 'alive' as a future source of organs." . . . And Professor Silver not only sees "nothing wrong, philosophically or rationally," with producing headless humans for organ harvesting; he wants to convince a skeptical public that it is perfectly O.K. (Krauthammer 76)

3. The human species is a rather difficult species to clone. Our scientists have developed a unique and efficient way to clone humans. This enables us to assure the highest quality clones for personal or business uses. Our clones' brains have been completely wiped of any bad habits, tendencies and memories of the original human donor. [. . .] Droids are popular and less expensive than a clone, but that problem of no emotions can wear on you after a while. Our clones can be trained to be loving, caring, responsible adults. ("Clone Inc." 1997)

4. The commission concluded that at this time it is morally unacceptable for anyone in the public or private sector, whether in research or clinical setting, to attempt to create a child using somatic cell nuclear transfer cloning. We reached a consensus on this point because current scientific information indicates that this technique is not safe to use in humans at this time. (Shapiro 195–96)

5. Cloning will be attractive because of some medical uses. Genetic replicas of geniuses might also benefit society. On the other hand, ruthless and egocentric despots may replicate themselves millions of times over. Cloning on a large scale would also reduce biological diversity, and the entire human species could be wiped out by some new epidemic to which a genetically uniform population was susceptible. (Mautner 68)

6. In most states, fertility clinics are observing a voluntary moratorium on human cloning, because they suspect that success rates would be low. [. . .] After all, of the 277 attempts by the Scottish embryologist Ian Wilmut to create a clone from an adult sheep's mammary cell, only one produced a live offspring—Dolly. Most people believe that it is unethical to subject humans to a procedure with those odds; it would also be prohibitively expensive. Few women now make their eggs available to fertility clinics, and when they do, they are paid approximately $2,000 per egg. No clinic is going to be able to acquire

277 eggs for use with a single patient; even if one did, 277 eggs at $2,000 apiece would require $554,000 for each child created through cloning. (Andrews B4–5)

7. The Church of Scotland has already stated that to clone human beings would be ethically unacceptable as a matter of principle. On principle, to replicate any human technologically is a violation of the basic dignity and uniqueness of each human being made in God's image, of what God has given to that individual and to no one else. (Bruce)

8. A moratorium on the cloning of animals would go well beyond what society needs in order to take stock. But a declared moratorium on human cloning is desirable, even though it carries with it a possibility that will worry those who wish to pursue such research: that legislators will consider the potential benefits but decide that the risks to society are too significant for it to be permitted at all. The history of technology suggests, however, that highly regulated human cloning will, after all, be found to be a tolerable way to proceed. ("Human Cloning Requires a Moratorium, Not a Ban" 1)

9. In medicine, scientists dream of using cloning to reprogram cells so we can make our own body parts for transplantation. Suppose, for example, you needed a bone-marrow transplant. Some deadly forms of leukemia can be cured completely if doctors destroy your own marrow and replace it with healthy marrow from someone else. But the marrow must be a close genetic match to your own. If not, it will lash out at you and kill you. [. . .] But suppose, instead, that scientists could take one of your cells—any cell—and merge it with a human egg. The egg would start to divide, to develop, but it would not be permitted to divide more than a few times. Instead, technicians would bathe it in proteins that direct primitive cells, embryo cells, to become marrow cells. What started out to be a clone of you could grow into a batch of your marrow—the perfect match. (Kolata 8–9)

ACTIVITY 15

In your notebook, consider each of the preceding nine passages. What conclusions do you think researchers should draw? How does this evidence connect with the main research question: "Should we permit research on cloning humans?" Try to answer for each whether the evidence is good. Is it relevant? Is it useful? If it is good—and especially if it isn't—why do you think so? This activity asks you for thoughtful answers, not necessarily "right" ones. Read the following discussion items and answer as many of the questions as you can in each item. Save for last your answer to the main question.

Item One: What would you say is Lee Silver's most important point in excerpt one? In his epigraph, he dedicates his book to his parents: "To Joseph and Ethel Silver for creating me the old-fashioned way." Is there any implied contradiction in that epigraph versus Silver's stand on human cloning throughout his book? Why, in your opinion, does Silver include his statement concerning IVF? What, if anything, can be inferred from his credentials: Lee Silver is a professor of molecular biology, ecology, and evolutionary biology at Princeton. Often quoted in articles, he is considered an expert in cloning research.

Item Two: Though President Clinton cut off all funds for research on human cloning in this country, other countries are working vigorously on this research. Recall that Dolly was born in Scotland. If it is going to happen anyway (in other countries) why not in America? Anyone who has read Silver's book Remaking Eden should believe that Silver is rational and ethical, but Krauthammer makes Silver appear unethical. How does Krauthammer do this? In your opinion, why does he do this? Can you explain whether, in your own judgment, a researcher should use the Krauthammer passage either for or against the question of human cloning?

Item Three: This passage is meant as satire. A by-line on the Internet page states "Los Angeles' Largest Outlet for Clones and Accessories" and "Cloning Humans for 30 Years." Do you see any connection between "the highest quality clones" and the research question: should we clone humans? Even if all this is intended as humor, can you think of any reason(s) for comparisons with "Droids"? Should a researcher use this item in a research paper? (Why or why not?)

Item Four: The commission that Shapiro mentions is the National Bioethics Advisory Commission that President Clinton mandated to review the issue of human cloning. In your opinion, would any of the researchers here be likely to disagree with the conclusion of the commission? From what you know about cloning, are you able to say whether it is more dangerous than in vitro fertilization or surrogate mothering? As far as we know, there has never been any research on human cloning in the United States (prior to NBAC). Can you think of any possible reason(s) for allowing such research? From a research point of view (in your opinion), what importance might there be in the conclusion of the commission?

Item Five: From what you know about cloning, is there anything in Mautner's logos that a researcher might challenge? On what grounds might a researcher agree or disagree with Mautner that genetic replicas of living geniuses might benefit society? Which genetic replicas of living geniuses would you especially hope to see? How or why does Mautner think that "the entire human species could be wiped out"? As a critical thinker why, do you suppose, has Mautner made his first statement so general?

The article contains brief information on Michael Mautner. He is a research professor of chemistry at the University of Canterbury in New Zealand. Can you say whether or how his credentials might affect his authority as a researcher?

Item Six: What is the first law of statistics? Are you able to surmise the effect of the numbers Andrews uses to describe Ian Wilmut's results—"of the 277 attempts [...] only one produced a live offspring"? Does your own understanding of cloning allow you to say what is "created through cloning"? As a researcher what effect do you believe Andrews achieves when she uses the phrase "each child created through cloning"?

Item Seven: Can researchers tell whether the second sentence in excerpt eight should be attributed to Robert Bruce or the Church of Scotland? In your own judgment, without necessarily getting into the morality of it, unless you wish to, what should researchers understand by the statement: "to replicate any human technologically is a violation of the basic dignity and uniqueness of each human being made in God's image"? Assuming for a moment that you are an advocate for Robert Bruce, can you explain his point of view? Would you say that Bruce or the Church of Scotland would apply the same complaint to IVF, surrogate mothering, and other means of "birth assistance"?

Item Eight: What is the meaning of <u>moratorium</u>? From what you know of the controversy surrounding human cloning, can you say whether the editorial in excerpt eight is fair-minded? Can you say whether research into human cloning shows that there are or may be dangers in human cloning? Is it clear to you whether science should or should not proceed with research into human cloning? Do you agree that American scientists should be required to work carefully under government regulations while scientists in other countries are free to work without such regulations? Without necessarily referring to the cloning controversy, do you think researchers should accept ethics as a branch of science?

<u>Nature</u> is a premier British journal of science. Does that fact have any influence on your reaction to the passage?

Item Nine: In your opinion, should medical science encourage research into the uses of cloning (uses other than assisted childbirth)? Because cloning operates at the cellular level, it might have important considerations for cancer: in your judgment is that fact significant enough to encourage human cloning research? Is there any basis for the fears of some people that any sort of cloning is a step onto the slippery slope?

Kolata is a well-respected science writer for the <u>New York Times</u>. She broke the story about Dolly's birth.

Summing Up the Evidence

The test case here shows that scientists have the technology to clone mammals and, therefore, probably humans. There may be medical reasons for doing it, including cloning organs and tissues. There are social, psychological, and moral arguments against doing it, as well as fears of it (injury, monstrosity, death), and suggestions for how to get past the arguments, such as government regulations. All things considered, researchers are left with a hard problem. As in a lot of research, these nine items don't leave you with a clear-cut answer, and as in many such cases, you must make a decision, form a critical judgment based on all the factors, the evidence plus your own understanding. In your own mind, given all you know about cloning, what seems to you a reasonable conclusion? Should human cloning be allowed or not? And why, or why not?

ACTIVITY 16

Please read Charles Krauthammer's <u>Time</u> article. Write your analysis and evaluation of the essay. Look for any insights, assumptions, and overgeneralizations. Is his thinking reasonable? Do you think well of his logos, pathos, and ethos? Should this essay be used in a project on the ethics of cloning? (2 to 4 pages)

Of Headless Mice . . . and Men: The Ultimate Cloning Horror: Human Organ Farms

Charles Krauthammer

Last year Dolly the cloned sheep was received with wonder, titters and some vague apprehension. Last week the announcement by a Chicago physicist that he is assembling a team to produce the first human clone occasioned yet another wave of Brave New World anxiety. But the scariest news of all—and largely overlooked—comes from two obscure labs, at the University of Texas and at the University of Bath. During the past four years, one group created headless mice; the other, headless tadpoles. 1

For sheer Frankenstein wattage, the purposeful creation of these animal monsters has no equal. Take the mice. Researchers found the gene that tells the embryo to produce the head. They deleted it. They did this in a thousand mice embryos, four of which were born. I use the term loosely. Having no way to breathe, the mice died instantly. 2

Why then create them? The Texas researchers want to learn how genes determine embryo development. But you don't have to be a genius to see the true utility of manufacturing headless creatures: for their organs—fully formed, perfectly useful, ripe for plundering. 3

Why should you be panicked? Because humans are next. "It would almost certainly be possible to produce human bodies without a forebrain," Princeton biologist Lee Silver told the <u>London Sunday Times</u>. "These human bodies with- 4 out any semblance of consciousness would not be considered persons, and thus it would be perfectly legal to keep them 'alive' as a future source of organs."

"Alive." Never have a pair of quotation marks loomed so ominously. Take 5 the mouse-frog technology, apply it to humans, combine it with cloning, and you become a god: with a single cell taken from, say, your finger, you produce a headless replica of yourself, a mutant twin, arguably lifeless, that becomes your own personal, precisely tissue-matched organ farm.

There are, of course, technical hurdles along the way. Suppressing the 6 equivalent "head" gene in man. Incubating tiny infant organs to grow into larger ones that adults could use. And creating artificial wombs (as per Aldous Huxley), given that it might be difficult to recruit sane women to carry headless fetuses to their birth/death.

It won't be long, however, before these technical barriers are breached. 7 The ethical barriers are already cracking. Lewis Wolpert, professor of biology at University College, London, finds producing headless humans "personally distasteful" but, given the shortage of organs, does not think distaste is suffi-cient reason not to go ahead with something that would save lives. And Profes-sor Silver not only sees "nothing wrong, philosophically or rationally," with producing headless humans for organ harvesting; he wants to convince a skep-tical public that it is perfectly O.K.

When prominent scientists are prepared to acquiesce in—or indeed encour- 8 age—the deliberate creation of deformed and dying quasi-human life, you know we are facing a bioethical abyss. Human beings are ends, not means. There is no grosser corruption of biotechnology than creating a human mutant and disemboweling it at our pleasure for spare parts.

The prospect of headless human clones should put the whole debate about 9 "normal" cloning in a new light. Normal cloning is less a treatment for infer-tility than a treatment for vanity. It is a way to produce an exact genetic replica of yourself that will walk the earth years after you're gone.

But there is a problem with a clone. It is not really you. It is but a twin, 10 a perfect John Doe Jr., but still a junior. With its own independent conscious-ness, it is, alas, just a facsimile of you.

The headless clone solves the facsimile problem. It is a gateway to the 11 ultimate vanity, immortality. If you create a real clone, you cannot transfer your consciousness into it to truly live on. But if you create a headless clone of just your body, you have created a ready source of replacement parts to keep you— your consciousness—going indefinitely.

Which is why one form of cloning will inevitably lead to the other. Cloning 12 is the technology of narcissism, and nothing satisfies narcissism like immortal-ity. Headlessness will be cloning's crowning achievement.

The time to put a stop to this is now. Dolly moved President Clinton to 13 create a commission that recommended a temporary ban on human cloning. But with physicist Richard Seed threatening to clone humans, and with headless animals already here, we are past the time for toothless commissions and meaningless bans.

Clinton banned federal funding of human-cloning research, of which there 14
is none anyway. He then proposed a five-year ban on cloning. This is not
enough. Congress should ban human cloning now. Totally. And regarding one
particular form, it should be draconian: the deliberate creation of headless
humans must be made a crime, indeed a capital crime. If we flinch in the face
of this high-tech barbarity, we'll deserve to live in the hell it heralds. (76)

Chapter 9

Documentation

Documentation refers to the method by which you tell your readers where you found your information. Because other researchers must be able to evaluate the quality of your work, it's important to be accurate and consistent in the way you give references. A reference note is information, such as a parenthetic name and page number, referring to an entry in your Works Cited or References bibliography at the end of your paper. Writers use various documentation styles today: MLA, APA, traditional footnotes, endnotes, and several others. If some problem should arise that isn't covered by the models in this chapter, you should make a reasonable adaptation from the most appropriate model. Although documentation is absolutely essential in research writing, you must not let it overwhelm or distract from your text. The most efficient documentation is to give attribution as part of your sentence:

> In <u>Clone</u>, Kolata raises an important question: "How much potential for evil can we tolerate to obtain something that might be good?" (5)

The full reference for Kolata should appear in your Works Cited or References at the end of your paper.

HOW MUCH DOCUMENTATION?

For most research you should have as much documentation as possible. In some other types of writing, source material may be kept to a minimum. Students writing about literature, for example, are sometimes asked to rely on their own ideas and not quote extensively from critics and authorities. But, for most research, you should have maximum documentation. In effect, your reference notes are your data. They point to the evidence in your research. It's normal for student research to use much source material summarized, paraphrased, or, occasionally, quoted from authorities. You might have too much documentation, but that's not likely. A string of quotes makes for hard reading (the string of pearls effect), but you can overcome this problem by paraphrasing more, summarizing the data in your own words, and working your evidence into a readable report. All such evidence, of course, would need reference notes.

RESEARCH PROBLEMS TO AVOID

The String of Pearls

Forcing the reader to read quote after quote, with little intervening explanation, is the string of pearls effect. Paraphrase and summarize in your own words to cut down on the number of direct quotes (but remember to document paraphrases and summaries). Although you are unlikely to have too much documentation, you <u>can</u> have too many quotes in your paper—use paraphrase instead.

Underresearched Paper

Make sure you have enough data. If you offer too little evidence, it will seem that you haven't done sufficient reading on the subject, that you have missed important books or articles. The general rule on how much is enough is to get all there is. Two dozen books and articles may seem like a lot to read, but if there are a hundred or more in the library, two dozen is less than 25% of the available material. You must make sure that your thesis is thoroughly supported and that you have covered all the aspects of your research question.

Overworking the Data

Don't use a single example to illustrate two different points if you can avoid doing so. That is, avoid citing lyrics in one paragraph as an illustration of "originality" but then citing the same lyrics again in a later paragraph as an illustration of "religious motif." Overworking the data suggests insufficient research. Find new examples for each new point you make, if possible.

Underdocumentation

If there aren't enough reference notes, you will seem to be quoting, paraphrasing, or plagiarizing without sufficient documentation. There shouldn't be undocumented information in your paper. It's better that every sentence have a reference note than to risk the appearance of "spotty" or casual documentation.

Plagiarism

Plagiarism is usually the result of improper or missing documentation. It amounts to stealing an author's work. In the world of copyright laws that protect writers' intellectual property as well as incomes, plagiarism is a serious crime. Then too, failure to document properly creates problems for your readers. There is no research when readers can't verify your sources.

Stolen or illegally purchased papers with your name on them (that is, handing in someone else's work as your own) can have serious consequences—such as being expelled from school, fired from your research position, or prosecuted for falsifying evidence in a government project, for example.

Copying itself is not the problem. Copying without crediting the original with quotation marks and a full reference is. In fact, every time you use someone else's work—including paraphrasing words, sentences, paragraphs, or even whole papers—there is a danger of either accidental or deliberate plagiarism.

The Original Material

Following is a paragraph from Page Smith's book.

Testimony to the bad consciences of universities about the sorry state of the teaching function is the widespread practice of awarding, with much fanfare, cash prizes to the "teacher-of-the-year." This is supposed to demonstrate the institution's commitment to "excellence in teaching." What it does, in fact, is to distort and demean the true nature of teaching. (218)

Correct Use of Borrowed Information in a Research Paper

Though today all kinds of prizes and awards are common enough (including trophies for outstanding athletes and Oscars for the "best" movie performance), there is at least one critic who does not think highly of them in education. Speaking of the "sorry state" of teaching, Page Smith criticizes "cash prizes to the 'teacher-of-the-year.' This is supposed to demonstrate the institution's commitment to 'excellence in teaching.' What it does, in fact, is to distort and demean the true nature of teaching" (218).

This writer correctly paraphrases by using her own words, using quotation marks to show what was borrowed, and giving a page reference to show the page from which the borrowed material came. The original author (Page Smith) is mentioned and need not be repeated in the page reference. In the Works Cited section at the end of her paper, the writer would provide a full reference to Page Smith's book.

Plagiarism, Accidental (Maybe)

Though today all kinds of prizes and awards are common enough (including trophies for outstanding athletes and Oscars for the "best" movie performance), there is at least one critic who does not think highly of them in education. Speaking of the "sorry state" of teaching, one critic has said, "cash prizes to the 'teacher-of-the-year'" are bad. "This is supposed to demonstrate the institution's commitment to 'excellence in teaching.' What it does, in fact, is to distort and demean the true nature of teaching."

One purpose of reference notes is to help readers find the material you have used. The other purpose is to give writers credit for their work. Writers are concerned about their intellectual property and can be both morally and legally upset by theft of their work. Here a student has correctly quoted from source material but omitted any reference to Page Smith or any page reference to his book. This looks like it could be an accidental omission (maybe) but it's a serious omission.

Plagiarism, Deliberate (Probably)

Though today all kinds of prizes and awards are common enough (including trophies for outstanding athletes and Oscars for the "best" movie performance), there is at least one critic who does not think highly of prizes in education. Speaking of the sorry state of teaching, a critic believes cash prizes to the teacher-of-the-year are supposed to demonstrate the institution's commitment to excellence in teaching. What it does, in fact, is to distort and demean the true nature of teaching.

This looks like it might be a deliberate theft of an author's property. Page Smith's exact words have been used, but this writer provides neither a citation nor quotation marks around the borrowed material. The writer admits the material is borrowed from "a critic," but without quotation marks readers cannot tell which are the borrowed words and which aren't. It looks as if the writer wants to take credit for these words. The basic crime of plagiarism is failure to document, and this looks like a deliberate case.

Plagiarism, Deliberate Theft

The idea behind prizes and awards is motivation: they are supposed to be motivating for those who get them and for those who want them. They are supposed to be rewards for excellence. However, awards in education don't have any such motivational effect. Financial gifts for good teaching don't motivate anyone and they don't tell much about anyone's excellence. Rewards in education just corrupt teaching, substituting money for the inherent motivation of a teacher's love of learning and dedication to teaching.

This writer has borrowed from Page Smith as surely as the others, but this plagiarism is worse: it is a deliberate theft of the original idea, worse than the others because this writer has tried to disguise the theft. A simple test of plagiarism is whether you can recognize the original under the disguise, be it ever so slyly camouflaged. It is both morally and intellectually offensive because writers have no need to do it. A simple reference identifying the original author in this case would avoid charges of plagiarism: (Smith 218) if the writer cites the Smith book at the end of the paper or (See Page Smith, <u>Killing the Spirit:</u> <u>Higher Education in America</u>, New York: Penguin, 1990: 218 for the idea that financial awards for teaching are corrupting).

REFERENCE NOTES

Many disciplines now use one of the in-text reference styles. Give a parenthetic reference in your paper, such as this: (Smith 83). The number 83 is a page reference, and your reader will find Smith's work in the References or Works Cited section at the end of your paper. Once the most popular style of documentation, footnotes and endnotes are less widely used today.

CONTENT NOTES

A content note is a note from you to your readers. (See chapter 6 for an example.) The note gives additional information or clarification. There is some bias against using notes; many researchers believe that any relevant or important information ought to be included in the body of the paper, and anything else should be omitted. However, researchers sometimes do use notes; the best advice is to use notes only when they are truly important but would seem intrusive in your paper. Avoid supplying all sorts of incidental information, "showing off" with content notes.

In the in-text documentation style, content notes (and only content notes) are treated as endnotes. Give a note number at the appropriate place in your paper, raised half a line. At the bottom of the page or the end of your paper, preceding your Works Cited or References page, list your content notes, with corresponding endnote numbers, on a Notes page. Student work should have few content notes: if you have more than three, you need to reconsider what you are doing. Possible content notes include the following:

<u>Cross-reference</u>	You direct readers to another part of your paper for additional information.
<u>Definition</u>	You define a term or add to the definition in your paper.
<u>Evaluation</u>	You comment on the relative quality of a source or compare one with another.
<u>Explanation</u>	You clarify a statement, especially as quoted from a source, by adding more information.
<u>Extension</u>	You refer the reader to other works, other sources for further information on a point.

Identification   You provide relevant information to identify a person, place, or object mentioned in your paper.

Opinion   You offer your own opinion, doubt, or denial where a reader might mistakenly assume you agree with ideas or words in source material.

WHAT TO DOCUMENT

Direct Quotations

Any words you copy from a source should be placed in quotation marks, followed by a parenthetical citation, followed by the sentence period.

> Wilmut wanted "to develop animals that could produce drugs for human use" (Kolata 24).

Words and Ideas from a Source

A word or two or a concept that you take from a source and incorporate into your own sentences should be documented.

> Parents should be able to control what happens to their children before birth. Silver calls this their "parental prerogative" (9).

Changing the words doesn't change your obligation to document. Ideas, interpretations, analyses, and concepts that might seem to be conclusions on your part should be documented. For example

> By one definition at least, we are told that human life ends when the brain stops functioning. So therefore, by reversing this definition, we should also be able to argue that the embryo or fetus is also not alive before its brain begins to function. Thus it is not possible to "kill" an unborn fetus.

This student seems to have thought of a novel way to turn the antiabortion argument around by reversing a definition of life so that it serves the opposing view. But without documentation, it looks like this writer is claiming the idea as his or her own. Unfortunately, the entire idea is plagiarized from Joseph Fletcher in "Ethical Aspects of Genetic Controls" (New England Journal of Medicine 30 Sept. 1971: 285). To avoid plagiarism and make sure readers understand the source of this idea, the writer should use a parenthetic note such as this:

> By one definition at least, we are told that human life ends when the brain stops functioning. Therefore, by reversing this definition, we should be able to argue

that the embryo or fetus is also not alive before its brain begins to function. Thus it is not possible to "kill" an unborn fetus. (See Fletcher for brain-activity as the determinant for the start of life as well as its end, precluding any "murder" of the unborn.)

The entire reference for Fletcher would then appear in the Works Cited at the end of the paper.

For most research it's both acceptable and desirable to document everything. You must avoid giving the impression that you are claiming, for your own, ideas borrowed from others. No researcher can afford the damage plagiarism does to credibility—to ethos.

Paraphrases and Restatements

When you change someone else's words, phrases, or ideas into your own language, you must still give a note:

> Eighty-seven years ago the United States were united as a country on the North American continent by people who wanted freedom for everyone in a nation based on the democratic thesis that no person should be superior nor inferior to anyone else. (Lincoln, Gettysburg Address)

Major Source

If you make many references to the same source—for example, if you are writing about a book, poem, play, or other source—you needn't keep documenting it. As long as it's clear to the reader that you are still discussing the same source, you may use only page numbers for references.

> In <u>Remaking Eden</u>, Silver describes a future scenario of humans cloned on a mass scale. He imagines that people will be classified into two groups: the "Naturals" and the "Gene-enriched" or "GenRich" (4). The GenRich will constitute 10% of the population, yet they will rule the world because they will be the smartest, the strongest, and the most creative (4). Scientists and those who control technology will be GenRich (5):
>
> > All aspects of the economy, the media, the entertainment industry, and the knowledge industry are controlled by members of the GenRich class. GenRich parents can afford to send their children to private schools rich in the resources required for them to take advantage of their enhanced genetic potential. In contrast, Naturals work as low-service providers or as laborers, and their children go to public schools. (6)
>
> At the end of his book, Silver returns to this scenario, suggesting that the GenRich and the Naturals will become different species—unable to cross-breed (241). Whether Silver's fantasy is possible or probable is up to readers to decide.

Source within a Source

Avoid using material you find quoted in a secondary source. Find the original source, if possible. If you find Smith quoting Jones, don't use the quote unless the original source is out of print or impossible to find. Only then should you refer to the secondary source:

MLA

Selzer marvels at the human body the way poet Marianne Moore marveled at a cherry: "What sap went through that little thread to make the cherry red!" (qtd. in <u>Down from Troy</u> 132).

APA

Selzer marvels at the human body the way poet Marianne Moore marveled at a cherry: "What sap went through that little thread to make the cherry red!" (as cited in <u>Down from Troy</u> 132).

WHAT NOT TO DOCUMENT

Common Knowledge

Common knowledge is information that most educated people are expected to know. You learn information from your friends, television, radio, movies, newspapers, magazines, and so on. You are surrounded by information. President Clinton was impeached but not convicted in 1999. That's common knowledge—"everyone" knows it, and you don't need a source for it.

Still it may be difficult for students to know what is or isn't common knowledge today. "Everyone" should know where the White House is: 1600 Pennsylvania Avenue, Washington, DC. Even if you don't know it, the address is so widely known that it should be considered common knowledge and doesn't require documentation. However, if you <u>copy</u> (or paraphrase) that information from an encyclopedia, atlas, or other source, you must document it. Who was secretary of state in President Clinton's administration? Surprisingly, many people do not know that Madeline Albright was America's first female secretary of state. (And Janet Reno was the first female attorney general.) But most educated people do know, and if you read the newspapers or pay attention to the nightly TV news, you too should know. Secretary Albright's name should be considered common knowledge. However, if you have to look it up, you should cite the source.

That Dolly was the first animal cloned from an adult cell can also be considered common knowledge; the information has been so widely reported that educated people <u>should</u> know it, even if some don't. Citing a source for this information should not be necessary. What is or isn't common, then, is largely the result of the audience to whom you are writing and your own expertise in the matter. A renowned scholar writing to other scholars may take much for granted. Students writing for a general audience should take little for granted. Thus, if you aren't sure whether information you use is common knowledge, give a source for that information.

Within the specialized area of your research, knowledge is common if it's readily available in most general reference works, such as encyclopedias and almanacs, or through the popular media—television, newspapers, and magazines. But the rule is, when in doubt, document.

ACTIVITY 1

Please read the following excerpt and analyze the statements in it. Using the researcher's rule—if you found it, cite it—indicate whether you think researchers would require reference notes for the numbered statements in the paragraph. Some statements may not require references. Explain why the statements do or don't need reference notes in your opinion.

(1) Running is not a miracle cure that keeps people healthy and happy. (2) Endorphins can cause runners to become addicted. (3) They run even when it is not healthy: "Addicted runners believe that they 'have' to run on a daily basis—in fact, that running is necessary to be able to function." (4) Often this compulsion to run causes runners to overlook safety and ignore injuries. (5) In fact, 80% of running injuries are caused by overtraining. (6) Running can increase bone mass density and prevent fractures; however, one study found that running can also cause hormone imbalances which result in low bone mass densities for as many as 50% of the women who train intensely. (7) This significantly increases the likelihood of stress fractures. (8) Sprains and strains also commonly accompany exercise. (9) Research has shown that 57% of people who train over 50 miles a week are injured each year—less than 30% of those who run under 10 miles a week get injured. (10) In addition, the more dedicated runners are less likely to see a doctor; they seek medical treatment only as a last resort because the prescription is often to stop running.

IN-TEXT RULES

The in-text documentation style here, based on the style of the MLA (Modern Language Association), uses references in the body of your paper itself. Give enough information in your paper so that readers can find the source in your Works Cited list. Thus, much documentation can be reduced to an author's name. If you cite specific information from the source, give a page number, too:

Schrof reports that more experiments are underway since Wilmut's success with Dolly (36).

Direct quotations can be identified with a parenthetic reference to name and page number:

> Cloning experiments with animals have continued since Dolly: "University of Wisconsin researchers said last week they had merged genetic material of pigs, rats, and monkeys with cow eggs" (Schrof, "Custom Cows" 36).

But don't use too many quotations. Unless there is some reason for copying from sources, it is better to paraphrase; use you own words as much as possible. In part research writing is a test of your writing skill as much as your ability to research. Incorporating information skillfully and readably is part of the test.

This in-text style is meant to keep documentation accurate but unobtrusive. Learn to incorporate documentation smoothly into your writing just as you learn to incorporate the words and ideas of your sources. Here are some guidelines.

Use Author's Name

Most of your references should give the author's last name in the text of your paper instead of in a parenthetical note at the end of a sentence, though it is customary to place page numbers at the end.

> According to Kolata, Wilmut and his colleagues at the Roslin Institute did not celebrate when Dolly was born (219–20).

In the name and date style (APA), include the publication date as well:

> "According to Kolata (1998, pp. 219–220), . . ."

In MLA style, if there are more than three authors, give the last name of the first author and "et al."

> Three authors, MLA style:
> Miles, Bertonasco, and Karns maintain that a writer's voice is a combination of persona and tone (210).

> Listed in your Works Cited:
> Miles, Robert, Marc F. Bertonasco, and William Karns. <u>Prose Style: A Contemporary Guide</u>. 2nd ed. Upper Saddle River, NJ: Prentice, 1991.

> More than three authors, MLA style:
> Campbell et al. published a cloning experiment that actually preceded Wilmut's, but none of Campbell's lambs survived.

Listed in your Works Cited:
> Campbell et al. "Sheep Cloned by Nuclear Transfer from a Cultured Cell Line." Nature 380 (1996): 64–66.

Alternative style, giving all authors' names:
> Campbell, K. H. S., J. McWhir, W. A. Ritchie, and Ian Wilmut. "Sheep Cloned by Nuclear Transfer from a Cultured Cell Line." Nature 380 (1996): 64–66.

Whichever way you choose, you must be consistent throughout your paper.

For the name and date (APA) style, when there are two authors, give both authors' last names every time you use them. For more than two authors (and up to five) give all authors in first reference to them.

> Campbell, Mcwhir, Ritchie, and Wilmut (1996) discovered a number of anomolies in their efforts to clone sheep.

Name and date style in your paper, more than two authors, second reference:
> According to Campbell et al. (1996), their team achieved an animal clone through nuclear transfer.

Name and date style in your references list, last names first:
> Campbell, K. H. S., McWhir, J., Ritchie, W. A., & Wilmut, I. (1996, March 7). Sheep cloned by nuclear transfer from a cultured cell line. Nature, 380, 64–66.

If there are six or more authors in APA style, give first author's last name and use et al. for all references.

> Bogel et al. (1984) have written a book for novice teachers.

In your reference list, for six or more authors in APA style, give all authors' last name and initials.

> Bogel, F. V., Carden, P., Cox, G. H., Davis, S., Freedman, D. P., Gottschalk, K. K., Hjortshoj, K., & Shaw, H. E. (1984). Teaching prose: A guide for writing instructors (F. V. Bogel & K. K. Gottschalk, Eds.). New York: Norton.

Use Name and Title

If there is more than one work by the same author in your bibliography, you must include the titles in your references, but you can shorten the titles.

> Kolata, a highly respected science writer for the New York Times, strives to be fair-minded, acknowledging benefits and disadvantages of what she reports. In 1998 she published one of the first books on cloning, Clone: The Road to

<u>Dolly</u>. Recently, she reported on a study a nine-year-old girl did that disproved the alternative medicine practice of therapeutic touch ("A Child's Paper").

Your Works Cited page would list alphabetically the second and any additional titles by the same author, with three hyphens in place of the author's name:

> Kolata, Gina. "A Child's Paper Poses a Medical Challenge." <u>New York Times</u> 1 Apr. 1998: A1.
> ---. <u>Clone: The Road to Dolly, and the Path Ahead</u>. New York: Morrow, 1998.

Use Shortened Titles

To keep references brief, shorten titles, but keep them unambiguous so that the reader can recognize the titles in your Works Cited. For example, suppose your paper contains two sources from Sharon Begley of <u>Newsweek</u>. References to her article "Little Lamb, Who Made Thee?" could be shortened:

> Many journalists explain the significance of Dolly's cloning and its possible consequences. Begley asks, "Will it take a few human-clone disasters to bring about a ban?" ("Little Lamb" 57).

References to the Bible should use standard abbreviations.

> "Let not mercy and truth forsake thee: bind them around thy neck; write them upon the table of thine heart" (Prov. 3.3).

For references to plays, poetry, or other works with numbered sections or lines, give all the relevant numbers that would help a reader find the source: section, part, act, scene, line. Don't use <u>l</u>. or <u>ll</u>. for <u>line</u>.

> "I must be cruel, only to be kind" (<u>Hamlet</u> III.iv.178).

This line is from Shakespeare's <u>Hamlet</u>, act three, scene four, line 178. In general avoid roman numerals, but the use of roman for plays is an exception.

> "An aged man is but a paltry thing, / A tattered coat upon a stick . . ." ("Byzantium" 9–10).

The lines are from Yeats's poem "Sailing to Byzantium," lines 9 and 10.

Use Page Numbers

When making reference to a specific part of a source, you must give a page number in the reference. MLA style does not repeat hundreds or thousands indicators: 17–19, 289–93, 1529–31; but note: 999–1002, 2997–3001—to avoid a possible ambiguity, supply the full page numbers. When the reference note comes at the end of your sentence, the sentence period should be placed after the parenthesis. Note that in MLA style, page numbers are not identified with "p." or other markers. If additional references are made to the same source, you need only the page number. Don't precede page numbers with a comma: (Harolton 97). The APA style, however, requires full numbers and uses "p." and "pp." for parts of chapters, essays, and other sections of edited books and for newspaper pages, including sections and divisions of the paper, if any. APA does not abbreviate numbers as MLA does: use full numbers (191–197) for APA style in your paper and in your References list.

MLA

> Many scientists object to governmental efforts to ban all research regarding human cloning (Kassirer and Rosenthal). Cloning human cells may provide great therapeutic benefits. One bill introduced by Senators Feinstein and Kennedy is acceptable, however. "That bill would ban the implantation of an embryo developed by the technology into a human uterus for the purpose of creating a child, but it would protect research [. . .] to clone molecules, cells, and tissues" (906). The bill also contains "a 'sunset' clause that would end the prohibition in 10 years" (906–07).

APA

> Many scientists object to governmental efforts to ban all research regarding human cloning (Kassirer & Rosenthal, 1998). Cloning human cells may provide great therapeutic benefits. One bill introduced by Senators Feinstein and Kennedy is acceptable, however. "That bill would ban the implantation of an embryo developed by the technology into a human uterus for the purpose of creating a child, but it would protect research . . . to clone molecules, cells, and tissues" (p. 906). The bill also contains "a 'sunset' clause that would end the prohibition in 10 years" (pp. 906–907).

BIBLIOGRAPHY

Always take bibliographic information from the title page and copyright page of your source, not from indexes or the card catalog.

Authors' Names

Take authors' names from the title page. In MLA style don't abbreviate or substitute initials when full names are given on the title page. (See the APA guidelines later in this chapter for a different rule.)

Titles

Give titles exactly as they appear on the title page. Include subtitles. Disregard articles <u>a</u>, <u>an</u>, and <u>the</u> when alphabetizing authorless titles:

> "Coffee Cups Are Crawling with Critters." <u>Morning Sun</u> [Mt. Pleasant, MI] 2 Apr. 1998:11.
> "A Stonehenge of Sorts Lies in the Sahara." <u>New York Times</u> 2 Apr. 1998, natl. ed.: A5.
> "The Teams That Made Milwaukee Famous." <u>New York Times</u> 1 Apr. 1998, natl. ed.: C5.

Place of Publication

Use only the first city if several are listed. For unfamiliar cities, or if there is likely to be some ambiguity (London, Ontario), give the state or province as well. Use postal abbreviations for state names: MI instead of Mich. Note that there may be some confusion about New York. In documentation, when giving the publisher's geographic location, "New York" is the name of the city and should be spelled out (not abbreviated). As a general rule, state names are seldom used, even if you think the city is unfamiliar, such as Sioux Falls—home of Brevet Press in South Dakota. Only if there may be some confusion about the city—as when there is more than one city with the same name—should you include the state, and then the state name should be given as its postal abbreviation. (There are cities named "Cleveland" in 19 different states: AL, AR, GA, MN, MO, MS, NC, ND, NM, NY, OH, OK, SC, TN, TX, UT, VA, WI, WV, and in that case it is probably wise to give the postal abbreviation for the state along with the city: Cleveland, AL, for example.) Use the abbreviation "n.p." (no place) when the title page shows no place of publication.

Shorten Publishers' Names

Writers and others in the publishing world quickly become familiar with the major publishers' names; it's usually not necessary to give the full name. Give that part of the name that people would use to look up the publisher's address. Thus, words and abbreviations such as <u>Company</u>, <u>Co.</u>, and <u>Inc.</u> can be dropped. Names formed from two names (Harcourt Brace, Houghton Mifflin, Prentice Hall, and so on) need only the first name: Harcourt, Houghton, Prentice. You can use UP for University Press, as in Oxford UP.

Professional organizations are frequently referred to by their initials (such as NCTE). You may list such publications by initials in your Works Cited list. (See the sample reference for a committee or group author.) But if the organization is likely to be unfamiliar to your readers, spell out the name in full: National Council of Teachers of English.

Some publishers have divisions with different names. Anchor is a division of Doubleday. Use a hyphen to separate a division name from a parent company: Anchor-Doubleday.

Copyright Date

The copyright date is frequently listed on the back of the title page. Copyright date is usually the date of the first edition, but it isn't necessary for you to include "First Edition" along with the date. Only editions other than the first need to be identified. For example, although Stephen Reid's book <u>The Prentice Hall Guide for College Writing</u> was first published in 1989, its latest edition was published in 2000. This would be the citation:

> Reid, Stephen. <u>The Prentice Hall Guide for College Writing</u>. 5th ed. Upper Saddle River, NJ: Prentice, 2000.

BASIC WORKS CITED MODEL, BOOK (MLA)

This basic bibliography form for books is standard for the MLA.

```
    A        B C                    D                        E F     G     H
Walker, Alice.  The Same River Twice: Honoring the Difficult.  New York:
    Scribner, 1996.
    I      J        K
```

A. Author's name in inverted order (only the first author's name is inverted).
B. Period after author's name.
C. Two spaces (after all end marks).
D. Full title, underlined.
E. Period.
F. Two spaces.
G. Place of publication.
H. Colon.
I. Second line double spaced, indented five spaces (hanging indent).
J. Publisher's name, followed by comma.
K. Copyright date followed by period.

BASIC WORKS CITED MODEL, PERIODICAL (MLA)

```
    A          B C      D                    E F     G    H      I       J K L
Alter, Jonathan.  "In the Time of Tolerance."  Newsweek 30 Mar. 1998: 29.
```

A. Author's last name first.

B. Period.

C. Two spaces.

D. Title of article in quotation marks.

E. Period within quotation mark.

F. Two spaces.

G. Title of magazine underlined.

H. One space.

I. Date in military order: day, month, year; no commas within.

J. Colon after date.

K. Page number without "p." or "pg." or other label.

L. Period.

BOOKS: MLA WORKS CITED MODELS

One Author

> Morrison, Toni. <u>Beloved</u>. New York: Knopf, 1987.
> Tan, Amy. <u>The Hundred Secret Senses</u>. New York: Putnam, 1995.
> West, Cornel. <u>Race Matters</u>. New York: Vintage-Random House, 1994.

List items in a bibliography in alphabetical order.

More Than One Book by Same Author

Don't repeat an author's name with subsequent books in MLA style. When you have two or more books by the same author, after the first book, use a string of three hyphens in place of the author's name. The hyphens for subsequent authors must indicate <u>exactly</u> the same authorship as for the first. As an example, here are two books by Peter Elbow:

> Elbow, Peter. <u>Embracing Contraries: Explorations in Learning and Teaching</u>. New York: Oxford UP, 1986.
> ---. <u>Writing with Power: Techniques for Mastering the Writing Process</u>. New York: Oxford UP, 1981.

Any different information about the authorship of subsequent books must be indicated. If, in a subsequent book, the author is an editor, translator, or served in any capacity different from that in the previous book, this new information must be included (---, ed.)

Note that this convention doesn't apply to coauthors. If Smith has written one book and coauthored another, don't use hyphens for Smith's name with the coauthored book.

Author of One Book, Coauthor of Another

Postman, Neil. <u>Teaching as a Conserving Activity</u>. New York: Delacorte, 1979.

Postman, Neil, and Charles Weingartner. <u>Teaching as a Subversive Activity</u>. New York: Delacorte, 1969.

Two or More Authors

Note that only the first author's name is inverted. The names of second and third authors are given in normal order.

Belanoff, Pat, and Marcia Dickson. <u>Portfolios: Process and Product</u>. Portsmouth, NH: Boynton/Cook, 1991.

Belenky, Mary Field, Lynne A. Bond, and Jacqueline S. Winestock. <u>A Tradition That Has No Name: Nurturing the Development of People, Families, and Communities</u>. New York: BasicBooks-Harper, 1997.

If there are more than three authors, use "et al." ("and others") unless you refer to the others by name in your text. For example, the title page of <u>Fields of Writing: Reading across the Disciplines</u> lists five authors: Nancy R. Comley, David Hamilton, Carl H. Klaus, Robert Scholes, and Nancy Sommers. In your Works Cited list, give the first author's last name first, followed by "et al."

Comley, Nancy R., et al. <u>Fields of Writing: Reading across the Disciplines</u>. 4th ed. New York: St. Martin's Press, 1994.

If you prefer, give all authors' names in your text and in your Works Cited, but be consistent:

Comley, Nancy R., David Hamilton, Carl H. Klaus, Robert Scholes, and Nancy Sommers. <u>Fields of Writing: Reading across the Disciplines</u>. 4th ed. New York: St. Martin's Press, 1994.

Committee or Group Author

National Academy of Engineering, Institute of Medicine. <u>On Being a Scientist: Responsible Conduct in Research</u>. Washington, DC: National Academy Press, 1995.

National Council of Teachers of English. <u>Trends and Issues in Postsecondary English Studies</u>. Urbana: NCTE, 1999.

Book with Editor(s)

Reynolds, Richard, and John Stone, eds. <u>On Doctoring: Stories, Poems, Essays</u>. New York: Simon & Schuster, 1991.

Walsh, Mary Roth, ed. <u>Women, Men, and Gender: Ongoing Debates</u>. New Haven: Yale UP, 1997.

Essay, Chapter, or Selection in Anthology, Edited Work

> Dickinson, Emily. "The Brain—is wider than the Sky." <u>Poetry: An Introduction</u>. Ed. Michael Meyer. Boston: Bedford Books of St. Martin's, 1995. 269.
>
> Rosener, Judy B. "Leadership and the Paradox of Gender." <u>Women, Men, and Gender: Ongoing Debates</u>. Ed. Mary Roth Walsh. New Haven: Yale UP, 1997. 294–97.

Translation, Author's Name First

Include the translator's name if it appears on the title page.

> Eco, Umberto. <u>The Island of the Day Before</u>. Trans. William Weaver. New York: Harcourt, 1994.

Translation, Translator's Name First

> Weaver, William, trans. <u>The Island of the Day Before</u>. By Umberto Eco. New York: Harcourt, 1994.

The translator's name should be first only if you are writing about the translator's work, such as the accuracy or style of the translation.

Multivolume Work

> Churchill, Winston S. <u>A History of the English-Speaking Peoples</u>. Collectors Edition. 4 vols. Norwalk, CT: The Easton Press, 1984–1986.

Part(s) of Multivolume Work

> Churchill, Winston S. <u>The Age of Revolution</u>. Norwalk, CT: The Easton Press, 1985. Vol 3. of <u>A History of the English-Speaking Peoples</u>. 4 vols. 1984–1986.

Churchill's work has individual titles and publication dates for each volume. Parenthetic references in your paper to part of a multivolume work must give volume and page number(s), for example: (3:91–92).

Reprint of Older Work

Give the original publication date first (after title) and then the reprint date (after the publisher's name).

> Morrison, Toni. <u>Song of Solomon</u>. 1977. New York: Plume-Penguin, 1987.
>
> Selzer, Richard. <u>Letters to a Young Doctor</u>. 1982. New York: Harvest-Harcourt, 1996.

Note the publishers' "imprints" in the examples above. Publishers may use various names: if the imprint appears on the title page along with the publisher's name, both should be given (hyphenated) in your Works Cited list.

Introduction, Preface, Foreword

Elbow, Peter. Foreword. <u>Portfolios: Process and Product</u>. By Pat Belanoff and
   Marcia Dickson. Portsmouth, NH: Boynton/Cook, 1991. ix–xvi.

Ruether, Rosemary Radford. Introduction. <u>Ethics for a Small Planet: New
   Horizons on Population, Consumption, and Ecology</u>. By Daniel C. Maguire
   and Larry L. Rasmussen. Albany: State U of New York, 1998. xi–xv.

Bible, Sacred Works

The Holy Bible. Authorized King James Version. New York: Harper, n.d.
<u>New American Standard Bible</u>. n.p.: Harvest House, 1993.

Don't underline titles of Holy Scripture such as the Bible or the Koran, except for other than authorized versions. Don't list the Bible in your Works Cited merely to cite (in text) a biblical passage. A listing for the Bible is required only when discussing the Bible itself (the Bible as literature, for example) or when citing other than the authorized version, the title of which should be underlined. Note: the abbreviation "n.d." means no date of publication; "n.p." means no place of publication.

Anonymous Works

The word <u>anonymous</u> indicates an unknown author but should not be used unless it appears on the title page. Modern works published with no author listed are not considered anonymous. (See Magazine Article, No Author Given.)

Dictionary

<u>Webster's New World College Dictionary</u>. 3rd ed. New York: Simon &
   Schuster, Macmillan, 1996.

In a paper about the dictionary itself, a complete bibliographic reference is appropriate. Don't cite the dictionary merely to define a word, but if you <u>copy</u> a dictionary definition, you must give a full bibliographic reference in your Works Cited list. Give the word you copy in quotes, include edition number if other than the first, omit publisher and place of familiar works. Many words have multiple meanings. Indicate which meaning you cite with appropriate numbers and letters if any: in <u>Webster's New World College Dictionary</u>, 3rd ed. (618), the meaning of "Have," definition 13, is "To be in a certain relation, as to <u>have</u> a brother."

Encyclopedia, Alphabetically Arranged Work

Page numbers are unnecessary for publications arranged alphabetically.

> "American Indian Languages." The New Encyclopaedia Britannica. 15th ed. 1998.
> "North American Indian Languages." The New Encyclopaedia Britannica: Micropaedia. 15th ed. 1998.

Many Britannica articles are "signed" with authors' initials. Find authors' names in Propaedia: Guide to Britannica.

Dissertation, Unpublished

> Shannon, Maureen. "Senior Learners: Motivations and Composition Strategies for Teaching Students 55+." Diss. Illinois State U, 1997.

Dissertation, Published

> Selby, Stuart Allen. The Study of Film as an Art Form in Secondary Schools. Diss. Columbia U, 1963. New York: Arno, 1978.

Article from **Dissertation Abstracts**, or **Dissertations Abstracts International**

> Edison, Marcia Irene. "Out of Class Activities and the Development of Critical Thinking in College." DAI 58 (1997): 03A. U of Illinois at Chicago.

Note: A, B, or C after DAI page numbers indicate humanities and social sciences (A), science and engineering (B), and other than United States (C).

PERIODICALS: MLA WORKS CITED MODELS

Weekly Magazine Article

> Gibbs, Nancy. "Day of Deliverance." Time 13 Apr. 1998: 44–51.
> Walsh, Kenneth T., and Marianne Lavelle. "The Clintons Rally." U.S. News & World Report 9 Feb. 1998: 20+.

Abbreviate months (except May, June, July): Jan., Feb., Mar., Apr., Aug., Sept., Oct., Nov., Dec. Use a period after each abbreviation. Note that the day precedes the month, and no comma is needed to separate the date from the title or the month from the year. However, APA style, by contrast, does not abbreviate months: (2000, April 2). The plus sign (+) indicates that there is more to the article following on discontinuous pages. The article, "The Clintons Rally," appears on pages 20 to 24 and (interrupted by full-page ads) page 28.

Magazine Article, No Author Given

"Big Stories, Scant Attention." <u>Sports Illustrated</u> 23 Mar. 1998: 18–20.
"Picturesque Charm: All Two Blocks of It." <u>U.S. News & World Report</u> 9 Feb.
   1998: 58.

No punctuation separates the date from the magazine title.

Monthly Magazine Article

Glaser, Ronald J. "The Doctor Is Not In." <u>Harper's</u> Mar. 1998: 35–41.
Riddle, Robert D., and Clifford J. Tabin. "How Limbs Develop." <u>Scientific
   American</u> Feb. 1999: 74–79.

Page numbers aren't identified by "page" or "p." or any other designator in this style. Also, note that magazine titles (<u>Harper's</u>, <u>Scientific American</u>) don't end with periods (whereas book titles do end with periods).

Newspaper Article

Beck, Joan. "Make It Boxing's Last Round." <u>Detroit Free Press</u> 13 Apr. 1998: A11.
Drinkard, Jim. "Union Chief Hand-Delivers $1M Check to Democrats." <u>USA
   Today</u> 8 June 2000: A1+.
Greene, Bob. "Higher Profiles and Diminished Voices." <u>Chicago Tribune</u> 29
   Mar. 1998, sec. 1: 2.

If an article appears in a newspaper with sections that begin with letters (as in the Beck and Drinkard examples), cite the letter followed by the page number. The Bob Greene example shows that this newspaper identifies its sections with numbers instead of letters. Use the abbreviation "sec." followed by the section number, a colon, a space, and the page number for such newspapers. The plus sign (+) in the Drinkard example indicates the rest of the article follows on a discontinuous page, A6 in this case.

Newspaper Article, Unsigned

"Munchies Brought on by Stress Linked to Hormone, Study Finds." <u>Chicago
   Tribune</u> 5 Apr. 1998, sec. 1: 12.

You may find titles of newspaper articles in lowercase letters except for the first word, such as "Lawyers ready to split tobacco billions." When you use the

MLA style, you should regularize the capitalization: "Lawyers Ready to Split Tobacco Billions."

Reviews, Signed and Unsigned: Books, Films, Music CDs

Farley, Christopher John. "Heading for the Light." Rev. of <u>Ray of Light</u>, by Madonna. <u>Time</u> 16 Mar. 1998: 75.

Maslin, Janet. "A Sly Lens on Corporate America." Rev. of <u>The Big One</u>, dir. Michael Moore. <u>New York Times</u> 10 Apr. 1998, natl. ed.: E1+.

Rev. of <u>Good Fences</u>, by Erika Ellis. <u>Publishers Weekly</u> 9 Mar. 1998: 47.

Smith, Barbara Herrnstein. "Is It Really a Computer?" Rev. of <u>How the Mind Works</u>, by Steven Pinker. <u>Times Literary Supplement</u> 20 Feb. 1998: 3–4.

Thompson, David. "A Dark Bright Light." Rev. of <u>The Truman Show</u>, dir. Peter Weir. <u>Esquire</u> May 1998: 46–49.

White, Armond. "Against the Hollywood Grain." Rev. of <u>Amistad</u>, dir. Steven Spielberg. <u>Film Comment</u> 34.2 (1998): 34–42.

In place of director (dir.) other appropriate titles may be abbreviated: prod., trans., ed., and so on. The plus sign (+) in the Janet Maslin example indicates that the rest of the article appears on discontinuous pages: it begins on page E1, but the rest of it (in this case) appears on page E27.

Editorial, Signed and Unsigned

"Men Doing Their Share." Editorial. <u>The Christian Science Monitor</u> 17 Apr. 1998: 16.

Zabludoff, Marc. "Fear and Longing." Editorial. <u>Discover</u> May 1998: 6.

Letter to the Editor

Eichhorn, Gunther L. Letter. <u>The New Yorker</u> 26 Jan. 1998: 9.

Moyers, Bill. Letter. <u>New York Times</u> 10 Apr. 1998, natl. ed.: A18.

Nelson, Carol. Letter. <u>Public Health</u> 113 (1998): 99.

Letters don't usually have titles, though editors may supply them, for example, "Penmanship Counts" found with the Eichhorn letter. Unless you know for certain that the title was part of the original letter, you should not use it.

Professional, Technical, or Specialty Journal, Each Issue Starting with Page 1

Farris, Phoebe. "Images of Urban Native Americans: The Border Zones of Mixed Identities." <u>Journal of American Culture</u> 20.1 (1997): 27–30.

Gaughan, John. "From Comfort Zone to Contact Zone." <u>English Journal</u> 87.2 (1998): 36–43.

Note volume and issue numbers—20.1 and 87.2—typically distinguish journals from magazines. For magazine citations don't use volume and issue numbers; use the date instead: day-month-year. See APA guidelines for a different treatment of volume and issue numbers.

Professional, Technical, or Specialty Journal, Pages Numbered Continuously throughout Volume

> Dolan, Liam, and R. Scott Poethig. "Clonal Analysis of Leaf Development in Cotton." <u>American Journal of Botany</u> 85 (1998): 315–21.
>
> Feig, Denice S., and C. David Naylor. "Eating for Two: Are Guidelines for Weight Gain during Pregnancy Too Liberal?" <u>The Lancet</u> 9108 (1998): 1054–55.
>
> Miller, Mike. "Telling Cells to Die: Apoptosis Research Takes Off." <u>Journal of the National Cancer Institute</u> 92 (2000): 793.

"Pages numbered continuously" means (for example) if the first issue ends on page 155 the next issue will start on page 156. These examples use only the volume number because issue numbers are not needed when pages are numbered continuously.

Titles and Quotes within Titles

To write about Hinton's article concerning John Steinbeck's <u>The Grapes of Wrath</u>, you should underline Steinbeck's title in the title of her article:

> Hinton, Rebecca. "Steinbeck's <u>The Grapes of Wrath</u>." <u>The Explicator</u> 56.2 (1998): 101–03.

Lent's title begins with the quoted phrase "I can relate to that . . . ." To include this article in your Works Cited list, you must enclose the entire title of the article in double quotation marks but change those around Lent's quoted phrase to single quotation marks:

> Lent, Robin. " 'I can relate to that . . . ': Reading and Responding in the Writing Classroom." <u>College Composition and Communication</u> 44 (1993): 232–40.

The general rule for quotation marks around titles within quotation marks is to change the original marks to single quotation marks and then add double quotation marks around the entire title. For example

> Trail, George Y. "Teaching Argument and the Rhetoric of Orwell's 'Politics and the English Language.' " <u>College English</u> 57 (1995): 570–83.

Underlined titles (books, plays, films, dramas, and so on) present a problem when they are included in a book title—as for example a book about one of

Shakespeare's plays or a book about a film, because the titles of such works are themselves usually underlined. One solution to this problem is to include those titles without underlining:

> Bridges, Herb. <u>Filming of</u> Gone with the Wind. Macon, GA: Mercer UP, 1998.
> Haley, David. <u>Shakespeare's Courtly Mirror: Reflexivity and Prudence in</u> All's Well That Ends Well. Newark: U of Delaware P, 1993.
> Kastan, David Scott, ed. <u>Critical Essays on Shakespeare's</u> Hamlet. New York: G. K. Hall; London: Prentice Hall International, 1995.

OTHER SOURCES

Handout or Unpublished Essay

> Hoefel, Roseanne. "English 320: Critical Theory." Course Syllabus. Alma College. Alma, MI: 8 Jan. 1999.
> Konopa, Don. "The Paradox of Zen." Research Paper Handout for English 101. Kalamazoo Valley Community College, 15 Nov. 2000.

Lecture, Speech, Public Address

> Donaldson, Sam. "The State of Television News." Lecture. Kansas State University, Manhattan, KS, 23 Nov. 1997.
> Strossen, Nadine. "Women Under the Law." Lecture. Alma College, Alma, MI, 17 Mar. 1998.

Film

> <u>Titanic</u>. Dir. James Cameron. Perf. Leonardo DiCaprio and Kate Winslet. Paramount, 1997.

Video Recording: Television or Film

> "The Field of Time." <u>Bill Moyer's The Language of Life</u>. Dir. David Grubin. Videocassette. Newbridge Communications, 1995.
> <u>Independence Day</u>. Dir. Roland Emmerich. Perf. Will Smith, Bill Pullman, and Jeff Goldblum. Videocassette. Twentieth Century Fox, 1996.

Play, Performance

> <u>Wait until Dark</u>. By Frederick Knott. Dir. Leonard Foglia. Perf. Marisa Tomei and Quentin Tarantino. Brooks Atkinson Theater, New York, 6 Apr. 1998.

Musical Performance

Clapton, Eric. Concert. Madison Square Garden, New York. 18 Apr. 1998.

Musical Composition

Beethoven, Ludwig van. Symphony no. 7 in A, op. 92.

Recording

Carpenter, Mary Chapin. <u>A Place in the World</u>. Sony, 1996.
London Chamber Orchestra. <u>LCO2</u>. Virgin Classics, 1989.

Individual Selection from a Recording

Carpenter, Mary Chapin. "Ideas Are Like Stars." <u>A Place in the World</u>. Sony, 1996.
London Chamber Orchestra. "The Lark Ascending." By Ralph Vaughan Williams. <u>LCO2</u>. Virgin Classics, 1989.

Television Show

"I.G. (Immune Globulin)." Narr. Mike Wallace. <u>Sixty Minutes</u>. CBS. 26 Apr. 1998.
"Mind's Eye." <u>The X-Files</u>. Fox. 19 Apr. 1998.

Work of Art

<u>Aphrodite</u> (the "Venus de Milo"). The Louvre, Paris.
Hopper, Edward. <u>Cape Cod Morning</u>. National Museum of American Art, Washington, DC.

Poem Published Separately

Stafford, William. "The Way It Is." <u>Hungry Mind Review</u> Spring 1998: 32.

Poem in a Collection

Harjo, Joy. "Anchorage." <u>Letters to America: Contemporary American Poetry on Race</u>. Ed. Jim Daniels. Detroit: Wayne State UP, 1995. 95–96.

Letter, Personal

Cavalieri, Grace. Letter to the author. 15 Dec. 1997.

Letter(s), Published

> Van Gogh, Vincent. <u>The Complete Letters of Vincent Van Gogh</u>. 3 vols. Greenwich, CT: New York Graphic Society, 1958.

Identify the state as well as the city only if there is a possible ambiguity. Use postal abbreviations for states. Supply names of foreign countries and Canadian provinces if necessary.

> Van Gogh, Vincent. Letter to Theo, No. 358. <u>The Complete Letters of Vincent Van Gogh</u>. Vol. II. Greenwich, CT: New York Graphic Society, 1958. 265–69.

Use the date of a letter, when available, along with any identifying number. If there is an editor, add (for example) "Ed. George Smith." after the title of the collection. To cite more than one letter from a collection, give a reference to the collection in your Works Cited and cite the various letters in your paper itself (Van Gogh 265–69).

Personal Interview

> Lee, Li-Young. Personal interview. 20 Nov. 1997.

Telephone Interview

> Clifton, Lucille. Telephone interview. 15 Jan. 2000.

Published Interview

> Percy, Will. "Rock and Read: Will Percy Interviews Bruce Springsteen." <u>DoubleTake</u> Spring 1998: 36–43.

A Chart, Diagram, Map, or Table

> "Major Soil Groups." Map. <u>Contemporary Atlas of the United States</u>. By Catherine M. Mattson and Mark T. Mattson. New York: Macmillan, 1990: 9.
> "Milestones in Recombinant DNA Technology." Table. <u>An Introduction to Recombinant Technology</u>. By Alan E. H. Emery. New York: Wiley, 1984: 2.
> "Send in the Clones." Diagram. "Little Lamb, Who Made Thee?" By Sharon Begley. <u>Newsweek</u> 10 Mar. 1997: 56–57.

A Cartoon

> Johnston, Lynn. "For Better or Worse." Cartoon. <u>Detroit Free Press</u> 15 Apr. 1998: D16.
> Ziegler, Jack. Cartoon. <u>New Yorker</u> 23 Mar. 1998: 71.

An Advertisement

> L. L. Bean. Advertisement. <u>Time</u> 7 Aug. 2000: 9.
> Saturn. Advertisement. <u>The Atlantic Monthly</u> Aug. 2000: 50–51.

ELECTRONIC SOURCES

Because Internet sources are subject to updating and editing, it is helpful, if possible, to give both the date posted and the date you access the source.

> National Bioethics Advisory Commission. <u>Report and Recommendations of the National Bioethics Advisory Commission</u>. June 1997. On-line. 20 Feb. 1998. <http://earthops.org/cloning_report.html>.

Occasionally Internet addresses may be too long to fit on a single line of your paper. You must not add hyphens nor allow your word processing program (such as Word or WordPerfect, for example) to add punctuation or arbitrary breaks. Divide Internet addresses only after a slash. See Nash entry.

Article from a Magazine

> Hivley, Will. "Worrying about Milk." <u>Discover</u>. Aug. 2000: 44–51. 4 August 2000 <http://www.discover.com/aug_00/gthere.html?article=featmilk.html>.
> Nash, Madeleine, J. "The Personality Genes." <u>Time</u>. 27 Apr. 1998: 14 pars. 15 Oct. 1999 <http://www.time.com/time/magazine/1998/dom/980427/ science.the_personality_8.html>.

Note that the Hivley entry contains page numbers while the Nash entry contains paragraph numbers. Ask your instructor if he or she has a preference about identifying page or paragraph numbers. Often you must be satisfied with whatever Internet sites provide.

Internet sites can be difficult to find. The more letters and numbers in the address (the URL), the more possibilities for difficulties. It may be easier to find the home page (http://www.pathfinder.com/time) and then use the links or the archives to seek out articles you need.

Article from an Online Newspaper

> Chaplin, Julia. "Quiz Shows Make Every Contestant a Video Gladiator." <u>New York Times on the Web</u> 16 Jan. 2000. 31 March 2000 <http://www.nytimes.com/library/style/weekend/ 011600quizshow-videogames.html>.
> Mishra, Raja. "Two More Birds Found with West Nile Virus." <u>Boston Globe Online</u> Sec. A:01. 5 Aug. 2000. 5 Aug. 2000 <http://www.boston.com/

dailyglobe2/218/metro/ Two_more_birds_found_with_West_Nile_
virus+.shtml>.

Article from a Professional or Technical Journal

Dobrin, Arthur. "How Do You Get to Carnegie Hall? Practice, Practice,
Practice." The Humanist 57.4 (1997): 43-45. 25 Apr. 1998
<http://web4.searchbank.com/infotrac/session/726/666/19280875w3/
9!xrn_8&bkm>.

Tener, Norton. "Information Is Not Knowledge." Childhood Education 72.2
(1995): 100. 25 Apr. 1998 <http://web4.searchbank.com/infotrac/session/
726/666/19280875w3/12!xrn_33&bkm>.

Article from an Encyclopedia

"Parks, Rosa—Women in American History." Britannica Online. 1999.
Encyclopaedia Britannica. 4 Apr. 2000 <http://women.eb.com/women/
articles/ Parks_Rosa.html>.

Online Book

Increasingly, entire books are being scanned onto the Net. Scanned means
photographic equipment ("scanners") can be used to copy entire documents,
articles, and even entire books onto the Internet, and you can read them online
or, in many cases, download them to your own computer. Often, this is a rapid
procedure (depending on the speed of your computer and browser) and you
need not fear spending hours downloading material you could easily find in your
own school or town library. Depending on your own software and the capacity
of your computer, a book in your computer could be searched, analyzed, and
compared relatively quickly and easily.

Shelly, Mary. Frankenstein. London, 1831. Electronic Text Center. Ed.
Judy Boss. 1994. U of Virginia Library. 25 Apr. 1998
<http://etext.lib.virginia.edu/modeng/modengO.browse.html>.

See also links to other full-text sites:

<http://promo.net/pg> (Project Gutenberg Homesite)
<http://purl.vt.edu/vtdocs/books/booklist>
<http://mitpress.mit.edu>
<http://digital.library.upenn.edu/books>
<http://www.csbsju.edu/library/books/online.html>
<http://www.selu.edu/Library/InternetRes/full-text.html>

CD-ROM

> The Columbia Granger's World of Poetry. CD-ROM. New York: Columbia
>   UP, 1995.
> Women in the Arts Collection. CD-ROM. Columbus, Ohio: McGraw-Hill
>   Home Interactive, 1997.

ACTIVITY 2

Edit the following MLA "Works Cited" page. Correct any errors of form or violations of MLA guidelines. Some entries may not contain any errors.

> Burfoot, Amby, and Marty Post. "Block Party." Runner's World Feb. 1998: p. 16.
> Richard C. Crandall. Running: The Consequences. Jefferson, NC: McFarland,
>   1986.
> Jones, Bruce H., David N Cowan, and Joseph J. Knapik. "Exercise, Training,
>   and Injuries." Sports Medicine Vol 18 No 3 1994: pp. 202–214.
> Kuipers, Harm. "How Much Is Too Much? Performance Aspects of
>   Overtraining." Research Quarterly for Exercise and Sport 67.3 (1996): 65+.
> Winters, Kerri M., et al. "Bone Density and Cyclic Ovarian Function in Trained
>   Runners and Active Controls." Medicine and Science in Sports and
>   Exercise 28.7 (1996): 776–85.

NAME AND DATE METHOD OF DOCUMENTATION: APA STYLE

The name and date method of documentation is based on the style of the American Psychological Association (APA). This method is often used in science, education, and business. Some researchers believe that references in the text are helpful because readers can identify authorities and dates of research immediately; the full references can be found at the end of the paper when additional source information is desired. If you plan to cite whole books and articles without quoting directly from them, this may be the preferred form of documentation, especially when the age of the research may be an important consideration:

> The experiments in animal cloning immediately raise intense questions
> concerning how soon we may have human clones (Bender, 1993; O'Connor,
> 1996; Pattison, 1995).

Such documentation indicates that all three sources contain this idea, thus lending emphasis for its use here. However, too many references on a page can become intrusive, sacrificing readability for documentation:

The experiment was "inherently flawed" (Brown, 1988, p. 12), and projects based on its results soon consumed millions of wasted dollars (Potter, 1991, pp. 19–20) and sidetracked projects for years afterward (Davis, 1994; Jacques, 1994; Nichols, 1996).

So many references so close together are bound to interfere with reading; a research paper is more than a collection of facts. You can reduce the clutter by giving some references in your text itself. See options in the following sections.

GUIDELINES FOR REFERENCES IN THE TEXT

At the most appropriate place in the text (often the end of a sentence), give the author's name, followed by comma, space, date, and page number if necessary.

> Wilmut and his colleagues at the Roslin Institute did not celebrate when Dolly was born (Kolata, 1998, pp. 219–220).

Option: As an alternative, the author's name can be given in the text, with only the date and pages (when needed) supplied in parentheses.

> According to Kolata (1998), Wilmut and his colleagues at the Roslin Institute did not celebrate when Dolly was born (pp. 219–220).

Option: Both the name and date can be incorporated into your text. In that case, only page numbers would be in parentheses, and only if you cite from specific pages.

> In her 1998 book about cloning, Kolata says Wilmut and his colleagues at the Roslin Institute did not celebrate when Dolly was born (pp. 219–220).

You must give a full description in your References list for such a note.

Extended Discussion

You needn't keep citing a source as long as no intervening source is introduced. If the discussion is lengthy, you may give just the name (Silver) where appropriate to remind the reader. Nevertheless, in general, it's better to give additional references than to risk ambiguous documentation.

Two or More Authors

For two authors, always give both authors' names (last names only). For three to five authors, give all authors' names in the first reference; thereafter use only the first author's name with "et al." For six or more authors, give only the first author's name and "et al." for all references. Use an ampersand in APA references.

First Reference

(Kassirer & Rosenthal, 1998)
(Campbell, McWhir, Ritchie, & Wilmut, 1996)
(Sagan et al., 1978) [6 authors]

Subsequent References

(Kassirer & Rosenthal, 1998)
(Campbell et al., 1996)
(Sagan et al., 1978)

Do not use the ampersand (&) in the text of your paper. If you give the names in the text of your paper, without parentheses, use "and" instead of the ampersand: Kassirer and Rosenthal (1998) or Campbell, McWhir, Ritchie, and Wilmut (1996).

No Author

If there is no author's name, use either the title or an abbreviated (but recognizable) form of the title: (New Technologies for Sports Medicine, 1998) or (New Technologies, 1998).

Author with Long Name

You may shorten or abbreviate lengthy names of groups or committees (NCTE, 1996) as long as the reader will be able to recognize the name in your References list: National Council of Teachers of English.

Two Authors with Same Name

Use initials to identify authors with the same last name:

(G. Kennedy, 1993), (J. Kennedy, 1996).

Same Author, Same Year

Two or more works by the same author published in the same year should be further identified in parentheses with lowercase letters:

. . . (Watts, 1999a, 1999b) . . .

In References List

In your References List these titles should be listed alphabetically by the title, after the date.

> Watts, J. (1999a). Experiment sparks cloning debate in Japan. <u>Lancet, 354,</u> 1801.
> Watts, J. (1999b). Japan set to make first legal prohibition on life-sciences research. <u>Lancet, 354,</u> 1885.

<u>Note:</u> Volume numbers are underlined for professional journals.

Multiple References

If you have more than one author in a reference, follow the order in your References list, usually alphabetical (Bowker, 1990; Lopez, 1993; Rozier & Henderson, 1992). References to the same author also follow the order in the References list—chronological rather than alphabetical (Sipka, 1988, 1992, 1994).

REFERENCES LIST: APA STYLE

Your References list should contain only those sources you actually cite in your paper. When you use the name and date style, the list is always called "References" (not "Bibliography," which might include sources not cited). The purpose of the References list is to help other researchers find the materials you have used, and you should provide complete and accurate information from the title page of a book (not the cover) or as the information appears in a journal, magazine, newspaper, or other source, not the table of contents or indexes. However, use only the initials of authors' first and middle names, even if the names are spelled in full in the source.

Reference models given here are the ones most often needed by students. Others may be inferred from those given here. Occasionally, you may find a source for which there is no exact model; in that case you must invent a reasonable application of these general principles.

BASIC REFERENCE FORM, BOOK (APA)

A   B   C D   E   F   G H   I

Hubbard, R., & Wald, E. (1993). <u>Exploding the gene myth</u>. Boston: Beacon Press.

J   K   L

A. Author(s) name(s), last name first (note that all authors' names are inverted). Use only initials for first and middle names, even if a full name is given on title page. Also, the first line is usually indented five spaces.

B. Ampersand in place of <u>and</u> (but use <u>and</u> when referring to authors in your paper: "Hubbard <u>and</u> Wald show the formula . . .").

C. Two spaces between name and date. (Two spaces after any end mark.) Period after initial serves as end mark.

D. Date of publication in parentheses (frequently given as "copyright" on title page), followed by period and two spaces.

E. Capitalize the first word and all significant words in journal and magazine titles. For other titles (books, articles, essays) capitalize only the first word and proper names. The first word of a subtitle after a colon or dash should be capitalized: <u>Women, men, and gender: Ongoing debate</u>.

F. Underline the titles of books, journals, magazines, and newspapers. Underline volume numbers in journal references. Don't put quotation marks around titles of articles. The only exception to this rule occurs when one title appears inside another:

> Trail, George Y. (1995). Teaching argument and the rhetoric of Orwell's "Politics and the English language." <u>College English, 57,</u> 570–583.

Note: APA Style does not abbreviate page numbers.

G. Period ending book title. Any explanatory information, such as (ed.) for edition is usually set off in parentheses.

H. Place (city) of publication. If the city may be ambiguous (London, Ontario) or unfamiliar (Upper Saddle River), add the postal abbreviation for the state (NJ), province, or nation.

> Reid, S. <u>The Prentice Hall guide for college writing</u>. (5th ed.). Upper Saddle River, NJ: Prentice, 2000.

List only the first city when more than one is given on the title page.

I. Colon and space between place and name of publisher.

J. Do not indent subsequent lines. However, as an alternative, you may indent the second and subsequent lines instead of the first if your instructor prefers.

K. Publisher's name: shorten publisher's name—Boynton instead of Boynton/Cook Heineman. Drop redundant information such as "Co." and "Inc."

L. Period at end of reference.

Page Numbers

Most references that would require a page number in MLA style will also require page numbers in the APA (name and date) style: specific page references, direct quotes, block quotes, paraphrases, and so on. The specific page numbers should appear in parentheses in your paper.

> A line from your paper:
>
> Pulitzer winner for distinguished commentary, Clarence Page (1989) makes certain that <u>Chicago Tribune</u> readers know he is black; the question of race, he says, "has some merit" (p. 373).

The corresponding entry in your References list:

> Page, C. (1989). The people's republic of Chicago. In K. J. Willis (Ed.), <u>The Pulitzer prizes</u> (pp. 373–396). New York: Touchstone.

Note that when you cite direct quotes from sources, you should use "p." or "pp." for page numbers of certain types of publications, namely newspapers, and chapters, essays, or other divisions within sources, especially parts of books with editors.

Note also that the page numbers "373–396" in the preceding model are complete. The APA style gives page numbers in full: it does not omit parts of numbers as in "373–96."

BASIC REFERENCE FORM, PERIODICALS (APA)

Periodicals include journals, magazines, newspapers, and other publications that are published "periodically."

>   A   B   C   D
> King, K. A. (1998). Should school uniforms be mandated in elementary schools? <u>Journal of School Health, 68</u>(1), 32–37.
>   E   F   G H I J K L

A. Author's last name, first and middle initials (even if full name is spelled out in the source).

B. Two spaces between author's name and date.

C. Date in parentheses, followed by period.

D. Title of journal article without quotation marks. Capitalize only the first word, proper names, and the first word of a subtitle after a colon. End with a period or other end mark.

E. Two spaces between title of article and title of journal.

F. Capitalize first and all significant words of journal title. Underline periodical titles.

G. Comma after periodical title.

H. Underline volume number. No space or separating mark between volume and issue number. Most journals number pages continuously and therefore don't require issue numbers: use a comma between volume number and page numbers in such cases.

> Reynolds, J. F. (1989, Summer). Concepts of memory in contemporary composition. <u>Rhetorical Society Quarterly, 19,</u> 245–252.

Note that the comma after the volume number is also underlined.

I. Issue number in parentheses for journals starting each issue on page 1. Most journals number continuously: if the first issue ends on page 328, the second issue will begin on page 329. Only when each issue begins on page 1 should you include an issue number. Do not underline issue numbers.

J. Comma after volume and issue number, if any.

K. Page numbers given last. Use "p." or "pp." for newspaper entries but not magazines or journals.

L. Period at end of reference.

REFERENCE LIST MODELS, APA STYLE: BOOKS

One Author

Walker, A. (1996). <u>The same river twice: Honoring the difficult</u>. New York: Scribner.

Note initials in author's name, capitalization in title, shortened name for publisher.

Morrison, T. (1987). <u>Beloved</u>. New York: Knopf.
Tan, A. (1995). <u>The hundred secret senses</u>. New York: Putnam.
West, C. (1994). <u>Race matters</u>. New York: Vintage-Random House.

Note alphabetical order for items in reference list.

More Than One Book by Same Author

Treat these books as if they were written by different authors with the same name. Don't use a string of hyphens. Chronological order is required.

Kennedy, G. A. (1963). <u>The art of persuasion in Greece</u>. Princeton, NJ: Princeton University Press.

Kennedy, G. A. (1972). <u>The art of rhetoric in the Roman world, 300 b.c.–a.d. 300</u>. Princeton, NJ: Princeton University Press.

Kennedy, G. A. (1980). <u>Classical rhetoric and its Christian and secular tradition from ancient to modern times</u>. Chapel Hill: University of North Carolina Press.

<u>Note:</u> Kennedy references—identify most states except those very well known or those identified in the publisher's name. Do not use "U" and "P" for University and Press, as in MLA style.

Author of One Book, Coauthor of Another

Postman, N. (1979). <u>Teaching as a conserving activity</u>. New York: Delacorte.

Postman, N., & Weingartner, C. (1969). <u>Teaching as a subversive activity</u>. New York: Delacorte.

Coauthored books should be listed after books with one author, regardless of the dates.

Two or More Authors

> Kass, L., & Wilson, J. Q. (1998). <u>The ethics of human cloning</u>. Washington, DC: AEI Press.
>
> Belenky, M. F., Bond, L. A., & Winestock, J. S. (1997). <u>A tradition that has no name: Nurturing the development of people, families, and communities</u>. New York: BasicBooks-Harper.

For APA style, your References list must give all authors' names, no matter how many. Don't use "et al." in your References list. However, to cite such a work in your paper use only the first author's last name, et al., and the date: (Comley et al., 1994). Add page numbers if needed (or after a block quote). Give explanatory information, such as edition number (if other than first edition), in parentheses. Invert all authors' names.

> Comley, N. R., Hamilton, D., Klaus, C. H., Scholes, R., & Sommers, N. (1994). <u>Fields of writing: Reading across the disciplines</u> (4th ed.). New York: St. Martin's.
>
> Sagan, C., Drake, F. D., Druyan, A., Ferris, T., Lomberg, J., & Sagan, L. S. (1978). <u>Murmurs of earth: The voyager interstellar record</u>. New York: Random House.

Committee or Group Author

> National Academy of Engineering, Institute of Medicine. (1995). <u>On being a scientist: Responsible conduct in research</u>. Washington, DC: National Academy Press.
>
> National Council of Teachers of English. (1999). <u>Trends and issues in postsecondary English studies</u>. Urbana, IL: NCTE.

Group authors and unsigned works are alphabetized according to the first significant word in the name or title: don't alphabetize under <u>A</u>, <u>An</u>, or <u>The</u>. <u>The Zuider Report</u> would be alphabetized as if it started with <u>Zuider</u>.

Book with Editor(s)

> Reynolds, R., & Stone J. (Eds.). (1991). <u>On doctoring: Stories, poems, essays</u>. New York: Simon & Schuster.
>
> Walsh, M. R. (Ed.). (1997). <u>Women, men, and gender: Ongoing debates</u>. New Haven: Yale University Press.

Chapter or Section in an Edited Work

> Rosener, J. B. (1997). Leadership and the paradox of gender. In M. R. Walsh (Ed.), <u>Women, men, and gender: Ongoing debates</u> (pp. 294–297). New Haven: Yale University Press.

Note that editor's name is not inverted, in contrast with the preceding entry Book with Editor(s), and no period appears between the book title and the parenthetical reference to pages.

Translation

> Eco, U. (1994). <u>The island of the day before</u> (W. Weaver, Trans.). New York: Harcourt.

Multivolume Work

> Churchill, W. S. (1984–1986). <u>A history of the English-speaking peoples</u> (Collectors Edition, Vols. 1–4). Norwalk, CT: Easton Press.

To cite this entire work in a parenthetic reference, use (Churchill, 1984–1986).

Part(s) of Multivolume Work

> Churchill, W. S. (1985). <u>The age of revolution</u>. Norwalk, CT: Easton Press, Vol 3. of <u>A history of the English-speaking peoples</u> (Vols. 1–4). 1984–1986.

Churchill's work has individual titles and publication dates for each volume. In-text references to part of a multivolume work must give volume number and page number, for example: (3:91–92).

Unsigned Work

> <u>The New York Times film reviews 1993–1994</u>. (1996). New York: Times Books & Garland Publishing.

Note that unsigned works, such as the preceding one, are listed by title and referred to in your text by an abbreviated but recognizable form of the title such as <u>Times film reviews</u>. An unsigned work is not considered "anonymous" unless that word appears on the title page.

Reprint of Older Work

> Agee, J., & Evans, W. (1966). <u>Let us now praise famous men</u>. New York: Ballantine. (Original work published 1939)
> Selzer, R. (1996). <u>Letters to a young doctor</u>. New York: Harvest-Harcourt. (Original work published 1982)

Parenthetic references to reprints should give both dates in your paper: (Agee & Evans, 1939/1966).

Edition

Reid, S. (2000). The Prentice Hall guide for college writers (5th ed.). Upper Saddle River, NJ: Prentice.

Introduction, Preface, Foreword

Elbow, P. (1991). Foreword. In P. Belanoff & M. Dickson, Portfolios: Process and product (pp. ix–xvi). Portsmouth, NH: Boynton/Cook.

Ruether, R. R. (1998). Introduction. In D. C. Maguire & L. L. Rasmussen, Ethics for a small planet: New horizons on population, consumption, and ecology (pp. xi–xv). Albany: State University of New York.

Dictionary

Neufeldt, V. (Ed.). (1996). Webster's new world college dictionary (3rd ed.). New York: Simon & Schuster.

Webster's third new international dictionary of the English language. (1986). (Unabridged.) Springfield, MA: Merriam-Webster.

Encyclopedia, Alphabetically Arranged Work

American Indian languages. (1998). The new encyclopaedia Britannica (15th ed.). Chicago: Encyclopaedia Britannica.

North American Indian languages. (1998). The new encyclopaedia Britannica: Micropaedia (15th ed.). Chicago: Encyclopaedia Britannica.

Dissertation, Unpublished

Shannon, M. (1997). Senior learners: Motivations and composition strategies for teaching students 55+. Unpublished doctoral dissertation, Illinois State University.

Article from Dissertation Abstracts or Dissertation Abstracts International

Edison, M. I. (1997). Out of class activities and the development of critical thinking in college. Dissertation Abstracts International, 58, 03A.

Note: "A" after a page reference indicates humanities, and "B" indicates sciences in Dissertation Abstracts. The title became Dissertation Abstracts International starting with volume 30.

REFERENCE LIST MODELS IN APA STYLE: PERIODICALS

Weekly Magazine Article

> Gibbs, N. (1998, April 13). Day of deliverance. <u>Time, 151,</u> 44–51.

Note that with APA style you should give volume numbers for magazines as well as for journals.

Magazine Article, No Author Given

> Picturesque charm: All two blocks of it. (1998, February 9). <u>U.S. News & World Report, 124,</u> 58.

Monthly Magazine Article

> Riddle, R. D., & Tabin, C. J. (1999, February). How limbs develop. <u>Scientific American, 280,</u> 74–79.

Significant words in the titles of the periodicals are capitalized, but not words in the titles of articles themselves. Also, months are not abbreviated (in contrast to MLA).

Newspaper Article

> Beck, J. (1998, April 13). Make it boxing's last round. <u>Detroit Free Press,</u> p. A11.
> Greene, B. (1998, March 29). Higher profiles and diminished voices. <u>Chicago Tribune,</u> sec. 1, p. 2.

For newspaper articles with discontinuous pages, separate the pages with commas

> Suskind, R. (1990, September 6). A lady lawyer in Laramie writes land-mark letter. <u>Wall Street Journal,</u> pp. A1, A6.

Note that the comma after a newspaper title should be underlined. Newspaper articles and sections of books require "p." and "pp." for "page" and "pages."

Newspaper Article, Unsigned

> Munchies brought on by stress linked to hormone, study finds. (1998, April 5). <u>Chicago Tribune,</u> sec. 1, p. 12.

Reviews, Signed and Unsigned: Books, Films, Music CDs

Farley, C. J. (1998, March 16). Heading for the light [Review of the album <u>Ray of Light</u>]. <u>Time, 151,</u> 75.

[Review of the book <u>Good fences</u>]. (1998, March 9). <u>Publishers Weekly,</u> <u>245,</u> 47.

Use brackets to describe the article. When there is no title, use the bracketed information and the brackets as the title.

Smith, B. H. (1998, February 20). Is it really a computer? [Review of the book <u>How the mind works</u>]. <u>Times Literary Supplement,</u> pp. 3–4.

Thompson, D. (1998, May). A dark bright light [Review of the film <u>The Truman show</u>]. <u>Esquire, 129,</u> 46–49.

White, A. (1998). Against the Hollywood grain [Review of the film <u>Amistad</u>]. <u>Film Comment, 34</u>(2), 34–42.

Wolkomir, R. (2000, February). [Review of the book <u>Mind of the raven</u>]. <u>Smithsonian, 30,</u> 150–152.

Editorial, Signed and Unsigned

Men doing their share. (1998, April 17). [Editorial]. <u>The Christian Science Monitor,</u> p. 16.

Zabludoff, M. (1998, September). [Editorial]. Fear and longing. <u>Discover,</u> <u>19,</u> 6.

Letter to the Editor

Eichhorn, G. L. (1998, January 26). Penmanship counts [Letter to the editor]. <u>The New Yorker,</u> 9.

Moyers, B. (1998, April 10). Addiction can be a disease and a behavior [Letter to the editor]. <u>New York Times,</u> p. A18.

Nelson, C. (1998, March/April). More on midwives [Letter to the editor]. <u>Public Health, 113</u>(2), 99.

Note that <u>The New Yorker</u> and a few other magazines have no volume numbers.

Professional, Technical, or Specialty Journal, Each Issue Starting with Page 1

Farris, P. (1997). Images of urban Native Americans: The border zones of mixed identities. <u>Journal of American Culture, 20</u>(1), 27–30.

Gaughan, J. (1998). From comfort zone to content zone. <u>English Journal,</u> <u>87</u>(2), 36–43.

Note that volume numbers are underlined. Page numbers are not preceded by "p." or "pp." for journal references. Newspapers or parts of books require "p." or "pp." for pages. Also note the issue number is in parentheses. Because each volume usually has several issues in it, readers need to know the issue number in order to find the referenced pages. There is no space between volume and issue numbers.

Professional, Technical, or Specialty Journal, Pages Numbered Continuously throughout Volume

Dolan, L., & Poethig, R. S. (1998). Clonal analysis of leaf development in cotton. American Journal of Botany, 85, 315–321.

Feig, D. S., & Naylor, C. D. (1998). Eating for two: Are guidelines for weight gain during pregnancy too liberal? The Lancet, 9108, 1054–1055.

Titles and Quotes within Titles

Hinton, R. (1998). Steinbeck's The grapes of wrath. The Explicator, 56, 101–103.

Lent, R. (1993). "I can relate to that . . . ": Reading and responding in the writing classroom. College Composition and Communication, 44, 232–240.

Trail, George Y. (1995). Teaching argument and the rhetoric of Orwell's "Politics and the English language." College English, 57, 570–583.

REFERENCE LIST MODELS IN APA STYLE: OTHER SOURCES

Handout or Unpublished Essay

Hoefel, R. (1999, January 8). English 320: Critical theory. Unpublished Course Syllabus. Alma College, Alma, MI.

Konopa, D. (1997, November 14). The paradox of Zen. Unpublished Research Paper, Handout for English 101. Kalamazoo Valley Community College, Kalamazoo, MI.

Lecture, Speech, Public Address

Donaldson, S. (1997, November 23). The state of television news. Lecture presented at Kansas State University, Manhattan, KS.

Strossen, N. (1998, March 17). Women under the law. Lecture presented at Alma College, Alma, MI.

Note that titles of public addresses are underlined in APA style.

Film

Cameron, J. (Director). (1997). <u>Titanic</u> [Film]. Paramount.

Video: Film or Television

Emmerich, R. (Director). (1996). <u>Independence day</u> [Videotape]. Beverly Hills: Twentieth Century Fox.

Grubin, D. (Producer and Director). (1995). The field of time. In <u>The language of life</u> [Videotape]. New York: Newbridge Communications.

Television Show

Carter, C. (Producer). (1998). Mind's eye. In <u>The x-files.</u> Fox.

Hamlin, J. (Producer). (1998). The piano man. In <u>Sixty minutes.</u> CBS.

Play, Performance

Knott, F. (1998). <u>Wait until dark.</u> (L. Foglia, Director). Brooks Atkinson Theater, New York.

Recording

Carpenter, M. C. (1996). <u>A place in the world</u> [CD]. New York: Sony.

Individual Selection from a Recording

Carpenter, M. C. (1996). Ideas are like stars. On <u>A place in the world</u> [CD]. New York: Sony.

Work of Art

<u>Aphrodite</u> (the "Venus de Milo") [Statue]. The Louvre, Paris.

Hopper, E. (1950). <u>Cape Cod morning</u> [Painting in oil]. National Museum of American Art, Washington, DC.

Poem Published Separately

Stafford, W. (1998). The way it is. In <u>Hungry mind review,</u> p. 32.

Poem in a Collection

> Harjo, J. (1995). Anchorage. In J. Daniels (Ed.), <u>Letters to America:</u> <u>Contemporary American poetry on race</u> (pp. 95–96). Detroit: Wayne State University Press.

Letter, Personal

Give all references to personal data in your text, not in your References.

> G. Cavalieri (personal communication, 1998, March 15).

[Or]

> (G. Cavalieri, personal communication, March 15, 1998)

Letter(s), Published

> Van Gogh, V. (1958). Letter to Theo (No. 358). In <u>The complete letters</u> <u>of Vincent Van Gogh</u> (Vol. 2). Greenwich, CT: New York Graphic Society.

Personal Interview

Treat as personal data. Unless or until it is published in some form, you should treat it like a personal letter: cite it in your text, not in your References.

> Lee. L. (personal interview, November 20, 1997 at Alma College, Alma, MI).

Published Interview

> Percy, W. (1998, Spring). Rock and read: Will Percy interviews Bruce Springsteen [Interview]. <u>DoubleTake, 4</u>, 36–43.

A Chart, Diagram, Map, or Table

A figure is a chart, map, or diagram, or any visual information other than columns of numbers (a table). A figure should have a citation at the bottom of the page on which it appears. The citation should appear as a footnote.

> Begley, S. (1997, March 10). [Diagram of Dolly cloning]. In Little lamb, who made thee? <u>Newsweek, 129</u>, 56–57.
> Mattson, C. M., & Mattson, M. T. (1990). Major soil groups [Map]. In <u>Contemporary atlas of the United States</u>. New York: Macmillan, 9.

A Cartoon

Treat a cartoon as a figure—something to look at for visual information. Cite in a footnote at the bottom of the page.

> Johnston, L. (1998, April 15). For better or worse [Cartoon]. <u>Detroit Free Press,</u> p. D16.
> Ziegler, J. (1998, March 23). [Cartoon]. <u>New Yorker,</u> 71.

An Advertisement

Treat an advertisement as a figure.

> L. L. Bean. (2000, August 7). [Advertisement]. <u>Time, 156,</u> 9.
> Saturn. (2000, August). [Advertisement]. <u>The Atlantic Monthly, 286,</u> 50–51.

REFERENCE LIST MODELS IN APA STYLE: ELECTRONIC SOURCES

Article from a Magazine

> Hivley, W. (2000, August). Worrying about milk. <u>Discover, 21</u>. Retrieved August 4, 2000, from http://www.discover.com/aug_00/gthere.html?article=feat-milk.html
> Nash, M. J. (1998, April 27). The personality genes. <u>Time, 15</u> Retrieved October 15, 1999, from http://www.time.com/time/magazine/1998/dom/980427/science.the_personality_8.html

Note that APA citations of electronic sources do not end with a period unless a period belongs at the end of a URL.

Article from an Online Newspaper

> Chaplin, J. (2000, January 16). Quiz shows make every contestant a video gladiator. <u>New York Times on the Web</u>. Retrieved March 31, 2000, from http://www.nytimes.com/library/style/weekend/011600quizshow-videogames.html
> Mishra, R. (2000, August 5). Two more birds found with West Nile virus. <u>Boston Globe Online</u> Retrieved August 5, 2000, from http://www.boston.com/dailyglobe2/218/metro/Two_more_birds_found_with_West_Nile_virus+.shtml

Article from a Professional or Technical Journal

Dobrin, A. (1997). How do you get to Carnegie Hall? Practice, practice, practice. The Humanist, 57(4) Retrieved May 8, 1999 from http://web4.search-bank.com/infotrac/session/726/666/19280875w3/9!xrn_8&bkm

Tener, N. (1995). Information is not knowledge. Childhood Education, 72(2). Retrieved November 14, 1998, from http://web4.searchbank.com/info-trac/session/726/666/19280875w3/12!xrn_33&bkm

Article from an Encyclopedia

Parks, Rosa—women in American history. (1999). Britannica Online Encyclopaedia Britannica. Retrieved April 4, 2000, from http://women.eb.com/women/articles/Parks_Rosa.html

Online Book

Shelly, M. (1831). Frankenstein. Ed. Judy Boss. 1994. University of Virginia Library Retrieved July 28, 2000, from Electronic Text Center http://etext.lib.virginia.edu/modeng/modengO.browse.html

CD-ROM

The Columbia Granger's world of poetry. (1995). [CD-ROM]. New York: Columbia University Press.

Women in the arts collection. (1997). [CD-ROM]. Columbus, Ohio: McGraw-Hill Home Interactive.

ACTIVITY 3

Edit the following APA References page. Correct any mistakes in form or violations of APA guidelines. Some items may not need editing.

Burfoot, A., and Post, M. (1998, Feb.). "Block party." Runner's World, p. 16.

Richard C. Crandall. Running: The Consequences. Jefferson, NC: McFarland, 1986.

Jones, B. H., Cowan D. N., & Knapik, J. J. (1994). Exercise, training, and injuries. Sports Medicine, 18(3), 202–214.

Kuipers, Harm. (1996). How much is too much? Performance aspects of overtraining. "Research Quarterly for Exercise and Sport," 67.(3), 65+.

Winters, Kerri M., et al. (1996). "Bone Density and Cyclic Ovarian Function in Trained Runners and Active Controls." Medicine and Science in Sports and Exercise, 28.7, 776–85.

LEGAL CITATIONS AND GOVERNMENT REFERENCES

Because there are so many cases, reporters, state and federal laws and abbreviations, we can present only a brief sampling of basic models. Students who need more than this will find the "Blue Book" an essential source. However, the Blue Book is designed for practicing members of the legal profession and is likely to be difficult for most students.

Then too, legal citations amount to their own, separate style sheet and should not be thought of as limited to either APA or MLA. However, appropriate, accurate legal references should be included in the bibliography at the end of your paper no matter which style you have used for your paper overall. For additional information about legal citations, see the <u>Blue Book: A Uniform System of Citation</u>, 16th ed (Cambridge: Harvard Law Review, 1996).

Citing a Case

To cite a case in your paper, use the names of the parties involved and the abbreviation "v." for versus: <u>Standard Oil Co. v. FTC</u>. Much abbreviating is common in legal citations (FTC is an abbreviation for the Federal Trade Commission here). The citation itself is an abbreviation for the full case name and other information, which must be found in your bibliography. Underline case names in your paper but not in your Works Cited or References bibliography. To save space, the citations are as abbreviated as possible, so it is helpful to understand the general form of legal citations, most of which, including their abbreviations, can be found in the Blue Book:

Model Case Citation for Your Bibliography

A   B   C   D   E   F   G   H
Standard Oil Co. v. FTC, 477 U.S. 23, 75 (1999).

A. Name of first party in case (not abbreviated).

B. Abbreviation for "versus."

C. Name of second party (Federal Trade Commission here).

D. Volume number of reporter.

E. Name of reporter (official "report" of case: abbreviation for U.S. Reports). (Full names of most reporters can be found in the Blue Book.)

F. First page of the case.

G. Specific page you cite, if any.

H. Date of decision.

Citing a Constitution

A   B   C
U.S. Const. amend. XIV, §1.
N.J. Const. art. VI, §4.

A. The name of the government: the U.S. Constitution; the New Jersey Constitution.
B. The part of the Constitution: Amendment 14; article 6.
C. Any sections: §1; §4.

Government Documents

Government publications have been rapidly changing formats along with changing technologies, and you can find many government documents on the Internet. One useful source for government listings is the <u>Congressional Record</u>, the
"official record" of the proceedings of the House and Senate. (Though it's "official," you may find more in the <u>Record</u> than actually occurred on the floor of
the House or Senate. Representatives and Senators are allowed to "expand" their
entries after the fact.)

  Cong. Rec. 10 Feb. 1998: H566–80.

Citing the <u>Congressional Record</u> takes the preceding brief form. The "H"
before a page number signifies the House of Representatives. "S" preceding
page numbers signifies the Senate. No title is given (even though the document
itself has a title "Human Cloning Prohibition Act").

  For other documents, give the name of the government followed by the
agency when the author of the document is unknown. Note that GPO stands
for Government Printing Office. If there are additional documents by the same
government (for example, United States or a state government), use three
hyphens for the government and an additional three for the name of the agency.
Include the type of document, if known.

> United States. Cong. House. <u>To Prohibit the Cloning of Humans</u>. 105th Cong.,
>   1st sess. H. Rept. 923. Washington: GPO, 1997.
> ---. Senate. <u>To Reform the Federal Election Campaign Laws Applicable to
>   Congress</u>. 106th Cong., 1st sess. S. Bill 16. Washington: GPO, 1999.
> ---. Dept. of Justice. <u>Sourcebook of Criminal Justice Statistics—1996</u>.
>   Washington: GPO, 1997.
> ---. Office of Technology Assessment. <u>Adult Literacy and the New
>   Technologies: Tools for a Lifetime</u>. Washington: GPO, 1993.
> ---. National Endowment for the Arts. <u>Cultural Centers of Color</u>. Washington:
>   GPO, 1996.

Government Document with Author's Name

Bass, Bernard M. <u>A New Paradigm of Leadership: An Inquiry into Transformational Leadership</u>. U.S. Army Institute for the Behavioral and Social Sciences. Alexandria, VA: 1996.

Gore, Albert. <u>Federal Welfare-to-Work Commitments: A Report to President Bill Clinton</u> by Al Gore, Vice President of the United States. Washington, DC: GPO, 1997.

Chapter 10

Writing Your Research Paper

RESEARCHERS AS WRITERS

Research and writing are closely connected. No matter what you intend to write, you will almost certainly find yourself gathering up notes and collecting information. Writers are researchers. Both writers and researchers must gather and select. For both, <u>drafting</u> often means "organizing" and working on the outline. As a research writer, you must synthesize information. Researchers, like other writers, have a responsibility to their readers, not only to be fair-minded and accurate but to be concise and readable.

No one can really tell you exactly how or what to write. But at the outset, when you are struggling with something new, learning to deal with impersonal, often technical subject matter—when all that is piled up in front of you, the task can be intimidating. For that reason, we present here, in a logical sequence, a procedure for students in which prewriting, collecting, drafting, organizing, synthesizing, and rewriting follow one another. In practice, these stages of research often overlap: like doing research, writing a research paper is more often a spiral than a straight line. However, to simplify the process, we present a chronological procedure. We leave it to you to decide where your own procedure spirals back to earlier stages of your research or writing.

For your reader's benefit, you should organize your research paper in a standard form. The standard form shortens the time readers must spend reading. Readers expect to find your thesis early in the paper; they shouldn't have to hunt for it. Research papers are written in plain English because most readers don't have time for artistic language. Nor do readers have time for dull, plodding language that anesthetizes the analytical mind. Readers are grateful to find the parts of your paper where they expect to find them. Some readers choose to skip to the end, to read the conclusion first, to see whether the research has any useful findings for their own work. They will find the conclusion readily when you follow a standard arrangement and label the parts of your paper. (We are aware, of course, that not all research is presented this way.)

WRITING A REPORT

Various forms of writing require you to state an idea and then give information to support your idea. Such writing can include proposals, explanations of projects or events (such as a witness's report of an accident), and even specialty forms such as the income tax forms used to "report" to the IRS. A report is an informational research paper.

Please read the following student paper and try to explain the way it is written.

Barber 1

Danelle Barber
English 101
8 April 1999

GHB: Great Bodily Harm

When she woke up, Julie Simmons couldn't figure out
how she'd made it back to her house in Los Angeles.
She looked down. She was naked, but she didn't recall
getting undressed. All she remembered was having
dinner in her date's apartment and then falling
asleep on his couch. (Moore 203)

When Julie confronted her date about the night, he claimed   1
she had too much to drink and he had driven her home. She knew
she'd only had a few beers, but she believed his story--for a
while anyway (203). A few weeks later a memory jolted free
from an unknown abyss. When she slipped in the shower, the
cold slap of the tile brought her back to that fateful night.
"She was on her hands and knees on the bathroom floor as her

date stood behind her. Then came a searing pain. The memory
was vivid and undeniable. Julie had been raped and, until that
moment, she hadn't even remembered it" (Moore 203). Julie was
poisoned with Gamma Hydroxy Butyric Acid--otherwise known as
GHB, the newest date-rape drug. But what exactly is GHB, and
how is it being used to render its victims helpless?

GHB has been identified by many different names: "grievous   2
bodily harm," "scoop," "saltwater," "liquid ecstasy," "Liquid
X," "cherry meth," "soap," "Easy Lay," "GBH," "Georgia Home
Boy," "Natural Sleep 500," and "Oxy-sleep" to name a few (U.S.
Dept. of Health 2). GHB can be made in a fine powder form or
as a concentrated liquid. Both are bought cheaply on the street
and are illegal in the United States (Gould 1-2). GHB is found
naturally in nearly every cell in the body, but when more is
ingested, the results can be deadly. This was the case for
Hillory Janean Farias. The 17-year-old Texas girl went with
friends to a dance club and only drank soda. It is believed
that GHB was sprinkled into her drink when she wasn't paying
attention. Within 24 hours, the straight-A, star athlete was
dead from a drug overdose (Gorman 1). The police found 27
milligrams of GHB per liter of blood (Fowkes and Dean 1).

Unfortunately, Hillory and Julie aren't the only ones who   3
have fallen victim to GHB. Police in Chicago faced a multiple
outbreak in 1997: seven people were found dazed and confused
outside a popular nightclub--all unknowingly drank GHB (Staten
1). New York and Texas alone received 69 reports of GHB
poisonings between August 1995 and September 1996 (U.S. Dept.
of Health 1).

Gamma Hydroxy Butyrate is increasingly popular at   4
fraternity parties, clubs, bars, and other social events in the
Unites States. Quietly slipped into a drink, the drug is
colorless, odorless, and nearly tasteless. An added bonus: all
traces of GHB leave the body after 12 hours. Within 5 to 20
minutes of ingestion, a teaspoonful of GHB causes the user to
take on many of the properties of someone who has been
drinking extreme amounts of alcohol: disinhibition, a false
sense of security, and low levels of consciousness result. The
user's heartbeat also slows and her blood pressure drops. In
extreme cases, she may stop breathing (Staten 1). Sometimes the
girl is said to go into a coma, but she actually lapses into a
state called "clonus"--a rapid "relaxation" and "contraction"
of muscles—or falls into deep tranquilization (Morgenthaler and

state called "clonus"--a rapid "relaxation" and "contraction"
of muscles—or falls into deep tranquilization (Morgenthaler and
Joy 2). In most GHB cases, not enough oxygen gets to the brain,
and the user becomes unconscious and loses her memory. "A
substance that knocks out the victim and leaves her with amne-
sia makes the perfect agent for date rape," says Michael Ellis,
director of the Southeast Texas Poison Center (Gorman 1).

GHB hasn't always been considered a date rape drug.   5
Introduced to Europe in 1961 by Dr. Henri Labont, the drug was
used as an anesthetic for surgery. It was used medically in Europe
for years before it surfaced in the United States. In the late
1980s, GHB was widely dispensed in health-food stores, hawked as a
growth hormone and sleep aid. Sales skyrocketed (Tennant 1-3).
Although Gamma Hydroxy Butyrate is still legally prescribed in
Europe, the United States has since found the drug to be harmful
(Taylor 2). In 1990, complaints surfaced about GHB's effects;
consequently, the FDA pulled the drug off the shelves (Tennant 1).
Med Watch News, a program that reports findings of the FDA to
health-care professionals, reported the following:

> Starting in 1990, FDA began an intense investigation
> of GHB distribution after numerous cases of
> GHB-related illness were reported. [. . .] Many of those
> injured required hospitalization, and some deaths have
> been linked to the consumption of GHB products. By the
> end of 1991, FDA and the Department of Justice had
> taken enforcement action against several firms and
> individuals involved in manufacturing, distributing,
> and promoting GHB. [. . .] These actions--along with
> embargoes, public education campaigns and other
> measures taken by state and federal authorities--
> appeared to temporarily diminish the distribution and
> abuse of GHB. ("FDA Re-Issues Warning" 1)

Or so the FDA thought. The use of GHB remains an extremely
serious problem.

Locally, is there a problem with GHB being used as a   6
date-rape drug? Samantha Reid, Detroit resident, died earlier
this year after drinking a soda sprinkled with Gamma Hydroxy
Butyrate. Four men are facing preliminary hearings in the
15-year-old's death. Renee Oradnik from the Delta County Alliance
against Violence and Abuse says she is currently counseling a
woman from my hometown area who was drugged and raped at

Michigan State University. These are the only local cases I
have heard about, but not everyone who has been victimized
by GHB comes forward; moreover, GHB poisoning is extremely
difficult to prove.

Escanaba Public Safety Det./Lt. Darryl McKnight says, "A   7
lot of the problem is when they [women] go to college. When
they go out to bars or go to parties, they [drugs] can be
slipped into any type of drink they're given and dissolved in
just about anything including soft drinks." Escanaba is
choosing to combat the problem through education. Special
sessions and programs specifically on date-rape drugs have
been started to keep the high school students informed and
educated (Barr A6). Wake Forest University is also testing
this technique on the college campus: WFU President
Kenneth Zick set up informational forums to educate students
there (1).

So how can you, personally, protect yourself from Gamma   8
Hydroxy Butyrate? Here are some suggestions to prevent
involuntary ingestion of GHB:

Never accept anything to drink from strangers--get them
directly from the bartender (Substance Abuse).

Do not leave your drink unattended EVER, and do not leave
it with anyone else. Always take your drink with you
wherever you go (Taylor 2).

Keep a close eye on your friends. If you notice
drunken-like behavior after one beer, call 911 and
get her out of there immediately. If it is possible,
try to take the spiked drink with you--it can be
tested for the presence of drugs (Gould 11).

NEVER leave a friend whom you suspect has been drugged!
("Rohypnol Alert" 1)

"It's something that scares me deeply," says a female   9
student in a Los Angeles bar, "because I don't like feeling
vulnerable" ("Campuses Warning" 1). GHB is definitely scary.
Michigan, along with most of the United States, has passed a
bill placing GHB into the Schedule I drug category (Tennant 4).
This enables stiffer penalties for Gamma Hydroxy Butyrate
suppliers, users, and abusers. But the availability of a recipe
on the Internet increases the number victimized. Unbeknownst to
a woman, GHB is manufactured in a kitchen, slipped into her
drink, and she becomes the man's prey. To some, GHB is a

Barber 5

substance used to get an "easy lay." To some, GHB is a drug
that renders women unconscious with no memory. To some,
GHB causes death. We all have a responsibility to be educated
on this drug and its effects; similarly, we all have a
responsibility to watch our drinks when we go out.

Barber 6

Works Cited

Barr, Nancy. "Lethal Combination: Sex, Drugs and Alcohol." The
    Escanaba Daily Press 25 Mar. 1999: A6.
"Campuses Warning Students about Rape Drugs." CNN Interactive.
    Cable News Network. 17 Mar. 1999 <http://www.cnn.com/US/
    9709/17/rape.drugs/index.html>.
Cohn, Michael. "GHB Supply FAQ." n.d. 27 Mar. 1999
    <http://uts.cc.utexas.edu/~laborit/supplynf.html>.
"FDA Re-issues Warning on GHB." Med Watch News 12 Mar. 1997.
    27 Mar. 1999
    <http://www.pharminfo.com/medwatch/mwrpt7.html>.
Fowkes, Steven, and Ward Dean. "GHB Madness, Two Years
    Later." Smart Drug News 18 Feb. 1996. 27 Mar. 1999
    <http://www.ceri.com/ghbmad2.htm>.
Gorman, Christine. "Liquid X." Time 30 Sept. 1996. 27 Mar. 1999
    <http://cgi.pathfinder.com/time/magazine/archive/1996/dom/
    960930/health.html>.
Gould, Eileen. "Rohypnol and GHB—'Date Rape' Drugs." Report by
    Texas Association against Sexual Assault. 27 Mar. 1999
    <http://www.taasa.org/currentissues/datedrugs.htm>.
Moore, Mary K. "The Date Rapist's Scary New Weapon."
    Cosmopolitan Feb. 1999: 203–05+.
Morgenthaler, John and Dan Joy. "GHB." Cognitive Enhancement
    Research Institute n.d. 27 Mar. 1999 <http://earthops.org/
    ghb_research.html>.
"Rohypnol Alert: The Date Rape Drug of Choice." n.d. 27 Mar.
    1999 <http://www.clark.net/pub/klaatu/rohypnol.html>.

Barber 7

Staten, Clark. "CPD Investigating GHB Ingestion/Overdose."
    <u>Emergencynet News Service</u> 1 Feb. 1997. 27 Mar. 1999
    <http://www.emergency.com/ghb1.htm>.
<u>Substance Abuse and Sexual Assault</u>. Washington DC: Hoffmann-La
    Roche Inc., 1999.
Taylor, Betsy. "Fact Sheet on Rohypnol and GHB." <u>Wake Forest</u>
    <u>Student Health Service</u> n.d. 27 Mar. 1999
    <http://www.wfu.edu/Student-Services/Student-HealthService/
    Rohypnol2.html>.
Tennant, Christopher. "Wonder Drug, Rape Aid." n.d. 27 Mar.1999
    <http://www.student.com/article/ghb>.
U.S. Department of Health and Human Services. "Gamma Hydroxy
    Butyrate Use in New York and Texas, 1995-1996." Apr. 1997.
    27 Mar. 1999 <http://www.emergency.com/ghb_2.htm>.
Zick, Kenneth A. "Letter from VP Ken Zick." <u>Wake Forest Student</u>
    <u>Health Service</u> 23 Feb. 1998. 27 Mar. 1999
    <http://www.wfu.edu/Student-Services/Student-Health-Service/
    KenZick.html>.

Danelle's report is a research paper that explains what GHB is for the bene-fit of readers who may not be familiar with the drug. Her paper doesn't present an argument: she presents a point of view. That is, Danelle does not present counterarguments nor make concessions; she does not analyze strengths or weak-nesses in arguments. Instead, she asks a question, which is the last sentence of her first paragraph: <u>But what exactly is GHB, and how is it being used to render its victims helpless?</u> Then she presents facts about GHB to answer it.

Danelle's report represents a popular research assignment: an objective presentation or analysis of an issue. In research papers of this type, writers usually don't state an arguable thesis; instead, they ask a question or state the point of their paper and then supply facts, examples, and rarely, arguments that support their point.

Consider using the following outline to structure an informational report of your own.

A Useful Pattern of Organization for Informational Reports

   I. Introduction

      A. Catch your reader's interest. (See Introductory Strategies in chapter 1.)

      B. Ask the thesis question you want to investigate. For example, "What is stem-cell research and what recent discoveries have been made through it?"

  II. Body
      A. Present some brief background to the problem: its history.
      B. Present—in some organized way—the information you have found.
There is no one right way to present and organize information: you
need to discover a way that best suits your purpose. Consider using
chronological order or order of importance. Consider using any of the
kinds of evidence or strategies of development explained in chapter 3:
examples, details, reasons; authorities, statistics; induction, deduction;
description, narration, comparison-contrast, classification, cause-effect,
definition.
  III. Conclusion
Answer the "So what?" question. Explain why the information you
have presented is important for readers to know.

ACTIVITY 1

Each paragraph of a research paper should contain only one main idea. Write
a sentence outline describing the main idea in each of Danelle's paragraphs
(which we have numbered). For an example of a sentence outline, see the
Outline of Sowell's Essay in chapter 2.

ACTIVITY 2

Evaluate the quality of Danelle's information: where did she find her facts? Can
readers find anything not factual in her paper (such as opinions, exaggerations,
or fallacies)? In your notebook write a page or so analyzing Danelle's use of
sources and facts. Bring your notebook to class to discuss.

ACTIVITY 3

In your notebook, evaluate Danelle's report by using A Critical Thinker's Guide
for Evaluating Writing at the end of chapter 1.

Although we have placed writing your research paper last, in fact you need to think about your paper all along the way. Research writing, as you may have realized by now, isn't like cooking or carpentry or other physical processes in which step by step you complete each act and then go on to the next. Writing is more like gardening: you must keep after it, returning to it again and again to water, fertilize, weed, hoe, prune, and finally, harvest the outcome. Many writers find themselves returning again and again to earlier thoughts, making changes, revising and editing, adding more information.

THE TWO-SIDED ARGUMENTATION PAPER

Shaping Your Thesis

A thesis is an implied promise to your readers: "If you read my paper, you'll know why the church finds cloning morally repugnant" or "If you read my paper, you'll know why so many investors are excited about the potential for profits in cloning." You can see why it might not be a good idea to shape your thesis before doing any reading. You need the background to help you avoid making promises you can't keep.

The Arguable Proposition

Your thesis must have two parts: a subject (we're using "cloning" for our example) and a proposition about the subject—a <u>what</u> and a <u>what about it</u>. Traditionally, the thesis is a statement that reasonable people can have different opinions about: a thesis is an "arguable proposition." A good thesis has two or more good sides, not one good and one bad side. Thesis statements don't usually contain "maybe" or "possibly," because few people are likely to argue that "Cloning <u>may be</u> immoral," for example.

A thesis can take different forms. In an argument paper a thesis is usually a statement, such as "Cloning is immoral." But your thesis can be worded as a question: "Is cloning immoral?" Your background reading should help you to find your working thesis.

Consider a possible thesis. In the cloning research you can find optimism for curing or preventing diseases and afflictions because many are the result of a missing or damaged gene. Genetic engineering will allow scientists to discover these flaws before the embryo is a day old. A little microsurgery snips out the flawed gene and replaces it with a healthy one. That sounds like it might make a workable thesis: "Genetic engineering will cure or prevent many genetic diseases and afflictions." However, remember the "growth phenomenon." This thesis may sound workable, but there are a few research problems in it.

1. It's true, of course, there has been much optimism about curing or preventing genetic flaws, but you would need to read the research to find out how much "optimism" there has been and how much research is available.
2. And further, about how many diseases and flaws are you talking? Five? Twelve? A hundred? What if there are many more than you imagined?
3. At what point does a "flaw" become a cosmetic choice—is a big nose a "flaw"?
4. And where does that "healthy" gene come from? What exactly is the procedure for replacing a defective gene with a healthy one?

It still sounds like a fair thesis—genetic engineering as a medical option—but you should read some research before committing to any thesis. It might turn out that, indeed, there is a good deal of optimism for genetic "cures" and "preventions," but what if there are other sides to this? What if there are dangerous side effects? What if some scientists, doctors, and others are hopping mad about it and fighting to prevent "interfering with nature"? Can you ignore that side of the thesis? If you include it, you will have to write a two-sided examination of the question: your project will double in size. And what about those three or four problems? Maybe you should pick one of them for your project.

Discovering Order

As you collect your notes (on notecards or on paper), you can begin sorting them in different ways. At first you should be guided by the notes themselves: avoid imposing order on your data—try to discover the inherent order of your notes. Label your notecards or paper (lightly in pencil) according to key ideas and main points. You need to spread out your cards, sort them into piles. At this point in the process you shouldn't concern yourself too much about the final plan for your paper. These early explorations should be tentative and experimental; look for whatever order may reveal itself in your notes. Even if you find a reasonable-looking plan at the outset, you should still experiment with other possibilities. A "good enough" plan isn't the goal. You need the best plan.

You needn't be committed to an iron-fast decision about organization. You must keep sorting and thinking, working with your notes until you find the organizational strategy that works best for the material you have and the audience you anticipate. The important point here is to have a plan. In your planning and revising cycles, before things settle into their final shape, keep experimenting, rearranging your notes, and trying different organizational ideas.

Continue working on your outline, your data, and your rough draft until they all begin to jell. At first, the early work controls your time—reading, note-taking, and outlining. But as you make progress, the later work begins to control your time—outlining, drafting, and polishing. From your rough draft you can give more consideration to your readers. You can start to check things such as your documentation, the logic of your paper, and the readability of your writing. Finally, when you think you have it all, you need to read with a critical eye, looking for <u>accuracy</u>, <u>clarity</u>, and <u>economy</u>, or the lack thereof.

Working through Your Project

Research projects involve stop and go, forward and backward movements. Many writers say they start with tentative ideas about their topic, tentative outlines, tentative sources and notes—things they keep returning to throughout the project. While working on your bibliography, you may also be thinking about your outline (revising it in your head) and at the same time thinking about how to write your introductory paragraph. Research is an open-ended, fluid process that can fit your own personality and work habits. The only constants that apply to all researchers is to keep reading and keep thinking about what you are reading.

Although you could go on and on collecting sources, reading and taking notes and revising, at some point you must make a decision: your research is finished when you have enough material, enough to establish your thesis, enough to persuade your readers. Knowing when to stop is part of the process. A good rule is to stop when you are not finding anything new, when the material gets repetitious, but beware of making that judgment too soon.

Understanding Audience

Usually, the audience for school papers is your instructor . . . and sometimes other students. Your readers will not wish to read a thin overview of your subject. The more experienced your audience is, the more they will expect you to follow standard procedures for research writing. You probably have your own ideas about writing for educated readers, but you must remember that no one likes a condescending writer. Sarcasm and misplaced humor are mistakes. The best advice is to take your assignment seriously, but don't overdo it. Refrain from poetic or creative word plays, and don't make claims about the subject you don't find in the research such as "Heroin has been the most terrible problem since the beginning of time." Exaggerations will certainly reduce your credibility: once lost, credibility is hard to get back.

Controlling Your Voice

Use your own voice in your research paper. Research writing requires correct grammar, but you shouldn't attempt to sound as if you were one of the authorities in the research. You should avoid slang, but, in general, your paper should sound like you. The sound of your personality should not be very different from your ordinary voice when you are being polite. An academic voice should be objective. You should stick to the subject in research writing, use factual evidence, testimony from authorities, good reasoning, and statistics. You still need to appeal to your readers' logos, pathos, and ethos.

Avoid pretentious writing, which occurs when writers pretend to be more important than they really are. One of the biggest mistakes for writers is to assume that educated readers will be impressed with big words and long sentences. Just sound natural, but be careful with your grammar and basic skills. You impress your readers with information, facts, details, not pretentious writing like this:

> The eventuality of a scientific investigation into the results of cloning a human individual is predicted to be an undeniable certainty within the ensuing decade if not sooner.

You must ask yourself (your readers certainly will), "Who in the world talks like that?" This writer sounds like he or she has swallowed a dictionary. The message under all the verbiage is simply that scientists predict someone may soon try to clone a human. Nothing is gained by so many big words, and a great deal is lost, particularly the good will of readers.

Through your voice, your readers hear your attitude toward them, toward the subject you are investigating, and toward yourself. You don't want to sound superior to your audience (and thus condescending). And you don't want to sound indifferent. If you are bored, your readers will be bored too. Research writers don't usually try to be amusing or entertaining; it's never good to be flippant (inappropriately or disrespectfully attempting to be humorous).

In general, clear, plain, simple English is the best approach. Be as concise as you can; avoid jargon when possible. It's permissible and often preferable to use the pronoun "I." What is not recommended is artificial, inflated language used to impress your readers. (For more on voice see interchapter 1.)

Presenting Your Evidence

You can lose everything in a hastily written paper. Like other aspects of research, writing the paper takes time and patience. Your paper usually can't wait until after everything else is done. As your project begins to take shape, the components will begin to influence each other. As your data begin to pile up, your outline begins to take shape (usually altered from your first conception of it), and the paper too begins to form in your mind. There usually isn't enough time to finish all your research before starting the paper. You must begin reading immediately, begin acquiring data, taking notes, organizing, making outlines, and trying drafts. The last-minute syndrome, in which writers attempt to throw together a paper the night before it is due, can have predictably unfortunate results.

Substantiating Your Data

You must help readers find your sources, check your facts. Substantiation makes the difference between research and other kinds of writing. Library research is a compilation of the available information, and somewhere between not enough and too many is an appropriate number of sources. You need as many references as is necessary to establish your thesis.

Citing research shows that you are well-read in your subject area and, therefore, have authority for your work. Substantiation tells your readers: "Who said so. How do you know this? Where did you get this information?" Substantiation is the research behind your research. It connects you to other researchers. Substantiation is the reason for documentation. Documentation is your References and your Works Cited: they show what you read, who wrote it, and where you found it. For that reason it's important to use a standard system of documentation. (See chapter 9, Documentation.)

THE FORMAL OUTLINE

Most research papers require a formal outline. The outline is useful to your readers: it shows at a glance the structure and development of your paper and reveals whether your material is clearly organized. Preliminary outlines can let your instructor (or a classmate) offer advice and assistance. Most of all, the outline focuses your attention on the logic of your paper, whether your ideas are arranged in sequence, following a plan that leads to your conclusion point by point.

As you collect your sources, you can begin to sort and organize them into major and minor points. Your outline isn't usually a simple plan that you can fill in with details from your reading. Like your paper itself, your outline should grow and develop until you begin to understand your data in terms of categories, points, and subpoints. The outline should not become an arbitrary blueprint you impose on the data. Instead of forcing data to fit into your outline, you must be prepared to alter the outline to accommodate the data. Even while you are writing the first draft of your paper, you may find yourself working back and forth, first shaping the paper to fit the outline and then altering the outline to fit the paper. This kind of creative give and take makes the outline a useful tool—it helps you understand what you are doing. When you finish, your paper and outline will agree with each other. The logic of both of them will show your analysis of the data.

Revising the Preliminary Outline

A formal outline should go beyond listing the main points. The finished outline that accompanies your paper should contain enough detail so that readers can see your main and minor points and the structure of your paper. At the outset, most research outlines look very similar:

I. Introduction
II. Body
III. Conclusion
IV. Works Cited

The following is a rough preliminary outline for a paper on human cloning.

I. Thesis statement
II. Recent technology leading to human cloning
III. Reasons against cloning
IV. Reasons for cloning
V. Evaluating the evidence
VI. Distribution of evidence for cloning

This is a satisfactory preliminary outline, but it doesn't have enough detail yet to tell much about the paper. It shows the main parts of the paper, but it doesn't tell much about the research. It really isn't much more than the standard headings for any outline. Still, it may be enough for a preliminary outline to get you started. It is consistent in its use of topics (you can use topical statements or full sentences, but not both). It avoids using obvious terminology such as "Introduction" and "Conclusion." You may use those terms if you wish, but it is generally more helpful to your readers if you use more descriptive headings for these two parts of your outline. Best of all, the preliminary outline is structured with the opposing view first—the paper will thus end with the writer's appeals and arguments.

With more reading and critical thinking, the writer can produce a more detailed and helpful outline:

THE FORMAL OUTLINE MODEL

A Review of Research on Cloning Humans [Working title]

by Julie Mitchell

I. The cloning problem [Avoids "Introduction"]
    A. Scenario of infertile couple
    B. Scenario of cloning Michael Jordan
    C. Thesis: Human beings should not be cloned until animal [Thesis]
       cloning is tested extensively and ethical questions are
       examined fully.
II. Technology leading to human cloning
    A. Definition of "cloning" [Useful clarification]
    B. In vitro fertilization and reproductive needs of infertile
       couples
       1. Increasing use of IVF
       2. IVF costs
    C. Cloning as an option for infertile couples
       1. Description of cloning from adult animal cells
       2. Likelihood that humans can be cloned if animals can

III. Reasons to clone humans   [Weaker view first]
  A. Potential medical benefits
    1. Growing bone marrow and tissues for transplants
    2. Growing organs now in short supply
    3. Reducing common genetic problems
  B. Reproductive rights of people in our country
    1. Silver's "parental prerogative" for parents to have children who carry their genes
    2. Allowing parents to replicate children who were killed
    3. Allowing single women and lesbian couples to have children
IV. Reasons not to clone humans   [Stronger view last]
  A. Need for more testing with animals first
    1. Wilmut's 276 failures before cloning Dolly
    2. Possibility that Dolly was not cloned from adult cell
    3. Failure to replicate Wilmut's cloning
    4. Disrupting genetic diversity
  B. Not trusting scientists not to abuse clones   [Counterarguments]
    1. Tuskegee Study
    2. Willowbrook Study
    3. Possible backfire of unethical experimentation
  C. Cloning as unnatural reproduction
    1. Against tradition of sexual intercourse
    2. Against God's will
    3. Not conceived normally, clones without souls
V. Evaluation of arguments for and against human   [Avoids "Conclusion"]
    cloning
  A. Opening door of human cloning
  B. Reviewing arguments for and against
  C. Ian Wilmut on both sides
  D. National Bioethics Advisory Committee
      recommendation   [Saved for end]
    1. Five-year ban on human cloning
    2. Reexamining cloning after more scientific developments
  E. Restatement of thesis
VI. Works Cited   [Sources]

Anyone reading this outline will get a clear understanding of the subject, the major and minor points, and the structure of the paper.

Writers don't always make outlines; however, the formal outline is usually required in research writing. You should make a flexible, preliminary outline, and then revise it and make it more detailed as you work on your paper. The outline helps you (and your readers) to think about the logos of your paper, its overall structure, coherence and clarity. A well-organized paper can also help your credibility—your ethos: it shows that you are a careful researcher-writer, aware of your readers.

ACTIVITY 4

After you have done some of your research—reading, note-taking, gathering ideas and data—prepare an outline for your research paper. Follow the form of the preceding example—a topic outline. Remember that your outline will be tentative—not finished until after you have completely written your paper. If you have finished writing your paper, making an outline will help you see and evaluate its structure and organization more clearly.

THE ABSTRACT

The abstract is a summary of your paper. Though not every paper requires an abstract, the longer and more technical your paper is, the more an abstract will help your readers. For casual readers, an abstract serves as a quick preview. For more serious readers, your abstract indicates the quality and significance of your work; it tells other researchers whether your paper may have relevance to their own research. An abstract helps you examine your project objectively. Though the abstract appears first—either before or after your outline—it is written last.

Many articles on the Internet now contain brief abstracts. Here is one for a 10-page article: "The Wisdom of Repugnance: Why We Should Ban the Cloning of Humans" by Leon R. Kass published in The New Republic (2 June 1997: 17–27).

Abstract: People should trust their initial repugnance about human cloning. Important human values, such as the profundity of sex, the sacredness of the human body, and the value of individuality are at stake. Human production must not be debased by turning it into mere willful manufacturing. (27 Feb. 1998 <http://web3.searchbank.com/infotrac/session/990/66/10326127w3/12!xrn_49&bkm>)

Here is another abstract—a more objective example—which accompanied a published paper "Upper Respiratory Infections: Treatment Selection for Active Patients" by Randall A. Swain and Barbara Kaplan in The Physician and Sportsmedicine (Feb. 1998: 85)

Abstract: Moderate exercise may reduce the risk of upper respiratory tract infections, but intense training can increase that risk. Though the average cold does not appear to hinder athletic performance, short-term symptomatic treatment consisting of topical decongestants and/or nasal ipratropium bromide may be useful for active patients. Vitamin C and zinc lozenges may reduce the duration of cold symptoms. Antibiotics are appropriate for treating such complications as acute bacterial sinusitis, otitis media, or pneumonia but are ineffective against viral infection. Some drugs are banned by sports organizations, and others, such as first-generation antihistamines, may impair performance.

Guidelines for <u>Dissertations Abstracts International</u> limit abstracts to no more than 350 words (about a page or so of double-spaced text). In all cases, because research now must be indexed and cataloged, you need to follow procedures for clarity and accuracy and use your most concise language. APA guidelines, for example, are highly restrictive, limiting the abstract to no more than 960 characters <u>and</u> spaces: approximately 120 words. APA recommends that your abstract should contain only the four or five important "concepts, findings, implications," starting with the most important (9). Much scientific writing calls for 250 to 350-word abstracts, or approximately one or one and a half double-spaced pages (if you use a 12-point font).

ACTIVITY 5

Write an abstract of your own research paper. Assume you will present your paper at a conference on undergraduate research, and the conference director wishes to compile abstracts into a program for the conference. Or, assume your abstract will appear in a professional journal that interests you. Follow the journal's guidelines for abstracts (usually in the front of the journal). If you can't find journal guidelines, limit your abstract to about a page, double-spaced.

THE TITLE

Some writers compose their title first; others wait until the paper is finished before deciding on the title. Because research papers must be indexed so that other researchers can find them, your title is an important research tool. The title of a research paper should be informative, clear, and specific. A title such as "Mysteries in the Sky" will not help researchers looking for material to use in their own research. Think of the way modern computers "search" for information. Computers cannot interpret language: they look for words that match the search terms. To help other researchers find your work, a better title might be "The UFO Phenomenon: A Review of Research." Often the thesis statement or question is the title. Avoid cute or amusing titles.

ACTIVITY 6

Evaluate the following titles for research papers of about 10 to 12 pages. Students were asked to look at two or more sides of an issue. Considering clarity, accuracy, and specificity, how well do you think these titles would help other researchers who are looking for information? How well does the title help readers to know what the paper will be about? Assign a number to indicate your evaluation of each title: 1 for "excellent," 2 for "more or less OK," and 3 for "needs work." Then explain your evaluations.

1. Lacking Social Interaction: Worried Teens and Depression
2. Is Hormonal Replacement Therapy Worth the Risk?
3. On the Usage of Cloning: Protecting Our Humanity
4. Society's Final Statement: Pros and Cons of Capital Punishment
5. Patriotic Civilian Militias: Democracy's Essential Shield
6. Prison Reform: Racism in America's Justice System
7. Is Marijuana Prohibition Working?
8. Does Mainstreaming Benefit Teachers and Exceptional Students?
9. A Brief History of Cocaine
10. An Argument against the Use of Animals in Testing Hazardous Substances

---

THE INTRODUCTION

In some scientific writing (reports not meant for publication) researchers may skip the formal introduction. However, most writing needs an introduction to catch reader interest, including scientific readers. Somewhere in your introduction you must make your thesis statement or ask your thesis question. Whether to use a statement or a question is the writer's choice. The thesis question is useful in some situations—as when you write a report. (Check with your instructor.) The thesis statement, however, announces from the beginning what your paper will illustrate and serves as a guide for some readers, especially researchers who want to know immediately what your paper will be about. ("This paper will review the research that shows genetic engineering can eradicate many genetic diseases.") Some instructors prefer to see the thesis as the first sentence, but others prefer to see it as the last sentence of the introduction. If your thesis finishes the introduction, it makes a good transition to the rest of the paper.

An introduction can be a single paragraph or longer, but it shouldn't delay the paper unnecessarily. The length of the introduction depends somewhat on your purpose. If you are writing a historical background or discussing the significance of your research question, the introduction may be a separate section of your paper, more than one-paragraph long. Avoid one-sentence introductions for research papers. Remove such sentences entirely; connect them to the next paragraph, or build them into more substantial paragraphs.

Also avoid empty introductions that wander vaguely around the subject. Not an ornament, the introduction is an important part of your paper and should provide the reader with useful information. Your introduction should not assume the reader knows the title of the paper, the assignment, or anything else. Even though you may be writing the paper at the direction of your instructor, the paper must stand on its own. Make no references to "the assignment" or anything else not in the research. For examples of introductory strategies, see chapter 1.

ACTIVITY 7

In your notebook compare the beginnings of these two student papers. We think they are both good, but see if you can find differences or similarities before expressing any evaluations or preferences of your own about them.

A. DNA Molecules of Truth: How Useful in Forensics?

Anne Griffith

> "Whenever you have excluded the impossible, whatever
> remains, however improbable, must be the truth."
> (Sir Arthur Conan Doyle, "The Adventure of the Beryl
> Coronet")

While Sir Arthur Conan Doyle was not addressing the issue   1
of forensic DNA analysis, his quote does provide an adequate
explanation of the theory behind this complex technique.
In October 1997, correctional officer Iran
Shuttlesworth was convicted of the kidnapping and
first-degree sexual assault of a Milwaukee woman.
As they do in many crimes, examiners from the FBI
Laboratory had compared the suspect's DNA to that of
a semen stain found on the victim's clothing. At
the trial, an examiner testified that the FBI had
identified Shuttlesworth as the source of the semen
stain. ("DNA Profiling Advancement" 1)

(box continues)

This situation in which a correctional officer was convicted of this horrible offense after DNA analysis linked him to the crime is only one example of Doyle's principle in action. DNA analysis is a recently developed forensic technique that aids law enforcement officials in their search for justice by linking samples of DNA found at a crime scene with possible suspects. DNA analysis may either conclusively lead to an acquittal or it can aid in the conviction process.

To understand the process and theory of DNA analysis, you must first understand the basic structure and function of DNA. Deoxyribonucleic acid (DNA) is a complex molecule located within every bodily cell. A single DNA strand takes the form of a twisted double helix. The double helix resembles a ladder—with each rung of the ladder representing a union between two molecules known as base pairs. There are four base pairs: adenine (A), guanine (G), cytosine (C), and thymine (T). These four bases adhere to strict pairing rules. A always bonds with T, and C always bonds with G. No exceptions! Chromosomes are comprised of DNA and function to transmit heritable information from cell to cell and from parent to child. Within every human cell, there are 23 pairs of chromosomes. On each chromosome, there is a particular sequence of these base pairs that acts as a code for a specific structure, function or feature of the body. This specific sequence is called a gene (McDonald 2). Due to the specific base pairing rules of DNA, these genes can copy themselves and perform their function as the director of protein synthesis within the body.

No two individuals--with the exception of identical twins-- have the exact same DNA code within their genes. However, the DNA code is the same in every individual cell of a single person, despite its origin. The premise of DNA profiling is that "At certain locations on human chromosomes, geneticists have discovered that the sequence of DNA varies in discrete intervals from person to person. [. . .] Comparing the sequences at several different chromosomal locations, or loci, generates an individual DNA profile" (George 2).

Because every person has a unique DNA blueprint, DNA profiling has often been referred to as DNA fingerprinting. This term is a misnomer. When examining fingerprints, one will find that even genetically identical twins will have individually unique fingerprints due to nongenetic events during development. Also, when examining fingerprints, the entire print of an individual is closely examined. When

(box continues)

performing DNA analysis, only a fraction of the tremendously long gene is examined for similarities. At best, DNA analysis can be compared to the examination of a partial fingerprint (Inman and Rudin 6).

B. Understanding Alzheimer's Disease: An Ongoing Challenge

Meagan Tripp

Taking the elevator, I could already smell the stale, dry, chemical aroma of the second floor. The doors creaked open, and I saw Grandma leaving the lunchroom. She happened to glance my way and stared for a moment before uttering, "Oh look . . . it's the one that goes to college." I was now in my grandmother's world; I no longer had a name.

I followed her slowly into her room. Next, I took down the calendar and wrote activities down in big capital letters. As I did, I slowly and deliberately went over the events with my grandmother. The rest of the visit was typical. For the hour I was there, we had the same four or five short conversations many times. To break up the endless repetition of stories, I decided to help her clear up some of the clutter on her dresser. After I had propped up a fallen picture frame, my grandmother pointed at the photograph inside and said skeptically, "Now who is that man next to me in that picture?" The question hurt deep inside, but I did not let that show as I answered her: "That's Grandpa Stillman, Grandma." The glazed-over, puzzled expression melted from her face, as my grandmother replied, "Oh yes . . . that's right . . . I met him a long time ago . . . at my first job I think. . . ."

My grandfather died of Alzheimer's disease when I was twelve. Even today, I remember the phone calls and how he struggled to keep track of which grandchildren lived with which of his sons. But it was distant then: my grandparents lived in Massachusetts. Now, I watch as my grandmother suffers from the very same terrible, unexplainable disease. My heart stirs with hate, confusion, anger, and sorrow. I struggle to understand,

(box continues)

> but I cannot. Moreover, knowing that there may be a genetic
> element of Alzheimer's disease, I cannot even begin to imagine
> watching my father suffer through this. Will he have
> Alzheimer's? Will I? Am I a carrier with the possibility of
> passing it onto my children? I needed an answer, so I set
> out to find it. Evidence that points out a definite genetic
> aspect of Alzheimer's disease does exist, but a significant
> history and other risk factors also come into play. The more
> people understand about the disease, the better, and the search
> is ongoing.

ORGANIZING YOUR PAPER

For most research writing, the simplest organizational patterns are usually the best.

Chronological

Often the simplest plan means chronological order: start at the beginning and proceed in order of events to the end. This plan works well for informational research papers (reports), but it may not work as well for argumentative papers in which you examine different sides of an issue.

> In in vitro fertilization (IVF), a woman's ovaries are stimulated with fertility drugs to produce multiple eggs. The physician monitors the woman's response by examining urine samples, blood samples, and ultrasound imaging. After giving her an injection to control the timing of the egg release, the physician retrieves the eggs. [. . .] After they are retrieved, the eggs are placed in separate glass dishes and combined with prepared spermatozoa from the woman's partner or a donor. The dishes are placed for 12 to 18 hours in an incubator designed to mimic the temperature and conditions of the body. If a single spermatozoon penetrates an egg, IVF has occurred. ("Reproductive Technologies" 2221)

Order of Importance

When you have more than one argument, more than one example, more than one detail, which one comes first? Which comes last? In an argumentative, persuasive paper, give the least important first and the most important last. That is, the structure of the paper ought to be based on "order of importance"—from least important to most. Such an organization is counterintuitive for many students, who prefer to give their most important information first. However, a research paper that becomes increasingly <u>less</u> important as it progresses will have the wrong effect on readers.

Still, the order of importance need not be applied mechanically. There should be enough flexibility in your structure to allow some variation, even within the overriding strategy. If you have, for example, two important points and two or three lesser points, you could choose the "covered wagon" strategy: place the weaker points in the middle, sandwiched between the stronger points. Overall, it is more important that you achieve the effect you want with your readers than that you follow rules and patterns of organization. Look at your outline: ask yourself why your points are arranged in this order. What effect are you trying to achieve?

Making Concessions

In an argumentative paper you should concede whatever must be conceded: you will bias your research if you report only the data you approve of. You can show yourself to be reasonable and unbiased if you concede points to readers who disagree with your thesis: when a point must be conceded (meaning, it is undeniable), you lose nothing by making the concession—and you gain credibility.

When you write about a controversy, when there are two or more sides to investigate, you must present yourself as an objective researcher. (See Remaining Impartial in chapter 8.) The best strategy is to present the opposing view first. If your research has convinced you that cigarette smoking causes cancer, you should first present the side of those who believe that cigarette smoking does not cause cancer. Presenting this side first, and presenting it well, helps you to convince your readers that you understand the issues and will establish your ethos as a fair and unbiased researcher. You are not the prosecutor but the judge—evaluating all evidence impartially. Putting your strongest argument last, in the strongest position, gives your paper a natural progression, ending with strength.

WRITING CLEAR PARAGRAPHS

A paragraph, by definition, should discuss only one idea. And both you and your readers should be able to see that idea clearly in each of your paragraphs. Loosely written, poorly developed paragraphs make hash of research. For example, read the following two versions of a paragraph. Which paragraph most suggests a careful writer who is trying to help readers? Which communicates more clearly? Why? What is wrong with the other paragraph?

> A. Cells are awesome. All living things are made up of cells. Everything inside of us is made up of cells. But cells can be destroyed. In order to understand cloning it is necessary to understand cells. Both animals and plants have cells.

A cell has a nucleus and cytoplasm. The nucleus carries genetic information of a life form. Cells are important because of DNA.

B. The basic living unit of biolife is the cell. All creatures large and small—from the blue whale and the giant sequoia to each of the billions of symbiotic bacteria that live inside your gut helping you digest your last meal—are composed of one or more of these microscopic entities. If you break a cell apart, the individual pieces that you obtain are no longer alive. They are just built-up molecular structures—combinations of atoms—and nothing more. Some cell fragments may be able to utilize energy to maintain their structure for brief times under special conditions, but they can't reproduce themselves. Thus, biolife cannot be reduced to any unit smaller than a cell, and the simplest cell possible is still inordinately complex. (Silver 24)

Topic Sentences and Details Strengthen Paragraphs

Lee Silver's paragraph communicates more clearly because it begins with an explicit topic sentence and is then supported with specific details and reasons. A well-developed paragraph has ample data, illustrates a single point, and is clearly and efficiently organized. The number and quality of details, the ease with which you can discuss the details, the skill with which you can incorporate details into your sentences—these make the difference between a merely average researcher and a truly superior research writer. Developing by detail is the chief strategy of much writing. The weaker paragraph, however, has no clearly focused topic sentence, and its support is more general than specific. The paragraph drifts from the universality of cells to the components of cells. Researchers tend to write underdeveloped paragraphs when they do not have sufficient information.

For each of your paragraphs, you must be able to answer the questions, What is this paragraph about? Why is it here: what function does it serve? You can use topic sentences to help you and help your readers to know whether a paragraph is unified. Not all paragraphs need a topic sentence, especially if you have made the paragraph absolutely clear, but if you can't think of a sentence that would incorporate all the supporting evidence in your paragraph, you should revise the paragraph.

A topic sentence can appear first, last, or in the middle of your paragraph. Its position is less important than the ease with which it fits into the paragraph—the logic of its position relative to your other sentences.

ACTIVITY 8

Examine the paragraphs in your research paper. Select a paragraph that might be used as an example of a carefully written paragraph. Write an informal outline for that paragraph: show how your sentences are related. Then write a page or less explaining why you think the paragraph works well, both internally and externally (in relation to the paragraphs that precede and follow it). If you can't find a good paragraph for this assignment, revise your paragraphs until you can find at least one good one.

Use Unifying Devices

When paragraphs are "not clear" or "don't stick to the subject," you can prevent confusion and strengthen your paragraphs with unifying devices such as transitional signals: <u>however</u>, <u>therefore</u>, <u>consequently</u>, <u>also</u>, and so on. You can also unify paragraphs by using pronouns, synonyms, and repetitions of concepts.

ACTIVITY 9

Examine the paragraph from <u>Remaking Eden</u> by Lee Silver. Notice his use of unifying devices. How often does he repeat "cell"? How often does he use pronouns that refer to cells? Then examine the paragraphs in your own research paper for unifying devices. Revise to improve unity where you can.

THE CONCLUSION

The conclusion of a research paper shouldn't be a mere summary; it should be the climax of your paper. There is important work to do in the conclusion. For example

- Review the key points for your readers.
- Evaluate the strengths and weaknesses in the arguments.
- Restate your thesis or answer your research question.
- End with something memorable (save something for the end).

So far, your paper has shown that there is a thesis statement or a research question and that there is evidence supporting it or contradicting it. Now you must answer your thesis question. It's a good idea to start your conclusion with a brief review of the arguments. The purpose of this review is to remind the reader of the basic positions in the research.

Inexperienced writers tend to write conclusions that are too short. You must remember that your readers haven't read the material in the library or on the Internet and haven't spent hours analyzing and organizing the data. Your conclusion may seem obvious to you, but it's your job to help the reader understand what you understand. Your paper must reach some closure: perhaps the evidence leads to a conclusion that one side of the argument makes more sense than the other. Or perhaps both sides make sense and you must take some middle position. Or perhaps there isn't enough evidence for any intelligent conclusion to be drawn. You must decide what the evidence does show, and then you must help your readers understand your conclusion. Perhaps the whole question hangs on some key point, as when, for example, the major underlying assumption is wrong.

Distinction between Presenting and Evaluating Data

It sometimes happens that writers get to the end of a paper and find they have nothing left to say. This problem may cause a researcher to write a brief summary and quit. But the cure for this problem is usually in the middle of the paper, where you may discover you have been drawing conclusions along with your presentation of evidence. Thus, here at the end you must return to the beginning of research and again make the distinction between facts and opinions, opinions and implications, evidence and assumptions.

You should adopt this rule: the middle section of a research paper is for presenting evidence . . . only. For example, suppose you found this paragraph in the middle section of a paper:

> Britannica Online lists an article from the <u>Nation's Health</u> which shows, among other things, that cigarette smoking, marijuana and alcohol use is increasing among 8th graders. Since all of these "recreational drugs" cost money, it is probably true that 8th graders have too much "discretionary" money. But worse than that is the fact that those who sell such products are preying on ever younger consumers, specifically children. ("Marijuana, Tobacco Use Still Increasing")

This paragraph contains a writing problem: it seems there won't be much left for the conclusion of this paper. The writer will have to conclude that adolescents are using more drugs—but that has already been said in the middle of the paper. Material that belongs in the conclusion has been used in the presentation of data. Only the first sentence of this little paragraph is a fact; only the first sentence belongs in the presentation of the data. All the rest is the writer's <u>conclusions</u>. The writer <u>infers</u> or <u>deduces</u> that children have too much discretionary money. The writer <u>assumes</u> that sellers are preying on children. These may be correct inferences, deductions, and assumptions, but their accuracy isn't the point. The point is they don't belong in the middle of the paper. Thus, when writers get to the conclusion of a paper such as this one, they may believe they have nothing left to say, but the truth is more likely that they have already said it.

The old writer's rule—"save something good for the conclusion"—means the conclusion is not just the end of the paper: it's the <u>point</u> of the paper. And deciding what the evidence means is the activity of the conclusion. Everything in the paper should aim at the conclusion, where you will tell the reader what the research means. In your conclusion you should show readers how an educated person should evaluate the data you have presented in the middle of your paper.

In addition to showing your reader the outcome of the argument, you must bring the paper to completion, give the reader a sense of ending. A good quote, some striking fact or statistic, a relevant personal note, or simply an especially well-worded final sentence can round off your ending. Frequently, research papers end with a call for more research, but you must avoid raising any new or irrelevant questions in the conclusion.

WORKS CITED OR REFERENCES

Different instructors may require different formats for documentation. Before handing in documented papers, find out which format is preferred. Footnotes and endnotes are no longer used in many disciplines. Preferred modern practice is to give an author's name and other information in your paper. These (fictitious) examples indicate various ways to give documentation:

> Smith's book <u>Cloning and Nature</u> may be old (1990) but still relevant.

However, for variety, you can also give citations at the end of sentences:

> In <u>Cloning and Nature</u>, 1990, Smith predicted that it would soon be possible to clone a human being (29).

> A few scientists predicted in <u>Cloning and Nature</u> that "human clones might appear as soon as the 1990s" (Smith 29).

At the end of the paper, your reader will find Smith's work listed in your bibliography. The two most widely used styles for in-text references are the MLA style and the name and date style of the APA. Both are illustrated in chapter 9.

If you write a short paper and use only a few references, you could give the full bibliographic information in the paper itself. For example

> According to Harold T. Shapiro in his article "Ethical and Policy Issues of Human Cloning" in <u>Science</u> 277.5323 (1997) 195–96, legislators should ban any attempts to clone humans.

Your bibliography is a useful part of your paper: it lets your readers see how recent your research is and shows whether you are aware of important publications. It's a measure of how thorough your research is, and it can be an aid to other researchers.

The Bibliography Rule

Never put anything into your master bibliography you haven't actually seen: you must not simply copy a bibliography from the indexes or print one from your school's electronic catalog. You must skim through each item to see that it is, in fact, related and likely to be useful before including it in a working bibliography. You must not include anything in your Works Cited or References lists that you haven't actually used in your paper: the bibliography must match your paper.

Follow the guidelines of your instructor. An <u>annotated</u> bibliography gives brief descriptions or evaluations of the sources; a <u>limited bibliography</u> contains just those works actually cited in your paper (that is, the bibliography matches your in-text references); a <u>selected bibliography</u> includes everything you read for your paper, regardless of whether you actually cited all of it in the paper. Both the MLA and the APA style always require the limited bibliography only, called <u>Works Cited</u> (MLA) or <u>References</u> (APA).

A MODEL TWO-SIDED PAPER

One of the most challenging tasks of research writers and readers is the evaluation of research. On what criteria can we determine the value of this kind of writing? You could decide that you like or dislike a text, but for research we need more objective criteria, criteria that other readers or writers could use. Are there any such "objective" criteria?

ACTIVITY 10

Read the following research paper carefully. Then in your notebook, evaluate the paper by using A Critical Thinker's Guide for Evaluating Writing at the end of chapter 1. Evaluate the paper's title, introduction, body, conclusion, and works cited. What are the paper's strengths and weaknesses? If there are weaknesses, can they be revised? What advice would you give this author?

Julie Mitchell
Professor DeVille
English 101
8 February 2000

Should Humans Be Cloned?

Imagine the near future: you and your spouse are infertile but
deeply desire a child of your own. You decide to clone. The
procedure is performed at a clinic. In nine months you have an
identical twin. The child grows up looking remarkably like you
but has a different personality. You realize your dream of
having a family. Or imagine a news bulletin on TV: police in
Guatemala have raided a colony of ten-year-old clones who look
like Michael Jordan. They have been bred to play basketball. If
only one becomes a star player, the investment of money and
time will have been worth it. Are these scenarios possible?
Yes, maybe. Many scenarios--positive and negative, ethical and
unethical--are possible. Although human cloning may provide
exciting medical and scientific benefits, much research
suggests humans should not be cloned until animal cloning has
been tested extensively and ethical questions have been
examined fully.

Technology Leading to Cloning

Before Dolly, the lamb cloned from an adult sheep cell by Ian
Wilmut and colleagues of the Roslin Institute in Scotland,
scientists had cloned plants for hundreds of years and only
within the last 40 years mice, frogs, monkeys, and cows. The
term <u>cloning</u> means to make a genetic replica of "a molecule,
cell, plant, animal, or human being" ("Cloning Isn't Sexy" 14).
Thus, Dolly is a twin of her mother with her exact same DNA.

Humans had always procreated through sexual intercourse
until Louise Brown, the first "test-tube baby," was born
in England on July 25, 1978. Since her birth, in vitro
fertilization (IVF) has provided infertile couples with the
technology to conceive children outside the womb. Scientists

put egg and sperm in glass dishes to fertilize the eggs. After an egg divides a few times, it is placed in a woman's uterus; the natural process of embryonic and fetal development then begins.

IVF has become an industry serving the needs of many infertile couples. Lee Silver, professor of molecular biology at Princeton University and author of <u>Remaking Eden: Cloning and Beyond in a Brave New World</u>, says that reproduction through IVF "exploded" from 337 IVF births reported in 1985 to 6,870 births reported in 1993 (69). Our country at present has nearly 300 IVF clinics (Andrews B4) and more than two million infertile couples (Silver 71). Yet most people cannot easily afford IVF; the technology is expensive. "At a typical IVF clinic, a couple may spend between $44,000 and $200,000 to achieve a single pregnancy," writes Silver (69). Physicians and reproductive biologists must be highly educated and skilled.

Cloning may be another option for reproduction. Based on Dolly's example, adult animal cells can be cloned through nuclear transfer. The process works this way: scientists remove the nucleus from an egg cell, then fuse that nucleus with a body cell (such as an udder cell in Dolly's case) through a jolt of electricity. The egg nucleus reprograms the genes in the cell to produce an embryo. Because the genes of different animals are remarkably similar, scientists predict that if sheep can be cloned, so can humans. Silver writes, "The cloning of Dolly broke the technological barrier. There is no reason to expect that the technology couldn't be transferred to human cells. On the contrary, there is every reason to expect that it <u>can</u> be transferred" (93). On February 27, 1997, an editorial in the science journal <u>Nature</u> stated, "Cloning humans from adults' tissues is likely to be achievable any time from one to ten years from now" ("Caught Napping").

Working for a company in Scotland called PPL Therapeutics, Ltd., Ian Wilmut and his colleague Keith Campbell claimed they developed their process of cloning to produce sheep milk with a protein that clots blood--useful for hemophiliacs. They had no intention to stir a worldwide debate about cloning humans. However, despite their medical and economic motives, an alarm rang around the world: should human beings be cloned?

Reasons Why Humans Should Be Cloned

Defenders of human cloning argue that cloning cells--without
cloning a complete human being--might provide important medical
benefits. People with leukemia could have their own cells
cloned and made to generate bone marrow which would be a
genetically perfect match. Dr. Stuart Orkin, a Harvard Medical
School professor, testified before a presidential ethics
commission that cloning to produce marrow was feasible (Kolata
234). Human cells could also be cloned to grow skin tissue for
burn victims, neural tissue for people with brain diseases like
Parkinson's (Nash), nerve tissue for regeneration of nerve
fiber (Kestenbaum), and heart muscle cells to repair damaged
hearts (Kiernan A17).

    Cloning human cells might enable doctors to grow organs
like kidneys, livers, and hearts. If this process worked, it
could replace efforts to transplant animal organs into humans.
Scientists do not know if genetic transfers from animals are
safe: animal viruses may develop within humans. But if humans
could grow their own organs with their own genetic blueprints,
their body would be less likely to reject the organs. Although
growing organs in test tubes sounds like science fiction, it is
now thought possible. Orkin, of Harvard, believes scientists
someday might be able to reprogram a cell's DNA so that
nuclear transfer (as happened with Dolly) would not be
necessary. A cell could then "differentiate into any sort of
cell that the scientists want" (Kolata 236-37). A cell could be
reprogrammed to grow into a kidney, presumably without growing
within a human body. The organ could be grown by itself and
later transplanted.

    There is a need for organs. "Between 1990 and 1995, an
average of 4,835 people each year donated organs after death,
according to the Health Resources and Services Administration.
[. . .] Nonetheless, approximately 48,000 people are now on the
waiting list for organs" (FDA 1). Animal transplantation of
organs is experimental and has not successfully met the needs
of long-term human survival. Human cloning of organs could help
solve this problem.

    Human cloning could reduce the number of genetic problems
such as Down's syndrome. Most birth defects are caused by an
abnormal number of chromosomes when an egg and sperm fertilize.

7

8

9

10

Mitchell 4

Because cloning does not involve the splitting and merging of
two different genetic blueprints, "the chance that mistakes of
this type will occur is greatly reduced" (Silver 104). Cloning
would also reduce other genetic abnormalities such as Tay-Sachs
disease, sickle cell anemia, and cystic fibrosis.

Defenders of human cloning argue that cloning should   11
be their reproductive right. Couples and individuals in our
society have the freedom to bear children. They have the
right to procreate naturally or to use in vitro fertilization. Cloning could be another option. Silver argues that
adults have a "parental prerogative" to procreate and produce
children who share their own genetic heritage (9). If they
can't conceive a child naturally and if they can't afford
IVF, then cloning could become an alternative. Cloning as
such could benefit infertile couples and help replace a child
or loved one who has died. Christopher Wills in <u>Discover</u>
magazine writes, "One can easily imagine a scenario in which
cloning might be a blessing. Suppose a couple has one trea-
sured child and they are unable to have more. Then the child
is suddenly killed in an accident. Should the couple be
allowed to clone the child and start over? Many of us would
say yes" (23).

Cloning would provide reproductive options for people   12
other than married heterosexual couples.

> Lesbian couples, in particular, would have a new way
> to share biological parentage of a child. One member
> of the couple could provide the donor cell, and
> either one could provide the unfertilized recipient
> egg. The newly formed embryo could then be
> introduced into the uterus of the genetically
> unrelated woman. The child that is born would be
> related by genes to one mother, and related by
> birthing to the other, so that both women could
> rightly call themselves biological parents.
> (Silver 116)

Single women could have one of their own cells cloned and   13
fused with one of their own unfertilized eggs. Older women past
menopause could bear children who were cloned. Men could also
clone themselves by providing their own donor cell--but they
would need to use a woman's unfertilized egg and a woman to
serve as a surrogate mother (117).

Mitchell 5

Reasons Why Humans Should Not Be Cloned

Opponents of human cloning argue that scientists have only
begun to test adult-cell cloning with animals. It took Wilmut
276 attempts before he succeeded in cloning Dolly. If you
believe that human embryos are fully human or have moral
status, then experimenting with human embryos is unethical.
Also, because cloning animals from adult cells has only
recently begun, we don't know how many clones will be deformed
or abnormal in some way. Are we willing to experiment with
humans like this?

14

        Despite the success of cloning Dolly and other sheep,
Wilmut and Campbell have not repeated their experiment as of
yet, and other laboratories have failed to duplicate their work
("Scientists Say"). Wilmut, in fact, admitted that it is
possible that Dolly was cloned not from an adult cell but a
fetus cell. He said, "We and everybody else had completely
overlooked it" ("Scientists Say"). Wilmut and his colleagues
also don't know how Dolly will age. If she was cloned from an
adult cell, will her cells grow old sooner than if she were
conceived naturally or cloned from an embryonic cell? Cloning
may also disrupt genetic diversity. If cloning were taken to an
extreme, inbreeding could occur, thus weakening the genetic
makeup of the clones.

15

        Another major argument against cloning humans is a
distrust of science. In her book <u>Clone: The Road to Dolly, and
the Path Ahead</u>, Gina Kolata points out precedents for abusing
people in the name of science. In the "Tuskegee Study of
Untreated Syphilis in the Negro Male" doctors observed the
effects of syphilis on 600 poor black men in Macon, Georgia,
from 1932 to 1972. Though doctors could have treated the men
with penicillin after WWII, they didn't (78). Doctors also
exploited defenseless mentally retarded children in the
Willowbrook Study in Staten Island, NY. To develop a vaccine
for hepatitis B, they infected the children with a liver virus
(78). How much should we trust scientists and doctors? Will
the desire to experiment with human cloning cause ethical
disasters? Will some scientists become like Frankenstein and
his monster or like Dr. Moreau and his half-human/half-animal
creations? Will the desire for money or fame, by cloning the

16

Mitchell 6

first human being successfully, drive some people to disregard
ethics and morals?

   A third argument against human cloning is that it is   17
"unnatural." It goes against the natural order of men and women
procreating through sexual intercourse and giving birth to
unique individuals. Is human cloning against God's will?
An editorial in <u>Commonweal</u> referred to human cloning as
a "commodification of procreation" in which humans are
manufactured, not begotten ("Cloning Isn't Sexy" 2). The
General Assembly of the Church of Scotland stated that "to
replicate any human technologically is a violation of the basic
dignity and uniqueness of each human being made in God's image,
of what God has given to that individual and to no one else"
(Bruce 3). Further, a principle of many religions is that the
soul is born at conception along with the embryo. If a clone
is not conceived, it may not have a soul. The idea that
cloning takes God out of the process of conception offends many
religious people. Leon Kass in "The Wisdom of Repugnance"
writes, "Enchanted and enslaved by the glamour of technology,
we have lost our awe and wonder before the deep mysteries of
nature and of life" (2). In 1997 a <u>Time</u>/CNN poll showed that
four out of five Americans considered human cloning "against
God's will" or "morally wrong" (Silver 105).

Evaluation of Arguments for and against Human Cloning

"Where once a door seemed closed, it now has opened," said   18
Floyd Bloom, editor of <u>Science</u> magazine (Garelik). The door of
human cloning is both exciting and frightening. But it cannot
be shut: we cannot erase our knowledge of how to clone. Yet we
can and must use our knowledge responsibly and ethically.

   Sound arguments exist for both sides of the cloning   19
question. Cloning human cells might provide important medical
benefits such as growing bone marrow and other organs now in
short supply. Cloning humans could offer new reproductive
options for infertile couples and individuals, including
homosexuals. However, human cloning is now too risky, given
that scientists have not conducted long-term studies on animal
cloning. We cannot trust that scientists won't exploit
defenseless humans through cloning. By religious standards,

human cloning is "unnatural" and interferes with traditional
views of God. Yet this last argument has been raised against
in vitro fertilization which now meets the needs of many
infertile couples.

Dr. Ian Wilmut himself embodies both sides of the cloning   20
argument. His aim with Dolly was to develop several sheep from
a clone genetically modified with a human gene to produce drugs
in their milk to benefit humans. After the cloning, Wilmut
intended for these sheep to breed naturally (Bruce). His plan
was never to produce human clones. He has said he is against
cloning humans: "I think now to contemplate using our present
technique with humans would be quite inhuman" ("Scientist Who
Cloned" 1). However, he has stated that cloning human cells for
medical uses is ethical: "It is something that I would consider
doing" (Kiernan A17). Wilmut's view is not contradictory. He
recognizes both the practical benefits and the possible abuses
of cloning humans. Wilmut's view reflects the consensus of the
National Bioethics Advisory Commission which President Clinton
called on to review "the legal and ethical issues" involved
with human cloning (NBAC 3). On June 9, 1997, the commission
recommended a five-year ban on human cloning, with the ban to
be reexamined based on scientific developments. This ban does
not restrict cloning human or animal cells for research with a
"therapeutic intent" (Wertz).

Although the ban makes sense, it has not been formally   21
approved by Congress. Like in vitro fertilization technology,
cloning probably will not be federally funded. However, the
private sector is now free to pursue human cloning, and some
scientists no doubt will. Within a year of Dolly's birth, a
physicist named Richard Seed vowed to clone humans. This
prompted anticloning bans not only in Congress but in several
states. It also prompted opponents of cloning like Leon Kass of
the University of Chicago to call for an international ban on
all human cloning for research purposes--including medical
research. He believes such cloning is a slippery slope that
will soon lead to cloning full humans.

Yet human cloning seems inevitable. An editorial in   22
Nature argues that "a declared moratorium on human cloning is
desirable." It also states, "The history of technology
suggests, however, that highly regulated human cloning will,
after all, be found to be a tolerable way to proceed" ("Human

Mitchell 8

Cloning Requires"). Lee Silver agrees. Because humans desire
their own children and because science is driven by curiosity
and profit, cloning will become "just another means of
alternative reproduction" (119). He believes that governments
can work together to control it as they have done to control
nuclear warfare and weapons of mass destruction (8).

The moratorium on cloning humans provides time for   23
examination of ethical questions that aren't easy to answer: At
what point are embryos fully human? Do embryos have rights
after conception—natural or artificial? When does human life
begin? Does a cloned embryo have a soul? Will human cloning
further undermine the traditional family unit of two parents
begetting and raising children? Will more single-parenting
hurt society? Some of these questions have existed since the
abortion debates and apply directly to in vitro fertilization.
If they have not prevented these procedures, they will not
likely prevent cloning.

We can predict that within the next few years more   24
scientists will experiment with animal cloning to produce
important drugs and organs for humans. Too, they will
experiment with cloning human cells to produce tissues and
organs to save human lives and to test cures for diseases like
AIDS. We can predict that some scientists will, if they have
not done so already, experiment with cloning complete human
beings. However, if the technology for cloning proves safe
and no less ethical than in vitro fertilization, we may well
clone human beings as a source of reproductive freedom. In the
meantime, it is clear that human beings should not be cloned
until animal cloning has been tested extensively and ethical
questions have been examined fully.

Mitchell 9

Works Cited

Andrews, Lori B. "Human Cloning: Assessing the Ethical and
    Legal Quandaries." <u>Chronicle of Higher Education</u> 13 Feb.
    1998: B4-5.

Mitchell 10

Bruce, Donald M. "1997 General Assembly Report—Cloning Animals
     and Humans." Society, Religion and Technology Project of
     the Church of Scotland. 22 May 1997. 27 Dec. 1997
     <http://www.srtp.org.uk/ga97clon.htm>.
"Caught Napping by Clones." Editorial. <u>Nature</u> 385 (1997): 753.
"Cloning Isn't Sexy." <u>Commonweal</u> 124.6 (1997): 5+. 27 Feb. 1998
     <http://web3.searchbank.com/infotrac/session/0/66/10326127w3/
     17!xrn_68&bkm_62>.
Food and Drug Administration. "Fact Sheet on Xenotransplantation."
     FDA Backgrounder 20 Sept. 1996. 28 Dec. 1997
     <http://www.fda.gov/opacom/backgrounders/ xeno.html>.
Garelik, Glenn. "Journal: 'Dolly' Is Breakthrough of the Year."
     <u>UPI Science News</u> 18 Dec. 1997. 27 Dec. 1997
     <http://biz.yahoo.com/upi/97/12/18/general_news/
     usbreak_3.html>.
"Human Cloning Requires a Moratorium, Not a Ban." Editorial.
     <u>Nature</u> 386 (1997): 1.
Kass, Leon R. "The Wisdom of Repugnance: Why We Should Ban
     the Cloning of Humans." <u>New Republic</u> 2 June 1997: 17+. 27
     Feb. 1998 <http://web3.searchbank.com/infotrac/session/
     990/66/10326127w3/ 12!xrn_49&bkm>.
Kestenbaum, David. "Cloning Plan Spawns Ethics Debate." <u>Science</u>
     279 (1998): 351. 27 Feb. 1998 <http://web3.searchbank.com/
     infotrac/session/990/66/10326127w3/3!xrn_10&bkm_4>.
Kiernan, Vincent. "Debate over Cloning Touches One of Society's
     Most Sensitive Nerves." <u>Chronicle of Higher Education</u> 27
     Feb. 1998: A16–17.
Kolata, Gina. <u>Clone: The Road to Dolly, and the Path Ahead</u>.
     New York: Morrow, 1998.
Nash, Madeleine J. "The Case for Cloning." <u>Time</u> 9 Feb. 1998:
     81. 25 Feb. 1998 <http://web3.searchbank.com/infotrac/
     session/248/364/10020965w3/13!xrn_3&bkm_3>.
National Bioethics Advisory Committee. "Cloning Human Beings:
     Report and Recommendations of the National Bioethics
     Advisory Committee." June 1997. 20 Feb. 1998
     <http://earthops.org./cloning_report.html>.
"Scientists Say Error Possible in Dolly Clone." Associated
     Press. ABCNEWS.COM 17 Feb. 1998 <http://www.abcnews.com/
     sections/living/DailyNews/clonecontroversy0217.html>.
"Scientist Who Cloned Sheep: Cloning Humans Would Be Inhuman."
     CNN Interactive. 12 Mar. 1997. 28 Dec. 97
     <http://www.cnn.com/HEALTH/9703/12/nfm/cloning/index.html>.

Mitchell 11

Silver, Lee M. <u>Remaking Eden: Cloning and Beyond in a Brave
      New World</u>. New York: Avon, 1997.
Wertz, Dorothy C. "National Bioethics Advisory Committee
      Recommends Cloning Ban." <u>Gene Letter</u> 2.1 Aug. 1997. 20
      Feb. 1998 <http://www.geneletter.org/0897/Cloningban.htm>.
Wills, Christopher. "A Sheep in Sheep's Clothing." <u>Discover</u>
      Jan. 1998: 22-23.

TYPING YOUR PAPER

MLA Guidelines

Our recommendations are adapted from the MLA guidelines. One-inch margins are required on all four sides, except for the first page, which optionally may have a half inch margin at the top and (optionally) a one inch margin for your identifying information.

1 inch margin above identifying information, single spaced

Stearly 1

¹/₂ inch top margin

```
John M. Stearly
Professor Shipers
English 101
8 Feb. 2000


            Is a Nuclear War Survivable?

              Living with the Bomb

     On August 6, 1945, the United States became the

most powerful nation ever to inhabit the earth when

it dropped the first atomic
```

The reason for typing or printing papers is to make them easy to read and to give your paper a professional appearance. If you're not sure about the quality of your printer, ask your instructor about it: clear, dark impressions that are easy to read are the standard.

1. Always type or use a computer printer for research papers. Use a standard size type (about 12-point or a "pica"): avoid very small type sizes. If you use a machine that requires a ribbon, make sure it produces sharp, dark images (invest in a new ribbon). Laser print is the highest quality and is recommended.

2. Use standard white typing paper, medium weight. Never use coated, easy-to-erase paper. Do not use computer paper (fan-fold paper with tractor edges). If you don't have a good printer, copy your work to a disk and take it to a place where you can print it on standard paper.

   If your instructor permits the use of computer paper (for rough drafts or homework perhaps) make sure to use only white paper and separate the sheets. Always remove the tractor edges (the strips with holes in them) before handing in computer paper. Type on one side of the paper only.

3. All text should be double-spaced, including indented quotes. Double-space your Works Cited or References pages, too. Ask your instructor for any alternatives.

4. Use one of the in-text styles: MLA or APA. Ask your instructor before using footnotes or endnotes.

5. Unless told otherwise, you may use headings and subheadings to label the sections of your paper.

6. Use a one-inch margin on all edges of your paper, except for the first page where you may use a half-inch top margin to accommodate your name and page number.

7. Title pages are optional in MLA style, but they are required in APA style. Ask your instructor. If no title page is desired, the MLA guidelines suggest that you put your name, your instructor's name, the course number, and the date in the upper-left (not right) corner of the first page of your paper. Check with your instructor if MLA style is not specified. If a title page is desired, center the title page information. Allow six to eight lines between the title and your name and six to eight lines between your name and other information.

8. Center the title of your paper at the beginning of the outline and again at the top of the first page of the paper itself, below any identifying information and the half-inch margin at the top of the page. All papers should have a title, but don't underline or put quotation marks around the title of your paper.

9. For school work, most instructors prefer that pages be stapled together. Don't pin, fold, or tear corners to fasten the pages together; they may come undone (and look unprofessional). Covers are not recommended: check with your instructor.

10. Number your pages. In both MLA and APA styles, number <u>every</u> page, including bibliography pages. In MLA style, number each page with an arabic numeral in the upper right-hand corner. Use your last name as a header: Smith 1. Don't write "page" or "p." or use anything other than your own name as a header. APA requires a running head (the first two or three words of your title) five spaces to the left of the page number.

11. Indent the first line of each paragraph five spaces. For long quotes in MLA, indent all lines ten spaces from your left margin (not the right margin); for long quotes in APA, indent five spaces from the left margin.

12. Student papers and any typed or printed manuscript should not contain words hyphenated to fit on a line. When a word is too long to fit on the line, insert a hard return and type the entire word on the next line.

13. Most printers do not have a "dash" key. It is standard procedure to use two hyphens to make a dash--it's an important distinction for well-educated readers. A single hyphen-like this-will cause confusion. Do not insert spaces before, between, or after hyphens or dashes.

14. Use two spaces between sentences.

15. Do not let your computer or typewriter "justify" the lines (stretch the lines so that they all look the same length). Ragged-right is the standard.

ILLUSTRATIONS AND TABLES

Use visual illustrations (line drawings, charts, diagrams, and so on) or a table of data wherever visuals could help readers understand your data.

Visual material should be kept simple and clear. All visual materials should be self-explanatory, but you should also provide a concise explanation. A figure is visual information. All visuals such as figures, charts, and diagrams should be carefully drawn. Type in all words and numbers: avoid printing by hand. See Figure 10.1. If you use a visual from a book or any source other than one created by your own hand, you must give a complete citation two lines below the figure.

Visuals should be introduced at the place in your paper where you mention them, if that is possible, or as close thereafter as practical. If there are too many figures, or if it's impossible to position them close to your mention of them, place them at the end of your paper in an appendix.

Label and number all figures and tables consecutively throughout your paper. If you have both figures and tables in your paper, label figures Figure 1, Figure 2, and so on; and label tables Table 1, Table 2, and so forth. The label and number for a figure or any kind of visual material are usually placed below the figure, followed by a caption on the same line (see Figure 10.1). The label and number for a table are usually placed above the table.

A table is columns of numbers and is not considered visual material. Capitalize all significant words in the title of a table, as you would a book title in a bibliography list. Indent the second line, if any. If the figure or table is one you found in a book or other source (not one you created yourself), it must have a source note two lines below the figure or table.

If you create a table using data from a published source, give a bibliographic reference immediately below your illustration. If your table needs explanation, use a raised alphabet letter after the title to cite the note, and place your explanatory note below the table (avoid notes if possible). Figures and tables

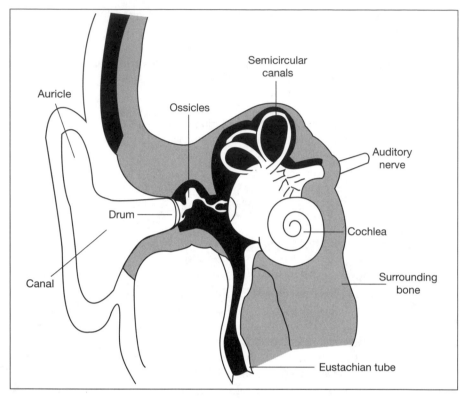

Figure 10.1. Simplified Drawing of Human Ear.
Source: "The Anatomy of the Human Ear," <u>Audio Hearing</u> 8 Feb. 2000 <http:www.audiohearing.co.uk/ear.html>.

TABLE 1   Marijuana, Cigarette, and Alcohol Use Among Adolescents[a]

Year	*M*	*C*	*A*	*M*	*C*	*A*	*M*	*C*	*A*
1996	11.3	21.0	1.0	20.4	30.4	21.3	44.9	34	31.3
1995	9.1	19.1	0.7	17.2	27.9		41.7	34	
		8th Grade			10th Grade			12th Grade	

[a] Marijuana use (M); cigarettes use (C); alcohol use (A): Alcohol use figures not available for 10th and 12th grade in 1995, but source indicates alcohol use for 1996 "remains about the same" (as 1995) for 12th graders.

Sample Table
Source: Britannica Online link to "Marijuana, Tobacco Use Still Increasing among Adolescents." <u>Nation's Health</u> 1 Jan. 1997 <http://www.britannica.com/bcom/magazine/article/0,6744,250156,00.html>.

should be self-explanatory, but you should explain them anyway in your text rather than in a note.

APA Guidelines

1. The title page is required. The page header should be an abbreviation of your title. The full title should be centered, and your name should be centered below the title, followed by your school or institution's name centered—all should start approximately half way down the page (that is, centered on the page).

     Student papers typically do not require a running head other than the page header. Running heads are required only for papers that are to be published in periodicals. If other identifying information is required (such as instructor's name, class name, or the date), place them after your school's name on the title page with the date last (see the accompanying model).

2. Use standard (20 pound) white paper. Do not use lightweight paper or easy-to-erase paper.

3. Type on one side only. Type all text double-spaced only. Do not single-space indented quotations or other text.

4. Use one-inch margins on all four edges of the paper, on every page except the title page (see the accompanying example). Do not make all lines of type the same length (do not use full justification).

5. Do not use *italics:* use <u>underlining</u> instead. The underline for periodical titles includes the volume numbers and commas: <u>U.S.News and World Report, 55</u>.

6. Indent the first line of each paragraph five spaces.

7. Use paragraph indents for the first line of each reference on your References page, unless you are directed to use hanging indents by your instructor.

8. Every page, starting with the title page, should be numbered. The number appears half an inch from the top of the page and one inch from the right edge of the page. The page header ends five spaces to the left of the number.

9. If an outline is required, it should follow the title page and should have a number and page header.

10. If your instructor requires an abstract, it should follow the title page or the outline, if an outline is required. The abstract page should have a number and page header, and it should be labeled "Abstract" centered on the next double-spaced line below the page header and number.

11. The title of your paper should be centered on the next double-spaced line below the page header and number.

12. Major sections of the paper (from the roman numerals on your outline) should be labeled and centered above each section.

Example Title Page Based on APA Guidelines

<u>Page header and number</u>   Politics of Starvation   1

<u>full title</u>   The Politics of Starvation in the Third World

<u>your name, with initial</u>   Victoria M. Solona

<u>your school</u>   Alma College

<u>date</u>   8 February 2000

<u>other information if required</u>

APA Page Models after Title Page

```
                         Politics of Starvation    2

           Outline
```

```
                         Politics of Starvation    3

           Abstract
```

```
                         Politics of Starvation    4

      The Politics of Starvation in the Third World
```

ACTIVITY 11

At the beginning of this book we gave you a ticket to notice things. Noticing is what critical thinkers do: you notice details, ideas, arguments. You notice appeals to logos, pathos, and ethos. You notice insights, assumptions, and overgeneralizations. And you notice words and sentences: how you say your message is part of what you say. Noticing leads to discovery, and your job as a critical thinker is to discover. In doing so you become more aware of your self and the world.

Please write in your notebook a page or more about your growth since the semester began. Give a candid analysis of changes you have noticed in your abilities to think, read, and write.

Concise Handbook on Grammar, Mechanics, and Usage

Ideas are composed of words: when the words are not accurate,
the ideas cannot be.

SENTENCES

Sentences are units of thought. In fact, one popular definition of a sentence is "a complete thought." We may write in paragraphs, essays, and longer units of text, but we create text one thought at a time, one sentence at a time.

Thoughts and ideas, like sentences, are composed of a subject—for example, "Thomas Edison." But what about Thomas Edison? To make a sentence, you need a statement about this subject. Here is one: "Thomas Edison inspired Henry Ford." If you wanted to support this sentence with specific evidence, you would then produce more sentences, such as this: "Ford admired Edison so much he obtained Edison's last breath bottled up in a test tube."

But there is much more to the story than that: one idea often leads to another. Then too, the event happened long ago; perhaps not everyone will know Edison's name. Should you add some identification—Thomas Edison, the great inventor? Or Thomas Edison, the inventor of the electric light?[1]

There are many possibilities for sentences and ideas, some better than others. In this section of the book, we will help you understand some of the common problems that distort writers' ideas and sentences.

---

[1]The story "Edison's Last Breath" is available on-line at <http://members.tripod.com/yakich/palmer.html> and also in a Bob Talbert column in the <u>Detroit Free Press</u> 28 January 1999: 6E.

What Is a Sentence?

When language is simple, it is easy to identify sentences; but in more complex language, the identification can be more difficult. When your thoughts are clear, your sentences should be too, but complicated thoughts and complex language can pose difficulties for writers.

ACTIVITY 1

What is a sentence and why is that important? If you're not sure exactly, simply write your best thought. Try to find the complete sentence in the following pairs. Try to explain what makes the other part of the pair not a sentence.

1. (A) The weather report daily on the Internet for most cities and all regions of the country. (B) The weather is reported daily on the Internet for most cities and all regions of the country.
2. (A) We have not only physical problems of duplicating living plants and animals, but also moral and philosophical questions. (B) The problems of cloning not only physical problems of duplicating plants and animals, including human animals, but also moral and philosophical questions.
3. (A) Successful cloning made Dolly the most famous sheep in experiments to clone a living animal from a donor cell. (B) Successful cloning Dolly the most famous sheep in experiments to clone a living animal from a donor cell.
4. (A) Fears that cloned animals would become involved in the meat and milk produced for consumption in the human food chain. (B) Many people fear that cloned animals could become involved in the meat and milk produced for consumption in the human food chain.
5. (A) Thomas Becket, in the twelfth century, became archbishop of the Catholic Church in England and was murdered as a result of the conflict between the king (the state) and the church. (B) Thomas Becket, in the twelfth century, archbishop of the Catholic Church in England and murdered as a result of the conflict between the king (the state) and the church.

Please don't read ahead until you have finished the activity.

A sentence is a complete thought containing a subject and a verb. Whether a thought is "complete" is partly a matter of grammar and partly a matter of culture. The grammar part requires that a sentence must have a subject and a verb and may also have other components. We recognize language patterns because we have become used to them: they are part of our culture. For example

Jack and . . . went . . .   After <u>and</u> most people expect to hear the rest of the pattern: <u>X</u> <u>and</u> <u>Y</u>, <u>Jack</u> "and" <u>Jill</u>. After <u>went</u> or <u>go</u> or other words of motion, we expect to hear a <u>how</u> or <u>why</u> or <u>where</u>: Jack and Jill "went" <u>up the hill</u>.

A sentence is complete when it has a subject and a verb and when its patterns meet our expectations. The importance of the subject is that it establishes what the verb can be, whether the verb must be <u>is</u> or <u>are</u> for example. Finding the subject is an important step in achieving agreement between the subject and its verb.

Finding the Subject of a Sentence

As long as we stick to Jack and Jill, most readers can easily find the subject of the sentence; however, we have deliberately included some more difficult sentences in Activity 1. In each of the pairs in Activity 1, one of the sentences is missing its verb, making it difficult to identify the subject and impossible to achieve agreement between subject and verb.

ACTIVITY 2

How can you find the subject of a sentence, and why is that important? If you aren't sure, write your best answer. Then see if you can underline the subject(s) for each of the following sentences.

1. Scientists are now able to produce identical animals through a process known as cloning.
2. When the golfing world discovered the young Tiger Woods, many athletic commentators in the late twentieth and early twenty-first centuries believed Woods was the finest golfer in the world.
3. In the men's artistic gymnastics in the 2000 Olympics, the gold medal for the parallel bars was awarded to Li Xiaopeng from China.
4. Even Dr. Ian Wilmut, whose team produced Dolly the sheep, believes cloning humans would be unethical.
5. Though many people assume children to be resilient and beyond the suffering of divorce, many children suffer as much as the adults.
6. Despite all the wonderful but so far mostly unrealized virtues of gene therapy, cloning humans remains a dangerous experiment.
7. Today's computers continue to gain in speed and power almost yearly, making your new machine obsolete before you get it.
8. At the present rate of consumption, the world's developed nations are soon going to exhaust the planet's ability to provide new resources.
9. Regardless of its strange appearance or its unusual hopping locomotion, the kangaroo continues to gain in numbers and has few enemies except people, who eat kangaroos.

10. Though old myths about animal behavior recommend against raising cats and dogs together, direct experience shows otherwise.

<u>Please don't read ahead until you have finished the activity</u>. The issue of subjects and verbs will be explained later.

———————

You can usually find the subject of a sentence by asking <u>who</u> or <u>what</u> is the actor in the sentence: who is (or was) doing the action of the sentence? The subject is often first or early in the sentence, but not always. For example: "Last night because of all the noise outside, I read <u>Moby Dick</u> until nearly dawn." Ask yourself, <u>who</u> is or was doing the action in the sentence (who was reading <u>Moby Dick</u>)?

In simple sentences the subject is often the first or second word. But as your writing matures, you may discover yourself adding modifiers and other sentence components, for example

Adjectives	<u>Young, attractive, lively</u> . . . Marla sang.
Adverb phrases	<u>Late in the program</u>, young, attractive, lively . . . Marla sang.
Verb complements	Late in the program, young, attractive, lively Marla sang <u>her school song</u>. [direct object]
Dependent clauses	Late in the program, young, attractive, lively Marla sang her school song <u>until she was exhausted</u>.

Theoretically there could be many other elements in a sentence in addition to the subject and verb. But few mature writers would pile up all sorts of elements in their sentences just to see how many they could have.

Then too, not all subjects need to be creatures that can "act" in the sense of doing something like singing. Some "actions" may be purely mental. Sentence "subjects" can be anything about which people talk. For example: "<u>Attributes such as intelligence</u> were once thought to be entirely genetic." The subject, "attributes such as intelligence," isn't really an actor, but if you rely on the test for subjects (ask who or what "were once thought to be entirely genetic") you can find even an abstract subject like this one. (See item 10 in Activity 2.)

Why Is Finding the Subject Important?

It is important for writers and readers to find the subject in a sentence because of the relation of the subject to the verb. The reader needs to know what you are writing about, and also the subject and verb must "agree." Whether the verb should be "were" or "is" depends on the subject. Plural subjects need plural verbs. The verb states what the subject is, was, or will be "doing." Many verbs express action or behavior such as go, speak, think, walk. Other verbs express a state of being: am, is, are, was, were, and so on. Regardless of the kind of verb you use, it must agree with the subject of your sentence.

Subject and Verb Agreement Problems

Any Verb Must "Match" Its Subject

A singular subject requires a singular verb; a plural subject requires a plural verb.

> The <u>sound</u> of the waves <u>puts</u> me to sleep. [singular]
> <u>Seymour</u> <u>wants</u> to clean his glasses. [singular]
> <u>Seymour and Buddy</u> <u>hope</u> to go hiking in Vermont. [plural]

How can you tell whether a verb is singular or plural? Most verbs (but not all) follow the same pattern for singular and plural. Study the following lists for a moment. Can you tell which are the singular and which are the plural verbs?

go	goes
have	has
think	thinks
do	does
invite	invites
contemplate	contemplates

A simple test reveals which are the singular and which are the plural verbs. Say <u>we</u> before the verb. <u>We</u> is a plural pronoun (so is <u>they</u>), and the verbs <u>go</u>, <u>have</u>, <u>think</u>, and so on are plural verbs. That is, if the sentence is correct English—we go, they have, we think—then the verb is plural: it <u>agrees</u> with its plural subject, <u>we</u> or <u>they</u>. To find a singular verb, say <u>he</u>, <u>she</u> or <u>it</u> before the verb: <u>he</u> <u>goes</u>, <u>she thinks</u>, <u>it has</u>. Only these three pronouns—he, she, it—take a different verb form. All other pronouns take the same verb form: <u>I go</u>, <u>you go</u>, <u>we go</u>, <u>they go</u>. Only <u>he</u>, <u>she</u>, or <u>it</u> changes the verb to <u>goes</u>, <u>has</u>, <u>thinks</u>, and so on. Use only <u>we</u> or <u>they</u> to find plural verbs (in our little verb test). Use only <u>he</u>, <u>she</u>, or <u>it</u> to find singular verbs.

Finding the correct subject and verb can be difficult enough with simple subjects, but agreement problems can be more difficult when the subjects are compound, that is, when they are joined by <u>or</u> and <u>nor</u> (as in Jack <u>or</u> Jill); or when joined by <u>either/or</u>, <u>neither/nor</u>, or <u>not/but</u>, or the indefinite pronouns such as <u>each</u>, <u>everyone</u>, and <u>everybody</u>.

ACTIVITY 3

See if you can select the correct verb for the subjects in these sentences. Try to say whether the verb is singular or plural. If you're not sure, give your best answers. We will discuss these subjects later.

1. Reynard and Oola (plans/plan) to develop their own software company.
2. Brazil or Argentina (is/are) where we would like to take our vacation.
3. The cheeses or the crackers (was/were) the cause of so much diarrhea at the party.
4. Neither the eel nor the glass snake (is/are) a true snake.
5. Neither peridots nor opals (is/are) precious gems but, rather, semiprecious.
6. Everybody (is/are) entitled to (her/their) own opinions.
7. Mothers who (is/are) trying to raise children must work hard.
8. Magazine articles that (is/are) political can be found in section P of the library.
9. Anyone who (is/are) ready to perform should attend the tryouts.
10. Neither the representatives nor the senators (was/were) able to provide answers to some questions from the audience.

Why is "agreement" so important? One answer is simply that there are many ways for subjects and verbs to go wrong. Another is that many people find agreement mistakes serious grammatical errors, serious enough to lead readers astray and to cast doubt on the writer's ethos and logos. Some writers believe that readers should not be aware of the writer's voice behind the words on the page, especially in fiction. Your sentences should flow along without hitches or sudden confusion that might cause your reader to stop and possibly backup to reread . . . trying to figure out what you are saying.

Agreement with Compound Subjects

Subjects Joined by <u>Or</u> or <u>Nor</u>. Singular subjects joined by <u>or</u> or <u>nor</u> take a singular verb. Plural subjects joined by <u>or</u> or <u>nor</u> require a plural verb.

> <u>Lori or Devonn is</u> available to take Sharon's place.
> <u>Neither he nor she has</u> been infected by the flu bug.
> Either the <u>women</u> or the <u>men are</u> supposed to decide the homecoming theme.

Using <u>Either . . . Or</u>, <u>Neither . . . Nor</u>, or <u>Not . . . But</u>. When <u>either . . . or</u>, <u>neither . . . nor</u>, or <u>not . . . but</u> joins a singular subject to a plural subject, the verb should agree with the closer one.

<u>Neither</u> the dog <u>nor</u> the cats <u>were</u> responsible for the mess in the garage.

<u>Not</u> the cats <u>but</u> the dog was responsible for the mess in the garage.

Each, Every, Everybody Require Singular Verbs. <u>Each</u>, <u>every</u>, <u>everybody</u>, and most other indefinite pronouns require singular verbs. (See Pronoun Agreement Problems.)

<u>Each</u> of the students <u>writes</u> an essay in an hour. [not <u>write</u>]

<u>Everyone</u> <u>is</u> concerned about the financial loss. [not <u>are</u>]

<u>Neither</u> of the book reviews <u>gives</u> a fair analysis. [not <u>give</u>]

Verbs and Who, Which, or That. After <u>who</u>, <u>which</u>, or <u>that</u>, the verb agrees with the word the pronoun identifies.

She is one of those <u>lawyers</u> <u>who</u> <u>earn</u> high salaries.
[<u>who</u> refers to <u>lawyers</u>; the verb <u>earn</u> must be plural]

Jerry is one of those <u>students</u> <u>who</u> <u>excel</u> in every class.
[<u>who</u> refers to <u>students</u>; the verb <u>excel</u> must be plural]

Terry is a <u>student</u> <u>who</u> <u>excels</u> in every class.
[<u>who</u> refers to a <u>student</u>; thus, the verb <u>excels</u> must be singular]

Pronoun Agreement Problems

Readers expect subjects and verbs to agree. And pronouns too can have agreement problems, both before and after the verb. Pronouns must agree with the words they refer to, whether they refer to the subject or object of the verb, object of a preposition, or an indirect object.

ACTIVITY 4

Try to determine whether the pronouns and verbs in these sentences agree. Underline anything that seems to be an error. Try to give a brief explanation of the error, such as "needs plural verb" or "needs singular subject" and so on.

1. Everyone has a hobby or some special activity they love to do.
2. When someone eats in a restaurant, they may need to worry about secondhand smoke, which causes cancer, heart disease, lung disease, and premature death.
3. None of the boys on the team was older than 13.
4. Everybody needs some kind of engine to provide drive in their life.

5. If people read Mitch Albom's book <u>Tuesdays with Morrie</u>, he or she will probably like it.
6. Elinore discovered that the telegram was for she.
7. Half the kids in the sixth grade was sick with the measles.
8. On the morning of August 6, 1945, everyone in Washington DC were notified that the <u>Enola Gay</u>, an American B-29, had dropped an atomic bomb named "Little Boy" on the Japanese city of Hiroshima.
9. Manoa discovered that the committee has selected her for president.
10. Some of the books in the children's library was deemed inappropriate for children.

Words such as <u>all</u>, <u>another</u>, <u>any</u>, <u>anybody</u>, <u>anyone</u>, <u>few</u>, <u>each</u>, <u>either</u>, <u>everyone</u>, <u>everybody</u>, <u>many</u>, <u>most</u>, <u>neither</u>, <u>none</u>, <u>no one</u>, <u>one</u>, <u>several</u>, <u>some</u>, <u>somebody</u>, <u>someone</u>, and <u>something</u> are called indefinite pronouns. In formal writing situations, these pronouns are generally used as singular words that require singular verbs and singular pronouns for agreement.

Incorrect:	<u>Everyone</u> needs positive reinforcement in <u>their</u> lives.
	[<u>Everyone</u> is singular but <u>their</u> is plural]
Revise:	<u>All people</u> need positive reinforcement in <u>their</u> lives.
	Or <u>Everyone</u> needs positive reinforcement in <u>his</u> life.
	Or <u>Everyone</u> needs positive reinforcement in <u>her</u> life.
	Or <u>Everyone</u> needs positive reinforcement in <u>his</u> or <u>her</u> life.
	(The Modern Language Association recommends against using his/her, him/her, and other split constructions. Try to rephrase your sentence instead: "We all need positive reinforcement.")

Incorrect:	Love makes a <u>person</u> who <u>they are</u>.
	[<u>person</u> is singular, but <u>they</u> is plural]
Revise:	Love makes <u>people</u> who <u>they</u> are.
	Or Love makes a <u>person</u> who <u>she</u> is.
	Or Love makes a <u>person</u> who <u>he</u> is.

In some cases, the correct sentence may sound awkward or unnatural. In that case, you need to revise your sentence until it sounds both correct and natural.

Incorrect:	<u>Everybody</u> will have <u>their</u> moment of fame.
	[<u>Everybody</u> is singular, but <u>their</u> is plural]
Revise:	"We will <u>all</u> <u>have</u> our moment of fame."

Exception to the Rule: The following pronouns agree with singular <u>or</u> plural verbs and other pronouns: <u>all</u>, <u>half</u>, <u>any</u>, <u>more</u>, <u>part</u>, <u>none</u>, and <u>some</u>. They agree with singular verbs when they refer to singular words but agree with plural verbs when they refer to plural words.

> <u>All</u> <u>patriots</u> <u>are</u> ready to surrender <u>their</u> lives for <u>their</u> country.
> <u>More</u> <u>women and children</u> <u>live</u> on welfare than any other people.
> <u>Some</u> of the <u>recruits</u> <u>were</u> in the service less than six months.
> <u>Some</u> <u>vandal</u> <u>has</u> broken in the window to the storeroom.

Other agreement problems concern collective nouns, clauses, pronouns as objects, and choices between <u>who</u> and <u>whom</u>.

Agreement with Collective Nouns

Though collective nouns identify groups (the <u>troop</u> <u>is</u> [not <u>are</u>] ready), treat them as singular, requiring singular verbs and pronouns for agreement: the <u>army</u>, the <u>band</u>, the <u>faculty</u>, the <u>corporation</u>. Words such as these require singular pronouns and verbs.

> The <u>company</u> <u>knows</u> what <u>it</u> <u>is</u> doing.
> [Not: The <u>company</u> knows what <u>they are</u> doing.]
> The <u>band</u> will record <u>its</u> first song next week.
> [Not: The <u>band</u> will record <u>their</u> first song next week.]
>
> <u>Scotland College</u> claims <u>its</u> athletes are scholars, and <u>its</u> scholars are athletes.
> [Not: <u>Scotland College</u> claims <u>their</u> athletes are scholars and <u>their</u> scholars are athletes.]

Clauses, Dependent and Independent

Before you can go much further with subjects and objects, you need a brief look at clauses. A clause is a group of words containing a subject and a verb—and it may have other components, such as objects. What pattern do you see in these clauses?

> When it snows . . .
> If it rains . . .
> Until we meet again . . .
> Though no one has said so . . .
> . . . even if we must stay home.

Every clause has a subject and verb. Each dependent clause is less than a complete sentence. Clauses may start a sentence, end a sentence or appear anywhere within a "complex" sentence, but dependent clauses alone are not full sentences. They do not make complete thoughts. They are called "dependent" clauses because they depend on some other clause to make the thought complete. The main clause contains the main subject and verb. Dependent clauses contain secondary subjects and verbs.

A sentence too is a clause because it also has a subject and a verb, and possibly other components. The difference between a clause and a sentence is this: a sentence is a clause that makes sense by itself; a sentence is a complete thought that can stand on its own—it is an "independent" clause. "When <u>it</u> <u>rained</u> . . ." is a clause because it has a subject and a verb, but it isn't a sentence— it is incomplete. It is called a dependent clause because it cannot stand alone— it <u>depends</u> on the rest of the sentence: "When it rained, <u>we all went home</u>." The clause "we all went home" is an <u>independent</u> clause: it could stand by itself. It contains the main subject and verb. A dependent clause cannot stand by itself; it is not a full sentence: "We all went home <u>when it rained</u>." Dependent clauses contain <u>secondary</u> subjects and verbs.

ACTIVITY 5

In the following items, try to determine how many clauses each sentence contains and whether they are dependent or independent or both. Try to draw a line under the main clause(s).

1. If it snows, we must stay home.
2. If it snows, we must stay home until it quits.
3. When an issue comes before Congress, the House and Senate will debate it until it is ready for the president's signature.
4. The days of studying in college are long and hard, but the rewards for so much work are worth the effort.
5. Though he was quite a young man, George Washington proved to be an able soldier, and he was also a superior politician, though he preferred the agrarian work of his home, Mount Vernon.

Sentences can have more than one independent clause and more than one dependent clause, each with its own subject and verb. For example, here are two dependent clauses: "<u>When the rain stopped</u> but <u>before the sun appeared</u> . . ."

Sentences may also have more than one independent clause (both of which could stand alone as an independent sentence):

The rain finally stopped, and we all went home.

After the rain stopped, <u>we decided</u> to go to the theater, but <u>we changed</u> our minds later when the rain started again.

In theory, there is no limit to the number of clauses a sentence might have. The preceding second example has four clauses. However, we do not recommend adding clauses just to see how many you can have.

Pronouns as Subjects and Objects in Clauses

Pronouns can be troublesome because they change spelling depending on how they are used in a sentence. Often your ear will tell you when a pronoun is incorrect: "Him is cleaning out the garage." But in more complicated sentences, it can be difficult to determine which is the correct form of a pronoun.

ACTIVITY 6

Select the pronoun you would use in each of these sentences, and then in a few words explain your selection: for example "subject pronoun" or "object pronoun."

1. (We/Us) guys were getting ready for a game of softball later in the day.
2. The general expected (we/us) new recruits would learn the drill quickly.
3. After conquering the Turks, Dracula ordered (they/them) to build (he/him) a fortress near the Arges river.
4. The police were certain it was "Light Fingers Maria" (who/whom) had opened the safe.
5. (Whoever/Whomever) has the loot is probably the one who stole it.

Pronouns can serve as subjects or objects in clauses. The form of a pronoun that is correct depends on how the pronoun is used in its clause. But if the form sounds awkward, even though "correct," you should revise your sentence.

Because only Jeremy would go, we sent <u>him</u>.

It was <u>he</u> <u>whom</u> we sent. [Technically this sentence is "correct," but it sounds so awkward and unnatural that you should revise it until it sounds both correct and natural: "We sent him."]

Merriam discovered the new puppy was for <u>her</u>, a birthday gift.

Using Subject Pronouns

<u>I</u>, <u>we</u>, <u>you</u>, <u>he</u>, <u>she</u>, <u>it</u>, <u>they</u>, <u>who</u>, and <u>whoever</u> are pronouns. In addition to using them as subjects, you should use these pronouns after the "being" verbs

of <u>am</u>, <u>is</u>, <u>are</u>, <u>was</u>, <u>were</u>, <u>be</u>, <u>being</u>, and <u>been</u>, including the future and perfect forms: <u>It will be she</u>; <u>It has been I</u>. After one of the "being" verbs, nouns and pronouns are technically not objects, because being verbs express no action. Therefore, after a "being" verb you should use a <u>subject</u> pronoun.

> It is <u>I</u>. [not <u>me</u>]
> The one they wanted was <u>she</u>. [not <u>her</u>]
> When the voice on the phone asked for Phil, he said, "This is <u>he</u>." [not <u>him</u>]
> This is <u>who</u>? [not <u>whom</u>]

But remember the rule against awkward sentences: your sentences must sound both correct and natural.

Using Possessive Pronouns. <u>My</u>, <u>mine</u>, <u>our</u>, <u>ours</u>, <u>your</u>, <u>yours</u>, <u>his</u>, <u>her</u>, <u>hers</u>, <u>its</u>, <u>their</u>, <u>theirs</u>, and <u>whose</u> are possessive pronouns.
    Note that pronouns do not use apostrophes: they indicate possession with a change in spelling.

> I once had a dog; it was <u>my</u> dog.
> Many people of poor countries are struggling for <u>their</u> survival.
> I gave my friend a cat: "Now that cat is <u>yours</u>," I said.

Using Object Pronouns. <u>Me</u>, <u>us</u>, <u>you</u>, <u>him</u>, <u>her</u>, <u>it</u>, <u>them</u>, <u>themselves</u>, <u>whom</u>, and <u>whomever</u> are object pronouns.
    The "object" receives the action of the verb:

> "We saw <u>him</u>." "We admired <u>her</u>."
> "The package was sent to <u>her</u> by Aunt Jane."

You can usually find the <u>object</u> (if there is one) by asking "what" after the verb. "I read the book."—read what? (the book).
    Prepositions too can have objects. In general, prepositions are followed by object pronouns:

> There were no secrets <u>between</u> <u>him</u> and <u>me</u>. [not <u>him</u> and <u>I</u>]
> He wrote, "Let's just keep this <u>between</u> <u>you</u> and <u>me</u>." [not <u>you</u> and <u>I</u>]
> She waved <u>at</u> Shannon and <u>me</u>. [not <u>Shannon</u> and <u>I</u>]

You can find the object of a preposition by asking "what" after the preposition:

> Benny fell into the well. [Into what? the <u>well</u>]
> We found a box of coins beneath the floor of the attic. [Beneath what? the <u>floor</u>].

As the name implies, most prepositions (but not all) are words of position. It will be helpful for you to become familiar with the following list of prepositions:

above	behind	inside	since
about	below	in spite of	through
according to	beneath	instead of	throughout
across	beside	into	to
after	between	like	toward
against	beyond	near	under
along	but	next to	underneath
amid	by	of	until
around	during	on	up
as	except	on behalf of	upon
aside from	for	out of	with
as to	from	outside	within
at	in	over	without

Who and Whom

For most writers the most difficult pronoun agreement problem is the problem of who and whom, whoever and whomever. Whom and whomever are slowly passing out of American English. Especially in oral English many people use only "who" for both subjective and objective cases. However, because whom and whomever are still recognized as a correct objective case by educated readers and writers, you need to know the differences between who and whom.

ACTIVITY 7

Try to select the correct pronouns in the practice sentences here. Try to explain in a word or two why you selected your answer (i.e., "who" is the subject; "whom" is the object). If you're not sure, don't worry; write down your best answers.

1. Annissa was not the person (who/whom) we expected to have the answer.
2. Anyone (who/whom) gives illicit drugs to a child should be punished.
3. (Whoever/Whomever) wants to go on the picnic should sign up before June 10.
4. (Whoever/Whomever) smokes should be aware of the serious dangers of tobacco.
5. (Who/Whom) we should send on the cruise is not easy to decide.

Please do not read on until you have finished the activity.

_____

Pronoun "case" helps to show how your pronouns are used, for example, as subjects, objects, or to show possession.

When your sentences are written in "normal" order, subject–verb–object, you can usually see how any of your pronouns are used. The subject usually comes early in the sentence; the object usually comes late in the sentence.

Subject	Verb	Object
The <u>student</u>	<u>wrote</u>	<u>the essay</u>.

The subject does the acting, the verb names the action, and the object receives the action. Not all verbs can take an object; however, if you substitute pronouns for the nouns in the preceding sentence, a subject pronoun must be chosen for the <u>student</u> and an object pronoun for the <u>book</u>: <u>She wrote it.</u>

However, writers don't always use "normal" order. <u>Who</u> and <u>whom</u> are often used in questions. And in that case, you may need to turn the sentence around (in your mind) until it makes a statement instead of a question.

Question	Turned into Statement
Did you see who was driving that car?	You did see who was driving that car.
Or	
	You did see [something]—[that] <u>she</u> was driving that car.

This analysis shows that the sentence requires a subject pronoun, such as <u>he</u> or <u>she</u>. <u>Who</u> is the correct subject form. <u>Who</u> is the subject of "was driving that car."

In other cases, the "who or whom" sentence may not be a question, but it is not quite in "normal" order:

Out of Order	Analyzed
We knew the ones whom the police were after.	We knew [something]—[that] the police were after <u>them</u>.

The analysis shows that the sentence needs an object pronoun, like <u>them</u> (object of the preposition <u>after</u>). <u>Whom</u> is the correct form. However, this is an example of a sentence that would read as well without <u>whom</u>. <u>We knew the ones [whom] the police were after.</u> Use the writer's rule for concise writing: delete unnecessary words.

ACTIVITY 8

For practice, see how well you can select the correct who/whom pronouns in these sentences. Try to explain your answer, for example: "<u>who</u> is the subject of <u>goes</u>"; or "<u>whom</u> is the object of <u>know</u>."

1. We knew the old man (who/whom) lived across the street.
2. The ones (who/whom) left the place in such a shambles were the gang.
3. The workers (who/whom) we asked to do the work were late.
4. The picture revealed (who/whom) was the one in the background.
5. (Who/Whom) we wanted for president, we were reluctant to say.

Appropriate Verb Tenses

Verb tenses indicate time. The simple tenses indicate past, present, and future events: <u>I go</u>, <u>I went</u>, <u>I will go</u>. The "perfect" tenses indicate on-going or customary action: past perfect time indicates one action was completed before another, and future perfect indicates events that will be completed before some other in the future:

Present Perfect:	I have talked about this for years.
Past Perfect:	I had talked for an hour before the exit bell rang.
Future Perfect:	After today, I will have talked to this group 20 times.

There are also "progressive" forms for ongoing actions. You can see at once the pattern of progressive forms.

I am talking	I have been talking
I was talking	I had been talking
I will be talking	I shall have been talking

ACTIVITY 9

Before we discuss various problems with verbs, try to underline the correct verbs in these sentences. Try to explain your choices.

1. Hiram's well-respected book on cloning (gave/had gave) a terse response to critics: "Nuts to them," he said.
2. This researcher (finds/found) that animals kept in below-zero temperatures quickly die.
3. It is essential that everyone (attend/attends) the meeting on resources and expenses.
4. The data (seem/seems) persuasive, but if we compare them with earlier results we may find them less convincing.
5. If it (was/were) possible to increase our budget by a million dollars, I would certainly attempt to do so.
6. Our experiments were not successful until we (begin/began) to include some ancient secrets.
7. It was clear that we lost all the ongoing experiments because the lab (burned/had burned) down.
8. <u>Time</u> magazine (presented/presents) one of the best articles on the life of the equidae.
9. The financiers asked, "Suppose the experiment (was/were) to fail, how would we get our money back?"
10. I first (introduce/introduced) a quart of highly acidic solution, and then (allow/allowed) it to give off toxic fumes until the experimental subjects (die/died).

<u>Please don't read on until you have finished the activity</u>.

The following "problems" or examples can help you understand verb usage.

Use the Past Tense to Describe What Happened in Your Research

We <u>implanted</u> hundreds of cells before producing one live embryo.
I <u>kept</u> oocytes alive in petri dishes.

Exceptions to the Rule: You may sometimes address the reader in the present tense, as if explaining your reasoning or speculating aloud:

If we [meaning researchers, or the reader and the writer] <u>produce</u> 277 failures before we <u>get</u> one live sheep embryo, what <u>is</u> the implication for human cloning?

Use the Present Tense to Quote from Books and Articles or to Refer to Source Material

Sharon Begley's <u>Newsweek</u> article "Little Lamb Who Made Thee?" <u>gives</u> a very clear description of the procedure and <u>shows</u> a simple diagram.

The Watson article in the <u>Atlantic</u> <u>is</u> an important discussion of the ethics and moral, social, and psychological problems of cloning human beings.

Use the Past Tense to Identify Source Material

Sharon Begley's <u>Newsweek</u> article on cloning <u>appeared</u> on March 10, 1997.

The <u>Atlantic Monthly</u>'s article "Moving Toward the Clonal Man" by James D. Watson <u>was</u> one of the earliest to discuss the ethics of human cloning—May of 1971. The Internet subsequently published the entire article.

When Some Events Occur Further Back in Time Than Others, Use <u>Had</u>

When some events occur further back in time than others, use <u>had</u> (the past perfect tense) for the earlier event:

Incorrect:	We knew the bird escaped when we saw that its cage door was open.
Revise:	We knew the bird <u>had</u> escaped when we that saw its cage door was open.

Because we <u>had assumed</u> that a human clone <u>was</u> impossible, we <u>made</u> no preparations for discussing the implications, and we <u>prepared</u> no documents for seeking grants or other financial support to conduct experiments.

Use <u>Were</u> and <u>Be</u> to Express Doubts, Wishes, Probability, Condictions Contrary to Fact, or Hypothetical Statements

If I <u>were</u> you, I would not get there too early.
He wished he <u>were</u> an astronaut.
Suppose the clone <u>were</u> injured, what then?
Be it ever so humble, there's no place like home.
We insist that you <u>be</u> present.

Avoid Unjustified Shifts in Tense

Make sure all other verbs in your sentences match tenses.

<u>Incorrect</u>:	In the play, Susan <u>is waiting</u> for the proper moment, but John suddenly <u>announced</u> he <u>was</u> leaving. [present and past tense mixed]
<u>Revised for Consistent Tense</u>:	In the play, Susan <u>waits</u> for the proper moment, but John suddenly <u>announces</u> he <u>is</u> leaving.
	Or
	In the play, Susan <u>waited</u> for the proper moment, but John suddenly <u>announced</u> he <u>was</u> leaving. [all in past tense]

Lie and Lay

Most verbs have four distinct forms. Some have alternate forms; a few have repeated forms. Regular verbs form their past and past participle with -d, or -ed: seized, wanted, sailed. Irregular verbs usually form their past and past participle with a spelling change: swim, swam, swum, swimming. The forms of a few verbs are listed here:

Present	Past	Past Participle	Present Participle
awaken	awakened	awakened	awakening
begin	began	begun	beginning
break	broke	broken	breaking
buy	bought	bought	buying
draw	drew	drawn	drawing
drink	drank	drunk	drinking

Lie and lay are three different verbs, each with its own four forms.

Lay	laid	laid	laying

This verb means to put or to set as in lay the plates on the table, and I laid the flowers on the table an hour ago. We have laid the plates for dinner.

Lie	lay	lain	lying

This verb means to recline as in lie down and rest awhile. I lay in bed all this morning. I have lain there for hours.

Lie	lied	lied	lying

This verb means to falsify as in to tell a lie.

The first two verbs, lie and lay, confuse people, especially writers. (You can disregard the third verb for now, because few people are confused about it.) It may be helpful to remember that lie and lay are different in meaning and they are also different in usage. The first one, lay always takes an object: you must lay something somewhere. The second, lie never takes an object; it is usually followed by a place expression—down in bed, on the table, on the ground, and so on.

ACTIVITY 10

In this activity you can ignore the verb that means to falsify. The activity concerns only lie (recline) and lay (put). See if you can underline the correct verb in these sentences. Try to explain your answer, for example "past tense of lie" or "present tense of lay" and so on.

1. Rover had (laid/lain) in the culvert for most of the day, hiding from the sun.
2. The newspaper had been (laying/lying) on the front steps all through the rain.
3. I (lay/laid) my best shotgun on the gun rack after every use.
4. Our librarians (laid/lay) the new books on the reading table.
5. Auntie Em had (laid/lain) Dorothy's blue dress on a hanger in the closet.
6. Uncle Charley (laid/lay) out in the hammock after hoeing through the corn plants for an hour.
7. The children were (laying/lying) bouquets on the teacher's desk.
8. I was so tired after work that I had to (lay/lie) down and rest before dinner.
9. The Shuttle crew actually launches the ship while (lying/laying) on their backs.
10. Our old tractor was (laying/lying) on its side, rusting in the sun.

Revise Faulty Parallelism

What pattern(s) do you see in the following sentences?

> Hunters in the North are on the lookout for deer, moose, elk, and bear.
> Many youngsters today enjoy swimming, scuba diving, and surfing.
> So far we have read novels, histories, short stories, and biographies.

<u>Please don't go on until you have at least a good guess about the pattern in these sentences</u>.

The pattern in each of the preceding sentences concerns "parallel construction." Sentence elements should be parallel if possible. Parallel construction means that elements in the sentences are structured the same way, using the same form for each item in the pattern. For example

| Incorrect: | I like reading and to write. |
| Revise: | I like <u>reading</u> and <u>writing</u>. |

| Incorrect: | The laboratory needed new equipment to improve instruction and which would expose students to new technology. |
| Revise: | The laboratory needed new equipment <u>to improve</u> instruction and <u>to expose</u> students to new technology. |

| Incorrect: | Dr. Brown is a person of beauty, of grace, and she is wise. |
| Revise: | Dr. Brown is a person <u>of beauty</u>, <u>of grace</u>, and <u>of wisdom</u>. |

If we interfere with the parallelism in the preceding examples, we might get results such as these:

> Hunters in the North are on the lookout for deer, moose, elk, and bears. [Note that each item uses the collective form except "bears" which uses a plural.]

> Many youngsters today enjoy swimming, scuba diving, and to surf.
> [Each item uses an -ing form except "to surf."]

Dangling or Misplaced Modifiers

You need to watch for modifiers that have nothing to modify or that seem to modify the wrong thing in your sentence: "Sleeping all afternoon, the cot was as comfortable as a bed." The writer knows what is intended, but for the reader, the sentence seems to say the cot was sleeping all afternoon.

ACTIVITY 11

What is a "dangling" or "misplaced" modifier? Even if you are not sure, give your best guess. We will soon explain the concept. Try to explain the errors (if any) in the following sentences.

1. Don't bite into apples with your teeth when they are dirty.
2. We had brought toys for the children in the trunk of our car.
3. We asked the waitress with the menus standing at our table to give us a minute.
4. The busboy cleaned off the table by the window covered with smears and dirt.
5. Coasting without a sail, the shoreline soon came into sight.
6. Feeling a sour stomach, the medicine Irene took was proving effective.
7. The monitor on Ellroy's computer made sparks after he dropped it.
8. The monkeys were kept by the zoo keepers in glass cages.
9. Those who exercise often injure themselves.
10. While pumping for water, the well suddenly ran dry.

The misplaced modifier is similar to the -ing dangling modifiers in items 5, 6, and 10. If a modifier has no subject, it is called a "dangling modifier." Who or what is "coasting without a sail"? Who or what is "feeling a sour stomach"? Who or what was "pumping for water"?

When the modifier is aimed at an improper or inappropriate subject, it is called a "misplaced" modifier. Who or what is the subject of "when they are dirty" in item 1?

If writers lose the sense of their sentences, words for people and objects can get misplaced. You may know what you are trying to say: your ideas may seem obvious to you, but your readers have only the words on the page to guide them. For example

Incorrect: We hid our gifts to surprise the assistants in our lab coats.

By placing the phrase in our lab coats next to assistants, the writer has made it seem that the assistants were wearing the coats. The sentence makes better sense if you get the coats away from the assistants:

Revise: To surprise the assistants, we hid our gifts in our lab coats.

Other examples

Incorrect: The audience applauded Hala's playing with enthusiasm. [Who or what is enthusiastic in this sentence: the audience or Hala's playing?]
Revise: The audience enthusiastically applauded Hala's playing.
Or The audience applauded Hala's enthusiastic playing.
Incorrect: People shouldn't eat fish when they smell bad.
[Who smells bad here, the people or the fish?]
Revise: Never eat fish that smell bad.

The modifier in Activity 11 item 9 "often" is called a "squinting" modifier, because it seems to aim at two words simultaneously: often exercise and often injure.

The main rule to remember is this: find or supply an appropriate subject for your modifiers. Place modifiers next to—or as close as possible to—the thing they modify. When they are placed next to some other word, the "misplacement" results. To revise these sentences you may need to supply an appropriate subject.

Incorrect: Sleeping without a heavy blanket, the room began to get cold.

The problem here is that there is no person who is "sleeping without a heavy blanket." The only noun your readers can find is "the room." Like many of these sentences, you must supply an appropriate subject for these "dangling" modifiers.

Revise: Sleeping without a heavy blanket, Jenny began to feel cold.
Or Jenny began to feel the room getting cold.

Avoid Sexist Language

Sexism is inappropriate. Writers should avoid a bias in words that indicate gender. For example, when a class contains both men and women, you should indicate that fact: <u>Each student</u> should bring <u>his</u> or <u>her</u> book to class.

Write in the Plural if Possible

<u>Students</u> should bring <u>their</u> books to class.

Sexist:	<u>A researcher</u> needs endurance if <u>he</u> hopes to finish <u>his</u> work on time. [Don't assume all researchers are male.]
Revise:	<u>Researchers</u> need endurance if <u>they</u> hope to finish <u>their</u> work on time.
Sexist:	Ask personnel to send an extra <u>workman</u> over. [Don't assume all workers are male.]
Revise:	Ask personnel to send an extra <u>worker</u> over.

Substitute Neutral Words When Either Gender Is Implied

<u>humankind</u> instead of <u>mankind</u>
<u>spokesperson</u> instead of <u>spokesman</u>
<u>chairperson</u> instead of <u>chairman</u>
<u>mail carrier</u> instead of <u>mailman</u>
<u>postal worker</u> instead of <u>postman</u>
<u>personnel</u> instead of <u>manpower</u>
<u>worker</u> instead of <u>workman</u>

Unless there are other clues to suggest you are talking about only one gender or the other, you should substitute neutral words.

ACTIVITY 12

Revise these sentences to remove gender bias.

1. Whoever is manning that ship is about to wreck it.
2. A fellow with a vulgar mouth is not what we want for our receptionist.
3. Make sure the surgeon gets his hands clean before putting on his gloves.
4. The damage must have been done by some guy with a grudge against the captain.
5. A secretary who can't spell won't keep her job for long.

PUNCTUATION

In interchapters 1 and 2, we presented semicolons, colons, dashes, underlining (italics), and parentheses as punctuation tools that help create your voice—the sound of your personality on the page. Used well, these various ways to join thoughts give your writing more power. They clarify your meaning and add emphasis. Imagine if you could use only periods—no other forms of punctuation. The possibilities for joining and emphasizing certain thoughts would shrink. In this section, we present other matters of punctuation that you can refer to as you edit your writing, trying to make it clear and free of errors.

Period

Use a Period at the End of a Complete Statement
Writing naturally generates critical thinking.

Note: Failure to end a sentence with a period makes a writer look careless.

Use a Period for Each Item in a Sentence Outline or List of Full Sentences

The student employees had a few minor complaints:

1. The working hours were too long.
2. The pay was too low.
3. The working conditions were too uncomfortable.
4. The boss was too arrogant.

In a list or outline of words or phrases rather than sentences, do not use periods.

The students had only these minor complaints:

1. Long working hours
2. Low pay
3. Uncomfortable working conditions
4. An arrogant boss

Use Periods with Most Abbreviations and Initials

e.g.   Inc.   pp.   Ms.   Mr.   Dr.   J.F.K.

Do not add an additional period when an abbreviation or initial comes at the end of a sentence.

We were set to go at 8:00 p.m. [Use small caps if your printer has them: P.M.]

After six years, Barb finally earned her PhD. [or Ph.D.]
Our list server is listserv@eff.org.

Many abbreviations of well-known organizations do not require periods.

FBI   NAACP   NFL   NOW   NRA

Comma Splices and Run-On Sentences

Comma splices and run-on (or fused) sentences are common sentence problems (see interchapter 1).

Comma splice: A comma splice is a sentence error in which only a comma divides two complete thoughts without any connecting word (such as <u>and</u>, <u>but</u>, <u>or</u>).

Run-on: A run-on sentence is a rear-end <u>collision</u>. One complete thought runs into another with no punctuation between them.
  Run-ons can be repaired various ways:

- By connecting both complete thoughts with a semicolon
- By connecting both complete thoughts with a comma and connecting word
- By connecting both complete thoughts with a colon or a dash
- By separating both complete thoughts with a period and starting a new sentence
- By combining into one concise complete thought

ACTIVITY 13

See if you can revise the errors in these sentences. Try to describe the errors (comma splices or run-on sentences).

1. Madeleine Albright was Secretary of State in the Clinton administration, she was the first woman ever to hold that position.
2. The F-22 Rapter Stealth Fighter was hailed as a great advance in modern weaponry it was virtually invisible to enemy radar.
3. Tchaikovsky's <u>Swan Lake</u> remains one of his popular ballets it features graceful and beautiful swanlike movements.
4. The boa constrictor is a fearsome snake, often huge, the snake kills its prey by squeezing and suffocating it.
5. The kangaroo is the world's largest marsupial, it is native to Australia, where people eat kangaroos.
6. Great Grandfather hid his money in trees and under rocks no one has ever found it.

7. George Washington wore ill-fitting wooden teeth, his lips protruded slightly.
8. Columbus set out for the New World with his three little ships, they were a gift from Queen Isabella of Spain.
9. Hemingway wrote several excellent novels <u>A Farewell to Arms</u> is one of his finest.
10. The nature of modern research can create difficulties for many students, few of them have the patience for statistics.

_____

Comma

Use Commas to Separate Sentences Joined by <u>And</u>, <u>But</u>, <u>Or</u>, <u>Nor</u>, <u>For</u>, <u>Yet</u>, <u>So</u>

Thousands of fans packed the stadium<u>, yet</u> they made hardly a sound as the performer sang.
I am not proud of this<u>, but</u> this is what I did. (Albom, <u>Tuesdays with Morrie</u> 27)
The skin from his wrist to his knuckles was dotted with age spots<u>, and</u> it was loose . . . . (Albom, <u>Tuesdays with Morrie</u> 35)

Note that the comma comes <u>before</u> the connecting word, not after.

ACTIVITY 14

Try to correct any comma errors (if any) in these sentences. See if you can explain the errors.

1. Hundreds of shoppers milled through the mall starting their Christmas shopping early but they seemed too preoccupied and hurried to enjoy the holiday season.
2. Too many reporters began asking too many tough questions so the Senators ended their televised session immediately.
3. Urban and suburban development increasingly encroaches on wildlife havens yet people are surprised to discover wild animals wandering through city streets.
4. A single classroom set of the new biology texts arrived and we quickly stowed them away on shelves in the closet.
5. Computers can already take dictation and, soon even little notebooks will be as powerful as mainframes.

_____

Use a Comma to Join Very Short Complete Thoughts if Similarly Constructed

I came, I saw, I left.
We sang, we laughed, we danced all night.

Use a Comma after Most Introductory Elements

Yes, the cells duplicated themselves.
First, we must organize a committee.
Besides Carol, Gene and Roseanne are going.
To think critically, you must see hidden differences and similarities.
"Whatever you really learn, you teach yourself." (Berthoff 9)

If a sentence begins with a long phrase, series of phrases, or an incomplete thought containing a verb, use a comma.

Looking at the sky, I noticed a hawk.
Rereading essays, underlining key ideas, memorizing definitions, I studied for my exam.
"While we are free to choose our actions, we are not free to choose the consequences of those actions." (Covey 90)

ACTIVITY 15

Decide whether these sentences are properly punctuated. If you see any punctuation problem(s), see if you can correct them. Try to explain any errors you find.

1. Reaching for the gravy Bud accidentally spilled it all over the table.
2. After the mixture comes to a boil you must carefully add the sodium.
3. When the bell rang the two battlers staggered toward each other.
4. Although apparently sober Jeeter was unable to convince the officers that he should be allowed to drive his car home.
5. Pine boards, various nails and screws, preconstructed building elements, wiring and plumbing, began to arrive early in the morning before the builders had arrived.

Use a Comma to Separate Items in a Series

I had stopped on my way from the airport at a nearby supermarket and purchased some turkey, potato salad, macaroni salad, and bagels. (Albom, <u>Tuesdays with Morrie</u> 48)

When a series of items is the subject of a sentence, do not insert a comma after the last item—do not separate the subject from its verb.

Dates, places, and the names of presidents were all she could remember.
Not: Dates, places, and the names of presidents, were all she could remember.]
Newspapers, magazines, and books covered Don's floor.
[Not: Newspapers, magazines, and books, covered Don's floor.]

Use a Comma between Movable Adjectives

If adjectives describe the same word and can be rearranged without loss of meaning, separate them with commas. A good test is to ask whether the word <u>and</u> could be inserted between them. If so, use commas.

It was an entertaining, unusual experience.
(It was an entertaining [and] unusual experience.)
The Victorian house reminds me of a sweet, old, charming lady.
(The Victorian house reminds me of a sweet [and] old [and] charming lady.)

Use Commas to Set Off a Group of Nonessential Words

Ernest Hemingway, author of <u>The Old Man and the Sea</u>, spent many years fishing off the coast of Havana. Hemingway is so famous that it is not necessary to identify him as the author (set off the identifying information).

Setting the descriptive phrase off this way indicates there is (was) only one Ernest Hemingway and the description is not necessary to identify him. If there were two Hemingways, you might need the descriptive, explanatory information to tell readers which one you mean. Other examples:

The young woman, the one we are discussing, entered MIT.
Katie, on the other hand, loved to dance.
The idea, it occurred to me, just might work.
The plan, or at least the latest version of it, was not well received.

<u>Note</u>: You can use dashes instead of commas for more emphasis.

Use Commas to Set Off Contrastive Elements

The issue concerns people, not politics.
He's a great guy, but spoiled.
Most students volunteered, yet some did nothing.

Use Commas to Separate Dialogue from the Rest of a Sentence

She asked, "How can you distinguish between the dancer and the dance?"
"It's not who wins," he said bitterly, "but how much you get paid."

Note: Commas and periods go inside quotation marks.

Use Commas Correctly in Dates and Addresses

Amber was born on May 16, 2000, at Greenville General Hospital.
Ann Arbor, Michigan, is still Spencer's permanent address.

(Notice especially the commas after 2000 and Michigan)
When the day precedes the month, no commas are required:

She was born 16 May 2000.

Use a Comma after Openings and Closings of Any Letter

Dear Mark,	Dear Mom,	Hi, Honey,
Sincerely,	Love,	With best wishes,

Use Commas for Clarity

Sometimes you may need to use a comma to prevent ambiguity or misreading.

Those who can teach the rest of us.   [?]
Those who can, teach the rest of us.
Having eaten the children went quietly to bed.   [?]
Having eaten, the children went quietly to bed.

Overuse of Commas

Use a comma before a word such as and, but, or only if the word joins two complete thoughts. The comma is a signal to readers. But with a compound verb, use no comma. For example: "She wrote and proofread her paper." Without the comma you tell your readers that you have written one sentence with a compound verb: wrote and proofread.

Bob typed his paper carefully and handed it in the next morning.
[Not: Bob typed his paper carefully, and handed it in the next morning.]
She shrugged her shoulders and walked away.
[Not: She shrugged her shoulders, and walked away.]
We found our way to the train station and called our host family.
[Not: We found our way to the train station, and called our host family.]

ACTIVITY 16

Try to fix punctuation errors, if any, in these sentences. Try to explain any errors you find.

1. <u>Time</u>, <u>Newsweek</u>, <u>USA Today</u>, were our favorite news sources.
2. The campus police impounded Rachelle's car, and took her to the Public Safety building.
3. Shakespeare the great English playwright wrote <u>Hamlet</u> and <u>King Lear</u>.
4. The politicians each asserted "My opponent is mistaken about the facts."
5. The children were told to send their letters to Mrs. Morgan at 665 Green Street, Saginaw Michigan.
6. There's no sense in using the bed for eating bread crumbs get all over the place.
7. The school was used for many other community activities not just education.
8. "Not me" Avol insisted "I'm not going in there for anything!"
9. The Snack Shop promised a soul-lifting simply divine malted milkshake.
10. Japanese aircraft attacked Pearl Harbor on December 7 1941 "A day that will live in infamy" according to then President Franklin Delano Roosevelt.

Semicolons and a Complex Series

Use semicolons to separate items in a series containing commas:

> The United States has several observatories, such as the Palomar, near San Diego, California; Mount Wilson, near Pasadena, California; McDonald, near Fort Davis, Texas; and Kitt Peak, near Tucson, Arizona.

> A report from the National Center for Clinical Infant Programs makes the point that school success is not predicted by a child's fund of facts or a precocious ability to read so much as by emotional and social measures: being self-assured and interested; knowing what kind of behavior is expected and how to rein in the impulse to misbehave; being able to wait, to follow directions, and to turn to teachers for help; and expressing needs while getting along with other children. (Goleman 193)

> This month, she has learned three things essential to being a human: she has learned to eat tiny occasional spoons of rice cereal, food other than mother's milk; she has learned to raise herself up straight on arms and toe points, in a push-up that allows her to look over the edge of her bassinet; and she has learned to laugh. (Erdrich 81)

Using semicolons to divide elements within in a complex list can involve phrases or complete thoughts between the semicolons.

Exclamation Mark

The exclamation mark is seldom used in formal writing. But in informal writing it can be used—usually in dialogue—to indicate excitement, shouting, or extreme emphasis.

> What a disgusting thing to say!

Using more than one exclamation mark at a time is seldom appropriate.

Parentheses

Use Parentheses to Set Off Clarifying Information

Parentheses set off clarifying information or information not grammatically connected to the sentence.

> The affliction (anorexia nervosa) is an eating disorder that strikes mostly girls and young women.
>
> Repeating <u>people</u> for emphasis, Lincoln wanted "a government of the <u>people</u>, by the <u>people</u>, for the <u>people</u>" (emphasis added).

The phrase "(emphasis added)" tells readers that you underlined the word <u>people</u> in the quote. The MLA recommends against underlining for emphasis in formal writing, especially adding emphasis to source material.

When it becomes necessary for one parenthetic element to fall within another, the first element is set off with dashes and the second with parentheses.

> The reader may forget the explanation too, or—as for tables (above)—may look at the figures before reading the text. (O'Connor, <u>How to Copyedit Scientific Books & Journals</u> 88)

Use Full Parentheses to List or Outline

> This method requires that: (1) the gene be properly constructed and inserted for expression because it is the protein targeted for detection, and (2) the protein be isolated and purified from its natural source, which is then used to raise antibodies. (Wong 86)

The half-parenthesis is not used in MLA or APA styles. Avoid punctuation such as the following:

> We knew that 1) there was too much salt, and 2) we could not account for any of it.

Brackets

Most computers and typewriters today have square brackets, but if yours doesn't, you should draw them in with a pen. Brackets set off clarifying material you insert into quotations.

> Four score [80] and seven years ago our fathers brought forth on this continent a new nation.

President Lincoln did not have the word "80" in his speech, and we do not have the right to alter his words. Therefore, we call attention to the fact that we are adding something to his speech, to clarify a term that is no longer familiar to many readers.

Use "Sic" to Indicate Errors in Quotes

To indicate an error in material you quote, use the word <u>sic</u>, meaning "thus the error was" in the original. In MLA style of documentation, use parentheses around <u>sic</u>.

MLA Style

> "Many people are anxious to continue with cloning research because they believe cloning will allow them to become immoral" (sic). [<u>sic</u> tells readers <u>immoral</u> was not your mistake; it was in the original]

> In his review of the film <u>American Beauty</u>, Jamey Houghton writes, "Some will enjoy the film merely for it's (sic) dead-on portrayal of a present day nuclear family." ["it's" means "it is"; "its" without an apostrophe is needed]

The APA style requires "sic" to be underlined and enclosed in brackets: [<u>sic</u>]. APA's rule is that if you find an error in something you are quoting, you are required to copy the error, but immediately after the error, in square brackets give [<u>sic</u>]. Note the placement inside the sentence period for both MLA and APA.

APA Style

> Our expedition found itself standard [<u>sic</u>] on the Galapagos islands until they realized we were late and sent a boat for us. [<u>sic</u> tells readers "standard" was not your error; it was in the original]

ACTIVITY 17

Try to correct any punctuation errors in these sentences. Give a very brief explanation for each error, such as "half-paren."

1. It is likely many scientists agree that a retrovirus is responsible for acquired immune deficiency syndrome (AIDS).
2. After the television show about the White House (<u>West Wing</u>) the show's producers received letters and phone calls from Miami, Florida, Phoenix, Arizona, Dallas, Texas, Los Angeles, California, and other cities all over the country.
3. We can see that there are at least three major fears about cloning: 1) dangers to the infant, physical fears and 2) psychological fears that the cloned child may grow up "different" from other children and 3) ethical fears, fears that cloning may be immoral—playing God.
4. MLA's style sheet helps readers of your paper on human cloning see that you aren't "cowning sic around."
5. We hold these truths to be self-evident that all men [all people] are created equal. . . .
6. Arturo worked night and day to finish his Ph.D..
7. The Connecticut Cooking Club prepared pies, and cakes for the workers repairing the old church.
8. Furthermore no one has been accused of filching here.
9. Until the children stop making so much racket the TV remains off.
10. Wieners, potato salad, burgers, and lemonade, were the picnic "fixins."

Quotation Marks: How to Quote from Sources

Quoting from sources is a serious activity, especially in research writing. It's important to get your quotations accurate by applying quotation marks properly.

ACTIVITY 18

See if you can fix errors concerning quotation marks in the following sentences. Don't worry if you are uncertain about your answers; we will review the rules after the activity. See if you can give brief explanations for any errors you find, for example "poem title."

1. "Newsweek" carried an article on the use of pig organs in human beings.
2. Amy Wu, in her essay, Stop the Clock, asserts that she "is a failure at housework.
3. The last word of the King James Bible is Amen.
4. We found an article called <u>The Last Word in Cloning</u> in an old copy of "Esquire."
5. Government of the people, by the people, and for the people, Lincoln said.
6. Speaking to a large crowd, Velva said, Never again shall we know the agonies of worldwide depression; she would have said more but the audience burst into applause at just that moment.

7. Over the faulty old public address system, the students heard the principal apparently saying, hot hogs and silly for bunch today.

8. In his article on gun control, Mitch Albom offered his theory that 'we live in an age of hair trigger-tempers—and that is no place for hair-trigger weapons'.

9. "My favorite poem is Robert Frost's Stopping by Woods on a Snowy Evening," Vonny said.

10. Ms. Remington asked the eighth graders, What is Poe's poem The Raven really about.

<u>Please don't read on until you have finished the activity</u>.

Copying and Quoting

Use Quotation Marks for Any Words You Copy from a Source

Quoting a word:	Sowell repeats "stampede" three times in his essay.
Quoting a phrase:	Tannen argues that we live in an "argument culture."
Quoting a sentence:	Tannen writes, "The argument culture urges us to approach the world, and the people in it, in an adversarial frame of mind."

Some Exceptions to the Quotation Rules

Indirect quotes give a report of what someone said, not the actual speech by that person.

Indirect:	The boss told us we would have to start looking for new jobs.
Direct:	The boss said, "You will all have to start looking for new jobs."

Rhetorical questions are questions asked for effect and are not intended to elicit answers. They can sometimes be a way to avoid harsh statements.

Harsh statement:	"No one can get a new job now."
Rhetorical question:	"Who can find new jobs under these conditions?"

Internal thoughts, monologues, and conversations with yourself need quotation marks.

"I wonder what they meant by that? Should I say something back? No, better simply to let it pass, I think."

Long Quotations Do Not Use Quotation Marks

MLA style requires writers to indent (set off or block display) quotations of four or more lines. APA style requires writers to set off (indent) any quotation longer than 40 words.

Indent all lines of a long quotation <u>10 spaces</u> from the left margin (APA says 5 spaces), and type the quote double-spaced. Do not indent from the right-hand margin; do not attempt to make all the lines the same length. To indent 10 spaces and to also use quotation marks around a long quote is redundant: use quotation marks for shorter quotes only.

Long quotations should be copied exactly as you find them, including any quotation marks you find <u>within</u> them. Parenthetic references come after the final sentence period in both MLA and APA styles.

Indented Quote

```
       Everyone should read Robert Pirsig's Zen and the Art of
Motorcycle Maintenance; it contains many insights. For exam-
ple, Pirsig writes:
               The real cycle you're working on is a cycle called
               yourself. The machine that appears to be "out there"
               and the person that appears to be "in here" are not
               two separate things. They grow toward Quality or
               fall away from Quality together. (319)
       This makes sense to me. I should care about my car and try to
       keep it running well, and I should care about my mind and body
       and try to keep them running well. Somehow we're connected.
```

When using a long quote (four or more lines), do not add quotation marks around it. Do not indicate the beginning of a single quoted paragraph with a paragraph indentation. However, if you display two or more full paragraphs, indent the first line of each paragraph an additional three spaces.

Vary the Way You Use Direct Quotes

Here is the first line of a paragraph in Deborah Tannen's <u>You Just Don't Understand</u> (97):

Not only men disparage an interest in the details of people's lives as "gossip."

Usually, you need only place the sentence in double marks to quote it; however, this sentence already contains text in double marks: "gossip." (It makes no difference how many words are involved but see Indented Quote.) To avoid having two sets of double marks, you must replace the internal double marks with single quotes.

In the following, note the single quotation marks around <u>gossip</u>, placement of comma inside all quote marks, and placement of citation inside the end-of-sentence mark (the period).

Direct Quote Begins a Sentence

"Not only men disparage an interest in the details of people's lives as 'gossip,' " Tannen writes (97).

Direct Quote Ends a Sentence

Tannen writes, "Not only men disparage an interest in the details of people's lives as 'gossip' " (97).

Direct Quote Interrupted

"Not only men," says Tannen, "disparage an interest in the details of people's lives as 'gossip' " (97).

<u>Note:</u> where to interrupt Tannen's sentence is not a random decision. You need to consider what the interruption will do to Tannen's style, the effect on the flow of her sentence, the distortion or emphasis on Tannen's thought, and the possible distraction for your reader.

Use Quotation Marks around Material Incorporated into Your Own Sentences

In a <u>Newsweek</u> essay, "Burned Out and Bored," Professor Ronald Dahl says one of the more disturbing problems for parents today may be the "rising rates of psychiatric problems among children and adolescents in our society" (18).

The quotation has been "incorporated" into the grammar of the sentence and does not require a comma. Incorporated means it is part of the sentence; if you didn't see it printed this way, you wouldn't hear where the quote marks go. There is no signal for the quotation.

Use Quotation Marks around Words Used in a Special Sense or Words Misused Intentionally

Seymour wondered if college ever involved "lower" education, not higher.
My "friend" took my credit card and never told me.

Use Quotation Marks to Indicate Dialogue

"Papa?"
"Yes, June."
"Tell me about the most-most."

> For an instant he did not remember. "Ah," he said, "you mean that club in New York where people are the most of everything."
> "That's the story." (Bellow 295–96)

Note that each change of speaker requires a new line and a paragraph indentation.

Use Quotation Marks for Titles of Short Works and Divisions within Longer Works

Essays: "Stop the Clock" by Amy Wu
Poems: "A Dream Deferred" by Langston Hughes

Titles of book-length poems such as <u>The Odyssey</u> are underlined.

> Short stories: "A Good Man Is Hard to Find" by Flannery O'Connor
> Newspaper articles: "Don't Shoot Holes in Gun Control Bills" by Mitch Albom, <u>Detroit Free Press</u>
> Magazine articles: "The Swooshification of the World" by Rick Reilly, <u>Sports Illustrated</u>
> Book chapters: "Different Words, Different Worlds"—chapter 1 in <u>You Just Don't Understand</u> by Deborah Tannen
> Popular songs and specific works on albums (record, tape, cassettes, CDs): "Every Breath You Take" by Sting

Commas and Periods Go inside the Quotation Marks

Commas and periods go inside the quotation marks, no matter how many quote marks you have—unless you cite a page number.

We heard the boy shout, "Don't you call me a 'pig.' "

Morrie did not want to be "useless."

Morrie did not want to be "useless," but he needed help from a live-in nurse.

But Note:

Morrie did not want to be "useless" (12).

Using Other Punctuation with Quotation Marks

Colons and semicolons always go outside quotation marks.

<u>Affect</u> means "to influence": e.g., the weather <u>affects</u> my mood.
Dale called her brief poem "Moonlight of Autumn"; it was sweet and romantic.
The article said, "We will soon have the ability to engineer in or out specific genetic attributes"; "how soon, then," Matt wondered, "before we decide all babies should be blue-eyed and blonde?"

Question marks and exclamation marks go either inside or outside the quotation marks, depending on the quoted matter.

Quoted Matter Is Not a Question

Are we going to follow the example of history: "If we <u>can</u> do it, we <u>will</u> do it"?

Quoted Matter Is a Question

The scientists wondered, "Is it possible to stop this madness?"

Both Quoted Matter and Not-Quoted Matter Are Questions

Do you know the song "Oh Where Has My Little Dog Gone?"

Exclamation

"No, the name of the Beatles reflects music, not insects!" I said.

Using Single Quotation Marks

Use single quotation marks around a word or group of words quoted within a sentence.

Cathy asked, "Have you read Salinger's story 'A Perfect Day for Bananafish'?"
"Harry is really being difficult," Lori complained. "He said, 'Do it yourself,' when I asked him to help me clean the room."
Mitch Albom writes about Morrie, "He was intent on proving that the word 'dying' was not synonymous with 'useless' "(12).

Theoretically, by alternating double and single marks, there might be no end to the number of embedded quotes you could write. But as a practical matter, you should probably rethink your sentence rather than have more than two or three sets of marks.

Can you explain the placement of the question mark in this sentence? Why is it placed after the single quote?

The survey asked, "Do you believe the statement, 'It is unethical and should be illegal for science to attempt to produce "better babies" '?"

Question Marks

Use a Question Mark after a Direct Question

Will cloning humans be all bad?
Did you cite page numbers after your quotes?

Indirect questions require no question mark:

She wondered why nobody liked her.

He asked whether she could help him with physics.

Use a Question Mark for a Question Embedded in a Statement

A democracy needs citizens who can understand complex political issues, philosophic principles, and social values (how else can we decide questions about abortion, equality, civil liberties, and all the rest?).

Ellipsis

Use an Ellipsis Enclosed in Brackets to Indicate Omission of Words

Use three ellipsis points enclosed in brackets to indicate you have omitted one or more words from quoted matter. The use of brackets tells readers the ellipsis dots do not appear in the original quote. The ellipsis requires a space before and after each of its three periods. When the ellipsis comes at the end of a sentence, the sentence period becomes the fourth point. The ending ellipsis can indicate a few words omitted, or it can indicate several sentences have been omitted.

Suppose you wanted to omit the words we underlined in the following quote from Tuesdays with Morrie.

Quoted Matter

He is a small man who takes small steps, <u>as if a strong wind could, at any time, whisk him up into the clouds. In his graduation day robe, he looks like a cross between a biblical prophet and a Christmas elf.</u> He has sparkling blue-green eyes, thinning silver hair that spills onto his forehead, big ears, a triangular nose, and tufts of graying eyebrows. Although his teeth are crooked <u>and his lower ones are slanted back—as if someone had punched them in</u>—when he smiles it's as if you'd just told him the first joke on earth. (3–4)

Quoted Matter with Ellipsis

He is a small man who takes small steps [. . .]. He has sparkling blue-green eyes, thinning silver hair that spills onto his forehead, big ears, a triangular nose, and tufts of graying eyebrows. Although his teeth are crooked [. . .] when he smiles it's as if you'd just told him the first joke on earth. (3–4)

Slash

Use a slash to incorporate two or three lines of poetry within your text: with a space on each side (/) to indicate line breaks. It is often better to "incorporate" a line or two than to set them off as a block quote. Incorporating them into your own sentence makes for smoother reading and less distraction for your readers. But you must use slashes to indicate the line breaks in poetry.

> Whitman begins "Song of Myself" with three memorable lines: "I celebrate myself, / And what I assume you shall assume, / For every atom belonging to me as good belongs to you." The lines not only grow in length but also in the speaker's connection with readers—with humanity.

ACTIVITY 19

Try to correct any errors of quotation marks or other associated punctuation errors in these sentences, including end-of-sentence errors. Add needed marks; underline unneeded marks. Try to explain your corrections.

1. One of Robert Frost's famous poems is 'The Road Not Taken'.
2. Estavon said Hello to everyone.
3. "I will tell you what it means:" after a short pause Janelle went on "It means there will be no dinner tonight!"
4. Wannetta insisted 'These are all mine' she was pointing at limes, lemons, oranges, all the citrus bins.
5. Doesn't everyone know President Kennedy's phrase ask not what your country can do for you, ask what you can do for your country?
6. On the witness stand, Lamar swore I have never met Noreen, let alone had a relationship with her.
7. It may be slang, but the word jerk (a person of little value) exactly describes the mentality of those who drive down freeways shooting strangers.
8. The Captain attested that no member of my troop is capable of falsehoods and she offered to prove it.
9. Ms. Deutch asked, "Wilhelm, did you just now say, I hate this stuff?"
10. One of the great tragedies of the twenty-first century was the sinking of the Russian nuclear submarine, <u>Kursk</u>, with the loss of "all 118 hands aboard."

Mechanics

Small matters count in writing. There have been court cases over misplaced or missing commas. Spelling, grammar, and punctuation can make a difference in meaning. Then, too, errors in basics can suggest things about you.

ACTIVITY 20

Try to correct any errors in mechanics in these sentences (apostrophes, hyphens, underlining, capitalization, abbreviations, and numbers). Explain your corrections, if you can. Don't worry about being right or wrong; use your best judgment. We will review mechanics after you try the activity.

1. Johns older sister was to be married in April.
2. The childrens' numerous toys were scattered everywhere.
3. Our governor alleged that there was not a dimes worth of difference between her opponents.
4. The president believes its appropriate to vote for the new fuel bill in congress.
5. The effect on Lancelot of Guineveres kiss' was said to be electrifying.
6. The Marines believed the secret new attack plans were the presidents strategies.
7. Ms Handerton was not prepared for an unannounced reunion with her exhusband.
8. Uncle Charley was of the opinion that postmodern art was delightful despite the opinions of others.
9. Most words beginning with "counter" are spelled without a hyphen as in the word countercharge.
10. For one good introduction to the subject of cloning, you should read Gregory Pence's book Who's Afraid of Human Cloning?
11. The USS Cole was attacked, and badly damaged by a presumed suicide terrorist attack that took the lives of several American sailors at the refueling port in the Gulf of Aden.
12. West Wing, one of the popular television shows of the year 2000 portrayed a liberal president and idealistic administration in the White House.
13. As the great liner pulled away from the dock, those on the shore gave many shouts of bon voyage, hasta la vista and other expressions of good will.
14. Whooping cough, caused by the bacterium, bordetella pertussis was contagious and rampant throughout the early half of the twentieth century.
15. Plato's student, Aristotle, one of the great minds of the ancient world, died in BC 322.

<u>Please finish the activity before reading on.</u>

Apostrophe

Use Apostrophes Correctly to Show Possession

Singular nouns, add **'s**   the boy's bike
a writer's notebook
Tim's video collection

Plural proper nouns ending in **s**, add only the apostrophe   the Joneses' house
the Jameses' dog

All singular proper nouns add apostrophe and <u>s</u>: Mr. Jones's house, Miss James's promotion.

Singular indefinite pronouns, add **'s**   one's options
anyone's problem

Personal pronouns (<u>I</u>, <u>we</u>, <u>us</u>, <u>you</u>, <u>he</u>, <u>she</u>, <u>it</u>) do <u>not</u> use apostrophes to show possession; instead each has a possessive form: <u>my</u>, <u>mine</u>, <u>our</u>, <u>ours</u>, <u>your</u>, <u>yours</u>, <u>his</u>, <u>hers</u>, <u>its</u>, <u>their</u>, <u>theirs</u>. The pronoun <u>it's</u> isn't possessive: it's a contraction of <u>it</u> and <u>is</u> or <u>has</u>:

It's cold out today. It's been cold all week. It's likely to stay cold.

Joint possession, add **'s** to the last owner named	Tom and Susan's computer
Individual ownership, add **'s** to each owner mentioned	Tom's and Susan's computers
Plural nouns ending in **s**, add only the apostrophe	the boys' bikes
the girls' school
Plural nouns not ending in s, add **'s**	the men's shoes
the women's rights
the children's toys
the people's faces
Abstract or inanimate nouns and familiar expressions follow the normal rules	a day's work
life's difficulties
five dollars' worth

Use Apostrophes to Show Omission of Letters in Contractions

Contractions give an informal tone to your writing: they are generally acceptable except in the most formal writing situations:

we're   she'll   you're   haven't   didn't   it's (it is)   isn't

Use Apostrophes to Show Plurals

Words referred to as words, abbreviations, and letters and numerals referred to as symbols form their plurals by adding **'s**.

p's and q's   C.P.A.'s   rpm's   if's, and's, or but's
I used to think 3's were erased 8's.

<u>Note:</u> Apostrophes are not required when dates are treated as collective nouns: 1900s, 1990s.

Hyphen

Use a Hyphen to Connect Compound-Word Modifiers before a Noun

deep-fried mushrooms   ill-conceived plan   well-written essay

Compound-word modifiers after a noun are not hyphenated.

The essay was well written.
The plan is ill conceived.

Hyphenate Words Formed with Certain Prefixes and Suffixes

Words that use the prefixes <u>all-</u>, <u>cross-</u>, <u>ex-</u>, <u>half-</u>, <u>ill-</u>, <u>well-</u>, and <u>self-</u> and the suffix <u>-elect</u> are usually hyphenated.

all-knowing   ex-president   self-conscious   governor-elect

When <u>self</u> is a word's root rather than a prefix, it is not hyphenated.

selfhood   selfish

The following prefixes and suffixes form words that are spelled without hyphens (<u>counterrevolution</u>, <u>extraordinary</u>, <u>twofold</u>, <u>postmodern</u>, <u>underrated</u>, <u>nonfattening</u>):

anti	intra	pro	super
co	like	pseudo	supra
counter	non	re	ultra
extra	over	semi	un

fold	post	sub	under
infra	pre		

<u>Exceptions:</u> Use a hyphen when one of these is attached to a proper noun:

un-American   anti-Communist   ex-New Yorker

Use a Hyphen for Two-Word Numbers

twenty-one   forty-five   three-fifths

Use a Hyphen to Avoid Ambiguity or Confusion

She was excited about the re-creation. [The hyphen is needed to distinguish between <u>re-creation</u> (a reenactment) and <u>recreation</u> (a diversion of some kind).]

Don't Use Hyphens to Divide Words at the End of Lines

Dividing words with hyphens at the end of lines is not accepted in MLA or APA style. When words are too long to fit on the line, move the entire word to the next line. Don't let your computer add hyphens.

Underlining (Italics)

Use Underlining or Italics for Titles of Long Works

Underline titles of most publications: books, booklets, pamphlets, magazines, newspapers, long poems, plays, albums (records, tapes, cassettes, CDs), operas, films, works of art, and the names of radio and television series. Do not underline titles of documents such as the Constitution or the Declaration of Independence.

Many people love the novel <u>The Catcher in the Rye</u>.
Did you ever see <u>X-Files</u> on TV?
I like to read the "My Turn" column in <u>Newsweek</u>.
Jane loves Edward Hopper's painting <u>Cape Cod Morning</u>.

Use Underlining for Words Used as Words

Mr. Spock's characteristic response to anything unusual was his utterance of the word <u>fascinating</u> without any indication of emotion at all, least of all fascination. What does the phrase <u>family values</u> really mean?

Underline Foreign Words and Phrases

I walked away, thinking to myself <u>c'est la vie</u>.
Now the creature has the appearance of a mulberry, and is called a <u>morula</u>, the Latin word for that which it resembles. (Selzer, <u>Letters</u> 160)

Underline the Names of Ships, Planes, and Trains

The <u>Titanic</u> was the largest and most luxurious ship ever built at the time. I like the sounds of the words <u>Nina</u>, <u>Pinta</u>, and <u>Santa Maria</u>.

Underline Scientific Names for Animals and Plants

The doctor announced that I had touched <u>Rhus toxicodendron</u>, poison ivy.

Underline Special or Technical Terms

The <u>hypothalamus</u>, which regulates body temperature, is in the forebrain.

Capitalization

Capitalize the First Word of a Sentence

The only way to become a writer is to write.

Capitalize the First Word of a Quotation

My grandfather told me, "The road is better than the inn."

Do Not Capitalize the First Word of an Incorporated Quote

After all the excitement about the cloned sheep Dolly, the press reported there was "a remote possibility that the cell came from a fetus rather than an adult."

Do Not Capitalize the First Word after a Colon

There is no way to prevent it: a scientist in Chicago announced that he would attempt to clone a human being.

The capitalization rules after a colon differ from one authority to the next. In general, don't.

However, do capitalize the first word after a colon if it begins a question or quote:

This is the question: Where will we find our evidence?
Patrick Henry stated his opinion clearly: "Give me liberty, or give me death."

Capitalize Names, Descriptive Names, and Nicknames

Susan   Homer Peabody   Babe Ruth, "the Sultan of Swat"
Thomas Edison, "the Wizard of Menlo Park"   Magic Johnson

Capitalize the Names of Nationalities and Ethnic Groups

Khmer   German   Tswana   Irish   Indian

Capitalize Words Formed from Proper Nouns

Proper nouns refer to specific things; common nouns refer to general things. Common nouns are not capitalized.

Proper Nouns	Common Nouns
Dr. Richard Selzer	medical doctor
Eureka College	college
Uncle Ernie	my uncle
Ford Ranger	truck
Orion	constellation

Capitalize the Names of Awards, Brand Names, Historical and Cultural Events

the Academy Awards   the Nobel Peace Prize   Labor Day   Rosh Hashana

Do Not Capitalize the Common Names of Most Plants and Animals

oak tree   lily   sparrow   rainbow trout

Do Not Capitalize Derived Words That Have Acquired Special Meaning

french fry   china closet   panama hat   india ink   brazil nut

Do Not Capitalize Generic Terms without Names

asteroid   moon   meteor

Do Not Capitalize a Generic Term When It Comes before a Name

the comet Kohoutek   the asteroid Ceres

Capitalize Religious Terms

Easter   Passover   Eucharist   Ramadan

Do Not Capitalize Religious Objects

rosary   menorah   crucifix

Capitalize Languages, Names with a Degree, Degree Abbreviations, Specific Courses

English   Spanish   French
Indira Nastalia, PhD (or Ph.D.)   Dr. Indira Nastalia
BA   MA   (or B.A.   M.A.)   Math 101

Do Not Capitalize Subjects Other Than Languages

history   social studies   economics

Do Not Capitalize a Degree without a Name

associate   bachelor's   master of arts   doctorate

Do Not Capitalize School Years or Rank

first-year student   sophomore   junior   senior

Capitalize Geographic Features, Places

Ohio   Grand Canyon   Mt. Rushmore   Center Street
Great Bear Lake   Big Two-Hearted River

Do Not Capitalize the Names of Seasons

winter   spring   summer   fall

Capitalize Geographical Areas, Not Directions

Capitalize <u>north,</u> <u>south,</u> <u>east,</u> <u>west</u> and their derivatives only when they refer to specific geographical areas, not when they refer to directions.

Bob lived in the South for 10 years before he moved to the East Coast.
From Canada we drove south to Bismark.
To find the drug store, go north two blocks and then west one block.

Capitalize Institutions, Organizations

the Red Cross   Department of Labor   Federal Bureau of Investigation
the Democratic Party   U.S. Congress   General Motors

Capitalize Military Groups, Battles, Wars

Vietnam War   Desert Storm   U.S. Army   U.S. Navy

Do Not Capitalize Informal References
to Military

army   navy   the armed services
Lester is joining the army, and I'm joining the marines.

Capitalize Heavenly Bodies

Mars   Jupiter   comet Halley   asteroid Juno

Capitalize the Names of Ships,
Planes, Trains

Titanic   the Shuttle   Atchison, Topeka, and Santa Fe

Capitalize Titles of Address,
Position, Rank

the Pope   the Queen   Mrs. or Ms. Clinton   Dr. Philip Truman

Do Not Capitalize Titles of Office
without Names or When the Name Comes First

the governor   Chris Brown, governor   Governor Chris Brown
the president   President Clinton
the senator   Senator Kennedy

Do Not Capitalize Family Members
Except in Place of/or with Names

my mother   your sister   Aunt Jane
We believe Mother will be elected to the task force.

Capitalize Important Words in Titles
of Publications, Documents

Capitalize the first word, the last word, and all significant words between, except articles (a, an, the), prepositions (in, to, of, from, by . . .), and conjunctions (and, but, or).

We read two stories by Flannery O'Connor: "A Temple of the Holy Ghost" and "The Life You Save May Be Your Own."

The journal article "The Uses and Ethics of Cloning" surprised me.

Robertson, John. "Human Cloning and the Challenge of Regulation." <u>New England Journal of Medicine</u> 339.2 (1998): 119–22.

Do Not Use "the" as Part of a Newspaper Title in Your Works Cited (MLA style)

Kolata, Gina. "A Child's Paper Poses a Medical Challenge." <u>New York Times</u>. 1 Apr. 1998: A1.

But use the full title in your text (MLA style).

I enjoy the film reviews in the <u>The New York Times</u>.
[see chapter 9 for APA style]

Abbreviations and Numbers

Abbreviate Titles before and after Names

Dr. Smith   Cathy Smith, PhD (or Ph.D.)   Ms. Jones   Martin Luther King Jr.
Rev. David Hooper   John Stone, MD (or M.D.)

Abbreviate Institutions, Companies, Agencies, Organizations

Public Broadcasting Corp.   PBS   YMCA   CIA   FBI

Abbreviate Time, Dates, and Measures with Specific Numbers

12:00 AM or A.M. (or A.M. [small caps] or a.m.)   3:00 PM or P.M. (or P.M. or p.m.)
500 BC [or B.C.]   AD 55 or A.D. 55 [note the order of BC and AD dates]

Other acceptable variations for BC are BCE and B.C.E. (before the common era).

12 qts.   No. 6   9 mm.

Latin abbreviations are still used by some writers. Ask your instructor about using them.

e.g. (for example)   i.e. (that is)   etc. (and so forth)

Robert De Niro has starred in many great films (e.g., <u>Taxi Driver</u>, <u>The Deer Hunter</u>, and <u>Raging Bull</u>).

Many readers are unfamiliar with these abbreviations and for them the English equivalents are generally preferable.

Spell Out Numbers Expressed as One or Two Words

twelve   sixty-eight   forty million

Use Numerals for Numbers Expressed as More Than Two Words

1,568   7,120,000 $3^{1}/_{2}$

Spell Out Numbers That Start Sentences

Two hundred and fifty-two students graduated.

Scientific writing generally prefers numbers:

The vial held 2 drops of solution.

The experiment required 12 mice as subjects.

ACTIVITY 21

Try to correct any errors in capitalization in these sentences. Explain your corrections, if you can.

1. Children enjoy the sounds of nursery rhymes like little miss muffett sat on a tuffet long before they are able to comprehend them.
2. Halley's comet is named for the british astronomer Edmund Halley, who died in the eighteenth century.
3. She is an excellent professor, about whom her students have said: "she has an excellent command of her subject."
4. Each branch of the military wants its own air force: could such redundancy of weaponry be one of the causes of our budgetary overruns?
5. After the speeches the audience was left somewhat puzzled: what, after all, was the point?
6. President Carter was commonly known as jimmy by most of the country.
7. I love visiting yellowstone national park.

8. The sparrows we have always, but the Robins arrive with spring each year, about mid-march.

9. A likely first-year student schedule would contain some math, english, history, and biology, and possibly a second language like french or german.

10. The great chief, sitting bull surprised and killed colonel custer and approximately 200 soldiers at the battle of little bighorn.

USAGE

"Usage" refers to customs and traditions of language use (or disuse) of certain words or word forms accepted by educated readers and writers. There may not be 100% agreement about some usage items; language use changes over time. For example, the word "ain't" was once considered polite usage, but today it is considered extremely illiterate and is seldom found in educated language.

<u>Note:</u> The authors regret the loss of the Usage Glossary from the book. The length of the book has made it necessary to cut the usage section. However, for instructor's benefits, we have included the missing usage material in the Instructor's Manual on-line. You are free to reproduce both the glossary and its activities for your students.

Bibliography

Ager, Susan. "Cool Comfort Steals Summer's Seasoning." Detroit Free Press 17 Aug. 1993: 1D.

---."Baby, Baby, Baby, Three Has Its Charms." Detroit Free Press 15 Nov. 1994: 1D.

Albom, Mitch. Tuesdays with Morrie. New York: Bantam Doubleday Dell, 1997.

---. "Don't Shoot Holes in Gun Control Bills." Detroit Free Press 19 Nov. 1997: 1F.

---. "Detroit Will Rue Its Deal with Devil." Detroit Free Press 1 Aug. 1999: 1G.

Alter, Jonathan. "Diana's Real Legacy." Newsweek 15 Sept. 1997: 60–62.

Andrews, Lori B. "Human Cloning: Assessing the Ethical and Legal Quandaries." The Chronicle of Higher Education 13 Feb. 1998: B4.

Baldwin, James. Notes of a Native Son. New York: Dial Press, 1963.

Barry, Dave. "The Evil Eye." In Dave Barry Is from Mars and Venus. New York: Random House/Alfred A. Knopf, 1997.

Bauby, Jean-Dominique. The Diving Bell and the Butterfly. New York: Knopf, 1997.

Beck, Joan. "Gore's Tear-Jerking Speech Belies Tobacco Background." Detroit Free Press 4 Sept. 1996: 9A.

Begley, Sharon. "Little Lamb, Who Made Thee?" Newsweek 10 Mar. 1007: 53–59.

Belenkey, Mary Field, Blythe McVicker Clinchy, Nancy Rule Goldberger, and Jill Mattuck Tarule. Women's Ways of Knowing: The Development of Self, Voice, and Mind. New York: Basic Books/HarperCollins, 1986.

Bellow, Saul. Herzog. New York: Viking Press, 1961.

Bennett, William. "Leave Marriage Alone." Newsweek 3 June 1996: 27.

Berry, R. J. "Between God and Darwin." The Christian Science Publishing Society 1999. <http://www.csmonitor.com/>.

Berthoff, Ann. Forming/Thinking/Writing. Portsmouth, NH: Boynton/Cook, 1982.

Best, Steve. "When Elephants Weep." Rev. of When Elephants Weep: The Emotional Lives of Animals, by Jeffrey Moussaief Masson and Susan McCarthy. New York: Delacorte, 1995. <http://www.uta.edu/english/dab/illuminations/best4.html>.

Blake, W. "A Poison Tree," in Laurence Perrine, Sound and Sense, 7th ed. New York: Harcourt, Brace, Jovanovich, 1987.

---. "Marriage of Heaven and Hell," in William Blake, ed. Michael Mason. Oxford: Oxford University Press, 1988.

"Blowing Smoke on Teens." USA Today 3 Jan. 1996: 10A.

Boyer, Ernest. "The Legacy of Ernest Boyer, 'Evangelist of Education.'" The Chronicle of Higher Education 5 Jan. 1996: A18.

Bruce, Robert. "1997 General Assembly Report—Cloning Animals and Humans." Society, Religion and Technology Project of the Church of Scotland 4 Apr. 1997. <http://www.srtp.org.uk/ga97clon.htm>

Bruner, Jerome. The Process of Education. Cambridge: Harvard UP, 1960.

---. Toward a Theory of Instruction. Cambridge: Belknap Press, Harvard UP, 1966.

---. On Knowing: Essays for the Left Hand. New York: Atheneum, 1971.

Butler, Declan. "Poll Reveals Backing for Xenotransplants." Nature 22 Jan. 1998: 315.

Cantor, George. "Internet No Substitute for Real Knowledge." Detroit News, 25 Jan. 1997: C6.

Carlson, Scott. "Lawsuit Pits Two Instructors against Anonymous 'Teacher Review' Postings." The Chronicle of Higher Education 1 June 2000.

Caston, Anne. Flying Out with the Wounded. New York: New York UP, 1997.

Charon, Mona. "Those Racist Cabbies." Jewish World Review 15 Nov. 1999. <http://www.jewishworldreview.com/cols/charen111599.asp>.

Chavez, Linda. "Why I Own a Gun." Jewish World Review 23 Sept. 1999 <http://www.jewish-worldreview.com/cols/chavez092399.asp>.

Chisholm, Shirley. Unbought and Unbossed. Boston: Houghton Mifflin, 1970.

Chitty, Mary. Rev. of Who's Afraid of Cloning?, by Gregory Pence. Library Journal Dec. 1997: 143.

Chopin, Kate. "The Story of an Hour," in The Complete Works of Kate Chopin. Baton Rouge: Louisiana State University Press, 1969.

Clifton, Lucille. "wishes for sons." In quilting: poems 1987–1990. Rochester, NY: BOA Editions, 1991.

---. "jasper texas 1998." In Blessing the Boats: New and Selected Poems 1988–2000. Rochester, NY: BOA Editions.

Clinton, Hillary. "Women's Rights Are Human Rights," Beijing 5 Sept. 1995. <http://www.white-house.gov/wh/eop/first_lady/html/china/plenary.html>

Coates, James. "Internet Is Thick with False Webs of Conspiracy." Chicago Tribune 10 Nov. 1996: 1. <http://archive.chicago.tribune.com>.

Coe, Richard. Process, Form, and Substance: A Rhetoric for Advanced Writers, 2d ed. Englewood Cliffs, NJ: Prentice Hall, 1990.

Cooper, Lane. The Rhetoric of Aristotle. New York: Appleton-Century-Crofts/Meredith Corp., 1932, 1960.

Courtney, Brian A. "Freedom from Choice." [My Turn Column]. Newsweek 13 Feb. 1995: 16.

Covey, Stephen. The Seven Habits of Highly Effective People. New York: Simon & Schuster, 1989.

Crumm, David. "Lives of Nun and Princess Defined by Difference." Detroit News and Free Press 6 Sept. 1997: 1A.

Cummins, Richard. "The Wide World Web and the Quality of Students' Research Papers." The Chronicle of Higher Education 10 Oct. 1997: B3, B12.

Cushman, Thomas. "Questioning a Proposed Dual Tract to Tenure." Letter to the editor. Chronicle of Higher Education, 18 Aug. 1995: B4.

Dahl, Ronald. "Burned Out and Bored." Newsweek 15 Dec. 1997: 18.

Deardorff, Julie, and Andrew Buchanan. "Many See Two Sides to Cloning Debate. Chicago Tribune 24 Feb. 1997.

Deutsch, Linda, and Michael Freeman, "Simpson's a Lying Killer, Lawyer Concludes." Associated Press 22 Jan. 1997: 5A.

Dewey, John. Democracy and Education: An Introduction to the Philosophy of Education. New York: Macmillan, 1924.

---. How We Think: A Restatement of the Relation of Reflective Thinking to the Educative Process. Chicago: Regnery, 1933.

Dillard, Annie. Pilgrim at Tinker Creek. New York: Harper's, 1974.

---. Teaching a Stone to Talk. New York: HarperCollins, 1982.

---. The Writing Life. New York: HarperCollins, 1989.

Dobson, James C. "Sounding the Alarm on Gambling." <u>Focus on Family</u> 1999
<http://www.family.org/cforum/hotissues/A00007064.html>.

Downie, N. M., and R. W. Health. <u>Basic Statistical Methods</u>. 2nd ed. New York: Harper & Row, 1965.

Duff, Nancy. Qtd. in Gina Kolata, <u>Clone: The Road to Dolly, and the Path Ahead.</u> New York: William Morrow, 1998.

Dybek, Stuart. <u>Brass Knuckles</u>. Pittsburgh: U of Pittsburgh Press, 1999.

---. <u>The Coast of Chicago</u>. New York: Knopf, 1990.

Elbow, Peter. <u>Writing without Teachers</u>. New York: Oxford UP, 1973.

---. <u>Writing with Power: Techniques for Mastering the Writing Process</u>. New York: Oxford UP, 1981.

---.<u>Embracing Contraries: Explorations in Learning and Teaching</u>. New York: Oxford UP, 1986.

Erdrich, Louise. <u>The Blue Jay's Dance</u>. New York: HarperCollins, 1985.

Estelman, Loren. "Conversations." <u>Detroit Magazine</u> 4 May 1986: 8.

"Gaming Industry Myths and Facts." Washington, DC: The American Gaming Association, n.d.

Garrow, David J. "Back to Birmingham." <u>Newsweek</u> 21 July 1997: 37.

Goldblatt, Mark. "We're Hard-Wired to Stereotype." <u>The New York Daily News</u> 9 April 1999.

Goleman, Daniel. "The New Thinking on Smarts." <u>USA Weekend</u> 8–10 Sept. 1995: 7.

---. <u>Emotional Intelligence</u>. New York: Bantam, 1995.

Goodman, Ellen. "In the Male Direction." <u>Keeping in Touch</u>. New York: Summit Books, 1985.

---. "On Being a Journalist." In <u>Close to Home</u>. Washington, DC: The Washington Post Co., 1979.

---. "Linking Crime, Abortion Rates Makes Everyone Queasy." <u>Boston Globe</u> 15 Aug. 1999: F7.

Gould, Stephen Jay. <u>Bully for Brontosaurua: Reflections in Natural History</u>. New York: Norton, 1991.

Graves, Donald. <u>Writing: Teachers & Children at Work.</u> Exeter, Eng.: Heinemann, 1984.

Gray, John. <u>Men, Women and Relationships</u>. New York: HarperCollins, 1993.

Greene, Bob. "His Name Was Eric; He Wouldn't Steal, So His Life Was Stolen." <u>Chicago Tribune</u> 20 Oct. 1994: 19D.

"Gun Control." The American Civil Liberties Union 1996
<http://www.aclu.org/library/aaguns.html>.

Haiman, Franklyn. "Even Ugly Speech Deserves Protection."
<http://www.trib.com/FACT/1st.oped.haiman.html>.

Harjo, Joy. "I Give You Back." In <u>She Had Some Horses</u>. New York: Thunder's Mouth Press, 1983.

Harris, Sydney J. <u>Winners and Losers</u>. Allen, TX: Argus, 1968.

---. "Hate Is Simple, Love Complex." In <u>Pieces of Eight</u>. Boston: Houghton Mifflin, 1982.

Hayakawa, S. I., and Alan Hawakawa. <u>Language in Thought and Action</u>, 4th ed. New York: Harcourt, 1978.

Hemingway, Ernest. "The End of Something." In <u>In Our Time</u>. New York: Charles Scribner's Sons, 1925.

Hickey, Dona J. <u>Developing a Written Voice</u>. Mountainview, CA: Mayfield, 1993.

"Hip Hop Homophobe: Armed and Dangerous." Triangle Foundation. <http://www.tri.org>.

Hovind, Kent. "Dr. Hovind's $250.000 Offer." Creation Science Evangelism.
<http://www.drdino.com/Articles/Article1.htm>.

Hughes, Langston. "That Word Black," from <u>The Return of Simple</u>. New York: Hill & Wang, 1994.

"Human Cloning Requires a Moratorium, Not a Ban." Editorial. <u>Nature</u> 6 Mar. 1997: 1.

"Induced Abortion." The Alan Guttmacher Institute 1998.

Jeans, James. "Why the Sky Is Blue." In <u>The Stars in Their Courses</u>. New York: Cambridge UP, 1931.

Johnson, Thomas H., ed. <u>The Poems of Emily Dickinson</u>. Cambridge, MA: The Belknap Press of Harvard University Press.

Kalb, Claudia. "Our Embattled Ears." <u>Newsweek</u> 25 Aug. 1997.

Kane, Gregory. "Selling Bodies and Souls." Detroit News 6 Nov. 1997: 33D.

King, Stephen. "Why We Crave Horror Movies." Playboy 1982: 15-54, 237-46.

Koestler, Arthur. The Act of Creation. New York: Dell, 1964.

Kolata, Gina. Clone: The Road to Dolly and the Path Ahead. New York: Morrow, 1998.

Kozol, Jonathan. Illiterate America. New York: Doubleday, 1985.

---. Savage Inequalities: Children in America's Schools. New York: Crown, 1991.

Krauthammer, Charles. "Of Healess Mice... and Men: The Ultimate Cloning Horror: Human Organ Farms." Time 19 Jan. 1998: 76.

LaPierre, Wayne. "Standing Guard." National Rifle Association of America.

Larrabee, John. "Advocates Say Animals Are More Than Property." USA Today 28 Aug. 1997: 1–2.

Laurence, William. "Atomic Bombing of Nagasaki." New York Times 9 Sept. 1945.

Lee, Li-Young. Rose. Rochester, NY: BOA Editions, 1986.

Levy, Seteven. "World Wide Wake." Newsweek 15 Sept. 1997: 66.

Macrorie, Ken. Telling Writing. New York: Hayden, 1970.

"Marijuana, Tobacco Use Still Increasing Among Adolescents." <http://www.britannica.com/bcom/magazine/0, 6744,250156,00.html>.

Mautner, Michael. "Will Cloning End Human Evolution?" Futurist Nov.–Dec. 1997: 68.

May, Rollo. The Courage to Create. New York: Bantam, 1975.

"McVeigh Attorney: Don't Be Swayed by Sympathy." Morning Sun [Alma, MI.] 30 May 1997: 13.

"Medicine Attacks Cold Virus." The Morning Sun [Alma, MI] 1 Oct. 1997: 2.

Medved, Michael. "Hollywood's Poison Factory." Imprimus Nov. 1992: 2.

Moffett, James. Coming on Center: Essays in English Education. Portsmouth, NH: Boynton/Cook, 1981.

Noyes, Dorothy. "Senior-Teener, A New Hybrid." ["My Turn" column] Newsweek 5 Sept. 1994: 15.

Nye, Naomi Shihab. Words under the Words: Selected Poems. Portland, OR: Far Corner Books, 1995.

O'Connor, Flannery. Mystery and Manners. New York: The Noonday Press/Farrar, Straus & Giroux, 1957.

Oech, Roger von. A Whack on the Side of the Head. New York: Warner Books, 1983.

Olds, Sharon. The Wellspring. New York: Knopf, 1996.

Orwell, George. "Politics and the English Language," from Shooting an Elephant and Other Essays. New York: Harcourt, 1946.

Paul, Richard. Critical Thinking: What Every Person Needs to Survive in a Rapidly Changing World. Santa Rosa, CA: Foundation for Critical Thinking, 1993.

Peck, M. Scott. People of the Lie: On the Hope for Healing Human Evil. New York: Simon & Schuster, 1983.

Pipher, Mary. The Shelter of Each Other. New York: Ballantine, 1996.

Pirsig, Robert. Zen and the Art of Motorcycle Maintenance. New York: Bantam Books, 1974.

Pitts, Leonard, Jr. "No Contest: Books Beat Sport Anytime." Detroit Free Press 30 Aug. 1996: 1F.

Plath, Sylvia. Crossing the Water. New York: HarperCollins, 1960.

"Popular Music under Siege" American Civil Liberties Union 1996. <http://www.aclu.org/library/pbr3.html>

Prescott, Jeffrey. "New Facts on Racial Profiling." The Christian Science Monitor 10 May 2000.

Prothrow-Stith, Deborah. Deadly Consequences. New York: HarperCollins, 1991.

Quindlen, Anna. "Whoever We Are, Loss Finds Us and Defines Us." Detroit Free Press 5 June 1994: 11A.

---. "The Problem of the Color Line." 13 March 2000. <http://www. Newsweek.com/nw-srv/printed/us/dept/lw/a17047-2000mar5.htm>.

"Race, Crime and Justice." The Christian Century 117, no. 11 (5 April 200): 379.

Reilly, Rick. "The Swooshification of the World." Sports Illustrated 24 Feb. 1997: 78.

"Reproductive Technologies." Encyclopedia of Bioethics. Vol. 4 New York: Simon & Schuster, 1995.

Rodriquez, Richard. "Complexion." Hunger of Memory: The Education of Richard Rodriguez. Boston: David R. Grodine, 1981.

Roethke, Theodore. The Collected Poems of Theodore Roethke. New York: Doubleday, 1942.

Root-Bernstein, Robert S. "For the Sake of Science, the Arts Deserve Support." The Chronicle of Higher Education 7 Nov. 1997: B6.

Rosa, Linda, Emily Rosa, Larry Sarner, and Stephen Barrett. "A Close Look at Therapeutic Touch," JAMA 279.13 (1998): 1005–10. http://www.Ama=assn.org/sci=pubs/journals/ archive/jama/vol_279/no_13/joc71352.htm>.

Rothenberg, Albert. "Creative Contradictions." Psychology Today June 1979: 55–62.

Rothenberg, David. "How the Web Destroys the Quality of Students' Research Papers." The Chronicle of Higher Education 15 August 1997: A44.

Safire, William. Fumblerules: A Lighthearted Guide to Grammar and Good Usage. New York: Dell, 1990.

Salinger, J. D. Catcher in the Rye. Boston: Little, Brown, 1951.

Sample, Ryan Grady. "Bigger, But Not Better." [My Turn column]. Newsweek 11 Jan. 1999: 14.

Schlessinger, Laura. "Legal Abortion Not the Salvation That Feminists Claim." <http://www.uexpress.com/ups/opinion/dolumn/dl/text/1999/04/dl9904024828.html>

Scott, Eugenie C. "Creation Science: A Continuing Threat to Education." Institute for First Amendment Studies, Inc. 1999 <http://www.ifas.org/fw/9409/ creationism.html>.

Scott, Herb. Groceries. Pittsburgh: U of Pittsburg Press, 1976.

Schoofs, Mark. "Fear and Wonder: How Genetics Is Changing Our Lives." Village Voice 30 Sept. 1997: 38.

---. "The Way We Were." Village Voice 14 Oct. 1997: 36–38.

---. "The Myth of Race: What DNA Says about Human Ancestry—and Bigotry." Village Voice 28 Oct. 1997: 35.

Schwartz, Harry. "Cloning Dolly May Be Biggest News of Our Lives." Detroit Free Press 28 Feb. 1997: 13A.

Selzer, Richard. Confessions of a Knife. New York: William Morrow, 1979.

---. Mortal Lessons: Notes on the Art of Surgery. New York: Simon & Schuster, 1987.

---. Down from Troy: A Doctor Comes of Age. New York: William Morrow, 1992.

---. Letters to a Young Doctor. New York: Harvest Book, Harcourt Brace & Company, 1996.

---. The Doctor Stories. New York: Picador USA/St. Martin's Press, 1998.

Shapiro, Harold T. "Ethical and Policy Issues of Human Cloning." Science 277 (July 1997): 195–96.

Silver, Lee. Remaking Eden: Cloning and Beyond in a Brave New World. New York: Avon Books, 1997.

Smith, Page. Killing the Spirit: Higher Education in America. New York: Penguin, 1990.

Sowell, Thomas. "Human Parasites Are Infesting Society." Detroit News 22 May 1992: 9A.

---"Aborted Knowledge." Creators Syndicate 14 May 1999.

---. "Mass Shootings and Mass Hysteria." Creators Syndicate 10 June 1999.

Stafford, William. Writing the Australian Crawl: Views on the Writer's Vocation. Ann Arbor: U of Michigan Press, 1978.

---. You Must Revise Your Life. Ann Arbor, U of Michigan Press, 1986.

---. The Way It Is: New and Selected Poems. Saint Paul, MN: 1998.

Stroud, Joe H. [editorial, "Causes of Less Crime"] Detroit Free Press 28 Nov. 1997: 16A.

Strunk, William, Jr., and E. B. White. Elements of Style. 3d ed. Boston: Allyn & Bacon, 1979.

Sullivan, Andrew. "Let Gays Marry." Newsweek 3 June 1996: 26.

Tannen, Deborah. You Just Don't Understand. New York: HarperCollins, 1990.

---. The Argument Culture: Moving from Debate to Dialogue. New York: Random House, 1998.

Thomas, Evan, and Christopher Dickey. "The Last Chapter." Newsweek 15 Sept. 1997: 39.

Tollefson, Stephen K. Grammar Grams. New York: Harper & Row, 1989.

Toullmin, Stephen. The Uses of Argument. New York: Cambridge UP, 1958.

Turkle, Sherry. The Second Self: Computers and the Human Spirit. New York: Simon & Schuster, 1984.

Twain, Mark. Adventures of Huckleberry Finn. Berkeley: The Mark Twain Library/U of California Press, 1985.

Underwood, Sharon. "I've Had Enough of Your Anti-gay Venom." Concord Monitor and New Hampshire Patriot 30 April 2000.

Wakoski, Diane. "The Mind, Like an Old Fish." In Smudging. Santa Barbara, CA: Black Sparrow Press, 1978.

Walker, Alice. In Search of Our Mothers' Gardens. San Diego: Harcourt Brace Jovanovich, 1974.

"Was Fetal Cell Used? Scientist Says Error Possible in Dolly Clone." <http://www.abcnews.com/sections/science>.

Watts, Alan. The Book: On the Taboo against Knowing Who You Are. New York: Vintage Books, 1972.

West, Cornel. Race Matters. New York: Vintage–Random House, 1994.

Whitaker, Barbara. "Owners Give $2.3 Million to Clone Dog." New York Times on the Web 27 Aug. 1998 <http://archive.nytimes.com/archive . . .?getdoc+allyears2+db365+193609+0++>.

White, E. B. "Death of a Pig." Essays of E. B. White. New York: Harper & Row, 1977.

---. "Will Strunk—Omit Needless Words." Essays of E. B. White. New York: Harper & Row, 1977.

---. "Once More to the Lake." Essays of E. B. White. New York: Harper & Row, 1977.

Whitehead, Alfred North. Modes of Thought. New York: Macmillan, 1938.

---. The Aims of Education and Other Essays. New York: Macmillan, 1959.

Whitman, Walt. "Song of Myself." Leaves of Grass, ed. Malcolm Crowley. New York: Viking Penguin, 1959.

---. "When I Heard the Learn'd Astronomer," in Laurence Perrine, Sound and Sense, 7th ed. New York: Harcourt, Brace, Jovanovich, 1987.

"Who Are You Taking to the Prom This Year?" The American Civil Liberties Union 2000. <http://www.aclu.org/issues/gay/prom.html>.

Will, George. "Sex amidst Semicolons." Newsweek 4 Oct. 1993: 92.

---. "A New Level of Worrying." Newsweek 22 July 1996: 72.

---."Torricelli's Larger Point." Newsweek 1 Sept. 1997: 78.

---. "A Week of Sheer Fakery." Newsweek 15 Sept. 1997: 84.

Williams, William Carlos. Paterson. New York: New Directions, 1946, 1963.

Winn, Marie. The Plug-In Drug. New York: Viking, 1977.

Wittgenstein, Ludwig. The Philosophy Foundation. <http://www.world.std.com/~socrates/quotes.html>.

Wong, Dominic W. S. The ABCs of Gene Cloning. New York: Chapman & Hall, 1997.

Wolf, Naomi. Fire with Fire. New York: Random House, 1993.

Wu, Amy. "Stop the Clock." [My Turn column] Newsweek 22 Jan. 1996: 14.

Yeats, William B. The Poems of W. B. Yeats: A New Edition. Ed. Richard J. Finneran. New York: Simon & Schuster, 1956.

"Young Women and Abortion." National Organization for Women 1999 <http://www.now.org>.

Credits

Various Chapters

Definitions from <u>Webster's New World College Dictionary</u>, Third College Edition. Reprinted by permission from Hungry Minds, Inc.

DOWN WITH TROY, by Richard Selzer. Copyright © 1992 by Richard Selzer. Reprinted by permission of George Borchardt, Inc., for the author.

<u>Mortal Lessons</u>, by Richard Selzer. Copyright © 1974, 1975, 1976, 1987 by Richard Selzer. Reprinted by permission of Georges Borchardt, Inc., for the author.

<u>Letters to a Young Doctor</u>, by Richard Selzer. Copyright © 1982 by David Goldman and Janet Selzer, trustees. Reprinted by permission of Georges Borchardt, Inc., for the author.

From <u>You Just Don't Understand</u> by Deborah Tannen. Copyright © 1990 by Deborah Tannen. Reprinted by permission of HarperCollins Publishers, Inc.

Chapter 1

Amy Wu. "Stop the Clock" ("My Turn" column). From <u>Newsweek</u>, 22 Jan. 1996. © 1996 Newsweek, Inc. All rights reserved. Reprinted by permission.

Brian Courtney. "Freedom of Choice" ("My Turn" column). From <u>Newsweek</u>, 13 Feb.1995. © 1995 Newsweek, Inc. All rights reserved. Reprinted by permission.

Excerpts from pages 9-10, 31, 45 from <u>Deadly Consequences</u> by Deborah Prothrow-Stith, M.D. Copyright © 1991 by Deborah Prothrow-Stith and Michaele Weissman. Reprinted by permission of HarperCollins Publishers, Inc.

From <u>Confessions of a Knife</u> by Richard Selzer. New York: William Morrow, 1979. Reprinted by permission.

Excerpts from <u>Language in Thought and Action</u>, Fourth Edition by S.I. Hayakawa, copyright © 1978 by Harcourt, Inc., reprinted by permission of the publisher.

Joan Beck. "Gore's Tear-Jerking Speech Belies Tobacco Background." © Tribune Media Services, Inc. All Rights Reserved. Reprinted with permission.

"McVeigh Attorney: Don't Be Swayed by Sympathy." Reprinted by permission from the Associated Press.

Bob Greene. "His Name Was Eric; He Wouldn't Steal So His Life Was Stolen." © Tribune Media Services, Inc. All Rights Reserved. Reprinted with permission.

"I Have a Dream" speech. Reprinted by arrangement with The Heirs to the Estate of Martin Luther King Jr., c/o Writers House, Inc. as agent for the proprietor. Copyright 1963 by Martin Luther King, Jr., copyright renewed 1991 Coretta Scott King.

Declan Butler. "Poll Reveals Backing for Xenotransplants." From <u>Nature</u>, 22 Jan. 1998, p. 315. Copyright © 1998 Macmillan Magazines Ltd.

Ryan Grady Sample. "Bigger, But Not Better" ("My Turn" column). From <u>Newsweek</u>, January 11, 1999. © 1999 Newsweek, Inc. All rights reserved. Reprinted by permission.

Mark Schrofs, "How Genetics Is Changing Our Lives" <u>The Village Voice</u>. Reprinted by permission from The Village Voice.

Lori B. Andrews, "Human Cloning: Assessing the Ethical and Legal Quandries," <u>The Chronicle of Higher Education</u>, 13 Feb. 1998. Reprinted by permission from the author.

Interchapter 1

Adapted from <u>Developing a Written Voice</u> by Dona J. Hickey. Copyright © 1993 by Mayfield Publishing Company. Reprinted by permission of the publisher.

Claudia Kalb. "Our Embattled Ears." From <u>Newsweek</u>, 25 Aug. 1997. © 1997 Newsweek, Inc. All rights reserved. Reprinted by permission.

"Medicine Attacks Cold Virus." Reprinted by permission from the Associated Press.

Letter to Mrs. Lydia Bixby from Abraham Lincoln and letter from Kaiser Wilhelm to a German mother from <u>A Treasury of the World's Greatest Letters</u>, edited by M. Lincoln Schuster. Copyright © 1940 Simon & Schuster, Inc., renewed 1968 by Simon & Schuster, Inc.

Chapter 2

"American Skin (41 Shots)" by Bruce Springsteen. Copyright © 2000 by Bruce Springsteen (ASCAP). Reprinted with permission.

William Stafford. "Detroit Will Rue Its Deal with Devil." © Tribune Media Services, Inc. All Rights Reserved. Reprinted with permission.

William Stafford. "Don't Shoot Holes in Gun Control Bills." © Tribune Media Services, Inc. All Rights Reserved. Reprinted with permission.

Eugenie C. Scott. "Creation Science: A Continuing Threat." Reprinted by permission from Eugenie C. Scott.

From <u>The Argument Culture</u> by Deborah Tannen. Copyright © 1998 by Deborah Tannen. Reprinted by permission of Random House, Inc.

From <u>Remaking Eden</u> by Lee M. Silver. Copyright © 1998 by Lee M. Silver. Reprinted by permission of HarperCollins Publishers, Inc. and Avon Books.

Thomas Sowell. "Mass Shootings and Mass Hysteria." By permision of Thomas Sowell and Creators Syndicate, Inc.

One sentence from web page called CJR: Editor's Welcome, 6/26/97. www.njr.org/welcome.html. Reprinted by permission from the rights holder.

Carl Rogers. "Communication: Its Blocking and Its Facilitation." Reprinted by permission from Northwestern University Press.

From <u>Illiterate America</u> by Jonathan Kozol. Copyright © 1985. Reprinted by permission from Doubleday, a Division of Random House, Inc.

Gregory Kane. "Selling Bodies and Soul." <u>The Baltimore Sun</u>. Reprinted by permission.

Wayne LaPierre. "Standing Guard." Reprinted with permission from the National Rifle Association of America.

Linda Chavez. "Why I Own a Gun." By permission of Linda Chavez and Creators Syndicate, Inc. Appeared in Jewish World Review.

ACLU. "Why Doesn't the ACLU Support an Individual's Unlimited Right to Keep and Bear Arms?" Reprinted by permission from The American Civil Liberties Union.

NOW. "Young Women and Abortion." Issue Report reprinted by permission of the National Organization for Women. This is a factual document (January 1999) and is not designed to be an opinion piece.

Interchapter 2

Chapter 3

Interchapter 3

Chapter 4

John Stone, "Death" in <u>All This Rain</u>, 1980. Reprinted by permission from Louisiana State University Press.

"Sally Forth" cartoon. Reprinted with special permission of King Features Syndicate.

From <u>A Whack on the Side of the Head</u> by Roger Von Oech. Copyright © 1983, 1990, 1998 by Roger Von Oech. By permission of Warner Books, Inc.

John Gray. <u>Men, Women, and Relationships</u>. Reprinted by permission from Beyond Words Publishing.

From <u>The Shelter of Each Other</u> by Mary Pipher, Ph.D. Copyright © 1996 by Mary Pipher, Ph.D. Used by permission of Putnam Berkeley, a division of Penguin Putnam Inc.

Mother Goose & Grimm cartoon, "When Cannonballs Swim." © Tribune Media Services, Inc. All Rights Reserved. Reprinted with permission.

Mother Goose & Grimm cartoon, "Your Human's Open." © Tribune Media Services, Inc. All Rights Reserved. Reprinted with permission.

Mother Goose & Grimm cartoon, "Sorry Buddy, I'm Baroque." © Tribune Media Services, Inc. All Rights Reserved. Reprinted with permission.

"The Body of a Flea Magnified 215 Times." <u>Off the Leash</u> by W. B. Park. Reprinted by permission from W. B. Park.

"Fish Drinking at a Bar." <u>Off the Leash</u> by W. B. Park. Reprinted by permission from W. B. Park.

Jokes reprinted with permission from the Sarkes-Kernis Company, on behalf of Steven Wright.

Jokes reprinted by permission from Phyllis Diller.

"I Have a Dream" speech. Reprinted by arrangement with The Heirs to the Estate of Martin Luther King, Jr., c/o Writers House, Inc. as agent for the proprietor. Copyright 1963 by Martin Luther King, Jr., copyright renewed 1991 Coretta Scott King.

From "Why the Sky Is Blue" from <u>The Stars in Their Courses</u> by James Jeans. Reprinted with the permission of Cambridge University Press.

From "The Mind Like an Old Fish" by Diane Wakoski. Reprinted by permission from Black Sparrow Press.

"Streets of Philadelphia" by Bruce Springsteen. Copyright © 1993 by Bruce Springsteen (ASCAP). Reprinted by permission.

Lucille Clifton: "wishes for sons" copyright © 1991 by Lucille Clifton. Reprinted from <u>quilting poems 1987–1990</u> with the permission of BOA Editions, Ltd., 260 East Ave., Rochester, NY 14604.

"Hate Is Simple, Love Complex" from <u>Pieces of Eight</u> by Sydney J. Harris. Copyright © 1975, 1976, 1977, 1979, 1980, 1981 by The Chicago Daily News, The Chicago Sun-Times, Field Newspaper Syndicate, and Sydney J. Harris. Copyright © 1982 by Houghton Mifflin Co. Reprinted by permission of Houghton Mifflin Co. All rights reserved.

Dorothy Noyes. "Senior-Teener, A New Hybrid." From <u>Newsweek</u>, 5 September 1994. © 1994 Newsweek, Inc. All rights reserved. Reprinted by permission.

Dave Barry. "The Evil Eye." From <u>Dave Barry Is From Mars and Venus</u>. Copyright © 1997 by Dave Barry. Reprinted by permission of Crown Publishers, Inc.

Interchapter 4

<u>Prose Style: A Contemporary Guide</u>, 2/e by Miles/Bertonasco/Karns, © 1991. Reprinted by permission of Prentice-Hall, Inc. Upper Saddle River, NJ.

Richard Paul. <u>Critical Thinking: What Every Person Needs to Survive in a Rapidly Changing World</u>. Reprinted by permission from Richard Paul and the Foundation for Critical Thinking.

David Rothenberg. "How the Web Destroys the Quality of Students' Research Papers." From <u>The Chronicle of Higher Education</u>. Reprinted by permission from David Rothenberg.

Letters to the Editor in response to essay by David Rothenberg. Copyright 1997, The Chronicle of Higher Education. Reprinted with permission.

Farewell at a Writer's Conference, copyright © 1986 by William Stafford. From <u>You Must Revise Your Life</u> (University of Michigan). Reprinted by permission of The Estate of William Stafford.

Chapter 5

Excerpts from LANGUAGE IN THOUGHT AND ACTION, Fourth Edition by S. I. Hayakawa, copyright © 1978 by Harcourt, Inc., reprinted by permission of the publisher.

Excerpt from CRITICAL THINKING: WHAT EVERY PERSON NEEDS TO SURVIVE IN A RAPIDLY CHANGING WORLD by Richard Paul. Reprinted by permission from Richard Paul and the Foundation for Critical Thinking.

"How the Web Destroys the Quality of Students' Research Papers" by David Rothenberg. From CHRONICLE OF HIGHER EDUCATION. Reprinted by permission from David Rothenberg.

Letters to editor in response to essay by David Rothenberg. Copyright © 1997, The Chronicle of Higher Education. Reprinted with permission.

Interchapter 5

From <u>Tuesdays with Morrie</u> by Mitch Albom, copyright © 1997 by Mitch Albom. Used by permission of Doubleday, a Division of Random House, Inc.

Chapter 6

"Farewell to a Writer's Conference" copyright © 1986 by William Stafford. From YOU MUST REVISE YOUR LIFE (University of Michigan). Reprinted by permission of the Estate of William Stafford.

"My Papa's Waltz," copyright 1942 by Hearst Magazines, Inc. from <u>The Collected Poems by Theodore Roethke</u>. Used by permission of Doubleday, a division of Random House, Inc.

"A narrow Fellow in the Grass." Reprinted by permission of the publishers and the Trustees of Amherst College from <u>The Poems of Emily Dickinson</u>, Thomas H. Johnson, ed. Cambridge, Mass.: The Belknap Press of Harvard University Press, Copyright © 1951, 1955, 1979, 1983 by the President and Fellows of Harvard College.

Leonard Pitts and Bob Greene. "No Contest: Books Beat Sport Anytime." © Tribune Media Services, Inc. All Rights Reserved. Reprinted with permission.

"Brute" from DOCTOR STORIES by Richard Selzer.

All lines from "Metaphors" from <u>Crossing the Water</u> by Sylvia Plath. Copyright © 1960 by Ted Hughes. Copyright Renewed. Reprinted by permission of HarperCollins Publishers, Inc. and Faber & Faber, Ltd.

Anne Caston, <u>Flying Out with the Wounded</u>.

"Root Cellar," copyright 1943 by Modern Poetry Association. from <u>The Collected Poems of Theodore Roethke</u>. Used by permission of Doubleday, a division of Random House, Inc.

From <u>The Wellspring</u> by Sharon Olds. Copyright © 1996 by Sharon Olds. Reprinted by permission of Alfred A. Knopf, a Division of Random House, Inc.

Li-Young Lee. "Early in the Morning" © 1986 by Li-Young Lee. Reprinted from <u>Rose,</u> by Li-Young Lee, with the permission of BOA Editions, Ltd.

"A Bird came down the Walk." Reprinted by permission of the publishers and the Trustees of Amherst College from <u>The Poems of Emily Dickinson</u>, Thomas H. Johnson, ed. Cambridge, Mass.: The Belknap Press of Harvard University Press, Copyright © 1951, 1955, 1979 by the President and Fellows of Harvard College.

"Famous" from <u>Words Under the Words: Selected Poems</u> by Naomi Shihab Nye, copyright © 1995. Used by permission of Far Corner Books.

"The Grocer's Children" from <u>Groceries</u>, by Herbert Scott, © 1976. Reprinted by permission of the author and the University of Pittsburgh Press.

Interchapter 6

Chapter 7

Chapter 8

Chapter 9

Chapter 10

Index